# Documents
### Relating to the
# Colonial History
### of The
# State of New Jersey,

First Series - Volume XXXVI

Calendar of New Jersey Wills,
Volume VII, 1786-1790

*Elmer T. Hutchinson*

Heritage Books
2008

# HERITAGE BOOKS
*AN IMPRINT OF HERITAGE BOOKS, INC.*

## Books, CDs, and more—Worldwide

For our listing of thousands of titles see our website
at
www.HeritageBooks.com

Published 2008 by
HERITAGE BOOKS, INC.
Publishing Division
100 Railroad Ave. #104
Westminster, Maryland 21157

Copyright © 1941 Elmer T. Hutchinson

Other books by the author:

*Documents Relating to the Colonial History of the State of New Jersey, Calendar of New Jersey Wills, Volume VI: 1781-1785*

*Documents Relating to the Colonial History of the State of New Jersey, Calendar of New Jersey Wills, Volume VIII: 1791-1795*

*Documents Relating to the Colonial History of the State of New Jersey, Calendar of New Jersey Wills, Volume IX, 1796-1800*

*Documents Relating to the Colonial History of the State of New Jersey, Calendar of New Jersey Wills, Volume X, 1801-1805*

*Documents Relating to the Colonial History of the State of New Jersey, Calendar of New Jersey Wills, Volume XI, 1806-1809*

*Documents Relating to the Colonial History of the State of New Jersey, Calendar of New Jersey Wills, Volume XII, 1810-1813*

*Documents Relating to the Colonial History of the State of New Jersey, Calendar of New Jersey Wills, Volume XIII, 1814-1817*

All rights reserved. No part of this book may be reproduced or transmitted in any form or by any means, electronic or mechanical, including photocopying, recording or by any information storage and retrieval system without written permission from the author, except for the inclusion of brief quotations in a review.

International Standard Book Numbers
Paperbound: 978-1-58549-784-3
Clothbound: 978-0-7884-7144-5

# Calendar of New Jersey Wills

**1786, Aug. 10. Aaronson, John,** of Mansfield Township, Burlington Co.; will of. Wife, Rebekah, all the goods she brought when we married, and £100. Son, Joseph, the plantation where I live, and ½ my cedar swamp; and he is to pay to his 3 brothers and sister, to wit: Samuel, John, George and Rebeka Aaronson, £200, to bring up said children. Son, Thomas, plantation where my son, Joseph, lives; also the Curtis meadow, which joins Thomas Curtis; and ½ the cedar swamp; and Thomas is to pay to my children, Samuel, John, George and Rebeka, £225, when they are 21. Son, Samuel, a meadow, called Gibbs Meadow. My 3 youngest sons to be put to trades, at the discretion of their mother. Executors—wife, Rebekah, and sons, Joseph, Thomas and Samuel. Witnesses—Peter Tallman, Joseph Talman, Benjamin Aaronson. Proved Aug. 24, 1785. Lib. M, p. 315.

**1790, March 31. Abit, Abdon,** of Pittsgrove Township, Salem Co., yeoman; will of. Sons, John and Abdon, plantation where I live. Daughter, Mary Garrison, wife of Ephraim, 5 shillings. Daughter, Elizabeth Sutton, wife of James, 5 shillings. Daughter, Sarah Atkinson, wife of Moses, 5 shillings. Daughter, Marther Abit, bed and cow. Daughter, Anna Peachey, wife of Benjamin, £4. Executor —son, John. Witnesses—David Mayhew, Sarah Mayhew, Eleazar Mayhew. Proved June 15, 1790.
1790, May 22. Inventory, £13.7.1, made by Eleazar Mayhew and David Mayhew. Lib. 31, p. 483.

**1787, Jan. 31. Aborn, George,** of Gloucester Co. Ward. Son of Jonathan Aborn, of said Co., deceased. Said Ward makes choice of Jonathan Harker as his Guardian.
1787, Jan. 31. Guardian—Jonathan Harker. Fellowbondsman—Franklin Davenport; both of Woodbury, said Co. Witnesses—Benjamin Whitall and Thomas Hodgson. Lib. 29, p. 121.

**1786, Feb. 21. Acken, John,** of Essex Co. Int. Adm'x—Phebe Acken, of said Co. Lib. 28, p. 425.

**1790, Jan. 20. Ackerman, Abraham,** of Bergen Co. Int. Adm'r—Garret A. Ackerman. Fellowbondsmen—John Van Buskerk and Andrew A. Hopper; all of said Co. Witnesses—Nehemiah Wade and William Reading. Lib. 31, p. 543.

**1786, Sept. 10. Acton, Benjamin,** of Salem, Salem Co.; will of. Wife, Hannah, house and lot where I live, and, at her death, to my son, John; and it is to include 1½ acres. Daughter, Hannah Acton, rest of my ground. Executors—wife, Hannah, and Edward Hall. Witnesses —John Maxwell, Lewis Owen, Thomas Clement. Proved Nov. 3, 1786.
Lib. 28, p. 146.

**1786, March 22. Adams, John,** of Newtown Township, Sussex Co.; will of. Eldest son, Thomas, 5 shillings. Wife, Catherine, rest of goods to bring up my children. Executors—wife, Catherine, and friend, Moses Morris. Witnesses—John Ryerson, Benjamin Hull, George Lance. Proved May 10, 1786.

1786, April 24. Inventory, made by Martin Ryerson and Benjamin Hull. Lib. 28, p. 458.

**1788, Aug. 15. Adams, Stophel,** of Hardwick, Sussex Co., yeoman; will of. Wife, Catharine, all real and personal estate; and my youngest son, Henry, and my daughter, Catharine, to live with her, and, what is left after wife's death, I give to said children, except to each of the other children, Jacob, Christiana, Hannah and Barbara, to have 7 shillings and 6 pence each. Executors—friends, George Kein and Martin Swartwelder. Witnesses—Charles Rhodes, Margaret Harker, Abraham Shaver. Proved Oct. 14, 1788.

1788, Sept. 6. Inventory, £86.13.0, made by Abraham Shaver and John Markel. Lib. 31, p. 146.

**1790, Jan. 15. Adams, William,** of Hopewell Township, Cumberland Co., yeoman; will of. Wife, Anne, what the law directs of my real and personal estate, with 30 shillings worth of goods. Children, Lemuel, Philathea, Elizabeth, William and John, rest of real and personal estate, when they are of age. William and John to be bound to trades. Daughters, Philathea and Elizabeth, to be under the care of my wife. Executors—James Sheppard and Jacob Mulford. Witnesses—David Gillman, Isaac Hawthorn, Almoran Waithman. Proved Sept. 30, 1790.

1790, Jan. 28. Inventory, £70.7.3, made by David Gillman and Reuben Wheaton. Lib. 30, p. 272.

**1786, March 23. Albertson, Isaac,** of Newton Township, Gloucester Co., yeoman; will of. Wife to have my moveable estate, except what Jacob Albertson owes me, and she is to have the use of the plantation till it is sold, and she is to bring up my children till they go to trades, and I desire that Isaac, Thomas and Reckliff, be put to trades at the age of 14. Son, Aaron, 2 lots on the mill pond; one I bought of Thomas Redman, and one of Jacob Albertson. Daughter, Rachel, £15. Son, Samuel, a colt, and £3. My woodland that lies between Jacob Albertson and Peter Thompson to be sold when Samuel is 21, and the money to be given to my sons, Samuel and Nehemiah. Son, Aaron, is mentioned in the residue. Executors—wife, Deborah, and my son-in-law, James Hurley. Witnesses—John Snuke, Keziah Albertson, Peter Thompson. Proved May 19, 1786.

1786, May 16. Inventory, £466.6.8, made by John Hurley and David Henry. Lib. 28, p. 106.

**1786, Jan. 19. Albertson, John,** of Gloucester Co. Ward. Son of Josiah Albertson, of said Co., deceased. Said Ward makes choice of Joseph Burrough as his Guardian.

1786, Jan. 19. Guardian—Joseph Burrough. Fellowbondsman—Samuel Webster; both of said Co., yeomen. Witness—Jonathan Williams. Lib. 28, p. 124.

**1787, March 7. Albertson, Mary and William,** of Newton Township, Gloucester Co. Wards. Children of Nathan Albertson, of said place,

CALENDAR OF WILLS—1786-1790 9

deceased. Said Wards make choice of Joseph Burrough as their Guardian. Witnesses—Joseph Hugg, Jr., and Aaron Albertson.
1787, March 7. Guardian—Joseph Burrough. Fellowbondsman— Samuel Burrough, Jr.; both of Waterford Township, said Co. Witnesses—George Fisher and Joseph Hugg. Lib. 29, p. 121.

**1790, Aug. 21. Allen, Andrew,** of Shrewsbury, Monmouth Co. Int. Adm'r—Joseph Bishop. Fellowbondsman—Josiah Shearman; both of said Co. Witness—Thomas Henderson. Lib. 30, p. 418.

**1786, May 9. Allen, David,** of Lower Alloways Creek Township, Salem Co.; will of. Wife, Sarah, ⅓ of the profits of my land, and ⅓ of the personal estate. Sons, Isaac, David, Erazamos Kent and James, my land, and, if the child my wife will have be a boy, it must have its share. Daughters, Sarah, Rachel, Mary and Sufphias, my moveable estate. Executors—wife, Sarah, and my brother-in-law, Erazamos Kent. Witnesses—Samuel Dick, Ralph Allen, Thomas Sayre. Proved March 15, 1787.
1786, June 3. Inventory, £140.18.6, made by William Smith and John Briggs. Lib. 29, p. 144.

**1788, March 6. Allen, James,** of Northampton Township, Burlington Co.; will of. Son, Samuel, 75 acres of land, to be taken off the south side of my plantation where I live, next to Jacob Prickitt; and he is to pay to my son, William, £20, when he is 21. Son, John, 53 acres, to be taken off the east end of my plantation. Son, James, 20 acres off the northeast part, which join Samuel Stokes and William Burr. Son, William, 30 acres off the northwest part; also £40, to be paid to him by my sons, Samuel and Thomas, in manner as is ordered in their bequest by his mother. Son, Thomas, the house where I live, and the rest of the land. Daughter, Dorithy Joice, £5, as she has been provided for. Executors—brother-in-law, Samuel Phillips, and my son, Thomas. Witnesses—Jacob Prickitt, Rachel Crammer, Josiah Foster.
1789, June 27. Codicil. Witnesses—Rachel Crammer, Josiah Foster. Proved Oct. 12, 1790.
1790, Oct. 11. Inventory, £79.12.5, made by William Burr and Job Collins. Lib. 32, p. 73.

**1786, Sept. 20. Allen, John,** of Hanover Township, Morris Co.; will of. Wife, Rebeca, ⅛ of the moveable estate. Son, Aaron, to be bound out for wages, for his clothing and the support of the children. Sons, Silas and Samuel, to be put to trades, and my daughters, Hannah, Abigail and Rachel, to be put out. Children to have what is left. Executors—Cap. James Keen and Cap. Daniel Gard. Witnesses— Gideon Howell, Jonathan Tichnor, Jacob Whitehead. Proved Oct. 4, 1788. Probate to James Keen, the surviving Executor.
1786, Oct. 27. Inventory, £45.14.6, made by Jacob Minton and Gershom Gard. Lib. 31, p. 177.

**1787, March 24. Allen, John,** of Burlington Co. Int. Adm'r— Bethuel Moore. Fellowbondsman—Jonathan Crispin; both of Evesham Township, said Co.
1787, March 22. Renunciation by Hope Allen, widow of John Allen, late of Evesham Township, carpenter, in favor of Bethuel Moore.
1787, March 7. Inventory, £66.14.0, made by Jonathan Crispin and Thomas Sharp. Lib. 29, p. 74.

10   NEW JERSEY POST-REVOLUTIONARY DOCUMENTS

**1789, March 25. Allen, John,** of Essex Co. Int. Adm'x—Sarah Allen. Fellowbondsman—Abner Bradbury; both of said Co.
Lib. 38, p. 96.

**1790, May 18. Allen, John,** of Evesham Township, Burlington Co. Int. Adm'r—Daniel Joyce. Fellowbondsman—William Burr; both of said Co. Witness—David Ridgway.
1790, April 30. Inventory, £702.19.2, made by Lawrence Webster and Caleb Austin.
Lib. 32, p. 94.

**1790, July. Allen, Joseph,** of Monmouth Co. Ward. Son of Samuel Allen, of said Co., deceased. Petition of Martha Allen, widow of said Samuel, praying that she may be made Guardian of her son, the said Joseph Allen.
1790, July 28. Guardian—Martha Allen. Fellowbondsman—John Knott; both of Shrewsbury Township, said Co. Witnesses—Rachel Henderson and Thomas Henderson.
Lib. 30, p. 420.

**1787, March 22. Allen, Mary,** of New Mills, New Hanover Township, Burlington Co.; will of. Daughter, Margery Rogers, the land where John Goldy lives, in New Mills, and bounded south by the road that leads from New Mills to Brown's saw mill, east and north by Joseph Budd, deceased, and west by John Stewart. Granddaughter, Rhody Rogers, silver shoe buckels. Granddaughter, Margaret Rogers, a case of drawers. Granddaughter, Kessiah Rogers, my pewter. Daughters, Margaret and Margery, my apparel. Son, Samuel Allen, a bond I have against Thomas Platt. Daughter, Margery Rogers, rest of estate. Executrix—daughter, Margery Rogers. Witnesses—John Lacey, Samuel Gaskill, Beriah Taylor. Proved Oct. 12, 1790.
Lib. 32, p. 72.

**1786, Dec. 7. Ambler, David,** of Salem, Salem Co.; will of. To my sister' son, William Forgason, my plantation in Cumberland Co. Sister's son, John Forgason, house and land in Salem where I live. Sister's daughter, Patience Forgason, my land in Manington, which joins Benjamin Smith's. Executors—friend, Thomas Hancock, and Hill Smith. Witnesses—William Goodwin, William Daniel, Elizabeth Goodwin. Proved Dec. 10, 1788.
Lib. 31, p. 39.

**1788, Feb. 21. Amerman, Isaac,** of Knowlton, Sussex Co. Int. Adm'x—Eleanor Amerman. Fellowbondsman—Abraham Swisher; both of said place. Witnesses—Obadiah Brown and George Ribbel.
[No date.] Inventory, £86.6.0, made by Abraham Swisher and Abraham Bescherer. "70 acres of land, valued at £37.10.0."
Lib. 31, p. 156.

**1787, Dec. 8. Anda, Martha,** of Amwell, Hunterdon Co. Int. Adm'r—Jeremiah Basset. Fellowbondsman—Charles McHenry; both of said Co.
1787, Dec. 7. Inventory, £22.15.10, made by William Schenk and Charles McHenry.
1789, Feb. 6. Account by Adm'r. "Paid John Runyan, for making coffin, £1.1.10. Paid laborers for searching after the property of the deceased amongst the ruins of her house, 10 shillings."
Lib. 29, p. 297.

CALENDAR OF WILLS—1786-1790    11

**1786, Feb. 21. Anderson, Abraham,** of Hopewell Township, Hunterdon Co. Int. Adm'r—Henry Mershon. Fellowbondsman—John Holder Mersellis; both of said place. Witnesses—Micajah Phillips and Benjamin Mershon.
1786, Feb. 18. Renunciation by Andrew Mershon and Francinah Mershon, in favor of their sons, Henry Mershon and Benjamin Mershon. Witness—Nicholas Hendrickson.
1786, Feb. 22. Inventory, £15.5.1, made by Stephen Titus and Elijah Hart. "A bond from Abraham Anderson, Jr., for £100."
1787, Sept. 18. Inventory, £16.11.1, made by Stephen Titus and Elijah Hart; it being a list unappraised. "Account against Micajah Phillips, £3.4.0. Note against Henry Pinkerton, £10.10.7."
1791, Feb. 7. Account by Adm'r. "A bond against Theophilus Phillips, for £23, not included in the appraisement. Rent received from Theophilus Phillips; also from Timothy Mershon. Paid an award in favor of Benjamin Mershon, £51.5.2."    Lib. 28, p. 248.

**1786, March 28. Anderson, Andrew,** of Chester Township, Burlington Co., yeoman; will of. Son, Isaac, 5 shillings. Son, Andrew, £10. Son, Aron, the plantation where I live. Son, Abel, £10, when 21. Daughters, Susanna Hammell, Mercy Anderson, Mary Anderson, Abigail Anderson and Anna Anderson, my moveable estate. Son, Aaron, is to pay to Abraham Hewlings, £100. Wife, Phebe, room in the house, and to have provisions. Executors—Sons, Andrew and Aaron. Witnesses—Daniel Cartey, Samuel Wallace, William Cox. Proved April 22, 1786.
1786, April 15. Inventory, £216.5.4, made by Daniel Cartey and Hezekiah Toy.    Lib. 28, p. 1.

**1789, June 16. Anderson, Jeremiah,** of Nottingham Township, Burlington Co.; will of. Son, Samuel, 100 acres on east side of my plantation; he paying to my son, Enoch, £200. Son, Josiah, 100 acres on west side of my plantation. Sons, Samuel and Josiah, to have rest of lands. Sons, Samuel, Joshua and Josiah, personal estate. Executors—sons, Samuel and Josiah. Witnesses—Obadiah Eldredge, George Anderson, Ely Anderson. Proved Nov. 3, 1790.    Lib. 32, p. 70.

**1786, April 22. Anderson, Phebe,** of Chester Township, Burlington Co., widow of Andrew Anderson; will of. Son, John Williamson, 20 shillings. Daughter, Elizabeth Williamson, rest of estate. Executors—friend, Hezekiah Toy, and my daughter, Elizabeth Williamson. Witnesses—Hezekiah Toy, Thomas Marshall, Uriah Brock. Proved Feb. 7, 1789.
1789, Feb. 7. Renunciation by Hezekiah Toy and Elizabeth Anderson, late Williamson. Witnesses—Thomas Marshall and Uriah Brock.
1789, Feb. 7. Adm'r—Aaron Anderson, of Chester, said Co. Fellowbondsman—Daniel Ellis, of said Co. Witness—Thomas Adams.
1789, Aug. 10. Inventory, £54.7.0, of the estate of Phebe Anderson, late Williamson, made by Abraham Huntsman and James Hammell, Jr.
    Lib. 31, p. 314.

**1786, May 3. Anderson, William,** of Amwell Township, Hunterdon Co.; will of. Wife, Jannett, a good support on this plantation with my grandsons, John Scott Anderson and Jacob Anderson, his brother. To my said grandsons, my homestead where I live, with a lot which

I bought of Abraham Smith, after my wife's widowhood. Granddaughter, Jane Anderson, £40. Son, James, £20. Daughter, Anne Higgins, £20. Daughter, Elizabeth Stout, £20. I paid my daughter, Sarah, £20. On hearing of the death of my daughter, Mary, I paid to her eldest son £20. Executors—John Griggs, Joakim Griggs and Samuel Hill. Witnesses—Peter Rockafellar, Elizabeth Rockafellar, Samuel Hill. Proved Nov. 18, 1789. Lib. 32, p. 44.

**1786, July 20. Andres, Christian,** of Greenwich Township, Sussex Co., yeoman. Int. Adm'rs—Catherine Andres, of said place, and Joseph Mackey, of Oxford, said Co. Fellowbondsman—George Lance, of Oxford, yeoman. Witnesses—William Kerr and Thomas Anderson.
1786, June 20. Inventory, £247.14.3, made by Peter Schultz and George Lance. Lib. 28, p. 469.

**1786, May 13. Andrews, Nehemiah,** of Deptford Township, Gloucester Co. Int. Adm'r—David Cooper. Fellowbondsman—Joshua Hopper; both of said place.
1785, Oct. 24. Inventory, £43.8.6, made by Jonas Cattell and Joshua Hopper. Lib. 28, p. 121.

**1788, Jan. 22. Antrim, Joseph,** of Mansfield Township, Burlington Co., yeoman; will of. The plantation that I bought of my brother, Isaac, and a meadow that I bought of Joseph Gibbs, and my personal estate, to be sold. Son, John, ½ the rest of my land. Daughters, the other ½. Children, Martha, Susannah, John and Hannah, the overplus. Executors—Joseph Shreve and Edward Rockhill, Jr. Witnesses—John Reynolds, Aaron Swain, Tallman Pennock. Proved April 8, 1788.
1788, April 8. Renunciation by Edward Rockhill, Jr. Witness—Tallman Pennock.
1788, April 5. Inventory, £544.18.4, made by Nathan Robbins and Lawrence Minor. Lib. 29, p. 544.

**1787, Oct. 14. Applegate, John,** of Middlesex Co.; will of. Children, William Applegate, Keziah Applegate and Elizabeth Jeffers, 5 shillings each. To my other children, and Jene Sheerman, daughter of my daughter, Elizabeth Jeffres, the money from the sale of the land, and given to my 3 sons and 3 daughters, and Jene Sheerman; the sons being, John, Samuel and Israel, and daughters, Sarah, Rebeckah and Hannah. Executors—son, John, and Aaron Bennet, Jr. Witnesses—Zebulon Applegate, Garret Voorhees, John Davison. Proved May 30, 1788.
1788, May 29. Inventory, £72.17.10, made by Samuel Longstreet and Stephen Vorhes. Lib. 31, p. 201.

**1789, Sept. 14. Applegate, Silas,** of Willingborough, Burlington Co. Int. Adm'rs—Samuel Ivins and Lydia Applegate. Fellowbondsman—Isaac Newton; all of said Co.
1789, Sept. 11. Inventory, £188.5.0, made by Pearson Fenimore and Isaac Newton. Lib. 31, p. 318.

**1787, July 28. Applegate, Thomas,** of Middlesex Co. Int. Adm'x—Ann Applegate. Fellowbondsmen—Henry Lott and Nicolas Schenck.
1787, Aug. 3. Inventory, made by James Patton and Cornelius Vanars Dall. Lib. 29, p. 365.

CALENDAR OF WILLS—1786-1790    13

**1786, Nov. 2. Applegate, William,** of Middlesex Co. Ward. Son of William Applegate, of said Co., deceased. Said Ward makes choice of Andrew Rowan as his Guardian.
1786, Nov. 2. Guardian—Andrew Rowan. Fellowbondsman—Noah Morford; both of said Co. Witness—William Sickles.   Lib. 28, p. 343.

**1787, March 1. Applegate, William,** of Middletown Township, Monmouth Co. Int. Adm'rs—Richard Applegate and Anthony Holmes. Fellowbondsman—John Stillwell; all of said Co. Witness—William Stillwell.
1787, Jan. 30. Inventory, £279.4.9, made by John Stillwell and Thomas Walling, Jr.   Lib. 29, p. 339.

**1787, Jan. 30. Armstrong, Ephraim,** of Northampton Township, Burlington Co.; will of. Wife, Elizabeth, use of plantation, until son, Samuel, is of full age. Daughters, Mary Haines and Alley Armstrong, one cow to each. Son, John, 5 shillings. Daughter, Elizabeth Eggman, 5 shillings. Sons, Ephraim, Joseph and Samuel, my plantation when Samuel is 21, and they are to provide provisions off the place. Executors—wife, Elizabeth, and son, Ephraim. Witnesses—John Moore, William Price, Uriah Woolman. Proved March 22, 1788.
1788, March 19. Inventory, £47.9.3, made by Samuel Kemble and Abraham Reeve.   Lib. 30, p. 6.

**1790, Sept. 4. Arnold, Henry.** Adm'r—Thomas Cooper, of New York City. Fellowbondsman—Charles De Kay, of Newark, Essex Co. Whereas, James Sacket and Sarah Arnold were appointed Executors of Henry Arnold, which will was proved by them, since which time James and Sarah have died intestate, and there is still some goods left not administered, which were of the said Henry; therefore the said Thomas Cooper is appointed Adm'r with will annexed.
Lib. 30, p. 359.

**1786, July 16. Aronson, Rebecca,** of Waterford, Gloucester Co., widow; will of. Daughter, Mary Woolman, ⅓ of the apparel. To Samuel Woolman, son of Mary Woolman, looking glass. To Sarah Woolman, ⅓ of the apparel. To Jane Woolman, wife to said Samuel Woolman, rest of apparel. To Abel Nicholson, my grandson, £5, to be paid by Isaac Burrough, Jr. To Rebecca Burrough, my granddaughter, £90. To Joseph Burrough, my grandson, £50. To Reuben Burrough, £50. Executor—grandson, Abel Nicholson. Witnesses—John Shivers, Sr., Joseph Collins, Jr. Proved Jan. 14, 1788.
Lib. 31, p. 34.

**1790, Sept. 2. Arrison, Ashfordby,** of Kingwood, Hunterdon Co. Int. Adm'x—Mary Arrison. Fellowbondsman—Richard Opdycke; both of said place.
1790, Aug. 21. Inventory, £358.18.7, made by Elijah Allen and Hezekiah Waterhouse.
1795, May 9. Account by Mary Arrison. "Land sold to William Goddard, £30; also to John Jobs, £0.11.4. Rent of the farm to Moses Fisher, £56.13.4. Rent of the homestead, £60. Paid the amount of the legacies due to Jonathan Curtis' children on the 27th of Sept. 1784, being the day of this accountant's marriage, £219.5.11. Paid for 10 years, 7 mo. and 13 days interest on £219.5.11, belonging to the children of Jonathan Curtis, £163.0.2. Paid for support of the young

## 14 NEW JERSEY POST-REVOLUTIONARY DOCUMENTS

children of the intestate, since his decease, viz., Euphame, 3 years and 3 mo., £48.5.0.; Elizabeth, 4 years, £60; Jonathan, 3 years, 5 mo., doctoring and nursing him during long illness, funeral expenses, etc., £51.5.0; Grace, an infant born after her father's decease, £67.10.0; for clothing furnished Richard, 3½ years of his apprenticeship, £20."
1797, Aug. 1. Petition of Mary Arrison that she may sell land to pay debts. It was ordered that she might sell a plantation of about 100 acres in Kingwood, now in the possession of Moses Fisher.
Lib. 30, p. 315.

**1789, May 12. Asa, John,** of Burlington Co. Int. Adm'x—Mary Asa. Fellowbondsman—Richard Cox; both of Northampton Township, said Co. Witness—Thomas Adams.
1789, May 11. Inventory, £102.11.11, made by Job Moore and Abner Rogers. Lib. 31, p. 318.

**1787, March 2. Atkinson, Aaron,** of Springfield Township, Burlington Co.; will of. To my wife, £15 a year, and £— in goods. Son, Benjamin, all this plantation, Daughter, Ann Atkinson, £50, and the chest that was her mother's. Son, John, rest of estate, and rents of plantation, till Benjamin comes of age. Executors—brother, John Atkinson, and my cozen, Benjamin Atkinson. Witnesses—Samuel Atkinson, James McGonigle, David Ridgway. Proved March 14, 1787.
1787, March 14. Renunciation by John Atkinson.
1787, March 12. Inventory, made by Samuel Atkinson and Solomon Thomas. Lib. 29, p. 34.

**1789, Nov. 2. Atkinson, Benjamin, Jr.,** of Burlington Co. Ward. Son of Aaron Atkinson, of said Co., deceased. Said Ward having real and personal estate, makes choice of Benjamin Atkinson, Sr., as his Guardian.
1789, Nov. 2. Guardian—Benjamin Atkinson, Sr. Fellowbondsman —William Cooper; both of said Co. Witness—Thomas Adams.
Lib. 31, p. 323.

**1788, March 12. Atkinson, Elizabeth,** of Springfield, Burlington Co., widow; will of. Daughter, Hannah, a bed. Son, Aden Atkinson, rest of estate. Executor—son, Aden Atkinson. Witnesses—Benjamin Matson, Margret Clutch, Joseph Pancoast. Proved April 4, 1788.
1788, April 1. Inventory, £133.1.0, made by Samuel Atkinson and John Ridgway. Lib. 30, p. 16.

**1790, Jan. 29. Atkinson, Elizabeth,** of Gloucester Co. Int. Adm'r— Thomas Hodgson, of said Co. Fellowbondsman—Isaiah Toy, of Burlington Co. Lib. 31, p. 476.

**1786, Jan. 12. Atkinson, Thomas,** of Amwell Township, Hunterdon Co.; will of. Land to be sold. Son, Joseph, all personal estate. Executors—son, Joseph, and friend, Joseph Moore. Witnesses— Samuel Hill, Sarah King, Hugh Hicks. Proved Feb. 4, 1789.
1789, Jan. 3. Inventory, £1,027.3.3, made by John Griggs and Hugh Hicks. Lib. 32, p. 13.

**1787, Oct. 23. Atkinson, William,** of Springfield Township, Burlington Co. Int. Adm'r—Adin Atkinson. Fellowbondsman—Joseph Pancoast; both of said place.

CALENDAR OF WILLS—1786-1790    15

1788, April 1. Inventory, £68.14.4, made by Samuel Atkinson and John Ridgway. Lib. 29, p. 76.

**1787, Feb. 26. Aumack, Stephen,** of Monmouth Co. Int. Adm'r— Benjamin Haviland. Fellowbondsman—David Cooper, of said Co. Witness—Jacob Burdg.
1787, Feb. 22. Inventory, £56.15.6, made by Jacob Burdg and William Stillwell. Lib. 29, p. 339.

**1787, March 20. Avise, John,** of Woolwich Township, Gloucester Co. Int. Adm'x—Agnis Avis. Fellowbondsman—Joseph Harker; both of said place. Witness—Samuel Cozens.
1787, March 19. Inventory, £155.17.6, made by Joseph Harker and James Avise. Lib. 29, p. 120.

**1787, Oct. 5. Avise, William,** of Woolwich Township, Gloucester Co. Int. Adm'x—Ann Avise, widow of William. Fellowbondsman— Joseph Harker; both of said place. Witness—Kezia Albertson.
1787, Sept. 26. Inventory, £156.4.6, made by Joseph Harker and James Avise. Lib. 29, p. 116.

**1789, July 31. Ayars, Phillip,** of Hopewell Township, Cumberland Co.; will of. I have passed the three score years of age. Wife, Sarah, that house and lot at Shilo that was hers before I married her; also the goods that were hers. Son, Phillip, my apparel. One-third of my moveable estate I give to my wife, ⅛ to my son, and ⅛ to my only daughter. Son, Phillip, ⅝ of my lands, and my daughter, Lidya, ⅜; and my daughter is to have the plantation on which I live, and my son the other lands. Executors—wife, Sarah, my son, Phillip, and my son-in-law, Job Ayars. Witnesses—Benjamin Lupton, David Parvin, David Randolph. Proved Dec. 31, 1789.
1789, Dec. 21. Inventory, £228.10.4, made by Elnathan Davis and Isaac Davis. Lib. 30, p. 142.

**1789, Dec. 15. Bacon, Ann,** of Salem Co. Ward. Daughter of Samuel and Mary Bacon, of said Co., both deceased. Said Ward makes choice of John Denn as her Guardian.
1789, Dec. 15. Guardian—John Denn. Fellowbondsmen—Samuel Stewart and Thomas Thompson; all of Salem said Co. Witness— Samuel Dick. Lib. 31, p. 359.

**1789, April 17. Badcock, John,** of Great Egg Harbor, Gloucester Co.; will of. Fifty acres of land that join land where Samuel Snell lives, to be sold. Wife, Christean, the use of my part of the saw mill and land where I live, for 3 years. Son, John, ⅓ of my land and part of my saw mill, and, at his death, to his son, Jacob. Sons, Jacob and Enoch, the rest of saw mill and lands, when they are 21. Daughters, Margret Corson and Rebekah Campbell, 40 shillings each. Grandsons, Samuel and John Indecut, 10 shillings each. Granddaughter, Mary Indecut, 20 shillings. Daughters, Mary and Sarrah, rest of moveable estate, when they are 18. Executors—wife, Christeen and Jacob Indecut. Witnesses—William Waer, John Bush, Joshua Smith. Proved June 18, 1789.
1789, June 18. Renunciation by Jacob Endecott.
1789, May 23. Inventory, £150.0.8, made by William Gwin and Joshua Smith. Lib. 31, p. 419.

**1789, Dec. 26. Badgley, Enoch,** of Essex Co. Int. Adm'rs—Joseph Scudder and Jane Badgley. Fellowbondsman—Marsh Miller; all of said Co. Witnesses—Elijah Squier and Alexander C. Macwhorter, Surrogate.
1789, July 27. Inventory, £103.6.8, made by Mathias Sayres and Thomas Woodruff, in Elizabeth Township. Lib. 30, p. 218.

**1786, March 11. Badgley, John,** of Essex Co. Ward. Son of John Badgley, of said Co., deceased. Said Ward, having an estate of £400, makes choice of John Hole as his Guardian.
1786, March 11. Guardian—John Hole, of said Co. Lib. 28, p. 428.

**1788, Jan. 17. Bailey, Peter,** of Middlesex Co.; will of. Wife, ¼ of lands and personal estate. Son, John, ¼. Daughters, Eloner and Hannah, rest. Executors—son, John, and son-in-law, James Voorhees. Witnesses—Charles Applegate, Rebeckah Story, R. W. Cheney. Proved Dec. 13, 1788.
1788, Jan. 25. Inventory, £182.2.7, made by Samuel Potts and John Anderson. Lib. 31, p. 203.

**1787, Nov. 14. Bainbridge, Mary,** of Hopewell, Hunterdon Co., widow; will of. Son, William, all that shall be due me from my dower. Daughters, Mary and Abigail, residue of estate. Executors—son, William Bainbridge, and friend, Foster Burrowes. Witnesses—Thomas Baldwin, John Guild. Proved Feb. 6, 1787. Lib. 29, p. 270.

**1786, May 2. Baker, Abner,** of Essex Co. Ward. Son of Henry Baker, of said Co., deceased. Said Ward having an estate of £300, makes choice of Isaac Hendricks, as his Guardian.
1786, May 2. Guardian—Isaac Hendricks. Fellowbondsman—Thomas Woodruff; both of said Co. Lib. 28, p. 428.

**1787, May 16. Baker, Barbara,** of Burlington Co. Ward. Daughter of John Baker, of said Co., deceased. Said Ward makes choice of John Vandegrift as her Guardian, she having real and personal estate that needs care.
1787, May 16. Guardian—John Vandegrift, of Bucks Co., Pa. Fellowbondsman—Joseph Fenimore, of Burlington Co. Witness—Thomas Adams. Lib. 29, p. 80.

**1787, March 30. Baker, Daniel,** of Essex Co. Ward. Son of Daniel Baker, of said Co., deceased. Said Ward, having an estate of £150, makes choice of Nathaniel Little as his Guardian.
1787, March 30. Guardian—Nathaniel Littell. Fellowbondsman—Kennedy Vance; both of said Co. Lib. 38, p. 97.

**1790, Aug. 30. Baker, John,** of Upper Precinct, Cape May Co.; will of. Daughter, Mary Baker, all my lands in said place, joining lands of Daniel Garretson, deceased, Samuel Garretson and Samuel Orum, when she comes of age; also personal estate. If she do not live, then to my brother, Daniel, and my sister, Martha Baker. Executors—father, John Baker, and my mother, Elizabeth. Witnesses—Enoch Hughes, James McCray, Elizabeth Baker. Proved Aug. 6, 1803. Lib. 40, p. 491.

CALENDAR OF WILLS—1786-1790

**1788, Oct. 27. Baker, Matthias,** of Hunterdon Co. Int. Adm'rs—Judith Baker and William Baker. Fellowbondsman—Timothy Baker, Jr.; all of said Co.
1788, Dec. 27. Inventory, £253.0.7, made by Noah Hunt and John Vankirk. Lib. 31, p. 141.

**1789, March 10. Baker, Matthias,** of Somerset Co.; will of. Wife, Catharine, £50 in goods, and interest of £600 yearly. Daughters, Janet Ten Eyck and Phoebe Edgar, silver spoons. Said £600 is to be in the hands of William Edgar. To the 4 daughters of my brother, Henry, deceased, namely, Sarah, Mary, Susannah and Mariam, £50. Brother, Cornelius, some apparel. Presbyterian Church at Rahway, £50. Real estate to be sold. Daughters, Janet Tan Eyck and Phoebe Edgar, residue. Executors—sons-in-law, Richard Ten Eyck and William Edgar. Witnesses—Jacob Bond, Benjamin Harris, Jonathan Ford Morris. Proved April 20, 1789. Lib. 31, p. 400.

**1787, Feb. 20. Baker, Thomas,** of Elizabeth Township, Essex Co., yeoman; will of. Son, William, has had his share by deeds and otherwise. Wife, Martha, all the goods she had when I married her, and £6 a year. Granddaughter, Hannah Baker, daughter to Daniel Baker, deceased, some household goods. Grandsons, Daniel Baker and Aron Baker, the land to the southeast of the road. To Daniel Baker the land northwest of the road. Executors—neighbors, Thomas Osborn and Moses Miller. Witnesses—Samuel Pangburn, Smith Osborn, Richard Marsh. Proved March 17, 1787.
1787, March 15. Inventory, £66.8.9, made by Samuel Potter and Benjamin Bonnel. Lib. 29, p. 406.

**1788, March 1. Baker, Thomas,** of Wallpack Township, Sussex Co., millwright; will of. Land to be sold. Wife, Ann, ⅓ of real and personal estate. Children, Jonathan, Henry, William, Daniel, John and Joshua, Mary, Sarah, Ann and Jude, rest of estate. Executors—son, Jonathan, and Nicholas Depue. Witnesses—Abraham Vancampen, Robert Lockerby, Henry Biles. Proved May 27, 1788.
1788, May 26. Inventory, £483.14.6, made by Abraham Vancampen and Robert Lockerby. Lib. 31, p. 147.

**1787, June 29. Baker, William,** of the Parish of Turkey, Essex Co.; will of. Wife, Rachel, some goods and £10 yearly. Eldest son, Thomas, hat, coat and shirts. Son, Abner, watch, horse and gun. Third son, Nathan, my Psalm book and coat. My youngest son, John, silver buckles. Nathan and John to be put to trades. Daughter, Sarah, pots, cow and the Great Bible; also the goods her mother (my wife) has use of. I also give Sarah £50, when she is 18. Land to be sold. Sons, Thomas, Abner, Nathan and John, the residue. Executors—friends, Nathaniel Littell and Mathias Sayr. Witnesses—Benjamin Pettit, Daniel Maxwell, Hannah Potter. Proved July 14, 1787.
Lib. 29, p. 377.

**1787, Feb. 25. Baldwin, Jabez,** of Essex Co. Int. Adm'x—Phebe Baldwin. Fellowbondsman—Joseph Davis; both of said Co.
1787, Feb. 3. Inventory, £40.3.0, made by Samuel Dodd and Joseph Davis. Lib. 29, p. 417.

**1786, May 2. Ball, David,** of Essex Co. Int. Adm'r—Jonathan I. Dayton. Fellowbondsman—David Ross; both of Elizabeth Borough, said Co. Lib. 28, p. 425.

**1790, July 11. Ballinger, Patience,** of Deptford Township, Gloucester Co., widow of Isaac; will of. To my nieces, the daughters of my sister, Hannah Clement, deceased, namely, Casandria, Ann, Elizabeth, Ruth and Sarah, £100 each. Nieces, the daughters of my sister, Mary Hackney, deceased, namely, Ann and Mary, £10 each. Nephew, Jacob Burrough, £10. Nephew and niece, John and Hannah Albertson, £10 each. To Elizabeth Cattle, daughter of Jonas Cattle, £20. To Sarah Ward, daughter of James Ward, my case of drawers, which were late the property of said James. Sister, Casandria Burrough, £50. To Elizabeth Bell, £10. To Woodbury Monthly Meeting, £10. Sister-in-law, Sarah Davis, and her son, James, all the rents they owe on the ground they occupy. Sisters, Sarah Webster, Keturah Townsend and Ann Jenings, and my cousin, Sarah Crimm, wife of Peter Crim, rest of estate. Executors—brother-in-law, Jacob Jenings, and my kinsman, Peter Crim. Witnesses—Joseph Clement, Thomas Redman, Proved Nov. 24, 1790.

1790, Nov. 24. Renunciation by Jacob Jenings.

1790, Nov. 24. Inventory, £1,039.17.10, made by John Tatum and James Whitall, Jr. Lib. 31, p. 421.

**1789, Sept. 10. Barkley, Robert,** of Bedminster, Somerset Co.; will of. Real and personal estate to be sold. Son, John, £30 and all apparel. Grandson, Samuel Little, son of my daughter, Isbel, £15, when 21. Daughter, Elizabeth, a horse. Daughter, Martha, a horse. Residue to my wife, my 4 daughters hereafter named, and to the sons and daughters that are now living (except Samuel Little, who is now provided for), or may be born of my daughter, Isbel; namely, wife, Christian, ⅙; daughter, Nancy, wife of John King, ⅙; sons and daughters now living, and may be born of my daughter, Isbel, the wife of Robert Little (except Samuel) ⅙ part, including the £15 to the elder brother, Samuel Little; to my daughter, Rebecca, wife of Thomas Walker, ⅙; my daughter, Elizabeth, wife of Benyou Dunham, ⅙; and to my daughter, Martha, wife of David Dunham, ⅙ part. Executors—son, John, my brother, Hugh, and Robert Blair. Witnesses—John Vk. Taylor, John Todd, James Cuff. Proved Feb. 6, 1790.

1790, Jan. 27. Inventory, £316.18.2, made by Thomas Berry and Thomas Alston. Lib. 31, p. 506.

**1790, Oct. 14. Barnet, William,** of Elizabeth Town, Essex Co.; will of. Brother, Olliver Barnet, all my real estate and the personal, after the debts are paid. He is to be liberal towards my wife, child and grandchildren. Executor—brother, Olliver. Witnesses—Abraham Clark, Tenrub Price, J. L. Chr. D'Anterroches. Proved Dec. 28, 1790. Lib. 30, p. 346.

**1789, June 18. Barrack, Peter,** of Amwell Township, Hunterdon Co. Int. Adm'r—Samuel Williamson. Fellowbondsman—Peter Williamson; both of said place.

1785, Oct. 17. Inventory, £83.10.7, made by John Lake and John Buchannan.

CALENDAR OF WILLS—1786-1790   19

1791, June 24. Account by Adm'r.
1803, Aug. (1st Tuesday). The Adm'r was cited to appear, and answer Tunis Case, and Sarah, his wife, Samuel Barrick, Mary Barrick and Elizabeth Barrick, the widow and heirs at law, and to render an Account. Lib. 32, p. 56.

**1790, April 9. Barracliff, John,** of Greenwich, Cumberland Co.; will of. Daughter, Ruth Shints, a case of drawers that was her mother's, and £150. To my old faithful housekeeper, Elenor Whitteker, £15. Son, George, rest of my estate. Executor—son, George. Witnesses—John Bacon, John Bacon, Jr., Job Bacon, Jr. Proved Oct. 12, 1790.
1790, Sept. 28. Inventory, £1,046.19.0, made by John Miller and Richard Wood, Jr. Lib. 30, p. 274.

**1788, Dec. 30. Barret, Jesse,** of Gloucester Co. Ward. Son of Elijah Barrot, of said Co., deceased. Said Ward makes choice of William Beaston as his Guardian. Witnesses—Richard Davis and David Davis.
1788, Dec. 30. Guardian—William Beaston, of Egg Harbor. Fellowbondsman—Thomas Doughty; both of said Co. Lib. 31, p. 38.

**1786, April 28. Barret, Sarah,** of Cumberland Co. Int. Adm'r—Caleb Barratt. Fellowbondsman—James Randolph; both of said Co. Lib. 28, p. 181.
**1788, Jan. 15. Bassett, William,** of Hunterdon Co. Int. Adm'r—John Bassett. Fellowbondsman—Isaac Bassett; both of Bethlehem, said Co., yeomen. Lib. 31, p. 141.

**1787, Nov. 17. Bassett, Davis,** of Manington, Salem Co., yeoman; will of. Daughter, Beuley Brown, the 100 acres that did belong to my father, Elisha Bassett, in Piles Grove Township, Daughter, Abigail Humphries, 100 acres of the plantation where I live. Son, Josiah, rest of land where I live, of 250 acres. My personal estate to said children. Executor—son, Josiah. Witnesses—James Riley, Christopher Morris, Richard Smith, Jr. Proved Jan. 25, 1788.
1787, Dec. 21. Inventory, £810.1.11, made by John Barnes, Jr., and Daniel Bassett, Jr. Lib. 31, p. 40.

**1786, June 22. Bassett, Elisha,** of Pilesgrove Township, Salem Co., yeoman; will of. Son, Davis, the place where I live, and the meadow on Salem Creek, containing 100 acres; subject to the payment of £100 to my grandsons, Joseph Bassett and David Bassett. Son, Isaac, £10 and my apparel. Daughter, Elizabeth Davis, £50. Granddaughters, Grace Whithers and Ann Bassett, £10 each. Grandson, Andrew Miller, £10. To Rebecca Barber, £5. Personal estate to said children. Executor, son, Davis. Witnesses—Charity Dunlap, Thomas Davis, Jacob Davis. Proved Jan. 6, 1787.
1787, Jan. 5. Inventory, £416.9.4, made by Jacob Davis and John Barnes. Lib. 29, p. 136.

**1787, Sept. 15. Beach, John,** of Mendham, Morris Co. Int. Adm'r —Benjamin Freeman, Jr. Fellowbondsman—Jacob Arnold; both of Morristown, said Co. Witnesses—Abraham Canfield, Jr. and William Campfield.

1787, Sept. 11. Renunciation by Sarah Beach, in favor of Benjamin Freeman, Jr. Witnesses—William Leddel and Jacob Arnold.
1787, Sept. 14. Renunciation by Gabriel Beach, in favor of Benjamin Freeman, Jr. Lib. 29, p. 474.

**1787, Sept. 24. Beach, Sarah,** of Morristown, Morris Co. Ward. Daughter of Epenetus Beach, of said place, deceased. Said Ward makes choice of William D'Hart, as her Guardian.
1787, Nov. 10. Guardian—William D'Hart, of said place. Fellowbondsman—John Ralsten, of said Co. Lib. 29, p. 475.

**1790, April 13. Beck, Aaron,** of Burlington Co. Int. Adm'rs—John Scholey Beck and Robert Sherrad. Fellowbondsman—Isaiah Reed; all of said Co. Witness—Daniel Coate.
1790, April 12. Inventory, £27, made by Daniel Coate and Thomas Smith. Lib. 32, p. 97.

**1786, Jan. 24. Beck, Aasa,** of New Hanover, Burlington Co. Int. Adm'r—William Warner, of Monmouth Co. Fellowbondsman—Joseph Lamb, of Burlington Co.
1786, Jan. 21. Renunciation by the widow, Hannah Beck. Witness—Mary Beck.
1786, Jan. 25. Inventory, £133.12.6, made by Tanton Earl and Thomas Earl. Lib. 28, p. 73.

**1788, May 31. Bedell, John,** of Essex Co.; will of. Wife, Martha, use of all moveable and fast estate, till my daughter, Catharine, is 10 years of age; after which time my widow is to have the use of ⅓ of my estate. Daughter, Chateren, the rest of estate, when she is 18; but, if she die, then her estate I give to my brother, Abraham, and sister, Elenar, as follows: to sons of Abraham and Elenar, ⅔ of said estate, and to their daughters, ⅓. Executors—wife, Martha, Nathaniel Littell and my brother, Abraham Bedell. Witnesses—Abraham Rutan, Ezekiel Sayre, John Hole. Proved June 10, 1788.
Lib. 38, p. 91.

**1789, March 9. Beekman, John,** of Roxbury, Morris Co., inn holder; will of. All real and personal estate to be sold, and money divided among my wife, Ariony, and sons, Cornelius, Garret and John. Executor—friend, John Hardenburgh, of Somerset Co. Witnesses—John Castner, Anna Tunison, Malm. McCourney. Proved June 13, 1789.
1789, May 6. Inventory, £1,116.14.6, made by Philip Van Arsdalen and Derick Middagh. Lib. 30, p. 227.

**1790, June 3. Beers, Daniel,** of Mendham Township, Morris Co. Int. Adm'rs—Azubah Beers and John Mills. Fellowbondsman—Joseph Beers; all of said Co. Witnesses—Silas Condict and Benjamin Pitney.
1790, May 24. Inventory, £890.15.5, made by Silas Condict and Joseph Beers. Lib. 30, p. 480.

**1786, April 8. Beesley, Ann,** of Lower Alloways Creek Township, Salem Co., widow; will of. Son, Johnson Beesley, the plantation in tenure of Isaac Stow, which was my maiden land, of 445 acres; also plantation where I live, that was bought of Daniel Hall. Daughter, Ann Stow, plantation where Yost Moncy lives, of 50 acres; also 45

CALENDAR OF WILLS—1786-1790 21

acres, called the Sawmill tract. Granddaughter, Hannah McLean, daughter of Sarah McLean, ½ of the plantation formerly Daniel Hall's, now in possession of Eaton Smith and Ananias Clark, when she is 21; but, if she die under 21, then to the children of my daughter, Catharine Smith; and my brother, Robert Johnson, shall have the care of the premises for the use of Hannah McLean and not her father. The other ½ of the plantation before mentioned to my daughter, Catharine Smith, the same to her and said Hannah McLean. To son, Johnson's daughter, Elizabeth, a table cloth. Executors—brother, Robert Johnson, and Job Butcher. Witnesses—John Stow, Abel Smith, William Smith. Proved Dec. 27, 1786.
1789, April 5. Adm'r—Eaton Smith. Fellowbondsman—Maurice Welsh; both of said Co. Both Executors have renounced.
1786, Dec. 18. Inventory, £283.1.10, made by Andrew Yorke and Edward Hall. Lib. 31, p. 354.

**1786, Nov. 6. Bell, Jabeth,** of Roxbury, Morris Co., yeoman; will of. Son, Abraham, the place where I live, except that the line is to run through, as Mr. King's fence now runs, to Stephen Brown's line, in order that my daughters, Hannah Kelsey, Mehitabel Clauson, Unice Moor, Susannah Heaton, Elizabeth Fearchild, Deliverance Brown, Catharine Coleman and Abigail Bell have the strip of land between the said line and Mr. Terry. To Samuel Salmon, £7, when 21. Executors—son, Abraham, and my son-in-law, Stephen Brown. Witnesses —Joshua Cook, Martha Cook, Malm. McCourney. Proved June 2, 1789.
1789, May 26. Inventory, £52.3.6, made by Nathaniel Terrey and Nathan Luse. Lib. 30, p. 225.

**1787, Jan. 30. Bell, John,** of Hunterdon Co.; will of. Wife, Abbigal, and my son, William, all real and personal estate, divided in such manner as the said Abigail and William Tenant Bell shall think proper. Executors—wife, Abigal, and son, William T. Bell, when he comes of age. Witnesses—Bernard Hanlon, James Mitchell, William Addams. Proved Nov. 24, 1788.
1788, Nov. 27. Inventory, £321.5.2, made by Bernard Hanlon and Samuel Anderson.
1789, Feb. 27. Inventory, £390.8.10, made by Samuel Anderson and Bernard Hanlon. "Money due John Bell as taken from the Ledger, by Isaac Marshall; William Mason; Thomas Wells; James Davis; Henry Wells; John Rogers; Isaac Sapp; John Done; William Thompson (Pilot); Joseph Conner (Pilot); William Green (Sailor); Dr. Henry (William); James Polk (son of James); Sarah Polk (widow of James); Col. George Corbin (of Va.); Capt. William Keath (of Philadelphia); Martin Pendergrass; Dr. William Smith. George Mitchell.
1791, March 26. Abigail Bell supposed there were two bonds in the hands of her brother, George Mitchell, but she believes they do not exist.
1789, Oct. 3. Account by Abigail Bell, Executrix.
1793, Aug. 26. Account by Abigail Bell, Executrix. "House and lot in Kent Co. was sold by Sheriff." Lib. 31, p. 94.

**1789, Jan. 23. Bennet, Idah,** of Monmouth Co. Ward. Daughter of William Bennet, of said Co. Said Ward has personal estate, bequeathed to her by her deceased grandfather, and she makes choice of her father, William Bennit, as her Guardian.

1789, Jan. 23. Guardian—William Bennit, of Middletown, said Co. Witness—Euphamia Clayton. Lib. 30, p. 189.

**1787, April 4. Bennit, William,** of Manasquan, Shrewsbury Township, Monmouth Co., yeoman; will of. Eldest son, William, 5 shillings. Son, Benjamin, £30. Daughter, Thankfull Bennit, £10. Daughter, Rachel Bennit, £10. Wife, Margret, rest of estate during her life. Executors—friends, David Cortis and Joseph Borden. Witnesses—Samuel Lawrence, Thomas Curtis, Thomas Tilton. Proved May 1, 1788.
1788, May 1. Adm'r—Benjamin Jackson. Fellowbondsman—Edward Patterson Cook; both of said Co. Witness—Peter Knott. Joseph Borden refused to act as Executor, and David Curtis is deceased, and the widow refused to act as Adm'x, and requested that Benjamin Jackson should act.
1789, Jan. 8. Inventory, £65.2.11, made by Lewis Ellison, John Curtis and David Brewer. Lib. 30, p. 82.

**1790, Sept. 16. Bennit, William,** of South Ward of Perth Amboy, Middlesex Co.; will of. Wife, Mary, household goods, and use of land to support my son, William. Son, William, all estate; but, if he die, then to my brother Hendrick's son, William, and my brother Jacob's son, William, and my brother-in-law Walter Hires' son, William. When my son comes of age, he is to pay to the three daughters of my wife, namely, Catharine, Altee and Sarah, £50. Executors—brother, Henderick, and friend, John Morgan. Witnesses—Isaac Buckelew, Joshua Warne, P. Schenck. Proved Oct. 21, 1790.
1790, Oct. 26. Inventory, made by William Hillyer and Joshua Warne. Lib. 30, p. 511.

**1787, March 14. Berny, Peter,** of Hunterdon Co. Int. Adm'r—Ephraim Darby. Fellowbondsman—John Reed. Witness—Peter Hunt.
1787, March 14. Inventory, $94.50, made by John Reed and Gershom Lee. Lib. 29, p. 297.

**1787, Jan. 3. Berry, Samuel,** of Morris Co.; will of. Wife to have estate during her life. Eldest daughter, Catalinety Berry, land where I live, and the lot south of Beavar Dam Brook, and woodland on the mountain, which I bought in partnership with Martin Vanduyn. Daughters, Sarah Roomer and Jemima Bartolf, 100 acres on the mountain, called Catluss' plantation. Executors—said daughters. Witnesses—Abraham Ryerson, John Ryerse, Sarah Ryerson. Proved Jan. 18, 1790.
1789, Dec. 22. Inventory, £471.4.0, made by Albert Terhune and Thomas Dods. Lib. 30, p. 440.

**1789, June 11. Bertolf, Abraham,** of Hackensack, Bergen Co.; will of. Wife, Marregreetie, use of real and personal estate. Son, Gyles, that part of the farm where he lives. Son, John, the rest of the farm. Daughter, Marietie, wife of Henry Wannemaker, £120. Daughter, Marretie Wannamaker, a negro wench which she now has. Executors—sons, Gyles and John, and my son-in-law, Henry Wanemaker. Witnesses—John Outwater, Adolph Waldron, Isaac Krank. Proved Jan. 12, 1790. Lib. 31, p. 537.

**1786, Dec. 12. Betson, Mary,** of Monmouth Co. Int. Adm'r—Jacob West. Fellowbondsman—James Wilson; both of said Co.
1786, Nov. 7. Inventory, £16.19.0, made by Benjamin Van Cleaf and James Wilson. Lib. 28, p. 291.

**1787, Nov. 6. Bevins, Matthew,** of Burlington Co. Int. Adm'x—Ann Bevins. Fellowbondsman—Lewis Evans; both of said Co.
Lib. 29, p. 78.

**1790, March 28. Bilderback, Charles,** of Manington Township, Salem Co., yeoman; will of. Eldest son, Charles, 2 horses and 2 cows, and rest of moveable estate to my wife, Sarah, and Susannah, John, Sarah and Malcom Bilderbacks, my children. My share from the sales of my brother's estate in Delaware to be put to use till my sons, John and Malcom, are 21, when they are to have the same. Eldest son, Charles, plantation where I live, of 153 acres. Executors—wife, Sarah, and my son, Charles. Witnesses—Clayton Robins, Robert Murphy, Jonathan Bilderback. Proved Dec. 16, 1790.
1790, April 26. Inventory, £1,251.15.5, made by Benjamin Shourds.
Lib. 31, p. 485.

**1789, July 8. Billings, William,** of Cape May Co. Int. Adm'r—Joshua Billings. Fellowbondsman—Philip Hand; both of said Co. Witnesses—Sarah Hand and Betsy Griffing.
1789, Oct. 19. Inventory, £151.14.9, made by Philip Hand and Benjamin Stites. Lib. 31, p. 370.

**1787, Oct. 18. Bills, Silvanus,** of Monmouth Co. Ward. Son of Thomas Bills, of said Co., deceased. Petition of Sarah Parker, mother of said minor, who is 11 years of age, praying for Thomas Parker to be made Guardian.
1787, Oct. 18. Guardian—Thomas Parker. Fellowbondsman—Joseph Thomson; both of said Co. Witness—Jonathan Combs.
Lib. 29, p. 341.

**1788, Jan. 19. Bird, Joseph,** of Elizabeth Borough, Essex Co.; will of. Wife, Ursula, the goods she had when we were married and £100. Son-in-law, Samuel Force, £20. Son, Jeremiah, the use of 10 acres of my plantation, with the house where he now lives, which is to bind the land of Joseph Lee, William Mills, John Craig, Hambleton Robinson and the highway; and, after the death of Jeremiah, the 10 acres are to be sold, and, of the money, I give ½ part to my daughter, Sarah, the wife of Samuel Force, Jr.; ⅛ to my grandson, Joseph, son of my son, Joseph, deceased, and the other ⅜ to 3 of my grandchildren, children of my son, Jeremiah, namely: Abigail, Charles and Samuel Bird. If Elizabeth, the wife of my son, Jeremiah, should outlive him, then I give to her the use of the 10 acres, while she is the widow of Jeremiah. Rest of real estate to be sold, or rented out till my youngest grandson, Joseph, is 21, and of the money I give ½ to my daughter, Sarah, wife of Samuel Force, Jr.; ⅛ to my grandson, Joseph Bird, and the other ⅜ to my grandchildren, Abigail, Charles and Samuel, the children of my son, Jeremiah. Executors—friends, Amos Morss and Anthony Morss. Witnesses—William Fletcher, Joseph Hatfield, David Jones. Proved Dec. 16, 1788.
1788, Nov. 29. Inventory, made by Timothy Craig and Jeremiah Clark. Lib. 33, p. 495.

**1789, March 24. Bishop, Isaac,** of Piscataway Township, Middlesex Co. Ward. Son of Moses Bishop, of said place, deceased. Said Ward makes choice of Samuel Fitz Randolph as his Guardian.
1789, March 24. Guardian—Samuel Randolph, of said place. Fellowbondsban—Dugal Ayers, of said Co. Lib. 31, p. 396.

**1789, July 29. Bishop, Robert,** of Great Egg Harbor, Gloucester Co. Int. Adm'r—Joseph Bishop. Fellowbondsman—Jonathan Lippincott; both of Burlington Co.
1789, Sept. 11. Inventory, £21.15.7, made by Elias Hammitt and Jonathan Lippincott. Lib. 30, p. 137.

**1788, Aug. 29. Blackwell, John,** of Burlington Co. Int. Adm'x— Ann Blackwell. Fellowbondsman—William Peter Sprague; both of City of Burlington. Lib. 30, p. 58.

**1787, May 2. Blair, Thomas,** of Knowlton, Sussex Co. Int. Adm'x —Jane Blair, of said place. Fellowbondsman—James Todd, of Hardwick, said Co. Witnesses—James Blair and Thomas Anderson.
1787, April 11. Inventory, £85.17.6, made by Samuel Kirkindall and Andrew Wagner. Lib. 29, p. 490.

**1787, June 22. Blaw, Michael,** of Somerset Co.; will of. Wife, Mary, the land I bought of Cornelius Blaw, while my widow. Rest of real estate to be sold, and money given to sons, John, Samuel, Michael and Cornelius, and my daughters, Mary Blaw, Sarah Blaw, Leah Blaw and Elizabeth Blaw; when they are of age. Executors —John Voorhees, Sr., of Blomborough, Jacob Schanck and David Covenhoven. Witnesses—William Bell, Peter Van Voorhees, Jost Hageman. Proved Aug. 3, 1787.
1787, June 30. Inventory, £260.4.3, made by Richard Stout and Hendrick Sortor. Lib. 29, p. 427.

**1786, March 20. Blew, Michael,** of Somerset Co. Ward. Son of Michael Blew, of said Co., deceased. Said Ward makes choice of David Covenhoven, as his Guardian.
1786, March 20. Guardian—David Covenhoven. Fellowbondsman— Isaac Blue; both of said Co. Witnesses—Getty Frelinghuysen and Fred Frelinghuysen. Lib. 29, p. 197.

**1789, Feb. 3. Blower, Francis,** of Hunterdon Co. Int. Adm'r— Isaac Barnes. Fellowbondsman—Maskell Ewing; both of Trenton, said Co. Witness—Isaac DeCow. Lib. 32, p. 54.

**1786, May 9. Bogart, Jacob,** of Bridgewater, Somerset Co. Ward. Son of Gisbert Bogart, of said place, deceased. Said Ward makes choice of Andrew Van Middlesworth, as his Guardian.
1786, May 9. Guardian—Andrew V. Middlesworth, of Hillsborough. Fellowbondsman—Cornelius Simonson; both of said Co. Witness— George Van Nist. Lib. 29, p. 197.

**1786, July 28. Boggs, Elizabeth and William.** Wards. Children of William Boggs, deceased. Petition of Ann Allen, the mother of said Wards, praying for Richard Kinnan, who is near of kin, to be appointed Guardian of said minors.

CALENDAR OF WILLS—1786-1790   25

1786, July 28. Guardian—Richard Kinnan. Fellowbondsman—Nathaniel Brittain; both of Monmouth Co. Witness—Richard Crawford, Jr. Lib. 28, p. 295.

**1786, June 14. Boice, Leonard,** of Piscataway, Middlesex Co. Int. Adm'x—Mary Boice. Fellowbondsman—Jacob Suidam; both of said Co.
1786, July 4. Inventory, made by David Coriell and Joel Dunn. Lib. 28, p. 341.

**1789, Feb. 19. Bokonnon, George,** of Hardyston, Sussex Co. Int. Adm'r—Caleb Fish. Fellowbondsman—James Brodrick; both of Newtown, said Co. Witness—Francis Price.
1789, Feb. 17. Inventory, £19.0.6, made by Francis Price and George Givens. Lib. 30, p. 200.

**1786, Sept. 12. Bollen, John,** of Hopewell, Hunterdon Co., innkeeper. Int. Adm'x—Unis Bollen. Fellowbondsman—Benjamin Yard.
1786, Sept. 13. Inventory, £300.8.6, made by Thomas Bullman, John Welling, Jr. and Ely Moore.
1792, Aug. 4. Account by Unis Bollen, Adm'x. Lib. 28, p. 245.

**1788, Jan. 23. Bonnel, Thomas,** of Hanover Township, Morris Co.; will of. Son, Henry, ½ of my land, joining Daniel Burnet and John Genung. Son, James, £20. Son, Benjamin, was given the house and land I bought of David Ward. Son, Joseph, rest of land. Daughters, Hannah Rague, Phebe Bonnel and Affa Bonnel, my moveable estate. Doct. John Regue is to have none I gave to Hannah. Executor—Son, Joseph. Witnesses—Aaron Carter, Moses Genung, John Roberts. Proved May 11, 1790.
1790, April 28. Inventory, £71.16.8, made by Gershom' Norris and Benjamin Genung. Lib. 30, p. 449.

**1788, May 28. Bonnell, James,** of Essex Co., yeoman; will of. Wife, Sarah, household goods and riding chair, and use of my negro. Sons, Stephen, Abraham and Daniel, plantation where I live; Stephen's part to be along land of John Smith Shotwell, of 80 acres; Abraham is to come next, and then Daniel. Grandson, Jonathan Price, land I bought of my son, Abraham, April 29, 1760. Grandson, Jacob Hearty, a note I have against David Broadwell, dated April 17, 1781. Granddaughter, Joanna Price, £10. Daughters, Jemima Hearty, Sarah Wilson, Abigail Blackford and Mary Blackford, £20 each. Residue to my said children. Executors—friend, William Darby, and my son, Abraham. Witnesses—William Elstun, John Marsh, William Coles. Proved Oct. 16, 1788.
1788, Oct. 1. Inventory, £289.18.5, made by John Darby and William Elstun. Lib. 36, p. 482.

**1790, June 17. Bordan, David,** of Bergen Co.; will of. Wife, Carstina, all real and personal estate while my widow. Son, John, some tools. Grandchildren, David Van Derbeck, Isaac Vanderbeck and John Van Derbeck, the house and lot where I live, they paying to my granddaughter, Annaetye, their sister, £25. My daughters and granddaughters, £110. My daughters and granddaughters are, Eva, Helena Giesy Van Saen and Rachel Bennit, who are to have the rest of

estate. The children of my daughter, Grietye, deceased, to have an equal share. Son, John, rest of lands. My father-in-law, Daniel Romyn, deceased, allotted to me a part of quitrent on land from Jury Westervelt, which my children and grandchildren are to pay. Executors—son, John, and Lucas Van Saen. Witnesses—John Romyne, Margarietje Romyne, Aert Cuyper. Proved Sept. 21, 1790.
Lib. 30, p. 248.

**1790, May 7. Borden, Joel,** of Shrewsbury, Monmouth Co.; will of. My plantation at Squancom, where I live, to be sold, and the money divided into 11 parts, 8 of which I give to my wife, Elizabeth, and my children, Lydia, Samuel and Sarah, and the other 3 parts to my son, Joel. My youngest daughters, Elizabeth, Mary and Hannah, the land near Rumson, that joins John Borden, of 23 acres, when they are 18. Executors—daughter, Lydia Borden, and my friend, Benjamin Corlies. Witnesses—Philip Cooper, Ezekiel Johnson, Peter Cook. Proved Sept. 7, 1790.
1790, Sept. 6. Inventory, £770.1.5, made by Ezekiel Johnson and Edward Patterson Cooke. Lib. 30, p. 385.

**1788, Nov. 15. Borden, Joseph, Jr.,** of Burlington Co. Int. Adm'r —Robert Dougherty. Fellowbondsman—Abraham Winner; both said Co.
1788, Nov. 13. Renunciation by Mary Borden, the widow, and Joseph Borden and Eliza Borden, the parents, in favor of Robert Dougherty. Witnesses—Joseph Potts and Mary Potts.
1788, Nov. 19. Inventory, £132.1.7, name by Joseph Potts and John Butler. Lib. 30, p. 60.

**1789, April 13. Borden, Richard,** of Gloucester Township, Gloucester Co.; will of. I give ½ of an acre of land, where the buryingground is now erected, for the use of burying, where I desire to be buried. Wife, Sarah, the goods she brought when we married; also a bond against Joseph Marshal; also £75; also the rent that is coming on a lease from Zacheus Test I give to her to bring up her children. Daughter, Rachel Borden, the plantation which my father purchased of John Tice, and 9 acres which I bought of Moses Branson, except that which is given for a burying-ground. Daughter, Hannah Borden, that land which I bought of David Herley, except that which I sold to Joseph Hillman. Daughter, Rebekah Borden, that land in Burlington Co. that my father gave me by his will. Daughter, Elizabeth Borden, ½ of the land in Burlington Co. which I bought of Joseph Brackney. Rest of estate to be sold. Executors—Joseph Burrough and Thomas Thorne, who are to be Guardians of my children. Witnesses—Moses Branson, Isaac Tomlinson, Ephraim Tomlinson. Proved Oct. 20, 1789.
1789, Oct. 19. Inventory, £918.5.0, made by Ephraim Tomlinson and Moses Branson. Lib. 30, p. 118.

**1788, July 25. Borden, Thomas,** of Shrewsbury, Monmouth Co.; will of. Wife, Mary, household goods and Bible. Granddaughter, Mary Borden, a hatchet. Son, Phillip, a bed. Son, Thomas, the use of the lot I bought of Thomas Chambers, if he lives on it; but, if he moves off, then to son, Thomas. Grandsons, Aaron, Amos and Thomas Borden, £5 each, when 21. Executors—son, Thomas, Thomas Morford

CALENDAR OF WILLS—1786-1790         27

and John Scott, son of Samuel. Witnesses—Mauritz DeHaert, Jr., Ann Webley, John Hance. Proved Sept. 6, 1788.
1788, Sept. 2. Inventory, £205.2.0, made by John Hance and William Pintard. Lib. 30, p. 93.

**1790, June 8. Borton, Josiah,** of Evesham Township, Burlington Co. Int. Adm'rs—Caleb Borton and Joshua Borton. Fellowbondsman—John Borton; all of said place. Witnesses—Thomas Adams and James Kinsey, Jr.
1790, June 7. Inventory, £319.3.3, made by John Borton and Caleb Austin. Lib. 32, p. 96.

**1790, Sept. 20. Bowen, Dan,** of Deerfield Township, Cumberland Co.; will of. Son, Mark, the plantation where he lives, of 167 acres. Son, Dan, the plantation where he lives, of 140 acres; also my cedar swamp on Green Branch, of 5 acres. Son, Abraham, and Abraham Robinson, the plantation where I live, of 200 acres, and my son, Abraham, is to take the west side, and pay to my son, Ephraim, £6, and to my daughter, Ruhamey Moore, £12. Grandsons, Hosea Robinson, Eli Robinson and Ellis Robinson, £5 each. Daughter, Rebeckah Robinson, £10. Daughters, Mary Nickol, Rebeckah Smith and Rachel Robinson, rest of moveable estate. Sons, Mark and Dan, hold their plantations by deeds of gift, which I confirm. Executors—son, Abraham, and Abraham Robinson. Witnesses—John Carll, Phebe Nickol, Ephraim Lummis. Proved Nov. 15, 1790.
1790, Nov. 9. Inventory, £100.13.3, made by Jonathan Harris and James Hood. Lib. 30, p. 277.

**1786, March 17. Bowen, Mason,** of Cumberland Co. Ward. Son of Enoch Bowen, of said Co., deceased. Said Ward having real and personal estate, makes choice of Amos Westcott as his Guardian.
1786, March 17. Guardian—Amos Westcott, yeoman. Fellowbondsman—John Bateman; both of said Co. Lib. 28, p. 183.

**1788, Dec. 12. Bowen, Samuel, Sr.,** of Stow Creek Township, Cumberland Co.; will of. Son, Samuel, 5 shillings. Daughter, Mary Loper, 5 shillings. Granddaughter, Lydea Bowen, one shilling and sixpence. Wife, Rebeckah, ½ my moveable estate, and the other ½ to my daughter, Rebeckah, when she is 17, but it is to be put to interest till she is 10, and then my wife may have the use of it till Rebeckah is 17. Grandson, Samuel Bowen, some use of the personal estate. Executors—wife, Rebeckah, and her uncle, John Mills, of Lower Alloways Creek Township. Witnesses—John Wood, Zacheus Brown, David Ayars. Proved Jan. 14, 1789.
1789, Jan. 10. Inventory, £127.9.4, made by Uriah Bacon and Jacob Brown. Lib. 30, p. 158.

**1790, Oct. 12. Bowers, John,** of Hanover, Morris Co. Ward. Son of Dr. John Bowers, of said place, deceased. Said Ward makes choice of John Cobb as his Guardian.
1790, Oct. 12. Guardian—John Cobb, of said place. Fellowbondsman—David Ford, of said Co. Witnesses—Mary Canfield and Jabez Campfield. Lib. 30, p. 481.

**1789, Oct. 13. Bowker, Jemima,** of Burlington Co. Int. Adm'r—
Isaac Farnham. Fellowbondsman—Uriah Thompson; both of New
Hanover Township, said Co.
1789, Oct. 19. Inventory, £33.3.5, made by Job Cook and Joseph
Willits. Lib. 31, p. 318.

**1786, Sept. 30. Bowker, John,** of New Hanover, Burlington Co.;
will of. Grandson, Uriah Bowker, 5 shillings, when 21. Wife,
Jemima, rest of personal and real estate. Executrix—wife, Jemima.
Witnesses—Uriah Thompson, Job Cook, Joseph Lamb, Sr. Proved
May 22, 1789. Lib. 31, p. 259.

**1786, Oct. 6. Bowman, Richard,** of Bridgewater, Somerset Co., cordwainer; will of. Wife, Hannah, all real and personal estate till my
youngest child is of age, and then the lands I give to my sons, Richard, Samuel and Edward. To my 5 daughters, all the moveable
estate; who are Ann, Hannah, Sarah, Elizabeth and Mary. Wife to
have her support. Executors—wife, Hannah, and my sons, Richard
and Samuel. Witnesses—Hendrick Sadam, Richard Drake, Jacob
Ten Eyk. Proved Dec. 9, 1789.
1789, Nov. 16. Inventory, £94.19.6, made by Jacob Ten Eyk, Sr., and
John Herriot. Lib. 31, p. 396.

**1788, Sept. 20. Bowne, Peter,** of Monmouth Co. Int. Adm'r—
Samuel Bowne. Fellowbondsman—Hendrick Hendrickson; both of
said Co. Witness—Rachel Henderson. Lib. 30, p. 103.

**1788, May 2. Bradway, Sarah,** of Elsinborough, Salem Co.; will of.
Son, Thomas Bradway, house and 6 acres in Salem. Grandson, Aaron
Bradway, house and lot on east side of Salem Street. Son, Edward
Bradway, £150. Son-in-law, Aaron Bradway, £25. Daughters, Sarah
Wadington and Hannah Bradway, rest of estate; except my 2 sons,
Richard and Hill Smith, and my daughter, Elizabeth Clement, to have
5 shillings each, and also my grandchildren, John, Benjamin, and
Hill Smith, to have 5 shillings. Executors—sons, Edward and Thomas
Bradway. Witnesses—Hannah Nicholson, Joseph Hacket, Peter Dole.
Proved May 20, 1788. Lib. 31, p. 41.

**1790, March 25. Brant, John,** of Essex Co. Int. Adm'rs—Sarah
Brant, widow of John Brant, deceased, Daniel Johnson and Edward
Earle. Fellowbondsman—Eliphalet Johnson; all of said Co. Witness
—Joseph Brown, Jr. Lib. 30, p. 360.

**1789, Feb. 16. Bratton,** of Mansfield Woodhouse, Sussex Co. Int.
Adm'r — William Harrison, of Newtown. Fellowbondsman — David
Bratton, of Hardyston; both of said Co.
1789, Feb. 27. Inventory, £67.1.9, made by Newbold Woolston and
Andrew Miller. Lib. 30, p. 201.

**1787, May 9. Bray, Andrew,** of Kingwood Township, Hunterdon
Co., tanner; will of. Wife, Sarah, £12 yearly, and goods and livestock. Son, John, ⅙ of my lands in Pennsylvania. Daughter, Anne
Jones, a discharge of all the debts against Thomas Jones. Daughter,
Huldah Commons, books. Daughter, Sarah Shaw, ⅓ of my lands in
Pennsylvania. Daughter, Deliverance Shurts, ⅓ my lands in Penn-

sylvania. Son, Thomas, "all my est Jersey Writs". Grandsons, Andrew Shurts, Andrew Shaw and Tulalon Bray, ⅙ my lands in Pennsylvania. My tanyard in Kingwood to be sold. To Andrew Bray Stout, £5, when 21. Grandson, Andrew Bray, 30 shillings. Executors —son, John Bray, of Lebanon, and Robert Cummins. Witnesses— Jesse Hall, Jacob Hall, John Richards. Proved July 29, 1789.
1789, July 14. Inventory, £1,308.5.10, made by John Snyder and Jonathan Woolverton.
1794, May 6. Account by Executors. Lib. 32, p. 35.

**1790, Aug. 13. Brearley, David, Esq.,** of Trenton, Hunterdon Co.; will of. Son, William, £5. Wife, Elizabeth, ⅓ of the real and personal estate. Son, Joseph, my small sword. Son, David, my Scotch pistols, inlaid with silver. Daughters, Elizabeth Brearley and Esther Brearley, and my sons, Joseph, David and George, rest of estate. Real and personal estate to be sold. Brother-in-law, Joseph Higbee, to be Guardian of my sons. Executors—brother, Joseph, and my friends, James Mott and Joseph Bloomfield. Witnesses—Aaron Dunham, George Woodruff, Ephraim Olden. Proved Sept. 18, 1790.
1790, Sept. 18. Inventory, £1,350.12.8, made by James Ewing and Charles Axford. "3 muskets and 2 bayonets, surveyor's compass, library, McMurray's York Town map". "One month and 16 days pay due the Testator at time of his decease, as Judge, £47.18.4."
Lib. 30, p. 24.

**1788, Nov. 23. Brewer, Abraham,** of New Barbadoes Township, Bergen Co., yeoman; will of. Real estate to be sold. Wife, Catharina, to have a comfortable support out of my estate. Sons, Peter and David, to have what my Executors see fit, when said sons are 21. Executors—wife, Catharina, Necausy Brinkerhoff, Jacob Bogert and Peter Wilson. Witnesses—John Zabriski, Jr., Harmanus Huysen, Peter Demarest. Proved Nov. 1, 1790. Lib. 30, p. 250.

**1787, Sept. 3. Briant, John,** late of Springfield, Essex Co., now of Morris Co.; will of. Eldest son, Cornelius, £5. Grandson, John Briant, son of Cornelius, £15. Son, Andrew, my land in Springfield. Grandson, John Briant, son of Andrew, £20. Daughter, Rachel, wife of Mathias Makuren, and to the heirs of her body by her former husband, £16. Grandson, Jonas Bedford, £10. Daughter, Mary, wife of William Parselow, £10. Daughter, Phebe, wife of Phineas Tuttle, £16. To Cathrine Swaim, for the attention on my deceased wife, £5. Executors—son, Andrew, and Caleb Russell. Witnesses—Andrew Dalrymple, Abiel Wheeler, Uriah Parson. Proved Dec. 29, 1787.
1787, Dec. 29. Inventory, £355.9.1, made by Samuel Gordon and Abiel Wheeler. Lib. 29, p. 469.

**1788, Feb. 26. Briant, Martha,** of Greenwich Township, Gloucester Co., wife of Thomas Bryant; will of. Granddaughter, Kezia Hufey, wife of John Hufey, all my lands, and household goods. Executrix— said Kezia Hufey. Witnesses—David Chew, George Stiles, James Handsey. Proved Feb. 6, 1790. Lib. 31, p. 415.

**1787, Jan. 25. Briggs, Abel,** of Northampton Township, Burlington Co. Int. Adm'rs—John Briggs, George Woolston and Isaac Budd. Fellowbondsmen—John Woolston and Henry Voorhees.

1787, Jan. 23. Inventory, £606.8.0, made by Jacob Woolston and Henry Voorhees. Lib. 29, p. 72.

**1786, Feb. 1. Bright, Thomas,** of Greenwich Township, Gloucester Co. Int. Adm'r—Brown Youngs, of Hopewell Township, Cumberland Co. Fellowbondsman—Joseph Vanneman, of Gloucester Co., yeoman. Witness—Joseph Hugg, Jr. Lib. 28, p. 120.

**1789, March 28. Bright, Valentine,** of Gloucester Co. Int. Adm'r—John Anderson, of Salem Co. Fellowbondsman—George Bright, of Gloucester Co. Witness—Francis Davenport, Surrogate.
Lib. 30, p. 137.

**1786, July 28. Bright, William,** of Downe Township, Cumberland Co.; will of. Wife, Elizabeth, ⅓ of my lands, and all the moveable estate, except £30, which I give to my daughter, Anna Bright. Oldest son, William, the plantation I live on, when he is 20. Son, Levi, the land I bought of David Page. Daughter, Anna, the marsh on Dividing Creek; also the cedar swamp on Morris River. Executors—wife, Elizabeth, and my friend, Gideon Heaton. Witnesses—Gabriel Glan, Jonathan Terry, Ichabod Lore. Proved Jan. 6, 1787.
1786, Sept. 15. Inventory, £259.10.0, made by Gabriel Glan and Jonathan Terry. Lib. 29, p. 175.

**1790, April 13. Briton, Charity,** of Trenton, Hunterdon Co.; will of. Son, Samuel Bellangeau, £50. Nephew, Henry Bellangeau, £50. Daughter, Jane Jenkins, £50. To Ann Bellvill, £30. To Charity, the daughter of my son, Joseph Briton, a bed. To Susannah Briton, wife of my son, Joseph, my girl, Cilinda. Real estate to be sold. To Samuel Bellangeau, Jane Jenkins and Ann Bellville, the residue. My sons, Joseph and Isaac Briton, one dollar each. Executors—Abraham Hunt and Alexander Chambers, Jr. Witnesses—Mark Thomson, William Lowrey, Richard Howell. Proved April 27, 1790.
1790, April 27. Inventory, £148.1.10, made by Benjamin Smith and William Tindall.
1792, Aug. 17. Account by Executors. Paid the Executors of William Tucker for amount of the Testatrix's purchase at the sale of Samuel Tucker's furniture, more than her proportion, £0.10.1.
Lib. 30, p. 311.

**1787, March 5. Brittin, Jacob,** of Morristown, Morris Co. Int. Adm'x—Elizabeth Brittin. Fellowbondsman—Kennedy Vance; both of said place. Witnesses—Sarah Campfield and Jabez Campfield, Surrogate.
1784, Oct. 11. Inventory, made by Cornelius Ludlow and Peter Layton. Lib. 29, p. 472.

**1786, Oct. 2. Broderrick, Thomas, Sr.,** of Burlington Co. Int. Adm'r—Thomas Broderrick, Jr. Fellowbondsman—Michael Burrows; both of said Co.
1786, Jan. 26. Inventory, £83.18.5, made by Eli Budd and Henry Reeves. Lib. 28, p. 74.

**1789, May 11. Brokaw, Isaac,** of Somerset Co.; will of. Wife, Cathrine, £12 yearly, and her support by my sons, Caspares, John,

CALENDAR OF WILLS—1786-1790   31

Isaac, Abraham and Bergon. Son, Bergon, use of the plantation where I live, and he is to board my daughter, Phebe, and my granddaughter, Jane. The plantation I give to my said sons after 2 years. To the children of my daughter, Sarah, £60, when they are 21. Daughter, Jenney, £60. Daughter, Catlintje, £60. Daughter, Anne, £60. Daughter, Phebe, £70. Executors—sons, Caspares, John, Isaac, Abraham and Bergon, and my cousin, Abraham Staats. Witnesses—William McDuffee, Simeon Van Noortwyck, Nelly Cosort. Proved Aug. 31, 1789. Lib. 31, p. 398.

**1789, May 26. Brokaw, Simon,** of Hillsborough Township, Somerset Co. Int. Adm'rs—Mary Brokaw and Peter D. Vroom. Fellowbondsman—Bergon Brokaw; all of said place.
1789, May 11. Inventory, £217.16.5, made by Jacobus Bergon, Isaac Brokaw and Jacob Covert. Lib. 31, p. 413.

**1786, Jan. 17. Brooks, Jonathan,** of Middlesex Co. Int. Adm'r— John Brooks. Fellowbondsman—Reuben Potter; both of said Co. Witness—William Sickles. Lib. 28, p. 342.

**1788, March 7. Brooks, Samuel,** of Elizabeth Township, Essex Co., yeoman; will of. Wife, Hannah, use of moveable estate, while my widow, and use of my plantation till my grandson, Samuel Brooks Miller, is 21 years of age; and then to have ½ of my farm, in order to bring up my grandsons, Eli Miller and Samuel Brooks Miller; and reserving to my daughter, Elizabeth Shotwell, the use of what my son-in-law, Benjamin Shotwell, may owe to my estate. Grandsons, Noah Miller, Eli Miller and Samuel Brooks Miller, some books. The homestead I live on, that came to me by heirship from my father, Philip Brooks, and that I bought of William Stits, John D. Hart, John Blanchard and Jacob Miller; also the land I bought of Simeon Briant's Executors, being nearly a three square piece of swamp; also the land I swapt for of Simeon Bryant, to my grandson, Samuel Brooks Miller. Nephew, Samuel Bryant, 17 acres of the land I bought of Simeon Bryant, and the mountain land and salt meadow, except 2 lots I lately purchased. Grandsons, Eli Miller and Samuel Brooks Miller, the out lots. The lot I bought of Benjamin Shotwell, 15 of Feb. 1788, and the one I bought of my grandson, Noah Miller, 13th of Feb. 1788, to be sold. Grandson, Samuel Brooks Miller, is to support his mother, Elizabeth Shotwell, if she should need it. Executors—Wife, Hannah, grandson, Samuel Brooks Miller, and friend, William Darby. Witnesses—Enoch Miller, Moses Miller, Enoch Miller, Jr. Proved May 3, 1788. Lib. 31, p. 226.

**1790, Jan. 6. Brown, Andrew,** of Monmouth Co. Int. Adm'r— Jacob Tice. Fellowbondsman—Peter Schenck; both of said Co. Witness—Peter Baird. Lib. 30, p. 417.

**1786, June 20. Brown, George,** of Monmouth Co. Int. Adm'r— Daniel Grandin. Fellowbondsman—Garrit Schanck; both of said Co. Witness—Samuel Forman. Lib. 28, p. 293.

**1786, July 10. Brown, George,** of Nottingham Township, Burlington Co.; will of. The ¼ acre lot that joins Henry Keens's lot, and also the acre in the rear of said lot, to be sold. Son, Richard, the land

that joins the lot that I have ordered sold, of ¼ acre. Daughter, Sarah Brown, £6. Daughter, Prudy Brown, £6. Son, George, my stone house and the ¼ acre of land, when he is 21. Executors—Hugh Runyan, Hill Runyan and Richard Brown. Witnesses—Lewis Evans, Samuel Slack, Daniel Gano. Proved March 16, 1787.
Lib. 29, p. 55.

**1786, Feb. 19. Brown, Henry,** of Wantage Township, Sussex Co.; will of. Eldest son, John, a horse. Son, Thomas, a mare. Daughters, Patience and Anne, household goods. Youngest son, Henry, residue. Executors—sons, Thomas and Henry, and James Cudaback. Witnesses—Dougold Smith, William Mott, George Backster. Proved March 10, 1786.
1786, March 2. Inventory, £268.14.5, made by George Backster and Edmond Martin. Lib. 28, p. 465.

**1787, March 23. Brown, James,** of Essex Co. Ward. Son of Joel Brown, of said Co., deceased. Said Ward, being out of Wardship of Hannah Brown, Guardian in soccage, and having an estate of £200, makes choice of Richard Townly as his Guardian.
1787, March 23. Guardian—Richard Townley. Witness—William Livingston, Jr., Surrogate. Lib. 29, p. 419.

**1787, April 24. Brown, Jeremiah,** of Monmouth Co. Int. Adm'r—Samuel Brown. Fellowbondsman—Stephen Fleming; both of said Co. Witness—John D. Covenhoven.
1787, March 14. Renunciation by Rachel Brown, in favor of her son, Samuel Brown. Witness—George Maxson.
1787, March 14. Renunciation by John Brown, in favor of his brother, Samuel Brown. Witness—David Harriott.
1786, March 20. Inventory, made by Stephen Fleming and Henry Lafferty.
1794, April 23. Adm'r—Theophilus Little. Fellowbondsmen—Barnes I. Smock and George Maxson. Samuel Brown, the Adm'r, is deceased.
Lib. 29, p. 339; Lib. 33, p. 425.

**1787, Jan. 8. Brown, Joel,** of Essex Co. Int. Adm'rs—Hannah Brown and Nathaniel Brown. Fellowbondsman—Richard Townley; all of said Co. Lib. 29, p. 417.

**1788, Dec. 12. Brown, John,** of Woodbury, Gloucester Co., formerly of Scotland, stone cutter. Int. Adm'r—George W. Campbell. Fellowbondsman—Benjamin Whitall; both of said Co.
1788, Dec. 23. Inventory, £9.13.0, made by Joshua Howell and Benjamin Whitall. "Note from John Mc [unintelligible]. Witnesses—Thomas Gregeon and Walter Dawson, none of them known". "An unsettled account between said intestate and the Managers of the Court House and Gaol". Lib. 31, p. 37.

**1790, April 24. Brown, Lyndon,** of Burlington, Burlington Co. Int. Adm'r—Benaiah Brown, of said City. Fellowbondsman—John Brown, of Mansfield Township, said Co. Witnesses—Thomas Adams and Thomas Hewlings.
1790, April 27. Inventory, £24.9.0, made by Daniel Bacon, Jr., and Israel Tonkin. Lib. 32, p. 96.

CALENDAR OF WILLS—1786-1790       33

**1787, June 11. Brown, Mary,** of Burlington Co. Int. Adm'r—Thomas Perry. Fellowbondsman—Hosea Eayre; both of said Co. Witnesses—Herbert McElroy, Surrogate, and Thomas Adams.
Lib. 29, p. 75.

**1780, April 22. Brown, Thomas,** of Woodbridge Township, Middlesex Co.; will of. Son, William, £10. Wife, Frances, £100. Daughter, Agness, £50. Daughter, Christian, many goods. Daughter, Ursula, goods. Daughter, Fanne, £50. Sons, John, James and Philip, rest of moveable estate and my lands, when they are of age. Son, William, to have a tract bought for him. Executors—sons, John and James. Witnesses—Asher Fitz Randolph, Nathan Bunn, William Connoly. Proved Nov. 26, 1781.
1781, Dec. 12. Inventory, £1,006.12.11, made by Daniel Moore and John Brown.
Lib. 24, p. 32.

**1788, Aug. 13. Browne, Joseph,** of Newark, Essex Co. Int. Adm'rs—Hannah Browne, Job Browne and Daniel Williams, Jr. Fellowbondsman—Eleazer Brown; all of said Co.
1788, Aug. 21. Inventory, made by Moses Osborn and Eleazer Brown.
Lib. 38, p. 96.

**1786, May 30. Brush, Benjamin,** of Gloucester Co.; will of. Son, Benjamin, 4 shillings. Daughter, Ann, 20 shillings. Daughter, Lorinah, 5 shillings. Daughter, Hannah, 5 shillings. Son-in-law, Samuel Ball, 10 shillings. Son-in-law, Samuel Deniack, 5 shillings. Daughter, Bashti, 10 shillings. Wife to have the use of ⅓ of real estate. Sons, Ard and Edward, rest of real estate. Executor—son, Ard. Witnesses—James Dickey, Matthew West, John Neal. Proved Dec. 29, 1786.
1786, Dec. 16. Inventory, £133.15.0, made by Simon Lucas and Gibson Ashcraft.
Lib. 28, p. 93.

**[No date]. Bryant, William,** of Trenton, Hunterdon Co., practitioner of physic; will of. Wife, Mary, the house in which I live, during her life; also £900 of a bond of £1,650, now owing to me from John Cox, Esq. My natural son, William Bryant, by Charity Murrow, £600, when he is 21; and his mother is to be furnished with this clause of my will. If he die under said age. then £50 to be paid to his mother, Charity Murrow, and the rest divided between the surviving children of Samuel and Mary Duffield, of Philadelphia, of Benjamin and Elizabeth Woodruff, of Westfield, of Elisha and Catharine Boudinot, now of Hanover, and of William Pitt Smith, now of Albany. Sister, Rebecca Deane, £150; also the interest of £600 to be paid her during her life, and, after her decease, ½ of the principal to be paid to her daughter, Mary Deane, and the other ½ to the child or children of said Benjamin and Elizabeth Woodruff. Nephew, Belcher P. Smith, my gold watch. Nephew, William Pitt Smith, £100. To Mary Deane, daughter of my sister, Rebecca Deane, £50. To William B. Duffield, eldest son of Doctor Samuel Duffield, of Philadelphia, £50. After death of wife, the house to be sold, and ½ of the proceeds to be paid to the surviving children of Samuel and Mary Duffield, and of Elisha and Catharine Boudinot. The other ½ to William Deane, second son of my sister, Rebecca Deane. Executors—brother-in-law, William P. Smith, and my nephew, Belcher P. Smith. Witnesses—John Singer, William Plasket, John Dixon. Proved June 2, 1786.
Lib. 28, p. 232.

**1786, April 7. Bryant, William,** of Hopewell Township, Hunterdon Co.; will of. Son, William plantation where he lives, of 150 acres. Son, Benjamin, plantation where he lives, as it now stands divided by David Price, between him and his brother, William, of 150 acres. Son, John, the plantation I live on of 150 acres; but my daughters, Ann and Elizabeth, are to have the use of part of the house while they are unmarried. Grandson, William Forster, £30. Grandson, Ralph Hunt, son of my daughter, Elizabeth, £30, when 21. Granddaughters, Mary, the daughter of my son, John, and Charity, daughter of my daughter, Elizabeth, each a cow. Children, William, Benjamin, John, Ann, Sarah, Rebecca, Mary and Elizabeth, rest of estate. Executors—sons, William, Benjamin and John. Witnesses—Benjamin Vankirk, Andrew Blackwell, Jacob Blackwell. Proved July 21, 1787.
1787, July 17. Inventory, £1,276.3.6, made by John Vankirk and Benjamin Vankirk. Lib. 29, p. 283.

**1787, May 5. Buck, Aaron,** of Toms River, Monmouth Co. Int. Adm'r—John Richmond. Fellowbondsman—Benjamin Haviland; both of said Co. Witness—Rachel Henderson.
1787, March. Renunciation by Margrett Buck, widow of Aaron. Witnesses—Abiel Akin and George Cook.
1787, March 7. Inventory, made by George Cook and Abiel Akin.
Lib. 29, p. 339.

**1790, March 9. Buckalew, Joseph, Anne and Elizabeth,** of Middlesex Co. Wards. Children of Frederick Buckalew, of said Co., deceased. Said Wards make choice of Thomas Errickson as their Guardian.
1790, March 9. Guardian—Thomas Errickson. Fellowbondsman—Daniel Sperling; both of said Co. Witness—William Hyer, Jr.
Lib. 30, p. 536.

**1788, Feb. 23. Budd, John,** of Northampton Township, Burlington Co.; will of, being old and infirm. Grandson, Samuel Gaskill, £7. Granddaughter, Sarah Gaskill, £7. Granddaughter, Theofela Gaskill, £7. Grandson, John Gaskill, owes me £20, and he is not in these parts, but, if he comes back and is able to pay, then I give the said money to his brothers and sisters, above named. Daughter, Deborah Haywood, in Virginia, £20. Grandson, Budd Haywood, my silver watch. To George and Deborah Haywood's other 10 children, £80, to be put in hands of their father till they are of age. Grandson, George McCully, £25. Grandson, William McCully, £25, when he is 21. The 2 last grandchildren are to have good schooling and put to trades. To my 6 grandchildren, the children of my daughter, Margaret McCully, all the rest of my estate. Executors—my cousins, George Langstaff and Joseph Budd Major. Witnesses—Earl Shinn, Buddell Shinn, Joseph Paxson. Proved April 30, 1789.
1789, April 22. Inventory, £713.13.7, made by Jacob Merrit and Abraham Lippincott. Lib. 31, p. 260.

**1786, Jan. 3. Buffin, Michael,** of Mansfield Township, Burlington Co.; will of. Cousin, William Carslake, the plantation where he lives; and he is to pay to my daughter, Mary Braddock, £50, and to my sister, Ann English, £50, and to my sister's children, Abraham, John, Joseph, Ashar and Clayton Brown, and Asa Ware, £50, and to

CALENDAR OF WILLS—1786-1790   35

my son, Richard's children, Penelopy, Abigail, Sarah and Michael, and Levina and Hannah Fox, widow of Patrick Fox, £50. My land at Black Horse, now in possession of James Fenimore, to be sold, and the money given to my son, Richard, and my daughter, Mary Braddock. Son-in-law, Adam Braddock, and his wife, my said daughter, Mary, the part of my plantation where I live, and, at their death, to their 2 daughters, Phebe and Tryvena Braddock, Son, Richard, rest of plantation. Executors—friends, William Satterthwaite, of Chesterfield, and Thomas Pancoast, of Mansfield. Witnesses— John Pope, Jacob Van Sciver, Jacob Wolcott.
1786, April 18. Codicil. Granddaughter, Trivenia Braddock, the best bed. Granddaughter, Abigail Carlslake, a bed. Daughter, Mary Braddock, a copper kettle. Witnesses—Jacob Van Sciver, Abigail Van Sciver, Jacob Wolcott.
1787, Jan. 14. Codicil. Sister, Ann English, a riding mare. To William Carslake, a cow. Granddaughters, Phebe and Trivena Braddock, £6. Daughter, Mary Braddock, a cow. Son, Richard, a heifer. To Hannah Fox, a heifer, and all the sheep I have at Amos Rockhill's. Witnesses—Adam Nutt, Thomas Newton, Jacob Wolcott. Proved Jan. 29, 1787.
1787, Jan. 23. Inventory, £372.1.0, made by Nathan Robbins and Barzillai Furman. Lib. 29, p. 41.

**1786, March 1. Bunnel, Gershom,** of Essex Co., weaver; will of. Only son, Jacob, £8. My land in the upper part of Westfield to be sold, as also my moveable estate, and the money given to my daughters, Susannah, Abigail, Phebe, Mary, Joanna and Hannah. Executors—friends, Isaac Clark and Caleb Maxell. Witnesses—William Baldwin, Garret Gray, Andrew Joline. Proved March 28, 1786.
Lib. 28, p. 366.

**1790, March 16. Burkitt, Wright,** of Gloucester Co. Int. Adm'r— John Ashley. Fellowbondsman—Stephen Collins; both of Philadelphia. Witness—Francis Davenport, Surrogate. Lib. 31, p. 476.

**1786, Jan. 10. Burr, Henry,** of Northampton, Burlington Co. Int. Adm'rs—John Burr and Thomas Burr, sons of said Henry. Fellowbondsman—Abraham Reeves; all of said place.
1786, Jan. 12. Inventory, £375.19.3, made by Hezekiah Jones and William Bishop. Among other things; "the remainder of his wearing apparel; the principal part being given to his brother, John Burr, £3".
Lib. 28, p. 78.

**1786, Feb. 14. Burr, Henry, Jr.,** of Burlington Co. Ward. Son of Henry Burr, of said Co., deceased. Said Ward, having real and personal estate, makes choice of Uriah Woolman, as his Guardian.
1786, Feb. 14. Guardian—Uriah Woolman. Fellowbondsman— Hezekiah Jones; both of said Co. Witness—Thomas Adams.
Lib. 28, p. 81.

**1786, Feb. 14. Burr, John, Jr.,** of Burlington Co. Ward. Son of Henry Burr, of said Co., deceased. Said Ward, having real and personal estate, makes choice of Uriah Woolman as his Guardian.
1786, Feb. 14. Guardian—Uriah Woolman. Fellowbondsman— Hezekiah Jones; both of said Co. Witness—Thomas Adams.
Lib. 28, p. 81.

**1790, April 27. Burrough, Gideon,** of Gloucester, Gloucester Co., house carpenter; will of. Son, John, all my estate, and he is to maintain my wife. Executor—son, John. Witnesses—Joseph Hugg, Jr., Robert Sparks, James Chattin. Proved May 15, 1790.

1790, May 8. Inventory, £280.15.6, made by John Brick and Edward Watson.
Lib. 31, p. 416.

**1789, Nov. 6. Burrough, Patience,** of Pitts Grove, Salem Co.; will of. Son, Joseph Burrough, 5 shillings. Son, John Burrough, 5 shillings. To Isaac Burrough, £3. To David Burrough, £5. Son, Youryah, £20. To Hannah Abit, book. To Sarah Rose, warming pan. A head stone to be put to the grave of my husband and myself. Rest of estate to Hannah Abit, and my daughter Elizabeth Van Mete's children, and Sarah Rose and Youriah Burroughs, and Elizabeth's children to draw one share. Executor—friend, Benjamin Van Meter. Witnesses—Mary Krom, David Dubois, Jr., Abraham Du Bois. Proved Dec. 1, 1789.

1789, Nov. 12. Inventory, £243.11.9, made by William Garrison and Cornelius Nieukirk. To thirds due from the estate of Isaac Burroughs, deceased, £117.
Lib. 40, p. 519.

**1790, April 6. Burrough, Samuel,** of Waterford Township, Gloucester Co., farmer; will of. Wife to have £20 yearly. Son, Benjamin, the money due on contracts of sale of back lands in Pennsylvania; also the land which I bought of Jacob Haines. Son, Joshua, my homestead. Executors—sons, Benjamin and Joshua, and my friend, Thomas Thorn, to advise them. Witnesses—Ann Cooper, Thomas Thorne, Samuel Allinson. Proved May 7, 1790.

1790, April 26. Inventory, £779.4.9, made by Joseph Burrough and Thomas Thorne.
Lib. 31, p. 417.

**1786, Feb. 16. Burroughs, Isaac,** of Pitts Grove, Salem Co.; will of. Wife, Patience, £75 in goods, and £20 yearly. Son, Joseph, ½ of plantation where I live. Son, Isaac, the plantation that lately belonged to Jacob Van Meter. Son, David, the rest of by plantation, that joins William Garrison's; except 5 acres at northwest corner. Son, Uriah, the said 5 acres. Son, John, £5. Daughters, Elizabeth Vanmeter, Hannah Abbet and Sarah Burroughs, £50 each. Grandson, Isaac Burroughs Vanmeter, £5. Son, Uriah, £150. The lands I bought of Cadwallader Morris to be sold. Executors—wife, Patience, and my son, Joseph. Witnesses—Benjamin Burroughs, John Stulls, John Nelson. Proved March 20, 1786.

1786, March 7. Inventory, £672.3.5, made by William Garrison and Benjamin Vanmeter.
Lib. 28, p. 125.

**1788, Aug. 28. Burrowes, Foster,** of Hopewell Township, Hunterdon Co.; will of. Son, Nathaniel, all my lands in this Township; he paying the legacies. Daughter, Sarah, £50, to be paid to her when Nathan is 21; also, while she is single, rooms in the house. Daughter, Fanny Lot, £30. Son, Ebenezer, £100, and he is to have a trade. Son, Nathan, £100, and to learn a trade. Executors—brother, Stephen, and my cousin, Stephen Burrowes, Jr., and son, Nathaniel. Witnesses—Benjamin Johnson, Ann Johnson, Neille McGill. Proved Feb. 11, 1789.

1789, Feb. 10. Inventory, £438.19.9, made by John Carpenter and John Welling.
Lib. 32, p. 10.

**1790, Dec. 9. Burrowes, Thomas,** of Amwell, Hunterdon Co. Int. Adm'rs—Hannah Burrowes, of said place, and John Hunt, of Hopewell, said Co. Fellowbondsman—Andrew Smith, of Hopewell.
1790, Dec. 8. Inventory, £440.3.3, made by Andrew Smith and Robert Laning. "Note against Joseph Ashton, Jr., for £16. Bond given to Hannah Burrowes by her brother, Joseph Ashton, to be paid her one year after her mother's decease, for £50."
1794, Feb. 6. Stephen Burrowes, Guardian of Eden Burrowes, one of the heirs of Thomas Burrowes, has John Hunt, surviving Adm'r, cited to render an account of the personal estate.
1794, July 29. Account by John Hunt, surviving Adm'r.

Lib. 30, p. 315.

**1786, March 13. Burt, Margaret,** of Bridge Town, Middlesex Co., widow; will of. Niece, Rachel Boggs, £300, when 21. Nephew, Daniel Barhight, £100. Niece, Elizabeth, wife of said Daniel Barhight, apparel. Daughter, Haster Morgan; my granddaughter, Margaret Morgan and niece, Rachel Boggs, apparel. Great-granddaughter, Margaret Burt Blanchard, a silver bowl. To St. John's Church in Elizabeth Town, £30. Daughter, Hester Morgan, and my granddaughter, Margaret Morgan, my real estate. Executors—son-in-law, Benjamin Morgan, and my friend, John Chetwood. Witnesses—James Haydock, Cowperthwaite Copland, Daniel Marsh. Proved July 20, 1786.

Lib. 28, p. 299.

**1786, March 20. Butcher, Aaron,** of Stow Creek Township, Cumberland Co. Int. Adm'rs—Phebe Butcher and Jonathan Butcher. Fellowbondsman—Richard Wood; all of said Co. Witness—David Peirson.
1786, March 16. Inventory, £752.11.2, made by Richard Wood and Joshua Ayars.

Lib. 28, p. 181.

**1790, Jan. 11. Butcher, Richard,** of Stow Creek Township, Cumberland Co.; will of. Son, Job, 130 acres of land where I live, joining to Richard Wood's line (formerly Anderson's); also a salt marsh in Stow Neck, that I bought of Jonathan Bradway; also a silver spoon, marked R.A.B. Grandsons, Jonathan and Thomas Butcher, the rest of said plantation; but if Thomas should die under age, then I give his part to my son, Job, and my grandson, Jonathan. Grandsons, Aaron and James Butcher, the lands I bought of Job Sayre, Richard Wood and John Wheaton; also 35 and ½ acres of marsh of my home place, along Richard Wood's line. My salt marsh in Stow Neck, that I bought of John Deviney, I give to my son, Job, and my said 4 grandsons. Son, Jonathan, my large Bible. Grandson, Thomas Butcher, a silver spoon, marked R.B. Granddaughter, Elizabeth Hancock, £50. Granddaughter, Rebecca Jefferys, £31. Granddaughter, Elizabeth Ware, £50. Granddaughters, Hannah Ware and Phebe Butcher, £50 each, when they are 18. Executors—son, Job, and grandson, Jonathan Butcher. Witnesses—Thomas Remington, Elnathan Davis, George Garnett Fiddiss. Proved Sept. 11, 1790.
1790, Sept. 8. Inventory, £390.12.11, made by Thomas Padgett and Elnathan Davis.

Lib. 30, p. 255.

**1786, April 8. Buxton, James,** of Evesham Township, Burlington Co. Int. Adm'x—Hannah Buxton. Fellowbondsman—Francis Austin; both of said Co.

1786, April 3. Inventory, £361.11.8, made by Seth Thomas and Thomas Gill. Lib. 28, p. 80.

**1786, March 11. Buzby, Mary,** of Willingborough, Burlington Co.; will of. Son, William Buzby, a bond which I have against Joseph Fowler for £16. Daughter-in-law, Susana Buzby, a gown and quilt. Granddaughter, Mary Buzby, walnut table and chairs. Granddaughter, Mary Haines, apparel. Granddaughter, Elizabeth Haines, silver tea spoons. Son-in-law, Samuel Haines, and his 5 sons, William, Aaron, Abel, Joseph and Samuel, ½ the residue; and the other ½ to my granddaughters, Mary and Elizabeth Haines. Executors—son-in-law, Samuel Haines. Witnesses—Moses Wills, Hannah Buzby, Aaron Wills. Proved May 12, 1786.

1786, March 22. Inventory, £228.4.0, made by Aaron Wills and Moses Wills. Lib. 28, p. 46.

**1786, Jan. 10. Bayard, Joseph,** of Hardwick, Sussex Co. Int. Adm'r —Thomas Allen, of said place. Fellowbondsman—Francis Price, of Newton, said Co. Witness—Samuel Price and Thomas Anderson.

1786, Jan. 18. Inventory, £18.16.2, made by Henry Buchner and Jacob Buchner. Lib. 28, p. 470.

**1788, March 15. Calaghan, John,** of Salem Co. Int. Adm'r—Francis Hill. Fellowbondsmen—Francis Redrake and Allen Congleton, Jr.; all of Lower Penns Neck Township, said Co. Witnesses—Sarah Dick and Samuel Dick Lib. 37, p. 424.

**1787, April 19. Callender, Katherine,** of Burlington, Burlington Co., widow; will of. To my Executors, £1,000, in trust, to place the same at interest, and interest paid to my daughter, Hannah Sansom, and to pay the principal at the request of my daughter; and, if my daughter die without disposing of the same, then it is to be paid to such of my grandchildren as may be living, and to the heirs of those deceased; and if they all be deceased, then to be paid to the children of my brother, Robert Smith. Daughter, Hannah Sansom, my dwelling house and lot in Burlington, and now in tenure of Andrew Craig. Son-in-law, Samuel Sansom, in trust, for my grandchildren, William Sarah, Joseph and Samuel Sansom, £800, to be divided to them when they come of age. Nephew, Robert Smith, and to my niece, Sarah Smith, £10 each. Cousins, Benjamin Smith, Mary Smith, Daniel Smith and Robert Smith, children of my nephew, Daniel Smith, £10 each. Cousins, William Allinson and Mary Allinson, children of my nephew-in-law, Samuel Allinson, £10 each. Son-in-law, Samuel Sansom, and my daughter, Hannah Sansom, land adjoining Elfreys Alley, in Philadelphia; also the rest of real and personal estate. Executors— nephews, Daniel Smith, Samuel Allinson and Robert Smith. Witnesses —John Hoskins, Daniel Bacon, Jr., Joseph Hoskins.

1787, April 19. Codicil. In my will I did also mention my relation, Samuel Allinson, as one of my Executors, but as he lives at a distance, I release him, and appoint my grandson, William Sansom, in his stead. Witnesses—John Hoskins, George Hulme, John Hoskins, Jr. Proved Dec. 24, 1789.

1790, May 11. Inventory, £2,459.19.5, made by Abbott Williams and Andrew Craige. Lib. 31, p. 264.

CALENDAR OF WILLS—1786-1790 39

**1786, Nov. 28. Calvert, Martha,** of Burlington Co. Int. Adm'rs—John Bispham and Peter Shiras. Fellowbondsmen—William Atkinson and John Black; all of said Co. Witness—Thomas Adams.
Lib. 28, p. 75.

**1787, Dec. 25. Cameron, Hugh,** of Hardyston, Sussex Co. Int. Adm'x—Elizabeth Cameron, widow, of said place. Fellowbondsman—Humphrey Martin, of Wantage, said Co., yeoman. Witnesses—Thomas Anderson and William Anderson.
1787, Dec. 13. Inventory, £281.19.8, made by Silvanus Addoms and Humphrey Martin. Lib. 29, p. 490.

**1788, March. Camp, Nathaniel,** of Newark, Essex Co.; will of. Grandson, Joseph Camp, my fresh meadow at Camps Point, of 4 acres; bounded by David Hayes, Isaac Peirsons, and my own land; also a meadow at Canfields Creek; also 8 acres lying to the south of David Brown, bounded by Caleb Camp; also land which I bought of John Roberts, lying in the Little Neck; and he is to pay to my wife, Mary, £8 yearly. Grandson, Stephen Camp, son of John Camp, a meadow that is near Maple Island, bounded by Job and Samuel Camp, William Burnet and other lots; also a lot of salt meadow at Maple Island Creek, which I bought of Aaron Richards. Son, Nathaniel, (he paying to my wife, Mary, £12 yearly), the rest of real estate; he also paying the legacies hereafter mentioned, as well as the said money to my wife, which is contained in a deed of settlement. Granddaughter, Hannah Kinney, wife of Abraham Kinney, £75. Granddaughter, Lydia Griffith, £75. Granddaughter, Elizabeth Griffith, £75. Granddaughter, Mary Camp, £10. Granddaughter, Elizabeth Tichenor, £10. Granddaughter, Hannah Camp, £10. Grandson, Nathaniel Camp Griffith, £100, and, if he die, then to his two sisters, Lydia and Elizabeth. Executors —son, Nathaniel, and Caleb Camp, Esq. Witnesses—John Ward, Lewis Baldwin, Jabez Pierson.
1789, May 26. Codicil. The legacies left to my granddaughters, Hannah Kinney and Elizabeth Burnet, are to be paid out of the money due me from Doctor William Burnet, their father. Wife, Mary, the provisions in the house. Witnesses—Eleazer Brown, Thomas Knapp, Joseph Camp. Proved June 23, 1789.
1789, June 25. Inventory, £1,582.6.½, made by Jotham Johnson and Caleb Parkhurst. Lib. 30, p. 205.

**1790, April 17. Camp, William,** of Newark, Essex Co. Ward. Son of Isaac Camp, of said Co., deceased. Said Ward, having real estate, makes choice of Robert Nichols as his Guardian.
1790, April 17. Guardian—Robert Nichols, of said place. Witness— James Thompson. Lib. 30, p. 363.

**1789, Dec. 25. Campbell, Catharine,** of Hackensack, Bergen Co.; will of. To William Campbell, all personal and real estate. Executor—William Campbell. Witnesses—Joast Demarest, Samuel Wood, Gerrit Zabriske. Proved March 20, 1790. Lib. 31, p. 542.

**1789, May 15. Canfield, Abraham,** of Morristown, Morris Co., merchant; will of. Wife, Sarah, £25 and the goods she brought to me when married. Daughter, Mary Canfield, £40 and some goods. Daughter, Sarah, wife of Clement Wood, £40. Son, Israel, £5. Daughter, Hannah, looking glass and cow. Son, Abner, oxen, horses, cows and sheep, and £80. Daughter, Phebe Canfield, bed and table. Daughter, Anna, cow and bed. Rest of personal and real estate to daughters, Mary, Hanna, Phebe and Anna, and Isaac, Abraham, Abner, and David Seely Canfield, my sons. Executors—friend, Dr. Jabez Campfield, and my sons, Israel, Isaac and Abner, who are to be Guardians of my young children. Witnesses—Caleb Howell, Joseph Little, Abner Fairchild. Proved Aug. 18, 1789.

1789, Aug. 18. Inventory, £287.19.11, made by Jonathan Stiles and Joseph Fairchild. Lib. 30, p. 221.

**1787, May 25. Carlile, Anne,** of Burlington, Burlington Co., widow; will of. £5 is to be spent for clothing for my brother, Samuel Smith, and delivered to him. Nephew, Thomas Smith, the south ½ of my lot on York St. in Burlington, on which lot he has a stable; also that part of the woodland in said City, which will remain after 18 acres is run off; and, after his death, to his son, Seth Smith, and, if he die under age, then to the next oldest son of Thomas; and, if there be no son, then to the next oldest daughter living at his decease. To Elizabeth Smith, daughter of my nephew, Thomas Smith, my gold sleeve buttons. Niece, Sarah Brorgard, wife of Doctor John Brorgard, the north ½ of the said lot, except that part of the dwelling built by Doctor Brorgard, which I have conveyed to him; also 18 acres of woodland to be run off, so as to include the east part, next to Robert Grubb's land; to hold the north part of my lot on York St., with the wooden building, where I lately resided, erected thereon; and, after her decease, to her son, John Smith Brorgard, when he is 21, but, if he die, then to the next oldest son, and, if no son living, then to the next oldest daughter. Nephew, Thomas Smith, and my niece, Sarah Brorgard, the rest of estate. Executor—cousin, Joseph Smith, of Burlington. Witnesses—Daniel Smith, William Smith, Jr., Thomas Quest. Proved Dec. **15, 1789.**

1789, Dec. 11. Renunciation by Joseph Smith.

1789, Dec. 15. Adm'r—Thomas Smith, of Burlington, Fellowbondsman—Richard R. Smith, of said City.

1789, Nov. 16. Inventory, £158.18.3, made by John Hoskins and Richard Smith. Lib. 31, p. 315.

**1786, June 20. Carll, Buckley,** of Cumberland Co. Ward. Son of Willian Carll, of said Co., deceased. Said Ward, having real and personal estate, makes choice of Jacob Mulford as his Guardian.

1786, June 20. Guardian—Jacob Mulword. Fellowbondsman—Eli Elmer; both of said Co. Witness—Samuel M. Shute. Lib. 28, p. 183.

**1790, May 15. Carll, Buckley,** of Cumberland Co. Ward. Son of William Carll, of said Co., deceased. Said Ward, having real and personal estate, makes choice of James Hunt as his Guardian.

1790, May 15. Guardian—James B. Hunt. Fellowbondsman—Enos Ewing; both of said Co. Witness—Samuel M. Shute. Lib. 30, p. 281.

**1789, Sept. 22. Carll, Mary,** late Mary Craig, of Salem Co. Int. Adm'r. Samuel McClong. Fellowbondsman—Daniel Russell; both of New Jersey. Lib. 31, p. 358.

# CALENDAR OF WILLS—1786-1790 41

**1788, Feb. 21. Carman, Samuel,** of Middlesex Co. Ward. Son of Stephen Carman, of said Co., deceased. Said Ward makes choice of Benjamin Manning as his Guardian.
1788, Feb. 21. Guardian—Benjamin Manning. Fellowbondsman—Samuel Walker; both of Piscataway, said Co. Witness—William Hyer, Jr.
Lib. 31, p. 225.

**1789, Feb. 26. Carman, Samuel,** of Middletown Township, Monmouth Co. Int. Adm'r—Samuel Carman. Fellowbondsman—Joseph Carman; both of said Place. Witness—John Stillwell.
1789, Jan. 21. Inventory, made by John Stillwell and Daniel Covenhoven.
Lib. 30, p. 188.

**1786, Jan. 18. Carman, Stephen,** of Middlesex Co. Int. Adm'x—Abigail Carman. Fellowbondsman—James Rowland; both of said Co. Witness—David Olden.
Lib. 28, p. 342.

**1788, April 9. Carney, Thomas,** of Upper Penns Neck, Salem Co.; will of. Son, Thomas, plantation where I dwell, of 490 acres; also ½ of the mill; also ½ of the 300 acres which I and John Somerlin bought of Samuel Burman, commonly known as Miller's Mill. Daughter, Ruth Carney, plantation I bought of Andrew Dalbow, in Lower Penns Neck; also plantation I bought of Andrew Corneilson; also 50 acres bought of Samuel Kean, in lieu of a legacy bequeathed to her by her grandfather, Abel Harris. Daughter, Hannah Carney, plantation I bought of George Dennis, in Piles Grove. Son, Thomas, plantation which his grandfather bought by Sheriff's sale, on Salem Creek. Daughter, Ruth Carney, 50 acres which her grandfather bought of Michael Miller; also land which joins William Lambson, Matthias Johnson, late the property of Thomas and John Allen; also the marsh I bought of Robert Kitts. Friends, William Dickeson and James Clark to be Guardians of son, Thomas, and daughter, Hannah, whom I also appoint my Executors. Witnesses—James Clark, Jr., George McFarland, John Savoy. Proved March 18, 1789.
1789, June 15. Inventory, £1,381.12.8, made by George McFarland and Brathwaite Tuft.
Lib. 31, p. 328.

**1789, June 17. Carpenter, John,** of Deptford Township, Gloucester Co. Int. Adm'r—David Eldridge. Fellowbondsman—Daniel Sutherland; both of said Co.
1789, June 18. Inventory, £308.6.1, made by Robert Parks and Jesse Chew. "A debt against Samuel Carpenter, for a cedar swamp, £5."
Lib. 30, p. 136.

**1790, May 17. Carr, Thomas,** of Pequannack Township, Morris Co.; will of. Wife, Martha, house and land where I live; also the moveable estate; and, at her death, to my friend Jacob Arnold's eldest son, Samuel. Executor—Jacob Arnold. Witnesses—Elijah Freeman, John Fields, Oliver Headey. Proved July 12, 1790.
1790, June 30. Inventory, £89.14.7, made by Elijah Freeman and Oliver Headey.
Lib. 30, p. 451.

**1789, June 17. Carter, Daniel,** of Deptford Township, Gloucester Co. Int. Adm'x—Elizabeth Carter. Fellowbondsman—Ephraim Cheesman.
1789, May 20. Inventory, £190.0.8, made by John Turner and Amos Collins.
Lib. 30, p. 137.

**1786, Oct. 3. Carty, Daniel,** of Chester Township, Burlington Co. Int. Adm'r—John Shivers, of Gloucester Co. Fellowbondsman— Nathaniel Middleton, of Burlington Co.
1786, Oct. 2. Inventory, £64.4.0, made by Abraham Hewlings and Nathaniel Middleton. Lib. 28, p. 76.

**1789, April 6. Cary, Joel,** of Morris Co. Int. Adm'rs—Hannah Cary and Beriah Cary. Fellowbondsman—Lebbeus Dod; all of Mendham, said Co. Witness—Jabez Gwinnup.
1789, March 23. Inventory, £92.16.10, made by Jehiel Day and Henry Burnet. Lib. 30, p. 234.

**1788, Nov. 29. Casner, Peter,** of Roxbury, Morris Co. Int. Adm'r— Mary Casner and Gabriel Sparks. Fellowbondsmen—Nathan Luse and David Cook; all of said place. Witnesses—David Brown and William Campfield.
1788, Nov. 24. Inventory, £27.6.3, made by Nathan Luse and David Cook. Lib. 31, p. 199.

**1787, April 19. Casten [Carson], Phillip,** of Hanover, Morris Co.; will of. Relations, John Hill and Phillip Miller, £6 each. Relations, Peter Hill, Samuel Hill, John Hill, Phillip Miller, Abigail Hill, rest of moveable estate. Executors—neighbor, Elisha Rolfe. Witnesses— Jonathan Fairchild, Daniel Dickerson. Proved June 4, 1787.
1787, May 3. Inventory, £24.19.2, made by Gideon Howell and Jonathan Fairchild. A debt due from Capt. James Keen.
Lib. 29, p. 445.

**1788, Jan. 12. Castner, Jacob,** of New Brunswick, Middlesex Co.; will of. Wife, Cathrine, all my estate for the support of my children. Executrix—wife, Catharine. Witnesses—Hendrick Highland, James Cawood, Daniel Castner, Sr. Proved March 14, 1788.
1788, March 15. Inventory, £88.10.0, made by Isaac Sillcock and Richard Jaques. Lib. 31, p. 205.

**1786, June 4. Castner, John,** of Bedminster, Somerset Co.; will of. Mother, Barbary Castner, house and lot where she lives, and moveable estate, for the support of my brother, Coonrod, and sisters, who are not able to support themselves. Brother-in-law, Peter Bockover, my blacksmith tools. Executors—mother, Barbary Castner, and my friend, John Boylan, merchant. Witnesses—Dan Castner, John Bockover, James Lowes. Proved June 28, 1786. Lib. 28, p. 507.

**1790, Jan. 31. Cave, Sarah,** of Cape May Co., widow; will of. Daughter, Sarah Paddon, 2 beds and chest, cash and apparel. Executor—friend, William Shaw. Witnesses—Joseph Beesley, Jacob Teal, Stillwill Shaw. Proved May 3, 1790.
1790, June 15. Inventory, £24.3.3, made by Jacocks Swain and Daniel Crowell. Lib. 32, p. 102.

**1789, May 25. Chamberlain, Joseph,** of Windsor, Middlesex Co.; will of. Plantation where I live to be rented out till my youngest son is of age, and then to be sold, and money given to my boys and girls. Daughters, Mercy and Lydia, to have £5 extra. Land joining James Robbins to be sold. Children to be put to trades. Executors—Jona-

than Combs, Allison Ely, and my son, John. Witnesses—George Hulit, Enoch Chamberlain, Thomas Ewing. Proved June 15, 1789.
1789, June 12. Inventory, £571.6.6, made by Timothy Hulit and John Mount.
1789, June 12. Inventory, £723.15.0, made by Timothy Hulit and John Mount. Homestead of 330 acres sold for £660. Land joining James Robbins of 51 acres sold for £63.15.0. Lib. 31, p. 373.

**1786, Jan. 4. Chambers, David R.,** of Hunterdon Co. Int. Adm'x—Susannah Chambers. Fellowbondsman—Alexander Calhoun; both of Trenton, said Co.
1785, —. —. Inventory, £59. 8. 4, made by Benjamin Hayden and John McCollum. Lib. 28, p. 248.

**1786, Nov. 25. Chambers, John,** of Middlesex Co. Int. Adm'rs—Rachel Chambers and Henry Leats. Fellowbondsman—Isaac Rogers. Witness—Aaron Longstreet.
[No date]. Inventory, made by Isaac Rogers and William Cubberley.
Lib. 28, p. 337.

**1787, Aug. 30. Champneys, Benjamin,** of Salem Co. Ward. Son of Joseph Champneys, Jr., of said Co., deceased. Said Ward makes choice of Samuel Nelson as his Guardian.
1787, Aug. 30. Guardian—Samuel Nelson, of Pitts Grove. Fellowbondsmen—Frederick Freas and Jesse Rambo; all of said Co.
Lib. 29, p. 153.

**1788, April 19. Chessman, Peter,** of Gloucester Township, Gloucester Co., yeoman; will of. Wife, Christian, £100, and the goods she brought. Son, Richard, the homestead where my house stands, being 2,000 acres which I bought of Samuel Miflin; and ½ my saw mill. Son, Thomas, the plantation in Waterford Township, where he lives, which I bought of my brother, William; and 400 acres by the same, lying near the head of Prodder's Pond, which I bought of David Roe, John McCollough and Ephraim Tomlinson; also ½ of my saw mill. Daughter, Mary Ann Jackson, 5 shillings. I gave her a deed of gift for 400 acres of land. Daughter, Deborah Peirce, wife of Henry Peirce, £60. Daughter, Margret Peirce, wife of William Peirce, £10. Grandson, Jacob Williams, son of John Williams, 150 acres of land in Deptford Township, to be surveyed off of land I bought of Richard Penn. Sons, Richard and Thomas, land called the Indian Branch survey, surveyed by Samuel Clement for 537 acres. Executors—sons, Richard and Thomas. Witnesses—Randel Morgan, Isaac Ellis, Isaac Tomlinson. Proved Aug. 25, 1788.
1788, June 28. Inventory, £382.10.8, made by Richard Cheesman and Isaac Tomlinson. Lib. 31, p. 28.

**1787, Feb. 9. Cheesman, Richard,** of Gloucester Township, Gloucester Co., yeoman; will of. Wife, Jemime, the goods in my house, and my son, Ephraim, to give to his mother, £15. Daughter, Drusilla Hillman, may live in the house while she is the widow of Joseph Hillman. Grandson, Alexander Cheesman, son of my son, Uriah, 5 shillings. Son, Richard, 5 shillings. Grandson, Elijah Cheesman, son of my son, John, the land where Lot Evans lately lived. Son, Ephraim, plantation where I live, except the piece that John Thorne has within fence; also the pine land near Four Mile Branch; also the cedar swamp which I bought in partnership with Henry Thorne, of Abraham Leeds; also 150 acres of the deed of rights which I bought of Hannah Sawer. Great-grandson, Joab Hillman, grandson of my daughter, Lettia, the land I bought of John Blackwood; and, if he die, I give the same to his sister, Priscilla. Grandson, Isaac Jones, son of my daughter, Tamer, 5 shillings. Son-in-law, John Thorne, that land excepted from my plantation; he paying thereout ⅔ of the value, ⅙ of which I give to my daughter, Deborah Smallwood, and ⅙ to my daughter, Drusilla Hillman. Daughters, Deborah Smallwood, Drusilla Hillman and Issabella Thorne, 150 acres each, of the land I bought of Hannah Sawer. Executors—son, Richard, and son, Ephraim. Witnesses—Charles Dennis, Joseph Williams, Isaac Tomlinson. Proved March 9, 1789.

1789, Feb. 7. Inventory, £202.3.2, made by John Hedger and Isaac Tomlinson. Lib. 30, p. 124.

**1788, Jan. 10. Chetwood, William,** of Essex Co. Int. Adm'r—George Ross. Fellowbondsman—Samuel Smith; both of said Co. The said George Ross is appointed Adm'r of the estate that was left unadministered by Margaret Chetwood. Lib. 31, p. 244.

**1786, March 14. Chew, Richard,** of Monmouth Co. Int. Adm'r—Tunis Vanderveer. Fellowbondsman—David Vanderveer; both of said Co. Witness—Rulef P. Schanck.

1786, May 10. Inventory, £46.2.10, made by John Reid and David Loyd. Lib. 28, p. 294.

**1787, Jan. 8. Church, Nathan,** of Lower Precinct, Cape May Co.; will of. Brothers and sisters, Silas Church, Thomas Church, Susannah Richardson, Neomi Ingrum, Patience Schillinger and Lydia Paige, daughter of my sister, Lydia, deceased, and children of my sister, Prudence Schillinger, deceased, the remainder after debts are paid. Executor—Jeremiah Eldredge. Witnesses—James Whilldin, James Schillinger, Abraham Ytes [Yates]. Proved Jan. 20, 1787.

1787, Feb. 8. Inventory, £283.17.0, made by Constantine Foster and Ellis Hughes, Jr. Lib. 29, p. 231.

**1787, Oct. 7. Clap, Austin,** of New Mills, Northampton Township, Burlington Co., cordwainer; will of. To John Clap, son of George Clap, deceased, £10. To Jonathan Clap, son of William Clap, deceased, £10, when 21. To Austin Jobes, son of David Jobes, £5, when 21. Brother, John Clap, residue. Executor—brother, John. Witnesses—Joseph Campion, Mary Campion, John Allen. Proved Nov. 26, 1787.

1787, Nov. 21. Inventory, £86.1.4, made by William Kempton and Curliss Shinn. Lib. 29, p. 25.

**1787, Nov. 26. Clark, Hannah,** of Deptford Township, Gloucester Co.; will of. Real and personal estate may be sold or otherways disposed of, to the advantage of the children of my deceased sister, Ann Rayworth, and Martha Johns, when they come of age. Executors—brother-in-law, Richard Johns, and my nephew, Isaac Henszey. Witnesses—John Dill, Loudwick Hurst, Frederic Shinefelt. Proved March 15, 1788. Lib. 31, p. 15.

CALENDAR OF WILLS—1786-1790        45

**1788, May 4. Clark, James,** of Pilesgrove, Salem Co., yeoman; will of. Eldest son, Thomas, 56 acres adjoining the new house on the creek. Sons, Peter and Carney, 110 acres which I purchased of Carmack. Son, James, 3 acres that I bought of Thomas Hoffman. Sons, Henry and James, all the old tract where I live. Daughter, Cathrine Clark, £150. Executors—sons, James and Henry. Witnesses—Thomas Clark, Robert Clark, Adam Louderback. Proved May 20, 1788.
1788, May 22. Inventory, £413.13.5, made by William Dickeson and Thomas Clark. Lib. 31, p. 42.

**1786, Feb. 17. Clark, John,** of Cohansey, Cumberland Co., shopkeeper; will of. All goods to be sold. Sister, Isabella Clark, and my sister-in-law, Elizabeth Smith, £50 each. Brother, Alexander Clark, the residue. Executor—friend, David Lapsley. Witnesses—William Kidd, John Fitzsimmons, Sary Fitzsimmons. Proved Feb. 28, 1786.
1786, Feb. 28. Inventory, £719.9.7, made by James Harris and James Clark. Lib. 28, p. 179.

**1787, March. Clark, Thomas, Sarah, Rebecca, Lydia and Jonathan,** of Gloucester Co. Wards. Children of William and Susannah Clark, of said Co. Their mother, Susannah Clark, desires that Caleb Attmore may be made their Guardian.
1787, March 27. Guardian—Caleb Attmore, of Philadelphia. Fellowbondsman—Henry Cliffton, of Hunterdon Co. Lib. 29, p. 121.

**1786, Jan. 28. Clark, William,** of Upper Penns Neck, Salem Co., weaver; will of. My estate to be sold and money put to interest, until my niece and nephew, Catherine and Noah Clark, are 21, and then the whole to be paid to them; but, if they die, then sister-in-law, Sarah Loutherback, to have £10, and rest to my brothers, George and John, and sister, Catherine, in Ireland. Executors—cousin, James Clark, Sr., and my sister-in-law, Sarah Loutherback. Witnesses—Elijah Peddrick, Rebeca Pedrick. Proved Feb. 15, 1786.
1786, Feb. 11. Inventory, £99.17.4, made by Isaac Pedrick and Elijah Peddrick. File No. 1865 Q.

**1787, April 26. Clarke, John,** of Middlesex Co. Int. Adm'r—Charles Clarke. Fellowbondsman—Thomas Clarke; both of said Co. Witness —William Hyer, Jr.
1787, April 24. Inventory, £204.3.8, made by Ezekiel Smith and Robert White. Lib. 29, p. 365.

**1790, June 1. Clemans, Enoch,** of Waterford, Gloucester Co., yeoman; will of. Wife, Elizabeth, is to put my son, Enoch, out to a trade, when he is 14. Wife to have the use of personal estate in order to bring up my said son, and, when he is 21, he is to have the said estate. Executrix—wife, Elizabeth. Witnesses—Samuel Hillman, David Davis. Proved Aug. 26, 1790.
1797, July 31. Inventory, £49.13.8, made by Joseph Hillman and John Middleton. Lib. 32, p. 190.

**1788, Dec. 8. Clemans, Judah,** of Waterford, Gloucester Co. Int. Adm'x—Esther Clemans. Fellowbondsmen—John Clemans and Enoch Clemans; all of said Co.
1788, Aug. 19. Inventory, £332.15.0, made by David Davis and Thomas Thorne. Lib. 31, p. 35.

**1790, Sept. 4. Clement, Martha,** of Gloucester Co. Int. Adm'r—Richard Gibbs, of Salem Co. Fellowbondsman—Ethen Lore, of Cumberland Co.
1790, Sept. 22. Inventory, £100, made by Lucas Gibbs and Gervas Hall. Lib. 31, p. 476.

**1788, April 16. Clement, Peter,** of Waterford Township, Gloucester Co.; will of. I have bought lands, and suffered my son, David, to take deeds in his own name; so now I give him £5. Wife, Mary, my personal estate, and the profits of my lands. Sons, William, John and Jacob, all my lands. Executors—wife, Mary, and my son, William. Witnesses—Edward Clemans, Balser Hatso, Joseph Stokes. Proved Aug. 20, 1789.
1789, Aug. 17. Inventory, £640.4.4, made by Joseph Champion and Joseph Stokes. Lib. 30, p. 113.

**1790, Nov. 29. Clifford, Edward,** of Bethlehem Township, Hunterdon Co. Int. Adm'rs—John Clifford, of Amwell, Joseph Beavers, of Alexandria, and John Martin, of Bethlehem, all of said Co. Fellowbondsman—Francis McShane, of Bethlehem.
1790, Nov. 8. Inventory, £447. 2. 5, made by Elias Wikoff and Francis McShane.
1811, May 8. Account by Joseph Beavers and John Clifford, surviving Adm'rs. "Debts yet due from estate of Edward Clifford."
Lib. 30, p. 315.

**1790, April 14. Cline, Jacob,** of Greenwich, Sussex Co.; will of. Daughter, Catharine, wife of Matthias Shipman, Jr., a bed and other goods. Rest of personal estate to be sold, and money divided among my wife, Elizabeth, my daughter, Catharine, and my son, Jacob. Brother, John, my apparel for the use of my son, Jacob, and my brother is to bring him up. Executors—brother, John, and my brother-in-law, Balser Damer. Witnesses—Mathias Shipman, John Fred Ernst, Valentine Bidleman. Proved Nov. 25, 1790.
1790, Nov. 10. Inventory, £188.7.1, made by Jacob Shipman and Valentine Bidleman. Lib. 35, p. 32.

**1787, Aug. 26. Coate, Henry,** of Kingwood, Hunterdon Co.; will of. My wife and children to continue on this plantation, and they shall share alike. What I gave to my two daughters, Hettey Crooks and Lucy, to be reckoned as so much of their legacy. Son, Robert, shall own what is called his, above his share. My wife and son, Robert, are to have advise of my friends, Jeremiah King, Robert Emley and Joseph King in the management of the place. Sons, John and Henry, to be educated till they go to a trade. Executors—wife, Deborah, and son, Robert. Witnesses—Robert Emley, Joseph King, Jeremiah King. Proved Sept. 27, 1787.
1787, Sept. 26. Inventory, £406.9.6, made by Samuel Kester and Aaron Furman.
1806, Aug. 8. Robert Coate and his wife, Sarah, object to the appointment of auditors. Lib. 29, p. 280.

**1786, April 25. Coate, John,** of Springfield Township, Burlington Co.; will of. Niece, Hester Earle, wife of Caleb Earle, a mare. Nephew, Caleb Earle, the rest of estate, personal and real; except a bond I

CALENDAR OF WILLS—1786-1790    47

have against my brother, Daniel Coate, which I give to Daniel. Executor—nephew, Caleb Earle. Witnesses—Samuel Bloomfield, John Gardiner, Jr., John Pope. Proved June 12, 1786.
1786, June 1. Inventory, £107.5.1, made by John Black and Henry Ridgway. Lib. 28, p. 11.

**1788, Sept. 13. Coate, William,** of Burlington Co. Ward. Son of Barzillai Coate, of said Co., deceased. Said Ward, having real and personal estate, makes choice of Samuel Evans, as his Guardian.
1788, Sept. 13. Guardian—Samuel Evans. Fellowbondsman—Thomas Hollinshead; both of Evesham Township, said Co. Lib. 30, p. 61.

**1786, March 2. Cochey, John,** of Burlington Co. Int. Adm'r—Joseph Ridgway. Fellowbondsman—William Ridgway; both of Willingborough, said Co.
1786, March 2. Renunciation by Miriam Cochey, widow of John, in favor of her brother, Joseph Ridgway.
1786, March 22. Inventory, £64.6.11, made by Amos Austin and Thomas Green. Lib. 28, p. 76.

**1788, Sept. 10. Codd, John,** of Greenwich Township, Gloucester Co.; will of. Daughters, Mary Helloms and Elenor Steelman, 5 shillings each. Eldest son, Joseph, a like amount. Sons, John and Jeams, all real and personal estate. Executors—sons, John and Jeams. Witnesses—Isaac Steelman, John Shute, Jr., Ebenezer Adams. Proved Oct. 6, 1788.
1788, Sept. Inventory, made by Ebenezer Adams and Daniel Sutherland. Lib. 31, p. 30.

**1786, May 9. Cogler, John,** of Chester Township, Burlington Co., yeoman; will of. To James Hollinshead, son of John and Ales Hollinshead, all real and personal estate, when he is 21; but, if he does not live till then, to be divided between his sisters, Hannah and Mary, and his brother, Edmund. Executors—Joshua Bispham, Jr., and Edmund Hollinshead. Witnesses—John Risdon, Abraham Wells, Edmund Hollinshead. Proved Feb. 25, 1790.
1790, Jan. 23. Inventory, £82.5.9, made by Jacob Hollinshead and John Risdon. Lib. 32, p. 89.

**1787, June 14. Coleman, Jeremiah,** of Roxbury, Morris Co. Int. Adm'r—William Coleman, Fellowbondsman—John Coleman; both of said place. Witnesses—Abraham Canfield, Jr., and Jabez Campfield, Surrogate. Lib. 29, p. 473.

**1790, March 4. Colle, James,** of Springfield, Elizabeth Township, Essex Co.; will of. Wife, Anna, the interest of my bonds. Sister, Hannah, wife of David Morehouse, some goods, after death of my wife; and, if my sister is deceased, the goods to go to her eldest daughter. Sister, Mary Hedgers, 12 shillings. Wife rest of goods. Brother, Daniel, said bonds, after wife's death. Executors—wife, Anna, and my friend, Walter Smith. Witnesses—John Woodruff, Noah Brookfield, Samuel Woodruff. Proved June 30, 1790.
Lib. 30, p. 344.

## 48   NEW JERSEY POST-REVOLUTIONARY DOCUMENTS

**1787, Feb. 3. Collier, Henry,** of Horsneck, Essex Co.; will of. Son, Isaac Collier, 102 acres, being a part of my old place, bounded east by Henry Francisco and Thomas Sanfort. Daughter, Elizabeth, wife of Josiah Gould, 98 acres, being the rest of said place. Daughter, Susannah Collier, 32 acres, bounded by Henry Spear and Tunis Spear. To the children of my son, Joseph, deceased, £7 and 10 shillings; that is, to Elizabeth, Jemima, Rachel, Mary and Margaret. To the children of my daughter, Eleanor, wife of Aaron Kierstead, deceased, £7 and 10 shillings. To the children of my daughter, Sophia, wife of Henry Spear, £7 and 10 shillings. Daughter, Susannah, a cow, Children, Isaac, Henry Spear, Aaron Kiearsted, Josiah Gould and heirs of son, Joseph, and Susannah Collier, the 5 children of my son, Joseph. Executors—son, Isaac, and Josiah Gould. Witnesses—Arie Consolyee, Samuel Gould, Encrease Gould. Proved May 24, 1788.

1788, April 2. Inventory, made by Encrease Gould and James Post.
Lib. 38, p. 94.

**1787, March 22. Colver, Ephraim,** of Roxbury, Morris Co. Int. Adm'rs Isaac Heaton and Susannah Heaton. Fellowbondsman—John Bell; all of said place. Witness—Hannah Canfield.   Lib. 29, p. 472.

**1786, March 8. Colver, Thomas,** of Roxbury, Morris Co.; will of. Sons, Amos, Simon and my grandson, son of my son, Ephraim, deceased, the place where I live. Son, Thomas, the 40 acres where he lives, and my daughter, Lydia Winkler, to have the 15 acres where she formerly lived. To Ephraim Tuttle, the 3rd, £5. Executors—sons, Thomas and Simon. Witnesses—Andrew Flack, Silas Drake, John Hager. Proved Sept. 27, 1786.

1786, Aug. 5. Inventory, £59.7.8, made by Andrew Flack and Robert Colver.   Lib. 28, p. 484.

**1786, Nov. 15. Compton, Cornelius,** of Freehold, Monmouth Co.; will of. All real and personal estate to be sold. Sons, Jacob and William, £10 each, more than my other children. Children, Luis, Jacob and William, and my daughters, Sarah Ferrell, Usilla Compton, Hannah Compton and Nancy Compton, the residue. Executors—friends, John Baird and David Baird. Witnesses—Jacob Smith, John Clayton, Jr., Nathaniel Ferrill. Proved March 11, 1788.

1788, March 7. Inventory, £349.15.6, made by William Dey and John Dey. Plantation of 100 acres, value £250.   Lib. 30, p. 64.

**1786, Feb. 25. Compton, Eliakim,** of Middlesex Co. Int. Adm'r—Joseph Fitz Randolph, of Piscataway. Fellowbondsman—Daniel Compton, of Woodbridge; both of said Co. Whereas, Eliakim Compton made David Crow and Gabriel Compton his Executors, and they have since deceased.   Lib. 28, p. 341. (For will, see Lib. L, p. 409).

**1789, March 2. Compton, Gabriel,** of Woodbridge, Middlesex Co. Int. Adm'r—William Manning, Jr. Fellowbondsman—James Compton; both of said place. Said William Manning, Jr., is Adm'r of goods left unadministered by Mary Compton, who is also dead.
Lib. 31, p. 395.

CALENDAR OF WILLS—1786-1790    49

**1787, Dec. 18. Conklin, Isaac,** of Bergen Co. Int. Adm'x—Elizabeth Conklin. Fellowbondsmen——Harmanus Van Tuyl and James Skatts; all of said Co. Witness—Catherine Miller.
1787, Dec. 17. Inventory, £36.14.0, made by John Van Horne and Simon Van Winkle.    Lib. 29, p. 536.

**1788, Sept. 13. Conklin, Stephen, Jr.,** of Morristown, Morris Co. Int. Adm'rs—Stephen Conkling and Job Brookfield. Fellowbondsman—Benjamin Lindsly; all of said place.
1788, Sept. 13. Renunciation by Rachel Conklin, widow of Stephen.
1788, Sept. 15. Inventory, £377.14.8, made by Elijah Peirson and John Mills.    Lib. 31, p. 199.

**1786, April 15. Connelly, Owen,** of Pittsgrove Township, Salem Co.; will of. To Owen Connelly, son of Briant Conely, a watch, and a desk which is at my brother's. To Temperance Conely, daughter of Briant Conely, now living with William Lippincott, a cow. Brother, Briant, my apparel. To Ephraim Conely, living with Christopher Rape, bayonet and gun. Executors—brother, Briant, and Daniel Stanton. Witnesses—Robert Tyrrel, James Love, Ruth Currey. Proved Jan. 15, 1787.    File No. 1949 Q.

**1786, Jan. 21. Connet, Elizabeth,** of Essex Co., widow; will of. Son, Daniel Connet, 5 shillings. Granddaughter, Abigail Connet, daughter of my son, Daniel, £6, when 18. Daughter, Rhoda Connet, rest of my estate; and, if she die without heirs, then to my son, Edward Connet. Grandchildren, Mary, Phebe, Rhoda and Betsy Connet, daughters of my son, Moses Connet, deceased, some apparel. Executors—son, Edward Connet, and my daughter, Rhoda Connet. Witnesses—Moses Ross, Joanna Ross, William Coles. Proved Feb. 23, 1788.
1787, June 13. Inventory, made by Thomas Marsh and Daniel Baker.
Lib. 31, p. 233.

**1786, Jan. 21. Connet, John,** of Bridgewater, Somerset Co. Int. Adm'rs—Anne Connet and David Kelly. Fellowbondsman—Benjamin Blackford; all of said Co. Witnesses—Henry H. Schenck and Nicholas Perine.
1786, Jan. 17. Inventory, made by Jacob Bond and Anthony Cosad.
Lib. 29, p. 196.

**1790, Jan. 1. Conrey, Peter,** of Middletown, Monmouth Co.; will of. Daughter, Nancey, some goods. Daughter, Peggey, a bed. Daughter, Nancy, to have charge of children under age, namely, Peggey, Amay, Peter, Caty and John. They are all to have the estate when they come of age. Executors—friends, John Stillwell, at Garrets Hill, and John Morgan, blacksmith, of South Amboy. Witnesses—John Cook, Samuel Hoffmire, Nicholas Clark. Proved March 23, 1790.
1790, Feb. 4. Inventory, £153.9.3, made by Stephen Van Brakel and Peter Johnston.    Lib. 30, p. 395.

**1786, Feb. 18. Conrow, Darling, Rebeckah, Jaleel and David,** of Burlington Co. Wards. Children of Jacob Conrow, of said Co., deceased. Guardian—Darling Conrow. Fellowbondsman—Nathaniel Middleton; both of Chester Township, said Co.    Lib. 28, p. 81.

50   NEW JERSEY POST-REVOLUTIONARY DOCUMENTS

**1788, April 14. Conrow, Darling,** of Chester, Burlington Co. Int. Adm'x—Sarah Conrow. Fellowbondsmen—John Warrington and George Elkinton; all of said Co.
1788, April 10. Inventory, £382.2.10, made by John Roberts and Nathaniel Middleton. Lib. 30, p. 56.

**1786, Aug. 5. Cook, Adilicia,** of Woolwich Township, Gloucester Co. Int. Adm'r—Robert Cook. Fellowbondsman—John Matts; both of said place. Witnesses—William Hugg, Jr., and Joseph Hugg, Surrogate.
1786, July 28. Inventory, £128.0.2, made by Solomon Lippincott and John Matts. Lib. 28, p. 123.

**1786, Aug. 14. Cook, Ebenezer,** of Woolwich Township, Gloucester Co.; will of. Mother, Elizabeth Cook, £10, and to have her support on the place. Brother, Robert, £3. Brother, Joseph, £20. The plantation to be sold at mother's death, and divided between my two sisters, Hannah Adams and Caseandre Cook. Executors—my mother, my friend, Ebenezer Adams, and Caseandre Cook. Witnesses—Robert Zane, Rachel Zane, William Wood. Proved April 4, 1788. Lib. 31, p. 24.

**1790, Feb. 6. Cook, Elizabeth,** of Woolwich Township, Gloucester Co.; will of. Grandchildren, 5 shillings each. Son, Robert, £10. Daughter, Caseandra Cook, the pewter. Son, Joseph Cook, rest of estate. Executors—sons, Robert and Joseph Cook. Witnesses—Simon Zane, Benjamin Zane, Jacob Gosling. Proved April 16, 1790.
1790, March 11. Inventory, £120.12.7, made by Simon Zane and William Wood. Lib. 31, p. 426.

**1786, Oct. 1. Cook, Henry,** of Maidenhead, Hunterdon Co.; will of. Brother, William Cook, 50 acres that join Captain Joseph Scudder's land. Son, Samuel, 50 acres, being the upper part of the plantation where he lives. Son, Aaron, 50 acres of the lower part, down by the corner of William, Samuel and Aaron Cook. The other 50 acres to be sold, and the money divided among my children, Elisha, Richard, Henry, Sarah, Abigail, William and Job. Wife, Eleanor, my personal estate, and to be provided for on that part of my plantation which I have given to my son, Aaron; and his mother is to live with him. To Elias Cook, £15. Son, Richard, to have 3 acres in some convenient place. Executors—sons, Elisha, Samuel and Henry. Witnesses—Joseph Phillips, Robert Furman, Joseph Scudder. Proved Nov. 26, 1786.
1786, Oct. 1. Inventory, £258.9.6, made by Aaron Vancleve and Robert Furman. Lib. 28, p. 217.

**1786, Jan. 9. Cook, Joannah,** of Newark, Essex Co.; will of. Brother, John Ward, £20. To Jesey Ward, £5. To Elexander Hambelton Marsh, £20. To Abraham Ward, rest of personal and real estate. Executors—Abraham Ward and Zebulon Jones. Witnesses—Aaron Young, William Cassels, Isaac Badwin [Baldwin]. Proved July 18, 1787. Lib. 29, p. 401.

**1789, March 18. Cool, John,** of Upper Penns Neck, Salem Co., yeoman; will of. Wife, Ann, ⅓ of my land during her life. Son, John, land where I live, and a marsh on Oldmans Creek in Gloucester Co. Daughters, Hannah and Kesiah Cool, rest of land, and moveable

CALENDAR OF WILLS—1786-1790   51

estate. Executors—son, John, and Henry Guest. Witnesses—William Shute, Henry Guest, Sarah Shute. Proved Dec. 21, 1789.
1789, Dec. 10. Inventory, £129.15.4, made by Leonard Stanton and James Hewes. Lib. 31, p. 331.

**1787, July 10. Cooper, Daniel, Jr.,** of Morristown, Morris Co. Int. Admr's—Peter Cooper and William Cooper. Fellowbondsman—John Cooper; all of said place. Witness—Benjamin Vail.
1787, July 10. Renunciation by Ann Cooper, widow of Daniel Cooper, Jr.
1787, June 27. Inventory, £450.14.8, made by Benjamin Vail and Ephraim Martin. Lib. 29, p. 472.

**1789, May 4. Cooper, James,** of Deptford Township, Gloucester Co.; will of. Son, Benjamin, all my lands at Alloways Creek, Salem Co. Son, James, my plantation and all lands adjoining. Daughter, Rebecca Cooper, my lots of land that I bought of John Sharp, lying in Woodbury; also ½ acre that I bought of James Brown. Son, William, the lower plantation on Mantua Creek, when he is 21. Son, John, the other land on Mantua Creek. Daughter, Rebecca, £400. Daughter, Esther, £400. Daughter, Esther Cooper, land in Woodbury, on west side of the great road. Sons, James, William and John, my cedar swamp. Son Benjamin's daughter, Mary Cooper, £50, if she lives with my family, when 18. Daughter, Rebecca, her mother's apparel. Wife to have £300, and otherwise provided for. The 4-acre woodlot, that I bought of John Sharp, to my sons, Benjamin and James. Executors——sons, James and William. Witnesses—John Tatum, Joseph Clement, James Whitall, Jr. Proved Jan. 8, 1790.
1789, Aug. 24. Inventory, £1,693.16.8½, made by John Tatum and Phinehas Lord. Lib. 31, p. 423.

**1789, Dec. 2. Cooper, James,** of Roxbury, Morris Co. Int. Adm'rs—Phebe Cooper and David Thompson. Fellowbondsman—Henry Cooper; all of said Co. Witness—Jabez Guinnup.
1789, Dec. 4. Inventory, £422.5.7, made by John Rolston and John Wright. Lib. 30, p. 232.

**1788, July 12. Cooper, Nathan,** of Roxbury Township, Morris Co.; will of. Sons, Henry and James, all lands in Roxbury, on south side of road from Mendham to Roxbury, bounded by James Hopkins and Daniel Seward, of 250 acres; also land on north of road bounded by Nathan Cooper, Jr., Samuel Wills and James Hopkins, of 200 acres. Son, Nathan, 5 shillings. Son, Davenpoort Cooper, £10. Daughter, Hannah Saterly, 5 shillings. Daughter, Mary Clover, 5 shillings. Executors—sons, Henry and James. Witnesses—David Thompson, Caleb Howell, Pain Brown. Proved Aug. 7, 1788.
1788, Nov. 29. Inventory, £8.13.0, made by Jacob Conine and Constant Victor King. Lib. 31, p. 179.

**1788, April 12. Cooper, Robert,** of Woolwich Township, Gloucester Co.; will of. Son, Samuel, plantation where I live, except woodland lying outside of the orchard fence, with the lane that leads to Mary Key's lot; also the old meadow of 5 acres, and 15 acres of cedar swamp. Daughter, Mary, 11 acres of meadow in Penns Neck, Salem Co.; also £100. Son, Joseph, the new meadow of 9 acres, and the

## 52 NEW JERSEY POST-REVOLUTIONARY DOCUMENTS

woodland excepted; also 10 acres of cedar swamp at the lower end; also 28 acres of woodland that I bought of Andrew Homan; when he is 21. Daughter Sarah, 7½ acres of meadow, opposite Andrew Matson's house. Son, Robert, my house and lot in Sand Town. Wife, Elizabeth, £200. Son, Samuel, goods. Executors—wife, Elizabeth, and my son, Samuel. Witnesses—Benjamin Rambo, Samuel Beckett, Peter Beckett. Proved April 29, 1788. Lib. 31, p. 22.

**1790, Jan. 18. Cooper, Thomas,** of Woolwich Township, Gloucester Co. Int. Adm'x—Ann Cooper. Fellowbondsman — Ebenezer Adams; both of said Co.
1790, Jan. 13. Inventory, £184.10.7, made by David Hendrickson and Ebenezer Adams. Lib. 31, p. 476.

**1787, April 27. Cooper, William,** of Newton Township, Gloucester Co.; will of. Wife, Abigail, the brick house on the side of the road where my ferry house stands, in which William Goodwin lately lived, while my widow. Son, Daniel, my ferry and ferry house, except what I give to my sons, Charles and Richard; also ½ of the lands on the south side of Coopers Creek; also all my ferry boats; he paying every year to my wife, £60, and allowing my son, Richard, to occupy the store house on the wharf. Son, Richard, the said brick house, after death or marriage of my wife, and the other ½ of the lands on this side of the creek, except what I devise to my son, Charles; he paying to my son, Charles, £100, when he is 21. Son, Charles, the house and lots that I bought of Robert Parish's assignees; also the lot bought of Andrew Forsyth, and house and lot in tenure of Martin Cox, blacksmith. Daughters, Mary and Sarah, all my real estate in Philadelphia. Wife, £300. Daughters, Mary and Sarah, £400, and to Elizabeth Turner, £15. Wife to have use of all, to bring up my children. My nail factory is to be completed. Executors—wife, Abigail, son, Daniel, and brother, James Whital. Witnesses—Rebecca Cooper, Benjamin Van Leer, Richard Howell. Proved May 17, 1787, at Timber Creek.
1787, May 27. Inventory, £2,989.12.4, made by John Hall and Samuel Harrison. Lib. 29, p. 104.

**1787, Oct. 27. Corcelius, Peter, Sr.,** of Newtown, Sussex Co. Int. Adm'rs—Peter Corcelius and Jacob Lance. Fellowbondsman—George Corcelius; all of said place. Witness—Francis Price.
1787, Oct. 23. Inventory, made by John Gustin and Francis Price.
Lib. 29, p. 400.

**1789, Oct. 28. Corgie, George,** of Lower Precinct, Cape May Co. Ward. Son of Robert Corgie, of said place. Said Ward is under 14 years of age.
1789, Oct. 28. Guardian—Robert Corgie. Fellowbondsmen—Constant Hughes and George Taylor; both of said place. Witnesses—Sarah Hand and Jesse Hand. Lib. 31, p. 371.

**1789, Oct. 28. Corgie, Robert,** of Lower Precinct, Cape May Co. Ward. Son of Robert Corgie, of said place. Said Ward is under 14 years of age.
1789, Oct. 28. Guardian—Robert Corgie. Fellowbondsmen—Constant Hughes and George Taylor; both of said place. Witnesses—Sarah Hand and Jesse Hand. Lib. 31, p. 371.

CALENDAR OF WILLS—1786-1790     53

**1789, Aug. 17. Corgie, Sophia,** of Lower Precinct, Cape May Co. Ward. Daughter of Robert Corgie, of said place. Said Ward is under 14 years of age.
1789, Aug. 17. Guardian—Robert Corgie. Fellowbondsmen—Constant Hughes and George Taylor; both of said place. Witnesses—Sarah Hand and Jesse Hand. Lib. 31, p. 371.

**1786, March 11. Corlis, John,** of Shrewsbury, Monmouth Co., yeoman; will of. Wife, Rachel, the goods which she brought, and wife and children to live on the lands, till my daughter, Ann, is 21. Son, Asher, ½ of my lands. Son, John, the other ½. Wife to have £300. Daughters, Elizabeth and Ann, £300 each. Executors—friends, Joseph Wardell, Jr., and Benjamin Corlies. Witnesses—Jacob Hance, David Hance, William Corlies. Proved Jan. 5, 1787.
1786, Nov. 13. Inventory, £854.3.3, made by William Parker and John Hartshorne. Lib. 29, p. 333.

**1786, Dec. 1. Cornel, Peter,** of Middlesex Co. Int. Adm'rs—Elenor Cornel and Roelof Cornel. Fellowbondsman—Barent Johnson; all of said Co.
1786, Nov. 29. Inventory, £107.8.11, made by Cornelius Vanderbilt and Jacob Meserol. Lib. 28, p. 338.

**1786, Sept. 21. Cornel, Roeloff,** of Middlesex Co. Int. Adm'x—Mary [Maria] Cornel. Fellowbondsman—William Ryder; both of said Co.
1786, Aug. 26. Inventory, made by Johannes Van Leuwe and Hermanus Cortelyou. Lib. 28, p. 339.

**1790, June 12. Cornell, Albart,** of Millstone, Somerset Co., yeoman; will of. Wife, Anne, all real and personal estate while my widow. Son. Barnt, farm where I live. Grandson, Albert Cornell, a watch. Daughter, Jannetje, £150. Daughter, Elizabeth, £150. Executors—son, Barnt, and my son-in-law, Peter Quick. Witnesses—Peter Wyckoff, Cornelius Cornell, Joseph Cornell. Proved Aug. 20, 1790.
1790, Aug. 19. Inventory, made by Joseph Cornell, Cornelius Cornell and Jacobus Gerritsen. Lib. 31, p. 511.

**1787, Jan. 13. Cornell, Benjamin,** of Hopewell Township, Hunterdon Co.; will of. Moveable estate, and 2 houses and lots in Pennington, in tenure of Thomas Bullman and Thomas Craven, to be sold. Niece, Martha, wife of David Baldwin, plantation where they live. To Rebeccah Fitch, and her daughter, Sarah, £25 each, for their care in keeping my house. As to the mills and mill lot between Ralph Hunt and me, I hold a mortgage against said Hunt for his part, which is to be given up to him when he pays £60. My ½ of mills and plantation where I live, I give to my nephews, Joseph and Samuel Cornell, and they are to pay £200, which is to be divided between my brother John's sons, William, Abraham, Benjamin and Jonathan. If they should die, then my brothers John's and Edward's children to have the same. Executors—friends, Thomas Bullman and David Baldwin. Witnesses—Ralph Hunt, Jona. Wood, Hezekiah S. Woodruff. Proved Jan. 27, 1787.
1787, Jan. 25. Inventory, £1,357.6.8, made by John P. Hunt and Hezekiah Stiles Woodruff.
1792, Oct. 30. Account by Executors. Lib. 29, p. 246.

**1787, Nov. 27. Cornish, James,** of Evesham, Burlington Co. Int. Adm'r—Levi Lippincott. Fellowbondsman—Jacob Wills; both of said place. Witness—Thomas Adams.
1787, Nov. 26. Inventory, £30.10.3, made by Jacob Wills and C. Evans. Lib. 29, p. 78.

**1786, Jan. 28. Corson, Darius,** of Cape May Co. Int. Adm'x—Martha Corson, widow. Fellowbondsman—John Goldin; both of said Co. Witnesses—Hugh Hathorn and Jacob Willets. Lib. 38, p. 79.

**1789, Aug. 3. Corson, Ellis,** of Cape May Co. Int. Adm'r—Eli Corson. Fellowbondsman—Jacob Corson; both of Upper Precinct, said Co. Witnesses—Richard Townsend and Parmenas Corson.
1789, March 9. Inventory, £77.9.1, made by Parmenas Corson and Jesse Corson. Lib. 31, p. 370.

**1787, April 12. Corwin, Benjamin,** of Roxbury Township, Morris Co.; will of. Wife, Mary, her thirds. Son, Abner, all land. Daughter, Experience Reeve, moveable estate. Daughters, Susannah Corwin and Sarah Corwin, moveable estate. Executors—wife, Mary, and my son, Abner. Witnesses—Abraham Dickerson, Susanna Luther, William Woodhull. Proved April 30, 1787.
1787, April 28. Inventory, £394.15.4, made by William Woodhull and William Corwin. Lib. 29, p. 456.

**1788, Jan. 7. Corwine, George,** of Amwell, Hunterdon Co. Int. Adm'x—Ruth Corwine. Fellowbondsman—Obadiah Hunt; both of said Co. Witnesses—Adrian R. Furman and Moore Furman, Surrogate.
1788, Jan. 4. Inventory, £217.14.10, made by John Reed and Obadiah Hunt. Lib. 31, p. 141.

**1786, Dec. 8. Cory, Abner,** of Rahway, Essex Co.; will of. Wife, Neomai, horse and chair, a bed and furniture. Rest of the moveable estate to be sold. Son, Aaron, ⅜ of my real estate, when he is 21. The other ⅝ to my daughters, Sarah Cory, Susannah Cory and Racheal Cory, when they are 21. Executors—brother, David Cory, and my brother-in-law, Joseph Freeman, Jr., and Daniel Marsh. Witnesses—Benjamin Cory, Isaac Ross, Joseph Lee. Proved Sept. 29, 1787.
1786, Dec. 21. Inventory, £295.17.8, made by Jacob Winans and Abner Sayre. Lib. 29, p. 405.

**1788, Feb. 5. Cory, Noah,** of Essex Co. Ward. Son of John Cory, of said Co., deceased. Said Ward makes choice of John Cory as his Guardian.
1788, Feb. 5. Guardian—John Cory. Fellowbondsman—Thomas Woodruff, Jr.; both of said Co. Lib. 38, p. 97.

**1789, Dec. 11. Cory, Samuel,** of Elizabeth Town, Essex Co.; will of. Wife, Nency, the use of my plantation. Mother, Rachel Cory, a hive of bees and pork. Brother, Abraham Cory, my land, at wife's death. To James Raymond, son of my eldest sister, Mary, my hat that I wear; and to Mary's son, Seth, a chest. Executors—brother, Abraham, and my friend, Nathaniel Broadwell, of Morris Co. Witnesses—Nathaniel Taylor, Samuel Woodruff, Richard Swaim. Proved March 6, 1790.
Lib. 30, p. 320.

CALENDAR OF WILLS—1786-1790 55

**1790, May 24. Cosad, Anthony,** of Bernards Town, Somerset Co.; will of. Wife, Catherine, use of my home place to bring up my children, until they go to trades. I also give her goods and stock. Rest of land to be sold. Son, Thomas, 5 shillings. Son, Samuel, a colt. Sons, Jacob, Aaron and John, and my daughters, Mary Compton, Elizabeth Cosad, Catherine Cosad and Hannah Cosad, each a share with my sons, Thomas and Samuel. Jacob, Aaron and John to learn trades. Executors—brother, Samuel, and friend, David Smally, and, if either die, then I appoint James Bishop. Witnesses—Stephen Coon, Benjamin Winans, James Bishop. Proved June 10, 1790.
1790, June 10. Inventory, £160.2.7, made by David Kelly and James Bishop. Lib. 31, p. 509.

**1786, Sept. 20. Couvenhoven, Pieter,** of Somerset Co.; will of. Eldest son, Nicholas, plantation which I bought from my brother, Garret, where Nicholas now lives, of 218 acres; also 8 acres of my homestead; also ½ of the salt meadow near the mouth of South River; and he is to pay £250 to my grandchildren, Peter Probasco, and Mary, wife of Abraham Hoogeland. Son, Joseph, my homestead of 300 acres, except the said 8; also ½ of the said salt meadow; and he is to pay £400 to my daughters, Mary and Elizabeth. Elizabeth Lampree is to live with my son, Joseph, during her life. Executors—sons, Nicholas and Joseph, and my friend, Abraham Staats. Witnesses—Gabriel Vandervoort, John Kells, John Aten. Proved March 29, 1788.
Lib. 31, p. 158.

**1789, June 27. Covenhoven, Alche,** of Monmouth Co. Ward. Daughter of David Covenhoven, of said Co., deceased. Said Ward makes choice of Tunis Vanderveer as her Guardian.
1789, June 27. Guardian—Tunis Vanderveer, son of Garrit. Fellowbondsman—David Covenhoven; both of said Co. Witness—Rachel Henderson. Lib. 30, p. 189.

**1786, Sept. 29. Covenhoven, David,** of Monmouth Co. Int. Adm'r—John Covenhoven. Fellowbondsman—Joseph Clayton; both of said Co. Witness—Elisha Walton.
1786, Sept. 27. Renunciation by Idah Covenhoven. Witness—David Covenhoven.
1786, Sept. 22. Inventory, £502.19.2, made by Joseph Clayton and Elisha Walton. Lib. 28, p. 291.

**1786, May 20. Covenhoven, Jacob,** of Monmouth Co. Ward. Son of Jacob Covenhoven, of said Co., deceased. Said Ward makes choice of Thomas Seabrook as his Guardian.
1786, May 20. Guardian—Thomas Seabrook. Fellowbondswoman—Tunis Vanderveer. Witness—Samuel Forman. Lib. 28, p. 296.

**1786, Nov. 18. Covenhoven, William A.,** of Freehold, Monmouth Co.; will of. I am bound for £100 for my son, Benjamin, which is to be paid. Son, Joseph, 150 acres of land. Son David's sons, John, David and Garret, place where my son, William, lives, and they are to pay to son, William, £200. Son, Isaac, use of the place he lives on, and, after his death, to be sold, and his son, Thomas, to have £100, and his daughters, Sarah, Elinor and Elizabeth, £50 each, and the remainder to the rest of Isaac's children. Son, William, farm I live on.

Grandson, Cornelius Covenhoven, son of Albert, £5. Granddaughter, Elizabeth, daughter of Isaac, a bed. To daughters, Hendrika, Ellinor, Elizabeth, and my daughter Mary's children, goods and livestock. Son, Benjamin, my son David's sons, my son, Joseph, my son, Isaac, my son, William, and my grandson, Cornelius, son of Albert, farming utensils. Executors—son, William, Garret Vanderveer and John Craig, merchant. Witnesses—Alexander Low, Stephen Heavland, John Craig. Proved March 19, 1790.

1790, March 17. Inventory, £183.9.2, made by Joseph Clayton, James Tapscott and Samuel P. Forman. Lib. 30, p. 400.

**1789, Jan. 28. Cowell, John,** of Hunterdon Co., doctor; will of. Wife, Mary, and my son, John, and my daughter, Mary Cowell, all real and personal estate. Children under age. Executrix—wife, Mary, and friend, Alexander Chambers, Jr. to be assistant. Witnesses—Elizabeth Smith, Eunice Cowell, Hannah Howell. Proved Feb. 9, 1789.

1789, March 10. Inventory, £2,679.4.9, made by Alexander Chambers and Benjamin Smith. Lib. 32, p. 8.

**1786, Feb. 11. Cowen, Robert,** of New Hanover Township, Burlington Co. Int. Adm'r—William Kempton. Fellowbondsman—Thomas Platt; both of said place.

1786, Feb. 7. Inventory, £23.1.7, made by John Goldy and Thomas Platt. Lib. 28, p. 78.

**1786, Jan. 27. Cox, John,** of Upper Freehold, Monmouth Co., son of James; will of. Wife, Mary, ⅓ the profits of the real estate. Son, William, farm south of Shrewbury, where I live, given to me by my father, and 10 acres which was released to me by my cousin, James Cox; but, if he die without heirs, then to my grandson, Joshua Cox, son of my son, James; and, if he die, to grandson, Abel Cox, son of James. Grandson, Elisha Cox, £6 yearly, till he has £50, and, if he die, then to Abel. Son, James, land north of Shrewsbury, and, after his death, to my grandson, Abel, son of James, and, if he die, to his brother, Joshua. Granddaughter, Willeminer Cox, £3. Daughters, Catherine, wife of Benjamin Loxley, of Philadelphia, and Mary, wife of Robert Jones, now in England, personal estate. Grandson, Robert Jones, 1,000 dollars. Granddaughter, Mary Jones, 1,000 dollars. Two eldest daughters of Benjamin Loxley, Mary and Jane, legacies. Executors—friends, Elisha Lawrence, Jr., Edward Taylor, and my sons, William and James. Witnesses—William Snowden, Esek Cox, Robert Lawrence. Proved Aug. 12, 1788.

1788, June 4. Inventory, £390.8.7, made by Peter Imlay and Peter Covenhoven. Lib. 30, p. 88.

**1790, March 12. Cox, Joseph,** of Middlesex Co. Ward. Son of Joseph Cox, of said Co., deceased. Said Ward makes choice of John Chamberlain as his guardian.

1790, March 12. Guardian—John Chamberlain. Fellowbondsman—Joshua Ely; both of said Co. Witness—William Hyer, Jr.
Lib. 30, p. 535.

**1786, Nov. 28. Cox, Moses,** of Deptford Township, Gloucester Co., yeoman; will of. Real estate to be sold. Wife, Mary, ⅛ of the personal estate, and interest of £250, and, after her death, the said £250

I give to my sons, Moses and David. My children, Jonas, Moses, David, Elizabeth, Sarah, Mary and Rebecca, rest of estate. Executors —wife, Mary, and James Wilkins. Witnesses—Joseph Cowgill, John Paul, John Stephens.
1788, May 15. Codicil. My wife is to have the produce from the farm. Witnesses—John Paul, Thomas Willson, John Stephens. Proved June 4, 1788.
1788, June 3. Inventory, £179.16.7, made by James Whitall, Jr. and John Stephens. Lib. 31, p. 20.

**1790, June 26. Cox, Rachel,** of Burlington Co. Int. Adm'rs—Lydia Cox and Seth Austin. Fellowbondsman—Thomas Buzby; all of said Co.
1790, June 3. Inventory, £140.12.9, made by Henry Jones and John Evans. Lib. 32, p. 94.

**1788, Feb. 20. Cox, Thomas,** of Greenwich Township, Gloucester Co. Int. Adm'x—Jane Cox. Fellowbondsman—Richard Gruff; both of said place. Witnesses—William K. Hugg and Joseph Hugg, Surrogate.
1788, Feb. 19. Inventory, £68.15.0, made by William Ford and John Groff. Lib. 31, p. 36.

**1787, Aug. 18. Coxe, Beulah,** of Burlington Co. Ward. Daughter of William Coxe, of said Co., deceased. Said Ward makes choice of Seth Austin as her Guardian.
1787, Oct. 30. Guardian—Seth Austin, Fellowbondsman—Samuel Stokes; both of said Co. Witness—Thomas Adams. Lib. 29, p. 81.

**1787, Jan. 19. Craig, Elias,** of Pitts Grove, Salem Co. Int. Adm'x— Mary Craig. Fellowbondsmen—James Dunlap and Frederick Freas; all of said Co.
1786, Sept. 28. Inventory, £288.16.3, made by William Garrison and Benjamin Vanmeter. File No. 1921 Q.

**1790, April 13. Craig, James,** of Westfield, Elizabeth Township, Essex Co. Int. Adm'r—Isaac Hendricks. Fellowbondsman—John Scudder. Witness—John Crane.
1790, April 14. Renunciation by Mary Craig, widow of James. Witnesses—John Crane and John Scudder.
1790, April 14. Inventory, £64.12.10, made by John Crane and John Scudder. Lib. 30, p. 362.

**1786, Feb. 7. Crandal, Thomas,** of Cumberland Co. Int. Adm'x— Rebecca Crandal. Fellowbondsman—James Hollinshead; both of said Co. Witness—John Peck, Jr.
1786, Feb. 4. Inventory, £153.8.5, made by James Hollinshead and William Peterson. Lib. 28, p. 180.

**1787, June 20. Crane, David,** of Elizabeth Town, Essex Co., joiner; will of. Sons, Elias and Drake Crane, all my estate; when they are 21. Wife, Jane, use of real and personal estate, till Elias is 21, and then ½ till Drake is 21, and use of ⅓ during her life. If both sons die before they are 21, then I give the same to David Crane, son of Nathaniel Crane, of Elizabeth Town. Executors—friend, William Woodruff, and my son, Elias. Witnesses—Thomas Woodruff, Jr., Daniel Barhyt, John C. Woodruff. Proved Feb. 27, 1788. Lib. 31, p. 235.

**1789, Jan. 4. Crane, Elias,** of Newark, Essex Co.; will of. Granddaughter, Abigail Smith, and granddaughter, Mary Smith, daughters of my daughter, Mary Smith, deceased, £5 each, when they are 18. Daughter, Sarah Tichenor, £10. Daughter, Phebe Cadmus, £15. Son, David, rest of personal and real estate. Executors—son, David, and Sayre Crane, son of John. Witnesses—Jedediah Johnson Nichols, Hannah Johnson, John Ogden. Proved Aug. 18, 1789.
Lib. 30, p. 215.

**1786, March 27. Crane, Elihu,** of Essex Co. Int. Adm'rs—Isaac Alling and Abiel Camfield. Witness—William Livingston, Jr., Surrogate. Lib. 28, p. 425.

**1786, April, 19. Crane, Elihu,** of Essex Co. Ward. Son of Elihu Crane, of said Co., deceased. Said Ward, having an estate of £300, makes choice of Isaac Allen as his Guardian.
1786, April 19. Guardian—Isaac Alling. Fellowbondsman — Abiel Camfield; both of said Co. Lib. 28, p. 429.

**1790, April 25. Crane, Elijah,** of Newark, Essex Co.; will of. Wife, Rachel, £20 and household goods. Son, Elijah, 3 lots of land on the hill, back of my dwelling house, and adjoining the Harbour road; also the lot I bought of Comfort Davies; also 5 acres of salt meadow on Morris Neck. My other son, Jonathan, rest of lands. Unmarried daughters, Phebe, Rebecca and Lucy, £20 each. Executors—my 2 sons, and my son-in-law, Jonathan Baldwin. Witnesses—Uzal Johnson, Moses Baldwin, Alexander C. MacWhorter. Provèd July 20, 1790. Lib. 30, p. 345.

**1789, Nov. 19. Crane, Joseph,** of Newark, Essex Co.; will of. All my real estate, except ½ of my dwelling house, I give to children: Phineas, Hannah, wife of John Gifford, James, Abigail, wife of Uriah James, John, Mary, wife of John Baldwin, and Sarah. The part of land of the value of £100 which my son, John, has a deed for, in the name of Alexander Eagles, is to be considered as part of his share. The land which my son, Phineas, is now possessed of, which formerly belonged to my brother, Jedediah, shall go to my son, Phineas, the value of which is £100. The profits of the part of my daughter, Abigail, is to be applied by her to bring up her children, and, on her death, her part is to go to her children. Wife, Elizabeth, to have ½ my dwelling house, and, after her death, to my children. Executors—sons, Phineas, James and John, and Alexander Eagles. Witnesses—David Crane, Alexander MacWhorter, Joseph Mun. Proved Aug. 9, 1789. (The foregoing has the above dates, as given). Lib. 30, p. 202.

**1786, March 11. Crane, Rebecca,** of Newark, Essex Co.; will of. To Daniel Beach, all real and personal estate, in trust, for the use of the children of my son, Jonas Crane, deceased, namely, John Haight Crane, Rebecca Crane and Paul Crane, as he thinks best. Granddaughter, Rebecca Crane, to have some curtains. Granddaughters, Sarah Croefoot and Catey Peirson, some goods. Executor—Daniel Beach. Witnesses—Juliana Pierson, Margaret Nichols, Elisha Boudinot. Proved July 2, 1787. Lib. 2, p. 399.

**1786, July 25. Crawford, Joseph,** of Essex Co. Int. Adm'r—John Condit. Fellowbondsman—Joseph Tomkins; both of said Co.
Lib. 28, p. 427.

## CALENDAR OF WILLS—1786-1790

**1790, Feb. 13. Cresse, Arthur,** of Upper Precinct, Cape May Co.; will of. Son, Zebulon, the land which is bounded by my son, Jacob, and Jacob Spicer. Son, Jacob, the other land. Daughter, Rachel, some goods. Daughter, Elizabeth, some goods, and the use of a 3-acre field, while they are single. Granddaughter, Mary Stites, a bed and bedding. Children; Zebulon, Jacob, Marcy, Mary, Rachel and Elizabeth, rest of estate. Executors——Jonathan Hildreth and Eli Eldredge. Witnesses—Thomas Scott, Ann Cresse, Nathan Cresse.
1790, Feb. 13. Codicil. Daughter, Rachel Cresse, a young mare. Daughter, Elizabeth Creen, a heifer. Grandson, James Corson, a hat. Witnesses—Richard Townsend, Thomas Keen, Reuben Townsend. Proved May 4, 1790.
1790, March 4. Inventory, £127.0.3, made by Richard Townsend and Elijah Townsend. Lib. 31, p. 544.

**1786, Dec. 14. Cresse, Daniel,** of Middle Precinct, Cape May Co., yeoman; will of. Wife, Mary, ⅓ of the moveable estate, and use of land till grandson, Cresse Townsend, is 21. Grandson, Cresse Townsend, son of Jotham Townsend, and Rachel Townsend, the land where I live, which joins land of David Townsend and wife, and Lewis Cresse, and is near the Delaware Bay; but, if he should die, then I give the same to Japhet Ireland, son of Thomas Ireland and Mary Ireland, of Great Egg Harbor, in Gloucester Co. Wife, Mary, rest of moveable estate. To Israel Cresse, son of Israel Cresse, and Hannah, his wife, £25. Executors—wife, Mary, and my friend, Philip Cresse. Witnesses—Jonathan Mills, Elizabeth Cresse, Eli Eldredge. Proved June 4, 1789.
1789, June 3. Inventory, £355.14.4, made by Humphry Stites and Eli Eldredge. Lib. 31, p. 359.

**1788, April 20. Cresse, John,** of Cape May Co.; will of. Wife, Rachel, ⅔ of my estate, and the other ⅓ to the Baptist Society of Cape May Co. Executors—wife, Rachel, and Amos Cresse. Witnesses—Thomas Pratton, Joseph Morris, John Dickinson. Proved June 26, 1788.
1788, June 10. Inventory, £224.17.7, made by Philip Hand and David Cresse. Lib. 31, p. 79.

**1788, Jan. 29. Cresse, Lewis,** of Cape May Co., yeoman; will of. Son, Daniel, all my lands. Granddaughter, Ellenner, daughter of my son, Daniel, £3, when 18; but, if she die, then to my grandson, Ebinnwzer Shaw, and grandson, Aaron Shaw, sons of Hosea Shaw. Son, Lewis, 15 shillings. Daughter, Abigail Shaw, a silk handkerchief, and rest of moveable estate. Executors—son, Daniel, and son-in-law, Hosea Shaw. Witnesses—David Cresse, Mathias Shaw, Nathan Shaw. Proved March 10, 1788.
1788, Feb. 27. Inventory, £294.0.7, made by John Cresse and David Cresse. Lib. 31, p. 77.

**1789, March 28. Croshaw, John,** of New Hanover, Burlington Co. Int. Adm'r—Isaiah Croshaw. Fellowbondsman—Daniel Hough; both of Springfield Township, said Co.
1789, April 4. Inventory, made by Samuel Shinn and William Fox. Lib. 31, p. 318.

**1787, July 30. Croshaw, Thomas,** of New Hanover, Burlington Co. Int. Adm'r—Joseph Croshaw. Fellowbondsman—Caleb Wright; both of said place.
1787, July 29. Renunciation by Hannah Croshaw, widow, in favor of Joseph Croshaw.
1787, July 25. Inventory, £70.5.0, made by John Goldy and Caleb Wright. Due from George Croshaw's widow, £2.9.5. Lib. 29, p. 74.

**1788, March 18. Cross, Bryan,** of Somerset Co.; will of. Brother, Robert, plantation I bought of Samuel Annin, of 101 acres. Brother, William, £60. Brothers, John, John Leferty, Joseph and James, £60 each. Sisters, Catherine, Martha and Mary, £30 each. Nephew, Bryan Cross, son of my brother, John, £25. Executors—father, Robert Cross and friend, Joseph Boyles. Witnesses—Joseph Annin, Benjamin Vail, Samuel Annin. Proved May 4, 1789.
1789, April 24. Inventory, £419.5.5, made by Nathaniel Ayers and Joseph Annin. Lib. 31, p. 402.

**1789, Feb. 5. Crow, Humphry,** of Cape May Co. Ward. Son of Josiah Crow, of said Co., deceased. Said Ward is under 14 years of age.
1789, Feb. 5. Guardian—Jacob Richardson. Fellowbondsman—Richard Shaw; both of said Co. Witness—Sarah Hand. Lib. 31, p. 373.

**1788, May 6. Crow [Crowell], Rachel,** of Cape May Co. Int. Adm'r—George Hand. Fellowbondsman—Levi Hand; both of said Co. Witnesses—Jeremiah Hand and Jesse Hand.
1788, Jan. 17. Inventory, £21.15.1, made by David Hildreth and Jeremiah Richardson. Lib. 31, p. 93.

**1786, June 30. Crowel [Crow], John,** of Cape May Co. Int. Adm'x—Experience Crowel. Fellowbondsman—Jedidiah Hughes; both of said Co. Witnesses—Jeremiah Eldredge and Abraham Woolson. Lib. 28, p. 187.

**1788, Aug. 14. Crowel, Ruth,** of Cape May Co. Ward. Daughter of Josiah Crowel, of said Co., deceased. Temperence Crowel, the mother of said Ruth, makes application to be made Guardian of her daughter, till she is 14.
1788, Aug. 14. Guardian—Temperence Crowel. Fellowbondsmen—Constant Hughes and George Taylor; all of said Co. Witnesses—Sarah Hand and Jesse Hand. Lib. 31, p. 94.

**1789, March 24. Crum, William,** of Pitts Grove, Salem Co.; will of. Son, William, plantation where I live, of 100 acres, which joins 60 acres which I deeded to my son, Isaac. Daughter, Susanna Crum, a bed and cow. Daughter, Elizabeth Crum, bed and cow. Youngest daughters, Mary and Abigal, a bed and cow to each when 21. Wife, Susanna, rest of personal estate. Executors—wife, Susanna, and my son, Isaac. Witnesses—Isaac Nieukirk, Ann Nieukirk, John Nelson. Proved April 4, 1790.
1789, April 15. Inventory, £146.16.0, made by Isaac Nieukirk and Benjamin Vanmeter. Lib. 31, p. 486.

## CALENDAR OF WILLS—1786-1790

**1790, March 29. Crusee, Henry,** of Middlesex Co. Int. Adm'x—Elizabeth Crusee. Fellowbondsman—Cornelius Crusee; both of said Co.
1790, Jan. 26. Inventory, £54.13.9, made by Garret Schenck and John Hight. "Debt due from Lukas Crusee, £5." Lib. 30, p. 534.

**1790, Sept. 15. Crusee, Henry,** of Middlesex Co. Ward. Son of Henry Crusee, of said Co., deceased. Said Ward makes choice of his mother, Elizabeth Crusee, as his Guardian.
1790, Sept. 15. Guardian—Elizabeth Crusee. Fellowbondsman—Jediah Higgins; both of said Co. Witnesses—William Sickels and William Hyer, Jr. Lib. 30, p. 536.

**1786, Jan. 22. Curry, Samuel,** of Newark, Essex Co.; will of. Wife, Hannah, use of real estate, except what is to be sold to bring up my children; also the goods she brought when we were married. My slaughter house to be sold. Sons, Israel and Samuel, my homestead, tanyard and shop. Son, Thomas, my land near Jonas Harrison, of 3 acres, and 10 acres of woodland. Son, David, my land over the Great Swamp, of 33 acres. To the child that my wife is pregnant with, if a son, a lot over Pierson's Creek, of 15 acres, and the woodland near Boiling Spring, of 4 acres; and, if a girl, £60. Daughter, Johanna, £60, when 21. Daughter, Betsey, £60. Daughter, Phebe, £60. My land over the mountain, the land near Springfield and 15 acres of salt meadow to be sold. Sister-in-law, Abigail Curry, £10, and the debts that are due on my brother Thomas' books. To the First Presbyterian Church of Newark, £25. My wife, Hannah, my brother-in-law, Nathaniel Canfield, and friend, Isaac Allen, to be Guardians of my children. Executors—wife, Hannah, Nathaniel Canfield and Isaac Alling. Witnesses—Uzal Johnson, Elisha Boudinot, Ichabod Gruman.
1788, Feb. 21. Codicil. Sons, Israel and Samuel, to have that lot at the Ferry, that was devised to me by my uncle, Timothy Crane, of 14 acres. My wife gave birth to a son. Witnesses—Stephen Hay, A. Crane, Nathaniel Andrass. Proved July 14, 1788. Lib. 31, p. 228.

**1786, June 27. Curtis, John,** of Chesterfield Township, Burlington Co. Int. Adm'r—John Curtis, of Mansfield. Fellowbondsman—John Taylor, of Nottingham Township; both of said Co.
1786, June 22. Inventory, £909.9.4, made by Isaac Cowgill and John Thorn. Lib. 28, p. 77.

**1786, June 8. Dacker, Dan,** of Sussex Co.; will of. Sons, Jerimiah and Moses, £2 each. Daughters, Sarah Green and Mary Williams, £2 each. Plantation to be sold. Daughters, Charity and Temprence Decker, my beds. Children, Dan, Aaron, Charity and Temperence, the money from sale. Sons, Dan and Aaron, my grist mill. Executors—friends, William Thompson and Evi Adams. Witnesses—Benjamin Dunning, Robert Boys, Hannah Shapard. Proved June 17, 1786.
1786, June 15. Inventory, £514.0.8, made by Ebenezer Owen and Benjamin Edsall. Lib. 28, p. 443.

**1788, April 21. Dalles, William, Jr.,** of Cumberland Co. Int. Adm'rs—Rebbekah Dalles and Jonathan Dalles. Fellowbondsman—David Lore; all of said Co. Witness—Samuel M. Shute.
1788, April 15. Inventory, £741.10.9, made by David Lore and Joshua Brick. Lib. 31, p. 76.

## 62   NEW JERSEY POST-REVOLUTIONARY DOCUMENTS

**1789, Aug. 27. Dalrimple, Joseph,** of Mendham Township, Morris Co.; will of. To Elizabeth Veal, the woman I now live with and own as my wife, ⅓ of my estate. Eldest son, Silas, ⅙ of the rest. Son, Malon, ⅙. Daughter, Hannah Dalrimple, ⅙. Son, Dennis, ⅙. Son, Joseph, ⅙. Son, William, ⅙. To eldest daughter of Elizabeth Hull, named Rachel Dalrimple, 5 shillings. Executors—friends, Hartshorn Fitz Randel, Nathaniel Doty and Artemas Day. Witnesses—Daniel Cook, Samuel Cosad. Proved June 9, 1790.
1790, June 9. Inventory, £78.18.5, made by James Johnston and Samuel Cosad. Lib. 30, p. 469.

**1786, Dec. 6. Daniel, Henry,** of Waterford Township, Gloucester Co.; will of. Son, James, a 10-acre lot on Burlington road, which joins land of Jacob Browning and Henry Crowel. Daughter, Elizabeth Deel, a chest of drawers. Son, Owen £3. Son, Charles, £3. Son, George, £3. Executors—sons, James and George. Witnesses—John West, John Erwin, Henry Wood. Proved Oct. 19, 1787.
1787, Oct. 18. Inventory, £136.4.0, made by James Sloan and Samuel Erwin. Lib. 29, p. 110.

**1787, Aug. 12. Daniel, Ruth,** of Lower Alloways Creek Township, Salem Co., widow; will of. Sister, Mary Shaphard, apparel. To Aron Daniel, £20. To Jonathan Dennis, £40. To Abot Sayrs, £30, and to his mother, Hannah Sayrs, £15. To Susannah Barber, £5. To Elizabeth Daniel, daughter of Aaron Daniel, a new chest, made by William Daniel. Rest of estate to Liddia Shephard, Ruth Fithen, Luse and Mary Shephard and Elizabeth Daniel. Executor—friend, Edward Bradway. Witnesses—Elizabeth Peddrick, Naomi Dennes, Hugh Peddrick. Proved Nov. 30, 1789. Lib. 40, p. 523.

**1789, May 24. Dare, Robert,** of Deerfield Township, Cumberland Co.; will of. That part of my plantation on the west side of the road that leads to Pilesgrove to be sold, which land joins Nathan Leak, late the property of Joseph Sneathen, and land formerly of Samuel Hannah. Wife, Mary, the use of the rest of the plantation, to bring up the children; and, after wife's death, to be sold, and the money divided among my sons and daughters. Sons, Robert and Jeremiah, to be put to trades, when 14. Executors—sons, John and Gamaliel. Witnesses—David Moore, David Dare, John Snethen. Proved Sept. 23, 1789.
1789, July 21. Inventory, £215.10.9, made by Samuel Ogden and David Moore. Lib. 30, p. 147.

**1789, Nov. 22. Darnel, Edward,** of Evesham, Burlington Co.; will of. Son, Samuel, the land where he lives, and the cedar swamp I bought of Isaac Evans, and ½ the pine land, which I bought of Samuel Clemens, situated in Gloucester Co., and 2 acres of cedar swamp I bought of John Brannon; provided he pays the following sums:— £100 due on bond to Gabriel Davis; £60 due to Hannah Prickett; £35 due to Caleb Attmore, £35 to William Haines, son of Jeremiah, late of Northampton, deceased, and £5 yearly to my wife, Jane. Son, Edmund, the land where I live, and all the rest of lands; provided he pays all other debts, and £10 yearly to my wife, Jane. Grandson, Edward Darnel, son of my son, Samuel, the profit of a bond of £26, due from Paul Troth. To Bathsheba and Selane Crispin, £9, provided

CALENDAR OF WILLS—1786-1790 63

they stay till that time. Executor—son, Edmond. Witnesses—Joseph Barton, Uriah Barton, James Griffitts. Proved Jan. 4, 1790.
1789, Dec. 23. Inventory, £798.19.10, made by Lawrence Webster and Thomas Ballinger, Jr. Lib. 32, p. 58.

**1789, Aug. 11. Daten, Freelove,** of Fairfield, Cumberland Co., widow; will of. Son, Ephraim Daten, all my salt marsh at West Point, and all my right in lands that formerly belonged to Leonard Daten; also ¼ of the land I bought of Timothy Elmer, Esq., which joins the plantation that was given to him by his father, Joseph Daten. Daughters, Mary Daten, Sarah Daten and Freelove Daten, rest of land bought of Timothy Elmer; also personal estate. Executors—daughters, Mary and Sarah Daten. Witnesses—Ephraim Harris, William Ayars, James Howell. Proved Nov. 6, 1789. Letters granted to Mary Daten and Sarah D. Clark.
1789, Oct. 20. Inventory, £274.11.3, made by Amos Westcott and James Howell. (See Dayton). Lib. 30, p. 150.

**1788, June 24. Davenport, Emanuel,** of Burlington Co. Int. Adm'rs—Mercy Davenport and Joseph Forsyth. Fellowbondsmen—Thomas Ashmoor and Joel Gibbs; all of said Co.
1788, June 21. Inventory, made by James Mathis and Thomas Ashmoor, at Lamberton. Lib. 30, p. 58.

**1788, Nov. 5. Davis, Arthur,** of Deerfield, Cumberland Co., yeoman; will of. Wife, Esther, ½ my moveable estate. Sons, Elijah, Daniel and Arthur, 5 shillings each. Son, Benjamin, plantation where I live, with two and ½ acres of salt marsh in Preston Marsh; also 2 acres of cedar swamp in Green Swamp, during his life, and to his heir, if he have a son, if not, then to my grandchild, Arthur, the son of my son, Arthur. Daughters, Martha Ogden, Ruth Garrison and Naomy Shull, £5 each. Rest of moveable estate to my sons, Benjamin and Abijah. Executors—sons, Elijah and Daniel. Witnesses—Othniel Davis, Levi Leake, Michael Hoshel. Proved Dec. 11, 1789.
1789, Nov. 27. Inventory, £329.11.1, made by Ephraim Foster and Preston Hannah. Lib. 30, p. 139.

**1786, Sept. 26. Davis, David,** of Cumberland Co. Int. Adm'r—Othniel Davis. Fellowbondsman—Ezekiel Foster; both of said Co. Witnesses—Moses Ayars and Samuel M. Shute. Lib. 28, p. 182.

**1786, Sept. 12. Davis, James,** of Trenton, Hunterdon Co., schoolmaster. Int. Adm'x—Mary Davis. Fellowbondsman—James Ewing; both of said place.
1786, Sept. 11. Inventory, £205.10.9, made by Samuel Tucker and James Ewing. Lib. 31, p. 142.

**1786, May 19. Davis, John,** of Gloucester, Gloucester Co. Int. Adm'rs—Earl Davis and Elizabeth Davis. Fellowbondsman—Robert F. Price; all of said place. Witness—James Hurley.
1786, May 15. Inventory, £942.12.11, made by Samuel Harrison and Jacob Albertson. Lib. 28, p. 122.

**1787, March 20. Davis, Jonathan,** of Burlington Co. Ward. Grandson of Isaac Davis, of said Co., deceased. Said Ward, having real and personal estate, makes choice of Aaron Ivins as his Guardian.

64 NEW JERSEY POST-REVOLUTIONARY DOCUMENTS

1787, March 20. Guardian—Aaron Ivins. Fellowbondsman—James Lawrie; both of Monmouth Co. Lib. 29, p. 80.

**1786, Aug. 23. Davis, Phineas,** of Piscataway, Middlesex Co. Ward. Son of Thomas Davis, of said place, deceased. Said Ward makes choice of Joshua Davis as his Guardian.
1786, Aug. 23. Guardian—Joshua Davis. Fellowbondsman—Samuel Drake; both of said place. Lib. 28, p. 342.

**1790, July 21. Davis, William,** of Burlington Co. Int. Adm'x— Lydia Davis, widow of said William. Fellowbondsman—Joshua Shreve; both of said Co.
1790, July 21. Inventory, £10.5.0, made by Job Gaskill and Joshua Shreve. Lib. 32, p. 97.

**1790, Jan. 22. Dawson, Richard,** of Gloucester Co. Int. Adm'rs— Lydia Dawson and Aaron Dawson. Fellowbondsman—Daniel Wills; all of said Co.
1790, Jan. 11. Inventory, made by Charles Lock and Daniel Wills. Lib. 31, p. 477.

**1789, Feb. 18. Day, John,** of Morristown, Morris Co. Ward. Son of Ezekiel Day, of said place, deceased. Said Ward makes choice of Aaron Ketchel as his Guardian.
1789, Feb. 18. Guardian—Aaron Kitchel, of Hanover. Fellowbondsman—Benjamin Lindsly; both of said Co. Witness—Nathan Reeve. Lib. 30, p. 235.

**1788, Oct. 14. Dayton, Ann,** of Cumberland Co. Ward. Daughter of Eli Dayton, of said Co., deceased. Having real and personal estate, said Ward makes choice of Norton Lawrence as her Guardian.
1788, Oct. 14. Guardian—Norton Lawrence. Fellowbondsman—Eli Elmer, Esq.; both of said Co. Witness—Samuel M. Shute. Lib. 31, p. 77.

**1786, Aug. 31. Dayton, Jonathan,** of Essex Co. Int. Adm'r—Elias Dayton. Fellowbondsman—Samuel Smith; both of said Co. Lib. 29, p. 417.

**1788, April 23. Dayton, William,** of Essex Co. Int. Adm'rs—Jacob Van Arsdalen and Thomas Salter. Fellowbondsman—Jona I. Dayton; all of said Co. Lib. 31, p. 243.

**1787, June 4. Deacon, George,** of Burlington Township, Burlington Co. Int. Adm'r—John Deacon, of said place. Fellowbondsman—Isaac Wetherill, of City of Burlington.
1787, June 2. Renunciation by Susannah Deacon, widow of George Deacon. Witnesses—George King and Diockesian King.
1787, June 6. Inventory, £527.9.8, made by John Antram and Josiah Haines. Lib. 29, p. 77.

**1790, Nov. 2. Deacon, Isaac, Rachel and Theodocia,** of Burlington Co. Wards. Children of George Deacon, of said Co., deceased. Guardian—Susannah Deacon, their mother. The said infants are under 14 years of age. Fellowbondsmen—Thomas Haines and Zacheriah Antram. Lib. 32, p. 98.

CALENDAR OF WILLS—1786-1790    65

**1787, Oct. 12. Dean, William,** of Greenwich Township, Gloucester Co. Int. Adm'r—Arthur Mcklewain. Fellowbondsman—Ward Perce; both of said place, yeoman. Witness—Kezia Albertson.
1787, Oct. 13. Inventory, £16.6.7, made by John Barns and Ward Perce. Lib. 29, p. 116.

**1788, Dec. 24. De Camp, Aaron,** of Essex Co. Int. Adm'rs—Mary De Camp and John DeCamp; both of said Co. Fellowbondsman—Nathaniel Littell, of Morris Co. Lib. 38, p. 97.

**1787, Feb. 21. Decker, Aaron,** of Hardyston, Sussex Co. Ward. Son of Dan Decker, of said place, deceased. Said Ward makes choice of Ebenezer Owens as his Guardian.
1787, Feb. 21. Guardian—Ebenezer Owens. Fellowbondsman—Duncan Mc Nicol; both of said place. Witnesses—Mark Thomson and James Hyndshaw. Lib. 29, p. 491.

**1786, Nov. 29. Decker, Temperance and Charity,** of Sussex Co. Wards. Daughters of Dan Decker, of said Co., deceased. Said Wards makes choice of Ebenezer Owen as their Guardian.
1786, Nov. 29. Guardian—Ebenezer Owen. Fellowbondsman—William Green; both of Hardyston, said Co. Lib. 28, p. 472.

**1786, Dec. 30. De Cow, Eber,** of Mansfield Township, Burlington Co.; will of. Grandson, Eber De Cow, son of my son, John, my plantation in Mansfield and Chesterfield, now in possession of my son, John, when he is 21; and he is to pay to his father, John De Cow, £100, and his mother, Sarah De Cow, £100. Grandson, Thomas De Cow, son of John, when he is 21, the land which I purchased of Stoffell Longstreet, situated in Upper Freehold, Monmouth Co. Grandson, John De Cow, son of John, my plantation in Sussex Co., near Pequest, which I bought of my brother, Jacob De Cow. Son, John, a mortgage against William Walton, and the use of the land bequeathed to my said grandchildren, till they are to receive the same. To each of the children of my son, Joseph, deceased, 5 shillings, as my said son has had his share. Executors—son, John, Witnesses— Moses Ivins, Cleayton Newbold, John Pope. Proved Feb. 26, 1787. Lib. 29, p. 66.

**1787, Jan. 2. De Cow, Joseph,** of Burlington Co. Int. Adm'rs—Isaac De Cow and John Satterthwaite. Fellowbondsman—John Taylor; all of said Co.
1787, Jan. 2. Renunciation by Achsah De Cow, widow of said Joseph, in favor of Isaac De Cow and John Satterthwaite.
1791, March 23. Adm'x—Achsah De Cow, of the estate of Joseph De Cow, left unadministered by Isaac De Cow and John Satterthwaite, who are also deceased. Fellowbondsman—Stacy Taylor, of said Co.
1787, Jan. 4. Inventory, £797.0.7, made by Joseph Pancoast and Cleayton Newbold. Lib. 29, p. 77; Lib. 32, p. 183.

**1787, Feb. 15. De Cow, Mary, Joseph and Clayton,** of Burlington Co. Wards. Children of Joseph De Cow, of said Co., deceased. Achsah De Cow, the mother of Mary, aged about 7 years, Joseph, about 5 years, and Clayton, about one year old, makes application to be appointed their Guardian.

66 NEW JERSEY POST-REVOLUTIONARY DOCUMENTS

1787, Feb. 15. Guardian—Achsah De Cow. Fellowbondsman—John Taylor, Jr.; both of said Co. Lib. 29, p. 80.

**1786, April 18. Dederer, Christian, Sr.,** of Bergen Co. Int. Adm'rs—Isaac Sherwood and Christian Dederer. Fellowbondsman—Barent Coles; all of said Co.
1786, May 2. Inventory, £164.12.7, made by Albert Westervelt and Jacob Bogert. Articles were taken away by the widow, who gave to her daughter, Sally, some other articles. Lib. 29, p. 223.

**1789, April 20. Demarest, Benjamin,** of Harington, Bergen Co.; will of. Son, Samuel, the cow he had when he first married, and the ½ of my land. Son, Jacobus, the other ½. The house goods to be divided between my daughters and my last wife's daughters.. Wife, Soekke, some goods in the house. Executors—sons, Samuel and Jacobus. Witnesses—Harmin Van Reype, Abraham Cadmes, Cornelius Fershee. Proved March 15, 1790.
1790, March 16. Inventory, £107.11.6, made by Harmen Van Reype and Gerrit Durie. Lib. 30, p. 545.

**1786, Feb. 8. Demarest, Benjamin P.,** of Hackensack, Bergen Co. Int. Adm'r—David B. Demarest. Fellowbondsman—Gerret D. Demarest; both of said place.
1786, Feb. 20. Inventory, £54.9.10, made by Johannes Westervelt and Gerret D. Demarest. Also signed by Peter Demarest and Johannes Demarest. Lib. 29, p. 223.

**1787, May 17. Demott, Claesye,** of Bergen, Bergen Co., widow of Michael Demott; will of. To all the children of my brother, John Winne, ½ of my real and personal estate. To the children of my brother, Lavynis Winne, the other ½. If my brother-in-law, Robert Sickelse, shall happen to die leaving my sister, Antye, a widow, then she is to have £6 a year. In case my brother-in-law, Garrebrant Garrebrantse, shall happen to die, leaving my sister, Marritye, a widow, then she is to have £6 a year. Executors—friends, John I. Vreeland and John I. Van Houte. Witnesses—Elias I. Vreland, Elizabeth Vreeland, Hessel Peterse. Proved Jan. 27, 1789. Lib. 30, p. 246.

**1790, March 24. Demott, Michael,** of Reading Township, Hunterdon Co.; will of. Wife, £60 and £24 yearly. Son, Derick, my apparel. Daughters, Sarah Decker, Stinety Williamson and Elizabeth Demott, ½ of my "linning." Grandchild, Catherine Demott, a bed and £160; her father is Derick Demott. The 14-acre lot on the west side of my meadow, joining lands of Peter Scamp, Derick Demott and Elizabeth Demott, to be sold. Executors—son, Derick, and my son-in-law, Cornelius Williamson. Witnesses—Cornelius Johnson, John Kinney, Elizabeth Johnson. Proved July 1, 1790.
1790, June 25. Inventory, £4,314, made by Cornelius Johnson and Peter Schamp.
1791, Sept. 13. Account by Executors. Lib. 30, p. 294.

**1787, April 4. Dennis, Garratt,** of South Amboy, Middlesex Co. Ward. Son of Joseph Dennis, of said place, deceased. Said Ward makes choice of John G. Wall as his Guardian.
1787, April 4. Guardian—John G. Wall. Fellowbondsman—Samuel Neilson; both of said Co. Lib. 29, p. 366.

CALENDAR OF WILLS—1786-1790 67

**1787, Aug. 15. Dennis, Joseph, Sr.,** of Wantage, Sussex Co. Int. Adm'r—Jesse Dennis. Fellowbondsman—Joseph Dennis; both of said place. Witness—Evi Adams.
1787, Aug. 15. Inventory, £250.15.3, made by Edmond Martin and Evi Adams. Lib. 29, p. 489.

**1786, July 1. Denton, Anthony,** of Middlesex Co. Int. Adm'x—Margaret Denton. Fellowbondsman—John Hatfield; both of said Co.
1786, June 30. Inventory, £177.5.0, made by Thomas McDowell and John Hatfield. Lib. 28, p. 340.

**1786, March 1. Derickson, William,** of Woolwich Township, Gloucester Co. Int. Adm'r—Thomas Derickson. Fellowbondsman—Isaac Zane; both of said place, yeomen.
1786, Feb. 23. Inventory, £278.19.6, made by Isaac Zane and Joseph Pinyard. Lib. 28, p. 122.

**1790, Dec. 20. Dewit, Elizabeth,** of Amwell Township, Hunterdon Co. Int. Adm'r—Samuel Ramsey, of Mansfield Township, Sussex Co. Fellowbondsman—John Coryell, of Amwell.
1790, Dec. 18. Inventory, £36.8.0, made by John Meldrum and William Acker. Irons claimed by Sarah Dewit. Lib. 30, p. 314.

**1786, Nov. 30. Dey, Theunis,** of Saddle River Township, Bergen Co.; will of. Son, Richard, my homestead with the lot of land marked on a draft No. 3. Son, Philip, 3 lots marked No. 4. Son, Peter, land marked No. 2. Son, David, land marked No. 1. Sons, Peter and David, part of land known as No. 1, in the Pacquanack Patent, which I bought of John Low. Son, John, lots in New York City in West Ward, and known on a draft thereof, as Nos. 1, 7, 8 and 12, and lying between Division Street and Dey's Slip; also the addition of water lot. Sons, Richard, Philip, John, Peter and David, a water lot. Son, Benamin, £800. Daughter, Esther, £363. Daughter, Jane, £500. Executors—sons, Richard, Philip, John, Peter, Benjamin and David. Witnesses—Gileam Jacobus, Cornelius Kip, Isaac Van Saun. Proved July 23, 1787.
Lib. 29, p. 491.

**1786, May 2. Dicker, Richard,** of Upper Alloways Creek, Salem Co.; will of. Daughter, Lydia Dicker, 5 acres of land that I bought of Henry Mulford. To my intended wife, Elizabeth Bradway, £10. Daughters, Hannah, Lydia and Elizabeth Dicker, rest of estate. Executor—friend, John Stewart, of Lower Alloways Creek. Witnesses—William Richmond, Sarah Vanculin, Samuel Stewart. Proved March 15, 1787.
1786, May 15. Inventory, £166.4.0, made by John Vanculin and Tyler Scoggin. Lib. 29, p. 148.

**1789, Sept. 25. Dickey, Alexander, Captain.** Inventory, £250 16.8, made by Peter Smith and Nathaniel Sebrey. File No. 6814 G.

**1787, Aug. 9. Dickinson, Peter and Caleb,** of Morristown, Morris Co. Wards. Sons of Philemon Dickinson, of said place, deceased. Said Wards make choice of Samuel Tyler as their Guardian.
1787, Aug. 9. Guardian—Samuel Tyler, of Elizabeth Town, Essex Co. Fellowbondsman—Isaac Badgley, of Morris Co. Lib. 29, p. 475.

**1787, July 30. Dils, Johannes,** of Lebanon, Hunterdon Co.; blacksmith; will of. Son, John, 5 shillings, he being the eldest son. Daughter, Anne, wife of Peter Rodenbogh, £100. Son, Harmanus, £100. Daughter, Elizabeth, wife of Mordecai McKinney, £100. Son, Peter, £100. Son, Joseph, £50. Daughter, Charity, wife of Casper Hendershet, £50. Grandson, Moraits, son of my daughter, Catherine, £15, when he is 21. If my daughter, Elizabeth, and my son, Peter, should not come to demand their legacies within 16 years, then they shall be divided among my other children. Executors—son, Harmanus, and my brother, Philip. Witnesses—Henry Swesey, John Forrester, William Lyons. Proved Nov. 27, 1789.

1789, Nov. 27. Inventory of "Honnis William Dils," £634.14.6, made by James Snyder and John Forrester.

1794, Feb. 6. Account by Harman Dils, acting Executor.

Lib. 32, p. 48.

**1786, June 16. Dils, John,** of Amwell Township, Hunterdon Co.; will of. Wife, Marey, all lands and moveable estate, together with my children, Jacob Dils, Elizabeth White, Georg Dils, Peter Dils and William Dils. The share of Elizabeth White to be given to her children, John Dils and Anna Dils, when they are of age. Mother, Mary Dils, to be supported. Executors—sons, George and William, and my friend, Jonas Chatburn. Proved Sept. 8, 1786.

1786, July 7. Inventory, £187.15.9, made by John Hull and Uriah Bonham.

1788, Nov. 13. Account by Jonas Chatburn, acting Executor. Paid for copy of settlement of estate of Peter Dils, deceased, 4 shillings.

1789, Aug. 7. Account by Jonas Chatburn, acting Executor.

1789, Oct. John Bodine took exceptions to the account.

Lib. 28, p. 230.

**1787, May 28. Diltz, Henry,** of Kingwood, Hunterdon Co. Int. Adm'x—Urie Diltz. Fellowbondsman—Lawrence Kemple; both of said Co. Witness—Crist Lawbaugher.

1787, May 22. Inventory, £329.5.3, made by Christopher Lawburgher and John Rockafellow.

1801, May. Petition. Henry Diltz had real estate, and died intestate, leaving heirs, John Bird, and Mary, his wife, late Mary Diltz; John Lear, and Sarah, his wife, late Sarah Diltz; Catherine Diltz; Peter Diltz; Jacob Henn, and Anna, his wife, late Anna Diltz, some of whom are under age, and we pray that the real estate may be divided. Signed, Jacob Henn and Ane Hen.

1801, Aug. 6. Report of Commissioners to divide real estate. There was set off to Julianna Stevenson, late Dilts, widow of Henry Dilts, who claims ⅓ of real estate, a lot of 29 acres. To Mary Bird, late Mary Diltz, wife of John Bird, and daughter of intestate, 19³⁄₁₀ acres; to Sarah Lair, late Sarah Dilts, wife of John Lair and daughter of intestate, lot of 12 acres; to Catharine Dilts, single woman, 18 acres; to Peter Diltz, 4⁷⁄₁₀ acres; to Anna Hann, wife of Jacob, 19 acres.

Lib. 29, p. 297.

**1788, Aug. 13. Dixson, Daniel,** of Fairfield Township, Cumberland Co.; will of. Wife, Hanah, £40, and the house and garden where I live, while my widow. Grandson, Daniel Dixson, my land east-southeast of a certain line; also my marsh at Abbett''s Island; also a cedar swamp in Buckshootem, that I bought of Jeremiah Nixon; also the house and land where I live, with all the land I bought of Lot Fithen, and all I bought of Adam Minch; but, if he die before 21, then the said lands are to be divided between my daughters and granddaughter, Mary Dixon. Son, Urban, the rest of my lands. Daughters, Mary, Elizabeth and Tamson, rest of moveable estate. Executor—son, Urban. Witnesses—John Lawrence, Hannah Dixson, Joseph Daniels. Proved March 18, 1789. Lib. 30, p. 154.

**1790, Sept. 21. Dixson, Hannah,** of Cumberland Co., widow. Int. Adm'r—Jeffrey Parvin. Fellowbondsman—Amos Westcott; both of said Co. Lib. 30, p. 280.

**1789, June 4. Dod, Joseph,** of Newark, Essex Co.; will of. Wife, Sarah, my moveable estate. Son, Matthias, ⅛ of my lands at Swinefill, except the piece I bought of Job Crane, which is to be sold. Son, Ebenezar, ⅛ of said lands. Son, Joseph, the other ⅛. Wife, Sarah, rest of lands during her life, to bring up my children. Sons, Moses and Alling, to have trades. Son, Daniel, homestead where I live, and ½ of the land near Jed. Lindsley's; and the other ½, and the land I bought of Mathew Condit, I give to sons, Moses and Alling. Son, Daniel, my land on the mountain. Sons, Daniel, Moses and Alling, my salt meadow. Daughter, Rachel Mun, £9. Daughter, Mary Williams, £6. Daughters, Lydia Dod and Abigail Dod, £50 each. Executors—wife, Sarah, and friend, Benjamin Williams, and son, Matthias. Witnesses—Thomas Williams, Caleb Williams, John Dod. Proved Feb. 25, 1790. Lib. 30, p. 321.

**1786, Jan. 4. Dole, Joseph,** of Great Egg Harbor, Gloucester Co.; will of. Wife, Sarah, use of ½ of my plantation. Son, Joseph, plantation where I live, except his mother's bequeath. Daughters, Hannah Ingersull, Rebecah Garwood, Sarah Scull, Mary and Surviah Dole, rest of real estate, except a salt marsh on Jonathan's Thorofair. Executors—wife, Sarah, and son, Joseph. Witnesses—Noah Smith, Jonathan Addoms, Mary Addams. Proved July 24, 1786.
1786, April 4. Inventory, £118. 8. 2, made by Jonathan Addoms and Noah Smith. Lib. 28, p. 90.

**1787, Dec. 10. Doremus, Cornelius J.,** of Persipining, Hanover Township, Morris Co.; will of. Wife to have a good living out of my estate. Son, David, all my lands in Preckinus. Son, Jacob, £17. Son, Abraham, 130 acres of the south side of my land. Son, Cornelius, rest of land. Son, Jacob, £200. Daughter, Orecha Doremus, £20. Daughter, Margaret Doremus, £20. Daughter, Rachel Doremus, £20.
1786, April 4. Inventory, £118.8.2, made by Jonathan Addoms and Cornelius. Witnesses—Joseph Grover, Thomas Baldwin, John Baldwin. Proved June 2, 1788.
1788, May 26. Inventory, £125.18.3, made by Michael Cook and Joseph Scott. Lib. 31, p. 181.

**1790, Jan. 19. Doremus, Peter,** of Pequanack Township, Morris Co.; will of. Wife to have the house and land where I live, while my widow. Son, Cornelius, £30. Son, Richard, my lands, except what lyes at Toms Point. Son, Jacob, £20. Son, Peter, £25, when 21. Daughters, Sarah and Polley, £20 each, when 18. The 25 acres at Toms Point I

give to children, Cornelius, Richard, Jacob, Peter, Sarah and Polley. Executors—wife, Mary, and brother, Thomas Doremus. Witnesses—John Dehart, John Dye, Simeon Doremus. Proved Dec. 21, 1790.
1790, Dec. 11. Inventory, £241.18.0, made by Thomas Dods and Henry Vanness. Lib. 30, p. 474.

**1786, April 8. Doty, Henry,** of Bernards Town, Somerset Co. Ward. Son of Isaac Doty, of said place, deceased. Said Ward makes choice of James Bishop as his Guardian.
1786, April B. Guardian—James Bishop. Fellowbondsman—Roberds Littell; both of said place. Witness—John Perrine. Lib. 29, p. 197.

**1786, Aug. 26. Douglas, James,** of Trenton, Hunterdon Co. Int. Adm'r—Conrad Kotts. Fellowbondsman—Moore Furman; both of said place. Witness—Ren Williams, Jr.
1786, Aug. 25. Inventory, £20.16.9, made by John Singer and Barnard Hanlon.
1790, Dec. 15. Account by Adm'r. Lib. 28, p. 245.

**1787, Sept. 1. Downney, Anne,** of Amwell Township, Hunterdon Co.; will of. Son, John Downney, house and land in New Brunswick, Middlesex Co. Daughter, Elizabeth Downney, house and lot where I live, and moveable estate. Executrix—said daughter. Witnesses—William Chamberlin, Enos Laning, Jacob Mattison. Proved Nov. 9, 1787.
1787, Nov. 2. Inventory, £22.10.6, made by William Chamberlain and Enas Laning. Lib. 29, p. 282.

**1786, April 2. Drake, Francis,** of New Brunswick, Middlesex Co.; will of. Gisebert Sutphen to have possession of my plantation for 4 years, and then to be sold. Brother, John Drake, ⅔ of rest of estate. To William Marinor and his children, ½ of the other ⅓. Children of Nathaniel Marinor, the other ½ of the third. Executors—friends, Guisbert Sutphen and Jonathan Combs, Jr. Witnesses—Charles Robertson, John Dehart, Jonathan Combs. Proved May 20, 1786.
1786, May 19. Inventory, made by Jonathan Combs and John Dehart.
Lib. 28, p. 329.

**1786, June 27. Drake, Samuel,** of Piscataway, Middlesex Co. Int. Adm'r—Samuel Drake. Fellowbondsman—Joseph Drake; both of said place. Witness—William Hyer.
1786, —.—. Inventory, made by John Ayers and Christianus Lupardus. Lib. 28, p. 340.

**1790, May 29. Drummond, Elias,** of Acquackanonk, Essex Co. Ward. Son of Robert Drummond, of said place, deceased. Said Ward, having real and personal estate, makes choice of Edward Thomas as his Guardian.
1790, May 29. Guardian—Edward Thomas. Fellowbondsman—Samuel Sayre; both of said Co. Lib. 30, p. 363.

**1787, Aug. 9. Drummond, Robert,** of Bergen Co. Int. Adm'r—William Drummond. Fellowbondsman—Garrit Ackerman; both of said Co. Witness—Caterine Miller.
1787, Aug. 20. Inventory, £26. 7. 11. Lib. 29, p. 535; 3183B.

**1787, March 22. Duell, John,** of Pilesgrove Township, Salem Co. Ward. Son of John Duell, of said place, deceased. Said Ward makes choice of John Kille as his Guardian. Witness—Joshua Cozens.
1787, March 22. Guardian—John Kille, Fellowbondsman—James Stratton; both of Woolwich Township, Gloucester Co. Witness—Joshua Cozens. Lib. 29, p. 121.

**1790, Nov. 23. Duglass, William,** of Chesterfield Township, Burlington Co. Int. Adm'r—Joseph Duglass. Fellowbondsman—John Thorn; both of said Co.
1790, Dec. 31. Inventory, £168.3.5, made by John Thorn (of Crosswicks) and John Thorn. Legacy in hands of William Biles, £45.12.3. Legacy in hands of William and Joseph Potts, £55.16.8. Lib. 32, p. 97.

**1787, June 1. Dukemaneer, Susannah,** of Gloucester, Gloucester Co., single woman; will of. To Mary, wife of John Glover, £40. To the children of the said John and Mary, namely, John, Isaac, Samuel, Joseph, Jacob, Rachel and Mary, £4 each. To Mary, Kitturah and Rhoda, the daughters of my brother, Samuel Dukemaneer, my apparel. Brother, Samuel, the residue. Executor—friend, Thomas Redman. Witnesses—James Hurley, William Hinchman, Jr. Proved Oct. 3, 1787.
1787, Aug. 24. Inventory, £65.8.7, made by John Glover and James Hurley. Lib. 29, p. 103.

**1789, Dec. 23. Dunham, Azariah,** of New Brunswick, Middlesex Co.; will of. Wife, Mary, house where I live. Eldest son, David, 2 lots in Piscataway; one is where he lives, which I bought of Benjamin Dunn, and the other lot of 20 acres was devised to me by my father, Jonathan Dunham. Son, Lewis, land in Woodbridge. Son, James, plantation at Mount Airy, in Hanover Township, Morris Co., which I bought of Jacob Tappan, Son, Jacob, land in Hanover Township, Son, William, house in New Brunswick. Daughter, Mary, wife of John Conger, of New York State, £780. Daughter, Jane, wife of Joseph Thixton, of Piscataway, 30 acres which I bought of Henry Sutton and Benjamin Foster. Daughter, Nancy Dunham, land bought of William Piatt. Daughter, Sarah, wife of James Hankinson, of Monmouth Co., legacy. Daughter, Hannah Dunham, £1,161. Son, James, and my friend, Andrew Kirkpatrick, the house where my son, John, now lives, and Ann, his wife, for their benefit. Son, William, and my daughter, Hannah, to be educated. Executors—sons, David, Lewis and James, and friend, Andrew Kirkpatrick. Witnesses—William Applegate, Moses Guest, William Lawson, Jr.
1790, Jan. 12. Codicil. To Hellen, the wife of my grandson, Azariah Dunham, a cow. Witnesses—William Applegate, William Lawson, Jr., Joseph Bonney. Proved Feb. 19, 1790.
1790, Feb. 19. Inventory, £1,262.18.0, made by John Bray and Cornelius Voorhies. Lib. 30, p. 481.

**1787, Feb. 26. Dunham, John,** of Bernards Town, Somerset Co. Int. Adm'x—Martha Dunham. Fellowbondsman—Abraham Dunham; both of said place.
1787, Feb. 22. Inventory, £45.9.3, made by John Oliver and Abraham Dunham. Lib. 29, p. 439.

**1789, Dec. 30. Dunham, Samuel,** of Stow Creek Township, Cumberland Co.; will of. Personal estate to be sold, debts to be paid, and, of the overplus, I give ⅓ to my wife, Amy, and the rest to my father, Frances Dunham, my brother, Hugh Dunham, and my brother, Hezekiah Dunham. Executors—brother, Hugh Dunham, and Joseph Bacon. Witnesses—Caleb Ayars, Ebenezer Davis. Proved Oct. 12, 1790.
1790, Jan. 14. Inventory, £56.13.4, made by Job Ayars and David Ayars. Lib. 30, p. 276.

**1790, Aug. 23. Dunn, Benjamin,** of Piscataway, Middlesex Co.; will of. Son, Justus, plantation where he lives. Son, John, £200. Son, Daniel, £250. Daughter, Catrine Smith, £70. Son, James Thomson Dunn, plantation where I live, formerly property of his grandfather, James Thomson, deceased; and he is to pay to my daughter, Christian Dunn, £230, after the death of their grandmother, Charity Thomson; also pay to my daughters, Rachel Dunn and Annah Dunn, £300. Grandson, Reune Dunn, £5. Executors—sons, Justus and James, and my friend, Thomson Stelle. Witnesses—Phineas Fitz Randolph, James Dunn, John Langstaff. Proved Oct. 19, 1790.
1790, Oct. 21. Inventory, made by Hugh Dunn and Oliver Stell.
Lib. 30, p. 508.

**1789, April 15. Dusinbery, John,** of Bethlehem, Hunterdon Co., yeoman; will of. Wife, Johanna, her apparel and bed. Eldest sons, John and William, £50 each. Sons, Samuel and Henry, all they owe me. Son-in-law, Joshua Opdyke, and his wife, Mary, what they owe me. Youngest sons, Silvanus and George, £100 each. Executors— wife, Johanna, and son, Henry. Witnesses—John Garrison, George Garrison, Samuel Eveland. Proved May 28, 1789.
1789, May 13. Inventory, £1,970. 12. 1, made by Thomas Bowlby and John Garrison.
1792, April 10. Inventory, of book debts, £694.0.6.
1792, April 11. Account by Henry Dusenbury, acting Executor.
1811, Feb. 11. Account by Henry Dusenbury. Lib. 32, p. 4.

**1787, Nov. 2. Earle, Edward,** of Seacoakes, Bergen Co.; will of. Son, Richard, £5. Wife, Close, to be supported. Son, John, my house and barn. Son, Richard, the little cedar swamp, and the 7 and ½ acres of upland that joins Daniel Smith. Son, Edward, £300, when he is 21. Daughter, Sicilia, the wife of Rodman Fields, £80. Daughter, Mary Earle, £80. Daughter, Sicilia, the wife of Rodman Fields, a negro wench. Executors—sons, Richard and John, and Isaac Vangeson. Witnesses—Job Smith, Enoch Smith, John Day. Proved Jan. 23, 1788. Lib. 31, p. 245.

**1788, July 5. Earle, Philip,** of Bergen Township, Bergen Co. Int. Adm'r—Rynier Earle. Fellowbondsman—John E. Earle; both of said place. Lib. 31, p. 257.

**1786, Feb. 22. Eayre, Thomas,** of Burlington, Burlington Co. Int. Adm'r—Asa Eayre, of Northampton Township. Fellowbondsman— Joseph Eayre, of Evesham Township; both of said Co.
1786, Feb. 22. Inventory, made by Samuel Eyre and Abraham Stockton. Lib. 28, p. 74.

CALENDAR OF WILLS—1786-1790    73

**1786, Jan. 25. Edwards, Philip,** of Shrewsbury, Monmouth Co. Int. Adm'x—Margaret Edwards. Fellowbondsman—Abier Edwards; both of said Co. Witness—John Brinley.
    1786, Jan. 21. Inventory, £117.1.6, made by John West and John Brinley. Lib. 28, p. 295.

**1786, June 27. Eldredge, Aaron,** of Cape May Co. Int. Adm'x—Elizabeth Eldredge. Fellowbondsmen—Persons Leaming and Jeremiah Eldredge; all of Lower Precinct, said Co. Witnesses—Matthew Whilldin, Jacob Hughes, Hugh Holmes and Aaron Hand.
    1785, Aug. 16. Inventory, £379.3.3, made by Jacob Hughes and Matthew Whilldin. Lib. 28, p. 187.

**1788, July 9. Eldredge, Abraham,** of Nottingham, Burlington Co.; will of. Wife to have the ⅛ of the profits of the lands, and the other ⅔ to bring up my children. My 3 sons to be put to trades when old enough. Eldest son, Obadiah, house where I live, and 250 acres, which is bounded by James Schooley. Second son, John, 100 acres on the Allintown road. Third and last son, Wilson, the place where Nathaniel Roszill lives. Daughter, Mary, £50. Daughter, Ann, £50. Daughter, Tobitha, £50. Daughter, Martha, £50; all when they are 18. Executors—friend, William West and David Cubberley. Witnesses—William Willgus, Abram Crequi, William Arwine. Proved Aug. 11, 1788.
    1788, Aug. 6. Inventory, £684.10.2, made by John Abbott and John Watson. Lib. 29, p. 540.

**1789, May 20. Eldredge, George,** of Cape May Co.; will of. My house and lands to be sold. Wife, Lydia, all estate. My friend, Jeremiah Eldredge, is to help her sell the land. Executrix—wife, Lydia. Witnesses—Nathaniel Foster, Andrew Higgins, Ephraim Wills. Proved June 27, 1789.
    1789, June 26. Inventory, £35.2.4, made by Jeremiah Eldredge and Eleazer Hand. Lib. 31, p. 361.

**1789, Dec. 29. Eldredge, Jonathan,** of Cape May Co., yeoman; will of. Son, Elijah, my gun. Wife, Prudence, use of lands, till my youngest child is 14. Wife to have ⅛ the personal estate, and rest to my daughter, Lois; son, John, and son, Nathan, when they are 21. Oldest son to have the land on the south side of the road; that is to say, to son, Elijah; and the land on the north side, I give to son, Jonathan. Executors—wife, Prudence, and David Hughes. Witnesses—William Schillinger, Matthew Whilldin, John Stites. Proved March 19, 1790.
    1790, Feb. 9. Inventory, £88.2.1, made by William Schellinger and John Stites. Lib. 32, p. 100.

**1789, Dec. 20. Eldredge, Levi,** of Cape May Co.; will of. Wife, Esther, ⅛ the personal estate. Son, Lamuel, part of my plantation, bounded by lands formerly of James Whilldin, Memucan Hughes, and to contain 100 acres. Son, Daniel, the lands I bought of my cousin, Ezekiel Eldredge. Son, Levi, the rest of lands; he paying to my son, Jacob, £25, when he is 21. Rest of moveable estate to children, Jacob, Daniel, Elizabeth Hand, Abigail Eldredge, Judeth Eldredge and Jean Eldredge. My son-in-law, Elihu Hand, is to bring up my sons, Lamuel, Jacob and Daniel, until they are 14, and my daughters,

Judith, Abigail and Jean, until they are 18; and I give Elihu the use of ⅔ of the land, until my son, Levi, is 21, which will be Oct. 14, 1797. Executors—wife, Esther, and Jeremiah Eldredge. Witnesses—Jonathan Eldredge, Theoda Buck, Philomola Schillinger. Proved Aug. 4, 1790.

1790, July 26. Inventory, £229.6.2, made by Robert Parsons and John Stites, Jr. Lib. 31, p. 547.

**1786, March 2. Eldridge, Abigail,** of Springfield Township, Burlington Co. Int. Adm'rs—Noah Eldridge and Caleb Haines; both of said place. Fellowbondsman—Samuel Shinn, of Hanover Township, said Co.

1786, March 3. Inventory, £1,267.16.7, made by Samuel Shinn and David Ridgway. Lib. 28, p. 76.

**1788, Feb. 20. Eldridge, Ezekiel,** of Gloucester Township, Gloucester Co. Int. Adm'x—Charity Woolson, of Burlington Co. Fellowbondsman—John Thorne, of Gloucester Township, yeoman. Witnesses—Elizabeth Hugg and Joseph Hugg, Surrogate.

Lib. 31, p. 35.

**1786, April 22. Eldridge, Jonathan,** of Springfield, Burlington Co.; will of. Nephew, John Eldridge, son of Noah Eldridge, my real estate, and he is to pay the following sums: To Hannah Eldridge, £50, when she is 21; to Elizabeth Eldridge, £50, when 21. Brother, Noah, a mare and riding chair. Executors—brother, Noah Eldridge, and John Atkinson. Witnesses—Caleb Conaroe, Patience Conaroe, John Allen. Proved May 27, 1786.

1786, May 25. Inventory, £239.2.6, made by Samuel Shinn and Silvanus Zelley. Lib. 28, p. 50.

**1789, Dec. 17. Eldridge, Obadiah, and John,** of Nottingham Township, Burlington Co. Wards. Sons of Abraham Eldridge, of said place, deceased. Having real and personal estate, they make choice of their mother, Amy Eldridge, as their Guardian.

1789, Dec. 17. Guardian—Amey Eldridge. Fellowbondsman—William Nutt and Alexander Adams; all of said place. Witness—Bowes Reed. Lib. 31, p. 321.

**1789, July 20. Elwell, Cornelius,** of Cumberland Co. Int. Adm'x— Mary Elwell. Fellowbondsman—Samuel Sherry; both of said Co.

1798, Jan. 6. Copy of the account as made by Nathan Austin(?) and Mary, his wife, Adm'x of Cornelius Elwell. "One child, a daughter, about 3 months old, at the time of its father's death, to be maintained out of the child's share." Lib. 30, p. 163.

**1788, Sept. 29. Elwell, Ellis,** of Gloucester Co. Int. Adm'r—Elias Thomas. Fellowbondsman—John Vandyke; both of said Co.

1786, April 6. Inventory, £7.0.2, made by John Vandyke and William Olcraft. Lib. 31, p. 36.

**1787, July 6. Elwell, John,** of Pitts Grove, Salem Co.; will of. Son, Allexander, the 80 acres where he lives, joining Samuel Elwell and Henry Paullin. Sons, Sawtel, Ammariah, Evin and Ephraim, rest of lands. Daughter, Lurainy, some goods. Daughter, Rebeka, some goods. Executors—sons, Sawtel, Amariah, Allexander. Witnesses— John Nelson, Samuel Nelson, Elizabeth Nelson. Proved Dec. 19, 1789.

CALENDAR OF WILLS—1786-1790 75

**1789, Nov. 11.** Inventory, £131.18.0, made by Abraham Elwell and Samuel Nelson. Lib. 31, p. 332.

**1789, Dec. 7. Ely, John,** of Middlesex Co. Ward. Son of John Ely, Jr., of said Co., deceased. Said Ward makes choice of Joshua Ely and William Ely, as his Guardians.
1789, Dec. 7. Guardians—Joshua Ely and William Ely. Fellowbondsman—Allison Ely; all of N. J. Witness—James Anderson.
Lib. 31, p. 396.

**1786, Sept. 20. Emans, Andrew,** of Readingtown, Hunterdon Co. Int. Adm'rs—Sarah Emans and Harmen Lane. Fellowbondsman—William Emans; all of said Co.
1786, Sept. Inventory, £186.4.2, made by Henry Schamp and James Emans.
1793, May 11. Account by Hermen Lane, acting Adm'r.
Lib. 28, p. 245.

**1786, Oct. 24. Emans, Andrew,** of Readingtown, Hunterdon Co. Ward. Son of Andrew Emans, of said place, deceased. Said Ward makes choice of James Emans as his Guardian.
1786, Oct. 24. Guardian—James Emans, of said place. Fellowbondsman—Andrew Verseilus. Lib. 28, p. 248.

**1788, Nov. 21. Embley, Ezekiel,** of Cumberland Co. Int. Adm'x—Sarah Embley. Fellowbondsman—Legget Smith; both of said Co. Witness—Samuel M. Shute. Lib. 31, p. 75.

**1788, April 25. English, David,** of Freehold, Monmouth Co. Ward. Son of Jonathan English, of said place, deceased. Said Ward makes choice of Doctor James English as his Guardian.
1788, April 22. Guardian—James English, of said place. Fellowbondsman—James R. English, of said Co. Witness—Tobias Hendrickson. Lib. 30, p. 104.

**1788, Feb. 20. English, Joseph,** of Burlington Co. Int. Adm'x—Mercy English, widow of said Joseph. Fellowbondsman—Joseph Talman; both of Mansfield Township, said Co. Witness—Joseph Hollinshead, Jr.
1788, March 6. Inventory, £939.7.16, made by Thomas Biddle, Sr., and Daniel Newbold. Lib. 30, p. 59.

**1786, Feb. 18. English, Moses,** of Mansfield Township, Burlington Co. Int. Adm'r—Joseph Craft, of said place. Fellowbondsman—James Craft, of City of Burlington. Lib. 28, p. 79.
**1788, Feb. 25. Ennis, William,** of Essex Co. Int. Adm'r—Garrit I. Speer. Fellowbondsman—Peter Degarmo; both of said Co.
Lib. 31, p. 243.

**1789, June 3. Erwin, Cornelius,** of Morris Co.; will of. Mother, Sarah Erwin, £40. Sister, Susanna, a cow. Children to be educated. Son, Peter, all real estate, when 21. Daughter, Perynetie, £50. If all die, then my estate to go to my brothers and sisters. Executors—uncle, Joseph Board, and my father-in-law, Peter Ward. Witnesses—Andrew Seamers, John Seamer, Isaac Haulenbeck, Anthony Kinner. Proved Dec. 28, 1790.

1790, July 17. Inventory, £270.16.6, made by Isaac Tomkins and Peter Sniter. Lib. 30, p. 466.

**1788, Feb. 16. Evans, Sarah,** of Evesham, Burlington Co., widow; will of. Son, William Evans, £50. Children, Hannah Eldridge, Esther Wilkins, Mary Morgan (deceased), Rebekah Andrews and Sarah Buzby, rest of estate. Executors—sons, Enoch and William Evans. Witnesses—Elizabeth Evans, William Roberts. Proved Jan. 11, 1790.
1789, Dec. 21. Inventory, £202.19.0, made by Joshua Lippincott and Samuel Evans. Lib. 32, p. 63.

**1789, Oct. 2. Evelman, Elizabeth,** of Upper Freehold, Monmouth Co.; will of. Daughter, Mary Woodward, all apparel. Granddaughters, Susannah Woodward and Elizabeth Woodward, £10 each. Granddaughters, Alice Woodward and Acsah Woodward, £10 each, when of age. Niece, Susannah Woodward, daughter of Thomas Forman, my riding chair. Grandson, Forman Woodward, a horse to be sold for him, and ½ the price to be given to his brother, John. Son, Robert Evelman, rest of moveable estate. Executor—son, Robert. Witnesses—Elizabeth Montgomery, Rachel Drummond. Proved Oct. 12, 1790.
1790, Aug. 4. Inventory, £834.8.0, made by [names not given].
Lib. 30, p. 387.

**1790, Oct. 9. Ewan, Israel,** of Gloucester Co. Int. Adm'r—Evan Ewan. Fellowbondsman—Timothy Leach; both of said Co.
1790, Aug. 14. Inventory, made by Timothy Leach and Arthur Wescott. Lib. 31, p. 477.

**1788, June 17. Ewing, John,** of Greenwich, Cumberland Co. Int. Adm'r—Abner Ewing. Fellowbondsman—Thomas Maskell; both of said Co.
1788, June 16. Inventory, £235.7.3, made by Thomas Maskell and Job Butcher. Lib. 31, p. 75.

**1788, Oct. 28. Eyre, Samuel,** of Burlington, Burlington Co., yeoman; will of. Son, George, the lot I bought of my brother, Jehu, deceased, and 5 and ½ acres that I bought of Barzilla Scott, which join John Neale. Son, Nathan, the land which I bought of my brother, Benjamin George Eyre, and the land I bought of Richard Wells, and the 4½ acres which I bought of John Roberts. Son, Samuel, house and lot where I live, which I had by will of my father, George Eyre; but, if he die under age, then I give the same to my sons, George and Nathan. Daughters, Elizabeth Eyre, Mary Eyre and Hannah Eyre, rest of personal estate. My son, Samuel B. Eyre, is not 19 yet. Niece, Margaret Beatson Adams, £5. Sister, Ann Adams, £5. Executors—sons, George and Nathan, and my friend, Andrew Craige; all of Burlington. Witnesses—James Craft, Ellis Wright, William Smith, Jr. Proved Dec. 4, 1788.
1788, Dec. 3. Inventory, £1,082.16.4, made by John Neale and Amos Hutchin. Lib. 30, p. 27.

**1789, Dec. 30. Fairchild, Abial,** of Hanover, Morris Co. Int. Adm'rs—Elizabeth Fairchild and Lemuel Mintun. Fellowbondsman—Elisha Wolfe; all of said place. Witnesses—Jacob Gard and Jabez Gwinnup.

CALENDAR OF WILLS—1786-1790          77

1789, Dec. 28. Inventory, £103.15.0, made by Jacob Mintun and Jacob Gard. Lib. 30, p. 234.

**1790, June 12. Fairchild, Matthew,** of Hanover, Morris Co. Int. Adm'rs—Caleb Fairchild and Jonathan Fairchild. Fellowbondsman—Elisha Rolfe; all of said Co. Witness—Stephen Fairchild.
1790, June 11. Renunciation by Rebecca Fairchild. Witnesses—Elisha Rolfe and Jacob Palmer.
1790, June 10. Inventory, £82.2.3, made by George Badgley and Elisha Rolfe. Lib. 30, p. 480.

**1787, Feb. 10. Farber, John,** of Morris Co.; will of. Son, Paul, £50 above an equal share with my other children. Granddaughter, Elizabeth Sackman, £50, the interest of which for 4 years is to be paid to Daniel Walling, for bringing her up. Sons, George, Paul and Philip, and daughters, Susannah, Elizabeth, and the children of Margaret, rest of estate. One-third of the share given to Margaret's children, to Peter Matthews, her oldest son, and the rest to the other three, James, Catharine and Nancy. Executors—son, Paul, George Bockoven and Daniel Walling. Witnesses—Jacob Knoup, Anne Kely, Agness Bedell. Proved March 28, 1787.
1787, March 31. Inventory, £81.11.3, made by Stephen Conkling and Philip Lindsly. Lib. 29, p. 442.

**1787, June 4. Farley, George,** of Hopewell, Hunterdon Co., shoemaker. Int. Adm'r—Peter Phillips. Fellowbondsman—Lott Phillips; both of said place.
1787, May 22. Inventory, £41.17.6, made by Henry Phillips and John Phillips.
1790, April 30. Account by Adm'r. Lib. 29, p. 296.

**1790, March 1. Farley, Mindart,** of Tewksbury Township, Hunterdon Co., yeoman; will of. Wife, Barbary, £200 and negro wench, Cumbo. Son, Joshua, to live on my homestead, till my wife dies, with my wife, and, after her death, the place to be sold. To my 5 children, Caleb, John, Isaac, Joshua and Mary, residue, share and share alike. Executors—sons, Caleb, John and Joshua. Witnesses—John Hoffman, John Forrester, Adam Apger. Proved April 6, 1790.
1790, March 22. Inventory, £697.18.10, made by John Hoffman and John Forrester.
1808, July 28. Account by Joshua Farley, one of the Ex'rs.
1808, Oct. 27. Exceptions made by Coanrod Apgar, Adm'r of Mary Apgar, to the account. Lib. 30, p. 289.

**1789, Nov. 2. Faitoute, Aaron,** of Essex Co. Int. Adm'rs—Jesse Clarke and John Dunham. Fellowbondsman—Christopher Denman; all of said Co.
1789, Oct. 30. Inventory, £41.6.0, made by John Scudder and Moses DeCamp. Lib. 30, p. 218.

**1789, April 27. Felt, John,** of Greenwich Township, Sussex Co., yeoman; will of. Daughter, Mary, wife of Jacob Minier, £10. Daughter, Catharine, £3. To Henry, Elizabeth, Mary and Peter, the children of my daughter, Catharine, and her late husband, Henry Dishan, deceased, £300, when they are 21. Son, Daniel, rest of estate. Executor—son, Daniel. Witnesses—John Winter, Peter Winter, Valentine Bidleman. Proved May 17, 1790. Lib. 30, p. 434.

**1790, Oct. 23. Felthansen, John,** of Bridgewater, Somerset Co. Int. Adm'r—Richard McDonald. Fellowbondsman—Joseph Arrosmith; both of said Co. Lib. 31, p. 531.

**1786, June 8. Fenimore, Benjamin,** of Springfield, Burlington Co.; will of. Son, Abraham, that part of my farm and cedar swamp that I bought of my brother, Joseph, when he is 21; also the land I bought of Daniel Haines and wife, Mary. Son, John Hutchin Fenimore, all that part of my farm and cedar swamp that was left me by my father; also land I bought of Edward Kemble. Wife, Mary, household goods. Daughter, Rebecca, spoons. Benjamin Fenimore, son of my brother, Thomas, 20 dollars. Daughter, Rebecca, £250, when she is 18. Abraham is to pay to his mother, £6 a year. Wife to have the rents of the real estate. Executor—brother, Thomas Fenimore. Witnesses—Thomas Enoch, Samuel Eyre, James Fenimore. Proved Aug. 18, 1786.

1786, Sept. 1. Inventory, £2,147.16.10, made by Thomas Enoch and David Ridgway. Lib. 28, p. 68.

**1789, April 3. Fenimore, Richard,** of Willingborough, Burlington Co.; will of, being aged and infirm. Grandson, Richard Cooper, son of my daughter, Elizabeth Cooper, 150 acres, to be laid off of my land, and to join Benjamin Ridgway and James Kelley. To said grandson, 5 acres that I bought of my brother, Joshua, adjoining Rainbow Island; also a cedar swamp that I bought of John Monrow, and one of 3 acres that I bought of Daniel Ellis. Grandson, Richard Heaton, 50 acres that was devised to me by my father, joining lands of Samuel Newton and David Stokes; also Rainbow Island, which I bought of Richard Cox. Daughter, Rebeckah Willmington, the plantation where I live; also the land on the point of Rancocus, with the Sedge Island; also the rest of the land I bought of my brother, Samuel; and, after her death, to her son, Fenimore Willmington. Granddaughter, Hannah Heaton, £150. Executors—son-in-law, Paul Willmington, and my daughter, Rebeckah. Witnesses—George Smith, William Hatcher, Daniel Ellis. Proved Sept. 17, 1789.

1789, Sept. 21. Inventory, £641.0.1, made by Isaac Newton and Pearson Fenimore. Lib. 31, p. 269.

**1789, Nov. 8. Fenton, Eleazar,** of Springfield, Burlington Co.; will of. Son, Eleazar, land in Salem Co. which I bought of Robert Herbeson, of 5 or 6 acres. Son, John, rest of land in Salem Co. where he lives, of 300 acres. Son, Samuel, a bed. Daughter, Hannah, wife of Jacob Shinn, Jr., £100. Daughter, Elizabeth Fenton, a bed. Wife to have the rest of personal estate, to enable her to provide for my daughter, Elizabeth. Executrix—wife, Elizabeth. Witnesses—James Fenimore, Daniel Zelley, Samuel Fenimore. Proved Nov. 27, 1789.

1789, Nov. 26. Inventory, £384.4.3, made by Thomas Fenimore and Daniel Zelley. Lib. 31, p. 272.

**1789, March 31. Fervier, Stephen,** of Shrewsbury, Monmouth Co. Int. Adm'r—John Tallman. Fellowbondsman—Stephen Tallman; both of said place.

1790, June 21. Adm'rs — James Tallman. Fellowbondsman — Thomas Seabrook; both of said Co. Witness—Peter Knott. John Tallman. The former Adm'r is also dead.
1789, March 31. Stephen Tallman, Joseph Tallman and Mary Tilton, on oath declared that Stephen Fervier had no written will, but he had declared that he wanted John Tallman, of Shrewsbury, to have his property. He had no relations in America, and he died in Nov., 1788. Lib. 30, p. 187; Lib. 30, p. 417.

**1790, May 10. Field, Benjamin,** of Piscataway Township, Middlesex Co.; will of. Wife, Margaret, her ⅓ and a wench. Son, Jeremiah, my land in Somerset Co. and 10 acres of my farm. Son, John, ⅓ of my farm, next to my brother Richard's land. Son, Benjamin, ⅓ of my farm. Son, Jacob, the lands at the Landing. Son, Richard, the same amount of acres, next to Tunis Ten Eyck's land. Executors—sons, Jeremiah and John. Witnesses—Richard Field, Jr., Richard Field, Dennies Field. Proved June 12, 1790. Lib. 30, p. 521.

**1788, Feb. 26. Field, Francis,** of Chesterfield, Burlington Co. Int. Adm'r—Isaac Field, of said place. Fellowbondsman—Okey Hoagland, of Burlington, said Co.
1789, June 25. Inventory, £17.7.7, made by Gervas Pharo and John Thorn. Lib. 30, p. 60.

**1787, Dec. 31. Fisher, Christopher,** of Amwell, Hunterdon Co. Int. Adm'rs—Mary Fisher and John Lequear. Fellowbondsman—Derick Sutphen; all of said place.
1787, Dec. 20. Inventory, £498.3.1, made by Derick Sutphen and Nathan Stout. "Bond against John Lequear, not due till 3 days after decease of his mother, £36.1.0."
1789, April 6. Additional Inventory, £9.19.4, made by Nathan Stout and Derick Sutphen.
1789, Nov. 10. Account by Adm'rs.
1791, Oct. 27. Petition for division of lands allowed. Daniel Griggs, and Elizabeth, his wife, late Elizabeth Fisher, daughter of Christopher Fisher, deceased, state that said Christopher had land in Amwell Township, of about 180 acres, and, dying intestate, left 4 children, of whom is still under age, and they pray that the lands may be divided. Lib. 29, p. 297.

**1790, May 2. Fithian, Ephraim,** of Deerfield Township, Cumberland Co.; will of. Wife to have a bed and £10. Son, David, 25 acres of land, beginning at a maple corner of Ephraim Russel, standing near the run of Cohansey Creek. Son, Wade, rest of land. Daughter, Pheby Loper, one dollar. Daughter, Seviah Chamberlain, one dollar. Daughter, Lovece Fithian, £10. Daughter, Elizabeth Fithian, £8. The overplus, to all my children, except son, Wade. Executors—sons, Wade and David. Witnesses—David Moore, Abel Griffith, Josiah Seeley. Proved ——————, 1700. File No. 6031 F.

**1790, May 12. Fithian, Isaac,** of Cumberland Co. Ward. Son of John Fithian, of said Co., deceased. Having real and personal estate, said Ward makes choice of Ebenezer Elmer as his Guardian.
1790, May 12. Guardian — Ebenezer Elmer. Fellowbondsman—Reuben Burgin; both of said Co. Lib. 30, p. 281.

**1788, July 2. Fithian, John,** of Bridge Town, Cumberland Co., doctor; will of. Son, Lot, my lands and marsh in Greenwich Township, which my father willed to my sister, Molly Wheaton, during her life; and now I desire my said son to have the house and shop, and said lands, and 15 acres of woodland, bounded by Thomas Maskill; also ½ of 26 acres, bounded by Jacob Mulford; also my right in that plantation which Samuel Fithian, by will, gave to my father, and my father by will to me. Son, John, the house, garden and barn lot where I live. Son, Isaac, the rest of the orchard lot, and the land I bought of Jonathan Coney, and 5 acres of woodland. Son, Thomas, the house that I bought of Jonathan Coney, and 5 acres of woodland; also 10 acres that join Uriah Davis. Son, William, the house near Greenwich, that is occupied by John Ayres; also rest of woodland joining Jacob Mulford. Son, Isral, the tract I bought of Ebenezer Harris. Son, Lot, John and Unis, each a cow. Daughter, Unis, £10. Daughter, Elizabeth, £10. Son-in-law, Ezekiel Looper, the use of the said premises, till each of my said sons are 21. Executors—sons, Ezekiel Loper and John Fithian. Witnesses—Stephen Miller, Hannah Donaldson, Abel Corson. Proved March 21, 1789. Lib. 30, p. 156.

**1788, May 15. Fitz Randolph, Agnes and Nathaniel,** of Middlesex Co. Wards. Children of Nathaniel Fitz Randolph, of said Co., deceased. Experience Coddington, late Experience Fitz Randolph, widow of Nathaniel Fitz Randolph, asks for Benjamin Manning to be appointed Guardian of said children.
1788, June 10. Guardian—Benjamin Manning. Fellowbondsman—James Dunn; both of said Co. Lib. 31, p. 225.

**1787, Aug. 16. Fitz Randolph, James,** of Perth Amboy, Middlesex Co. Inventory, £142.10.8, made by George Harriot and Thomas Edgar. File No. 7111 L.

**1788, Jan. 19. Fitz Randolph, Samuel,** of Hardyston, Sussex Co.; will of. Wife, Elizabeth, £100. To Marcey Marlett, daughter of Sarah Dunn, £25. To Elizabeth Dunn, £25. All land, except a tract in Dismel, in Piscataway Township, to my children, Jephtha Fitz Randolph, Rosanah Fitz Randolph and Reuben Fitz Randolph, when they are of age. Said tract in Dismel to be sold. Executors—wife, Elizabeth, Machack Hull, of Bethlehem Twp., Hunterdon Co. and Evi Adams. Witnesses—John V. Anglen, Simeon Smith, Humphrey Martin. Proved May 7, 1788.
1788, May 5. Inventory, £244.14.3, made by Humphrey Martin and Azariah Martin. Lib. 31, p. 151.

**1788, Sept. 9. Fleming, James,** of Monmouth Co. Ward. Son of Jacob Fleming, of said Co. Said Ward had an estate left him by his grandfather, James West, and he makes choice of his father, Jacob Fleming, as his Guardian.
1788, Sept. 9. Guardian—Jacob Fleming. Fellowbondsman—Elisha Shepherd; both of said Co. Witness—Margret Williams.
Lib. 30, p. 105.

**1788, July. Fleming, Joseph, Stephen W., Jacob, Sarah and John West,** of Monmouth Co. Wards. Children of Jacob Fleming, of said Co., who states that their grandfather, James West, bequeathed to them personal estate, and he wishes to be made their Guardian.

CALENDAR OF WILLS—1786-1790 81

1788, Sept. 9. Guardian—Jacob Fleming. Fellowbondsman—Elisha Shepherd. Witness—Margaret Williams. Lib. 30, p. 105.

1789, May 28. **Flesebaorn [Flesebaron], Jacobus,** of Bergen Co. Int. Adm'rs—Jacob Merseles and Harmon Blauvelt. Fellowbondsman—Jacob Flesebaorn; all of said Co. Witness—Fredericus Haring. Lib. 30, p. 248.

1789, Sept. 28. **Flock, Andrew,** of Roxbury, Morris Co. Int. Adm'rs—Phillip Flock and John Flock. Fellowbondsman—Matthias Tufford; all of said place. Witness—Sally Gwinnup.
1789, Sept. 28. Renunciation by Margaret Flock, widow of Andrew. Witness—William Woodhull.
1789, Sept. 18. Inventory, £258.7.3, made by Christopher Keon and Matthias Tufford. Lib. 30, p. 233.

1790, March 8. **Fogg, Elijah,** of Salem Co. Ward. Son of Samuel Fogg, of said Co., deceased. Said Ward makes choice of Abot Sayre as his Guardian.
1790, March 8. Guardian—Abot Sayre. Fellowbondsmen—Edward Keasbey and Edward Bradway; all of said Co. Lib. 31, p. 505.

1786, Sept. 20. **Fogg, Joseph,** of Lower Alloways Creek, Salem Co. Int. Adm'x—Mary Fogg fellowbondsmen—Edward Bradway and David Adams; all of said Co. File No. 1887 Q.

1789, Nov. 3. **Folwell, Elizabeth,** of Woolwich Township, Gloucester Co.; will of. The £100 that was left me by my husband, to be applied to the use of my 2 youngest daughters, Mary Folwell and Ann Folwell, for their schooling and clothing. On the 17th of Jan., 1787, Jacob Jones, and his wife, Reginah, conveyed to me land, which I give to my son, Nathan Folwell; and he is to pay £300 agreeable to my husband's will. My 4 youngest children are to have the cloath at the weaver's. Daughter, Elizabeth Lippincott, my bonnets. Daughter, Mary Folwell, my saddle. Daughter, Ann Folwell, a bed. Youngest daughters, Mary and Ann Folwell, clothing. To William Folwell's daughter, Elizabeth, my large Bible. To William Lippincott's daughter, Elizabeth, rest of books. Mary Folwell is to have her home with her brother, Nathan Folwell. Son, William Folwell, is to take care of my youngest daughter, Ann, and the 2 youngest boys, John and Thomas Folwell. Executor—son, Nathan Folwell. Witnesses—Samuel Beckett, John Atkinson, Rachel Davis. Proved Jan. 1, 1790.
1789, Dec. 28. Inventory, £184.18.3, made by David Brown and John Jessup. Lib. 31, p. 427.

1787, Jan. 5. **Folwell, Thomas,** of Rackoon, Woolwich Township, Gloucester Co.; will of. Wife, Elizabeth, £100. Son, William, 5 shillings. Sons, Samuel, Nathan, John and Thomas, £40 each. Daughter, Elizabeth Lippincott, £10. Daughters, Mary and Ann Folwell, £40 each. Wife to have the residue. Executors—friend, Samuel Tonkin, and my son, William. Witnesses—Samuel Beckett, Mary Tonkin, Caleb Marlack. Proved Feb. 26, 1787.
1787, Jan. 30. Inventory, £1,122.12.5, made by John Jessup and Benjamin Rambo. Lib. 29, p. 115.

**1787, May 5. Force, Benjamin,** of Morristown, Morris Co.; will of. Wife, Abigail, real and personal estate. "To the second of my name, nefew and son of Squire Force, all at expiration of widow." Executor—Canady Vance. Witnesses—William Calwall, Abraham Caldwell, Uzal Johnson. Proved June 19, 1787.
1787, June 11. Inventory, £130.3.11, made by William Calwall and Benjamin Pettit. Lib. 29, p. 449.

**1790, April 23. Ford, John,** of Maidenhead, Hunterdon Co. Int. Adm'x—Elizabeth Ford, of said place. Fellowbondsman—John Johnson, of Western Precinct of Somerset Co.
1790, March 30. Inventory, £202.6.0, made by Jonathan Hunt and John Johnson.
1792, Oct. 20. Account by Adm'x. To the Trustee of Maidenhead Church, £12. Lib. 30, p. 318.

**1786, July 4. Forman, Rebekah,** of Bordentown, Burlington Co.; will of. Sisters, Mary, Amy, Abigail and Hannah, or their daughters, my furniture and clothing. Brother, Joshua Potts, £50. Friend, Polly Moore, if unmarried at my decease, £20. To Effy, Caty, Mary and Ursila, the daughters of Lewis Forman, £50. To Ursilla, Lucy, Lydia and Elizabeth, daughters of George Walker, £50. As my brother, Thomas Potts, has by law inherited the greater part of my mother's estate, he must not think that for want of affection I leave his son only £3. To my four sisters, the rest of my estate. Executors—sister, Amy Taylor, Oakey Hoagland and John Van Emburgh. Witnesses—John Oliver, John McGalliard, Rebecca McGalliard. Proved July 27, 1786.
1786, July 28. Inventory, £1,003.17.1, made by John Edwards and Tunis Probasco. Lib. 28, p. 32.

**1786, March 2. Fort, John,** of Burlington, Burlington Co.; will of. Son, John, of Northampton, £20. Grandson, Joseph Fort, son of my son, John, £20. I have a bond of my son, Marmaduke, for £200, which he gave me for my real estate, for which I gave him a deed, and he is to pay to my 5 daughters, Anne, Hannah, Lettice, Levinia and Jean, £160. Executors—my brother, Marmaduke, and my friend, John Goldy. Witnesses—Joab Dobbins, Nathan Folwell, Moses Kempton. Proved Nov. 18, 1786.
1786, Nov. 18. Inventory, £215.13.6, made by John Roberts and Joab Dobbins. Lib. 27, p. 523.

**1786, Feb. 13. Fortenor, Jonathan,** of Cumberland Co. Int. Adm'x —Drusilla Fortenor.
1786, Feb. 8. Inventory, £43.11.10, made by Davod Lore and William Price. Note against Joseph Sheldon. File No. 901 F.

**1786, June 23. Foss, Daniel,** of Lebanon Township, Hunterdon Co. Int. Adm'rs—Philip Foss and Daniel Foss. Fellowbondsman—Fredrick Miller.
1786, June 8. Inventory, £179.18.6, made by Fredrick Miller and Thomas Force. Lib. 28, p. 244.

**1787, Feb. 24. Foster, Ezekiel,** of Deerfield Township, Cumberland Co.; will of. Real and personal estate to be sold, and money divided into 6 parts. Son, Ezekiel, one part. Son, Jeremiah, two

CALENDAR OF WILLS—1786-1790   83

parts. Daughters, Patience, Martha and Elisheba, each one part. Executor—son, Ezekiel. Witnesses—Ephraim Foster, David Moore, Patience James. Proved May 14, 1788. Lib. 31, p. 60.

**1789, Jan. 28. Foster, George,** of Cape May Co. Int. Adm'x— Rachel Foster. Fellowbondsmen—Constantine Carll and Robert Edmunds; all of Lower Precinct, said Co. Witnesses—Margaret Goleker and Persons Leaming.
1789, Jan. 17. Inventory, £128.18.2, made by Constantine Carll and Robert Edmunds. Lib. 31, p. 370.

**1786, March 18. Foster, Joseph,** of Hanover, Morris Co. Int. Adm'r—Ransellor Foster. Fellowbondsman—Allehanson Foster; both of said place. Witnesses—Paul Lee and William Campfield.
Lib. 28, p. 487.

**1789, Oct. 28. Foster, Reuben, Jr.,** of Cape May Co. Ward. Son of Reuben Foster, of said Co., deceased. Petition of Salathiel Foster, Sr., to have a Guardian appointed.
1789, Oct. 28. Guardian—Salathiel Foster. Fellowbondsman—John Newton; both of Lower Precinct, said Co. Witnesses—Elijah Hand, Jr. and John Hand. Lib. 31, p. 372.

**1786, April 4. Fowler, Moses,** of Middletown Township, Monmouth Co. Int. Adm'x—Elizabeth Fowler. Fellowbondsman—Moses Shepherd; both of said Co. Witness—Jonathan Forman. Said Elizabeth is widow of Moses.
1786, Feb. 22. Inventory, £96.1.3, made by Charles Gordon and Moses Shepherd. Lib. 28, p. 294.

**1786, March 25. Fox, Jonathan,** of New Hanover, Burlington Co. Int. Adm'r—William Fox, Jr. Fellowbondsman—Samuel Shinn; both of said Co.
1786, March 22. Inventory, £54.10.10, made by Samuel Budd and Samuel Shinn. Lib. 28, p. 80.

**1790, May 20. Foy, Patrick,** of Shrewsbury, Monmouth Co. Int. Adm'r—John Lewis. Fellowbondsman—William Lewis; both of said place.
1790, Sept. 15. Inventory, £61.10.0, made by John Richmond and Aaron Brewer. Lib. 30, p. 419.

**1787, June 16. Francis, Robert,** of Freehold, Monmouth Co.; will of. Wife, Susannah, use of all estate. Sons, John, Robert, David and Nehemiah, all lands, when Nehemiah is 21. Daughters, Martha and Susannah, personal estate. Executors—wife, Susannah, and friend, John Richmond. Witnesses—Richard Rogers, Samuel T. Forman, Thomas Henderson. Proved Oct. 11, 1787.
1787, Sept. 12. Inventory, £391.0.6, made by Hugh Newel and Samuel T. Forman. Lib. 29, p. 310.

**1789, Sept. 6. Frederick, Hendrick,** of Ramapough, Bergen Co., yeoman; will of. Son, Henry Frederick, all my lands. Daughters, Margaret and Rachel, a bond of Adrian Post, for £80, one of Jacobus Koch and John Bartolf, of £16, one of Thomas L. Van Buskirk, of

£25, and an account against Lewis Conklin, of £8. Executors—son, Henry, and John Conklin, Jr. Witnesses—John Conklin, John Conklin, Jr., Adulphy Shurte. Proved April 24, 1790.
Lib. 31, p. 540.

**1789, Jan. 10. Freeman, Benjamin,** of Hanover, Morris Co.; will of. Wife, Esther, goods, a negro and bond against Henry Freeman for £100. Sons, Gilman, Jacob and Samuel. To my son, Benjamin 5 shillings, and my daughters, Elizabeth Johnson and Rachel McCurry. Son Samuel's son, Benjamin, a cow. Son Jacob's daughters, Phebe and Elizabeth, some linen. Executors—friends, Samuel Tuthill and David Fairchild. Witnesses—Benjamin Woodruff, Josiah Lambert, Nathaniel Beers. Proved Jan. 24, 1789.

1789, Jan. 24. Adm'rs—Jacob Freeman and Malcolm McCorrey. Fellowbondsmen—Nathaniel Terry and James Pitney, Jr.; all of Morris Co. Witness—Jonas Phillips.

1789, Jan. 22. Renunciation by Esther Freeman, widow of Benjamin. Witnesses—Hannah Cutter, Jacob Freeman, Samuel Freeman.

1789, Jan. 22. Renunciation by Benjamin Freeman, son of Benjamin.

1789, Jan. 22. Renunciation by Samuel Freeman, son of Benjamin.

1789, Jan. 20. Renunciation by Gilman Freeman, son of Benjamin. Witnesses—Jacob Freeman and Samuel Freeman.

1789, Jan. 19. Renunciation by Samuel Tuthill and David Fairchild. Witness—Samuel Tuthill, Jr.

1789, Jan. 17. Inventory, £1,346.14.10, made by Jonas Phillips and Silas Hyers.
Lib. 30, p. 229.

**1787, June 7. Freeman, Esther,** of Hanover, Morris Co.; will of, being the wife of Benjamin Freeman. Daughter, Sarah Tucker, ⅙ of personal estate. Daughter, Elizabeth Bird, also ⅙. Daughter, Mercey Bald, ⅙. Daughter, Jane White, ⅙. Daughter, Hannah Cutter, ⅙. Son-in-law, Samuel Cutter, ⅙. Executors—Kelsey Cutter and Samuel Cutter. Witnesses—William Johnes, Timothy Johnes. Proved Jan. 30, 1789.

1789, Jan. 31. Inventory, £233.11.3, made by Jonas Phillips and Silas Ayers.
Lib. 30, p. 231.

**1790, Dec. 13. Freeman, Frederick,** of Essex Co. Int. Adm'r—Joseph Tompkins.
Lib. 30, p. 361.

**1787, May 2. Freeman, James,** of Middlesex Co. Ward. Son of Jonathan Freeman, of said Co., deceased. Said Ward makes choice of Robert Ross, Jr., as his Guardian.

1787, May 2. Guardian—Robert Ross, Jr. Fellowbondsman—Robert Ross; both of said Co.
Lib. 29, p. 366.

**1790, Dec. 13. Freeman, Jedediah, Jr.,** of Essex Co. Int. Adm'r—Joseph Tomkins. Fellowbondsman—Amos Freeman; both of said Co.

1791, March 8. Inventory, made by Isaac Freeman and Jedidiah Freeman.
Lib. 30, p. 361.

**1789, April 1. French, Jemima,** of Moorestown, Burlington Co., widow; will of. Daughter, Sarah Brown, a bill I have against her son, George French. Granddaughter, Unea Keen, a wheel. Sons, Edward, Uriah and George, 10 shillings each. Rest to my four

## CALENDAR OF WILLS—1786-1790 85

children and said granddaughter, Unea. Executor—son, Edward French. Witnesses—Joseph Newton, John Cox. Proved May 13, 1789.

1789, April 15. Inventory, £74.0.10, made by John Cox and Joseph Newton. Lib. 31, p. 274.

**1790, July 5. Friend, Laurence,** of Gloucester Co. Int. Adm'r—David Harker. Fellowbondsmen—John Daniels and Samuel Davenport; all of said Co.

1790, July 28. Inventory, £46.3.8, made by John Daniels and Samuel Davenport. Lib. 31, p. 477.

**1789, Nov. 4. Frost, James,** of Middletown Township, Monmouth Co.; will of. Wife, Mary, to have a decent living. My daughter, Sarah Hoppins, land along George Taylor and Daniel Covenhoven. Grandson, James Frost, ½ of the woodland along John Stillwell. To said Sarah Hoppins and her heirs she hath by Samuel Hoppins a meadow. Granddaughter, Esther Frost, £100, to be paid by her brother, James Frost. Executors—friends, Samuel Hoppins, James Frost and Esther Frost. Witnesses—John Stillwell, Zephaniah White, Samuel Tunis. Proved Nov. 16, 1789.

1789, Nov. 14. Inventory, made by Thomas Seabrook and John Stillwell. Lib. 30, p. 170.

**1789, April 25. Furman, Agar,** of Hunterdon Co. Int. Adm'r—Jonathan Smith. Fellowbondsman—Enoch Smith; both of Maidenhead, said Co.

1792, April 12. Account by Adm'r. Lib. 32, p. 55.

**1788, Feb. 16. Furman, Josiah,** of Maidenhead, Hunterdon Co.; will of. Wife, Mary, negro girl, Dina. Granddaughter, Harlot Smith, said wench, after wife's death. Wife, Mary, ⅓ of the residue. Son, Agur, ⅓. Daughter, Sarah Johnson, ⅙, and daughter, Mary Smith, ⅙, after wife's death. Executors—sons-in-law, John Johnson and Jonathan Smith. Witnesses—David Price, James Taylor, Absalom Price. Proved March 3, 1788.

1788, Feb. 27. Inventory, £222.15.6, made by Nathan Moore and David Price.

1790, Oct. 9. Account by both Executors.

1792, April 12. Account by both Executors. Lib. 31, p. 102.

**1787, May 19. Furman, Zelika,** of Cape May Co. Ward. Daughter of Jonathan Furman, of said Co., deceased. Said Ward, having real and personal estate, makes choice of William Hand as her Guardian. Witnesses—Jesse Hand and Sarah Hand.

1787, May 19. Guardian—William Hand. Fellowbondsman—Benjamin Taylor; both of said Co. Witnesses—Sarah Hand and Sarah Hand, Jr. Lib. 29, p. 242.

**1786, May 19. Gagle, Jacob Fredrick,** of Cape May Co. Int. Adm'r—Joseph Wheaton. Fellowbondsman—Henry Y. Townsend; both of said Co. Witnesses—Elijah Townsend and Parmenas Corson. Lib. 38, p. 79.

86 NEW JERSEY POST-REVOLUTIONARY DOCUMENTS

**1787, Aug. 29. Gano, Daniel,** of Nottingham, Burlington Co. Int. Adm'r—Samuel Stout, of Hunterdon Co. Fellowbondsman—James Drake, of Burlington Co. Witness—Thomas Adams.
1787, Aug. 28. Inventory, £71.7.10, made by Lewis Evans and James Drake. Lib. 29, p. 76.

**1788, March 12. Gard, Daniel,** of Hanover, Morris Co. Int. Adm'x—Charity Gard. Fellowbondsman—Gideon Howell; both of said place. Witnesses—Job Gard and Abram Canfield, Jr.
1788, March 13. Inventory, £146.2.0, made by Jacob Mintun and Jonathan Tichnor. Lib. 31, p. 199.

**1787, Feb. 10. Gardiner, James,** of Salem Co. Ward. Son of James Gardiner, of said Co., deceased. Said Ward makes choice of his brother, Joseph Gardiner, as his Guardian.
1787, Feb. 10. Guardian—Joseph Gardiner. Fellowbondsman— George Colsen; both of said Co. Lib. 29, p. 153.

**1786, March 5. Gardner, William,** of Morristown, Morris Co.; will of. Daughter, Mary Wood, £12. Daughter, Affe Norris, £5. Son, Christopher, £10. Sons, Christopher, Jeniah and William, rest of estate. Executors—son, Christopher, and Daniel Wood. Witnesses— Daniel Brown, Abraham Ludlum, John Rose. Proved June 18, 1787.
Lib. 29, p. 461.

**1790, May 7. Garrabrants, Christopher,** of Essex Co. Int. Adm'r— John Garrabrants, Jr. Fellowbondsman—James McGinnis; both of said Co.
1790, May 8. Inventory, £0.3.6, made by James McGinnis and Garrabrant A. Garrabrants. Lib. 30, p. 362.

**1790, April 10. Garrison, David,** of Deerfield, Cumberland Co.; will of. Son, Joel, one acre on the south side of the lot where he lives; also 2 acres of woodland of the northeast side of my land in Russels Neck. Daughter, Mary Paris, one acre of land joining the Parsonage land. Daughter, Elizabeth Garrison, one acre on the north side of the last mentioned lot. Sons, David Ogden Garrison, Josiah Garrison and Azel Garrison, all my other lands, when they are 21. Wife, Mary, use of all lands, to bring up my children; also various goods. Rest of goods to be sold. Executors—wife, Mary, and Ezekiel Foster. Witnesses—Ogden Harris, Hannah Davis, Eunice Davis. Proved Sept. 30, 1790.
1790, April 23. Inventory, £90.9.1, made by Ephraim Foster and Daniel Davis. Lib. 30, p. 270.

**1790, March 12. Garrison, John,** of Cumberland Co., Reverend. Int. Adm'r—Levi Heaton. Fellowbondsman—Nathaniel Lore; both of said Co.
1790, March 10. Inventory, £70.14.9, made by Nathaniel Lore and Daniel Tullis. Lib. 30, p. 280.

**1786, Jan. 27. Garritse, Garret H.,** of Acquackanonk, Essex Co., yeoman; will of. Wife, Catriena, £6, and the goods she had from her father. Wife to use real and personal estate while she is single, and, after her death or marriage, my daughter, Ebegel, is to have the estate. Executors—uncle, Henry Gerretse and John El Vreeland, and my wife, Catriena. Witnesses—Garret Van Ryper, Jerry Van Ryper, Hassel Peterse. Proved June 13, 1786. File No. 6344 G.

**1786, Jan. 7. Garton, David,** of Cumberland Co. Int. Adm'r—Dan Bowen, Jr., Fellowbondsman—Abraham Bowen; both of said Co. Witness—John Peck, Jr.
1786, Jan. 3. Inventory, £153.15.0, made by Mark Bowen and David Sheppard. Bills against Philip Waiscot, Jonathan Garton and Hunagal Weck. Lib. 28, p. 180.

**1789, March 10. Garwood, Dorothy,** of Evesham Township, Burlington Co. Int. Adm'r—Jonathan Hilyard. Fellowbondsman—John Hilyard; both of Northampton Township, said Co. Witness—Thomas Adams.
1789, March 14. Inventory, £113.4.8, made by Thomas Gill and Jacob Hollinshead. Lib. 31, p. 319.

**1787, Feb. 22. Garwood, Hannah,** of Burlington Co. Int. Adm'r—Japheth Garwood. Fellowbondsman—Lawrence Webster; both of Evesham Township, said Co.
1787, Feb. 22. Inventory, £295.6.4, made by Lawrence Webster and Jonathan Crispin. "A legacy in the hands of Jacob Haines for £42.8.0. A legacy in the hands of Nemiah Haines for £153. A legacy in the hands of Isaac Haines for £100." Lib. 29, p. 74.

**1787, Sept. 6. Gauntt, Samuel,** of Springfield, Burlington Co.; will of. Wife, Hannah, £100, and Uz and Elihu are to pay her £12 a year. Son, Uz, ½ of my Propriety that I bought of my father, which may be seen in the deed dated 1690. Son, Asher, 4 acres, son, Elihu, rest of land, and other ½ of Propriety Right. Son, Peter, land that Jos Wright rents, and the oyster bed, bought of Robert Ridgway. Son, Reubin, £200. Daughter, Sarepta, £50. Daughters, Hannah Crosher and Sarah Shin and Elizabeth Shreve, £10 each. Executors—sons, Uz and Asher. Witnesses—John Karr, Mary Ridgway, Jennings Gaskill. Proved Nov. 30, 1787.
1788, Feb. 17. Inventory, made by Henry Ridgway, Samuel Stockton and Job Stockton, Jr. Lib. 29, p. 36.

**1790, Feb. 18. Gee, Joseph,** of Kingwood, Hunterdon Co. Int. Adm'r—James Thatcher. Fellowbondsman—William Thatcher; both of said place.
1786, Aug. 19. Inventory, £45.5.0, made by Jeremiah Thatcher and Gabriel Hoff, at the house of James Thatcher. Note against Bartholomew Thatcher, £3. Lib. 30, p. 315.

**1789, June 27. Gerretse, Rachel,** of Bergen Co. Int. Adm'r—Jacob Gerretse. Fellowbondsman—Adoniah Schuyler; both of said Co. Witness—John Neafis. Lib. 30, p. 247.

**1789, April 17. Gerretse, Rem,** of Hillsborough, Somerset Co. Int. Adm'r—Samuel Gerritson. Fellowbondsman—Hendrick Willson; both of said place. Lib. 31, p. 413.

## 88 NEW JERSEY POST-REVOLUTIONARY DOCUMENTS

**1786, April 17. Gerritsen, Ram,** of Somerset Co.; will of. Wife, Mary, plantation where I live, and the moveable estate, while my widow. Daughters, Mary and Anne, £100 each. Only son, Garrit, the said land of 100 acres when wife is done with it, if he is 21. Executors—brother, Samuel Garretsen and brother-in-law, Peter Pumyea, and my wife, Mary. Witnesses—James Van Duyn, Cornelius Van Duyn, Fulcert Buys. Proved Dec. 18, 1786.

1786, Dec. 18. Inventory, made by James Van Duyn and Abraham Staats. Lib. 29, p. 189.

**1787, April 4. Gibb, James,** of New Brunswick, Middlesex Co. Ward. Son of John Gibb, and grandson of Richard Gibb, both of said place, deceased. Said Ward makes choice of John Henry as his Guardian.

1787, April 4. Guardian—John Henry, of said place. Fellowbondsman—Robert Harris, of said Co. Witness—William Hyer, Jr.
Lib. 29, p. 365.

**1788, April 15. Gibbs, Hannah,** of New Hanover Township, Burlington Co. Int. Adm'r—Abel Gibbs, of Middlesex Co. Fellowbondsman—Nathan Wright, of Monmouth Co.

1788, April 18. Inventory, £269.1.2, made by John Ridgway and Alexander Howard. Lib. 30, p. 59.

**1789, March 31. Gibbs, Joseph,** of Mansfield Township, Burlington Co. Int. Adm'x—Elizabeth Gibbs. Fellowbondsman—William Carslake; both of said Co.

1789, April 2. Inventory, £136.11.0, made by Abel Starkey and Jonathan Barton. Lib. 31, p. 319.

**1787, May 24. Gibbs, Joshua,** of New Hanover, Burlington Co.; will of. Wife, Hannah, all real and personal estate, to enable her to support and educate my children. Executrix—wife, Hannah. Witnesses—Joseph Bullock, Nathan Wright, Samuel Steward. Proved June 22, 1787.

1787, June 20. Inventory, £586.15.2, made by Joseph Bullock and John Lawrie. Lib. 29, p. 40.

**1788, Feb. 4. Gibson, James, Sr.,** of Sussex Co. Int. Adm'rs— James Gibson, Jr. and William Harrison. Fellowbondsman—Archibald Stewart; all of Newtown, said Co. Witness—William Anderson. Lib. 31, p. 156.

**1790, Aug. 30. Gibson, Sarah,** of Gloucester Township, Gloucester Co. Int. Adm'r—John Haines. Fellowbondsman—Solomon Haines; both of Burlington Co.

1790, Aug. 30. Inventory, £50.18.3, made by Solomon Haines and Levi Kemble. Lib. 31, p. 477.

**1789, Dec. 30. Gildersleeve, John,** of Newark, Essex Co.; will of. Son, Joseph, my house, barn and the land; also ½ of the salt meadow. To the 2 sons of my son, Daniel, deceased, the land on the mountain; and the use of the same to my son, Joseph, and his son, John, till Daniel's 2 sons are of age. Daughters, Sara, Ruth, Lois and Phebe, moveable estate. My sons are to take care of my wife. Daughters, Sara and Lois, ½ of the salt meadow. Executors—

CALENDAR OF WILLS—1786-1790   89

sons, Joseph and Ezra, and my son-in-law, Moses Osborn. Witnesses—Uzal Ball, Briant Durant, Elijah Durant. Proved June 21, 1790.
1790, June 14. Inventory, made by Recompence Crowell and Henry Squier. Lib. 30, p. 351.

**1788, May 12. Giles, Hezekiah,** of Middlesex Co. Int. Adm'r—James Giles. Fellowbondsman—John Marselis; both of said Co.
1788, May 26. Inventory, £35.9.9, made by John Sebring, Jr., and Peter Runyon, Jr. Lib. 31, p. 223.

**1787, Feb. 17. Giles, Samuel,** of Hardwick, Sussex Co. Int. Adm'r—John Morris. Fellowbondsman—Isaac Coursen; both of said place, yeomen. Witness—Daniel Case.
1787, Feb. 19. Inventory, £18.19.2, made by Thomas Hazen, Jr. and Henry Silverthorn. Lib. 29, p. 488.

**1786, Jan. 29. Glasset, Susanah,** of Greenwich Township, Gloucester Co.; will of. Son, Isaac Lord, all my real estate, and, at his death, to my grandson, Isaac Lord (son of James Lord). To my 4 grandchildren, the children of James Lord, my personal estate. If my grandson, Isaac Lord, should happen to die, then the real estate is to descend to my great-grandson, Benoni Lord. Executors—son, Isaac Lord, and my friend, Joseph Estlack. Witnesses—John Packer, Basheba Packer, Uriah Paul. Proved March 9, 1790.
1790, Feb. 25. Renunciation by Isaac Lord, of Greenwich Township. Witnesses—Jonathan Fisher and Hannah White.
1790, Feb. 23. Inventory, £41.0.6, made by David Brown and Francis Robenson. Lib. 31, p. 429.

**1790, Jan. 26. Godden, David,** of Hanover, Morris Co.; will of. Wife, Elizabeth, part of the personal estate. Daughters, Hopestill and Providence, rest of personal estate. Sons, John and Joseph, my real estate. Son, Abraham, £60. Son, David, £5. Executors—sons, John and Joseph. Witnesses—Ebenezer Stiles, Ebenezer Stiles, Jr., Stephen Charlot. Proved Feb. 12, 1790.
1790, Feb. 11. Inventory, £112.17.7, made by Silas Ayers and Jonas Phillips. Lib. 30, p. 442.

**1790, April 24. Godown, Evans,** of Amwell, Hunterdon Co. Int. Adm'rs—John Godown and Jacob Godown. Fellowbondsman—Andrew Larason; all of said place.
1790, April 19. Inventory, £85.10.6, made by Andrew Larason and John Lake.
1791, April 22. Account by Adm'rs. Lib. 30, p. 316.

**1790, May 6. Godown, Hannah,** of Amwell, Hunterdon Co. Ward. Daughter of Evans Godown, of said Co., deceased. Said Ward makes choice of Thomas Godown as her Guardian.
1790, May 6. Guardian—Thomas Godown. Fellowbondsman—Daniel Thatcher; both of said place. Lib. 30, p. 319.

**1789, Dec. 2. Golden, John,** of Hopewell Township, Cumberland Co.; will of. Eldest son, Alpheus, the land I bought of James Loper, Jr., and ½ of the meadow below Thomas Brown, and ⅛ of the woodland in Deerfield Twp., and ⅛ of the cedar swamp at Lebanon and Greenbranch; also the use of the house where he lives, for one year after my death. Son, Joseph, that part of the place where I live, to extend west as far as the schoolhouse lot; also ⅛ of the woodland in Deerfield, and ¼ of the marsh below Thomas Brown, and ⅛ of the cedar swamp at Lebanon and Greenbranch. Son, David, rest of lands where I live, and rest of meadow and cedar swamp and woodland. Wife, Joanna, ⅓ of the moveable estate, and £10 towards the schooling of my young children. Daughters, Elizabeth, Ledreme and Joanna, moveable estate. Executors—son, Alpheus, and son-in-law, Benjamin Keen. Witnesses—William Biggs, Samuel Goulden, Elnathan Davis. Proved Dec. 28, 1789. Lib. 30, p. 141.

**1788, Feb. 22. Golder, Ellendes,** of Somerset Co., gentlewoman; will of. Son, John Voorhees, silver spoons; and he is to be put to a trade when 16. Daughter, Polly Skilman, apparel; but, if she die, then to my sister, Catherin Golder. Sister, Catherin Golder, silver spoons. Executors—friends, Abraham Golder and Henry Wilson. Witnesses—Isaac Blue, Aaron Manly, John Blue. Proved March 29, 1788.

1788, March 24. Inventory, made by Jacob Schenck and Abraham **Voorhees.** Lib. 31, p. 161.

**1790, April 24. Goldsmith, Samuel,** of Pittsgrove, Salem Co.; will of. Wife, Mary, all real and personal estate. Executrix—wife, Mary. Witnesses—Artis Seagrave, Sawtel Elwell, John Nelson. Proved June 15, 1790. Lib. 40, p. 526.

**1786, Dec. 21. Gordon, Jemima,** of Pequanock, Morris Co. Int. Adm'r—Timothy Canfield. Fellowbondsman—Joseph Conger; both of said Co. Witnesses—William Campfield and Abram Canfield, Jr.
Lib. 28, p. 488.

**1786, April 15. Gould, David,** of Hunterdon Co., Doctor of physick. Int. Adm'r—Thomas Anderson, Esq., of Sussex Co. Fellowbondsman—Moore Furman, of Hunterdon Co. Witness—John Anderson. Lib. 28, p. 247.

**1786, Oct. 20. Gouverneur, Nicholas,** of Newark, Essex Co.; will of. Wife, Mary, the use of my house at Newark where I live; also my homestead adjoining, my horses, stock, plate and goods; also some negros. She is to have the plate, goods, pictures and landscapes formerly belonging to the estate of Col. Peter Schuyler, deceased; also £100 yearly. Son, Isaac, £70 yearly. Brother, Isaac, knee buckles, of gold. Daughter, Gertruyda Burnet, the family pictures, except the one of Mrs. Winkle, of Batavia, deceased, which I give to my grandson, Anthony Rutgers. Granddaughter, Alida Gouverneur, my silver bread basket. Grandson, Nicholas Gouverneur Rutgers, my gold watch. Grandson, Herman Gouverneur Rutgers, gold headed cane. To the above grandsons all my right to lands on the west side of Lake Champlain, and on the Island in the said lake, caled Grand Isle, granted to me by deeds, one from Thomas Rhodes and Christopher Duyckinck, and the other from Elkanah Deane and his wife, Elizabeth. Granddaughter, Alida Gouverneur, my right in land in Lyman Township, New Hampshire,

## CALENDAR OF WILLS—1786-1790

which was laid out in the right of Abraham Angur, who was one of the Patentees in the Charter of said Township, and is numbered 4, and was conveyed to me from John Wendell, of Portsmouth, N. H. One-sixth of the money which shall be due to me from the estate of Anthony A. Rutgers, deceased, unto my daughter, Gertruyda Burnet; ⅙ to my grandson, Anthony Rutgers; ⅙ to my grandson, Nicholas G. Rutgers; ⅙ to my grandson, Herman G. Rutgers; ⅙ to my granddaughters, Mary Rhea and Cornelia Gale, and ⅙ to the 2 sons of Gertruyda, named Isaac Burnet and Staats Gouverneur Burnet. Rest of lands may be sold. Executors—wife, Mary; brother, Isaac; and nephews, Nicholas Low, Nicholas Gouverneur, Jr., Isaac Gouverneur, Jr. and Lewis Ogden. Witnesses—Sarah Wallace, Uzal Ogden, Robert T. Kemble. Proved April 17, 1787.
Lib. 29, p. 366.

**1790, March 30. Graff, Sarah,** of Waterford Township, Gloucester Co., widow; will of. Sister-in-law, Katherine Von Phull, wife of William Von Phull, of Philadelphia, one moiety of a house and lot in Queen Street, Lancaster, Penna., she paying yearly ¼ of the rents to her niece, Sarah Crugh, daughter of Valentine and Eve Crugh, of Lancaster, and, when the house is sold, she is to pay to said Sarah, when she is 18, ¼ of the said moiety the house may sell for. Cousin, Sarah Maule, during her life, a ground rent of £6 on a lot in Southwark, Philadelphia, and, at her death, to my brother, Benjamin Swett. Sister, Mary Swett, such clothing as she may want. To my kinswoman, Ann Odell, £25, and to her son, William Odell, my books. Friend, Easther Zantzinger, wife of Paul, £50. Nephew, Joseph Cooper Swett, £25, when 21. Sarah Graff, daughter of Sebastian Graff, my saddle. Brother, Benjamin Swett, rest of estate. Executor—brother, Benjamin Swett. Witnesses—John Price, Anna Giffard, Isabel Price. Proved April 19, 1790.

1790, April 3. Inventory, £744.4.9, made by John Gill and Thomas Redman.
Lib. 31, p. 430.

**1790, June 24. Grandin, Daniel,** of Freehold, Monmouth Co.; will of. Daughter, Mary, wife of Cornelius Clark, 20 shillings. This is not to affect any of my other children. Executors—my children, William, Sarah and Rachel Grandin. Witnesses—Rachel Henderson, Euphamia Clayton, Thomas Henderson. Proved Oct. 28, 1790.
Lib. 30, p. 380.

**1788, April 8. Gray, John,** of Hunterdon Co. Int. Adm'rs—Elizabeth Gray and Isaac Gray, Jr. Lib. 31, p. 142.

**1789, April 14. Green, Charles D. and James,** of Maidenhead, Hunterdon Co. Wards. Sons of George Green, of said place, deceased. Said Wards make choice of Rev. John Woodhull and Jonathan Phillips as their Guardians.

1789, April 14. Guardians—John Woodhull, of Monmouth Co. and Jonathan Phillips, of Hunterdon Co. Fellowbondsmen—Aaron Van Cleve and James Moore. Witness—David Johnes. Lib. 32, p. 57.

**1786, May 25. Green, George,** of Hardwick, Sussex Co. Int. Adm'r—Adam Green. Fellowbondsman—John Moore; both of said place. Witness—Charles Rhodes.

1786, Aug. 17. Inventory, made by Josiah Dyer and Francis Glover. "Meadow lot, 20 shillings per acre. Upland lot, 20 shillings per acre."
Lib. 28, p. 470.

**1790, April 23. Green, Jacob,** of Hanover, Morris Co., Reverend; will of. To wife, 4 score Spanish dollars, and ⅛ of my real estate. Son, Calvin, the place where he lives, bounded by Ellis Cook, William Cook, Thomas Eckley, Ezekiel Tucker and John N. Cummings, of 80 acres. Son, Ashbel, land on the road between Moses Fairchilds and his mother's, of 50 acres; also my right which is ⅔ of the grist and saw mills on Whipening River, with 25 acres; and he is to pay to my son, John W. Green, all that John owes him for his education, and Ashbel shall sell a mill, and, if it brings more than 1,330 dollars, he shall give ⅛ of the surplus to his brother, Calvin, and ⅛ to educate my grandson, Ashbel Green, son of Pierson Green, and ⅛ to educate my grandson, John B. Cooker. To Elijah Squire, Enoch Beach and Darling Beach, for the property of the family of my son, Pierson Green, a part of my plantation in Essex Co., bounded by Joseph Green, William Ely and Samuel Parrot, of 75 acres, for the support of said family. Sons, Pierson, Ashbel, Calvin and John Wickliffe, my clothing. Son, John W. Green, rest of the Willow meadow place. Daughter, Dorothy, 210 dollars. Daughter, Elizabeth, 240 dollars. Daughter, Keturah, 210 dollars. To children of my daughter, Abigail, deceased, 160 dollars. Executors—friends, Stephen Monson, Aaron Kitchel and David Bedford. Witnesses—John Ougheltree, Noah Beach, John Woodruff. Proved June 17, 1790.

1790, June 15. Inventory, £503.19.9, made by David Tuttle and Enoch Beach.
Lib. 30, p. 455.

**1786, Feb. 27. Green, John,** of South Amboy, Middlesex Co.; will of. House where I live, and goods therein, and the lands about it, to be for the use of my wife, until my 3 children, James, Mary and Anne, come of age, when it is to be divided between them. To my mother, the cow and the goods that belong to her. Executors—my wife, and John Morgan, son of William. Witnesses—William Hillyer, Abraham Buckelow, Christopher H. Shinemann. Proved April 24, 1786.

1786, April 9. Inventory, £41.11.9, made by Thomas Smith and William Hillyer.
Lib. 28, p. 334.

**1789, Nov. 11. Green, Richard Montgomery,** of Hunterdon Co. Ward. Son of George Green, deceased. Said Ward makes choice of John Woodhull and Jonathan Phillips as his Guardians.

1789, Nov. 11. Guardians—John Woodhull, of Freehold, Monmouth Co. and Jonathan Phillips, of Maidenhead, Hunterdon Co. Fellowbondsman—John Rozell, of Trenton, Hunterdon Co.
Lib. 32, p. 58.

**1788, Feb. 22. Gregory, Ebenezer,** of Morris Co. Int. Adm'rs—Seth Gregory and Silas Ayers. Fellowbondsman—Moses Johnson; all of said Co. Witness—Silas Condict.

1788, Feb. 7. Inventory, £65, made by Moses Johnson and Silas Condict.
Lib. 31, p. 200.

CALENDAR OF WILLS—1786-1790    93

**1787, Oct. 2. Grinslade, John,** of Chester, Burlington Co., yeoman; will of. Wife, Elizabeth, ½ of my personal estate, and the use of a room in the east end of the house on my plantation, which was lately bought of Samuel Lippincott, of Pilesgrove. Daughter, Elizabeth Grinslade, rest of personal estate, when she is 18. Son, John, my plantation, when he is 21. Executors—son, John, and my friend, William Roberts. Witnesses—John Hunt, Samuel Coles, John Collins. Proved Nov. 26, 1787.

1788, Sept. 22. Renunciation by John Grinslade, son of John Grinslade, late of Moorestown, deceased.

1787, Nov. 12. Inventory, £1,288.13.11, made by John Roberts and John Collins.    Lib. 29, p. 18.

**1789, April 12. Griscom, William,** of Haddonfield, Gloucester Co., sadler; will of. Daughter, Deborah, £4, to make her equal with my daughter, Hannah. Daughters, Deborah and Hannah, the rest of personal estate; also rents of 7 acres which I bought of Samuel Lippincott, in Newton Twp., and, at their deaths, I give the said land to my grandson, William Clement. Daughters, Deborah and Hannah, rest of lands. Executrixes—daughters, Deborah and Hannah. Witnesses—John Gill, Thomas Githens, Thomas Redman. Proved Jan. 30, 1790.

1790, Jan. 27. Inventory, £474.17.10, made by Thomas Redman and Thomas Githens.    Lib. 31, p. 431.

**1786, Dec. 1. Groom, Moses,** of Windsor Township, Middlesex Co. Int. Adm'x—Mary Groom. Fellowbondsman—Stacy Groom; both of said Co. Witness—William Sickles.

1786, Nov. 24. Inventory, £3.16.11, made by Joseph Story and Elisha Cook.    Lib. 28, p. 337.

**1787, April 9. Guild, John,** of Hopewell, Hunterdon Co., clerk; will of. Eldest son, John, £50. Second son, Ralph, the plantation where I live. Youngest son, Benjamin, £50. Daughters, Esther, wife of John Welling; Margarye (?), wife of John P. Hunt; Mary, wife of John Howell; Mercy, wife of Jesse Christopher, and Phebe and Charity, who are single, each an equal share, after Polly Howell and Mercy Christopher, with my 2 youngest daughters, have as much as to make them equal to their eldest sisters. Land which I bought of Joshua Bunn to be sold. Executors—son, Ralph, and sons-in-law, John Welling and John P. Hunt. Witnesses—John Davison, Henry Baker, Benjamin Woolsey. Proved Aug. 8, 1787.

1787, Aug. 2. Inventory, £363.14.11, made by John Carpenter and Henry Baker.    Lib. 29, p. 286.

**1789, July 27. Gumersall, Thomas,** Captain in the late Second Battalion of the Royal Regiment of New York; will of. Wife, Mary, all real and personal estate in Great Britain. Executrix—wife, Mary. Witnesses—Daniel Maxwell, Surgeon Poplar; James Staffon, hair dresser, Lime house. Proved Jan. 20, 1790, by Samuel Brook, who said he knew the hand writing. Letters granted to Mary Gumersall, now Mary Radford.

1790, Jan. 20. Inventory, £258.4.4, made by Silas Howell and Joseph Lewis.    Lib. 30, p. 439.

**1787, July 27. Hacket, David,** of Elsinborough Township, Salem Co., yeoman; will of. Wife, Elizabeth, use of personal and real estate, to bring up my children. Children, John, Richard and Thomas, (and if my wife have another child), the plantation in Manington Township, when they are 21. Sons to be put to trades when they are 14. Executors—wife, Elizabeth, and my friend, William Wilson. Witnesses—Ebenezer Howell, Thomas Thompson, William Wilson. Proved Nov. 15, 1787. Lib. 29, p. 122.

**1790, Jan. 12. Hackett, Elizabeth,** of Morris Co. Int. Adm'r— Augustine Reid. Fellowbondsman—Silas Howell; both of said Co. Witness—John Reid.
1790, Jan. 16. Inventory, £67.10.6, made by John Wurts and Isaac Starke. Lib. 30, p. 235.

**1790, Jan. 11. Hackett, Samuel R.,** of Hacketts Town, Sussex Co.; will of. To my kinswoman, Mrs. Mary Halsted, daughter of the late Rev. Mills, and my aunt, Mary Mills, for her kindness to my mother in her last illness, all my plate, except 2 pieces; also the bed and bedding that is now at my uncle Augustine Reid's. Kinswoman, Mrs. Gruson, daughter of my uncle, Patrick Hackett, a silver pint, now in possession of Major Helms, and one now with my said uncle Reid. Kinsman, Doctor Reading Beaty, a silver bowl. Friend, Miss Gainer Potts, £100. The bulk of my fortune will be in the hands of my uncle, Augustine Reid, if he keeps the plantations purchased by him at Sheriff's sale and pays the mortgage, which I would like him to do, but my Executors are to settle with him, so as not to injure him. To the Presbyterian Church of Independence, £40. To Miss Mary Reid, daughter of my uncle, Augustine Reid, my bed. To Sarah Young, £6, if she nurse me until my death. Kinsman, Montgomery Reading, rest of estate. If Miss Potts die, then I give her legacy to the eldest son of my kinsman, Major Samuel Reading, when he is of age. Executors—friends, Doctor John Beaty, of Princeton, and William Helms. Witnesses—Robert Cummins, Jonathan Sutten, William Crosby. Proved Jan. 29, 1790.
Lib. 30, p. 424.

**1790, Nov. 23. Hagerman, Jacobus,** of Windsor Township, Middlesex Co.; will of. My brother, Nice Hagerman's son, Garret, who is my heir-at-law, £4. Wife, Ruth, rest of real and personal estate. Executors—friends, Jonathan Combs, Koert Voorheis and William Smith. Witnesses—Thomas Savage, Mary Smith, Samuel Pullen. Proved Dec. 28, 1790.
1790, Dec. 23. Inventory, £210.6.6, made by John Bergen and Matthias Mount. Lib. 30, p. 500.

**1789, Nov. 25. Hagerty, Michael,** of Gloucester Co.; will of. Brother, Robert Hagerty, my personal estate; but, if he is not living, then to his 2 sons, Robert and John. To John Hagerty, son of William, 5 shillings. Nephews, Robert and John Hagerty, sons of my brother, Robert, all my lands in Harrison Co., Virginia, which I bought of Richard Mason. Executors—friends, Peter Thompson and Henry Bradshaw. Witnesses—Samuel Tallman, Sarah Bradshaw, Richard Snowden. Proved Jan. 28, 1790.
1790, Jan. 16. Renunciation by Peter Thompson.
1790, Jan. 28. Inventory, £30.5.2, made by William Eldridge and Samuel Tallman. Lib. 31, p. 433.

CALENDAR OF WILLS—1786-1790 95

**1790, Nov. 25. Haines, Elizabeth,** of Burlington Co. Ward. Daughter of Jeremiah Haines, of said Co., deceased. Said Ward makes choice of her uncle, William Haines, as her Guardian.
1790, Nov. 25. Guardian—William Haines. Fellowbondsman—Daniel Ellis; both of said Co. Witness—William Griffith, Surrogate.
1791, June 13. Inventory of bonds and notes, as the estate of Jeremiah Haines to the use of one of his children, Elizabeth Haines, under Guardianship of her uncle, William Haines, made by Peter Shiras and Thomas Bispham. Lib. 32, p. 554.

**1790, July 21. Haines, John,** of Northampton Township, Burlington Co. Int. Adm'rs—Rachel Haines and Jonathan Haines. Fellowbondsmen—Thomas Haines, Sr., and William Haines; all of said place.
1790, July 5. Inventory, £242.6.6, made by Jonah Woolman and Barzillai Deacon. Lib. 32, p. 94.

**1789, Nov. 24. Haines, Josiah,** of Burlington Township, Burlington Co.; will of. Real and personal estate to be sold, and divided as follows:—wife, Mary, one part; son, Caleb, one part; daughter, Hannah Bispham, one part; daughter, Sarah Haines, one part; daughter, Abigail Haines, one part; daughter, Mary Haines, one part; daughter, Catherine Haines, one part; and daughter, Elizabeth Haines, one part. Executors—son, Caleb, and my son-in-law, Thomas Bispham. Witnesses—Elizabeth Jones, Mary Jones, David Ridgway. Proved Dec. 31, 1789.
1789, Dec. 12. Inventory, £832.7.8, made by David Ridgway and John Rogers. Lib. 31, p. 281.

**1787, Aug. 20. Haines, Nathan,** of Evesham, Burlington Co., yeoman; will of. Son, Nathan, land to be taken off of my plantation where I live, as by a certain line; also a cedar swamp of 2½ acres, which I bought of William Evans. Wife, Dorcas, rest of my estate, personal and real, during her life. Son, Henry Pendergrass Haines, rest of my plantation, after his mother's death. Son, Joseph, 301 acres in the Forks of Susquehanna, near Chillasquaka Hills, in Pennsylvania. Daughter, Elizabeth Fowler, £5. Executrix—wife, Dorcas. Witnesses—William Stockton, Benjamin Stockton, Joseph Griffith. Proved Aug. 12, 1790.
1790, Aug. 9. Inventory, £722.17.1, made by Thomas Hollinshead and Joseph Roberts. Lib. 32, p. 90.

**1788, Nov. 24. Haines, Nathaniel,** of Northampton, Burlington Co.; will of. Son, John, ½ of my plantation, on the west side, and ½ of the cedar swamp. Son, William, the other ½ of the plantation, and other ½ of the cedar swamp. Wife, Mary, £40, and son, John, is to provide for her, and son, William, to give her £6 yearly. Daughter, Sarah Cox, £5. Granddaughter, Mary Lippincott, £10, when 18, and the high case of drawers, which her mother had in keeping. Executors—sons, John and William. Witnesses—Jonah Woolman, William Rogers, Jr., Joseph Kimble, Jr. Proved Dec. 27, 1788.
1789, Jan. 10. Inventory, £449.4.7, made by Jonah Woolman and Barzillai Deacon. Lib. 30, p. 41.

**1789, April 4. Haines, Samuel,** of Chester Township, Burlington Co., single man; will of. Real and personal estate to be sold. Brother, John Haines, £500, he paying to James Hopkins £75 for a stalion I bought of him. Brother, Ephraim Haines, £500, when 21. Mother, Hannah Buzby, £250. Friend, Elizabeth Rodgers, £500. Executors—brother, John Haines, and uncle, John H. Stokes (Doctor). Witnesses—Joseph Hunt, William Coates, Joseph Stokes. Proved June 11, 1789.
1789, June 9. Inventory, £184.5.2, made by John Cox and Joseph Stokes. Lib. 29, p. 331.

**1787, Nov. 11. Halladay, James,** of Manington, Salem Co., farmer; will of. Eldest son, Samuel, 2 shares of my estate. Son, James, 2 shares. Wife, Marey, one share. Son, John, one share. Daughter, Marey, one share. Daughter, Susannah, one share. Son, **Samuel,** one share more. Children to have trades. Executors—Neighbor, Jonathan Bilderback, and my son, Samuel. Witnesses—Tarver Seagrave, William Hiles, William Gregory. Proved March 15, 1788.
1788, Jan. 3. Inventory, £555.3.6, made by William Philpot and Joshua Pedrick. Lib. 31, p. 45.

**1787, May 2. Halsey, Ananias,** of Hanover, Morris Co. Int. Adm'x—Margret Halsey. Fellowbondsman—William Ford; both of said place.
1787, April 30. Inventory, £175.3.2, made by Ebenezer Sayre and David Bedford. Lib. 29, p. 474.

**1788, Nov. 29. Halsey, Isaac,** of Essex Co. Int. Adm'rs—Joseph Halsey, Jedidiah Swan and William Darby. Fellowbondsman—Ichabod Halsey; all of said Co.
1788, Dec. 2. Inventory, made by Isaac Clark and Mathias Sayres. Lib. 38, p. 96.

**1790, Sept. 21. Halsey, Jacob,** of Essex Co. Ward. Son of Isaac Halsey, of said Co., deceased. Ichabod B. Halsey, an elder brother of said Jacob, asks for Jedidiah Swan to be appointed Guardian of said infant.
1790, Sept. 21. Guardian—Jedidiah Swan, of said Co.
Lib. 30, p. 363.

**1787, March 13. Hamilton, Archable,** of Manington, Salem Co.; will of. Sons, Isaac and Jacob, my lands; but, if they die without issue, then to my son, William. Son, Abraham, £10. Daughter, Margaret Bishop, a cow. Daughters, Mary, Susanna and Ann Hamilton, moveable estate. Granddaughter, Elizabeth Hamilton, daughter of Charles Hamilton, 5 shillings. Executors—son, Isaac, and Mary Hamilton. Witnesses—Christopher Smith, John Smith, John Kamstar. Proved Aug. 19, 1789.
1789, Jan. 16. Inventory, £217.15.9, made by William Walmsley and Christopher Smith. Lib. 31, p. 334.

**1789, March 13. Hamilton, Arthur,** of Woodbury, Gloucester Co.; will of. Wife, Prissilla, the interest of my estate, until my daughter, Deborah Hamilton, is 16, and then to be divided among my wife and my children, Arthur, John, James, Sarah and Deborah. Execu-

tors—wife, Priscilla, and my friend, Benjamin Heritage. Witnesses—
John Blackwood, Aaron Hewes. Proved March 27, 1789.
1789, March 27. Renunciation by Benjamin Heritage.
Lib. 30, p. 112.

**1786, Feb. 16. Hammell, Hannah, late Coberly [Cubberley],** of Burlington Co. Ward. Daughter of William Coberly, of said Co., deceased. Said Ward, having real and personal estate, makes choice of William Coverly as her Guardian.
1786, Feb. 16. Guardian—William Cubberley, of Nottingham Township, said Co. Fellowbondsman—Amos Hutchin, of City of Burlington. Lib. 28, p. 81.

**1786, May 25. Hampton, Abraham,** of Essex Co. Int. Adm'r— Jedidiah Swan. Fellowbondsman—Isaac Clark; both of said Co.
1786, May 22. Renunciation by Susanna Hampton, widow of Abraham. Lib. 28, p. 427.

**1787, March 14. Hamson, Daniel,** of Newtown, Sussex Co. Int. Adm'r—Robert Hamson. Fellowbondsman—Michael Ayers; both of said place. Witness—Silas Hopkins.
1787, March 15. Inventory, £59.11.0, made by John Ryerson and William Perine. Lib. 29, p. 489.

**1786, May 18. Hancock, Samuel,** of Burlington Co. Ward. Son of Godfrey Hancock, of said Co., deceased. Ann Antram, late Ann Hancock, widow and Executrix of said Godfrey Hancock, states that she lately intermarried with Thomas Antram, and, there being some estate of her late husband to be divided among his several children, some of whom are under age, prays that her son, Isaac Hancock, may be appointed Guardian of such of the said children, till they can choose for themselves.
1786, May 18. Guardian—Isaac Hancock. Fellowbondsman—William English; both of said Co. Lib. 28, p. 81.

**1789, Nov. 12. Hancock, Sarah,** of Lower Alloways Creek Township, Salem Co., widow of William; will of. The land in Elsinborough Township, which I bought of Richard Smith, to be sold to pay debts; but, if personal estate should pay all, then the said land to my son, John; and, if he die, then to Sarah Sinnickson. Executors—friend, Thomas Sinnickson, and my son, John. Witnesses— Andrew Yorke, John Hancock, Eleanor Yorke. Proved Jan. 6, 1790.
Lib. 31, p. 490.

**1787, Feb. 15. Hand, Daniel,** of Cape May Co., gentleman; will of. Daughter, Hannah Holmes, wife of Nathaniel Holmes, the part of the plantation where I live, along Christopher Ludlam's line, and to contain 50 acres, and at her death to go to her son, Nathaniel Holmes. One hundred pounds are to be in the hands of my son-in-law, Nathaniel Holmes, and he shall pay yearly to my son, Daniel, £10, but if Daniel die before all is used up, then it is to be divided between my daughters, Hannah, Martha and Sarah. Son, Seth, the rest of the plantation; also the cedar swamp I bought of Ephraim Jenkins, lying in the Upper Precinct, on the most southerly side of the Cedar swamp bridge. Daughter, Martha Hand, wife of Absolam Hand, that part of my land in Jo More's Neck; provided she and her

98   NEW JERSEY POST-REVOLUTIONARY DOCUMENTS

husband will quitclaim all their right to my daughter, Sarah, to that land that is on the upper side of the road, except 10 acres which lies on Savage's line, which he is to retain, and, if they refuse to quitclaim, "that all my interest in Jo More's Neck be equally divided between my two daughters, the said Martha and Sarah, to hold to my said daughter, Martha, her heirs and assigns forever, and to my daughter, Sarah, for and during her natural life; remainder to my granddaughter, Elizabeth Stites, to her, her heirs and assigns forever." Daughter, Sarah Stites, £25, and two lots of cedar swamp in the Upper Precinct, at the Peach orchard. Son, Jesse, the son of Mary Teel, my plantation in Middle Precinct, at Horse Neck, which I bought of Elijah and Shamgar Huet; also the cedar swamp on the northeast side of Cedar Swamp Bridge, in the Upper Precinct, near Leonard's Causeway, which swamp I bought of Jacob Spicer. One hundred pounds is to be placed in the hands of my friend, Philip Hand, to bring up and educate my two children, Jeremiah and Ezekiel, sons of Mary Teel, and I appoint the said Philip Hand and Nathaniel Holmes to be Guardians of said children. Daughters, Deborah Hand and Elizabeth Hand, land in Lower Precinct of Cape May, at New England, that I bought of Christopher Foster. Executors—friend, Philip Hand, my son, Seth Hand, and my son-in-law, Nathaniel Holmes. Witnesses—Benjamin Ingrum, Jeremiah Hand, Amelia Ludlam. Proved Aug. 9, 1787.
1787, May 7. Inventory, £516.12.6, made by Rev. Artis Seagreave and Philip Cresse. Lib. 29, p. 235.

**1790, Aug. 31. Hand, Elijah,** of Cape May Co. Int. Adm'x—Rachel Hand. Fellowbondsmen—Nathan Hand and Sarah Leamyng; all of Cape May and Cumberland Counties. Witnesses—Elijah Hand and Philip Stites. Lib. 32, p. 106.

**1788, Feb. 2. Hand, Elizabeth,** of Cape May Co., widow of Henry Hand; will of. Son, Eleazar Hand, £10, and that in goods such as his sister, Hannah Hand, shall point out to him to take. Daughter, Hannah Hand, rest of estate. Executrix—daughter, Hannah. Witnesses—Nezer Swain, Catherine Swain, John Leake. Proved Jan. 27, 1789.
1789, Jan. 6. Inventory, £453.4.11, made by Jeremiah Eldredge and Ellis Hughes, Jr. Lib. 31, p. 362.

**1789, Feb. 11. Hand, Elizabeth,** of Cape May Co. Ward. Daughter of Nathan Hand, of said Co., deceased, and Rachel, now wife of Shamgar Huet.
1789, Feb. 11. Guardian—Shamgar Hewit. Fellowbondsman—Thomas Shaw; both of said Co. Witnesses—Jeremiah Hand and William Treen. Lib. 31, p. 372.

**1786, Dec. 2. Hand, Ezra,** of Cape May Co. Int. Adm'x—Mary Hand. Fellowbondsmen—Timothy Hand and Ellis Hughes, Jr.; all of said Co. Witnesses—Henry Hand and Elizabeth Richardson.
1786, Oct. 27. Inventory, £194.17.1, made by Henry Hand and Ellis Hughes, Jr. Lib. 28, p. 249.

**1787, Aug. 21. Hand, Henry, Esq.,** of Cape May Co.; will of. Son, Eleazar, the plantation I bought of Cornelious Schellenger, at Cold Spring; also the use of the plantation where I live, and all other

CALENDAR OF WILLS—1786-1790   99

land for the time being, and, after his death, to his heirs. Wife, Elizabeth, the use of ½ of my lands. Daughter, Hannah, the use of part of the house, if she remain single. Wife to have ⅛ of the moveable estate. Daughter, Hannah, £150. Son, Eleazar, my apparel. Executors—wife, Elizabeth, son, Eleazar, and daughter, Hannah. Witnesses—Abijah Reeves, John Taylor, Sr., Elijah Hughes. Proved Oct. 20, 1787.
1787, Oct. 20. Inventory, £961.3.5, made by Jeremiah Eldredge and Ellis Hughes, Jr. Lib. 29, p. 232.

**1790, June 1. Hand, John,** of Cape May Co. Int. Adm'rs—Mary Hand and Jacocks Swain. Fellowbondsman—Richard Townsend; all of said Co. Witnesses—Judith Smith and Jesse Hand.
1790, June 12. Inventory, £155.12.8, made by Jacob Hughes and Daniel Crowell. Lib. 32, p. 104.

**1790, Feb. 10. Hand, Jonathan,** of Cape May Co. Int. Adm'r—Eli Townsend. Fellowbondsman—Richard Townsend; both of said Co. Witnesses—Sarah Hand and Lydia Hand.
1790, April 12. Inventory, £580.0.11, made by James Godfrey and Richard Townsend. Lib. 32, p. 107.

**1787, March 20. Hand, Mary,** of Cape May Co., widow. Int. Adm'r—Constantine Hughes. Fellowbondsman—Ellis Hughes, Jr.; both of said Co., gentlemen. Witnesses—Sarah Hand and Rachel Hawk.
1787, June 29. Inventory, £136.5.4, made by Thomas Buck and Elijah Hughes. Lib. 29, p. 240.

**1790, May 1. Hand, Nathan,** of Cape May Co. Ward. Son of Nathaniel Hand, of said Co., deceased. Said Ward makes choice of Jeremiah Hand as his Guardian.
1790, May 1. Guardian—Jeremiah Hand, of Middle Precinct. Fellowbondsman—Jacob Richardson, both of said Co. Witnesses—Sarah Hand and Jesse Hand. Lib. 32, p. 107.

**1790, March 19. Hand, Rachel,** of Cape May Co. Int. Adm'r—David Hand. Fellowbondsman—Levi Eldredge; both of Lower Precinct, said Co., gentlemen. Witnesses—William Schillinger and John Stites.
1789, Dec. 3. Inventory, £47.5.9, made by Levi Eldredge and John Stites. Lib. 32, p. 106.

**1788, Oct. 14. Harden, Joseph,** of Haddonfield, Gloucester Co., taylor. Int. Adm'x—Mary Harden. Fellowbondsman—John Rowand; both of said Co.
1788, Oct. 11. Inventory, £190.15.2, made by Thomas Redman and John Rowand. Lib. 31, p. 37.

**1789, June 20. Hardin, Benjamin,** of Gloucester Co. Int. Adm'rs—Redeca [Rebecca] Hardin and John Johnson. Fellowbondsman—Jeptha Abbott; all of said Co.
1789, May. 4. Inventory, £79.7.11, made by John Earley and Jeptha Abit. Lib. 30, p. 137.

100   NEW JERSEY POST-REVOLUTIONARY DOCUMENTS

**1788, April 1. Hardong [Harding], Jeremiah,** of Greenwich, Cumberland Co.; will of. Son, Isaac, house and lot where I live, except the shop. Son, John Harding, one acre of land joining David James. Daughter, Hannah Harding, an equal share of the moveable estate with the rest of the children, when she is 18. Richard Harding the rest of the lot. Son, Samuel Harding, and my daughter, Sarah Harding, their equal share of the moveable estate. Wife, Dorothy, her share of the moveable estate. If another child be born, it is to have its share. Wife to have the use of the house until my son, Isaac, is 21. Executors—wife, Dorothy, and my friend, David Elwell. Witnesses—Richard Wood, Peter Andrews, Richard Wood, Jr. Proved May 14, 1788.
1788, May 14. Inventory, £156.17.2, made by John Miller and Richard Wood.   Lib. 31, p. 61.

**1788, Jan. 1. Hardy, Mary,** of Burlington Co. Int. Adm'r—Isaac Cowgill. Fellowbondsman—Amos Hutchin; both of said Co.
1789, Jan. 17. Inventory, £83.13.0, made by John Butler and Robert Dougherty. "Sale of house and lot in Bordentown, sold by John Hollinshead, late Sheriff, at the suit of John Taylor, £78. Due from James Hardy, for house rent since her death, £4.15.0. Due from Jeremiah Mahaney, for house rent since her death, 18 shillings."
   Lib. 30, p. 57.

**1789, April 21. Haring, John G.,** of Harington, Bergen Co.; will of. Wife, Rensye, my land during her life, except the land at Pascack. Son, Garrit, £3, and the lands where I live. Daughter, Margritie Haring, my 2 lots on Hackensack River. Land at Pascack to be sold. Rest to my 2 children, when they are of age. Executors—father-in-law, Garrit Eckerson, and two brothers, Peter and Jacobus. Witnesses—Cornelius Eckerson, Frederick Haring, James Perry.
1789, April 21. Codicil. Witnesses—Garret Smith, Johannis Haring, James Perry. Proved June 6, 1789.   Lib. 30, p. 236.

**1789, April 30. Harris, Francis,** of Burlington Co. Int. Adm'x—Euphania Harris. Fellowbondsman—John Canned; both of said Co. Witness—Thomas Adams.   Lib. 31, p. 319.

**1790, Feb. 22. Harris, George,** of Hacketts Town, Sussex Co.; will of. My property "to be divided among her [no name given] and my children, at the discretion of John McCarter and my wife, except my wife's bed, which I give to her." Executor—John McCarter. Witnesses—Arthur Hazen, Daniel Stuart. Proved Feb. 26, 1790.
1790, Feb. 25. Inventory, £92.12.5, made by Obadiah Ayers and Daniel Stuart.   Lib. 30, p. 423.

**1789, Jan. 5. Harris, Isaac,** of Fairfield, Cumberland Co. Int. Adm'x—Mary Harris. Fellowbondsmen—Jonathan Bowen and David Bowen; all of said Co.
1789, Jan. 2. Inventory, £100, made by Amos Westcott and James Howell. Inventory, £15, for a pair of oxen, which came to hand since the above.
1787, April 27. Bond. I, Isaac Harris, of Fairfield, Cumberland Co., yeoman, am bound unto Jonathan Bowen and David Bowen, Adm'rs of Elijah Bowen, of said Co., deceased, in the sum of 201 pounds and four pence. Whereas, the said Elijah Bowen died intes-

tate, and the said Jonathan and David Bowen administered on the estate, and Elijah did have, at the time of his death, 6 children, Elijah, Seth, David, Rebecca, Mary and Abigail; and Whereas, three of the said children, to wit:—Seth, Rebecca and Abigail, being helpless and not of ability to support themselves, it is agreed among the other 3 children that Elijah should have £7, and give a receipt, being the eldest son, and that the rest of estate, after paying the debts and the widow her dower, should be equally divided between his son, David, and his daughter, Mary; provided they should keep and support the 3 helpless children from ever becoming chargeable to the public; and Whereas it is agreed between his son, David, and his daughter, Mary, with the approbation of the Adm'rs, that David should keep and support his brother, Seth, and that Mary should keep and support her sisters, Rebecca and Abigail; and Whereas, the whole of the estate to be divided between the said David and his sister, Mary, (after paying the debts, the widow's dower and his son, Elijah) amounted to 201 pounds and 4 pence; and Whereas, the said Isaac Harris, since the decease of Elijah Bowen has intermarried with the said Mary Bowen, daughter of Elijah Bowen, deceased, who consents to the said divisions of the estate, that he will in consideration of the above sum to him paid by the said Jonathan and David Bowen, acknowledged by his and his wife's receipt, to keep and support the said Rebecca and Abigail, during their lives. Signed by Isaac Harris, in the presence of Temperence Billings and David Bowen, Jr. Lib. 30, p. 163.

**1788, Oct. 14. Harris, John,** of Bridgwater, Somerset Co. Ward. Eldest son of John Harris, of said place, deceased. Said Ward being out of wardship of Mary Kain, makes choice of John McCarter as his Guardian.

1788, Oct. 14. Guardian—John McCarter. Fellowbondsman—John Logan; both of Mendham, Morris Co. Lib. 31, p. 201.

**1787, June 30. Harris, Mary,** of Woolwich Township, Gloucester Co. Int. Adm'rs—George Katts and Meriam Harris. Fellowbondsman—John Smith; all of said place. Lib. 29, p. 117.

**1788, June 28. Harris, Noah,** of Cumberland Co. Ward. Son of Noah Harris, of said Co., deceased. Said Ward, having real and personal estate, makes choice of Henry Mulford as his Guardian.

1788, June 28. Guardian—Henry Mulford. Fellowbondsman—Jonathan Bowen; both of said Co. Lib. 31, p. 77.

**1790, May 7. Harris, Thomas,** of Tewksbury, Hunterdon Co. Int. Adm'rs—Thomas Harris and Francis Drake, of Tewksbury and Bridgewater. Fellowbondsman—Jacob Kline, of Tewksbury.

1790, May 3. Inventory, £214.13.4, made by Thomas Berry and Jacob Kline.

1796, June 4. Account by both Adm'rs. Lib. 30, p. 317.

**1788, May 16. Harrison, Caleb,** of Newark, Essex Co.; will of. Wife, Abigail, as much in value as she brought when I married her. Daughter, Azuba, all the goods called hers. Daughter, Mary, 5 shillings. Son, George, ½ the residue. Son, Isaac ¼, and to daughter, Phebe, ¼ the residue. Executors—sons, George and Isaac, and my son-in-law, Edward Earle. Witnesses—James Thompson, John Dod, Jr., James Farrand. Proved June 3, 1788. Lib. 38, p. 93.

**1786, March 28. Harrison, Isac,** of Newark, Essex Co.; will of. Wife, Martha, my household goods for her disposal as she sees fit among my daughters. Son, Thomas, £100. Sons, James and Samuel, all my lands, after their mother is done with them. Son, Amos, £100, and he is to have a trade. If any of my sons die under age, then their portion to go to their brother and sisters. Executors—brother, Simeon, and my son-in-law, Josiah Quinby. Witnesses—Moses Quinby, Dadok Baldwin. Proved Nov. 24, 1786. Lib. 28, p. 418.

**1788, April 10. Harrison, William,** of Middlesex Co. Int. Adm'r—Frederick Van Dike. Fellowbondsman—Henry Lupp; both of said Co. Witness—William Hyer, Jr. Lib. 31, p. 223.

**1788, Sept. 9. Harrison, William,** of Woodbridge, Middlesex Co.; will of. Wife, Elizabeth, all she had when we married, and £50. Son, George, £60. Son, William, £100. Son, Robert, £100. Son, Jonas, £30. Granddaughter, Elizabeth, the daughter of my son, Isaac, £20. Grandson, Frazee Harrison, son of my son, George, deceased, land which George in his lifetime bought of Matthias Halsted. Daughters, Arabella and Rachel Harrison, to have their share of money. Executors—sons, George and William. Witnesses—William Martin, Margaret Kinsey, Joseph DeCamp. Proved April 12, 1790.

1790, March 30. Inventory, £375.9.4, made by John Thorp and William Martin. Lib. 30, p. 514.

**1788, Jan. 15. Harsel, Anthony,** of Hunterdon Co. Int. Adm'r—Christopher Harsel. Fellowbondsman—Tunis Tunison; both of Lebanon, said Co. Witnesses—Rowland Hall and Morris Robeson.

1788, Jan. 2. Inventory "of Anthony Harshel," £261.8.11, made by William Housel, Philip Dils and Tunis Tunison.

1791, Dec. 22. Account by Adm'r. Lib. 31, p. 143.

**1790, Nov. 3. Hart, Elijah,** of Hunterdon Co. Int. Adm'rs—Kesiah Hart and Enoch Hart. Fellowbondsman—Nathaniel Hart; all of Hopewell, said Co.

1784, Aug. 4. Inventory, £133.17.6, made by Daniel Howell and Moore Scott.

1791, Nov. 2. Account by Adm'rs. Lib. 30, p. 814.

**1787, Aug. 27. Hart, Mary,** of Hunterdon Co. Ward. Daughter of Ralph Hart, of said Co., deceased. Said Ward makes choice of John P. Hunt as her Guardian.

1787, Aug. 27. Guardian—John P. Hunt. Fellowbondsman—Peter Gordon. Witness—William Tindall. Lib. 29, p. 299.

**1786, Jan. 28. Hartley, Thomas,** of Elsinborough Township, Salem Co.; will of. Son, Thomas, my house and lot, and he is to pay to his brother, Mark, £30, when Mark is 21. Wife, Esther, may live in the house. Son, Samuel, 10 acres in Lower Alloways Creek. Daughter, Susannah, all her late mother's (Catharine's) apparel. Personal estate to wife and daughters, Elizabeth, Susannah and Mary, and my son, Mark. Executors—wife, Esther, and Samuel Stewart. Witnesses—Joseph Swabey, Anthony Hartley, John Smith. Proved Aug. 25, 1788.

1788, April 15. Inventory, £355.5.7, made by William Goodwin and John Thompson. Lib. 31, p. 46.

## CALENDAR OF WILLS—1786-1790

**1788, June 9. Harvey, Benjamin,** of Salem Co. Ward. Son of William Harvey, of said Co., deceased. Said Ward makes choice of James Slape as his Guardian.
1788, June 9. Guardian—James Slape. Fellowbondsmen—James Mason and Job Shreve; all of Manington, said Co.  Lib. 29, p. 153.

**1789, Feb. 21. Harvey, Hannah,** of Middletown, Monmouth Co.; will of. Brother, Samuel Harvey's daughter, Margreat Harvey, £20, when 21. To Margaret Harvey, daughter of Thomas Harvey, the son of Samuel Harvey, £15, when 18. To Hannah Harvey, daughter of Thomas Harvey, son of Samuel Harvey, £15, when 18. To Hanner Hance, the daughter of John Tone, rest of estate. Executor—friend, John Robins. Witnesses—John Morris, James Morris, William Taylor. Proved March 9, 1789.
1789, March 4. Inventory, £311.9.7, made by Thomas Lloyd and Garrit Bennet.  Lib. 30, p. 177.

**1787, Harvey, William,** of Salem Co. Ward. Son of William Harvey, of said Co., deceased. On petition of James Slape, the maternal grandfather, he is appointed Guardian.
1787, March 12. Guardian—James Slape. Fellowbondsmen—James Mason and Job Shreve; all of Manington, said Co.  Lib. 29, p. 153.

**1786, March 10. Hathaway, Isaac,** of Morris Co. Int. Adm'r—Jacob Tappen, of Hanover. Fellowbondsman—William Leddel, of Mendham; both of said Co.
1786, March 10. Renunciation by Sarah Hathaway, widow of Isaac, in favor of Jacob Tappen. Witnesses—James Young and Robert Young.  Lib. 28, p. 486.

**1788, July 25. Havens, John,** of Shrewsbury, Monmouth Co.; will of. Sons, John and Jacob, all my lands. Son, Daniel, £10. Son, Moses, £20, if he comes after it in 10 years. Son, Jesse, £5, if he comes home in 4 years; if not, to be put to use till his daughter, Anna, comes of age. Daughter, Eavis, £10. Daughter, Elizabeth, £10. Grandson, Jesse Havens, £50. Grandsons, John Davis and Jesse Havens, £5 each. Rest to Moses, Eavis, John and Jacob Havens and Elizabeth Davis. Executors—son, John, and son-in-law, William Davis. Witnesses—Jonathan Curtis, Walter Curtis, Margret Price. Proved Oct. 30, 1788.
1788, Sept. 1. Inventory, £533.12.10, made by Jonathan Curtis and Lewis Ellison.  Lib. 30, p. 98.

**1789, April 2. Haviland, Joseph,** of Monmouth Co. Int. Adm'r—Stephen Haviland. Fellowbondsman—James Johnson; both of said Co. Witness—Euphamia Clayton.
1789, March 23. Inventory, £24.11.0, made by Samuel Hayes and James Johnson.  Lib. 30, p. 188.

**1789, Oct. 17. Haviland, Martha,** of Elizabeth Town, Essex Co.; will of. My little niece, Jane Haviland, daughter of my brother, Benjamin Haviland, bedstead and the curtains. Niece, Jane Tooker, daughter of my sister, Sally Tooker, a bedstead and curtains. Niece, Sarah Morris, daughter of my sister, Mary Tharp, a bed. Niece, Sally Higgins, blankets. Brother, Benjamin's wife, a petticoat, and to her daughter, Jane Haviland, a silver tea spoon. To Mary Jones a cloak.

Niece, Abigail Haviland, daughter of John Haviland, rest of silver. My negro woman, Rose, I give to my brother, Benjamin; and the legacy that my brother, William Haviland, deceased, left me, I give to my brother, Benjamin Haviland, to be kept for his son, Benjamin Winans Haviland. Executors—brother, Benjamin Haviland, and John Beers. Witnesses—Lewis Tooker, Mary Hatfield. Proved Dec. 18, 1790. Lib. 33, p. 390.

**1790, Dec. 28. Haviland, Thomas,** of Essex Co. Ward. Son of John Haviland, of said Co., deceased. Said Ward makes choice of Benjamin Haviland as his Guardian.

1790, Dec. 28. Guardian—Benjamin Haviland. Fellowbondsman—William Brown Higgins; both of said Co. Lib. 33, p. 396.

**1790, Dec. 28. Haviland, William, Benjamin Winans, Jane and John,** of Essex Co. Wards. Children of Benjamin Haviland, of said Co. The father asks to be appointed Guardian.

1790, Dec. 28. Guardian—Benjamin Haviland, the father of said minors. Fellowbondsman—William Brown Higgins; both of said Co.
Lib. 33, p. 396.

**1789, May 12. Hawk, George,** of Windsor Township, Middlesex Co.; will of. Wife, Catharine, the goods she brought, and use of land I bought of Isaac Clarke. Son, Jacob, use of said land. Granddaughter, Elizabeth Antrum, £15, when 18. Son, Frederick, personal estate. Grandson, George Hawk, son of Jacob, said land. Executors—friends, Ezekiel Smith and William Covenhoven, son of Minicus. Witnesses—Israel Clarke, Stephen Johnes, Jr., William McGalliard. Proved June 12, 1789.

1789, June 10. Inventory, £123.19.9, made by John Flock and James McGalliard. Lib. 31, p. 376.

**1790, Oct. 12. Hawkins, Joseph,** of Bergen Co. Int. Adm'r—Job Smith. Fellowbondsman—Adam Boyd; both of said Co. Witness—Albert C. Zabrisky. Lib. 31, p. 543.

**1790, Oct. 12. Hawkins, Sarah,** of Bergen Co. Int. Adm'r—Job Smith. Fellowbondsman—Adam Boyd; both of said Co. Witness—Albert C. Zabrisky. Lib. 31, p. 543.

**1786, March 16. Hays, John,** of Chesterfield, Burlington Co.; will of. Friend, Marmaduke Watson, all real and personal estate, in trust, to pay £— to my granddaughter, Mary, when she is 18, and the rest to my daughter, Hannah Douglass, it being my will that my son-in-law, John Douglass, shall have no power over it. Executor—said Marmaduke Watson. Witnesses—Levi Carson, Rebeckah Gray, John Oliver. Proved April 21, 1786. Lib. 28, p. 49.

**1788, Dec. 25. Hazen, Daniel,** of Independence, Sussex Co. Int. Adm'r—Arthur Hazen, yeoman. Fellowbondsman—Samuel Landon, Sr.; both of said place.

1788, Dec. 21. Inventory, £262.6.3, made by Samuel Landon and Thomas Hazen. Lib. 31, p. 156.

CALENDAR OF WILLS—1786-1790 105

**1787, Feb. 17. Headdle, James,** of Burlington Co. Int. Adm'r—Schuyler Bradford. Fellowbondsman—Joshua M. Wallace; both of City of Burlington. Witnesses—Thomas Adams and Herbert McElroy.
Lib. 29, p. 79.

**1786, Feb. 25. Heard, John,** of Essex Co. Int. Adm'rs—Ellis Barron and Andrew Elston. Fellowbondsman—James Edgar, of Middlesex Co. Lib. 28, p. 424.

**1789, Aug. 8. Heaton, Benjamin,** of Independence Township, Sussex Co.; will of. Wife, Rebekah, all goods necessary, during her life. Son, Jonathan, my lands, and he is to support his mother; and, if he die without issue, then to his sister, Ann. Daughter, Ann, £40. Daughter, Rachel, £30. Son, John, £50. Daughters, Mercy Willson and Rebekah Lundy, 20 shillings. Executors—son, Jonathan, daughter, Ann, and friend, Jonathan Lundy. Witnesses—Jacob Lundy, Mordecai Willson, Jacob Lundy, Jr. Proved May 6, 1790.
1790, April 20. Inventory, £300.13.3, made by Jacob Lundy and Jonathan Wilson. Lib. 30, p. 427.

**1788, March 28. Heaton, Gideon,** of Downs Township, Cumberland Co.; will of. Wife, Anna, use of plantation where I live, and use of plantation from which I lately moved, where John Kelsay lives, till my sons, Daniel and Gideon, are of age. Son, Samuel, plantation he lives on. Son, Daniel, the land on south side of Dividing Creek, being the plantation I live on. Son, Gideon, the plantation where John Kelsay lives, and the place at Morris River, which I bought of the Sheriff. Daughter, Anna Heaton, land at Roadstown. Executrix—wife, Anna. Witnesses—Nathaniel Lore, John Lore, Levi Heaton.
1788, March 31. Codicil. Daughter, Anna, a white cow. Witnesses—same as above. Proved Sept. 22, 1788.
1788, June 30. Inventory, £473.18.0, made by Levi Heaton and Gabriel Glan. Lib. 31, p. 63.

**1789, Dec. 12. Heaton, Samuel,** of Downs Township, Cumberland Co., yeoman; will of. Wife, Mary, use of my lands, till my sons are of age; and then she is to have the use of the lot I bought of Daniel Tullis. Son, Aula, the west end of my plantations when 21. Son, Seth, the east end of the same; also lot I bought of Daniel Tullis. If both sons die, then I give the said lands to my brothers, Daniel Heaton and Gideon Heaton. Executors—wife, Mary, and my uncle, Levi Heaton. Witnesses—John Lore, John Henderson, Anna Henderson. Proved Sept. 30, 1790. Lib. 30, p. 265.

**1789, Aug. 18. Heaviland, John,** of Amwell Township, Hunterdon Co., cordwainer; will of. Wife, Rebecah, all real and personal estate, to bring up my children, who are, Nathan, my only son, and my daughters, Hannah, Grace, Elizabeth and Lettea. Wife is to take care of my aged mother, Mary Heaviland. Children to have what is left when wife is done with it. Executors—wife, Rebeccah, and my friend, Samuel Hill. Witnesses—Samuel Griggs, John Lowe, Jacob Mattison. Proved Nov. 18, 1789.
1789, Oct. 1. Inventory, £249.17.10, made by John Griggs and Samuel Griggs.

1794, March 31. Inventory, £54.18.9, of goods found in the hands of his Executrix, Rebeckah Heaviland, deceased, made by Samuel Griggs and James Clark.
1798, May 30. Account by Samuel Hill, Executor of John Heaviland. Lib. 32, p. 46.

**1787, Jan. 31. Helmes, Haunce,** of Woolwich Township, Gloucester Co. Int. Adm'r—William White. Fellowbondsman—Ebenezer Adams; both of Greenwich Township, said Co., yeomen. Witness— Isaac S. Hugg.
1787, Jan. 30. Inventory, £863.0.1, made by David Hendrickson and Ebenezer Adams. Lib. 29, p. 119.

**1787, Oct. 9. Hendershot, John, Jr.,** of Oxford, Sussex Co. Int. Adm'rs—Rachel Hendershot and John Hendershot. Fellowbondsman—Mathias Shipman; all of said Co. Witnesses—Mary O. Anderson and Thomas Anderson.
1786, Sept. 1. Inventory, £373.14.6, made by Mathias Shipman and Balser Domar. Lib. 29, p. 489.

**1786, June 14. Hendershot, Michael,** of Sussex Co.; will of. Grandson, Moses Moris, the black mare and colt. Children, John, Elizabeth Bemer, Cateren Denis, Casper, Jacob, Wilam, Sarah Roof, Suffiah Roof, rest of estate. Executor—Daniel Pridmore. Witnesses—John Casaday, Abraham Courssen, John Predmore. Proved Nov. 11, 1786.
1786, Nov. 23. Inventory, £152.10.8, made by Henry Johnson and William Perine. Lib. 28, p. 464.

**1788, Oct. 25. Henderson, David, Elizabeth, Hannah and Jemima,** of Hunterdon Co. Wards. Children of John Henderson, Jr., of said Co., deceased. Petition by Sarah Henderson, widow of John Henderson, Jr., praying that she may be made Guardian of said children. Witnesses—Aaron Watson, William Runkle, David Hagerty and Robert Hagerty.
1788, Oct. 30. Guardian—Sarah Henderson, Fellowbondsman— Aaron Watson; both of Bethlehem, said Co. Lib. 31, p. 146.

**1788, March 12. Henderson, John,** of Bethlehem, Hunterdon Co., yeoman; will of. Wife, Mary, ⅓ of the moveable estate, and £12 a year while my widow. To the children of my son, John, deceased, £20 a year, to be left in the hands of my Executors. To Alexander McCrea, my son-in-law, 160 acres of land, which join Aron Watson and Samuel Johnson. To Jean McCrea, my granddaughter, £30 when of age. Grandson, John Henderson, son of David, deceased, 160 acres joining Robert Embley at the west end; and John is to pay to John McCrea, son of Alexander, £60. Grandson, David, son of my son, John, deceased, 180 acres at the east end of plantation, and is to pay his sisters, £90; that is, £30 to each, and to Archebel McCray, son of Alexander, £20. Executors—son-in-law, Alexander McCrea and Thomas Bowlby. Witnesses—William Runkle, Samuel Large, David Hagerty. Proved May 30, 1788.
1788, May 9. Inventory, £270.2.1, made by James Henderson and Samuel Large.
1790, May 5. Account by Executors. Lib. 31, p. 106.

**1788, Nov. 17. Henderson, John,** of Hunterdon Co. Ward. Son of David Henderson, of said Co., deceased. Petition of John Richey and Elizabeth, his wife, widow of David Henderson, that they may be made Guardians of said minor. The last Term of Court ordered that Alexander McCrea be appointed, but the mother desires that it may be reversed.

1789, Feb. 5. Guardians—John Richey and Elizabeth Richey. Fellowbondsman—Benjamin Opdycke; all of said Co. Witnesses—Jacob Smith, Richard Leacy, Sr. and Joseph Parke. The said Alexander McCrea applied to be made Guardian, saying that John Henderson, of Bethlehem, by his will dated 12 of March, 1788, left his grandson, John Henderson, son of David, deceased, being about 8 years of age, 160 acres in Bethlehem; also 180 acres to his grandson, David Henderson, son of John, deceased, being about 6 years of age, and made his son-in-law, the said McCrea, his Executor. Said petition of McCrea is dated Oct. 28, 1788. Lib. 32, p. 57.

**1789, June 12. Henderson, Mary,** of Hunterdon Co., widow of John Henderson, Sr.; will of. To Peter Waycoff, ¼ of my apparel. To Mary Reemmer, ¼. To Jean Opdike, ¼. To Hannah Longer, ¼. Rest of estate to be equally divided between my 6 children, and Peter Waycoff is to have an equal share with the rest. Executors—friends, Thomas Bowlby and William Runkle. Witnesses—Robert Hagerty, David Hagerty, Jane McCray. Proved Oct. 24, 1789.

1789, Sept. 7. Inventory, £49.5.0, made by Lawrance Updike and John Updike, Sr.

1805, Feb. 6. Account by Executors. Lib. 32, p. 34.

**1786, June 20. Hendrickson, Abraham, Sr.,** of Monmouth Co. Int. Adm'r—Jacob Hendrickson. Fellowbondsman—Koert Schenck, Sr.; both of said Co. There are goods left unadministered by Abraham Hendrickson, Jr. Lib. 28, p. 293.

**1786, Oct. 6. Hendrickson, Abraham, Jr.,** of Freehold, Monmouth Co. Inventory, £83.2.10, made by Kert Schenck, cordwainer, and George Smock. File No. 5681 M.

**1788, July 31. Hendrickson, Daniel,** of Middletown, Monmouth Co. Int. Adm'x—Cathrine Hendrickson, widow of said Daniel, and Hendrick Hendrickson, son of said Daniel; both of said place. Witnesses—Garrit Hendrickson and Thomas Hendrickson.

1788, Aug. 12. Inventory, £1,259.0.3, made by Garrit Hendrickson and John Stillwell. Lib. 30, p. 102.

**1790, June 16. Hendrickson, Henry,** of Greenwich Township, Gloucester Co. Int. Adm'r—William White. Fellowbondsman—Daniel Sutherland; both of said Co.

1790, June 14. Inventory, £79.8.3, made by Charles Lock and David Hendrickson. Lib. 31, p. 478.

**1786, June 20. Hendrickson, John,** of Monmouth Co. Int. Adm'r—Jacob Hendrickson. Fellowbondsman—Koert Schenck, Sr.; both of said Co.

1786, Oct. 6. Inventory, £60.3.7, made by Koert Schenck and George Smock. Lib. 28, p. 294.

**1786, May 12. Hendrickson, Moses,** of Woolwich Township, Gloucester Co.; will of. Brother, Henry, all the land that falls to my share of my brother, John. To my sister's daughter, Catrenah Hendrickson, the place that joins my brother, Henry. Sister-in-law, Mary Hendrickson, £10. To Mathew Lord, £5. Executor—friend, Ebenezer Adams. Witnesses—David Hendrickson, Ebenezer Adams, Edy Hendrickson. Proved June 16, 1786.
1786, May 20. Inventory, £40.15.11, made by David Hendrickson and Henry Hendrickson. Lib. 28, p. 104.

**1789, May 18. Henry, George,** of Hunterdon Co. Ward. Son of Samuel Henry, of said Co., deceased. Said Ward makes choice of Bernard Hanlon as his Guardian.
1789, May 18. Guardian—Bernard Hanlon. Fellowbondsman—John Singer; both of Trenton, said Co. Lib. 32, p. 56.

**1788, May 13. Henry, John.** Account by Thomas Joslin, Adm'r.
Dr.
1787 Amount of Inventory of personal estate, £105.13.3.
Money received from Isaac Nixon, £0.7.6.
Money received from Thomas Earl, £0.3.3.
Amount of Inventory of personal estate of Rhoda Henry, deceased, £10.6.10.
Sundries not appraised, £1.5.0.
Due the Accomptant, £1.7.10.
Cr.
1787 Cash paid Samuel Husted for crying vendue, £0.7.6 (March 23).
Sept. 27 Benjamin Simkins and Martha McGee, for keeping Thomas Henry, infant of said deceased, £3.12.0.
Nov. 20 Diament Whitaker for keeping a child, £2.12.0.
Paid accounts against Rhoda Henry, dec., £10.9.3.
Clothing for the children, £1.10.0.
Joseph Conner for bringing up a child, £8.
Diament Whitaker, Do. for 3 years, £10.
File No. 6209 F.

**1788, Feb. 22. Henselbecker, Johannes,** of Bergen Co. Int. Adm'r—Johannes Henselbecker. Fellowbondsman—Albert Van Voorhase; both of said Co. Witness—Catherine Miller. Lib. 31, p. 257.

**1790, Feb. 15. Heretage, Joshua,** of Kingwood, Hunterdon Co. Int. Adm'rs—Mary Heretage and Absalom Runyan. Fellowbondsman—Stephen Gano; all of said place.
1790, Feb. 15. Inventory, £123.15.0, made by Pallmer Phillips and James Danily.
1791, Jan. 12. Account by William Hannah and Mary, his wife, late Mary Heretage, widow of Joshua Heretage. Lib. 30, p. 317.

**1789, June 15. Hewes, Aaron,** of Woodbury, Gloucester Co., tanner and currier. Int. Adm'rs—Jane Hewes and Josiah Hewes. Fellowbondsman—David Cooper.
1789, July 27. Inventory, £2,640.15.7, made by John Wilkins and Thomas Redman. "A legacy is due from the estate of Joseph Hewes, of North Carolina, deceased, value uncertain." Lib. 30, p. 137.

CALENDAR OF WILLS—1786-1790   109

**1786, Sept. 26. Hewes, Lydia,** of Woolwich, Gloucester Co., spinster; will of. Brother, Caleb Hewes, a bed. Sister, Rebecca, the bed which fell to me by the death of my sister, Elizabeth. Brothers, William Hewes, Isaac Hewes, Caleb Hewes, Aaron Hewes, George Hewes, Samuel Hewes, and my sister, Rebecca, the residue, except the silver spoons, which I give to my sister, Rebecca. All which I gave to my brother, John Hewes, I give to my brother, Samuel. Executors—brothers, Isaac and Caleb. Witnesses—Mary Lawrance, Catharine Wiser, Matthew Gill, Jr. Proved March 20, 1787.
1787, March 12. Inventory, made by Isaac Zane and Matthew Gill, Jr. Lib. 29, p. 92.

**1790, July 17. Hewitt, John,** of Gloucester Co. Int. Adm'r—Francis Eastlack, of Salem Co. Fellowbondsman—Thomas Claypool, of Gloucester Co. Lib. 31, p. 478.

**1788, Aug. 22. Hiels [Hiles], Jacob,** of Oxford Township, Sussex Co. Int. Adm'rs—Anne Hiles and Jacob Hiles, Jr., both of said place. Fellowbondsman—John Wheeler, of Newtown, said Co. Witness—William Lodor.
1788, April 4. Inventory, £180.2.9, made by John Kinney and William Lodor. Lib. 31, p. 157.

**1786, Aug. 17. Higbee, John,** of Galloway, Gloucester Co., blacksmith and husbandman; will of. Wife, Mary, the use of my farm. Sons, Edward, Isaac and John, shall have their proportion of my real estate, where they are now seated. Son, Absalom, the place where Samuel Strickland, deceased, did live; also the salt meadow which I bought of Robert Smith, Sr. Son, Josiah, 14 acres of the home estate. Sons, Samuel, William, Richard and Charles, their shares of real estate, and their younger brothers, Samuel, William, Richard and Charles, their shares. Executors—wife, Mary; son, Edward, and John Smith. Witnesses—Robert Leeds, Enoch Leeds, George Edwards. Proved Nov. 7, 1786. Lib. 28, p. 84.

**1789, Feb. 6. Higgens, Joseph,** of Amwell Township, Hunterdon Co.; will of. Wife, Elizabeth, some goods, and all she had when I married her. Son, Michael, the saw mill and lot; and a meadow at Little Egg Harbor. Grandsons, Andrew and Joseph Higgins, plantation where I live; and Andrew is to pay £50 to Richard Green. Executors—son, Michael, grandson, Andrew Higgins, and my wife, Elizabeth. Witnesses—Cornelius Hoppock, Jacob Holcomb, Henry Lott. Proved July 3, 1790.
1790, July 8. Inventory, £374.4.3, made by Cornelius Hoppock and Jacob Holcomb. Lib. 30, p. 310.

**1786, Aug. 25. Higgins, Edward,** of Middlesex Co. Int. Adm'r—John Thomson. Fellowbondsman—William Burnet; both of said Co. Lib. 28, p. 339.

**1790, Dec. 28. Higgins, James,** of Essex Co. Ward. Son of Nathaniel Higgins, and Elizabeth, his wife, of said Co. Said Ward makes choice of Benjamin Haviland as his Guardian.
1790, Dec. 28. Guardian—Benjamin Haviland. Fellowbondsman—William Brown Higgins; both of said Co. Lib. 33, p. 396.

**1789, Feb. 5. Hildreth, James,** of Cape May Co. Ward. Son of James and Martha Hildreth, of said Co., deceased. Said Ward is under the age of 14.
1789, Feb. 5. Guardian—Joseph Hildreth. Fellowbondsman—Jonathan Leaming; both of said Co. Witnesses—Sarah Hand and Jesse Hand. Lib. 31, p. 372.

**1789, Feb. 10. Hildreth, James,** of Cape May Co. Int. Adm'r—Joseph Hildreth. Fellowbondsman—Jonathan Leaming; both of said Co. Witnesses—Sarah Hand and Jesse Hand.
1790, Feb. 13. Inventory, £393.5.3, made by Thomas Shaw and Jotham Townsend. Lib. 31, p. 370.

**1790, Aug. 9. Hildreth, James,** of Cape May Co. Ward. Son of Joshua Hildreth, of said Co., deceased. Said Ward is under the age of 14.
1790, Aug. 9. Guardian—David Hildreth. Fellowbondsman—Joshua Hildreth; both of said Co. Witnesses—Sarah Hand and Jesse Hand.
Lib. 32, p. 107.

**1788, Jan. 9. Hildreth, Jonathan,** of Cape May Co. Int. Adm'x—Dorcas Hildreth. Fellowbondsman—David Hildreth; both of Middle Precinct, said Co. Witnesses—Sarah Hand, Jr. and Jesse Hand.
1788, April 10. Inventory, £254, made by Philip Cresse and Eli Eldredge. Lib. 31, p. 93.

**1790, Aug. 9. Hildreth, Joshua,** of Cape May Co. Ward. Son of Joshua Hildreth, of said Co., deceased. Said Ward is under the age of 14.
1790, Aug. 9. Guardian—David Hildreth. Fellowbondsman—Joshua Hildreth; both of said Co. Witnesses—Sarah Hand and Jesse Hand.
Lib. 32, p. 107.

**1789, Feb. 10. Hildreth, Martha,** of Cape May Co. Ward. Daughter of James Hildreth, and Martha Hildreth, of said Co., deceased. Said Ward is under the age of 14.
1789, Feb. 10. Guardian—Joseph Hildreth. Fellowbondsman—Jonathan Leaming; both of said Co. Witnesses—Sarah Hand and Jesse Hand. Lib. 31, p. 372.

**1788, May 13. Hile, Christian,** of Lebanon, Hunterdon Co.; will of. My estate to be sold. Wife, Cathrene, to have 2 shares of the money to my sons one. My 10 children to have the rest; each son to have 2 shares, and each daughter one. Sons, Henry, Christophel and John, to be paid at the end of a year. Sons, Thomas and Christian, to have their shares at the end of one year. Son, Peter, to have his share when he is 21. Daughter, Hannah, to have her share at the end of a year. Daughters, Elizabeth, Mary and Margret, to have theirs when 18. Executors—friends, William Hazlitt and Thomas Vanbuskark. Witnesses—John Bell, John Hockenbery, Hester Vanbuscark. Proved June 3, 1788.
1788, May 19. Inventory, £183.3.5, made by John Bell and John Hockenbery.
1791, May 4. Account by William Hazlett, Esq. Lib. 31, p. 105.

**1790, Aug. 16. Hill, Charles,** of Essex Co. Int. Adm'r—David Banks. Fellowbondsman—Jesse Baldwin, of Newark, said Co. Witness—Elias Boudinot.
1790, Aug. 16. Inventory, £273.11.1, made by Abiel Canfield and Jesse Baldwin.
1790, Nov. 30. Inventory, £227.1.1, made by the Adm'r, of the papers in his hands. "A deed from Samuel Arnet, and his wife, to William and James Hill, for land on which the house stands, where John Burnet lives. William Hill's will." Lib. 30, p. 362.

**1789, Nov. 7. Hill, James,** of Newark, Essex Co.; will of. To my natural child, James Hill, the son of Sarah McCormick, which child now lives with his mother in Ireland, ½ of my real and personal estate. Brothers, Charles Hill and Samuel Hill, rest of estate. Executors—William Hill, of New York, and my brother, William Hill. Witnesses—John Bard, Daniel McElkeran, David A. Ogden. Proved Jan. 4, 1790. Probate to William Hill, of New York, the surviving Executor, Oct. 19, 1790.
1790, Feb. 17. Inventory, £108.7.4, estate of William and James Hill (deceased), by Robert Johnston and Daniel McElkeran.
Lib. 30, p. 330.

**1790, Dec. 18. Hill, James,** of Middlesex Co. Inventory, made by Andrew Applegate and Joseph Applegate. Benjamin Cole, Adm'r.
File No. 7589 L.

**1786, July 1. Hill, Martin,** of Weasel, Essex Co. Inventory, £109.12.1, made by Dr. Ebenezer Blachly and John Burnet.
File No. 6992 G.

**1787, Jan. 10. Hill, Samuel,** of Amwell, Hunterdon Co.; will of. Son, James, the plantation where he lives, in Sussex Co. Two youngest sons, Charles and John, a horse to each, when they are 21. Eldest daughter, Elizabeth, to have an outset equal to her sister, Phebe. Wife, Bearsheba, ⅓ the profits of my real estate. At death or marriage of my wife, the real estate to be sold, and money divided into 7 parts. Eldest son, Paul, to have 2 parts. Daughters, Elizabeth and Phebe, and Samuel and Charles and John, one part each. Executors—Paul Hill, Jacob Young and John Stout. Witnesses—John Stout, Nathan Stout, Samuel Danbury.
1787, Feb. 26. Codicil. Son, Charles, has not served all his time. Witnesses—John Stout, Mary Stout, Nathan Stout. Proved April 1; and Codicil proved Oct. 11, 1788, by John Stout, son of Nathan.
1788, March 28. Inventory, £516.13.8, made by Derick Sutphen and William Chamberlain. "One Militia Note, signed Nathaniel Hunt, £5.3.9. One Soldier Note, signed John Pierce, £30. One State note, signed Silas Condit, £30.12.0. One State note, signed William Verbryck, £0.16.8."
1791, July 28. Account by Paul Hill and Jacob Young, acting Executors. Lib. 31, p. 109.

**1789, March 27. Hill, Thomas,** of Trenton, Hunterdon Co. Ward. Son of James Hill, of said place, deceased. Said Ward makes choice of his mother, Sarah Hall, as his Guardian.
1789, March 27. Guardian—Sarah Hall. Fellowbondswoman—Mary Chambers; both of said place. Lib. 32, p. 57.

**1790, Dec. 11. Hilliard, John,** of Burlington Co. Int. Adm'rs—Frances Hilliard, Jonathan Hilliard and William Ridgway. Fellowbondsmen—William Haines and Andrew Craig. Witness—James Kinsey, Jr.
1790, Dec. 14. Inventory, £1,084.7.3, made by Thomas Haines and John Rogers. Lib. 32, p. 96.

**1789, March 28. Hilliard, Uriah,** of Burlington Co. Ward. Son of John Hilliard, of said Co., deceased. Said Ward makes choice of Richard Edwards as his Guardian.
1789, March 28. Guardian—Richard Edwards. Fellowbondsman—Thomas Ellis; both of Northampton Township, said Co.
Lib. 31, p. 322.

**1789, May 6. Hinchman, John,** of Evesham, Burlington Co., yeoman; will of. Wife, Elizabeth, £50 in goods. Sister, Hannah Stokes, and her children, Hannah Buzby, Sarah Gill, Mary Wilkins, Judith Middleton, Samuel Stokes, John Hinchman Stokes; and my sister, Elizabeth Hatkinson, and her children, John Bispham, Joseph Atkinson, John Atkinson, Mary Stokes, Elizabeth Butcher and Ann Rossell; and the 3 following children of my sister, Sarah, namely, Benjamin Bispham, Thomas Bispham and Elizabeth Bispham, all the money that may be due in Great Britain. Nephew, Hinchman Bispham, son of my sister, Sarah, all of my plantation in Evesham Township, and all my right under a deed of Trust, and Bond and Warrant of Attorney, made to me by John Hinchman Stokes, dated May 12, 1788, he to hold forever, paying as follows:—to my nephew, John Hinchman, £100; my nephew, James Hinchman, £50; my granddaughter, Judith Jenings, £150; my nephew, Charles French, £30; and to my nephews and niece, Benjamin Bispham, Thomas Bispham and Elizabeth Bispham, £70. He is also to pay to my wife £30 a year. I give to my wife a bond from Joseph Rigby, dated Nov. 7, 1788. Executors—nephews, John Hinchman Stokes, Joseph Atkinson and Hinchman Bispham. Witnesses—Nathan Cliffton, Thomas Porter, Thomas Redman. Proved July 18, 1789.
1789, July 6. Inventory, £518.8.11, made by Thomas Hollinshead and John Roberts. Lib. 31, p. 279.

**1786, March 6. Hinds, John,** of Philadelphia. Adm'r—John Esdale, of City of Burlington. Fellowbondsmen—John Lee and James Mason; both of Mount Holly, Burlington Co. Whereas John Hinds, of Philadelphia, made his will, dated March 11, 1775, wherein he appointed his wife, Mary Hinds, as his Executrix, and she hath lately departed this State, and gone beyond the sea, and the estate of said John Hinds stands in need of care; therefore the said James Esdale is made Adm'r, with will annexed. Lib. 28, p. 77.

**1780, May 2. Hinds, Richard,** of Amwell Township, Hunterdon Co.; will of. Son, Richard, £20, if he lives longer than his mother. Youngest son, Joseph, £5. Daughter, Mary, wife of Joshua Stout, £5. To the heirs of my daughter, Rebeckah, deceased, £5. Daughter, Elizabeth, £100. Son, James, rest of estate. Executor—son, James. Witnesses—Samuel Paddon, John Mounteer, David Parker. Proved Aug. 6, 1789.
1789, July 4. Inventory, £188.10.6, made by Thomas Holcomb and Joshua Laing.

CALENDAR OF WILLS—1786-1790    113

1789, May 7. Citation to Margaret Hinds, widow of Richard Hinds, deceased, and Joseph Hinds, son of said Richard, and Elizabeth Hinds, daughter of said Richard, to appear in Court, as the proving of the will is opposed by Joshua Stout and Mary, his wife, daughter of said Richard.   Lib. 32, p. 29.

**1787, March 15.  Hiner, Christopher,** of Alexandria Township, Hunterdon Co.; will of. Wife, Susanna, a bed, and rest of estate to be sold, and money divided among my wife and children, Margaret Hiner, Harbert, William, John, Charity Hiner, Mary Hiner and Catherine Hiner. Each child to have its share when of age. Executors— friends, John Hiner and William Smith. Witnesses—Henry Gulick, Peter Haughawout, William Mettler. Proved March 27, 1787.

1787, March 27. Inventory, £321.19.11, made by Henry Gulick and John Tomson.

1805, Nov. 13. Account by Executors.   Lib. 29, p. 273.

**1790, Feb. 15. Hoff, Gabriel,** of Kingwood, Hunterdon Co. Int. Adm'rs—Mary Hoff, John Leigh and Absalom Runyan. Fellowbondsman—Hezekiah Waterhouse; all of said place.

1790, Feb. 4. Inventory, £334.9.7, made by Richard Opdyke and Hezekiah Waterhouse.

1813, Feb. 1. Account by Mary Hoff and John Leigh, surviving Adm'rs.   Lib. 30, p. 313.

**1789, Jan. 2. Hoff, Jacob,** of Kingwood Township, Hunterdon Co. Int. Adm'rs—Thomas Hoff and Isaac Hoff. Fellowbondsman— Cornelius Hoff; all of said Co.

1789, Jan. 1. Renunciation by Lydia Hoff, widow of Jacob.

1788, Dec. 23. Inventory, £468.8.8, made by Richard Opdycke and Gabriel Hoff.

1789, Nov. 28. Account by Adm'rs. "Wearing apparel to be divided among the children, £17.8.0."   Lib. 32, p. 55.

**1790, Sept. 4. Hoff, John,** of Independance Township, Sussex Co. Int. Adm'rs—Elizabeth Hoff, widow, and Joseph Hoff, Jr. Fellowbondsman—Montgomery Reading; all of said place. Witness—John Ware.

1790, Sept. 2. Inventory, £161.2.0, made by John Ware and Abraham Johnson.   Lib. 30, p. 439.

**1789, Jan. 16. Hoff, Lydia, Ann and John,** of Hunterdon Co. Wards. Children of Jacob Hoff, of said Co., deceased. Their mother, Lydia Hoff, prays to be appointed their Guardian. Petition signed at Alexandria.

1789, Feb. 5. Guardian—Lydia Hoff. Fellowbondsman—Thomas Hoff; both of Kingwood, said Co. Witnesses—Joseph Sherrerd and William Lowrey.   Lib. 32, p. 57.

**1787, Jan. 17. Hogland [Hoagland], Abraham,** of Middlesex Co. Int. Adm'rs—Mary Hogland and Peter Probasco. Fellowbondsman— John Longstaff; all of said Co.

1787, Inventory, made by John Arnold and John Longstaff.
   Lib. 29, p. 364.

**1786, Sept. 2. Holeman, Robert,** of Windsor, Middlesex Co. Int. Adm'r—Joseph Holeman. Fellowbondsman—Jacob Holeman; both of said Co.
1786, Sept. 2. Renunciation by Elizabeth Holeman, widow of Robert, in favor of her brother-in-law, Joseph Holeman.
1786, July 25. Inventory, £525, made by Isaac Perine and Thomas Dye. Lib. 28, p. 340.

**1790, June 2. Holeman, Robert,** of Middlesex Co. Int. Adm'x—Margret Holeman. Fellowbondsman—Jacob Holeman; both of said Co.
1790, May 24. Inventory, made by Jacob Jemson and Isaac Bilyew. Lib. 30, p. 535.

**1788, July 28. Hollfday, John,** of Finns Point, Lower Penns Neck, Salem Co., yeoman; will of. Daughter, Sarah, £100. Daughter, Rebecca, £100, when 18. Son, John, £400, when 21. Wife, Catharine, £150. To the child yet unborn, £100. The place where I live to be for the support of my children, who are young. Sister, Sarah Connor, £5, and to James Smith, £4. Brother, James, £5, and to his sons, John, William and Joseph, £12. Executors—wife, Catharine, and William Bilderback. Witnesses—Richard Brown, Isaac Fowler, Jesse Newark. Proved Aug. 24, 1788. Lib. 31, p. 43.

**1786, April 13. Hollinshead, Hugh,** of Chester Township, Burlington Co. Int. Adm'rs—Eleanor Hollinshead and Jacob Hollinshead. Fellowbondsman—Charles French; all of said Co. Witness—Thomas Adams, Surrogate.
1786, April 6. Inventory, £623.4.7, made by Thomas Hollinshead and Moses Wills. Lib. 28, p. 80.

**1788, Aug. 1. Hollinshead, John,** of Chester, Burlington Co., son of Edmund. Int. Adm'x—Alice Hollinshead. Fellowbondsman—John Risdon; both of said Co.
1788, July 9. Inventory, £369.0.1, made by Jacob Hollinshead and Edmund Hollinshead. Lib. 30, p. 58.

**1788, Oct. 29. Holloway, Joseph,** of Chesterfield, Burlington Co. Int. Adm'x—Isabella Holloway. Fellowbondsman—James Esdale; both of said Co.
1788, Nov. 1. Inventory, £186.11.2, made by Nathan Middleton and Joseph Brown. Lib. 30, p. 60.

**1786, March 19. Holme, Esther,** of Waterford, Gloucester Co.; will of. To Haddonfield Monthly Meeting, £12. Daughter, Phoebe Bate, apparel. Granddaughter, Sarah Rate, my bed and Bible; and her sister, Sibillah Bate, 20 shillings, and sister, Esther Bate, 15 shillings. Granddaughter, Esther Lanning, formerly Camble, my warming pan. Grandson, Thomas Bate, my slave; and his brother, Japhet Bate, 20 shillings. Executor—friend, John Gill. Witnesses—Jacob Horner, John Gruffyth. Proved June 16, 1788. Lib. 31, p. 18.

**1788, March 26. Holme, Mary,** of Haddonfield, Gloucester Co., widow; will of. Daughter, Kezia Cox, silver spoons. Daughter, Hannah Royl, silver buckles. Son, Samuel, my Bible. Such part of my goods as will be convenient to my said daughters, they living

CALENDAR OF WILLS—1786-1790   115

near Bedford, Penna. Executors—son, Samuel, and friend, Thomas Redman. Witnesses—John Parkam, Rebecah Hartley. Proved April 30, 1788.   Lib. 31, p. 16.

**1786, May 3. Holmes, John,** of Newton Township, Gloucester Co. Int. Adm'x—Mary Holmes, widow of said John, of said place. Fellowbondsman—Benjamin Cozens, of Waterford Township, said Co., yeoman.
1786, April 29. Inventory, £100.2.0, made by Samuel Eastlack and Joseph Hillman.   Lib. 28, p. 121.

**1786, Jan. 27. Holmes, Jonathan,** of Freehold, Monmouth Co. Int. Adm'r—John Van Der Veer. Fellowbondsman—Asher Holmes; both of said Co. Witness—Samuel Forman.
1796, July 27. Adm'r—John Stoutenborough. Fellowbondsmen—Stephen Van Brakel and Peter Johnston; all of said Co. The said Jonathan Holmes was son of Daniel.
1797, Dec. 19. Inventory, of goods left unadministered by the late Adm'r, John Vanderver, deceased.
   Lib. 28, p. 292; Lib. 35, p. 384.

**1786, April 8. Holmes, Jonathan,** of Cumberland Co. Int. Adm'x—Rachel Holmes. Fellowbondsman—Thomas Brown; both of said Co. Witness—Ame Brewster.
1786, April 8. Inventory, £292.17.9, made by Jonathan Bowen and Thomas Brown.   Lib. 28, p. 181.

**1789, Feb. 8. Holmes, Rachel,** of Cumberland Co. Int. Adm'r—Ebenezer Elmer. Fellowbondsman—Thomas Brown; both of said Co.
   Lib. 30, p. 164.

**1786, Jan. 27. Holmes, William,** of Freehold, Monmouth Co. Int. Adm'r—John Van Der Veer. Fellowbondsman—Asher Holmes. Witness—Samuel Forman.
1796, July 27. Adm'r—John Stoutenborough. Fellowbondsmen—Stephen Van Brakel and Peter Johnston; all of said Co. Witness—Caleb Lloyd. He is Adm'r of what is left by former Adm'r, John Vanderveer.   Lib. 28, p. 291; Lib. 35, p. 384.

**1787, Jan. 30. Holton, John,** of Woolwich Township, Gloucester Co.; will of. Daughter, Deborough Holton, my silver buckles and spoons, when she is 18. Rest of goods to be sold and money divided between my 3 sons, Andrew, William and James, as they come of age. Executor—friend, Andrew Matson. Witnesses—Jacob Archer, Jr., John Kerns, James Russel. Proved Feb. 13, 1788.
1787, Feb. 24. Inventory, £41.10.0, made by James Russel and Jacob Archer.   Lib. 31, p. 27.

**1787, Feb. 13. Homan, William,** of Woolwich Township, Gloucester Co., yeoman; will of. Sons, William and Vanderver Homan, all my lands and live stock. Daughter, Precillah, the wife of Peter Lock, £100. Executors—sons, William and Vanderver. Witnesses—Thomas Denny, Ebenezer Adams, John Lock. Proved May 9, 1787.
1787, May 8. Inventory, £648.5.7, made by Daniel Sutherland and Ebenezer Adams.   Lib. 29, p. 91.

**1788, Feb. 19. Hommer, Adam,** of Lebanon, Hunterdon Co. Int. Adm'rs—Elizabeth Hommer and Harbert Hommer. Fellowbondsmen— Peter Young and George Gearhart; all of said Co. Witness—Moore Furman.
1788, Jan. 24. Inventory, £318.19.1, made by Tunis Tunison and George Gearhart.
1797, Feb. 8. Account by Elizabeth Hummer and Herbert Hummer, Sr.; Adm'rs. "Paid Herbert Hummer, Jr., £0.10.0."
Lib. 31, p. 142.

**1790, Feb. 9. Hood, William,** of Salem Co.; will of. To be buried in the Churchyard in Salem, and to have a headstone. Son, William, all real and personal estate; but the interest to be paid to Sawrah Cookes till he is 21; but, if he dies, then she is to have all estate. My younger brother, James Hood, living in County of Tayrone, in Parish of Ardstaw, in north of Ireland, my watch. Executors— friends, Edward Forest and Robert Humes. Witnesses—Luke Kine, Peter Downey. Proved Sept. 20, 1790.
Lib. 40, p. 527.

**1790, Jan. 5. Hooper, Margaret,** of Hunterdon Co. Int. Adm'r— Robert L. Hooper. Fellowbondsman—Samuel W. Stockton; of Trenton, said Co.
Lib. 30, p. 318.

**1786, June 17. Hopkins, Drial, and Hester,** of Knowlton, Sussex Co. Wards. Son and daughter of Nathan Hopkins, and his wife, Hannah Hopkins, now Hannah Baker, and grandchildren of Jonathan Hopkins, of Knowlton.
1786, June 17. Guardians—William Hopkins, of Roxbury, Morris Co., and Joshua Swayze, of Oxford, Sussex Co. Fellowbondsmen— Caleb Swayze, of Oxford, and William Armstrong, of Hardwick.
Lib. 28, p. 471.

**1788, Dec. 12. Hopper, Charity,** of Bergen Co. Ward. Daughter of John Hopper and Altye Hopper, of said Co., deceased. Said Ward makes choice of her brother, John I. Hopper, as her Guardian.
1788, Dec. 12. Guardian—John I. Hopper. Fellowbondsman—Gerret Hopper; both of said Co. Witness—Anne Westervelt.
Lib. 31, p. 257.
**1788, March 20. Hopper, John,** of Bergen Co. Int. Adm'r—John J. Hopper. Fellowbondsman—Gerret Hopper; both of said Co.
Lib. 31, p. 257.

**1787, Sept. 3. Horn, John,** of Amwell, Hunterdon Co. Int. Adm'r— Thomas Horn. Fellowbondsman—Abner Hixson; both of said Co. Witness—Daniel Willson.
1787, Aug. 17. Inventory, £85.11.3, made by William Hoogland and Daniel Willson.
1790, Feb. 9. Account by Adm'r.
Lib. 29, p. 296.

**1786, Oct. 23. Horner, Content,** of Monmouth Co. Int. Adm'x— Mary Guisbertson. Fellowbondsman—Richard Francis; both of said Co. Witness—Bartholomew Apelgate.
1786, Oct. 14. Renunciation by Hugh Horner, son of Content. Witnesses—George Cook and Richard Francis.
1786, Oct. 14. Renunciation by Sarah Horner, widow of said Content.

## CALENDAR OF WILLS—1786-1790

1786, Oct. 14. Inventory, £31.4.10, made by Richard Francis and George Cook. Lib. 28, p. 292.

**1790, June 1. Hornner, William,** of Kingwood Township, Hunterdon Co. Int. Adm'r—William Hornner. Fellowbondsman—John Gardner; both of said place.
1790, June 8. Inventory, £114, made by John Gardner and William McClean.
1791, Sept. 29. Account by Adm'r. Lib. 30, p. 313.

**1789, Aug. 20. Hornor, Joshua,** of Upper Freehold, Monmouth Co.; will of. Wife, ⅓ of moveable estate. Son, Benjamin, £3. Son, Job, a cow. Son, James, 12 acres where he lives. Son, Fuller, and my son, Joshua, rest of estate. Executor—son, Fuller. Witnesses—William Hornor, Samuel Johnson, Zebedee Collins. Proved Oct. 7, 1789.
1789, Oct. 5. Inventory, £145.11.3, made by Benjamin Hornor and John Harker. Lib. 30, p. 166.

**1788, Sept. 23. Horseman, Jeremiah,** of Knowlton, Sussex Co. Int. Adm'r—John Hartman. Fellowbondsman—Abraham Swisher; both of said place.
1788, Sept. 23. Inventory, £23.8.6, made by Abraham Bescherer and Abraham Swisher. Lib. 31, p. 156.

**1790, Aug. 12. Hosher, Robert,** of Trenton, Hunterdon Co. Int. Adm'r—William Hosher. Fellowbondswoman—Jane Hosher; both of said place. Lib. 30, p. 316.

**1788, April 9. Houston, William C.,** of Trenton, Hunterdon Co.; will of. Wife to have £250. If my wife bring up my children she may have such articles as are needful. Son, George, £50. Son, Churchill, my library. My 5 children to have my personal estate, not given herein. Real estate to be sold. Executors—Isaac Collins, James Mott and Maskell Ewing, the younger; my true friends. They are to be Guardians of my children. Witnesses—Benjamin Smith, John Singer, Job Moore. Proved Aug. 22, 1788.
1794, Jan. 4. Renunciation by James Mott, who was appointed in the will of William Churchill Houston, as one of his Executors.
1788, Sept. 13. Inventory, £355.0.5, made by James Ewing and Benjamin Vancleve.
1794, June 3. Account by Maskell Ewing, one of the Executors. "Cash paid James Ewing, Treasurer of the Trenton Academy, for wood for George Houston, £0.3.9. Cash paid Thomas Hunt, for George S. Houston, £0.6.6." Lib. 31, p. 112.

**1787, June 22. How, Samuel,** of Burlington, Burlington Co. Ward. Son of Samuel How, Esq., of said place, deceased. Said Ward, having real and personal estate, makes choice of Daniel Ellis as his Guardian.
1787, June 22. Guardian—Daniel Ellis. Fellowbondsman—Robert P. Jones; both of said City. Witness—Thomas Adams.
Lib. 29, p. 80.

**1789, Dec. 21. Howard, Sheffield,** of Essex Co. Int. Adm'x—Anne Bingham, wife of Charles Bingham. Fellowbondsman—Elias Boudinot, of Newark, said Co. Witness—W. Griffith. Lib. 30, p. 219.

**1790, May 25. Howell, Daniel,** of Amwell, Hunterdon Co. Int. Adm'r—Reading Howell, of Philadelphia. Fellowbondsman—Uriah Bonham, of Kingwood, said Co.
1790, May 25. Inventory, £236.14.9, made by Uriah Bonham and William Rettinghous.
1791, Dec. 5. Account by Adm'r. "Paid A. Williamson for going to Philadelphia, respecting Daniel Howell, son of Joseph, and on business of that estate, £0.15.0." Lib. 30, p. 317.

**1787, April 2. Howell, Israel,** of Kingwood Township, Hunterdon Co.; will of. Wife, Susannah, all my lands in this Township; that is to say, my tavern and lots; also the moveable estate. Daughter, Mary Howell, £600, when she is 18. Brother, Absolom, my watch. Executors—wife, Susannah, and my brother-in-law, Benjamin Fleming. Witnesses—Aaron Forman, John Brown, Henry Cleffton. Proved April 21, 1787.
1787, April 9. Inventory, £1,377.16.3, made by Samuel McFarson and Aaron Forman. Lib. 29, p. 265.

**1787, Dec. 22. Howell, Rednap,** of Hunterdon Co. Int. Adm'r—John Woolverton. Fellowbondsman—Samuel Green; both of said Co. Witness—Richard Throckmorton.
1787, Dec. 21. Inventory, £7.17.9, made by Samuel Green and John Melrose. Lib. 29, p. 294.

**1786, Nov. 27. Hoy, Michael,** of Somerset Co.; will of. John Brown, and Catharine, his wife, use of house and lot near Queens Town, for their kindness to me; and, after their deaths, to their children, William and Mary Brown. Executors—friends, John and Joseph Schenck, sons of John. Witnesses—Arthur Keefe, John Totten, Lucretia Keefe, Anna Keefe. Proved April 1, 1787.
1787, April 7. Inventory, £31.19.11, made by Jacob G. Bergen and Joseph Olden. Lib. 29, p. 424.

**1787, March 8. Huddy, Catharine,** of Monmouth Co. Int. Adm'r—Jacob Hart. Fellowbondsman—Hendrick Vanderveer; both of said Co. Witness—Peter Holsart.
1787, March 3. Inventory, £238.3.10, made by Peter Holsart and Joseph Throckmorton. Lib. 29, p. 340.

**1789, Sept. 25. Hudson, Isaac and Joseph,** of Cumberland Co. Wards. Children of Obed Hudson, of said Co., deceased. Providence Ludlam, kin of said infants, requests that Guardians may be appointed.
1789, Sept. 25. Guardians—David Sheppard and John Sheppard, Jr. Fellowbondsman—Providence Ludlam; of Greenwich Township, said Co. Witnesses—Sally Watson and Rachel Ludlam. Lib. 30, p. 163.

**1787, Aug. 30. Hudson, Obed,** of Greenwich, Cumberland Co., yeoman; will of. Wife, Phebe, use of real and personal estate while she lives, in order to bring up my sons, Isaac and Joseph till they are 14. Eldest daughter, Sally, £15. Daughter, Anna, £75. To

CALENDAR OF WILLS—1786-1790    119

Richard Miller, son of my present wife, £10. To Sally Miller, her daughter, £5. Sons, Isaac and Joseph, rest of real and personal estate, after death of my wife. Executors—wife, Phebe, and my friends, Job Butcher, John Miller and Job Tyler. Witnesses—Isaac Sparks, Isaac Hawthorn. Proved Nov. 18, 1787.
 1787, Nov. 15. Inventory, £806.17.0, made by John Miller and Job Butcher.  Lib. 29, p. 178.

**1789, May 12. Hudson, William,** of Middlesex Co. Int. Adm'r—Ford Cutter. Fellowbondsman—Thomas Goodfellow; both of Piscataway, said Co.  Lib. 31, p. 393.

**1789, March 7. Huet, Azariah,** of Cape May Co. Ward. Son of Azariah Huet, of said Co., deceased. Said Ward is under the age of 14.
 1789, March 7. Guardian—Philip Hand. Fellowbondsman—Jonathan Leaming; both of said Co. Witnesses—James Smith and Archibald Stewert.  Lib. 31, p. 372.

**1789, March 7. Huet, Humphrey,** of Cape May Co. Ward. Son of Azariah Huet, of said Co., deceased. Said Ward is under the age of 14.
 1789, March 7. Guardian—Philip Hand. Fellowbondsman—Jonathan Leaming; both of said Co. Witnesses—James Smith and Archibald Stewert.  Lib. 31, p. 372.

**1788, April 15. Hughes, James,** of Great Egg Harbor Township, Gloucester Co.; will of. To my 3 daughters, a cow and calf to each. Wife to have rest of estate to bring up my children. Sons, James and Robard, my lands. Witnesses—Timothy Brandriff, Reuben Ireland, Elizabeth Brandroff. Proved Feb. 18, 1789.
 1789, Feb. 18. Adm'x—Ruth Hughes. Fellowbondsmen—Reuben Ireland and Richard Westcott; all of Gloucester Co. James Hughes in his will did not appoint any Executors.  Lib. 30, p. 106.

**1790, May 26. Hughes, Jedediah,** of Cape May Co. Int. Adm'r—John Hughes. Fellowbondsman—Thomas Shaw; both of said Co. Witnesses—Persons Leaming and Eli Eldredge.
 1790, June 14. Inventory, £283.16.5, made by Thomas Shaw and Eli Eldredge.  Lib. 32, p. 105.

**1787, Nov. 20. Hughes, Mary Magdelane,** of Mount Holly, Burlington Co.; will of. Daughter, Martha Hughes, to have two lower rooms of the new building, joining to this house, and, after her death, the same shall become the property of my son, Charles John Hughes; and also the house I live in. Daughter, Martha, various silver articles. Daughter. Elizabeth Hugg, interest of some money. Son, Samuel Hughes, silver spoons. Grandchildren, Samuel and Mary Magdalene Bonnel, a large silver spoon to each, which I brought with me from Europe. Daughter, Elizabeth Hugg, my apparel. To my daughter, Martha, my daughter, Elizabeth, and her step-daughter, Sarah Hugg, apparel. Executor—son, John Charles Hughes. Witnesses—Samuel Spraggs, Mary Spraggs, Sarah Farquar. Proved Jan. 5, 1788.
 1788, Jan. 10. Inventory, £81.12.9, made by Moses Kempton and Zach. Rossell.  Lib. 30, p. 18.

**1788, June 20. Hughes, William,** of Gloucester Co. Ward. Son of John Hughes, of said Co., deceased. Said Ward makes choice of Jacob Middleton as his Guardian.
1788, June 20. Guardian—Jacob Middleton. Fellowbondsman—Isaac Flaningam; both of said Co. Lib. 31, p. 38.

**1788, July 19. Huie, Robert,** of Mendham Township, Morris Co.; will of. Wife, Pierses, all goods, horse and cow. Rest of personal and real estate to be sold, and money lodged in the hands of my Executors, and of the interest my wife is to have a support, and after her death, the money to be divided among my son, James, my daughter, Elizabeth, wife of David Kanine, and my daughter, Jane, wife of Amos Day. Executors—friends, David Thompson and Nehemiah Day. Witnesses—Sarah Huie, James McVicker, John McCarter. Proved Sept. 23, 1788.
1788, Sept. 24. Inventory, £49.16.6, made by James McVicker and Daniel Babbit. Lib. 31, p. 187.

**1790, April. Hulit, Daniel and Michael,** of Freehold, Monmouth Co. Wards. Son of Daniel Hulit, of said Co. Thomas Hulit prays to be made Guardian of said minors until they are 14.
1790, May 15. Guardian—Thomas Hulit. Fellowbondsman—Samuel Forman; both of Shrewsbury, said Co. Lib. 30, p. 420.

**1790, March 30. Hull, Benjamin,** of Southward of New Brunswick, Middlesex Co. Int. Adm'r—James Hull. Fellowbondsman—Hopewell Hull; both of said Co.
1788, Nov. 22. Inventory, £103.19.3, made by Jonathan Combs and James Perine. Lib. 30, p. 534.

**1786, Sept. 28. Hummer, Cort,** of Amwell, Hunterdon Co. Int. Adm'rs—Mary Hummer and Phillip Yawger. Fellowbondsman—Francis Persong; all of said place.
1786, Sept. 14. Inventory, £314.10.4, made by George Trimmer and Francis Persong.
1792, Oct. 25. Account by Mary Hummer and Philip Yawger.
Lib. 28, p. 245.

**1786, April 9. Hummer, Jacob,** of Lebanon Township, Hunterdon Co., yeoman; will of. After 2 years the personal and real estate to be sold, and money divided among my children, Jacob, Ann, Elizabeth, Mary, Margrit and Sara. Executors—son-in-law, John Low, and my brother, Herbert Hummer. Witnesses—Abraham Couwenhoven, Philip Grandin, Cornelius Low. Proved Sept. 27, 1788.
1788, Sept. 24. Inventory, £127.14.0, made by George Gearhart and Peter Young. "An old Psalm book and Bible in the Dutch language."
1793, May 9. Account by both Executors. "Paid for board of Jacob Hummer, son of Testator, £8."
1803, Aug. 4. Account by John Low, surviving Executor. "Cash retained by me in full of my wife's share, £107.3.0. To George and Elizabeth Pickle, for their share, £107.3.0. To Peter and Mary Huffman, for her share, £107.3.0. To Mathias Gearhart and Margaret, his wife, for her share, £107.3.0. To Isaac and Sarah Loder, for her share, £107.3.0. To Jacob Hummer, as his share, £214.5.0."
Lib. 31, p. 108.

**1788, March 17. Humphreys, Stephen,** of Hopewell Township, Hunterdon Co. Int. Adm'r—Peter Gordon. Fellowbondsman—John P. Hunt; both of said place.
1788, March 14. Renunciation by Sarah Humphreys, widow. Witness—Andrew Smith.
1788, March 14. Renunciation by John Humphreys, Nancy Humphreys and Mary Humphreys, children of said Stephen Humphreys, in favor of Peter Gordon. Witness—Andrew Smith.
1788, March 14. Inventory, £785.11.11, made by John P. Hunt and Andrew Smith.
1789, June 15. Account by Adm'r. Lib. 31, p. 142.

**1786, March 10. Hunt, Edward,** of Greenwich, Sussex Co., Esquire; will of. Wife, Mary, £40 per annum during her life. Daughters, Ann, Rebecca, Catura, Amelia and Hannah, rest of personal estate. Sons, Edward, William and John, plantation where I live, when 21. Daughters, Amelia and Hannah, £20 each. To Edward Vann a horse and saddle, if he lives with my sons until he is 21. The part given to daughter, Rebecca, is for her life; after which, it is to go to her children, Eleanor, Thomas, Ann, William and Edward. Executors—son, Edward, and friends, Aaron Yeomans and Benjamin McCullough. Witnesses—Richard Bennet, Peter Sharps, John Daniel Jaquet.
1786, March 10. Codicil. Two-thirds of the rents of my real estate to be divided between my 5 daughters, until son, William, is 21. Enough money is to be used to school my sons, William and John, and my grandsons, Edward Vann and Thomas Sprowl. Witnesses—same as above. Proved April 11, 1786.
1786, March 30. Inventory, made by David Johnston and Mark Thomson. Lib. 28, p. 429.

**1787, Oct. 15. Hunt, John,** of Stow Creek Township, Cumberland Co. Int. Adm'rs—Anne Hunt and John Peck. Fellowbondsman—Samuel Brewster; all of said Co. Witnesses—Hezekiah Bonham and Esther Hunt.
1787, Oct. 29. Inventory, £222.12.1, made by David Ayars and John More. Lib. 31, p. 76.

**1786, Jan. 7. Hunt, Samuel,** of Burlington Co. Int. Adm'r—Robert Pearson, Jr. Fellowbondsman—John Lawrence; both of City of Burlington. Witness—Thomas Adams. Lib. 28, p. 79.

**1789, Nov. 13. Hunt, Thomas,** of Amwell Township, Hunterdon Co.; will of. Advanced in years. Grandson, Henry Reading, son of my daughter, Abigail, 160 acres of land, being part of my homestead, and butted as in the 3 deeds by which I purchased; one I bought of Thomas and Richard Penn, of 67 acres; one of John Reading, of 49 acres, and one of George Green, of 50 acres; when he is 21. The rest of my homestead, of 200 acres, to be sold. But ¼ of an acre to be reserved for a burying-ground, and it is to have a good stone fence. Grandson, Edward Hunt, for his birthright, 20 shillings. Money to the children of my daughter, Abigail, except Henry Reading, who is not to have any part. Son, Samuel, my daughter, Abigail Reading, and all my grandchildren now alive, except children of my son, Samuel, but his eldest daughter by his first wife; also Elizabeth and Mary, the daughters of Mary Robins; also Mary, daughter of my son, Edward, deceased; also Jane, daughter of my son, John, deceased; also Mary Lowrey, John Lee, Thomas Lee, Joseph Lee, Levi Lee, Gershom Lee, Nathan Lee, Rebecca Rowze and Hannah, being children of my daughter, Rebecca Lee, which excepted persons are not to have any part of the residue. Grandson, Edward Hunt, is to pay to his sister, Parmela, £15. Executors—son-in-law, Charles Reading, and neighbors, Samuel Hill and Francis Berson. Witnesses—George Trout, John Buchannan, Paul Kuhl. Proved March 12, 1790. Probate to Charles Reading, Samuel Hill and Francis Berson.

1700, March 10. Inventory, £2,802.16.1, made by Thomas Reading and Paul Kuhl.

1793, May 8. Account by all Executors. Wearing apparel delivered to Samuel Hunt, by consent of legatees, £4.15.0. Lib. 30, p. 298.

**1790, Jan. 7. Hussey, Johannes,** of Deptford, Gloucester Co.; will of. Eldest son, John Michael Hussey, 5 shillings. Eldest daughter, Eve Cathrine Hussey, 5 shillings. Daughters, Christeen and Hannah Hussey, a bed for each when married. Wife, Urcilla, plantation where I live, of 300 acres, during her life, and after to my youngest sons, Samuel and John. Daughters, Susanah, Cathrine, Elizabeth and Hannah Hussey, the goods, after death of wife. Executors—friends, Samuel Hazlitt and William Dilkes. Witnesses—Walter Swoop, John Ware, Edward Collins. Proved June 15, 1790.

1790, June 14. Renunciation by Samuel Hazlitt.

1790, June 10. Inventory, £160.10.8, made by Enoch Sharp and Isaac Flaningam. Lib. 31, p. 436.

**1789, Jan. 6. Husted, Abigail, Joseph N., Mirabeth and William,** of Cumberland Co. Wards. Children of Moses Husted, of said Co., deceased. Petition of Moses Husted, brother and next of kin of William Husted, Joseph Newcomb Husted and Mirabeth Husted, infants under 14, praying that a Guardian may be appointed for said infants.

1789, Jan. 6. Guardian—Bayse Newcomb. Fellowbondsman—Isaac Brown; both of said Co. Lib. 30, p. 163.

**1786, March 29. Husted, Jeremiah,** of Cumberland Co. Int. Adm'x —Mary Husted. Fellowbondsman—John Bateman; both of said Co.

1786, March 27. Inventory, £89.1.11, made by Hampton Moore and John Bateman. Lib. 28, p. 181.

**1788, Feb. 23. Husted, Moses,** of Fairfield, Cumberland Co.; will of. Wife, Content, my lands, while my widow. Sons, Moses, William and Joseph, my lands. Daughter, Elizabeth, 5 shillings. Daughters, Ruth, Rachel, Anne, Abigil and Moraby, moveable estate. Sons are to have a marsh at Eagel Island, when they are of age. Executrix—wife, Content. Witnesses—John Powell, Bayse Newcomb. Proved April 25, 1788.

1788, March 27. Inventory, £227.4.0, made by Jeremiah Nixon and Reuben Powell. Lib. 31, p. 64.

**1788, Feb. 26. Hutchin, Ann,** of Monmouth Co. Ward. Daughter of Hugh Hutchin, of said Co., deceased. Said Ward having real and personal estate, makes choice of Nathan Robins as her Guardian.

1788, Feb. 26. Guardian—Nathan Robbins, of Mansfield Township. Fellowbondsman—Levi Nutt; both of Burlington Co. Witness—Thomas Adams. Lib. 30, p. 61.

CALENDAR OF WILLS—1786-1790      123

**1789, Feb. 14. Hutchins, Thomas,** of Piscataway, Middlesex Co.; will of. Brother, John Hutchins, my apparel. Sisters, Anna French and Mary Harris, goods. Executors—brother, John, and my friend, James Voorhees. Witnesses—Benjamin Wilson, John Linberger, John Runyon. Proved April 8, 1789.
1789, April 6. Inventory, made by John Ross and William Degroot.   Lib. 31, p. 378.

**1790, July 10. Hyer, Jacob,** of Middlesex Co. Int. Adm'r—William Hyer. Fellowbondsman—Elizabeth Hyer; both of said Co. Witness—Catharine Hyer.   Lib. 30, p. 535.

**1789, Jan. 22. Ilor, Catherine,** of Pilesgrove Township, Salem Co., widow; will of. Daughter, Hannah Ilor, my bed. Granddaughter, Mary Dickeson, the bed that her mother now has, when she is 18. Children, Henry Ilor, Elizabeth Smith, Cathrine Dickeson, Hannah Ilor, George Ilor and Jacob Ilor, rest of estate. Executor—friend, William Wallace. Witnesses—Enoch Ballinger, John Peak, Joseph Stonebanks. Proved March 18, 1789.
1789, Jan. 26. Inventory, £194.14.3, made by Isaiah Shinn and Joseph Stonebanks.   Lib. 40, p. 529.

**1787, Oct. 15. Inglish, Nathaniel,** of Greenwich Township, Gloucester Co. Int. Adm'r—Charles Thompson. Fellowbondsman—Daniel Sutherland; both of said place. Witness—Kezia Albertson.
Lib. 29, p. 116.

**1788, Dec. 9. Inskeep, Benjamin,** of Waterford Township, Gloucester Co. Int. Adm'x—Hannah Inskeep. Fellowbondsman—Parr Willard; both of said Co.
1788, Nov. 27. Inventory, £158.11.0, made by William Cox and Thomas Stokes.   Lib. 31, p. 37.

**1790, March 16. Inskeep, Isaac,** of Deptford Township, Gloucester Co. Int. Adm'rs—Samuel Inskeep and George Sparks. Fellowbondsman—Peter Crim; all of said Co. Witness—Franklin Davenport.
1790, March 20. Inventory, £769.11.9, made by James Wilkins and John Stephens.   Lib. 31, p. 478.

**1789, Nov. 4. Ivins, Barzillai, Thomas, Elizabeth, Mary, Margaret and Ann,** of Burlington Co. Wards. Children of Isaac Ivins, of said Co. Said Isaac Ivins prays that he may be appointed Guardian of said children, until they are 14 years of age.
1789, Nov. 4. Guardian—said Isaac Ivins. Fellowbondsman—John Thorn; both of Chesterfield Township, said Co.   Lib. 31, p. 323.

**1786, Aug. 11. Ivins, Isaac,** of Chesterfield, Burlington Co.; will of. Wife, Ann, £40 and all she brought with her. Grandson, Samuel Ivins, plantation where I live. Granddaughters, Mary and Sarah Ivins, daughters of my son, Samuel Ivins, deceased, £200. Grandson, Job Davis, £400, when 21. Grandson, Jonathan Davis, plantation I bought of Richard Kirby. Grandchildren, William, Abigal and Ivins Davis, £450, to be paid them by their brother, Jonathan. Son, Aaron, plantation I bought of William Kirby, in Hanover, he paying to my granddaughters, Mary, Meribah and Hannah Davis, £600. Daughter, Mary Davis, £10, yearly for 10 years. Son-in-law, John Robbins, plantation I bought of Robert Hutchenson, in Monmouth Co., and he is to pay to my granddaughter, Hannah Ivins, daughter of my son, Barzillai, £200. Granddaughter, Ann Davis, £200. Son, Isaac, house and lot I bought of Benjamin Bunting, lying near Burdentown, called the Red House; also a meadow I bought of Robert Hutchenson, in Monmouth Co., joining to Isaac Antrim and my son, Isaac. Grandson, Isaac Davis, £50. Rest of money to my children and grandchildren and my son's (Barzillai's) widow, Margaret Ivins. Executor, son, Aaron. Witnesses—Joseph Wildes, John Platt, John Earl. Proved Aug. 28, 1786.

1800, April 28. Adm'rs—Aaron Ivins and Isaac Ivins, Jr., both of Burlington Co. Fellowbondsmen—Isaac Ivins, Sr., of Gloucester Co., and Joel Middleton, of Burlington Co. Witness—Charles Kinsey. "Whereas Isaac Ivins made will and appointed Aaron Ivins as his Executor, and he also died."

1786, Aug. 19. Inventory, £4,345.15.9, made by Richard Potts and Isaac Bullock. Lib. 28, p. 27; Lib. 39, p. 73.

**1787, Feb. 27. Ivins, Samuel,** of Burlington Co. Ward. Son of Samuel Ivins, of said Co., deceased. Said Ward having real and personal estate, makes choice of John Platt as his Guardian.

1787, Feb. 27. Guardian—John Platt. Fellowbondsman—Gervas Pharo; both of said Co. Lib. 29, p. 80.

**1786, Dec. 18. Ivins, Sarah,** of Burlington Co. Ward. Daughter of Solomon Ivins, of said Co., deceased. Said Ward, having real and personal estate, makes choice of Daniel Hancock as her Guardian.

1786, Dec. 18. Guardian—Daniel Hancock. Fellowbondsman—Daniel Ellis; both of said Co. Witness—Thomas Adams. Lib. 28, p. 82.

**1786, April 4. Jaques, Nathan,** of Middlesex Co. Int. Adm'r—Jonathan Jaques. Fellowbondsman—Samuel Jaques; both of Woodbridge, said Co.

1786, April 6. Inventory, made by John Thorp and Samuel Jaques. Lib. 28, p. 341.

**1788, April 11. Jarman, Eleanor,** of Cumberland Co. Ward. Daughter of Beriah Jarman, of said Co., deceased. Said Ward, having real and personal estate, makes choice of Jonathan Jarman as her Guardian.

1788, April 29. Guardian—Jonathan Jarman. Fellowbondsman—John Burgin; both of said Co. Lib. 30, p. 163.

**1786, June 22. Jay, Joseph,** of Kingwood, Hunterdon Co. Int. Adm'r—James Thatcher. Fellowbondsman—Jeremiah Thatcher; both of said Co. Lib. 28, p. 246.

**1790, Sept. 25. Jeffery, John,** of Shrewsbury, Monmouth Co. Ward. Son of James Jeffery, of said place, deceased. Said Ward makes choice of Robert James as his Guardian.

1790, Sept. 25. Guardian—Robert James. Fellowbondsman—Joseph Thomson; both of Freehold, said Co. Lib. 30, p. 420.

**1790, Feb. 16. Jenkins, Deborah,** of Cape May Co. Int. Adm'rs—Nicholas Stillwill and Christopher Ludlam. Fellowbondsman—David Johnson; all of said Co. Witnesses—Sarah Hand and Jesse Hand.
Lib. 32, p. 106.

**1788, June 25. Jenkins, Nicholas,** of Lower Penns Neck, Salem Co.; will of. To Sarah Stark's sons, George and Paulin, whom I further name George and Paulin Jenkins, plantation where I live; but, if they die, then my cousin, Joseph Elwill and my friend, William Wright, to have the same. Sarah Stark is to have the use of said plantation during her life, and ⅛ of personal estate. Executors—William Wright and Sarah Stark. Witnesses—Margaret Elwill, George Moore, Andrew Sinnickson. Proved Nov. 4, 1789.

1789, June 7. Inventory, £163.16.4, made by John Jaquett and Allen Congleton, Jr. Lib. 31, p. 335.

**1787, April 7. Jennings, Priscilla,** of Hardwick, Sussex Co.; will of. Daughter, Elizabeth, my chest, and all my beds. Other goods to be sold, and money given to children, John, Elizabeth, Anne, Margaret and Benjamin. Daughter, Helena, had her share at her marriage. Executors—daughter, Elizabeth, and my friend, William Hankinson. Witnesses—Charles Rhodes, William Hankinson. Proved April 17, 1788.

1787, Sept. 18. Inventory, £53.2.3, made by [no names given].
Lib. 31, p. 149.

**1787, Feb. 10. Jobes, Isaac,** of Burlington Co. Int. Adm'x—Hannah Jobes, of Hanover Township, said Co. Fellowbondsman—James Craft, of Burlington, said Co.

1786, Aug. 11. Inventory, £172.2.0, made by Francis Harris. "25 acres of land, £100." Signed Nov. 7, 1787, by Hannah Cannady, late Hannah Jobes. Lib. 29, p. 79.

**1789, Feb. 19. Jobs, Elizabeth,** of Montague, Sussex Co. Ward. Daughter of Joseph Jobs, of said place, deceased.

1789, Feb. 19. Guardian—Wilhelmus Westbrook. Fellowbondsman—Abraham Chambers; both of said place; yeomen. (Said Ward is under 14). Witness—James Bonnell. Lib. 30, p. 201.

**1788, Jan. 15. Johnson, Andrew,** of Maidenhead, Hunterdon Co. Int. Adm'rs—Azubah Johnson and Thomas Blackwell. Fellowbondsman—Jonathan Hunt; all of said Co.

1788, Jan. 11. Inventory, £500.2.0, made by William Binge and Jonathan Hunt.

1789, Feb. 7. Account by Richard Bainbridge and wife, Azubah, late Azubah Johnson, Adm'x of Andrew Johnson.

1795, Sept. 21. Account by Richard Bainbridge and wife, Azubah, for all that came to their hands in trust for Mary, Hannah and Sarah Johnson, daughters of deceased. "Paid the amount of Hannah's funeral expenses, £4."

1796, Feb. 13. Account by Adm'rs.

1795, Oct. Term. Nathaniel Hunt, Jr., and Mary, his wife, late Mary Johnson, daughter and heir of Andrew Johnson, deceased, who took exceptions to the account of Richard Bainbridge and Azuba, his wife, late widow of Andrew Johnson. Lib. 31, p. 143.

**1789, March 7. Johnson, Anna,** of Hanover, Morris Co. Int. Adm'rs—Thomas Vail and Joseph Johnson. Fellowbondsman—Noah Vail; all of said place. Witness—Sally Pierson. Lib. 30, p. 234.

**1787, March 24. Johnson, Elizabeth, Mary, Sarah,** of Alexandria, Hunterdon Co. Wards. Daughters of Jacobus Johnson, of said place, deceased. Said Wards make choice of Hugh McAlister as their Guardian. Witness—David Everitt.
1787, March 24. Guardian—Hugh McAlister. Fellowbondsman—Andrew Keephart; both of said place. Lib. 29, p. 298.

**1790, Aug. 14. Johnson, Elizabeth,** of Amwell, Hunterdon Co. Int. Adm'r—Peter Johnson. Fellowbondsman—Cornelius Quick; both of said place.
1790, Aug. 11. Inventory, £66.4.7, made by John Price and Peter Kisler. Lib. 30, p. 316.

**1786, Jan. 31. Johnson, Lambert,** of Middletown, Monmouth Co.; will of. Son, Henry, all lands. Grandson, John Johnson, £10 when 21. Daughter, Margaret Johnson, 3 cows. My wife to have a good support by my son, Henry. Daughters, Margaret and Rachel, household goods. Wife, Idah, to have a cow. Executor—friend, Peter McLeese. Witnesses—James Lloyd, Jacob Burdge, John McCleese. Proved Dec. 26, 1786. File No. 5707 M.

**1790, Aug. 16. Johnson, Lawrence,** of Cumberland Co. Int. Adm'r—Enos Johnson. Fellowbondsman—Nicholas Johnson, the elder; both of said Co. Witness—William R. Cozens. Lib. 30, p. 281.

**1787, Jan. 30. Johnson, Margaret,** of Woolwich Township, Gloucester Co. Int. Adm'r—Benjamin Johnson. Fellowbondsman—Joseph Harker; both of said place, yeomen. Witness—Isaac S. Huff.
1787, Jan. 30. Inventory, £43.15.11, made by Joseph Harker and Joseph Rice. Lib. 29, p. 119.

**1786, April 29. Johnson, Matthias,** of Little Egg Harbor Township, Burlington Co. Int. Adm'r—Isaiah Haines. Fellowbondsman—John Hollinshead; both of said Co.
1786, April 28. Renunciation by Dorrity Johnson, widow of said Matthias, in favor of Isaiah Haines, of Evesham Township, said Co., principal creditor. Lib. 28, p. 80.

**1789, Jan. 6. Johnson, Samuel,** of Turkey, Elizabeth Borough, Essex Co., yeoman; will of. Wife, Lidia, the use of goods. Son, Samuel, £5 and no more, as he has had his share signed to him by a deed, for ½ of my homestead. Son, John, ¼ of rest of land. Son, Nathaniel, ¾ of the land. Executors—son, Samuel, and Ephraim Tucker. Witnesses—Levi Willcocks, Jeremiah Reding, William Willcocks. Proved Nov. 19, 1789.
1789, March 4. Inventory, made by William Wilcocks and Mathias Sayres. Lib. 30, p. 210.

**1788, April 9. Johnston, James,** of Hunterdon Co. Int. Adm'r—Samuel Johnston. Fellowbondsman—Joseph Lewis; both of said Co.
1788, March 29. Renunciation by David Johnston, eldest brother of James, deceased. Witnesses—Jacob Freese and George Garrison.
1789, Aug. 8. Adm'r de Bonis non—Joseph Scudder, Esq., of Freehold, Monmouth Co. Fellowbondsman—David Frazer, Esq., of Lebanon, Hunterdon Co.

CALENDAR OF WILLS—1786-1790   127

1788, April 9. Inventory, £37.12.0, made by Joseph Lewis and John Garrison, Sr.
1789, April 15. Citation. David Frazer, Guardian of Philip Johnson, deceased, had citation issued to Samuel Johnson, Adm'r of James Johnson, deceased, to file a perfect inventory.
1789, Aug. 5. Additional Inventory, £100.19.0, filed by Samuel Johnston.
1789, Nov. 12. Joseph Scudder, Adm'r de Bonis non of James Johnston, objects to the account of Samuel Johnston, late Adm'r of said James Johnston. Objection is made that he has not charged himself to 2 Militia pay notes of the value of £9.
1789, Aug. Term. Letters of Adm. to Samuel Johnston are revoked.
1789, Sept. 5. Account of Samuel Johnston, Adm'r.
Lib. 31, p. 143; Lib. 32, p. 56.

**1788, Feb. 14. Johnston, Maria, Nancy (Anne) and Elizabeth,** of Hunterdon Co. Wards. Children of Phillip Johnson, of said Co., deceased. Said Wards make choice of David Frazer as their Guardian.
1788, Feb. 14. Guardian—David Frazer, of said Co. Fellowbondsman—John Bray. Lib. 31, p. 225.

**1786, Sept. 29. Johnston, Mathew,** of Essex Co. Int. Adm'r—John Tuttle, of said Co. Lib. 28, p. 47.

**1790, June 16. Jones, Edward,** of Essex Co. Int. Adm'x—Sarah Jones, widow of said Edward Jones. Fellowbondsman—Abraham Sandford, of Bergen Co. Lib. 32, p. 511.

**1790, Sept. 27. Jones, Francis,** of Essex Co. Int. Adm'r—Joseph D'Camp. Fellowbondsman—Daniel Marsh; both of said Co.
Lib. 30, p. 361.

**1787, Sept. 22. Jones, Jacob,** of Woolwich Township, Gloucester Co., farmer; will of. Daughter-in-law, Mary Jones, £7. Granddaughter, Elizabeth Jones, £5. Wife, Regenah, and my son, Thomas, my bonds. Executors—wife, Regenah, and my son, Thomas. Witnesses—Joseph Adams, Samuel Adams, Benjamin Adams. Proved Jan. 1, 1788. Lib. 31, p. 12.

**1787, March 23. Jones, James,** of Mansfield, Burlington Co. Int. Adm'r—Ezra Black. Fellowbondsman—Thomas Taylor; both of Chesterfield, said Co. Witness—Thomas Adams.
1787, April 30. Inventory, £61.4.9, made by Nathan Robbins and Edward Rockhill, Jr. Lib. 29, p. 76.

**1786, March 2. Jones, John,** of Burlington Township, Burlington Co.; will of. To my 4 children, all personal estate, except some articles which my wife, Martha, is to have. Children, Thomas, John, Elizabeth and Martha, to have equally, when John is 21. Executor—friend, Joseph Cooper. Witnesses—Abraham Hewlings, Jr., John How, Dr. John Brognard. Proved March 8, 1786.
1786, March 8. Inventory, £277.12.0, made by William Deacon and Thomas Rogers, Jr. Lib. 28, p. 14.

**1788, March 31. Jones, Joseph,** of Greenwich, Gloucester Co.; will of. Wife, Hannah, the goods she brought with her, and to draw 2 shares of my estate. One share to each of my children, William, Rebekah, Isaac, Joseph, Sarah, Elizabeth and Aaron. Son, William Jones, to be under the care of Benjamin Wetherby till he is 21. The rest of my children, except Elizabeth and Aaron, to be in the care of Aaron Hews. Daughter, Sarah, my pewter. Executor— friend, Aaron Hews. Witnesses—Daniel Sutherland, Joel Paul, William White. Proved Oct. 8, 1788.
1789, Oct. 9. Adm'r—Samuel Paul. Fellowbondsman—William White; both of Gloucester Co. Aaron Hewes died after the will was proved.
1788, May 3. Inventory, £396.5.7, made by Daniel Sutherland and William White. Lib. 30, p. 138; Lib. 31, p. 13.

**1790, May 16. Journey, James,** of South Amboy, Middlesex Co.; will of. Wife, Massay, as much as she brought, and to have her living out of the place. Daughter, Ann, wife of John Baley, £50. Daughter, Audry, wife of William Brand, £50. Youngest daughters, Cateron and Lidia Journey, £60 each. Sons, Peter, Samuel, Joseph and John, my lands, when 21. Executors—son-in-law, John Baley, of Monmouth Co., and friend, John Embley, of Middlesex and William Dey, of Monmouth. Witnesses—John Dey, William Davison, Cornelius Sutton. Proved June 22, 1790.
1790, June 18. Inventory, £1,160.16.0, made by Samuel Longstreet and John Dey. Lib. 30, p. 522.

**1786, May 2. Katcham, John,** of Hopewell, Hunterdon Co.; will of. Wife, Wintiah, £600. Son, Levi, plantation where I live. Grandson, John Katcham, £50., when he is 21. Grandson, Elijah Mattison, £50. To Elizabeth Berean, who I am bringing up, a support. Daughters, Penelope and Sary, moveable estate. To Enoch Katcham, apparel. To Levi, ½ of the house, and the other ½ to Penelope and Elizabeth, for a home. Executors—son, Levi, and son-in-law, John Mattison. Witnesses—Hezekiah S. Woodruff, Thomas Craven, Thomas Bullman. Proved July 25, 1786.
1786, July 24. Inventory, £2,036.13.11, made by Henry Baker and Hezekiah S. Woodruff.
1786, Sept. 13. Account by Executors. Lib. 28, p. 207.

**1788, March 10. Kay, John,** of Woolwich Township, Gloucester Co. Int. Adm'r—Benjamin Ford. Fellowbondsman—James Lord; both of said place, yeomen. Witness—Joseph Kay. Lib. 31, p. 35.

**1790, Oct. 4. Kay, Mary and Patience,** of Gloucester Co. Wards. Daughters of Job Kay, of said Co., deceased. A petition was presented for a Guardian of said minors.
1790, Oct. 4. Guardian—Ebenezer Adams. Fellowbondsman— Thomas Thompson; both of said Co. Lib. 31, p. 482.

**1790, Jan. 14. Keatsley, Frederick,** of Gloucester Co. Int. Adm'r— James Hinchman. Fellowbondsman—Benjamin Whitall; both of said Co.
1790, Jan. 25. Inventory, £35.13.2, made by Ephraim Bee and James Jagard.
[Name is sometimes spelled Frederick Cashley]. Lib. 31, p. 478.

**1788, Sept. 29. Keen, Peter,** of Pilesgrove Township, Salem Co.; will of. Wife, Cathrine, £150 and many goods. Grandson, Samuel Keen, £15. Granddaughter, Rebeah Keen, £10, when 18. Sons, Elijah and Daniel, and my daughter, Elizabeth Bassett, wife of Samuel, and my daughter, Sarah Bassett, wife of William, rest of personal estate. Executors—wife, Cathrine, and son, Elijah. Witnesses—Henry Baly, Priscilla Ellis, John Mayhew. Proved July 29, 1789.
1788, Oct. 15. Inventory, £538.7.9, made by Abraham Richman and William Richman. Lib. 31, p. 339.

**1789, March 23. Kelsay, Robert,** of Stow Creek Township, Cumberland Co., clerk; will of, being advanced in age. To be buried by the side of my wife, with a stone as she has, and inscription thereon. Son, William, the use of my lot of land till his son, Robert, is 24. Son, Joseph, some money which he owes me. Son, David, some goods. Daughter, Miriam Bowen, some goods. Grandson, Robert Kelsay, the land I bought of Seth Bowen, when he is 24. To all grandchildren a Bible. Grandson, Robert Kelsay, son of Joseph, some goods. Sons, William and David, rest of estate. Executors—sons, William and David. Witnesses—Benjamin Peck, Daniel Kelsay, Robert Kelsay, Jr. Proved June 5, 1789.
1789, June 4. Inventory, £102.1.4, of personal estate of Reverend Robert Kelsay, made by David Gillman and Aulay McCalla.
Lib. 30, p. 148.

**1786, Dec. 29. Kemble, Samuel,** of Burlington, Burlington Co.; will of. Sons, William, Thomas and Samuel, my apparel. To Sarah Palmer, a bed. To Sarah Whitas, £10. Daughter, Susanna Stockton, the land I bought of Samuel Allinson. Rest of land to be sold. Executors—sons, William, Thomas and Samuel, and my son-in-law, Abraham Stockton. Witnesses—John Neale, Thomas Smith, Abraham Hewlings, Jr. Proved March 16, 1787.
1787, March 14. Renunciation by Abraham Stockton.
1787, Aug. 6. Renunciation by Thomas Kemble.
1787, March 12. Inventory, £131.19.8, made by Abraham Hewlings, Jr., and John Neale. Lib. 29, p. 1.

**1789, Dec. 3. Kenaday, John,** of Burlington Co. Int. Adm'r—John Allen. Fellowbondsman—Joshua Shreve; both of Springfield Township, said Co. Witness—Thomas Adams. Lib. 31, p. 319.

**1787, Jan. 7. Kennedy, John,** of Gloucester Co., laborer; will of. My executors are to collect the money of my bond on David Ridgway, and several sums that I put in the hands of Aquilla Jones, of Newton, to be converted into gold, and sent to Richard Butterfield in Rogerstown, within 4 miles of Callen, in the County of Kilkenny, in Ireland, and he is to give £30 to my brother, Thomas Kenady, in Callen, and the rest to Bridget Kenny, of Callen. Executors—Israel Morris, merchant in Philadelphia, and Thomas Heston, merchant at Samuel Cooper's ferry. Proved Jan. 15, 1787, by John Benson and Christian Grinder, who said they heard the will read to John Kenady, and he approved of the same, but he expired so suddenly as not to be able to sign the same.
1788, July 19. Inventory, £218.13.8, made by John Blackwood and Richard Howell. Lib. 29, p. 96.

**1787, Jan. 10. Kennedy, John,** of Gloucester Co., laborer. Int. Adm'r—Daniel Parke. Fellowbondsman—Samuel Driver; both of Greenwich Township, said Co. Witness—Joseph Hugg, Jr.
Lib. 29, p. 119.

**1787, Dec. 3. Kennedy, Samuel,** of Bernards Town, Somerset Co. Int. Adm'rs—Samuel Kennedy, of Sussex Co. and Henry Southard, of Somerset Co. Fellowbondsman—Gauin McCoy, of Somerset Co.
1787, Dec. 3. Renunciation by Jemima Kennedy, in favor of Doctor Samuel Kennedy and Henry Southard.
1787, Nov. 6. Inventory, made by William Conkling and Gauin McCoy. Lib. 29, p. 439.

**1788, Oct. 14. Kent, Helmer,** of Pequanack, Morris Co. Int. Adm'rs—Sarah Kent and Peter Cook. Fellowbondsman—Abraham Kitchel; all of said Co.
1788, Oct. 8. Inventory, £150, made by Abraham Kitchel and Aaron Biglow. Lib. 31, p. 200.

**1790, May 27. Key, Joseph,** of Gloucester Co., yeoman; will of. Wife, Sarah, household goods and a walnut table now in the possession of Jacob Featherer; also the goods she had when we were married. My wife is to maintain my children. Sons, John, William and Joseph, my plantation, at wife's death, which place I bought of John Key. Executors—brothers, Benjamin Ford and Thomas Key. Witnesses—Joshua Lord, Andrew Strang, Matthew Gill, Jr. Proved Nov. 22, 1790.
1790, Nov. 18. Inventory, made by Joshua Lord and Peter Beckett.
Lib. 31, p. 439.

**1786, March 17. Kimble [Kemble], Edward,** of Springfield Township, Burlington Co. Int. Adm'r—Thomas Fenimore. Fellowbondsman—David Ridgway; both of said Co.
1786, March 17. Renunciation by Hannah Kembel [Kemble], widow of Edward Kemble, in favor of Thomas Fenimore.
1786, March 16. Inventory, £163.10.2, made by Thomas Enock and David Ridgway. Lib. 28, p. 74.

**1790, Jan. 30. Kimble, James,** of Newtown, Sussex Co. Int. Adm'r—Caleb Kimble. Fellowbondsman—George Grimes; both of said place. Witness—Francis Price.
1790, Jan. 27. Inventory, £40.17.0, made by Francis Price and James Brodrick. Lib. 30, p. 438.

**1787, Jan. 11. Kingsland, Aaron,** of Bergen Co. Int. Adm'r—John Jordan, of Essex Co. Fellowbondsman—Joseph Kingsland, of Bergen Co.
1787, Jan. 14. Inventory, £5.0.9, made by Gilburt Van Emburgh and Jacob Weidman. Lib. 29, p. 535.

**1790, Dec. 4. Kitt, John,** of Burington Co. (otherwise called John Oselwean). Int. Adm'rs—Daniel Joyce and William Burr. Fellowbondsman—Phineas Kirkbride; all of said Co.
1790, Dec. 3. Inventory, £24.5.1, made by Hosea Eayre and Phineas Kirkbride. Lib. 32, p. 95.

## CALENDAR OF WILLS—1786-1790

**1790, March 23. Kline, Godfrey,** of Greenwich Township, Sussex Co. Int. Adm'r—John Kline, Jr. Fellowbondsman—William Kitchen; both of said place. Witnesses—Jonathan Willis and William Alexander Anderson.
1790, March 22. Inventory, £250.9.11, made by William Kitchen and Valentine Bidleman. Lib. 30, p. 437.

**1788, Jan. 19. Kline, John,** of Reading Township, Hunterdon Co.; will of. Wife, Jenny, use of plantation and £60. Estate to be divided among my children, Harmon, my daughters, and the child yet to be born; sons to have 2 shares, and daughters, Catee, Polly, Anne, Rachel and Lidia, one; when all come of age. Executors—John Simonson and Peter Schamp. Witnesses—John Wyckoff, Simon Wyckoff, James Snedeker. Proved Feb. 27, 1788.
1788, Feb. 26. Inventory, £537.2.1, made by John Wyckoff and Simon Wyckoff.
1799, Oct. 23. Account by Executors. "Paid the Executors of Herman Kline, deceased, for a legacy given to Joseph Bishop's wife, £31.11.8." Lib. 31, p. 114.

**1788, Jan. 30. Knott, David,** of Shrewsbury, Monmouth Co. Int. Adm'rs—Peter Knott and Thomas Henderson. Fellowbondsman—David Knott; all of said Co. Witnesses—Euphamia Clayton and Rachel Henderson.
1788, Jan. 28. Renunciation by Anna Knott, the widow.
1788, Jan. 28. Renunciation by Eliza Merryman, David Knott and Abigail Knott, children of David, deceased, in favor of Peter Knott and Dr. Thomas Henderson.
1788, Feb. 8. Inventory, £817.17.6, made by Benjamin Jackson and Edward Patterson Cook. Lib. 30, p. 101.

**1790, Nov. 24. Lacy, Joseph,** of Morris Co. Int. Adm'r—Jacob Lacy. Fellowbondsman—Daniel Lindsly; both of said Co. Witness—Jabez Gwinnup. Lib. 30, p. 481.

**1787, Nov. 26. Ladner, Benjamin,** of Hanover, Morris Co. Int. Adm'r—David Ward. Fellowbondsman—John Miller; both of said Co. Witness—Aaron Carter.
1787, Sept. 6. Renunciation by Mary Ladner, widow of Capt. Benjamin Ladner, John Ladner, his son, Phebe Carter, his daughter, and George Carter, her husband. Witnesses—Aaron Carter and David Ward, Jr.
1785, Jan. 7. Inventory, £123.9.11, made by David Ward, Jr., and John Miller, Trustees to said estate, and appraised by David Bruen and James Burnet. Lib. 29, p. 475.

**1786, June 23. Lafler [Lefler], Peter,** of Hillsborough Township, Somerset Co. Int. Adm'rs—Peter Lefler and Coonrod Lafler. Fellowbondsman—Derick Sutphen.
1786, June 12. Inventory, made by Derick Sutphen and Jacob Yung. Lib. 29, p. 195.

**1789, Dec. 24. Lake, Eleanor,** of Bethlehem Township, Hunterdon Co., widow of Thomas Lake; will of. Eldest son, Abraham, 10 shillings. Daughter, Eleanor, 10 shillings. Son, Jacob, 10 shillings. Son, Joseph, 10 shillings. Granddaughter, Sarah, daughter of son, Abraham, 10 shillings. Daughter, Hannah, my apparel and personal estate. Executrix—daughter, Hannah Lake. Witnesses—Joseph Hagaman, Richard Leacy, Sr., William Hazlitt. Proved March 19, 1790.

1790, March 16. Inventory, £69.16.6, made by Richard Leacy, Sr., and Joseph Hagaman. Lib. 30, p. 302.

**1787, July 30. Lake, Garret,** of Amwell, Hunterdon Co., yeoman; will of. Wife, Sarah, the profits of my farm and a lot in the swamp, joining John Heath. Son, Garret, said lands at his mother's marriage or death, if he is 21. Son, Thomas, land I bought of John Lewis, except a lot that Loman Sergent lives on. Daughter, Jean Heath, £30. Youngest son, Garret, stock. Executors—wife, Sarah, and my brother, John Lake. Witnesses—Peter Hoppock, Hopewill Hull, Cornelius Lake. Proved Sept. 26, 1787.

1787, Dec. 6. Inventory, £435.15.11, made by John Hull and Peter Hoppah. Lib. 29, p. 243.

**1787, Feb. 28. Lake, Thomas,** of Bethlehem, Hunterdon Co.; will of. Advanced in years. Wife, Elender, use of homestead, and ⅓ the personal estate; other ⅔ to my children, Elender and Hannah, except a Bible I give my son, Abram. Son, Jacob, Lectures on the 51st Psalm. Granddaughter, Sarah, a bed. Sons, Abram, Jacob and Joseph, my lands. Executor—son, Abram. Daughter, Hannah, to have £80, and granddaughter, Sarah Lake, £20. Witnesses—Richard Leacy, Sr., Joseph Laning, Thomas Bowlby. Proved April 25, 1787.

1787, April 24. Inventory, £123.6.10, made by Richard Leacy and Joseph Laning. Lib. 29, p. 266.

**1789, Oct. 9. Land, Charles and Louisa,** of Gloucester Co. Wards. Children of Henry Land, of said Co., who is appointed Guardian of his said children, until they are 14 years of age. Fellowbondsman—Benjamin Whitall, of said Co. Lib. 30, p. 139.

**1789, Feb. 6. Langstaff, Henry,** of Middlesex Co. Int. Adm'r—John Morgan. Fellowbondsman—James Drake; both of said Co. Lib. 31, p. 395.

**1787, April 3. Langstaff [Longstaff], Mary,** of Piscataway, Middlesex Co. Int. Adm'r—John Arnold. Fellowbondsman—Edward Griffith; both of said place.

1786, Jan. 20. Inventory, made by Lewis F. Randolph and Edward Griffith. Lib. 29, p. 364.

**1786, June 6. Laning, Isaac,** of Hunterdon Co. Int. Adm'x—Altye Laning. Fellowbondsman—Joseph Hagaman; both of Bethlehem, said Co.

1786, June 2. Inventory, £421.19.3, made by Thomas Bowlby and Joseph Hagaman.

1787, May 22. Account by Adm'x. Lib. 28, p. 247.

**1790, Sept. 25. Lanning, John,** of Evesham, Burlington Co. Int. Adm'r—Thomas Hollinshead. Fellowbondsman—Joseph Stokes; both of said Co. Witness—George Githens and James Kinsey, Jr.

1790, Sept. 20. Renunciation by Amey Lanning, widow, in favor of her friend, Thomas Hollinshead.

## CALENDAR OF WILLS—1786-1790 133

1790, Sept. 18. Inventory, £181.7.7, made by William Stockton and Joseph Stokes. Lib. 32, p. 95.

**1787, April 10. Lare, Garet,** of Bethlehem, Hunterdon Co.; will of. Wife, Elizabeth, household goods and livestock. Oldest daughter, Mary Lare, bed and chest. Youngest daughter, Anna Lare, bed and chest. Personal estate to children, Samuel, Mathias, Garret, Andrew, Mary, and Anna. Children to have schooling. Executors—John Chamberlin and William Lare. Witnesses—John Stiers, James Wilson, James Brown. Proved April 27, 1787.
 1787, April 25. Inventory, £259.8.0, made by Abraham Bonnel and John Crawford.
 1789, Feb. 15. Account by William Lear, Executor.
 1799, May 7. Account by William Lear, Executor. Lib. 29, p. 254.

**1787, Feb. 23. Larew, David,** of Amwell, Hunterdon Co., farmer. Int. Adm'r—Freegift Stout. Fellowbondsman—James Stout; both of said place. Witness—Peter Hunt.
 1782. March 23. Inventory, £99.19.6, made by Franklin Gordon and Cornelius Williamson. Lib. 29, p. 296.

**1790, April 12. Lawrence, Hannah,** of Middletown. Monmouth Co. Ward. Daughter of William Lawrence, Jr., of said place, deceased. Said Ward makes choice of Edmund Williams as her Guardian.
 1790, April 12. Guardian—Edmund Williams, of Shrewsbury, said Co. Fellowbondsman—William Lawrence, of said Co. Witness— Peter Baird. Lib. 30, p. 420.

**1789, Dec. 12. Lawrence, James,** of Upper Freehold, Monmouth Co.; will of. Son, James, the farm where William Rogers lives. Son, John, farm where I live; and he is to pay to my daughters, Rebecca and Mehetable, £100 each. Daughter, Rebecca Lawrence, some goods. Daughter, Mehetable Lawrence, some goods. Son, James, negros. Son, John, negros, and my share in the Arneys Town library. One hundred acres of the farm devised to son, James, to be sold; also 200 acres of that devised to son, John. Rest of land to be sold, except Proprietary Rights, as by virtue of a deed given to me by Col. Elisha Lawrence, which is to be conveyed back to him. Grandchildren, James Taylor and Elizabeth Taylor, money from sales of land, when they are of age. Executors—friends, James Lawrie and Robert Montgomery. Witnesses—Gilbert Smith, Joseph Holmes, John Lawrence. Proved Jan. 6, 1790.
 1789, Dec. 28. Inventory, £1,743.15.3, made by Gilbert Smith and Joseph Holmes. Lib. 30, p. 407.

**1788, Nov. 26. Lawrence, Jonathan,** of Deerfield, Cumberland Co. Int. Adm'x—Mary Lawrence. Fellowbondsmen—Norton Lawrence and James Burch; all of said Co.
 1788, Dec. 3. Inventory, £1,327.16.6, made by David Moore and Ephraim Foster. Lib. 31, p. 76.

**1788, May 15. Lawrence, Robert.** Int. Adm'x—Susanna Lawrence. Fellowbondsman—Elisha Newell; all of New Jersey. Witness— Rachel Henderson. Lib. 30, p. 13.

**1786, Feb. 28. Lawrie, Thomas,** of Nottingham Township, Burlington Co. Int. Adm'r—John Gardiner, Jr. Fellowbondsman—Samuel Hough; both of Springfield Township, said Co.
1786, March 8. Inventory, £79.5.7, made by John Watson and John Abbott. Lib. 27, p. 13.

**1790, March 20. Layton, Safty,** of Shrewsbury Township, Monmouth Co.; will of. Son, James, 10 shillings. Wife and daughter, Rebecah Layton, and my 3 youngest sons, Joseph, Thomas and Safty, rest of personal and real estate. Thomas and Safty to be put to trades. Executor—friend, Benjamin Jackson. Witnesses—Oliver Sherman, James Sherman, Edmond Lafetra. Proved May 8, 1790.
Lib. 30, p. 378.

**1787, Oct. 29. Leahy, John,** of Kingwood, Hunterdon Co. Int. Adm'x—Penelopy Leahy. Fellowbondsman—John Clifford; both of said place.
1787, Oct. 18. Inventory, £135.12.1, made by David Everitt and John Tenbrook. Also, Quarter-Master and Militia Certificates, total $896.
Lib. 29, p. 296.

**1787, Dec. 10. Leamyng [Leaming], Christopher,** of Cape May Co., gent.; will of. Wife, Sarah, use of ½ my lands. Son, Jacob Leamyng, those tracts of land I bought of Abraham Bennet and Samuel Jones, and wife, Sylvia, at the Neck; also ½ of a beach, called Two Mile Beach, and to be taken at the east end. Son, Christopher, ½ the plantation where I live, which was left me by my father, to be taken off the west end, joining land of Zebulon Swain. Son, Humphrey, ½ of the plantation where I live, to be taken off the east end, next to land of Jesse Hand. I give my cedar swamp to my sons, Spicer, Jacob, Christopher and Humphrey. My wife has right in certain lands, the fee simple whereof is vested to her; therefore I direct that my son, Allinson Leamyng, be kept at school by his mother, until he is 14. Son, Spicer, will have lands devised to him by my wife, and I desire him to pay £60 for paying legacies to my daughters; now I give him ½ of low ground in the Neck on the west side of the Rode, and along land of Aaron Eldredge, deceased. Son, Jacob, is to pay £60, when he is 22 years of age, to my Executors. Son, Christopher Leaming, also to pay £60. Son, Humphrey Leamyng, also to pay £60. If my sons do not make the payments, then I direct their lands to be equally divided among my daughters, Deborah Leaming, Hannah Leaming, and Esther Leaming. I give ⅔ of my personal estate to my said daughters, and ⅓ to my wife. My lands at Dennis's Neck to be sold. Executors—wife, Sarah, and my son, Spicer, and friend, Elijah Hughes. Witnesses—Elisha Hughes, Reeves Iszard, John Swain. Proved Sept. 10, 1788.
1788, April 18. Inventory, £341.6.8, made by Eli Townsend and Henry Y. Townsend. Lib. 31, p. 82.

**1786, April 6. Lee, Thomas,** of Cumberland Co. Ward. Son of Thomas Lee, of said Co., deceased. Said Ward, having real and personal estate, makes choice of Isaac Wheaton as his Guardian.
1786, April 6. Guardian—Isaac Wheaton. Fellowbondsman—Ebenezer Elmer; both of said Co. Lib. 28, p. 184.

CALENDAR OF WILLS—1786-1790 135

**1787, April 30. Leeds, Jonathan,** of Galloway, Gloucester Co., husbandman; will of. Sons, Robert, Enoch, Daniel and Solomon, all my lands and cedar swamps, and my ½ part of the fishery at the Fishing place, called also Swimming-over. Sons, Robert, Enoch, Daniel and Solomon, and my daughter, Rebekah, moveable estate. Daughter, Rebekah, £10. Executors—sons, Robert, Enoch and Solomon. Witnesses—Jeremiah Higbee, Robert Smith, Christian Holston. Proved Oct. 30, 1787.
1787, Oct. 6. Inventory, £93.6.2, made by Nehemiah Leeds and Jeremiah Higbee. Lib. 29, p. 111.

**1788, June 11. Leeds, Philo,** of Northampton, Burlington Co. Int. Adm'r—Samuel Leeds. Fellowbondsman—John Burr, Jr.; both of said place. Witness—George Painter.
1788, June 10. Renunciation by Sarah Leeds, widow of said Philo, in favor of her son, Samuel Leeds.
1788, June 9. Inventory, £59.1.8, made by Abner Rogers and John Burr, Jr. Lib. 30, p. 58.

**1790, June 4. Leek, John,** of Burlington Co. Int. Adm'x—Martha Leek. Fellowbondsman—Samuel Leek; both of Little Egg Harbor, said Co. Witness—James Kinsey, Jr.
1790, May 26. Inventory, £106.1.6, made by Samuel Loveland and John Forman, Jr. Lib. 32, p. 96.

**1787, July 7. Lefferty, Bryant,** of Bedminster, Somerset Co. Int. Adm'x—Rachel Lefferty. Fellowbondsman—John Boylan; both of said place. Lib. 29, p. 439.

**1787, May 17. Leforge, David,** of Piscataway, Middlesex Co.; will of. Wife, Catherine, £200 and many goods. Son, David, my plantation. The land I bought of Nicholas Leforge to be sold, and money to go to son, Peter, and my daughter, Mary Clawson. Son, Benjamin, £200. Executors—son, Benjamin, and my son-in-law, Cornelius Clawson. Witnesses—Samuel Whitehead, Jacob Boice, John Runyon. Proved June 6, 1787.
1787, May 31. Inventory, made by Benjamin F. Randolph.
Lib. 29, p. 356.

**1788, June 30. Leigh, Ichabod,** of Somerset Co., yeoman; will of. Estate to be sold. Wife, Anna, all she brought and £75. Grandson, Ichabod Leigh, £5. Granddaughter, Anna, £5. Eldest son, Samuel, £90. Son, Joseph, £60, and Bible. Son, Daniel, £70. Son, Eljiah, £60. Son, Zebulon, £50. Son, Isaack, £40. Son, John, £40. Daughter, Neomi, £40. Daughter, Elizabeth, £50. Daughter, Anna, £50. Daughters, Elizabeth and Anna, may live in the house for 4 years. Executors—Zebulon Stout, Jr., Samuel Leigh and Joseph Leigh. Witnesses—Peter Voorhees, Isaac Vanzant, Abraham Voorhees. Proved May 4, 1789.
1789, May 1. Inventory, made by John Voorhees and Abraham Voorhees. Lib. 31, p. 403.

**1787, Feb. 9. Leonard, James,** of Eastern Precinct, Somerset Co. Int. Adm'rs—Sarah Williams, of Philadelphia, and Daniel Perrine, of Eastern Precinct, Somerset Co. Fellowbondsman—Archibald Mercer, of Hillsborough, Somerset Co. Lib. 29, p. 438.

**1787, Sept. 26. Leonard, Paul,** of Hanover, Morris Co. Int. Adm'r—David Leonard. Fellowbondsman—Moses Kitchel; both of said Co.
1787, Sept. 20. Renunciation by Abegeal Leonard, widow of Paul. Witnesses—Stephen Leonard and Moses Leonard.
1787, Jan. 12. Inventory, £57.11.6, made by Jacob Gould and Phinehas Kitchel. Lib. 29, p. 473.

**1790, March 10. Leonard, Samuel,** of Shrewsbury, Monmouth Co.; will of. The article I made with James Throckmorton is to be fulfilled. My right in the saw mill tract to be sold; also my land over Squan River, joining David Ketcham and Abraham Gifford, of 30 acres. Daughter, Mary, £50. My sister, Hughs, £20. Daughters, Mary, Lucy and Susannah, goods. Children, Mary, Deborah, Lucy, Susannah and Samuel, rest of personal and real estate. Executors—daughter, Deborah Holmes; friend, Joseph Holmes, and my brother-in-law, Joseph Throckmorton. Witnesses—John Hyers, Jarrald Jeffery, Edmund Williams. Proved June 9, 1790.
1790, June 8. Inventory, £1,143.3.8, made by Denise Denise and William Grandin. Lib. 30, p. 392.

**1790, May 31. Leonard, Sarah,** of Monmouth Co. Ward. Daughter of Joseph Leonard, of said Co., deceased. Said Ward makes choice of Moses Shepherd as her Guardian.
1790, May 31. Guardian—Moses Shepherd. Fellowbondsman—Esek Hartshorne; both of said Co. Lib. 30, p 420.

**1786, Sept. 8. Leslie, William,** at present of Hillsborough, Somerset Co., late of New York City, physician; will of. Niece, Elizabeth Ten Eyck, wife of Coanrod, my chair and horse. Nephew, Coanrod Ten Eyck, my colt. Nephew, Benjamin Thompson, son of William and my sister, Elizabeth, deceased, rest of personal estate. My 407 acres of land in Reading Township, Hunterdon Co., now in tenure of Matthias Smock and Rynier Smock, and 60 acres in said place, in tenure of William Hellebrant, and 7 acres of woodland, in rear of Michael Demott's land, to be sold, and money given to my nephew, Benjamin Thompson, and my friend, John Shaw, of New York City, merchant, to be receiver of the money from said sale. Executors—friends, Frederick Frelinghuysen and Abraham Staats. Witnesses—Peter Stryker, Abraham Schenck, Jonathan Dunn. Proved Nov. 14, 1786. Lib. 29, p. 184.

**1787, Dec. 10. Lewis, Eliphalet,** of Mendham, Morris Co. Int. Adm'r—Samuel Cosad. Fellowbondsman—Abraham Lewis; both of said place.
1787, Dec. 6. Renunciation by Jene Lewis, widow, and by the heirs, Abraham Lewis, Elijah Lewis, Joseph Lewis, John Lewis, and my daughters, Mary Olifer and Jane Lewis. Witnesses—Abraham Lewis and Lebbens Dod.
1787, Nov. 28. Inventory, £98.0.6, made by Nathaniel Doty and Ebenezer Cook. Lib. 29, p. 474.

**1787, Jan. 20. Lewis, Jacob,** of Burlington Co. Int. Adm'r—Joseph Lewis, of said Co. Fellowbondsman—Joseph Sharp, of Salem Co.
1786, Nov. 20. Inventory, £218.10.0, made by Benjamin Haines and John Sharp. Lib. 29, p. 72.

## CALENDAR OF WILLS—1786-1790

**1786, Feb. 15. Lewis, Lawrence,** of Essex Co. Ward. Son of Mathew Lewis, of said Co., deceased. Said Ward, being out of wardship of Elizabeth Lewis, and having an estate of £200, makes choice of Benjamin Lyon as his Guardian.
1786, Feb. 15. Guardian—Benjamin Lyon, of said Co.
Lib. 28, p. 429.

**1789, March 2. Lewis, Thomas,** of Gloucester Co. Int. Adm'r—Isaac Lewis, of Salem Co. Fellowbondsman—James Kaighin, of Gloucester Co.
1789, Feb. 28. Inventory, £77.1.10, made by Joseph Kaighin and James Kaighin.
Lib. 30, p. 138.

**1787, Aug. 21. Light, John,** of Woolwich, Gloucester Co.; will of. Wife, Agnes, goods enough to keep house, and £25 yearly for 5 years, and, after that time, £18. Daughter, Mary Light, rest of estate, when 21. If she die, then to my sister, Catharina Lantis, in the Valley of Lieningen, near City of Greenstadt, in Germany, and her children. David Green, of Woolwich Township, owes me money on a mortgage, and, from his conduct, he intends to defraud; therefore my Executors are to prosecute the said David Green, and Jacob Green, if necessary, in Chancery. Executors—friends, Robert Brown and Matthew Gill, Jr. Witnesses—Henry Ridgway, Michael Ross, George Ross. Proved Feb. 19, 1788.
Lib. 31, p. 32.

**1789, Nov. 7. Linberger, John,** of Middlesex Co.; will of. Wife to hold the real and personal estate, and my children, John and William, and those unborn that my wife is pregnant with, to have the same, when youngest is 21. Executors—friends, John Hutchins and Joseph Ross. Witnesses—John Ross, John Ross, Jr., John Steele. Proved Dec. 24, 1790.
1789, Dec. 22. Inventory, made by John Ross and William Harris, Jr.
Lib. 31, p. 384.

**1787, Oct. 10. Linch, Michael,** of Chester Township, Burlington Co.; will of. Wife, Rachel Lynch, all the money that is due to me from Samuel Coles, and the goods which she needs. Son, Jesse, the rest of personal and real estate, and he is to take good care of his mother. Executors—son, Jesse, and my friend, Samuel Coles, of Moorestown. Witnesses—Reece Edwards, Morgan Hollinshead, John Cox. Proved June 23, 1789.
1789, June 22. Inventory, £986.3.0, made by Morgan Hollinshead and Reece Edwards.
Lib. 31, p. 283.

**1790, March 29. Lindsly, Jabez,** of Hanover, Morris Co. Int. Adm'x—Jemima Lindsly. Fellowbondsman—David Bedford; both of said place. Witness—Hannah Campfield.
1790, March 25. Inventory, £177.9.3, made by Stephen Day and John Blanchard.
Lib. 30, p. 480.

**1786, March 14. Lindsly, Timothy,** of Hanover Township, Morris Co. Int. Adm'r—Benjamin Lindsly. Fellowbondsman—Jonathan Stiles; both of Morristown, said Co.
1785, June 9. Renunciation by Elizabeth Lindsly, widow of said Timothy. Witness—Jonas Phillips.
1785, June 9. Inventory, £91.2.10, made by Jonas Phillips and Silas Ayers.
Lib. 28, p. 487.

**1787, July 17. Lines, John,** of Franklin Township, Bergen Co.; will of. Son, Abraham, all land, as in a Release, dated July 25, 1772, and given by Anthony Beam and Daniel Lines. Wife, Elenor, goods, except such as were given to him by his mother. Executors— friends, Frederick Frederickson, of Morris Co. and Henry Van Waggoner, of Saddle River, of Bergen Co. Witnesses—Anthony Bartrim, Joseph Bartrim, John Collins. Proved Sept. 29, 1787.

1787, Aug. 21. Inventory, £231.14.10, made by Joost Beam and Adrian Post. Lib. 29, p. 531.

**1789, Oct. 24. Lippincott, Aquilla,** of Chester Township, Burlington Co. Int. Adm'r—John Inskeep. Fellowbondsman—Samuel Coles; both of said Co.

1789, Oct. 22. Inventory, £33.1.1, made by Samuel Coles and Edmd Hollinshead. Lib. 31, p. 320.

**1789, Sept. 12. Lippincott, John,** formerly of Chester Township, now of City of Burlington, Burlington Co.; will of. Wife, Elizabeth, the profits of plantation in said Chester, where I formerly lived, with 3 acres of meadow, and which John Lippincott purchased of Thomas Styles, which plantation was devised to me by my father, and contains 110 acres. Daughters, Mary Lippincott, Beulah Lippincott and Hannah Lippincott, the plantation of 110 acres, and the lot of meadow, after their mother's death; also 10 acres of meadow in said Township, which join lands of John Stokes and Samuel Roberts, Jr. My grist mill may be sold, which is in Philadelphia Co., Penna. Children are to be educated. Executors—wife, Elizabeth, and my brother-in-law, John Elton, of Burlington, and my cousin, Samuel Shute, of Chester. Witnesses—William Borradaill, Daniel Smith, Abraham Gardiner.

1789, Nov. 16. Codicil. My wife is to have £200. Witnesses— William Borradaill, Daniel Smith. Proved Dec. 8, 1789.

1789, Dec. 7. Inventory, £213.8.6, made by William Borradaill and Abraham Gardiner. Debts due from Paul Crispin, Revel Elton, Alexander McMullen and Thomas Bennett. Lib. 31, p. 285.

**1790, Nov. 2. Lippincott, Martha, Hope and Rebecca,** of Burlington Co. Wards. Children of Seth Lippincott, of said Co., deceased. Their mother, Hope Lippincott, prays that she may be made their Guardian.

1790, Nov. 2, Guardian—Hope Lippincott. Fellowbondsmen—George Eyre and Hannah Kay; all of said Co. Lib. 32, p. 98.

**1787, Aug. 30. Lippincott, Nathaniel,** of Waterford, Gloucester Co., farmer; will of, being advanced in age. Wife, Mary, is provided for. Son, Caleb, the land which I bought of Richard Haines, on Coopers Creek, and bounded by Amos Haines and Samuel Stokes. Grandson, Wallace Lippincott, the place where I live, and land in tenure of William Bell; and, if he die, then to my grandson, John Lippincott; he paying to each of his brothers £100. Grandson, Jesse Lippincott, the other ½ of said plantation, he paying to my son Seth's daughters, £75 each. Grandson, Jesse Lippincott, the land which I gave to his father in his lifetime; but, if he die, then to his brother, Joshua. Grandson, Aquilla Lippincott, a lot in Moorestown, of 2 acres, which descended to me from my father; and he is to pay to my granddaughters, Abigail and Martha Borton, £50 each, and to

CALENDAR OF WILLS—1786-1790   139

my niece, Phebe Burr's daughter, Sarah, £50. Grandson, Nathaniel Buzby, £130. Granddaughters, Ann and Mary Buzby, my house in 5th street, a little above Arch, in Philadelphia, which I bought of Lazarus Pine; but, if they die under age, then the survivors of my daughter, Grace's children shall take the same; and I appoint their father, Jabez Buzby, trustee for his children. Granddaughter, Mary Haines, my clock. Grandsons, Benjamin and Nathaniel Buzby, sons of my daughter, Grace, £10 each. To Haddonfield Preparative Meeting, £5 to repair the graveyard. Grandson, Nathaniel Buzby, son of my daughter, Martha, and to my granddaughters, Ann Buzby, Mary Buzby, Abigail Borton and Martha Borton, rest of estate. Executors—sons, Caleb and Joshua. Witnesses—Thomas Stokes, Samuel Allinson, William Allinson.

1788, July 22. I exchanged some land with Samuel Allinson, which I give to my grandson, Wallace Lippincott. Witnesses—Samuel Allinson, Mary Allinson, Jane Siddons. Proved Aug. 16, 1790.

1790, July 31. Inventory, £507.7.7, made by Thomas Stokes and Nathaniel Borton. Lib. 31, p. 441.

**1786, March 11. Lippincott, Richard,** of Chesterfield Township, Burlington Co. Int. Adm'r—John Lippincott, of said place. Fellowbondsman—Daniel Hancock, of Mansfield Township, said Co.

1786, July 29. Inventory, £12.4.1, made by John Hall and Aaron Taylor. Lib. 28, p. 75.

**1786, May 24. Lippincott, Seth,** of Chester Township, Burlington Co. Int. Adm'rs—Caleb Lippincott, of Gloucester Co. and John Lippincott, of Burlington Co. Fellowbondsman—Abraham Heulings, of Burlington Co.

1786, May 22. Renunciation by Hope Lippincott, widow of Seth, in favor of Caleb Lippincott and John Lippincott. Witnesses— Thomas Marshall and Joseph Heulings.

1786, May 22. Inventory, £740.14.3, made by Abraham Heulings and Joseph Morgan, Jr. Lib. 28, p. 78.

**1790, Nov. 3. Lippincott, Wallace and Hannah,** of Burlington Co. Wards. Children of Seth Lippincott, of said Co., deceased. Said Wards make choice of their mother, Hope Lippincott, as their Guardian.

1790, Nov. 3. Guardian—Hope Lippincott. Fellowbondsmen— George Eyre and Hannah Kay; all of said Co. Lib. 32, p. 98.

**1788, March 19. Lishman, Henry,** of Springfield, Burlington Co.; will of. Wife, Sarah, £100, and some goods. Daughter, Hannah Lishman, £100. Son, Jacob, rest of estate. Executors—wife, Sarah, and son, Jacob. Witnesses—Samuel Atkinson, Elizabeth Atkinson, John Ridgway. Proved April 4, 1788.

1788, March 31. Inventory, £597.15.0, made by Samuel Attkinson and John Ridgway. Lib. 30, p. 10.

**1788, May 29. Lister, William,** of Hunterdon Co. Int. Adm'r— William Tindall. Fellowbondsman—Isaac Barnes; both of Trenton, said Co. Lib. 31, p. 143.

**1790, May 28. Littell, Andrew,** of Essex Co., yeoman; will of. Wife, Mary, the profits of my real and personal estate. Daughter, Tem-

perance Valentine, my loom. Rest of estate to my children, William Littell, Survia Frazee, Mary Vansickle, Rachel Masters, Ephraim Littell, Hannah Heddy, and Temperance Valentine. Executors—friend, George Brown, my son, William, and my son-in-law Joseph Valentine. Witnesses—Ebenezer Lyon, John Beach, William Coles. Proved June 14, 1790.
1790, June 1. Inventory, made by John Darby and Ezekiel Sayre. "A note against Zachariah Van Sickle." Lib. 30, p. 342.

**1789, July 8. Little, David,** of Morris Co. Int. Adm'r—Peter Smith. Fellowbondsman—Stephen Day; both of said Co. Witness—Jabez Gwinnup. Lib. 30, p. 233.

**1789, Sept. 18. Livingston, Philip,** of New York City. Adm'r—Brockholst Livingston, Esq., of said City. Fellowbondsman—Elisha Boudinot, Esq., of Essex Co. Whereas, said Philip Livingston, of New York City, merchant, made his will, and the Executors renounced, and Letters of Administration were granted to Philip Philip Livingston, son of said Philip Livingston, and whereas, the said Philip Philip Livingston is also deceased, leaving part of the estate unadministered; therefore the said Brockholst Livingston is appointed Adm'r. Lib. 30, p. 218.

**1788, Feb. 11. Lloyd, Bateman, Esquire,** of Salem, Salem Co.; will of. Son, Bateman, and my daughter, Rebecca Clarke, wife of Joseph Clarke, 3 Loan Office certificates. Son, Jacob, rest of estate. Executor—son, Jacob. Witnesses—Samuel Thompson, John Cope, William Wilson. Proved Aug. 15, 1790. Lib. 40, p. 536.

**1786, Oct. 17. Lock, Enos,** of Gloucester Co. Ward. Son of Andrew Lock, of said Co., deceased. James Carr, and Catharine Carr, the mother of Enos Lock, a minor under 14, made request that Doctor James Stratton, might be made Guardian of said minor.
1786, Oct. 17. Guardian—James Stratton, of Greenwich Township. Fellowbondsman—Jonathan Harker, of Deptford Township; both of said Co. Witness—Joseph Lippincott. Lib. 28, p. 124.

**1787, Jan. 4. Lock, Sarah,** of Cumberland Co. Int. Adm'r—Thomas Earl. Fellowbondsman—Reuben Husted; both of said Co., yeomen. Witness—Joel Husted. Lib. 29, p. 183.

**1789, March 12. Locke, Elizabeth,** of Hunterdon Co. Ward. Daughter of Francis Locke, of said Co., deceased. Said Ward makes choice of John Armstrong and Archibald Stinson, Jr. as her Guardians.
1789, March 12. Guardians, John Armstrong and Archibald Stinson, Jr. Fellowbondsman—George Armstrong; all of Hardwick, Sussex Co. Witnesses—Samuel Kennedy and Joseph Reeder.
Lib. 30, p. 201.

**1789, March 12. Locke, Francis, Jr.,** of Hunterdon Co. Ward. Son of Francis Locke, of said Co., deceased.
1789, March 12. Guardians—John Armstrong and Archibald Stinson, Jr. Fellowbondsman—George Armstrong; all of Hardwick, Sussex Co. Witnesses—Samuel Kennedy and Joseph Reeder. Said Ward is under 14 years of age. Lib. 30, p. 201.

CALENDAR OF WILLS—1786-1790   141

**1789, March 12. Locke, John,** of Hunterdon Co. Ward. Son of Francis Locke, of said Co., deceased.
1789, March 12. Guardians—John Armstrong and Archibald Stinson, Jr. Fellowbondsman—George Armstrong; all of Hardwick, Sussex Co. Witnesses—Samuel Kennedy and Joseph Reeder. Said Ward is under 14 years of age.   Lib. 30, p. 201.

**1789, Aug. 11. Long, Thomas,** of Cape May Co. Int. Adm'x—Eleanor Long, of said Co. Fellowbondsman—John Champion, of Gloucester Co. Witness—James Willets.
1789, Aug. 3. Inventory, £162.9.8, made by William Tomlin and James Willets.   Lib. 31, p. 371.

**1787, Jan. 17. Longstreet, Cornelius, Aaron and Helena,** of Middlesex Co. Wards. Children of James Longstreet, of said Co., deceased.
1787, Jan. 17. Guardian—Cornelius Ten Broeck, Jr. Fellowbondsman—John Voorhees, Jr.; both of said Co.   Lib. 29, p. 366.

**1788, May 19. Longstreet, Elias,** of Freehold, Monmouth Co. Int. Adm'rs—Rebecah Longstreet and Hendrick Voorhees; both of said Co.
1788, May 30. Inventory, £29.19.8, made by William B. Covenhoven and Jonathan Rhea.   Lib. 30, p. 102.

**1787, Feb. 20. Longstreet, Gilbert,** of Upper Freehold, Monmouth Co.; will of. Wife, Helena, use of all money, and what should remain to my daughter, Elenor Longstreet, when 21. If Eleanor die, then all to my wife, and my nephew, William Longstreet, son of John. Executors—brother, Daniel, and friends, Elisha Lawrence and Richard Cox. Witnesses—William Lloyd, Jacob Coward, Ann Kerr. Proved Nov. 27, 1787.
1787, Oct. 27. Inventory, £1,302.11.3, made by Richard Kinnan and William Lloyd.   Lib. 29, p. 324.

**1787, March 11. Lord, Constantine,** of Deptford Township, Gloucester Co., yeoman; will of. Son, Benjamin, my house and lot where I live, with 10 acres of woodland adjoining lands of Joshua Lord, deceased, Zephenia Brown and James Rambo; also 8 acres bought of James Rambo. Son, James, rest of my lands, when he is 21. Wife, Sarah, and daughters, Elizabeth and Sarah Lord, the moveable estate. Peter Crim and Phinehas Lord to be Guardians of my son, James. Executors—wife, Sarah, and Daughter, Elizabeth. Witnesses—William Keais, Samuel Paul, Sarah Keais. Proved Sept. 4, 1790.
1790, Oct. 24. Inventory, £434.1.4, made by Phineus Lord and Joshua Lord.   Lib. 31, p. 446.

**1786, Dec. 29. Lore, Daniel,** of Downs Precinct, Cumberland Co.; will of. Wife, Eve, use of lands and moveable estate. Son, Ethan, all my lands, after his mother is deceased; except 10 acres of woodland, joining to Whitlock Paullin. To Leusey Lore, £30, when she is 21. To daughter, Hannah Lore, £30, when 18. Daughter, Phebe Shaw, ½ of the Whitlock Paullin plantation, and ½ of said 10 acres. The other ½ I give to my daughter, Rachel Lore, when she is 21. Executors—Gideon Heaton and Nathaniel Lore. Witnesses—Ambrose Ladow, Jonathan Socwell, William Low. Proved Sept. 25, 1787.
   Lib. 29, p. 181.

**1788, March 16. Lore, Jonathan,** of Downs Township, Cumberland Co.; will of. Wife, Temprance, all that was agreed on in an article between us when married. Oldest son, Dan, ½ of the land in Bear Swamp, and ½ of my cedar swamp, and ½ of the out land. Son, David, £10. Grandson, John Lore, plantation I live on, and rest of lands. Grandson, Jeremiah Lore, £15. To son David's children, Anna Lore and John Lore, £15 each. Executors—son, Dan, and grandson, John Lore. Witnesses—Gideon Heaton, Hosea Sheppard, Mary Campbell. Proved March 24, 1788.

1788, April 10. Inventory, £310.14.4, made by Nathan Clark and Hoseah Sheppard. Lib. 31, p. 67.

**1787, July 2. Lore, Richard,** of Cumberland Co.; will of. To Andrew Garrison, £18, which Abraham Rogers owes me. To Elizabeth Garrison, daughter of Cornelius Garrison, rest of moveable estate. The money that is coming from John Brock is to pay charges. Elizabeth Garrison, wife of Cornelius, to have the use of the moveable estate during her life. Executor—Abraham Rogers. Witnesses—Edward Shropshire, Jehu Passons. Proved July 24, 1787.

1787, July 16. Inventory, £33.11.9, made by Edward Shropshire and Jehu Passons. Lib. 29, p. 180.

**1788, Feb. 1. Lowrance, Adam,** of Roxbury, Morris Co. Int. Adm'rs—Margaret Lowrance and John Maine. Fellowbondsman—Robert Colver; all of said place. Witness—John Jacob Faesch.

1788, Jan. 19. Inventory, £65.19.6, made by Robert Colver and Thomas Mane, Jr. Lib. 31, p. 200.

**1788, May 14. Lucas, Edward,** of Burlington Co. Ward. Son of Seth Lucas, of said Co., deceased. Said Ward, having real and personal estate, makes choice of Robert Lucas as his Guardian.

1788, May 14. Guardian—Robert Lucas, of Willingborough Township. Fellowbondsman—Jacob Perkins; both of said Co.
Lib. 30, p. 61.

**1789, April 20. Ludlam, Deborah,** of Cape May Co. Ward. Daughter of Reuben Ludlam, of said Co., deceased. Said Ward, having real and personal estate, makes choice of Christopher Ludlam as her Guardian.

1789, April 20. Guardian—Christopher Ludlam, of Middle Precinct, said Co. Fellowbondsman—Henry Townsend, of said Co. Witnesses—Sarah Hand and Sarah Hand, Jr. Lib. 31, p. 373.

**1788, Sept. 25. Luther, Lewis, Jr.,** of Mendham, Morris Co. Int. Adm'x—Perthana Luther. Fellowbondsman—Daniel Wright; both of said place.

1788, June 24. Inventory, £29.4.2, made by David Beman and Josiah Beman. Lib. 31, p. 200.

**1788, April 6. McBride, Dennis,** of Cape May Co.; will of. The chest of clothes and the cloth that was my wife's shall be kept for my 3 girls, Mary McBride, Elizabeth and Naamah; ½ to my oldest daughter, Mary, and the other ½ to Naamah and Elizabeth. Rest of estate to be sold. Son, John, to be put out to a tailor trade. Children, John, Mary, Naamah and Elizabeth, rest of estate. Executors—

CALENDAR OF WILLS—1786-1790  143

William Hawkins and Elijah Townsend. Witnesses—Daniel Stites, Hance Peterson. Proved Aug. 3, 1789.
1789, June 6. Inventory, £129.6.3, made by Richard Townsend and Hance Peterson. Lib. 31, p. 363.

**1787, Nov. 6. McClain, John,** of Nottingham, Burlington Co. Int. Adm'x—Diannah McClain. Fellowbondsman—Abraham Woglum; both of said Co.
1787, Oct. 26. Inventory, £75.15.5, made by Abraham Woglum and James Mathis, Jr. Lib. 29, p. 77.

**1788, Aug. 13. McClane, Diana,** of Lamberton, Nottingham Township, Burlington Co.; will of. Sister, Jane Brown, of Morristown, my apparel. To Diana Ferguson, spoons. To Zuba Gearing, spoons. To Mary Woodruff, wife of Simeon Woodruff, of Lamberton, £10. To Eleanor Ashmore, daughter of James Ashmore, deceased, £10, when she is 18. To Charles Higbee, son of Joseph Higbee, of Trenton, my lot of land in Lamberton, of ½ acre, and the house thereon. To Charles Higbee, the rest of estate. Executors—Charles Higbee. Witnesses—John Watson, Joseph Morris, Joseph Palmer. Proved Aug. 30, 1788.
1788, Aug. 27. Inventory, £15.16.9, made by Looe Baker, Sr., Anthony Ashmore and Looe Baker. Lib. 29, p. 543.

**1787, June 7. McClong, James,** of Upper Alloways Creek, Salem Co.; will of. To James McClong, son of William, the plantation where I formerly lived, and, if he die, then to my granddaughters, Mary and Hope, daughters of said William. Son, Samuel, use of said place for 6 years; he paying £12 a year to the widow of my son, William. Daughter, Jane, wife of Daniel Russel, some goods. Grandsons, James and William Russel, ⅛ of money due bonds. To James and William Craig, sons of my daughter, ⅛ of money. Son, Samuel, ⅛ of money, and wind mill, and, after his death, to his sons, William and Samuel. Executor—son, Samuel. Witnesses—Hosea Lawrence, John Nealy, Samuel Johnson. Proved March 15, 1788.
1788, Feb. 28. Inventory, £113.17.3, made by John Nealy and Hosea Lawrence. Lib. 31, p. 47.

**1790, May 31. McCollister, Charles,** of Pilesgrove Township, Salem Co., yeoman; will of. Wife, Rachel, moveable estate. When the children are of age, they are to have what remains. Executors—wife, Rachel, and John McCollister, Jr. Witnesses—Harmon Richman, Samuel Sharp, John Erwin. Proved July 24, 1790.
1790, June 14. Inventory, £234.17.3, made by Robert Peterson and David Paullin. Lib. 40, p. 525.

**1788, April 30. McCoy, Edward,** of Greenwich Township, Gloucester Co., husbandman; will of. Wife is to have some goods, and Executors are to rent a house in Philadelphia for wife and children, and children to be put to trades. They are to have the money given to them at suitable times. Executors—brother, Lawrence McCoy, and Daniel Sotherlin. Witnesses—James McConel, John Egan, Samuel Mickle.
1788, May 5. Codicil. My wife, Mary, and my brother, Lawrence, have agreed to live together during their lease at Long Point, leased of Joseph Ellis. Witness—Samuel Mickle. Proved Dec. 17, 1788.

144    NEW JERSEY POST-REVOLUTIONARY DOCUMENTS

1788, Aug. 5. Inventory, £160.19.3, made by William White and Samuel Mickle. Lib. 31, p. 27.

1789, June 13. McCullough, Benjamin, of Mansfield Woodhouse, Sussex Co. Int. Adm'r—William McCullough, of said place. Fellowbondsman—William Kerr, of Newtown, said Co. Witness—Henry Chery. Lib. 30, p. 200.

1790, Dec. 22. McCullough, Catura, of Sussex Co., late Catura Hunt, who was the wife of William McCullough. Int. Adm'r—William McCullough, of Mansfield Woodhouse, Sussex Co. Fellowbondsman— William Kerr, of Newtown, said Co. Lib. 30, p. 438.

1788, Sept. 10. McDonald, Hugh, of Newtown, Sussex Co. Int. Adm'r—John Kirkpatrick, of Hardwick. Fellowbondsman—John Salmon, of Newtown, both of said Co. Witness—John King. 1788, Sept. 10. Inventory, £54.14.4, made by John King and John Salmon. Lib. 31, p. 157.

1788, April 9. McElrath, Thomas, of Bridgewater Township, Somerset Co.; will of. Wife, Sarah, all real and personal estate during her life, and, after her death, ⅔ to the children of my sisters, Janet Thompson and Mary McDuffy, Thomas McElrath, son of Samuel McElrath, and Thomas McElrath, son of Archibald Campbel. My wife may dispose of ⅓. Executors—wife, Sarah, and friends, Joseph Annin and Jonathan Ford Morris. Witnesses—James Campbell, Margaret Thompson, Jonathan F. Morris. Proved April 18, 1788. 1788, May 10. Inventory, £427.16.8, made by John Latourette and David Howel. Lib. 31, p. 163.

1789, Dec. 24. McElroy, Herbert, Esq., of City of Burlington. Int. Adm'x—Mary McElroy. Fellowbondsman—John Neale; both of said place. Witness—John McElroy. Lib. 31, p. 320.

1786, Aug. 26. McFarlin, Samuel, of Essex Co. Int. Adm'r— Thomas McFarlin. Fellowbondsman—Robert Johnston; both of New York City. Lib. 28, p. 426.

1788, Sept. 30. McFarson, Nathaniel, of Kingwood, Hunterdon Co., yeoman; will of. Wife, Anne, £20, and use of my plantation, to support my children. Daughter, Rebecca McFerson, £50, when 21. Daughter, Elizabeth McFerson, £50, when 21. Son, Daniel, £100, when 21. Sons, Samuel McFerson and Daniel McFerson, rest of estate, when 21. Son, Daniel, is now a cripple. Executors—David McFerson and Reuben McFerson. Witnesses—Samuel McFarson, Uriah Bonham, David Brewer. Proved Jan. 19, 1789. 1789, Jan. 12. Inventory, £167.5.1, made by Aaron Forman and Samuel McFarson. 1791, Feb. 3. Account by Executors. Lib. 32, p. 19.

1788, Aug. 12. McGee, Ann, of Middlesex Co. Ward. Daughter of Robert McGee, of said Co., deceased. Said Ward makes choice of James Patton as her Guardian. 1788, Aug. 12. Guardian—James Patton. Fellowbondsman—Henry Waggoner; both of said Co. Lib. 31, p. 225.

CALENDAR OF WILLS—1786-1790   145

**1780, April 8. McGhee, Lydia,** of Middlesex Co. Ward. Daughter of Robert McGhee, of said Co., deceased.
1789, April 8. Guardian—Henry Waggoner. Fellowbondsman—James Patton; both of said Co.   Lib. 31, p. 396.

**1788, Aug. 12. McGhee, Mary,** of Middlesex Co. Ward, Daughter of Robert McGhee, of said Co., deceased. Said Ward makes choice of Henry Waggoner as her Guardian.
1788, Aug. 12. Guardian—Henry Waggoner. Fellowbondsman—James Patton; both of said Co.   Lib. 31, p. 225.

**1788, April 3. McKean, Thomas B.,** of Bordentown, Burlington Co.; will of. Sister, Letitia McKean, all real and personal estate, but, if she die before she is 21, then I give the same to my cousins, Joseph B. McKean, Robert McKean, Elizabeth McKean, Letitia McKean and Ann McKean, children of Thomas McKean, Esq., of Philadelphia. Executors—my relations, Joseph B. McKean, of Philadelphia, and Robert McKean, of Bordentown. Witnesses—Joseph Kirkbride, David Greenman, Hugh Jackaway. Proved May 3, 1788.
   Lib. 30, p. 32.

**1788, April 15. McKee, Alexander,** of Upper Freehold, Monmouth Co. Int. Adm'r—Nathaniel Imlay. Fellowbondsman—John Craig; both of said Co.
1788, April 28. Inventory, £330.2.3, made by Luke Dewidt and Arthur Lefferson.   Lib. 30, p. 104.

**1789, July 6. McKnight, Joseph,** of Hopewell Township, Hunterdon Co. Int. Adm'r—Hezekiah Stiles Woodruff. Fellowbondsman—Thomas Bullman; both of said place.
1789, July 6. Renunciation by Andrew Hoff and Elizabeth, his wife, and the daughter of Joseph McKnight. Witness—Abraham Atchley.
1789, June 29. Inventory, £18.11.5, made by Jesse Knowles and Cornelius Hoff.   Lib. 32, p. 54.

**1790, Oct. 27. McMichael, James,** of Hunterdon Co. Int. Adm'rs—William Bryant, Jr., and Susanna Bryant; both of Hopewell. Fellowbondsman—Cornelius Vannoy, of Maidenhead, all of said Co.
1791, April 1. Inventory, £864.2.10, made by the Administrators. "8 Certificates against the United States £751.12.9. Interest thereon received and accounted for by Capt. Beatty, late attorney to the deceased, £157.17.2, Paper Currency of Pennsylvania, equal to £112.10.2."
1791, April 2. Account by Adm'rs. "Paid Capt. E. Beatty, in Philadelphia £14.4.3. Paid Doctor John Beatty, Guardian of Nancy McMichael, toward her share of the estate, £58.6.10."   Lib. 30, p. 314.

**1790, Oct. 27. McMichael, Nancy,** of Hunterdon Co. Ward. Petition of Susanna Bryant, showing that her late husband, James McMichael, died in Ireland some time in the year 1786, and that his and her daughter, the said Nancy, is under 14, and she prays that Doctor John Beatty may be appointed Guardian of said Ann.
1790, Nov. 16. Guardian—John Beatty, of Princeton, Middlesex Co. Fellowbondsman—Alexander Colhoun, of Trenton, Hunterdon Co.
1801, July 2. Account by John Beatty, Guardian.

1793, May 8. McMichael, Nancy, of Hunterdon Co. Ward. Daughter of James McMichael, of said Co., deceased. Said Ward makes choice of Cornelius Vannoy as her Guardian.
1793, May 8. Guardian—Cornelius Vannoy, of Maidenhead. Fellowbondsman—James Willson, of Amwell; both of said Co.
Lib. 30, p. 319; Lib. 33, p. 314.

**1789, Nov. 16. McMicken, Benjamin,** of Middlesex Co. Int. Adm'x— Elizabeth McMicken. Fellowbondsman—Alexander McMicken; both of Piscataway, said Co.
1789, Nov. 7. Inventory, £111.8.3, made by William Degroot and John Sebring, Jr.
Lib. 31, p. 394.

**1789, Feb. 17. McPeak [McPeach], Dennis,** of Bergen Co. Int. Adm'x—Jane McPeak. Fellowbondsman—John Joraleman; both of New Barbadoes, said Co.
Lib. 30, p. 247.

**1787, March 28. McPherson, John,** of Burlington Co. Int. Adm'x— Hester McPherson. Fellowbondsman—John Abbott; both of Nottingham Township, said Co. Witness—Thomas Adams.
1787, March 21. Inventory, £209.17.0, made by John Abbott and William Nutt.
Lib. 29, p. 74.

**1786, Sept. 22. Mackay, Charlotte,** of Salem Co. Ward. Petition of John Barclay, of Philadelphia, praying that he may be appointed Guardian of Charlotte Mackay, daughter of William and Charlotte Mackay; he having married the sister of said Charlotte, deceased, and the father of said infant is an improper person to have the Guardianship.
1789, May 12. Guardian—John Barclay, of Philadelphia, being Guardian of the daughter of William Mackay, who is living, and Charlotte Mackay, late of Cumberland Co., deceased. Fellowbondsman—Robert Johnson, of town of Salem.
Lib. 31, p. 359.

**1786, Oct. 16. Maghee, Robert,** of Middlesex Co. Int. Adm'r—William Maghee. Fellowbondsman—John Maghee; both of said Co. Witness—Joacham Gulick.
1786, Oct. 16. Inventory, made by John Wetherill and Joacham Gulick.
Lib. 28, p. 338.
1789, June 3. Maghee, Robert, of Middlesex Co. Ward. Son of Robert Maghee, of said Co., deceased. Said Ward makes choice of James Patton as his Guardian.
1789, June 3. Guardian—James Patton. Fellowbondsman—Henry Waggoner; both of said Co. Witness—William Hyer, Jr.
Lib. 31, p. 396.

**1786, Dec. 28. Mandeville, Henry,** of Pequanack, Morris Co.; will of, being old. Son, Peter, who is the eldest son, 7 shillings, and that land where he lives; also 27 acres west of his home lot; and, after his death, to his eldest son, Henry. Son, Henry, my homestead; also the lot west of my son Peter's; also 50 acres along the mountain. Son, William, 50 acres he lives on. Son, David, the 50 acres where he lives. Grandson, Henry Mandevel, son of Henry, my Dutch Bible. Grandson, Henry Spear, only son of my daughter, Elizabeth Spear, 12½ acres, called the Moyack, which joins land of John Mead. To my 6 daughters, and the children of my daughter, Elizabeth, de-

ceased, my moveable estate; that is, to daughters, Elizabeth Berry, Marey (or Marcy) Bertholf, Ann Francisco, Lea Kip, Clawsey Mandevel, Areyantye Lambert, and children of daughter, Elizabeth Spear. Executors—sons, Henry and David. Witnesses—George L. Reyerson, Roelef Jacobus, Nicolas Jones. Proved Dec. 28, 1790.
Lib. 30, p. 462.

**1787, Jan. 25. Mapes, Joseph,** of Great Egg Harbor, Gloucester Co., husbandman; will of. Wife, Mary, the northeast side of plantation where I live, from the Bay up to the great road from James Somer's line to the old ditch in the Cove. Daughter, Melicent Winner, the plantation where I live, after her mother is done with it, during her life, and then the plantation and a piece of old cedar swamp at the foot of Blackman's Branch, to my grandson, Joseph Winner. Daughter, Melicent, the rest of real estate. Granddaughter, Mary Mapes, daughter of my son, Edmund, deceased, £100, when she is 21. Executors—wife, Mary, and John Winner, my son-in-law. Witnesses—Samuel Risley, Samuel Smith, William Murphey.
1787, Sept. 3. Codicil. My wife is to have a good living out of my estate. Witnesses—Noah Smith, John Somers. Proved Dec. 6, 1787.
1787, Nov. 13. Inventory, £543.11.6, made by Noah Smith and John Somers. Lib. 29, p. 100.

**1789, Sept. 18. Marsh, Alexander Hamilton,** of Essex Co. Ward. Son of Moses Marsh, of said Co. Said Moses applied to be made Guardian of said infant, until he is 14 years of age.
1789, Sept. 19. Guardian—said Moses Marsh, Jr. Fellowbondsman—David Whitehead; both of said Co. Lib. 30, p. 219.

**1786, April 17. Marsh, Jabez,** of Elizabeth Town, Essex Co. Int. Adm'rs—John Wood and Benjamin Marsh. Fellowbondsmen—Jeremiah Clark and James Marsh; all of said Co.
1786, April 10. Renunciation by Mary Marsh, widow of said Jabez, in favor of John Wood and her brother-in-law, Benjamin Marsh. Lib. 28, p. 426.

**1790, Nov. 7. Marshall, Thomas,** of Gloucester Township, Gloucester Co.; will of. Wife, Anne, the use of the lower room that fronts my saw mill. Son, John, my house, saw mill and land thereto belonging; except the room referred to for his mother; also 200 acres of the tract joining to George Green. John is to provide for his mother, and also for my 2 youngest sons, William and Thomas, until they are 15. Son, Randall, 50 acres next to John's tract. Son, David, 50 acres next to Randall's. Son, William, 50 acres next to David's. Son, Thomas, 50 acres next to William's. Son, John, and my brother, John, to pay the debts. Executors—son, John, and my brother, John. Witnesses—Joseph Bolton, Joseph Marshal, John Rodgers. Proved Dec. 14, 1790.
1790, Nov. 29. Inventory, £638.1.7, made by Moses Branson and Ephraim Tomlinson. Lib. 31, p. 448.

**1788, Oct. 31. Marthews, Martha,** of Cape May Co. Ward. Daughter of Samuel Marthews, of said Co., deceased. Landal Bowen desires to be made Guardian of his sister's child, the said Martha Marthews.

1788, Oct. 31. Guardian—Landal Bowen, of Cumberland Co. Fellowbondsmen—Jonathan Leaming and Jesse Hand; both of Cape May Co. Witnesses—Eli Eldredge and George Norton.
Lib. 31, p. 94.

**1788, Oct. 31. Marthews, Temperence,** of Cape May Co. Ward. Daughter of Samuel Marthews, of said Co., deceased. Landal Bowen desires to be made Guardian of his sister's child, the said Temperence Marthews.
1788, Oct. 31. Guardian—Landal Bowen, of Cumberland Co. Fellowbondsmen—Jonathan Leaming and Jesse Hand; both of Cape May Co. Witnesses—Eli Eldredge and George Norton. Lib. 31, p. 94.

**1787, April 23. Martin, David,** of Sussex Co. Int. Adm'r—Hugh Hughes. Fellowbondsman—Valentine Biddleman; both of Greenwich Township, said Co. Witness—Godfrey Kline. Lib. 29, p. 491.

**1787, Sept. 13. Martin, Elizabeth,** of Burlington Co. Int. Adm'r—Burgiss Allison. Fellowbondsman—Joseph Bloomfield; both of said Co. Witness—Thomas Adams.
1787, Sept. 17. Inventory, £171.12.11, made by John Butler and Thomas Moore. Lib. 29, p. 78.

**1789, Dec. 29. Martin, Hannah,** of Bridge Town, Woodbridge Township, Middlesex Co., widow of Mulford Martin, late of Ash Swamp, in Essex Co., deceased, and only surviving daughter of John Trembley, deceased; will of. Daughters, Constant, Phebe, Anne and Betsey, my apparel. Daughter, Phebe, interest of £15. Land where I live to be sold; also, after the death of Mary, the widow of my brother, Joseph Trembley, all my share of house and land where said Mary lives, and of what money is left I give my son, William Martin, ½, and the rest to two of my daughters, Anne Martin and Betsey Martin. If William die under age, then his share I give to my two daughters, Anne and Elizabeth, who are the youngest. Executors—son, Benjamin Spinning, and friend, Henry Marsh. Witnesses—Joseph Craven, John Spinning, Joseph D'Camp. Proved April 6, 1790.
1790, Jan. 13. Inventory, £1,763.8.10, made by Cowperthwaite Copland and Esek Fitz Randolph. Lib. 30, p. 517.

**1789, Aug. 20. Martin, Joseph,** of Woodbridge, Middlesex Co. Int. Adm'rs—Clarkson Martin and Nathan Martin. Fellowbondsman—Robert Ross, Jr.; all of said Co.
1789, Aug. 8. Inventory, £47.0.2, made by Samuel Compton and Robert Ross, Jr. Lib. 31, p. 394.

**1786, Sept. 20. Martin, Joseph, Jr.,** of Bernards Township, Somerset Co.; will of. Wife, Hannah, use of all estate until my son is 21. If my son die, my wife shall have ⅓, and my brother, Nathan, ⅔. Executors—wife, Hannah, and friend, Anthony Cosad. Witnesses—Azariah Coon, Isaac Grant, James Bishop. Proved Nov. 5, 1786.
Lib. 28, p. 512.

CALENDAR OF WILLS—1786-1790          149

**1787, Feb. 23. Martin, Mary,** of Sussex Co. Ward. Daughter of Stewart Martin, of said Co., deceased. Said Ward being out of wardship of Elizabeth Downing, makes choice of Jacob Arnold, as her Guardian. Witness—Dillon Downing.
1787, March 26. Guardian—Jacob Arnold. Fellowbondsman—Silas Howell; both of Morristown, Morris Co. Witness—Joseph Lindsley.
Lib. 29, p. 475.

**1788, Feb. 6. Martin, Mulford,** of Essex Co. Int. Adm'rs—Hannah Martin and Meric Martin. Fellowbondsman—Moses Jaques; all of said Co. Lib. 31, p. 243.

**1786, Aug. 24. Martin, William,** of Cape May Co. Int. Adm'r—Christopher Leaming. Fellowbondsman—Zebulon Swain; both of Middle Precinct, said Co. Witnesses—Amos Cresse and Thomas Yates.
1786, Aug. 24. Inventory, £32.10.12, made by Zebulon Swain and Amos Cresse. Lib. 28, p. 249.

**1788, Dec. 11. Marvin, Daniel,** of Hardyston, Sussex Co. Int. Adm'x—Catherine Marvin, of said place, widow. Fellowbondsman—Henry Schoonover, of Hardwick, said Co. Lib. 30, p. 200.

**1786, April 15. Mason, John,** of Elsinborough, Salem Co., farmer; will of. Daughter, Sarah Brown, house and lot where Thomas Clements lives. House and lot in Salem, where Edward Siddens lives, and 13 acres of meadow at Windom, to be sold. Wife, Susanah, farm where I live, to bring up my children and paying the rent due my aunt, Grace Fisher, until my son, Thomas, is 21. Son, Thomas, ½ my farm, he paying to his sisters, Mary and Elizabeth Mason, £100 each. Son, John, the other ½, he also paying £100 to Mary, Ann and Elizabeth. Daughters, Mary, Ann and Elizabeth, the salt marsh in Lower Alloways Creek Township, on Stow Creek. Executors—wife, Susanah, and her brother, John Goodwin. Witnesses—Ignatius Grafenperger, Rebecca Conover, Edward Jones. Proved May 10, 1786.
1786, May 15. Inventory, £641.14.8, made by Richard Smith and Aaron Thompson. Lib. 28, p. 153.

**1790, March 7. Matlack, Hannah,** of Haddonfield, Gloucester Co., widow; will of. Daughters, Amie and Sarah, my apparel. Daughters, Mary, Hannah and Sarah, £100. Granddaughter, Elizabeth Fortener, £50. Grandson, Samuel Middleton, at the death of his mother, my clock. Granddaughter, Agnees Lippincott, widow of Aquilla, 6 sheep, which are at Thomas Lippincott's. Grandson, Thomas Lippincott, £50. Grandsons, Thomas Lippincott, William Ellis and Aaron Ellis, rest of estate. Executor—grandson, Thomas Lippincott. Witnesses—John Middleton, Jr., Thomas Redman. Proved June 15, 1790.
1790, June 3. Inventory, £840.9.4, made by John Gill and Samuel Kenard. Lib. 31, p. 450.

**1786, Sept. —. Matlack, Joseph,** of Woodbury, Gloucester Co.; will of. Son, James, all my real estate. Younger son, Richard and Joseph, my public securities. Wife, Hannah, and daughter, Mary, rest of my estate. Executors—wife, Hannah, and my friend, Franklin Davenport, Esq. Witnesses—Joel Westcott, Samuel Folwell. Proved Oct. 19, 1786.

1786, Oct. 20. Inventory, £1,240.7.10, made by Isaac Flaningam and Aaron Hewes. Lib. 28, p. 101.

**1788, Dec. 9. Matlack, Rebecca,** of Gloucester Co., the elder. Int. Adm'r—Samuel Matlack. Fellowbondsman—Bark Baldwin; both of said Co. Witness—Franklin Davenport.
1788, Dec. 8. Inventory, made by John Middleton and Joseph Hillman. Lib. 31, p. 37.

**1789, Aug. 24. Matthews, Richard,** of Cape May Co., weaver; will of. Son, Richard, all my lands, when he is 21. Daughters, Elizabeth, Judith, Bethiah, Sarah and Charlotte, 20 shillings each, when they are 18. Wife, Judith, rest of moveable estate and use of lands, till my son is 21. He is to be put to a trade when he is 14. Executrix—wife, Judith. Witnesses—Thomas Hand, Elizabeth Hand, Constantine Carll. Proved Jan. 4, 1790.
1789, Sept. 23. Inventory, £182.5.4, made by Isaac Matthews and Constantine Carll. Lib. 31, p. 550.

**1788, April 10. Mattocks, Robert,** of Cape May Co.; will of. I give the use of my old tract of land, at the Blue Anker, to my wife and children, who shall remain with her, for the term of 5 years. All my land that was purchased since is to be sold, and the old tract after 5 years. One fourth of the saw mill, and ¼ of the 77 acres of cedar swamp, and two other tracts held by deed from Richard Fry and wife, bearing date July 6, 1765; also 314 acres, and the tract of 35 acres of cedar swamp, which are both described in a deed of Robert Mattocks, Jr.; also 3 other lots of cedar swamp, one lot of which was bought of John Golder and Burr, and one was surveyed by Thomas Denny, and the other by Richard Somers; all to be sold. One half of the 100 acre tract on the south side of White Oak, I give to John Martial, and the other ½ to John Inskep, if the right is found to be good. Thirty-five acres, over White Oak, I give up to Richard Somers. All other lands to be sold. Wife, Sarah, household goods. Daughter, Rebecca, a negro girl, which she raised from a child. My sail boat and rest of moveable estate to be sold. If my son, Luke, clears my estate from any incumbrance about Morris Beasley's estate, then there is to be paid to him £200. The rest of the money I give to my daughters, but those who are married must allow what is on account. Executors—son, Jesse, and John Martial [Marshall]. Witnesses—George Norton, Abijah Smith, John Cresse. Proved June 7, 1788.
1788, June 7. Inventory, £435.11.4, made by John Hedger and John Hider. Lib. 31, p. 86.

**1786, June 26. Mattson, Jacob,** of Woolwich Township, Gloucester Co. Int. Adm'x—Rebecca Mattson, widow. Fellowbondsman—Daniel Adams; both of said place. Witnesses—Sarah Hugg and Joseph Hugg, Surrogate.
1786, June 20. Inventory, £27.14.7, made by Ebenezer Adams and Daniel Adams. Lib. 28, p. 124.

**1787, March 30. Maul, Jeremiah,** of Deerfield Township, Cumberland Co.; will of. Eldest sons, David Maul and John Garrison Maul, that part of my farm where I live, down to the road; which road is to be the division line between my sons and brothers, William and

CALENDAR OF WILLS—1786-1790   151

Alexander Maul. I also give them 7½ acres of cedar swamp, on the head of Parvin's Branch; also 2 acres of meadow on Cohansey Creek; when they are 21. Youngest son, Jeremiah, £20. Brother, William, 68 acres where he lives. Brother, John, £20. Brother, Benjamin, £10. Brother, Robert, £10. My 2 youngest brothers are to be paid their legacy (£20) due to them from their deceased father's estate, namely, Benjamin Maul and Robert Maul. Wife, Rachel, ½ of the profits of the land. Executors—wife, Rachel, and William Garrison; and wife is to have the residue. Witnesses—Jonas Keen, Reuben Jay, Jemima Smith. Proved April 21, 1787.
1787, April 18. Inventory, £142.7.3, made by Jonas Keen and Ephraim Lummis. Lib. 29, p. 168.

**1789, June 6. Maul, William,** of Deerfield Township, Cumberland Co. Int. Adm'x—Phebe Maul.
1789, June 3. Goods sold at vendue to Jeremiah Sayre, Joseph Garrison, John Garrison, Phebe Maul, John Maul, Stephen Davis, Ezekiel Loper, William Loder, Aaron Moore, Jacob Joslin, Alexander Maul, Daniel Garrison and Fithian Stratton.
1789, June 6. Inventory, £101.4.6.
1792, July 22. Agreement between Phebe Maul and Jonathan Smalley, and he is to take possession of all estate that was William Maul's, deceased, and to take good care of the same, and, if he should not do so, the estate is to be taken from him, and put into whose hands that John Garrison pleases; but, if he is careful, he shall have the same till Garrison Maul is 21, he paying £20 out of the estate that is behind, and, when the said Garrison Maul is of age, then Jonathan Smalley shall give up ⅔ of the land; and said Smalley shall give the two boys learning. Signed by Jonathan Smalley. Witnesses—John Garrison and Marcy Gee.
1790, Feb. 23. Received of Phebe Maul, Adm'x of William Maul, £20, it being for a legacy left me by my brother, Jeremiah Maul. Signed John Mall, in presence of Israel Davis.
1790, May 24. Received of Phebe Maul, Adm'x of William Maul, £20, being a legacy due to Benjamin and Robert Maul, from their father, John Maul, deceased estate, and paid agreeable to the will of Jeremiah Maul, who was their Guardian. Signed Jonathan Smith and William Garrison, Executors; in presence of John Garrison.
1795, April 13. Received of Jonathan Smalley and Phebe, his wife, Adm'x of William Maul, 7 pounds and 15 shillings, in part of a legacy due to me from said William Maul, given by the will of Jeremiah Maul. Signed Benjamin Maul. File No. 6216 F.

**1786, June 3. Maxson, Nathan,** of Monmouth Co. Int. Adm'r—George Maxson. Fellowbondsman—Samuel Pease; both of said Co. Witness—Rachel Henderson.
1786, May 12. Renunciation by Elizabeth Maxson, widow of deceased, in favor of her son, George Maxson. Witness—Thomas Little.
Lib. 28, p. 293.

**1790, Feb. 8. Mearing, Peter,** of Sussex Co. Int. Adm'rs—George Mearing and Mary Mearing. Fellowbondsmen—Daniel Struble and Peter Smith; all of said Co.
1790, Feb. 6. Inventory, £93.13.6, made by Daniel Struble and Peter Smith. Lib. 30, p. 437.

**1789, March 1. Meeker, Aaron,** of Essex Co.; will of. Wife, Hannah, £100. The land that joins Jonathan Williams may be sold to pay debts. Sons, James, Henry, Job, Aaron, and the infant unborn (if a son), my lands. Executors—wife, Hannah, David Crane and my brother, James Meeker. Witnesses—Peter Fish, David Rogers, Lidya Cornish. Proved March 10, 1789.

1789, March 10. Renunciation by Hannah Meeker. Witness—David Rogers. Lib. 34, p. 33.

**1787, June 15. Meeker, David,** of Elizabeth Borough, Essex Co., yeoman; will of. Daughters, Elizabeth Meeker and Mary Meeker, use of the house, while they are single, and a cow to each; also £30 each. Son, John, £5. Grandson, Daniel Meeker, 5 shillings. Grandson, Samuel Meeker, 5 shillings. Daughter, Susanah Ayres, £5. Son, Michael, my lands. Executors—friends, Benjamin Scudder and Captn Jonas Wade. Witnesses—Matthias Meeker, David Headly, Thomas Woodruff. Proved Oct. 22, 1787. Lib. 29, p. 386.

**1788, April 26. Meeker, John,** of Elizabeth Town, Essex Co.; will of. Wife, Hannah, use of real and personal estate, to bring up my children. The 3 acres that I bought of William Brittin to be sold. Executrix—wife, Hannah. Witnesses—John Hendricks, Michael Woodruff, Alexander Gale. Proved July 1, 1788. Lib. 33, p. 214.

**1788, May 11. Meghee, Priscilla,** of Middlesex Co.; will of. To Priscilla Westlake, ½ of my apparel. To Lidia Meghee, the other ½. To the Presbyterian Church of Cranbury, residue. Executors—John Wetherill and Matthew Rue. Witnesses—Peter Ervin, Matthew Rue, William Meghee. Proved May 19, 1788.

1788, May 17. Inventory, made by John Wetherill and William Meghee. Lib. 31, p. 207.

**1788, July 17. Melick, Christion,** of Woodbridge, Middlesex Co. Int. Adm'r—Samuel Jaques, Jr. Fellowbondsman—Andrew Elston; both of said Co. Witness—William Hyer, Jr.

1788, July 8. Inventory, made by Andrew Elston and Jonathan Bloomfield. Lib. 31, p. 224.

**1788, April 4. Mellet, William,** of Somerset Co.; will of. Wife, Charity, ⅛ of the estate, and the rest to my children, William, Thomas, and my daughters, Charity Mellet, Elizabeth Mellet and Rebecca Mellet. Executors—wife, Charity, my son, William, Capt. John Little and Thomas Wiggins. Witnesses—John Little, Thomas Wiggins, Robert White, Hannah White. Proved Sept. 5, 1789.
Lib. 31, p. 405.

**1786, Jan. 27. Merrell, Benjamin,** of Hopewell Township, Hunterdon Co. Int. Adm'rs—John Merrell and Peter Gordon. Fellowbondsman—Samuel Stout; all of said place. Witness—Nathan Beakes.

1786, Jan. 23. Inventory, £334.0.9, made by Samuel Stout and Joab Houghton.

1790, May 13. Account by Adm'rs. Lib. 28, p. 247.

**1788, March 24. Merrick, John,** of Trenton, Hunterdon Co. Int. Adm'rs—John Armitage and Gershom Moore. Fellowbondsman—Isaac Barnes. Witness—William Smith.

## CALENDAR OF WILLS—1786-1790    153

**1788, March 24.** Renunciation by Sarah Merrick, widow of John Merrick. Witness—John Armitage.
**1788, March 26.** Inventory, £44.1.3, made by William Smith and Isaac Barnes. Lib. 31, p. 144.

**1788, Jan. 15. Merriot, John Rhodes,** of Hopewell Township, Cumberland Co. Int. Adm'r—Jonathan Youngs. Fellowbondsman—Brown Youngs; both of said Co. Witness—Levi Heaton.
**1788, March 3.** Inventory, £79.7.4, made by David Ayars and Caleb Ayars. Lib. 31, p. 76.

**1790, Aug. 10. Merrit, Isaac, Jr.,** of Burlington Co. Int. Adm'r—William Kempton. Fellowbondsman—Thomas Platt. Lib. 32, p. 95.

**1790, Nov. 20. Mickle, Elizabeth Estaugh,** of Gloucester Co. Int. Adm'rs—John S. Whitall and John Blackwood. Fellowbondsman—Joel Westcott; all of said Co. Lib. 31, p. 479.

**1790, Dec. 18. Mickle, Hannah,** of Gloucester Co. Ward. Daughter of John Mickle, of said Co., deceased. Said Ward makes choice of John S. Whitall as her Guardian.
**1790. Dec. 18.** Guardian—John S. Whitall, of Woodbury. Fellowbondsman—Benjamin Whitall; both of said Co. Lib. 31, p. 482.

**1789, May 23. Mickle, William,** of Greenwich Township, Gloucester Co.; will of, Wife, Sarah, the profits of plantation until son, David, is of age, and she is to bring up my children, Joshua, David, George and Sibbea Mickle. Sons, Joshua, David and George, plantation where I live. Daughter, Sibbea Mickle, £200. Wife, Sarah, rest of moveable estate. Executors—wife, Sarah, and Joshua Lord. Witnesses—Ann White, Abishai Chattin, William White. Proved Aug. 12, 1789.
**1789, June 26.** Inventory, £526.8.9, made by David Brown and William White. Lib. 30, p. 128.

**1787, Sept. 8. Middleswaert, Henry V.,** of Raritan, Somerset Co., yeoman; will of. Wife, Neltje, use of 100 acres. Oldest son, Teunus, £10. Daughters, Femmetje and Jeneke, a wench to each. Daughters, Ariantje, Susanna, Femmetje and Jeneke, £150. To Henricus, Neeltje, Antje and Jannetje, children of Teunus, £150. Sons, Andrias and John, rest of estate. Executors—sons, Andrias and John, and my son-in-law, Peter Staats. Witnesses—Samuel Beekman, Jacob Van Derbilt, Teunes V. Middleswart. Proved Jan. 10, 1788.
**1788, Jan. 8.** Inventory, £775.19.7, made by Samuel Beekman, Teunis I. Van Middleswart and Peter D. Vroom. Lib. 31, p. 172.

**1788, Jan. 7. Miller, Catharine and George,** of Salem Co. Wards. Children of George Miller, of said Co., deceased. Said Wards, having real and personal estate, make choice of Simon Souder as their Guardian.
**1788, Jan. 7.** Guardian—Simon Souder. Fellowbondsman—John Dilshaver; both of Cumberland Co. Witnesses—William Hains and Philip Souder. Lib. 31, p. 77.

**1786, Oct. 17. Miller, David,** of Elizabeth Town, Essex Co.; will of. Sons, Abraham and Ichobad, my apparel. Grandson, David, son of my son, Ichobad, shoe buckels. Wife to have use of goods. Daughter, Susannah Scudder, £5. Daughter, Hannah Clark, £15. Daughter, Phebe Walker, £30. Daughter, Sarah Stanberry, £15. Granddaughter, Phebe Scudder, £5. Son, Benjamin, a lot of land that joins land of Samuel Robinson, deceased. Son, Jonathan, part of the plantation. Wife to have the use of the land that I bought of Abner Sayre. Rest of land to be sold, and money given to my sons, Abraham, John, Ichobad, Jonathan and Benjamin. Executors—sons, Abraham and Ichobad, and friend, William Darby. Witnesses—Hannah Miller, Sally Clark, Abraham Clark. Proved Feb. 23, 1787.
Lib. 29, p. 383.

**1787, Jan. 5. Miller, Hannah,** of Cumberland Co. Ward. Daughter of Michael Miller, of said Co., deceased. Said Ward, having real and personal estate, makes choice of Jacob Miller as her Guardian.
1787, Jan. 5. Guardian—Jacob Miller. Fellowbondsman—John Dilshaver; both of said Co. Lib. 29, p. 184.

**1787, July 23. Miller, Jacob,** of Hopewell Township, Cumberland Co.; will of. Wife, Cathrine, furniture, horse, cows and ⅓ of the real estate. Sons, Jacob and George, the plantation where I live, and 20 acres of woodland in Deerfield Township. Sons, Michael and Andrew, my place in Deerfield, and 20 acres of meadow joining John Haun. Son, John, £150, and a meadow, lying between the fludgate and flying sluce, of 3 or 4 acres. Daughters, Barbary Miller and Margreat Miller, £100 each, when 18. If my sons die under 21, then their lands to go to my son, John. Executors—wife, Cathrine, and Peter Minch. Witnesses—John Trenchard, Joseph Irelan, Arthur Clark. Proved Sept. 24, 1787. Lib. 29, p. 174.

**1789, Oct. 30. Miller, John,** of Elizabeth Town, Essex Co.; will of. Son, John, ½ of the real and personal estate. Daughter, Betsey, wife of Thomas Barrett, ¼ of same. Grandson, John Miller Barret, son of said Thomas and Betsey, the other ¼. But my housekeeper, Mary Longworth, is to have £100. Executors—Aaron Lane and James Chapman. Witnesses—Edmund D. Thomas, Thomas Sullivan, Samuel Harriman, John Donington. Proved Jan. 5, 1790.
1790, Jan. 5. Renunciation by Aaron Lane and James Chapman. Witness—Samuel Harriman.
1790, Jan. 5. Adm'r—Thomas Barrett. Fellowbondsman—John Miller; both Executors having renounced. Lib. 30, p. 324.

**1790, Jan. 8. Miller, Samuel,** of Morristown, Morris Co. Int. Adm'r—Mose Miller. Fellowbondsman—Naphlah Byram; both of said Co.
1789, May 20. Inventory, £12.6.0, made by John Miller and George Carter. Lib. 30, p. 479.

**1786, Oct. 14. Mills, James,** of Essex Co. Int. Adm'rs—James Mills and John Craig; both of said Co. Lib. 28, p. 427.

**1789, May 20. Mills, Samuel,** of Fairfield Township, Cumberland Co., freeholder; will of. Wife, Mary, all real and personal estate, during her life, and, at her death, all lands to her son, William Machesny. Executrix—wife, Mary. Witnesses—Joel Husted, Mary Husted, Alexander Stephens. Proved March 29, 1790. Lib. 30, p. 275.

CALENDAR OF WILLS—1786-1790         155

**1790, Jan. 6. Mintis, George,** of Northampton, Burlington Co. Int. Adm'r—John Mason. Fellowbondsman—Thomas Platt; both of New Hanover, said Co.
1790, Jan. 5. Inventory, £33.12.6, of George Mintis, a negro, made by Thomas Platt and William Norcross.  Lib. 32, p. 93.

**1788, Aug. 23. Moffett, Abraham,** of Bernards Town, Somerset Co. Int. Adm'r—William Moffett, Jr. Fellowbondsman—Isaac Van Tuyl; both of said place.
1788, Aug. 18. Inventory, £36.15.5, made by David Kelly and Isaac Van Tuyl.  Lib. 31, p. 176.

**1789, Aug. 31. Monfoort, Abraham,** of Reading Township, Hunterdon Co. Int. Adm'rs—Nelle (Eleanor) Monfoort and Peter Monfort. Fellowbondsman—John Voorhees; all of said Co.
1789, Aug. 27. Inventory, £587.6.10, made by John Taylor and Tunis Melick.
1792, Feb. 6. Account by Peter Monfort, one of the Adm'rs. Paid William Graham, on account of a legacy given him by his grandfather's will, of which the intestate was Executor, £9.12.0.
1792, Feb. 8. Account by Peter Monfort. Balance of £106.18.1, which ⅓ belongs to the widow, and rest to the nine children, 4 of which have been supported by the widow and this accountant upwards of 2 years, of which no allowance has been granted.
1792, Feb. 4. Petition of Mary, Margaret, Hannah and Abraham Monfort, heirs of Abraham Monfort, stating that he had 2 lots of land, one of 157 acres, and other of 70 acres, the former in Readingtown, and the latter in Tewksbury, and we depend on the profits of the land for our support, which falls short, and there are 5 heirs besides us, and the mother is entitled to her dower; therefore we pray that Nelly Monfort and Peter Monfort, the Adm'rs, be directed to sell our right to the lands, as we are infants under 21. (Signed): Mary Monfort, Margaret Monfort, Hannah Monfort, Abraham Monfort.
We, heirs and Adm'rs of Abraham Monfort, agree that the prayer may be granted. (Signed): Nellie Monfort, Adm'x., Peter Monfort, Adm'r., Isaac Monfort, Cornelius Couwenhoven, Nelley Couwenhoven, Sarah Monfort, Cornelius Lane, Siny Lane, wife of C. L.
The lot of 157 acres was sold to Ephraim Bush, for £340. The lot of 70 acres was sold to Morris Creater, for £141.15.0. Lib. 32, p. 56.

**1788, Feb. 28. Monroe, Margaret,** of Northampton Township, Burlington Co., widow; will of. Daughters, Rebecah Shinn and Sarah Budd, and my granddaughters, Mary and Margaret, the daughters of Job Stockton, all my estate. Executors—sons-in-law, Earl Shinn, Job Stockton and Stacy Budd. Witnesses—Zacha Rossell, Samuel Spraggs, Richard Cox. Proved May 17, 1788. Lib. 30, p. 50.

**1786, May 6. Monrow, John,** of Northampton, Burlington Co.; will of. Wife, Margaret, ½ of the household goods and £200, and the use of my plantation now under lease to Elias Wilson, and 80 acres of woodland bought of Robert Smith. Granddaughter, Margaret Monrow, the said plantation, after wife's decease. Grandson, Edward Mullin, the house and lot where I live, that I bought of Thomas Reynolds, and the meadow which I bought of Joshua Evins; also a lot I bought of James Dobbins. Daughter, Rebeccah Shinn, £300, and I release my son-in-law, Earl Shinn, from paying the money he owes me, except a note of £89; and my daughter is to have the interest of £600, which after her death is to go to her children, except Thomas, John and Samuel. I also give her the house where she lives, and the goods I bought of the Trustees appointed to sell the same for the use of Earl Shinn's creditors; and, after her death, I give the same to my grandsons, Thomas and John Shinn. Grandson, John Stockton, the plantation which I bought of Preserve Brown, during his life, provided he shall return and live in New Jersey within 3 years after my death, and, after his death, to his heir, and, if he leave no heir, then it is to be sold, and the money given to my daughter's (Nancy Stockton's) children, only Monrow Stockton is to have 3 shares. Grandsons, Jonathan and William Stockton, my saw mill, and 320 acres that I bought of Joseph Ong and wife, and 100 acres of William Smith, and 230 acres, being part of 286 (BB. 121), 200 bought of Zebulon Webb, 86 acres in BB. pg. 120, 9 acres in S No. 6, pg. 148, 42 acres, pg. 146, 84 acres in L, pg. 184. Grandson, Monrow Stockton, the plantation where Ezekiel Job lives, which joins Joseph Lamb's plantation. Daughter, Sarah Budd, plantation which I bought of Joseph Budd; also the lots I bought of the Iron Work tract; also the Black meadow, by the 4 acres of meadow which I bought of Abraham Leeds, now occupied by my brother, George; also 11 acres I bought of Samuel Atkinson; also 13 acres of meadow I bought of Josiah Southwick; also 7 acres of cedar swamp bought of Joseph Burr; also plantation I bought of Joseph and Thomas Leonard; also a meadow bought of Tanton Earl; also land I bought of Executors of John Atkinson and William Calvert, joining land of Christopher Shuff. Grandsons, Thomas and John Shinn, rest of the 126 acre swamp. Granddaughter, Elizabeth Shinn, £10 yearly. Brother, George, apparel, and use of plantation where he lives, and, after his death, to my grandson, Samuel Shinn. Of my share of Long Beach at Little Egg Harbor, I give ⅕ to the sons of my daughter, Rebeccah Shinn, ⅕ to the sons of my daughter, Nancy Stockton, ⅕ to the sons of my daughter, Sarah Budd, ⅕ to my grandson, Edward Mullen, ⅕ to my granddaughter, Margaret Monrow. The rest of my land I give as follows:—¼ to the sons of my daughter. Nancy Stockton, ¼ to Thomas, John and Samuel Shinn, children of my daughter, Rebeccah Shinn, ¼ to my daughter's (Sarah Budd's) 2 eldest sons, Mahlon and Stacy Budd, and ¼ to my grandson, Edward Mullen. My Propriety Rights I give as follows:—¼ to my grandson, Edward Mullen, ¼ to my grandson, Jonathan Stockton. ¼ to my grandson, Thomas Shinn, and ¼ to my grandson, Mahlon Budd. Executors—sons-in-law, Job Stockton, Earl Shinn and Stacy Budd. Witnesses—Zachariah Rossell, Edward Black, Richard Cox, Jr. Proved Nov. 8, 1787.

1787, Nov. 1. Inventory, £4,692.5.1, made by Zachariah Rossell, Aaron Smith, and Mose Kempton. Lib. 29, p. 7.

**1788, March 11. Montanye, Joseph,** of Roxbury Township, Morris Co.; will of. Son, Abraham, 1/7 of my lands. Son, John, 1/7. Son, Joseph, 1/7. Son, Bergon, 1/7. Daughter, Rebecca Schoonover, 1/7. Daughter, Jane Vanwey, 1/7. Grandchildren, children of son, Isaac, deceased, 1/7. My sisters, Rebecca and Jane, some moveable estate. Executors—son, Bergon, and friend, James Skinner. Witnesses—Lemuel Fordham, Peter Brown, William Woodhull. Proved April 14, 1788.

## CALENDAR OF WILLS—1786-1790

**1788, March 31.** Inventory, £204.5.10, made by Peter Brown and Amos Leek.
Lib. 31, p. 188.

**1787, April 16. Moody, Thomas,** of Middlesex Co. Int. Adm'x—Hannah Skelton. Fellowbondsman—Ezekiel Smith; both of said Co. Witness—William Hyer, Jr.
Lib. 29, p. 364.

**1787, Nov. 10. Mooney, John,** of Essex Co. Int. Adm'x—Elizabeth Mooney. Fellowbondsman—Jonathan Miller; both of said Co.
Lib. 29, p. 418.

**1786, June 9. Moore, Anne and Sarah,** of Cumberland Co. Wards. Daughters of Joshua Moore, of said Co., deceased. Petition of Sarah Coles, aunt and next of kin of said infants, who are under 14; and she asks that a Guardian be appointed for said minors.
1786, June 9. Guardian—Jonathan Bowen. Fellowbondsmen—Alexander Moore, Jr., and Ebenezer Howell; all of said Co. Witness—Eli Elmer.
Lib. 28, p. 184.

**1790, Jan. 24. Moore, Benjamin,** of Trenton Township, Hunterdon Co., yeoman; will of. Son, Israel, the plantation I bought of my father, of 147 acres; also a £25 bond due from George Bright. Son, William Sacket, plantation I live on, of 33¾ acres, which I bought of Isaac Reeder; also 96 acres which I bought of Elnathan Davis; also 31 acres which I bought of Isaac Reeder; also 3 acres which I bought of Joshua Jones; also 25 acres on each side of Jacobs Creek, which I bought of John Gershom Mott. Grandson, Aaron Moore, to give my negros freedom. Daughter, Sarah Moore, £260. Executors—sons, Israel and William Sacket. Witnesses—Joseph Moore, Elizabeth Clifford, William Campbell. Proved July 13, 1790. Probate to Israel Moore and William Sacket Moore.
1790, June 26. Inventory, £488.6.1, made by John Carpenter and Joshua Jones.
Lib. 30, p. 286.

**1788, April 3. Moore, Eber,** of Evesham, Burlington Co. Int. Adm'r—Joseph Moore. Fellowbondsman—Joshua Bates; both of said Township.
1788, April 1. Renunciation by Sarah Moore, widow of Eber Moore, in favor of her brother-in-law, Joseph Moore. Witness—Joshua Bates.
1788, April 1. Inventory, £88.1.1, made by Bethuel Moore and Joshua Bates.
Lib. 30, p. 57.

**1787, June 8. Moore, Enoch, Jr.,** of Cumberland Co. Ward. Son of Enoch Moore, of said Co., deceased. Petition of Rebecca Moore, sister and next of kin of Enoch Moore, Jr., who asks that a Guardian may be appointed for said minor.
1787, June 8. Guardian—John Ewing. Fellowbondsmen—Isaac Smith, Esq., and Enos Woodruff; all of said Co. Witness—Amos Fithian.
Lib. 29, p. 184.

**1786, April 4. Moore, Fanny, and Rachel,** of Bergen Co. Wards. Daughters of Thomas Moore, Esq., of said Co., deceased. Said Wards make choice of Samuel T. Moore as their Guardian.
1786, April 4. Guardian—Samuel T. Moore, Fellowbondsman—Jacob Moore; both of said Co. Witness—Abraham Blauvelt.
Lib. 29, p. 224.

158  NEW JERSEY POST-REVOLUTIONARY DOCUMENTS

**1786, April 4. Moore, Helena,** of Bergen Co. Ward. Daughter of Thomas Moore, of said Co., deceased. Thomas T. Moore and Jacob T. Moore made application in behalf of their sister, Helena Moore, a minor under 14 years of age, praying that the said Jacob Moore may be made Guardian until said minor is 14.
1786, April 4. Guardian—Jacob Moore. Fellowbondsman—Samuel Moore; both of said Co. Witness—Abraham Blauvelt.
Lib. 29, p. 224.

**1789, Sept. 14. Moore, Isaac,** of Woodbridge, Middlesex Co. Int. Adm'x—Martha Moore. Fellowbondsman—Nathaniel Heard; both of said place.
1789, Sept. 9. Inventory, £291.14.0, made by Isaac Freeman and Nathaniel Heard. Lib. 31, p. 394.

**1786, April 1. Moore, Joseph,** of Evesham Township, Burlington Co., yeoman; will of. Wife, Patience, various goods. Daughter, Patience Wane, house in Mount Holly, bought of Joseph Hemsey. Son, Uriah, a meadow at the north end of my plantation, of 8 acres; also a meadow at the northeast corner of land I bought of John Small, joining the lot bought of my brother, Benjamin. Sons, Uriah, John and Cyrus, my landing lot. Son, John, the plantation where he lately lived. Son, Cyrus, land by line of my son, John; also my share of pine land by line of my son, John; also my share of pine land, being ¼ part of 200 acres, surveyed to myself, brother, Benjamin, Caleb Haines and Carlile Haines. Son, John, the land near Robert Engle. Son, Uriah, rest of plantation where I live, and he is to provide for his mother. Executors—sons, Uriah and John. Witnesses—Joseph Moore, Charity Small, Uriah Woolman. Proved June 7, 1786.
1786, Oct. 7. Inventory, £299.16.0, made by Bethuel Moore and Robert Engle. Lib. 28, p. 3.

**1789, Nov. 30. Moore, Thomas,** of Bordentown, Burlington Co., tanner; will of. Wife, Lydia, all household goods. That part of the land which is not sold, which I bought in company with my father-in-law, John Taylor, from Isaac Ivins, deceased; also land which I bought from Jason Emley, joining lands of Amy Potts, Thomas Potts and others, to be sold. Wife and children to be supported till the latter are 21, and then the overplus to be paid to children, James, John and Thomas. Executors—father-in-law, John Taylor, and my wife, Lydia. Witnesses—John Thorn, Thomas Thorn, Charles Burton. Proved Aug. 24, 1790.
1790, Aug. 21. Inventory, £717.17.0, made by John Thorn and Thomas Thorn. Lib. 32, p. 68.

**1790, Jan. 9. Moore, Uriah,** of Evesham, Burlington Co. Int. Adm'r—Cyrus Moore. Fellowbondsman—Uriah Woolman; both of said Co. Witness—Thomas Hewlings.
1790, Jan. 26. Inventory, £251.8.7, made by Bethuel Moore and Joseph Engle. Lib. 32, p. 93.

**1787, March 12. Moore, William,** of Downs Township, Cumberland Co.; will of. Oldest son, William, the land I bought of Reuben Lore, which joins his land. Son, Dicason, and son, Edward, the land where I live, and that where son, Dicason, lives. Edward to have

his land when 21. Grandchildren, the children that my daughter, Mary Ray had, £3 each. Grandson, John Hamlinton, £3. Executors— sons, William and Dicason. Witnesses—Gideon Heaton, Henry Fennemore, Margaret Hamilton. Proved Sept. 21, 1787.
1787, March 22. Inventory, £80.1.5, made by Gideon Heaton and William Young. Lib. 29, p. 164.

**1787, Feb. 9. Moores, James,** of Middlesex Co. Int. Adm'r—Israel Thornal. Fellowbondsman—Samuel Crow; both of Woodbridge, said Co. Witness—William Hyer, Jr. Lib. 29, p. 364.

**1789, April 30. Morgan, David,** of Gloucester Co., yeoman; will of. Daughter, Margret Morgan, a bed. Son, John, my apparel and books. Real estate to be sold, and money put to interest till my children are 21; and then my eldest son, John, to have 2 shares, daughter, Margret Morgan, and my sons, Joseph, Randle and David, the other 4 shares. Three younger sons to be put to trades when 14; and sons to live where they are now till that age; son, Joseph, with his uncle, Joseph Blackwood, son, Randle, with his cousin, Randle Morgan, and son, David, with Ephraim Cheesman. Executors—friends, George Morgan, Jonathan Morgan, Joseph Blackwood and Ephraim Cheesman. Witnesses—Drusilla Hillman, Charles Dennis, Isaac Tomlinson. Proved June 17, 1789. Lib. 30, p. 111.

**1790, April 19. Morgan, Griffith,** of Waterford Township, Gloucester Co., yeoman; will of. Wife, Rebekah, enough goods to furnish 2 rooms, and the rents from a meadow in Newton Township, on Pettys Island; bounded by Samuel Cooper, Marmaduke Cooper, Andrew Hodge and the Delaware River, which contains about 21 acres, as by an Indenture executed June 1, 1784, by Samuel Cooper and his wife, Prudence; all which I give my wife in order to take care of my daughter, Ann, till she is 18. After death of wife, I give the said meadow to my daughters, Agness Eldridge, Rebekah Cooper and Ann Morgan. Executors—uncle, Benjamin Morgan, and my son, James Morgan. Witnesses—Benjamin H. Tallman, Joseph Branson, James Sloan. Proved Oct. 5, 1790.
1790, April 29. Inventory, £826.5.0, made by Joseph Cooper and Joseph Champion. Lib. 31, p. 451.

**1787, Oct. 30. Morgan, Randall,** of Gloucester Co. Int. Adm'rs— James Jaggard and Michael Morgan, who are Adm'rs of Amy Morgan, of Deptford Township, said Co., who was Adm'x of Randall Morgan, deceased. Fellowbondsman—Henry Roe; all of said Twp. Witness— Kezia Albertson. Lib. 29, p. 116.

**1786, July 15. Morris, James,** of Essex Co. Int. Adm'r—Dennis Bacorn. Fellowbondsman—Caleb Hetfield; both of said Co.
Lib. 28, p. 428.

**1786, June 28. Morris, Job,** of Shrewsbury, Monmouth Co., yeoman; will of. Wife, Mary, all real and personal estate, and, after her death, to be sold, and divided among my children, Jeams Morris, Silfe Morris, Mary Morris and Lida Morris; except 10 shillings I give to my daughter, Rebekah Jackson. Executors—wife, Mary, and son, Hue Jackson. Witnesses—Jacob Laing, Samuel Lippincott, Edward Patterson Cook. Proved Aug. 25, 1786.

1786, Aug. 25. Inventory, £233.15.0, made by Edward Patterson Cook and George Parker. Lib. 28, p. 273.

**1788, Feb. 15. Morris, John,** of Woodbridge, Middlesex Co. Int. Adm'rs—Reuben Morris and Thomas Goodfellow. Fellowbondsman—Henry Sutton; all of N. J.
1788, Feb. 13. Inventory, made by John Conger and Henry Sutton. Lib. 31, p. 224.

**1789, April 4. Morris, John,** of Shrewsbury, Monmouth Co. Int. Adm'x—Anna Morris, widow of John. Fellowbondsman—Joseph Thomson; both of said Co. Witness—Margaret Forman.
1789, Feb. 27. Inventory, £129.7.8, made by Thomas Morford and William Lipencot. Lib. 30, p. 189.

**1789, March 19. Morris, Mary,** of Chester, Penna., wife of Richard Morris; will of. After the death of my husband, I give my plantation and several tracts of land in Gloucester Co., N. J., to my mother, Mary Cooper, during her life, and, after her death, to my brothers, William and John, and my sister, Esther; and they are to pay £100 to my step-sister, Rebecca Cooper; but if they all die, then to the children of my cousins, Warner Mifflin and Daniel Mifflin. Witnesses—Margaret Morris, Deborah Morris, Deborah Hicks. Proved Oct. 19, 1790.
1790, Aug. 21. Adm'r—Richard H. Morris, of Pennsylvania. Fellowbondsman—Aaron Hewes Middleton, of Gloucester Co., N. J. Mary Morris, late Mary Mifflin, made her will, and did not appoint any Executor. Lib. 31, p. 474.

**1790, Dec. 28. Morris, Sarah,** of Essex Co. Ward. Daughter of Nathaniel Morris, deceased, and Mary Thurston (late Mary Morris), his wife, of said Co. Said Ward makes choice of Benjamin Haviland as her Guardian.
1790, Dec. 28. Guardian—Benjamin Haviland. Fellowbondsman—William Brown Higgens; both of said Co. Lib. 33, p. 396.

**1790, May 17. Morrison, Jacob,** of Hardyston, Sussex Co. Int. Adm'rs—Morris Morrison and Henry Morrison. Fellowbondsmen—Isaac Tomkins and Matthias Winans; all of said place.
1790, May 17. Inventory, £114.17.11, made by Matthias Winans and Isaac Tomkins. Lib. 30, p. 439.

**1786, March 25. Morss, Amos,** of Essex Co.; will of. Wife, Susanah, my riding chair and a negro. Eldest son, Amos, negros. Son, Anthony, negros. Wife to have ½ the profits of plantation. Son, Amos, land I bought of Robert Morss; also salt meadow on line of John Spinning, deceased; and he is to pay to my granddaughter, Susannah Winans, £60. Son, Anthony, the place where I live, bounded by land of my brother, Joseph, deceased; and he is to pay to my daughter, Sarah, wife of Jonathan Olliver, £40, and to my grandson, Jonathan Olliver, son of said Sarah, £25; also to my granddaughter, Susanah, wife of Abraham Tooker, £15; and to my great-granddaughter, Phebe Tooker, daughter of said granddaughter, Susannah Tooker, £5. Daughters, Anne Brant and Elizabeth Clark, and my younger son, Anthony, the rest of moveable estate. Executors—sons, Amos and Anthony. Witnesses—Jacob Tremblee, William Oliver, Jr., Isaac Morss. Proved June 11, 1787. Lib. 29, p. 372.

CALENDAR OF WILLS—1786-1790   161

**1790, Nov. 25. Morss, Daniel,** of Galloway Township, Gloucester Co. Int. Adm'r—Daniel Morss. Fellowbondsman—Moses Burnet; both of said Co.
1790, Nov. 12. Inventory, not complete, made by Andrew Adams and Cornelius McCollum. Lib. 31, p. 479.

**1789, Dec. 23. Morss, Robert,** of Gloucester Co., Esq. Int. Adm'r—Nehemiah Morss. Fellowbondsman—Moses Burnet; both of said Co.
1789, Nov. 27. Inventory, £80.6.1, made by Adrial Clark and Cornelius McCollum, in Galloway Township, said Co. Lib. 30, p. 138.

**1788, Jan. 1. Morton, John,** of Waterford Township, Gloucester Co., weaver; will of. Wife, Ann, 10 acres of woodland in Chester Township, Burlington Co.; also the use of the house and land in Coles Town, which is to be sold after her death, and of the money I give ½ to Rachel Crusher, daughter of Thomas Crusher, and out of the other ½ I give to my supposed daughter, Deborah Ward, £50, and the rest to my relation, William Terrell, son of William Terrell. If Rachel Crusher die before my wife, then I give her share to the children of Joseph Weaver. Wife, Ann, the residue. To Ann Weaver, daughter of Thomas Weaver, £10. To John Taggert, son of Jacob Taggert, my apparel. Executors—wife, Ann, and my friends, Samuel Roberts and Reuben Marlack. Witnesses—Jacob Stokes, Joseph Githens, Joseph Stokes.
1789, Sept. 6. Codicil. I now order my apparel to be given to Joseph Weaver, my wife's brother. Witnesses—Joseph Stokes, David Williamson. Proved Oct. 17, 1789.
1789, Oct. 12. Inventory, £263, made by John Roberts and Joseph Stokes. Lib. 30, p. 121.

**1790, Nov. 24. Morton, Mary,** of Gloucester Co., late Mary Price. Int. Adm'r—George Morton, of Philadelphia. Fellowbondsman—Joshua Cooper, of Newtown, N. J.
1791, May 24. Inventory, £326.7.9, made by George W. Campbell and Elisha Clark. Bond from George Ward to Mary Price. Bond from Andrew Hunter to Mary Price. Bond from Hannah Matlack to Mary Price. Bond from Joshua Cooper to Jonathan Morgan, assigned to Mary Price. Lib. 31, p. 479.

**1786, Sept. 14. Mott, James,** of Middletown, Monmouth Co.; will of. Son, James, all lands; and he is to pay to my son, John, £5, and to Mary Mott, daughter of my son, Gershom, £300, when she is 21, and to Cornelia Mott, daughter of son, Gershom, £300, when she is 21. Son, James, ½ of residue, and the other ½ to my grandsons, James Holmes, son of my daughter, Sarah, and James Saltar, son of my daughter, Huldah. Executors—son, James, and my sister's son, Asher Holmes. Witnesses—Obadiah Holmes, John Holmes, Jr., Ezekiel Lewis. Proved Feb. 27, 1787.
1787, March 2. Inventory, £932.8.11, made by Joseph Dorsett and Hendrick Hendrickson. Lib. 29, p. 309.

**1789, May 15. Mott, Sarah.** Ward. Daughter of Gershom Mott, of Wilmington, deceased. Said Ward, having real and personal estate, makes choice of Anne Mott as her Guardian.
1789, May 15. Guardian—Anne Mott, of Burlington Co. Fellowbondsman—William Lowrey, of Hunterdon Co. Witness—Richard Throckmorton. Lib. 31, p. 322.

162    NEW JERSEY POST-REVOLUTIONARY DOCUMENTS

**1787, Nov. 8. Mount, Catharine,** of Burlington Co. Ward. Daughter of Richard Mount, of said Co., deceased. Said Ward makes choice of her brother, Mathias Mount, as her Guardian. Witness—Richard Throckmorton.
1787, Nov. 8. Guardian—Matthias Mount. Fellowbondsman—Joseph Disbrow; both of said Co.    Lib. 29, p. 81.

**1787, Jan. 24. Mount, James,** of Upper Freehold, Monmouth Co. Int. Adm'x—Jean Mount. Fellowbondsman—Jesse Mount; both of said Co. Witness—William Johnson.
1787, Jan. 16. Inventory, £424.18.0, made by William Mount and Joseph Holman.    Lib. 29, p. 340.

**1787, Nov. 8. Mount, Mary, Joseph and Rebecca.** Wards. Children of Richard Mount, of Burlington Co. Lydia Mount and Matthias Mount, widow and son of Richard Mount, deceased, make choice of Joseph Disbrow, as Guardian of said Wards.
1787, Nov. 8. Guardian—Joseph Disbrow, of Nottingham Township, Burlington Co. Fellowbondsman—Matthias Mount, of Windsor Township, Middlesex Co. Witness—Matthias Mount.    Lib. 29, p. 81.

**1787, March 15. Mount, Richard,** of Nottingham Township, Burlington Co. Int. Adm'rs—Joseph Disbrow and Matthias Mount; both of said place. Fellowbondsman—Joseph McCracken, of said Co.
1787, March 14. Inventory, £187.17.7, made by Joseph McCracken and William Ford.
1787, April 12. Inventory, £206.15.6, made by William West and William Foord.    Lib. 29, p. 73.

**1786, Aug. 29. Mourison, Hendrick,** of Pequanack Township, Morris Co.; will of. Son, Jacob, land where he lives. Son, Mouris, land where he lives. Son, Henry, land where I live. Daughter, Mary Frederick, household goods. Executors—sons, Jacob and Henry, and Cornelius Peer. Witnesses—John Stiles, Jared Root, Ephraim Stiles. Proved July 25, 1787.
1787, July 5. Inventory, £65.19.6, made by John Stiles and Abraham Davinport.    Lib. 29, p. 447.

**1790, Jan. 27. Mowerson, Frederick,** of Bridgewater Township, Somerset Co.; will of. Nephew, Peter Kinny, son of my sister, Angleche Kinney, deceased, to have nothing, only £5. Wife, Elizabeth, farm where I live. The farm where Christopher Stryker lives to be sold, and money given to my wife, and my nephew, George Hall, son of George. Rest of estate to wife. Executors—wife, Elizabeth, and friends, George Hall, son of George, and Richard Hall. Witnesses—William Hall, Derik Demott, Abraham Hall, Joseph Van Doren. Proved Aug. 21, 1790.
1790, Aug. 28. Inventory, £123, made by Edward Bunn and William Hall, together with Joseph Van Doren.    Lib. 31, p. 513.

**1786, Aug. 9. Mowra, Philip,** of Oxford Township, Sussex Co.; will of. Eldest son, Jacob, plantation I live on; he paying to my son, Philip, £200. Sons, Jacob and Philip, all other estate; they paying the legacies. Daughter, Marylis, £50. Daughter, Leah, £50. Daughter, Catherine, £50. Daughter, Elizabeth, £50. Executors—friends, Abraham McMurtrie and David Vanderen. Witnesses—Jacob Bower, John Scott, Peter Shoemaker. Proved Sept. 21, 1786.

CALENDAR OF WILLS—1786-1790        163

1786, Sept. 30. Inventory, £164.8.6, made by John Miller and John McMurtrie. Lib. 28, p. 455.

**1789, Nov. 24. Mulford, Barnabas,** of Roxbury, Morris Co. Int. Adm'x—Temperance Mulford. Fellowbondsman—Eleazer Lindsley; both of said place. Witness—Sally Pierson.
1789, Nov. 17. Inventory, £115.12.9, made by Eleazer Lindsly and Amos Leek. Lib. 30, p. 233.

**1787, Sept. 22. Mulford, Enoch,** of Cumberland Co. Ward. Son of David Mulford, of said Co., deceased. Said Ward, having real and personal estate, makes choice of John Mulford as his Guardian.
1787, Sept. 22. Guardian—John Mulford. Fellowbondsman—Eli Elmer; both of said Co. Witnesses—Jonathan Elmer and Timothy Elmer. Lib. 29, p. 184.

**1786, Mulford, Ezekiel,** of Cumberland Co. Int. Adm'x—Jemima Mulford, widow.
1787, Jan. 6. Account of Jemima Mulford. (Henry Sharp married the widow; lives in Cape May, near Henry Young).
1786, May 1. Bond. Between Persons Leaming, of Cape May Co., of one part, and Ezekiel Mulford, of Cumberland Co., of other part. The 1st part grants to 2nd part land in Cumberland Co., near the mouth of Maurice River, known by the name of Erexon Point, for the term of 3 years, for £15 a year, on 250 acres. Payments were made on the above lease, June 5, 1787, by Jemima Mulford, for £7.11.0, and also Oct. 26, 1787, by said Jemima Mulford, for £3.
File No. 6055 F.

**1786, March 2. Mulford, Isaac and Sarah,** of Cumberland Co. Wards. Children of Isaac Mulford, of said Co., deceased. Petition of Abraham Smith, next of kin of said orphans, who are under 14, for a Guardian to be appointed.
1786, March 3. Guardian—Henry Mulford. Fellowbondsmen—Isaac Smith and Job Tyler; all of said Co. Witnesses—Peter Andrews and John Reeve, Jr. Lib. 28, p. 183.

**1790, Feb. 19. Mulford, Jacob,** of Cape May Co.; will of. Wife, Phebe, use of ½ of my plantation, and £300. Grandson, John Mulford, all lands in Cape May Co.; but he is to give his brother, Jonathan Mulford, a title to land in Roadstown, in Cumberland Co., late the property of their father. If John should die, then I give said lands to all my children and grandchildren. Wife, Phebe, ⅓ of my personal estate, and the other ⅔ to my children, William Mulford, Jacob Mulford and Lovica Lummes, except 15 shillings, which I give to my youngest daughter, Jane. Executors—wife, Phebe, and my sons, William and Jacob. Witnesses—Ebenezer Newton, Alice Newton, Phebe Bencroft. Proved May 17, 1790.
1790, April 12. Inventory, £175.19.1, made by Nezer Swain and Ebenezer Newton. Lib. 32, p. 99.

**1787, March 28. Mulford, Jonathan,** of Elizabeth Borough, Essex Co.; will of. Sons, Jonathan and Cornelius, my apparel. Son, Jonathan, the plantation where I live, which joins Joseph Crane, deceased, John Bedell, Isaac Crane and Pursaick (Passaic) River; also the land I bought of Reverend Jonathan Elmer, of 8 acres. Son, Cornelius, land I bought of Thomas Baker, deceased; also land I bought of Ezekiel Sayre. Daughter, Esther Ball, some goods. Daughters, Deborah Bedell and Esther Ball, and my granddaughter, Deborah Willcoks, rest of moveable estate. The grandchildren, of my daughter, Mary Volintine, deceased, to have their equal share. Executors—sons, Jonathan and Cornelius. Witnesses—Benjamin Bonnel, Samuel Potter, Thomas Osborn. Proved Oct. 23, 1789.

1789, Oct. 21. Inventory, £53.16.0, made by Nathaniel Littell and Ezekiel Sayre. Lib. 30, p. 216.

**1789, Oct. 26. Mulford, Lewis,** of Elizabeth Town, Essex Co.; will of. Daughter, Anne, as much as will make her equal to my daughter, Hannah. Son, Lewis, £75. Granddaughter, Mary, daughter of my son, David, deceased, £30. Wife, Anne, use of real and moveable estate. Daughters, Hannah and Anne, moveable estate, after wife is done with it. Son, Thomas, the land where he lives, that formerly belonged to Elijah Davis; also 5 acres of my plantation. Sons, Benjamin and John, rest of my plantation. Sons, Thomas, Benjamin and John, 30 acres of land at Turkey, which I bought of Elijah Davis, which binds on land of Silvainus Oakley. Sons, Lewis and John, a salt meadow in the Great Meadows. Sons, Thomas and Benjamin, a salt meadow which was bought of William Trotter and Nathaniel Price; also the salt meadow I bought of Samuel Norris. Grandson, Stephen Mulford, son of my son, David, deceased, the land I bought of Aaron Lane. Son David's widow to have wood and grain. Executors—son, Thomas, and my son-in-law, Benjamin Cory. Witnesses—Gabriel Barton, Moses Meeker, John Barton. Proved March 29, 1790. Lib. 30, p. 333.

**1789, Aug. 27. Mulford, Mary,** of Cape May Co. Int. Adm'r—James Mulford. Fellowbondsmen—Charles Allen and Richard Shaw; all of said Co. Witnesses—Philip Hand and Aaron Hand.

1789, Aug. 27. Inventory, £40.2.7, made by Jeremiah Richardson and Richard Shaw. Lib. 31, p. 371.

**1787, March 12. Mulford, Thomas,** of Roxbury, Morris Co.; will of. Wife, Mary, ⅛ of the land, during her life, as well as the moveable estate; and, at her death, the goods I give to my daughters, Mary and Marcy. Son, Barnabas, said land during his life, and then to his son, Thomas; but, if Thomas die, then to his sisters. Son, Ananias, £1. Daughter, Mary, £5. Daughter, Marcy, £5. Executors—sons, Barnabas and Ananias. Witnesses—Henry Ludlam, Thomas Leek, Nathan Cooper, Jr. Proved April 28, 1787.

1787, April 26. Inventory, £52.2.3, made by Stephen Conkling and James Haines. Lib. 29, p. 455.

**1789, March 20. Mulford, Thomas,** of Hanover, Morris Co. Int. Adm'r—Moses Kitchel. Fellowbondsman—Benjamin Kitchel; both of said place. Witnesses—Jacob Thompson and John Smith.

1788, July 1. Citation. To Hannah Mulford, Peremiah Mulford, Jeremiah Mulford and Benjamin Mulford. You are notified that Letters of Administration will be granted to any person who may appear by July 12, 1788.

1789, March 20. Inventory, £4.15.6, made by David Bates and Benjamin Kitchel. **Lib. 30, p. 234.**

**1787, March 12. Mullen, John,** of Northampton Township, Burlington Co.; will of. Son, Samuel, the house and lot in Mount Holly, which was given to me by the will of my father, Edward Mullen; also the land I bought of Josiah White; also ½ of the meadow that I bought of the Trustees of the Iron Works Company; also ½ of my meadow that joins my brother, Joseph Mullen, Thomas Reynolds and others; and Samuel is to pay to my wife, Jean, £3 yearly, and £3 to each of my eldest daughters, Sarah Platt, Mary Hollingshead and Kezia Hilliard. Son, John, house and lot at Mount Holly, that I bought of Samuel Farrington; also ½ of the meadow I bought of said Trustees; also ½ the meadow that joins my brother, Joseph. Daughter, Elizabeth Mullen, £25. Daughter, Sarah Platt, a bed. Son, John, is to pay to his mother, £4 a year. Wife, Jane, household goods, cow, wood, etc. Executors—son, Samuel, and wife, Jane. Witnesses—John Clark, Aaron Smith, Haren Brian, Jonah Woolman. Proved May 22, 1788. Lib. 30, p. 1.

**1789, Dec. 8. Munday, Moses,** of Piscataway, Middlesex Co. Int. Adm'r—John Runyon. Fellowbondsman—David Blackford; both of said place.
1789, Dec. 8. Inventory, £4.10.0, made by Gilbert Molleson and David Blackford. Lib. 31, p. 394.

**1786, Feb. 24. Munday, Robert,** of Piscataway Township, Middlesex Co.; will of. Wife, Isabel, the goods she had at our marriage. Eldest daughter, Sophia, all the goods I had before I married my present wife. Real estate to be sold. Eldest sons, Israel, Asher and Robert, to be put to trades. Youngest son, Thomas, to be put to school. Daughter, Margaret, to be learned to read. My wife is pregnant, which child is to be taken care of. Executors—brothers, Thomas and Abraham, and friend, John Runyon. Witnesses—John Monday, Joshua Mundy, John Ross. Proved May 18, 1786.
1786, May 15. Inventory, made by James Pyatt and John Munday. Lib. 28, p. 331.

**1786, Dec. 28. Munson, John,** of Hanover, Morris Co.; will of. Son, Daniel, £5. Daughter, Elizabeth Fairchild, £5. Daughter, Anna Minton, £5. Daughter, Marget Munson, and my son, John, when he is 21, all moveable estate, and my lands. Witnesses—Joseph Lindsly, David Cory, Jemima Lindsly. Proved April 5, 1788.
1788, April 5. Adm'rs—Nathaniel Fairchild and Elizabeth, his wife, and Joseph Lindsly. Fellowbondsman—Gershom Gard; all of said place. Witness—Jemima Lindsly. The Testator neglected to appoint Executors.
1788, March 25. Inventory, £49.7.9, made by Jacob Mintun and Gershom Gard. Lib. 31, p. 197.

**1786, Feb. 14. Munyan, John,** of Upper Penns Neck, Salem Co., yeoman; will of. Land and moveable estate to be sold. My granddaughter, Siddonia Munyan, £10. Children, Joseph, Joice, John, Sarah, Mary, and grandchildren, the children of Thomas Munyan, deceased, residue. Executors—son, John, and my son-in-law, Thomas Shoot. Witnesses—Jacob Seers, William Cook, Isaac Pedrick. Proved May 13, 1786.
1786, April 1. Inventory, £432.6.6, made by Joshua Peddrick and Isaac Pedrick. Lib. 28, p. 134.

**1786, Oct. 31. Murdock, John,** of Woodbury, Deptford Township, Gloucester Co., silversmith. Int. Adm'x—Sarah Murdock. Fellowbondsman—John S. Whitall; both of said Township. Witnesses—Aaron Hewes and Joseph Hugg, Surrogate.

1786, Nov. 7. Inventory, £295.16.8, made by Joel Westcott and Jonathan Harker. Lib. 28, p. 123.

**1786, Nov. 28. Murfin, Mary,** of Nottingham Township, Burlington Co., widow; will of. Advanced in age. My plantation in Kingwood Township, of 349 acres, now in tenure of Samuel Kester, to be sold. Daughter, Ann Lawrie, £20. Grandson, Joseph Murfin Lawrie, £20. Cousins, Mary Ivins and Mary Bunting, daughters of Phineas Bunting, £5 each. Granddaughter, Amelia Stevenson, wife of John, and granddaughter, Mary Lawrie, rest of estate. Executors—grandson, Joseph Murfin Lawrie, and said John Stevenson. Witnesses—James Holloway, William Arey, William Cowperthwaite, Daniel Smith. Proved Nov. 28, 1788. Lib. 30, p. 52.

**1788, Jan. 21. Murrell, Joseph,** of Waterford Township, Gloucester Co.; will of. Wife, Ann, all real and personal estate, but, if she marry, £500. If my sons, Joseph and Franklin, should die then my wife is to have the disposal of my estate. If my wife and said sons should die, then I give my estate to Henry Pendegress Haines, Joseph Haines, Nathan Haines, Jr., Sarah Haines, Marian Haines and Kesiah Haines. Also my brother, and sister, Rachel Murrell, to have £100. Executors—wife, Ann, and friend, Thomas Hollinshead. Witnesses—Rachel Murrel, Marion H. Haines, Samuel Bloomfield. Proved March 11, 1789.

1789, March 11. Renunciation by Thomas Hollinshead.

1789, Feb. 13. Inventory, £639.6.1, made by John Griffyth and Thomas Stokes. Lib. 30, p. 105.

**1786, May 16. Muysinger, Conrad,** of Franklin Township, Bergen Co. Int. Adm'x—Margaret Muysinger. Fellowbondsman—Nicholas Muysinger; both of said place. Witness—Antye Westervelt.

1786, Aug. 30. Inventory, £119.19.0, made by James Christie and Deirck Wannamaker. Lib. 29, p. 223.

**1787, Feb. 5. Nealon, Hannah,** of Burlington Co. Int. Adm'r—John Wood. Fellowbondsmen—John Black and Joseph Newbold; all of said Co. Witnesses—Caleb Newbold and Anthony Sykes.
Lib. 29, p. 73.

**1786, Nov. 15. Neat, William,** of London, merchant. Adm'r—Henry Chapman, of New York City. Whereas, the said William Neat made his will 10th of April, 1775, and appointed John Platt, Henry Appleton, Samson Wright, Henry Chapman and John Rothero, his Executors, who are beyond the seas, except Henry Chapman.
Lib. 28, p. 426.

**1788, Sept. 16. Neely, Joseph,** of Pittsgrove, Salem Co., yeoman; will of. Son, John Nealy, 174 acres that join William Garrison, Samuel Swing and others. Wife, Elizabeth, the 180 acres where I live. Personal estate to said Elizabeth and John. Executrix—wife, Elizabeth. Witnesses—Abraham DuBois, David DuBois, Jr., Thomas DuBois. Proved June 5, 1789.

1789, April 14. Inventory, £846.14.7, made by Abraham DuBois and Samuel McClong. Lib. 31, p. 343.

**1788, Dec. 13. Nevius, John,** of Readingtown, Hunterdon Co. Int. Adm'rs—Deborah Nevius and Abraham Nevius. Fellowbondsman—Albert Nevius.
1788, Nov. 20. Inventory, £358.6.6, made by John Mehelm and Albert Nevius.
1790, May 25. Account by Adm'rs. Lib. 31, p. 144.

**1790, March 27. Newbold, Joseph,** of Chesterfield Township, Burlington Co.; will of. To my son, whom I adopt, by the name of Charles Newbold, eldest son of Martha Stevenson, plantation where I live, which is bounded by the place where Mathias Swen lives, and by Cleayton Newbold's, when he is 21. To my son, whom I adopt, by the name of John Newbold, 2nd son of said Martha, the plantation where Thomas Newbold lives. To my brother and sister's children, my nephews and nieces, the money of the abovesaid lands, if they should be sold, after the deaths of my said 2 sons, that is, if they die before 21. My brother, Cleayton Newbold's heirs, rest of my estate. My nephew, Joseph Hough, £200. Niece, Charlotte Hough, £100. My friend, Dinah Middleton, £50, but, if she die, then to her daughter, Patience Middleton. Friend, Meriam Middleton, goods. To Margaret Stevenson, mother of said Charles and John Newbold, £15 a year. To Michael Newbold, son of Thomas, £50. To Joseph Newbold, son of said Thomas, silver buttons. Executors—brother-in-law, Samuel Hough, and my cousin, Thomas Newbold, son of William. Witnesses—Francis Bowes Sayre, Caleb Newbold, John Lawrence. Proved May 19, 1790.
1790, April 13. Inventory, £2,438.5.11, made by Samuel Sykes, John Black, Jr. and Caleb Newbold. Lib. 32, p. 84.

**1789, Oct. 17. Newbold, Mary,** of Chesterfield Township, Burlington Co.; will of. Son, Samuel, my pine lands in Gloucester Co., which were left me by my father, Samuel Coles. Daughter, Rachel Newbold, silver tankard. Daughter, Martha Reeve, tea table, etc. Daughter, Ann Offley, goods. Cousin, Rachael Newbold, £20. Daughters the rest of estate. Executors—son, Samuel, and my brother-in-law, Cleayton Newbold. Witnesses—William Black, Jr., William Satterthwaite, Nathan Rockhill. Proved March 16, 1790.
1790, Feb. 27. Inventory, £2,436.0.7, made by William Satterthwaite and Nathan Rockhill. Lib. 32, p. 66.

**1786, Dec. 21. Newbold, Thomas,** of New Hanover Township, Burlington Co. Int. Adm'rs—Ann Newbold, Joshua Shreve and Joseph Lamb, Jr. Fellowbondsman—Joseph Lamb, Sr.; all of said Co.
1787, Jan. 30. Inventory, £149.15.4, made by Job Cook and John Wright. Lib. 28, p. 75.

**1786, Aug. 28. Newkirk [Nieukirk], Garrit,** of Upper Alloways Creek, Salem Co.; will of. Son, Cornelius, plantation where he lives, of 160 acres, also 40 acres of my new land. Son, Matthew, place where I live, with the grist mill, when he is 21. Grandson, John Nieukirk, the plantation joining Capt. Nieukirk, William Hampton and that of Cornelius, of 165 acres. Personal estate to be sold. Daughter, Elizabeth Patterson, £150. Daughter, Margaret Rambo,

£150. Daughter, Sarah Vanmeter, £150. Executors—sons, Cornelius and Matthew. Witnesses—Matthew Nieukirk, Tamar Martain, John Nelson. Proved Nov. 20, 1786.
1786, Sept. 13. Inventory, £429.13.3, made by William Garrison and Benjamin Vanmeter. Lib. 28, p. 151.

**1789, Nov. 7. Newton, Elizabeth,** of Cape May Co.; will of. Son, John Newton, land which I bought of Jacob Spicer. Daughter, Margaret Ware, my apparel. Rest to said children. Executors—son, John Newton, and my daughter, Margaret Ware. Witnesses— Ebenezer Newton, Elihu Hand, John Bridges. Proved Nov. 16, 1789.
1789, Nov. 14. Inventory, £294.9.9, made by Ebenezer Newton and Robert Parsons. Lib. 31, p. 365.

**1786, Feb. 25. Nicholas, Richard,** of Elizabeth Town, Essex Co.; will of. Friend, Johanah Moore, 3 acres along the road, against Benjamin Willis. Sister, Catharine, £7 a year. My other sisters to have rest of moveable estate. Nephew, John Nicholas Oliver, rest of plantation. Executors—nephew, John Nicholas Oliver, and friend, Enoch Moore. Witnesses—David Brant, Josiah Willson, Michael Bedeal. Proved April 4, 1786. Lib. 28, p. 360.

**1787, Aug. 11. Nicholson, Thomas,** of Greenwich Township, Gloucester Co. Int. Adm'r—Andrew Cox, yeoman. Fellowbondsman— Samuel Bowen, joiner; both of said place. Lib. 29, p. 118.

**1787, March 17. Nieukirk, John,** of Salem Co. Ward. Son of John Nieukirk, of said Co., deceased. Petition of Susannah Nieukirk, praying that Cornelius Nieukirk, may be appointed Guardian of said infant.
1787, March 17. Guardian—Cornelius Newkirk. Fellowbondsmen— William Garrison and Benjamin Vanmeter; all of said Co.
Lib. 29, p. 153.

**1786, July 12. Nixon, Catharine,** of Hardwick Township, Sussex Co.; will of. Sons, Allen Nixon and Patric Nixon, £5 each. Rest of estate to my 7 children, Mary Courson, William Nixon, Grace Fields, John Nixon, Mary Man, Allen Nixon and Patrix Nixon. Executors— sons, Allen and Patrick. Witnesses—John Armstrong, George Armstrong. Proved March 4, 1788.
1788, March 4. Adm'rs—Jacob Coursen and John Mann; both of Hardwick. Fellowbondsman—James Morrow, of Newton; all of Sussex Co. Allen Nixon and Patric Nixon, the Executors appointed, have both removed out of the United States.
1788, March 11. Inventory, £11.9.0, made by Francis Glover and John Green. Lib. 31, p. 155.

**1789, June 26. Nixon, Vavasar,** of Cumberland Co.; will of. To my mother and sister, Margret and Mary Nixon, £30. Sister to have hers when 18. To Oliver and Ephraim Nixon, rest of estate, as they come of age. Executor—Jeremiah Nixon. Witnesses—John Soullard, Ephraim Buck, Jeremiah Nixon. Proved Sept. 26, 1789.
1789, July 8. Inventory, £145.19.0, made by Abraham Sayre and Ephraim Buck. Lib. 30, p. 153.

CALENDAR OF WILLS—1786-1790     169

**1787, May 6. Nixson, Robert,** of Greenwich Township, Gloucester Co., yeoman; will of. Friend, Eli Wilson, all my goods. Executor—said Eli Wilson. Witnesses—William Ford, Thomas Thomson. Proved Nov. 19, 1787.     Lib. 29, p. 114.

**1786, April 24. Noble, William,** of Woolwich Township, Gloucester Co.; will of. Wife, Sarah, all that is left after paying my debts, in order to bring up my youngest children. Executors—friends, Robert Brown and Samuel Huling. Witnesses—Thomas Key, Elener Strang, Samuel Hulings. Proved May 10, 1786.
1786, May 8. Inventory, £114.7.6, made by John Kille and Thomas Key.     Lib. 28, p. 113.

**1787, Sept. 22. Noe, Samuel,** of Essex Co. Int. Adm'r—Nathaniel Leonard, of Middlesex Co. Fellowbondsman—Abraham Terrel, of Essex Co.     Lib. 29, p. 418.

**1790, March 13. Norbury, Joseph,** of Cape May Co. Int. Adm'x—Mary Norbury. Fellowbondsman—Abijah Smith; both of Middle Precinct, said Co. Witnesses—Sarah Hand and Jesse Hand.
1790, March 24. Inventory, £81.0.2, made by Thomas Shaw and Eli Eldredge.     Lib. 32, p. 105.

**1790, Dec. 11. Norcross, Samuel,** of Burlington Co. Ward. Son of Joshua Norcross, of New Hanover, said Co., deceased. Said Ward having real and personal estate, makes choice of Joseph Biddle as his Guardian.
1790, Dec. 11. Guardian—Joseph Biddle. Fellowbondsman—Daniel Ellis. Witness—James Kinsey, Jr.     Lib. 32, p. 98.

**1786, May 26. Norcross, Theodocia,** of New Hanover Township, Burlington Co.; will of. Daughter, Anne King, £50, and my share of a bond given to me and my said daughter, by Thomas Platt, and also one given by Eli Budd. Son, Jacob Norcross, £15, when he is 21. Son, Samuel Norcross, £15 when he is 21. Son, William Norcross, rest of estate. Executors—son, William, and my friend, Isaac Budd. Witnesses—Samuel Goldy, Jr., Levi Budd, Isaac Cowgill. Proved Feb. 27, 1787.
1787, Feb. 26. Inventory, £532.2.2, made by Thomas Platt and Levi Budd.     Lib. 29, p. 61.

**1789, May 23. Norris, Thomas,** of Princeton, Somerset Co. Int. Adm'x—Mary Norris. Fellowbondsman—James Norris; both of said place.
1789, April 4. Inventory, £115.19.6, made by James Hamilton and John Barlow. Articles were disposed of between the time of her husband's death and the above Inventory, by the widow, to the value of £30.3.6.     Lib. 31, p. 414.

**1790, May 9. Ogden, Abraham,** of Newark Township, Essex Co.; will of. My wife and my daughter, Mary, the use of ⅛ of my lands. Son, Abraham, bed, horse and steers. Grandson, Moses Osborn, £70. Daughter, Lydia Baldwin, £60. Granddaughter, Rachel Baldwin, £10. Grandson, Abraham Baldwin, £8. To Elizabeth Vincent, £5. Sons, Eleazar and Abraham, my lands at the Great Swamp. Executors—son, Eleazar, and my son-in-law, Josiah Baldwin. Witnesses—

Stephen Harrison, Elias Osborn, John Dod, Jr. Proved May 22, 1790.
1790, May 26. Inventory, £471.12.10, made by Stephen Harrison and John Lindsley.
Lib. 30, p. 351.

**1790, Feb. 1. Ogden, Benjamin,** of South River, Middlesex Co.; will of. Eldest son, David, the 10-acre lot where he lives. Rest of lands to be sold, and wife, Leah, to have ⅛ the money, and rest to sons, David and John, and my daughters, Jane Drake, Sarah Duley, Mary Machet and Ann Ryder, allowing ½ share to my grandson, Henry Luup, and 5 shillings to my daughter, Cathrine Coeks. Executors— son, David Ogden, and John Ogden. Witnesses—William Van Duerson, David Service, Jacob Dunham. Proved March 1, 1790.
1790, March 4. Inventory, £181.13.0, made by Jacob Dunham and William Van Duerson.
Lib. 30, p. 532.

**1790, Aug. 10. Ogden, David,** of Newark Township, Essex Co.; will of. To brothers and sisters, Thomas Ogden, Swain Ogden, Molly Dod, Sarah Edison, Susannah Williams, Hannah Bebout, Phebe Brundage, all real and personal estate. Brother, John, is to have no share. Executors—Joseph Harrison and Thomas Ogden. Witnesses—Joel Condit, Josiah Steele, Enos Williams. Proved Oct. 23, 1790.
1790, Oct. 15. Inventory, made by Aaron D'Camp and Abram Noe.
Lib. 30, p. 357.

**1790, Dec. 28. Ogden, Eliakim,** of Essex Co. Int. Adm'r—Daniel Ogden. Fellowbondsman—Ichabod Grumman; both of said Co.
Lib. 30, p. 360.

**1788, Jan. 28. Ogden, Gabriel,** of Essex Co. Int. Adm'rs—Moses Ogden and Charles Ogden, of Newark, and Lewis Ogden, of New York City. Fellowbondsman—Benjamin Johnson, of Newark.
Lib. 31, p. 243.

**1790, April 3. Ogden, Jonathan,** of Essex Co. Int. Adm'x—Phebe Ogden, widow of said Jonathan. Fellowbondsman—Ezekiel Ogden, of said Co.
1790, April 7. Inventory, £70.0.6, made by Richard Townley and Andrew Wilson.
Lib. 30, p. 363.

**1787, June 2. Ogden, Oliver,** of Mendham, Morris Co. Int. Adm'x— Kesiah Ogden. Fellowbondsman—James Young; both of said place. Witness—James P. Lasey.
1787, May 29. Inventory, £68.19.11, made by James P. Lasey and Moses Lindsly.
Lib. 29, p. 473.

**1786, June 9. Ogden, Samuel and Sarah,** of Cumberland Co. Wards. Children of Samuel Ogden, of said Co., deceased. Petition of James Ogden, next of kin, who desires that a Guardian be appointed for said minors.
1786, March 2. Guardian—James Ogden. Fellowbondsmen—Jedidiah Ogden and Amos Westcott; all of said Co. Witnesses—Joanah Ogden and Rhodah Wescoates.
Lib. 28, p. 184.

**1790, March 22. Ogden, Simeon,** of Newark Township, Essex Co.; will of. Wife, Catharine, the use of ⅛ of the land, and the goods she had before marriage. Son, Swain, my apparel. To my child or children, as the case may be, the real and personal estate. Execu-

tors—Capt. William Gould and Enos Williams. Witnesses—Samuel Tompkins, John Davison, Josiah Smith. Proved Nov. 18, 1790.
1790, April 8. Inventory, made by Joseph Harrison and Samuel Tompkins. Lib. 30, p. 358.

**1790, Dec. 28. Ogden, Theodorus,** of Essex Co. Int. Adm'r—Daniel Ogden. Fellowbondsman—Ichabod Grumman; both of said Co.
Lib. 30, p. 361.

**1787, March 20. Okly, Silvanus,** of New Providence, Essex Co., carpenter; will of. Wife, Mary, some household goods; but, if she marry, then my youngest daughter, Elizabeth, is to have them. Wife may have the use of some land. The grist mill, house and 4 acres; also 15 acres that I bought of Abraham Price; also ½ of a plantation in Sussex Co., to be sold to pay the debts; and, if it should not be enough, then my sons, Ephraim and John, are to pay the rest. If there is overplus money, then I give the same to my four youngest daughters, Hester, Mary, Nancy and Elizabeth. Sons, Ephraim and John, plantation where I live. Youngest son, David, my part of my land in Morris Co. Sons, Ephraim, John and David, my house and lot in New York City. Executors—Isaac Woodruff and Obadiah Vallentine. Witnesses—Jonathan Valentine, David Campbell, William Willcocks. Proved May 28, 1787. Lib. 29, p. 379.

**1787, April 6. Oldden, Elizabeth,** of Windsor Township, Middlesex Co.;_will of. Friend, William Clarke. an axe and hoe. To Esther Clarke, daughter of William, a washing tub. To Julia Clarke, a chest. Friend, Ursilla Hews, a gown. Friend, Hannah Clarke, widow of John, a bed, and rest of goods. Executor—William Clarke. Witnesses—Joseph Clarke, William Clarke, Jr., Hannah White. Proved Feb. 14, 1788.
1787, Oct. 10. Inventory, £21.12.0, made by Robert White and Ebenezer Wright. Lib. 31, p. 212.

**1786, Nov. 25. Olden, Jephtha,** of Deptford Township, Gloucester Co.; will of. Mother, Elizabeth Olden, the profits of my estate, which I leave in Trust to my friend, Aaron Hewes, of Woodbury, who is to have the same after my mother's death. Executor—said Aaron Hewes. Witnesses—George Ward, Nathan Folwell, Jacob Wood. Proved Dec. 22, 1786.
1786, Dec. 20. Inventory, £182.17.0, made by Samuel Mickle and George Ward. Lib. 28, p. 96.

**1789, Nov. 24. Olden, Joseph,** of Princeton, Middlesex Co.; will of. Sons, Ephraim and Job, all real estate, after death or marriage of widow, to whom I give use of ½ of the real. Son, Joseph, the debt he owes me. Wife to have £5 yearly, out of my house now in possession of Thomas Stockton. Wife and my daughters, Amey and Ann, rest of personal; taking out of Amey's share what she had at marriage. Executors—wife and sons, Ephraim and Job. Witnesses—David Olden, Jr., Thomas Olden, Jr., William Sickels. Proved April 13, 1790.
1790, March 13. Inventory, £617.13.11, made by Joseph Hornor and Samuel Oldden. Lib. 30, p. 526.

**1787, April 12. Oliver, Benjamin,** of Essex Co. Int. Adm'rs—Jeremiah Clark and Isaac Morse; both of said Co. Lib. 29, p. 416.

**1787, Feb. 23. Oliver, George,** of Cape May Co., pilot. Int. Adm'r—Thomas Buck. Fellowbondsman—Henry Stites; both of said Co. Witnesses—Samuel Springer and Sarah Hand.
1787, March 14. Inventory, £41.12.5, made by Elijah Hughes and Ebenezer Newton. Lib. 29, p. 242.

**1788, Dec. 31. Oliver, Joseph,** of Elizabeth Borough, Essex Co., miller; will of. Youngest children, John, Kelsey and William Oliver, my moveable estate. Son, Joseph, that land and salt meadow which I bought of my father, John Oliver; also ½ of the land I bought of Samuel Betts. Son, Jacob, the land which Samuel Scudder devised to his son, Moses Scudder, and he conveyed to me, with other land which his father conveyed to him by deed of gift. Son, Jacob, ½ of the land I bought of Samuel Betts; also the salt marsh that I bought of Moses Scudder. Son, John, the land I bought of Potter; also a salt meadow that I bought of Joseph Bird, deceased. Sons, Kelsey and William, the land I bought of the Adm'rs of George Ross. Wife, Elizabeth, the use of land; and she is to bring up my 3 youngest sons, John, Kelsey and William. Executors—brother-in-law, William Fletcher, and friend, Joseph D'Camp, of Rahway. Witnesses—John Scudder, James Youmans, Jeremiah Bird. Proved Nov. 14, 1789. Lib. 30, p. 208.

**1790, Aug. 10. Opdycke, Albert,** of Bethlehem Township, Hunterdon Co. Int. Adm'r—Benjamin Warne, of Greenwich Township, Sussex Co. Fellowbondsman—Joshua Corshon, of Amwell, Hunterdon Co. Witness—John Brooks.
1790, Aug. 12. Inventory, £99.12.0, made by Thomas Bowlby and Aaron Watson.
1791, Feb. 2. Acount by Adm'r. Lib. 30, p. 313.

**1788, Dec. 1. Opdyke, Joshua,** of Kingwood Township, Hunterdon Co.; will of. Son, Richard, 5 shillings. Son, Luther, 5 shillings. Daughter, Sarah, 5 shillings. Daughter, Elizabeth, 5 shillings. Daughter, Margrit, 5 shillings. Wife to have all my goods, while my widow, and afterwards to be sold and divided in 3 parts. To daughter Francese's 4 children, that is, to Henry Hoguland, Joshua Hoguland and John Hoguland, and Egnus Hoguland, when they come of age, one part; daughter, Hannah, one part; daughter, Caty, one part. Executors—son, Richard, of Kingwood, and Amos Hogland, of Amwell, mason. Witnesses—John Besson, Margaret Besson, Jacob Risler. Proved May 6, 1789.
1789, May 1. Inventory, £240.6.2, made by William Coolbagh and Absalom Runyan.
1793, May 10. Account by Richard Opdyke, Acting Executor. Legacies paid to Luther Opdyke, Sarah Allen and Margaret Glover. Lib. 32, p. 33.

**1788, Dec. 12. Oppie, William, Sr.,** of Somerset Co.; will of. Son, William, £150. Son, John, a bond of £50 against the estate of Peter Sedam. Sons, Isaac and Benjamin, some livestock, when they are 21. My 2 single daughters to have outsets. Daughters, Mary, Elizabeth, Grace and Nancy, and sons, Isaac and Benjamin, rest of estate.

Brother, Benjamin, house and lot at Rocky Hill, where he lives. Wife to have her living. Executors—sons-in-law, John Vactor and Abraham Voorhees, my son, John, and my wife. Witnesses—Thomas Swiney, John Honeyman, Samuel Brittan. Proved March 10, 1789.
Lib. 31, p. 406.

**1789, May 4. Orr, Arthor,** of Hanover, Morris Co. Int. Adm'rs.—Amy Orr and Lemuel Hedges. Fellowbondsman—Uzal Kitchel; all of said place.
1789, April 20. Inventory, £73.1.5, made by Uzal Kitchel and Timothy Tuttle.
Lib. 30, p. 233.

**1790, Dec. 4. Oselwean, John,** of Burlington Co., otherwise called John Kitt. Int. Adm'rs—Daniel Joyce and William Burr. Fellowbondsman—Phinehas Kirkbride; all of said Co.
1790, Dec. 3. Inventory, £24.5.1, made by Hosea Eayre and Phinehas Kirkbride.
Lib. 32, p. 95.

**1790, April 29. Otto, Catharine,** of Gloucester Co. Ward. Daughter of Bodo Otto, Jr., of said Co., deceased. Said Ward makes choice of Reverend Andrew Hunter as her Guardian.
1790, April 29. Guardian—Andrew Hunter. Fellowbondsman—Thomas Hendry; both of said Co.
Lib. 31, p. 482.

**1788, June 16. Otto, Jacob and Daniel,** of Gloucester Co. Wards. Sons of Bodo Otto, of said Co., deceased. Frederick Otto, their uncle and nearest of kin, desires that John Wilkins may be made their Guardian, until they are 14.
1788, Aug. 5. Guardian—John Wilkins. Fellowbondsman—John Sparks; both of Deptford Township, said Co. Witness—Joseph Hugg, Jr.
Lib. 31, p. 38.

**1788, July 23. Otto, John,** of Gloucester Co. Ward. Son of Bodo Otto, Jr., of said Co., deceased. Said Ward makes choice of John Wilkins as his Guardian.
1788, July 28. Guardian—John Wilkins, of Deptford Township. Fellowbondsman—John Sparks; both of said Co. Lib. 31, p. 38.

**1789, Jan. 3. Paine, Mary,** of Middlesex Co.; will of. Daughter, Mary, wife of Phinehas McCarty, £5. Daughters, Elizabeth, Rachel and Hannah, clothing and household goods. Sons, Abraham and Peter, and my daughters, Elizabeth, Rachel and Hannah, all the rest. Executors—friends, Melanthon Freeman and Alpheus Freeman. Witnesses—Isaac Freeman, Joseph Freeman, Charles Jaques. Proved May 12, 1790.
Lib. 30, p. 525.

**1788, March 16. Parker, Ammariah,** of Morristown, Morris Co.; will of. Wife, Tamor, many articles and some livestock, and, at her death, to daughters, Catharine and Nancy. Oldest son, David, 5 shillings; and to his oldest son, Solomon, £5. Son, Abraham, 5 shillings. My 3rd son, Stephen, 10 acres of my land near the Hammer Bridge. My 4 youngest sons to be put to trades. Wife to have use of house where John Crowel lives. Sons, Stephen, John, Isaac, Jacob and Moses, rest of land. Executors—wife, Tamor, and my friend, Samuel Oliver. Witnesses—Thomas Miller, Ebenezer Sturges, Rodah Sturges.

1788, March 21. Codicil. Knowing the lameness and age of my son, John, I give him 10 acres of land. I appoint Jonathan Stiles an Executor. Witnesses—same as above. Proved May 12, 1788.
1788, May 7. Inventory, £146.12.9, made by Ebenezer Sturges and Seth Crowell. Lib. 31, p. 190.

**1786, Nov. 9. Parker, Hannah,** of Shrewsbury, Monmouth Co., widow of Nathaniel; will of. Daughter, Elizabeth, £30. Daughter-in-law, Deborah Parker, some goods. To William Parker, Jacob Parker and Hannah Parker, my grandchildren, the children of my son, Jacob, and to Hannah Cook and Susanah Cook, the children of my daughter, Mary, the residue. Executors—daughter, Elizabeth Parker and my friend, William Chadwick, the elder. Witnesses—Robert White, trader, Nathan Jackson, Josiah Holmes. Proved Feb. 12, 1787.
1786, Nov. 22. Inventory, £74.2.0, made by Thomas Chadwick and John White. Lib. 29, p. 308.

**1790, June 2. Parker, Joseph,** of Shrewsbury, Monmouth Co. Int. Adm'r—William Parker. Fellowbondsman—Jonathan Rhea; both of said Co. Witness—Thomas Henderson, Surrogate. Lib. 30, p. 417.

**1786, Oct. 27. Parker, Michael,** of Shrewsbury, Monmouth Co. Ward. Son of Miln Parker, of said place, deceased. Said Ward makes choice of Joseph Throckmorton as his Guardian.
1786, Oct. 27. Guardian—Joseph Throckmorton, of said place. Witness—Samuel Forman. Lib. 28, p. 296.

**1787, March 17. Parrot, Thomas,** of Essex Co. Ward. Son of William Parrot, of said Co., deceased. Said Ward, being out of wardship of Abigail Parrot, and having an estate of £2,000, makes choice of Kennedy Vance as his Guardian.
1787, March 17. Guardian—Kennedy Vance, of Morris Co. Fellowbondsman—Benjamin Pettit, of Essex Co. Lib. 29, p. 419.

**1786, Jan. 23. Passel, Stephen,** of Elizabeth Town, Essex Co., cooper; will of. Wife, Phebe, some household goods. Daughter, Mary, wife of Charles Tooker, 2 silver spoons. Daughter, Sarah Mulford, 2 silver spoons. Daughter, Ann, wife of Alexander Scott, £7. Daughter, Abigail, wife of William Stiles, £7. Wife, Phebe, use of rest of personal and real estate. That lot of salt marsh in the Great Meadows, that was devised to me by my father-in-law, Nathaniel Crane, may be sold to pay debts; and, if any money is left, my wife is to have the use of it, and, after her death, to my son, Abner. After death of wife I give my house and land where I live, of 5 or 6 acres, to my sons, Abner and Stephen. Executors—wife, Phebe, and my friend, William Woodruff. Witnesses—Johnson Shotwell, Joseph Crane, John Chetwood. Proved July 27, 1786.
Lib. 28, p. 389.

**1789, Oct. 29. Patterson, John,** of Greenwich, Sussex Co. Int. Adm'r—Samuel Sherrerd, of said place. Fellowbondsman—William Kerr, of Newtown, said Co.
1789, Sept. 18. Inventory, £197.13.7, made by John Skillman and Valentine Bidleman. Lib. 30, p. 200.

## CALENDAR OF WILLS—1786-1790

**1786, Nov. 6. Paulin, Henry,** of Pittsgrove Township, Salem Co.; will of. Wife, Cathrine, horse, cow, sheep and goods; and to be supported on the place. Son, Nathan, £15, when 21. Daughters, Ruth Sheppard, Elizabeth Paullin, Margret Elwell, Rachel Nelson and Hannah Paullen, rest of personal estate. Sons, David and Henry, my plantation. Executors—wife, Cathrine, and sons, David and Henry. Witnesses—John Mayhew, Joseph Paullin, Uriah Paullin. Proved Aug. 20, 1787.

1786, Nov. 24. Inventory, made by William Brick and John Mayhew. Lib. 29, p. 131.

**1787, Feb. 13. Peacock, John,** of Evesham, Burlington Co., house carpenter; will of. Mother, Margaret Peacock, wife of my father, Abner Peacock, £20. Sister, Margaret Peacock, £15. Brothers, Thomas, Isaac, William, Abner, Daniel, Amos, Hooton and Abram, rest of estate. Executor—brother, William Peacock. Witnesses—Abraham Matlack, Thomas Hooton, Deborah Hooton. Proved March 8, 1787.

1787, March 5. Inventory, £269.6.2, made by Abraham Matlack and Thomas Hooton. Lib. 29, p. 33.

**1790, Aug. 7. Peacock, John,** of Evesham Township, Burlington Co., blacksmith; will of. Wife, Susanna, to be provided for by my son, John. Son, Joshua, a piece of land at the lower end of my place, along land of Zachariah Prickitt and Lawrence Webster; also 50 acres joining Charles Reed. Son, John, rest of lands, and he is to bring up my 4 unmarried children like the married ones were. Those unmarried are, Aletheia, Rachel, Elizabeth and Sarah. And to my married daughters, Hannah, Susanna, Mary and Lydia, 5 shillings each. John is to bring up and school my granddaughter, Hannah Peacock, till she is 18. Executor—son, John. Witnesses—Melchizedek Peacock, Levi Peacock, Joshua Sharp. Proved Nov. 6, 1790.

1790, Nov. 16. Inventory, £939.17.0, made by Melchizdek Peacock and Samuel Sharp. Lib. 32, p. 77.

**1786, April 26. Peake, Sarah,** of Monmouth Co. Int. Adm'r—James Rogers. Fellowbondsman—David Rhea; both of said Co. Witness—Elisha Walton.

1786, April 24. Inventory, £30.4.0, made by Alexander Montgomery and David Rhea, of the goods that were left unsold by seizure for rent. Lib. 28, p. 293.

**1787, March 14. Pearce, Henry,** of Horsneck, Essex Co., yeoman; will of. Daughter, Elizabeth, £10. Wife, Elizabeth, all real and personal estate, and, after her death, to my 4 sons, Henry, Edward, Andrew and George, my old homestead. Younger daughter, Charlott, £50. Executrix—wife, Elizabeth. Witnesses—Timothy Ward, Harman Masear, Encrease Gould. Proved April 30, 1789.
Lib. 38, p. 86.

**1789, May 6. Pearson, John,** of Burlington Co. Int. Adm'x—Sarah Pearson. Fellowbondsman—John Abbott; both of said Co.
Lib. 31, p. 321.

**1790, Jan. 16. Peirce, Samuel,** of Gloucester Co. Int. Adm'r—Joseph Marshall. Fellowbondsman—Benjamin Whitall; both of said Co.

1790, Jan. 19. Inventory, £67.13.7, made by Richard Cheesman and John Hedger. Lib. 31, p. 479.

**1788, Sept. 15. Peirson, Daniel,** of Newtown, Sussex Co. Int. Adm'r—Daniel Peirson, Jr., of said place. Fellowbondsmen—John Holmes and John Peirson; both of said place. Witness—Wright Redding.
1788, Sept. 16. Inventory, £265.11.4, made by Henry Johnson and Samuel Hill. Lib. 31, p. 157.

**1790, June 28. Peirson, David,** of Westfield, Elizabeth Township, Essex Co. Int. Adm'r—Squire Peirson. Fellowbondsman—Isaac Hendricks; both of said Co. Witness—Ezekiel Ball, Jr.
1790, June 30. Inventory, £38.4.3, made by Noah Clark and Isaac Hendricks. Lib. 30, p. 362.

**1786, May 24. Perce, John,** of Deptford Township, Gloucester Co., yeoman; will of. Sons, John and Ammariah, all my lands. Wife, some goods. Daughter, Hannah Andrews, 7 shillings and 6 pence yearly, while she lives where she lives now and no longer. Daughter, Margret, £5. Daughter, Mary, £30, and a home while she is single. Executors—sons, John and Ammariah. Witnesses—Paul Andrews, John Ferrol, Samuel Ladd. Proved Aug. 5, 1786.
1786, Aug. 3. Inventory, £99.1.4, made by Benjamin Ward and Jonas Cattell. Lib. 28, p. 92.

**1786, Oct. 20. Perkins, John,** of Deptford Township, Gloucester Co. Int. Adm'rs—Samuel Perkins, cordwainer, and Jonathan Harker, wheelwright; both of said place. Witness—Joel Westcott.
1786, Oct. 19. Inventory, £69.19.9, made by Joel Westcott and Samuel Wood. Lib. 28, p. 122.

**1790, Jan. 8. Perkins, Samuel,** of Deptford Township, Gloucester Co.; will of. Mother, Rachel Ward, £5. Brother, William Perkins, apparel. Wife, Mary, my land adjoining my father-in-law's lot, and rest of estate. Executors—wife, Mary, and my friend, Jacob Wood. Witnesses—Samuel Laning, Jr., Samuel Marshall, James Chattin. Proved April 14, 1790.
1790, April 7. Inventory, £136.7.6, made by John Sharp and Joel Westcott. Lib. 31, p. 453.

**1787, Sept. 4. Perry, Thomas,** of Middlesex Co. Int. Adm'r— Thomas Perry. Fellowbondsman—John Arnold; both of said Co.
1787, Feb. 7. Inventory, made by Jacob Compton and John Arnold. Lib. 29, p. 363.

**1787, April 16. Peterson, Aaron,** of Upper Precinct, Cape May Co. Int. Adm'r—Thomas Peterson. Fellowbondsmen—David Goff and John Goff; all of said place. Witnesses—Aaron Peterson and Sarah Hand.
1787, April 7. Inventory, £79.17.10, made by David Goff and John Goff. Lib. 29, p. 241.

**1790, Nov. 30. Peterson, Garret,** of Hillsborough, Somerset Co., yeoman. Int. Adm'rs—Andrew Van Middleswart and Abraham Vanarsdalen. Fellowbondsman—John Van Arsdalen; all of said place.

CALENDAR OF WILLS—1786-1790 177

1790, Nov. 8. Inventory, £585.5.4, made by Dirck Low and Peter Staats. Lib. 31, p. 60.

**1790, Dec. 28. Peterson, Thomas,** of Greenwich, Sussex Co. Int. Adm'x—Mary Peterson. Fellowbondsman—William Gardner, yeoman; both of said place. Witness—Benjamin Youmans.
1790, Dec. 6. Inventory, £176.5.9, made by Benjamin Youmans and Peter Wyckoff. Lib. 35, p. 47.

**1790, Nov. 5. Pettit, Amos,** of Newtown, Sussex Co. Int. Adm'rs— Esther Pettit, John Pettit and Jonathan Willis. Fellowbondsman— John Kelsey; all of said place. Witness—William Willis.
1790, Nov. 2. Inventory, £206.6.2, made by Samuel Lundy and John Kelsey. Lib. 30, p. 438.

**1787, Jan. 12. Pettit, Isaac,** of Hardwick Township, Sussex Co.; will of. Wife, Mary, may live on the place with the children, Rachil, John, Elizabeth, Deborah and Jonathan, until they are 14, when all is to be sold for their benefit. Executors—wife, Mary, and my brother, Jonathan. Witnesses—Abraham Shaver, John Moore, Mary Nixon. Proved Jan. 23, 1787.
1787, Jan. 22. Inventory, £33.14.10, made by Aaron Hankinson and John Moore. Lib. 29, p. 476.

**1789, Jan. 15. Pettit, Mary,** of Kingwood Township, Hunterdon Co.; will of. My husband, Jonathan Pettit, deceased, by his will gave me £100, which I give as follows:—to son, John Pettit, 5 shillings; daughter Susannah Combes' children, £24; daughter, Mary Green Sway, 5 shillings; daughter, Hannah Funk, £24; son, Aaron Pettit, £24; grandson, Jonathan Pettit, 5 shillings; daughter, Sarah Forker, £24. If my granddaughter, late Elizabeth Marshal, now Slaght, do sign a discharge of demands, which she has against the estate of my husband, then I give £40 out of the legacies above mentioned, except John Pettit's, Mary Green Sway's and grandson Jonathan Pettit's. Executors—son-in-law, Thomas Combs, of Kingwood, and my son, Aaron Pettit. Witnesses—John Johnson, Elizabeth Johnson. Proved Feb. 25, 1790.
1790, March 3. Inventory, £323.18.2, made by John Snyder and John Johnson.
1792, Feb. 23. Account by Aaron Pettit. Lib. 30, p. 281.

**1790, May 20. Pharo, Sikee, Samuel, Ann, Robert and Hannah,** of Burlington Co. Wards. Children of Timothy Pharo, of said Co., who makes petition that he may be appointed Guardian of said children.
1790, May 20. Guardian—Timothy Pharo. Fellowbondsmen— Josiah Gaskill and Gervas Pharo; all of said Co. Lib. 32, p. 98.

**1788, Oct. 21. Philips, Margaret,** of Hunterdon Co. Int. Adm'r— Archibald William Yard. Fellowbondsman—Job Moore; both of Trenton, said Co.
1788, Oct. 21. Renunciation by Pamelia Yard, niece of Margaret Philips, of Maidenhead, deceased. Lib. 31, p. 144.

**1790, March 13. Phillips, Peter,** of Amwell, Hunterdon Co. Int. Adm'rs—John Phillips, of said place, and Lott Phillips, of Hopewell. Fellowbondsman—Theophilus Moore, of Amwell, said Co.

1790, March 8. Inventory, £251.16.0, made by William Runk and Jacob Holcomb.
1790, March 12. Renunciation by Thomas Phillips, eldest son of Peter Phillips. Lib. 30, p. 318.

**1790, Feb. 9. Phillips, Theophilus,** of Hunterdon Co. Int. Adm'r—Palmer Phillips, of Kingwood. Fellowbondsman—Micajah Phillips, of Hopewell; both of said Co. Lib. 30, p. 318.

**1790, March 24. Philpot, Francis,** of Lower Penns Neck, Salem Co., yeoman; will of. Daughters, Rebeckah Philpot, Edith Jaquett, Hannah and Anne Philpots, plantation where I live, and marsh in Manington. My lands called Turnip Hill, in Alloways Creek Township, to be sold. Grandson, John Pedrick, £60, when 21. To my wife, £50. Executors—daughter, Rebeckah, and my friend, Jacob Pedrick. Witnesses—Peter Hickman, Samuel Griffee, Allen Congleton, Jr. Proved May 13, 1790.
1790, May 1. Inventory, £164.15.7, made by Peter Hickman and Braithwaite Tuft. Lib. 31, p. 488.

**1789, Nov. 12. Pickle, Henry,** of Readingtown, Hunterdon Co. Ward. Son of Baltis Pickle, of said place, deceased. Said Ward makes choice of Abraham Pickle as his Guardian.
1789, Nov. 12. Guardian—Abraham Pickle. Fellowbondsman—Baltus Pickle; both of said place. Witness—Margret Pittenger.
Lib. 32, p. 58.

**1790, June 30. Pierson, Isaac,** of Morristown, Morris Co.; will of. Wife, Rhoda, my personal estate; and she is to pay to my daughter, Phebe, £50. Wife to have use of lands till sons are of age. Sons, Darius and Jacob, my homestead of 140 acres. Sons, John and Abraham, the Keese lot. Daughter, Tahpenis, 20 shillings. Daughter, Eunice, £10. Daughter, Phebe, £50. Executors—wife, Rhoda, my son, Darius, and son-in-law, David Lindsly. Witnesses—Ezekiel Munson, Jonathan Goble, William Campfield. Proved Sept. 13, 1790.
1790, Sept. 7. Inventory, £268.13.6, made by Elijah Pierson and Jonathan Thompson. Lib. 30, p. 472.

**1789, Dec. 9. Pierson, Jonathan,** of Elizabeth Township, Essex Co.; will of. Wife, Sarah, use of ⅛ of the lands. Oldest daughter, Mary, the bed which her mother brought to me, and ½ of her mother's clothing, which is now at her grandfather's, Cornelius Ludlow; also £65; all when she is 21 or marries. Oldest son, Sineus, ½ of the land which joins Jacob Crane and David Chandler; also a salt meadow joining the Great Island, which I bought of Stephen Chandler; also a tract between the two Miammies, which Ezekiel Ludlow bought for me. Daughter, Elizabeth, ½ of her mother's clothing, and £65. Son, Ludlow, ½ of the land that joins Elihu Pierson and Timothy Woodruff; also ½ of the land in Newark Township that I bought of Lewis Mulford. Youngest son, Jonathan, the house I live in, and the acres on which it stands, which I bought of Lewis Mulford. Land is to be sold to educate the children. Executors—friends, Benjamin Ludlow, John Pierson and Ezekiel Woodruff, Jr. Witnesses—Wessels Tucker, Elihu Pierson, Andrew Wilson. Proved Jan. 29, 1790.
Lib. 30, p. 327.

CALENDAR OF WILLS—1786-1790 179

**1790, May 28. Pierson, Samuel,** of Hanover, Morris Co. Int. Adm'x—Rebecca Pierson. Fellowbondsman—David Garrigus; both of said place.
1790, May 19. Inventory, £106.5.3, made by David Garrigus and Ebenezer Stiles. Lib. 30, p. 480.

**1787, Sept. 28. Pinkerton, Henry,** of Hopewell, Hunterdon Co.; will of. Wife, Keziah, a living out of the profits of the plantation. Son, John, £40. Grandson, Henry Smith, £15. Granddaughter, Hannah Smith, and granddaughter, Elizabeth Smith, £10 each. Granddaughter, Cleary Moore, £16. Daughter, Polly Jones, 5 shillings. To the Hopewell Methodist Church, £10. Daughters, Elizabeth Hankins and Mehetabel Smith, rest of estate. Executors—Henry Baker, and my son-in-law, Richard Hankins. Witnesses—Cornelius Hoff, George Prall, Neille McGill. Proved April 1, 1788.
1788, March 25. Inventory. £40.11.10, made by Cornelius Hoff and Ishi Vancleave.
1799, Feb. 23. Account by Henry Baker, surviving Executor.
Lib. 31, p. 115.

**1790, May 18. Pinyard, Joseph,** of Greenwich, Gloucester Co.; will of. Wife, Sarah, use of lands where I live, which I had by will of my grandfather, till my youngest child, Joseph, is 21, if he live so long; otherwise till the death of granny, Jane Pinyard. After Joseph is 21, all my estate to be sold, and of the money I give my wife one share and a half, and to my eldest son, John, one share and a half, and to the rest of my children, Mary, Sarah, William and Joseph, one share to each. Executors—wife, Sarah, and my friend, Samuel French. Witnesses—Enoch Eldridge, John Pinyard, Jacob Gosling. Proved June 19, 1790.
1790, May 29. Inventory, £121.17.4, made by John Pinyard and Jacob Gosling. Lib. 31, p. 455.

**1786, Jan. 13. Pipet, Isaac,** of Northampton, Burlington Co. Int. Adm'rs—Hannah Pipet and George Woolston. Fellowbondsman—Job Moore; all of said place.
1786, Jan. 14. Inventory, made by Job Moore and Abel Briggs.
Lib. 28, p. 79.

**1790, Aug. 17. Pittenger, John and Joseph,** of Readingtown, Hunterdon Co. Ward. Sons of Joseph Pittenger, of said place, deceased. Said Wards make choice of John Simonson as their Guardian.
1790, Aug. 17. Guardian—John Simonson. Fellowbondsman—James Vanhorn; both of Bridgewater, Somerset Co. Lib. 30, p. 319.

**1786, Feb. 25. Plum, Joseph,** of Essex Co. Int. Adm'x—Joanna Plum. Fellowbondsman William Burnet; both of said Co.
Lib. 28, p. 424.

**1786, Feb. 17. Polemus, Leffert,** of Upper Freehold, Monmouth Co.; will of. Sister, Mary Polemus, £30, and rest of estate to brothers and sisters, Perthenia Vanskoyke, James Johnson, Mary Polemus, Tobias, Benjamin and Arthur Polemus. Half sister, Sarah Barrikelow, a half share. Executors—uncle, Arthur Lefferson, and James Lawrence, the elder. Witnesses—Richard James, Cornelius Barcalow, Abram Hendricks. Proved March 17, 1786.

**1786, March 7.** Inventory, made by Richard James and Derick Barcalow. Lib. 28, p. 282.

**1786, Jan. 14. Pool, Lawrence,** of Newtown, Sussex Co. Int. Adm'x—Catherine Pool. Fellowbondsman—Peter Crandlemire; both of said place.
**1786, Jan. 3.** Inventory, £71.16.0, made by Cornelius Flummerfelt and Benjamin Horton. Lib. 28, p. 469.

**1788, March 29. Porter, Elizabeth,** late Elizabeth Dumont (?), of Somerset Co. Int. Adm'r—John Porter. Fellowbondsman—John Ludlow; both of said Co. Lib. 31, p. 177.

**1786, Dec. 31. Porter, Richard,** of Hunterdon Co.; will of. Real and personal estate to be sold. Wife, Cathrine, £20 a year. Daughter, Nancy McCrea, £30. Daughter, Cathrine Faulkner, £80. Sons, William, James, Nathaniel and John, rest of estate. Executors—my 4 said sons. Witnesses—Thomas Berry, Mathias Lane, John Taylor. Proved April 26, 1787.
**1787, April 12.** Inventory, £413.17.9, made by John Taylor and Thomas Berry. Lib. 29, p. 253.

**1787, June 9. Post, Peter A.,** of Acquacanonk Township, Essex Co.; will of. Sister, Elseye, widow of Albert Bertholf, £20. Wife, Jacomeinty, use of land. Son, Adrian, my land, after death of wife. Daughter, Maike, £9. Peter and Abraham, children of my daughter, Margrit, £23. Executors—friends, John I. Post, Simeon Van Winkel, Jr., and Cornelius Van Winkle. Witnesses—Jane Stanton, Rachel Houten, Hessel Peterse. Proved Aug. 16, 1787. Lib. 29, p. 403.

**1789, Jan. 26. Post, William,** of New Shanneck, Somerset Co., yeoman; will of. Son, William, £5. I gave my son, Christopher, a deed for 138 acres of land. The 12 acres of land where my son, William, lives, my daughter, Idah, and her husband, Thomas Cock, shall have the use of it during their lives, and then to their heirs. Son, Teunis, farm where I live, of 267 acres. Daughter, Maria, wife of Daniel Perrine, £60. Executors—Richard Cock and John Vanderipe, son of Jurrie. Witnesses—Peter Stryker, Lucas Hoagland, Benijah Stout. Proved Feb. 16, 1790. Lib. 31, p. 516.

**1786, Dec. 19. Potter, Henry,** of Middlesex Co. Int. Adm'r—Ellis Potter. Fellowbondsman—Reuben Potter; both of Woodbridge, said Co. Lib. 28, p. 338.

**1789, Nov. 7. Powelson, Mina,** of Bridgwater, Somerset Co.; will of. Personal and real estate to be sold. Wife, Catharine, the goods she brought when I married her, and other goods; and rest to my wife, and children when of age. Children, John, Isaac, and the child my wife is pregnant with. Executors—brother, Cornelius, and friend, Robert Blair. Witnesses—John Voorhies, Abraham Powelson, Elener Voorhies. Proved Nov. 30, 1789.
**1789, Nov. 24.** Inventory, made by Guisbert Sutfen and John Voorhies. Lib. 31, p. 408.

**1790, Jan. 20. Prall, Cornelius, Catharine, Isaac and Lewis,** of Middlesex Co. Wards. Children of Isaac Prall, of said Co., deceased.

The Adm'rs of Isaac Prall ask for Guardians to be appointed for said minors.
1790, Jan. 20. Guardians—Lewis Prall, John Thorp and Robert Ross, Jr. Fellowbondsmen—Robert Ross, Sr., and Japheth Bishop; all of said Co. Witness—John Lyle, tertius. Lib. 30, p. 536.

**1790, Jan. 4. Prall, Isaac,** of Woodbridge, Middlesex Co. Int. Adm'rs—Lewis Prall and Robert Ross, Jr. Fellowbondsman—Daniel Hampton; all of said Co.
1790, Jan. 5. Inventory, £216.5.8, made by John Brown and Daniel Hampton. Lib. 30, p. 533.

**1786, Nov. 30. Preston, William,** of Monmouth Co. Int. Adm'x— Elizabeth Preston. Fellowbondsman—Joseph Preston, both of said Co. Witness—Robert McKnight.
1786, Nov. 16. Inventory, £60.11.9, made by Robert McKnight and Adam Woolley. Lib. 28, p. 291.

**1787, April 3. Price, Mary,** of Gloucester, Gloucester Co., widow; will of. Mother, Elizabeth Sparks, all my estate. Executrix—said mother. Witnesses—Thomas Sanders, John Brick, Isaac Burrough, Jr. Proved July 30, 1787.
1787, Sept. 7. Inventory, £31.7.6, made by William Eldridge and John Brick. Lib. 29, p. 107.

**1786, May 4. Price, Obadiah,** of Hunterdon Co. Ward. Son of Joseph Price, Jr., of said Co., deceased. Said Ward makes choice of Isaac Howell, of said Co., mason, as his Guardian. File No. 1356 J.

**1786, Aug. 15. Price, Robert F.,** of Gloucester, Gloucester Co., yeoman; will of. Wife, Mary, all real and personal estate. Executors— friends, John Brick and George Sparks, joiner. Witnesses—John Forrest, David Branson, Joseph Perry. Proved Oct. 9, 1786.
1786, Oct. 9. Inventory, £342.14.11, made by William Eldridge and Samuel Clement. Lib. 28, p. 87.

**1790, Jan. 2. Probasco, Christopher,** of Eastern Precinct, Somerset Co. Int. Adm'r—Garrit Probasco, of Bridgewater. Fellowbondsman—Robert R. Henry, of Bedminster.
1791, July 22. Inventory, made by Peter Sutfin and Abraham Voorhees. Lib. 31, p. 531.

**1786, Oct. 20. Probasco, John,** of Somerset Co. Ward. Son of Rem Probasco, of said Co., deceased. Said Ward makes choice of Abraham Staats, as his Guardian.
1786, Oct. 20. Guardian—Abraham Staats. Fellowbondsman— Jeremiah Van Liew; both of said Co. Witness—Elbert Monfort.
Lib. 29, p. 197.

**1789, April 16. Probasco, John,** of Middlesex Co.; will of. Wife, Dinah, profits of estate, for support of my youngest son, Jacob. Son, Jacob, my plantation, and 10 acres near Rariton Landing in Somerset Co., when 21. Son, Simon, and my daughter, Martha Probasco, the wife of Peter Probasco, rest of land in Somerset Co. Granddaughter, Catey, daughter of my son, Jacob, deceased, £25. Executors—wife, Dinah, and friend, Henderick Berger. Witnesses—Moses Scott, Jacob Hunt, John Bray. Proved June 17, 1789.

182   NEW JERSEY POST-REVOLUTIONARY DOCUMENTS

1789, June 8. Inventory, £1,404.4.5, made by John Boice and Ephraim Pyatt. Lib. 31, p. 385.

**1786, July 8. Provost, David,** of New York City. Adm'r with will annexed—Daniel Ludlow, of said City. Fellowbondsman—Abraham Ogden, of New Jersey. Whereas, the said David Provost made his will, dated Sept. 1, 1781, and appointed David Mathews of said City as his Executor, and the said Mathews is beyond the sea; therefore this appointment. File No. 6414 G.

**1788, April 8. Pryor, Thomas,** of Burlington, Burlington Co. Int. Adm'x—Hannah Pryor, of said City. Fellowbondsman—Thomas Redman, of Gloucester Co. Witness—Herbert McElroy, Surrogate.
1787, March 9. Inventory, £62.7.11, made by James Verree and Abbott Williams. Lib. 30, p. 60.

**1787, Jan. 20. Purviance, Mary,** of Pittsgrove, Salem Co.; will of. Granddaughters, Nansey and Susannah Eakin, daughters of Mary Greenman, ½ of my estate, when they are 18. Grandson, the son of my daughter, Mary Greenman, £10. [£10 was crossed out]. Grandson, Hazlehurst, £10. [£10 was crossed out]. Daughter, Mary Greenman, £20. Granddaughter, Sarah Purviance, daughter of my son, Andrew Purviance, deceased, 10 shillings. Daughter, Joannah Hazlehurst, and my granddaughter, Mary Hazlehurst, rest of estate. Executor—friend, Benjamin Vanmeter. Witnesses—William McKinney, Ezekiel Rose. Proved Dec. 10, 1788. Lib. 31, p. 49.

**1786, Dec. 17. Pyne, William,** late of the Parish of Heavytree, County of Devon, but now of Burlington, Burlington Co., gentleman; will of. Wife, Anna Pyne, all my estate. Executrix—wife, Anna. Witnesses—Eliza Peake, Rachel Smith. Proved July 3, 1788.
Lib. 30, p. 20.

**1788, Dec. 27. Quest, Rebecca,** of Burlington, Burlington Co.; will of. Niece, Rebecca McCollin, wife of Allen McCollin, my house and lot on High St., where I live, and the corner lot at High and Pearl Streets, and, at her decease, to her children. Sister, Dinah Bickham, and my niece, abovesaid, my goods. Niece, Rebecca Brooks, 3 silver spoons. Brother John's children, Thomas Quest, Edward Quest and Rebecca Quest, £30. To children of my sister, Rachel, wife of John Butler, to wit:—James, Rebecca, Joseph, Samuel and Israel, £4 each. To the children of my said niece, Rebecca McCollin, to wit:—Ann, John, Mary, Rachel, William and Rebecca, £5 each. Sister, Dinah Bickham, the residue. Executors—sister, Dinah Bickham, and my brother-in-law, John Butler. Witnesses—Daniel Smith, Robert Smith, George Hulme. Proved June 12, 1789.
1789, June 12. Inventory, £203.13.8, made by George Hulme and Abraham Gardiner. Lib. 31, p. 292.

**1790, Feb. 19. Quick, Cornelius,** of Amwell, Hunterdon Co.; will of. Wife, Mary, to be provided for by my son, Cornelius. Goods to be sold and money given to wife and my daughters, Cathrine Runyan and Mary Prall. Grandson, Cornelius Quick, £5. Son, Cornelius, my lands. Executors—John Lequear and Peter Prall. Witnesses—Nathan Stout, John Quick, John Price. Proved June 11, 1790.

CALENDAR OF WILLS—1786-1790   183

1790, June 9. Inventory, £329.13.2, made by Joseph Ott and Azariah Higgins. Lib. 30, p. 297.

**1786, July 3. Quick, Francis,** of Amwell, Hunterdon Co. Int. Adm'x—Ruth Quick. Fellowbondsman—Nathan Stout; both of said place.
1786, June 3. Inventory, £106.0.11, made by Nathan Stout and Jacob James Johnson. Lib. 28, p. 246.

**1789, June 12. Quick, John,** of Kingwood, Hunterdon Co., yeoman; will of. Wife, Mehetabel, my moveable estate, and use of lands until my son, John, is 25. Son, John, the south part of my plantation, at corner of Solomon Mott and Cornelius Huff; and he is to pay to my daughter, Sarah Quick, £30. Daughter, Martha Quick, £30. Daughter, Hannah Quick, all my land that lays to the north of said corners; also the land where John Warman lives. Executors—wife, Mehetabel, and my son, John. Witnesses—Cornelius Huff, Gershom Mott, Uriah Bonham. Proved Nov. 18, 1789.
1789, Nov. 16. Inventory, made by Cornelius Huff and Nathan Higgins. Lib. 32, p. 41.

**1789, Dec. 3. Quick, Thomas,** of Newtown, Sussex Co. Int. Adm'rs—Clara Quick and Peter Smith. Fellowbondsman—William Kerr; all of said place.
1789, Nov. 17. Inventory, £50.9.3, made by William Current and Peter Simons. Lib. 30, p. 199.

**1787, Feb. 16. Quicksall, Daniel,** of Greenwich Township, Gloucester Co. Int. Adm'r—Aaron Quicksall. Fellowbondsman—Ebenezer Adams, yeomen; both of said place. Witness—Joseph Lippincott.
1787, Feb. 15. Inventory, £174.0.9, made by John Daniels and Ebenezer Adams. Lib. 29, p. 120.

**1787, Jan. 22. Quicksall, Thomas,** of Burlington Co. Int. Adm'r—Joel Taylor. Fellowbondsman—John Curtis; both of said Co.
1787, Jan. 9. Renunciation by Daniel Quicksall, brother of said Thomas, in favor of Joel Taylor. Witness—Thomas Adams.
1787, Jan. 23. Inventory, £14.1.1, made by Edward Brooks and Caleb Carman. Lib. 29, p. 75.

**1787, March 3. Rambo, John,** of Greenwich Township, Gloucester Co.; will of. Son, William, and my grandchild, Elizabeth Chester, £12.10.0, each, if they should demand it within 10 years; but, if not, then to my 2 daughters. Sons, Jesse and Champneys, £25 each. My 2 daughters, £37.10.0, each. Sons, Jacob and Peter, to be bound out as their mother thinks fit. Son, Gabriel, a lot at Swedesborough. Son, Jacob, the Thoroughfare lot, of 20 acres. Son, Peter, 30 acres at Billings Port, on the Delaware River. Son, John, my plantation on Little MantuaCreek, and 5 acres on Little Ease Branch, and my Propriety Rights. Wife to have £150 and goods. Son, Gabriel, £40, when he is of age. Son, Peter, £60, when he is 21. If any of my children die under 21, then their share to be divided among the survivors of my last wife's children. Executors—wife, Elizabeth, and my son, Jesse. Witnesses—Uriah Paul, John Stephens, Rebeckah Orin. Proved March 30, 1787.

1787, March 28. Inventory, £658.17.9, made by James Wilkins and John Stephens. Lib. 29, p. 94.

1786, June 10. **Ramsey, Hugh,** of Salem Co. Ward. Son of Hugh Ramsay, of said Co., deceased. Petition of Joseph Nealy, grandfather of said minor, asking that John Holme may be appointed Guardian.
1786, June 10. Guardian—John Holme, of Alloways Creek. Fellowbondsman—Anthony Keasbey, of Salem. Lib. 28, p. 157.

1787, Aug. 10. **Ramsay, Hugh,** of Salem Co. Int. Adm'r—John Holme. Fellowbondsmen—William Dickeson and Adam Saul; all of said Co. This Adm'r is appointed on all left unadministered by Margaret Ramsay, who is also deceased. Lib. 29, p. 152.

1787, March 26. **Randolph, Simeon,** of Eastern Precinct, Somerset Co. Int. Adm'x—Elizabeth Randolph. Fellowbondsman—James Drake; both of said place. Witness—John Bray. Lib. 29, p. 438.

1787, March 26. **Range, John,** of Crane Town, Essex Co.; will of. Wife, Elizabeth, use of real and personal estate. She may sell a salt meadow of 4 acres in order to pay Thomas Codimus. Daughters, Elizabeth and Mary, the real and personal estate, after death of wife; and, if they die unmarried, then my wife's 3 daughters are to have ½, and the other ½ to be given to the Church of Orange. Executors—wife, Elizabeth, and my friends, Joseph Baldwin, of Crane Town, and Joseph Crane, of same place. Witnesses—Justus Burnett, Moses Dod, William Crane.
1787, March 31. Codicil. Witnesses—Justus Burnett, Oliver Crane, Zadock Crane. Proved July 24, 1787. Lib. 29, p. 388.

**1789, July 7. Rapelye, George, Jr.,** of Communipaw, Bergen Co. Int. Adm'r—George Rapelye. Fellowbondsman—John Rapelye; both of said Co.
1789, Dec. 10. Inventory, £144.1.6, made by Cornelius Garrabrants and Garrabrant Garrabrantse. Lib. 30, p. 248.

1788, April 7. **Rarick, Conrad,** of Roxbury Township, Morris Co.; will of. Wife, Anna, ½ of the household goods, and ⅓ of the lands, while my widow. Son, Henry, £70. Son, John, 2 horses. Son, William, 2 horses. Daughter, Mary Margaret Flock, some sheep. Children, Henry Rarick, Conrad Rarick, John Rarick, William Rarick, Mary Margaret Flock, Mary Catharine Waldorf, Anna Savereen, Mary Cous and Catharine Allpock, rest of moveable estate. Sons, John and William, my lands. Son, Henry, £50. Son, Conrad, £50. Daughter, Mary Margaret Flock, £50. Daughter, Mary Catharine Waldorf, £5. Daughter, Anna Sovereen, £50. Daughter, Mary Cous, £50. Daughter, Catharine Allpock, £50. Executors—friends, John Waldorf and William Allpock, and my son, John. Witnesses—John Darbe, Jr., Philip Dormer, William Woodhull. Proved May 7, 1790.
1790, April 29. Inventory, £475.16.10, made by William Woodhull and Philip Criter (Krider als) Lib. 30, p. 444.

**1786, April 7. Ray, George,** of Newtown, Sussex Co. Int. Adm'r—John Hepburn. Fellowbondsman—Edward Dunlop; both of said place. Witness—Richard Byron. Lib. 28, p. 471.

## CALENDAR OF WILLS—1786-1790

**1787, May 7. Ray, William,** of Salem Co. Int. Adm'rs—Rhoda Ray and David Elwell. Fellowbondsmen—Joseph Heward and David Moore; all of said Co. File No. 1957 Q.

**1790, Jan. 29. Raymond, Seth,** of Elizabeth Town, Essex Co.; will of. Mother, Christiana Raymond, ½ of my house and land, of 40 acres. Daughter, Abigail, whom I had by and is the daughter of Rachel Ross, the other ½ of house and land, when she is 18; but, if she die before that age, then to my brother, James Raymond, and my 3 sisters. Executors—mother, Christiana Raymond, and my friend, Amos Potter. Witnesses—John Winans, Abraham Lacy, Samuel Woodruff. Proved March 29, 1790. Lib. 30, p. 331.

**1788, Jan. —. Read, Andrew,** of Cape May Co. Int. Adm'r—Jacob Cresse. Fellowbondsman—Philip Hand; both of said Co., gentlemen. Witness—Aaron Hand.
1788, Aug. 5. Inventory, £25.12.9, made by Matthias Woodruff and Jesse Hand. "His joiners tools, £20.0.3." Lib. 31, p. 93.

**1788, May 7. Reading, William,** of Kingwood, Hunterdon Co. Int. Adm'r—Joseph Reading. Fellowbondsman—Lot Rettinghous; both of Amwell, said Co.
1788, May 5. Renunciation by Ann Reading, widow of William. Witnesses—John Longley and Grace Reily.
1788, April 26. Inventory, £181.17.6, made by William Hoogland and Lot Rettinghous. Lib. 31, p. 144.

**1788, June 2. Reeder, John,** of Trenton, Hunterdon Co.; will of. Wife, Taphath, to be supported by my sons, Andrew and Amos; and they are to bury her wherever she chooses, and, if she is buried by me, they are to set up grave stones with her name and age on them. Son, John, 20 acres of land, bounded by John Moore, widow Green and John Howell. Son, Abner, £10. Sons, Absalom and Abner, 40 acres on the east side of the great road, that I bought of George Green. Son, Amos, 124 acres. Son, Andrew, 10 acres next to Daniel Scudder; also the upper part of my plantation, joining Benjamin Moore and Benjamin Titus. Daughter, Fanny Chambers, £10. Daughter, Leticia Kruson, £30. Daughter, Hannah Hartley, £50. Daughter, Abigail, £60. Youngest daughters, Mercy and Elizabeth, £60 each, when 18. Grandson, Charles Reeder, son of my son, Isaac, £50, when 21. Executors—sons, Andrew, John and Absalom. Witnesses—Neille McGill, John Guild, William Campbell. Proved Aug. 22, 1788.
1788, Aug. 21. Inventory, £883.4.5, made by Ebenezer Rose and John Howell. Lib. 31, p. 120.

**1788, Oct. 16. Reeve, Mark,** of Fairfield, Cumberland Co.; will of. Wife, Hannah, 80 acres at the upper end of my plantation, at Alloways Creek, and 10 acres of woodland that joins it. Son, Josiah, rest of the plantation; but he is to pay the bonds due to John Wood. Son, Mark, land along Sheppard's line; also the salt marsh and lease of land that I have of Mary Sheppard. Son, William, my 2 tenements and land in Back Neck. Sons, Josiah and William, the cedar marsh at Morris River. Executors—sons, Josiah, Mark and William. Witnesses—Job Butcher, Samuel Reeve, Phebe Bates. Proved Sept. 11, 1790. Lib. 30, p. 258.

**1786, April 8. Reeves, Arthur,** of Deptford Township, Gloucester Co., yeoman; will of. To my wife the lower end of my land, starting at the lower corner, and running up to James Hinchman's land, and to the Second Branch, then to the great road against Biddle Reeves' house, and along his land to Joseph Cowgill's land, to a corner of Joshua Lord and Thomas Reeves; which she is to have while my widow. After that it is to be divided amongst my sons and daughters. Rest of estate to be sold, and divided amongst my sons and daughters. Sons, Arthur, Mark, Aaron and William to be bound to trades. Executors—brothers, Joseph and Thomas Reeves. Witnesses—Joseph Cowgill, George Elkines, Biddle Reves. Proved May 2, 1786.

1786, May 2. Inventory, £382.14.4, made by John Wood and Joseph Cowgill. John Wood proved the Inventory on Jan. 9, 1787, at which time Joseph Cowgill was dead. Lib. 28, p. 111.

**1786, Jan. 12. Reid, Deborah,** of Middlesex Co.; will of. Son, John Reid, £2. Son, James, £2. Son, Richard Reid, £2. Son, George Reid, £2. Daughter, Jane Johnson, ½ of my apparel. Daughter, Deborah Reid, rest of apparel. Son, William Reid, and my daughter, Deborah Reid, residue. Executors—sons, Richard and William. Witnesses—Joseph Journy, William Dey. Proved April 21, 1788.

1788, April 19. Renunciation by Richard Reid.
1786, Jan. 28. Inventory, made by William Dey and Jacob Smith.
Lib. 31, p. 213.

**1787, April 4. Reid, Lucretia, and Rhoda,** of Middlesex Co. Wards. Children of Joseph Reid, of said Co., deceased. Petition of David Riggs, Jr., that a Guardian may be appointed for said minors.

1787, April 19. Guardian—David Riggs, Jr. Fellowbondsman—Phinehas Riggs; both of said Co. Witness—William Hyer, Jr.
Lib. 29, p. 366.

**1787, March 5. Remington, Moses,** of Greenwich, Cumberland Co.; will of. Daughters, Rachell, Hannah and Sarah, 5 shillings each. Wife, Theodotia, rest of personal and real estate. Executrix—wife, Theodotia. Witnesses—Peter Andrews, Job Tyler, Richard Wood. Proved April 9, 1787. Lib. 29, p. 165.

**1790, Jan. 11. Remington, Sarah,** of Cumberland Co. Ward. Daughter of Moses Remington, of said Co., deceased. Said Ward makes choice of John Sheppard, Jr., as her Guardian.

1790, Jan. 11. Guardian—John Sheppard, Jr. Fellowbondsman—John Sheppard; both of said Co. Witnesses—Richard Wood, Jr. and Richard W. Sheppard. Lib. 30, p. 281.

**1790, June 15. Remington, Thomas,** of Greenwich Township, Cumberland Co., yeoman; will of. Wife, Sarah, £220. Son, Mark, all my lands. Daughter, Sary Remington, a chest of drawers, and articles in the care of Isaac Wheaton. Son-in-law, David Sheppard, books that were his father's. Son, Mark, rest of estate. Executors—friends, Thomas Padgett and Howel Watson. Witnesses—Samuel Smith, Thomas Butcher, George G. Tiddiss. Proved Sept. 28, 1790.

1790, June 24. Inventory, £744.19.6, made by James B. Hunt and Samuel Smith. Lib. 30, p. 263.

CALENDAR OF WILLS—1786-1790

**1789, Oct. 24. Remsen, William,** of Freehold, Monmouth Co. Int. Adm'rs—Agnes Remsen and Elias Conover. Fellowbondsman—John Covenhoven; all of said place. Witness—John Forman.
1789, Dec. 5. Inventory, £3,488.8.1, made by John Van Der Veer and John Lloyd. Lib. 30, p. 189.

**1788, June 10. Reves, Biddle,** of Deptford, Gloucester Co.; will of. Wife, Ann, use of my tavern and lot near Timber Creek Bridge, where Josiah Hillman lives; also house and lot where Jane Cox lives; and, after her death, I give each of them to my son, Clement Reves. Son, Thomas, my upper lot of swamp on Rambo's Run, and my 2 small stills, and £300. Daughters, Mary Groff and Ann Moffit, £200. Younger daughters, Desire, Sarah and Elizabeth Reves, £600. In addition to what I gave Josiah Reves after marriage, and for his services done for me, I give him £50. Son, Biddle, rest of estate, except what I will give to my son, Joseph, which is the lower part of my plantation, which is bounded by David Chew, Thomas Reves, Sr., and the Salem Road; also give him the meadow on Rambo's Run, extending to that of my son, Biddle; also the house and lot where Archibald Fitz Patrick lives; also the large still. If Clement should die under 21, then his share is to be vested in all my daughters. Son, Biddle, the land on my plantation where I live, long since inclosed and used for a grave yard for our family, in Trust, for the use of all the blood relations descended of my father, Thomas Reves, deceased. Executors—wife, Ann, and son, Biddle. I revoke a will by me made the 5th of June, 1788, and witnessed by Thomas Reeves, Rachel Brown and John Stevens. Witnesses—Mary Adams, Jedediah Line, Richard Howell. Proved March 2, 1789.
1789, Feb. 2. Inventory, £690.3.0, made by James Wilkins and John Jessup. Lib. 30, p. 131.

**1789, Oct. 21. Rhea, Catherine,** of Monmouth Co. Int. Adm'x— Anna Bower. Fellowbondsman—Alexander Low; both of said Co.
Lib. 30, p. 189.

**1789, May 26. Rhodes, William,** of Hardwick, Sussex Co. Int. Adm'rs—Anna Rhodes, Charles Rhodes and Peter B. Shaver. Fellowbondsman—Charles Rhodes, Jr.; all of said place. Witness—Jonathan Willis.
1789, April 18. Inventory, £137.8.4, made by William Hankinson and George Wintermut. Lib. 30, p. 200.

**1788, April 23. Richards, Thomas,** of Essex Co. Int. Adm'rs— Stephen Baldwin and Elizabeth Richards. Fellowbondsman—Ebenezer Ward; all of said Co. Lib. 31, p. 244.

**1786, April 18. Richards, William,** of Nottingham, Burlington Co., merchant; will of. Wife, Elizabeth, all real and personal estate. Executors—wife, Elizabeth, and Major Isaac Budd Dunn. Witnesses—John Clunn, Thomas Ashmoor, John Watson. Proved June 17, 1787.
1787, March 27. Inventory, as returned by the Executors. Dry goods in the store. Land at Lamberton, 284 feet fronting the River, and 420 feet deep, including the street of 66½ feet, with a frame house of 6 rooms and a loft. Ground in East Jersey, within 8 miles

of New York, on the Hackinsack River, of about 186½ acres. The following debts:—Francis Coddington, of Georgia, in the care of Majr Berrien, £100. Doct, Robert Wilson, of So. Carolina, £60. Doct. Henry Stuber, of Lancaster, £63.3.3. Patience Montgomery, the widow of Doct. Montgomery, of Accomack, Virginia, £36.6.7. The estate of Doct. William Ellis, £44.3.5. Lib. 29, p. 57.

**1787, March 25. Richman, William,** of Pittsgrove, Salem Co.; will of. Wife, Experience, horse, cows, hogs, furniture and £50. Real estate in Salem and Cumberland Counties to be sold, and money divided between my children, Jacob, Jonathan, Harman, Joseph, William and Priscilla Richman, when they come of age. Executors— David Moore and Israel Read. Witnesses—John Low, William Worth, John Nelson. Proved June 2, 1789.

1789, May 5. Inventory, £845.19.5, made by Fratrick Tentelpeck and John Mayhew. Lib. 31, p. 346.

**1788, Oct. 27. Richmond, Jonathan,** of Nottingham Township, Burlington Co.; will of. Real and personal estate to be sold. Wife, Emmy, ⅛ of my estate. Niece, Sally James, daughter of my sister, Mary Watley, 20 shillings. Nephew, Samuel Wooley, son of my sister, Catharine Wooley, rest of estate. Executor—said Samuel Wooley. Witnesses—Charles Higbee, Abraham Woglum, Renseeler Williams. Proved April 6, 1789.

1789, April 7. Inventory, £549.16.4, made by Lewis Yard and Joseph Rickey. Lib. 31, p. 298.

**1788, April 29. Ridgway, Henry,** of Woolwich Township, Gloucester Co. Int. Adm'rs—David Ridgway and Henry Burr, Jr.; both of Burlington Co., yeomen. Fellowbondsman—Samuel Ogden, of said Woolwich, tanner.

1788, April 29. Inventory, £376.10.3, made by Samuel Ogden and John Smith. Lib. 31, p. 35.

**1789, Sept. 21. Ridgway, Robert,** of Little Egg Harbor Township, Burlington Co.; will of. Son, Joseph, my farm, and my lands in Stafford Township, Monmouth Co., at Barnagate. To Friends' Meeting at Little Egg Harbor, £15. Daughter, Hannah Pharo, £100. Grandsons, Samuel Pharo and Robert Pharo, and granddaughters, Kesier, Ann and Hannah Pharo, rest of personal estate. Executor— son, Joseph. Witnesses—Jonathan Pettit, Peter Lippincott, Israel Penington. Proved **Nov. 4, 1789.**

1789, Oct. 27. Inventory, £459.4.9, made by Jonathan Pettit, John Gaunt and Israel Penington. Lib. 31, p. 296.

**1788, Aug. 9. Ridgway, Solomon,** of Burlington Co.; will of. Son, Henry, my plantation in Springfield, where he lives, provided he pays a certain debt to William Lovett Smith, and pays £250 to my 5 children, Solomon, Abigail, Lydia, Miriam and Daniel. Son, Solomon, my 3 tracts near the province line;\ also ½ part of 3 tracts where James Ker lives. Son, Benjamin, when he is 21, my plantation in Willingborough, he allowing to his mother, Mary Ridgway, ½ the profits, and paying, after her decease, to his brother, Daniel, £80, and to my granddaughter, Mary Maginnis, £15 when she is 21. Sons, William and Joseph, had conveyances from me, which I confirm. Executors—wife, Mary, and my sons, Henry and William. Witnesses—Stacy Budd, Beulah Ridgway, John Ridgway. Proved Oct. 6, 1788.

1788, Sept. 18. Inventory, £1,035.5.6, made by Samuel Haines and Thomas Buzby. Lib. 30, p. 44.

**1788, Nov. 16. Ridgway, Susannah,** of Springfield Township, Burlington Co.; will of. Daughter, Beulah Ridgway, some goods. Daughter, Susannah Ridgway, some goods. Son, Daniel Ridgway, some goods, and he is to pay to his brother, Freedom Ridgway, £5. Son, Freedom, some goods. Granddaughter, Susannah Ridgway, daughter of my son, Lot Ridgway, some goods. Granddaughter, Elizabeth Ridgway, daughter of my son, Lot Ridgway, some goods. Son, Daniel Ridgway, some goods. Executors—daughter, Beulah Ridgway, and my cousin, John Ridgway. Witnesses—William Ridgway, Jonathan Taylor, Hephzibah Tonkin. Proved Dec. 22, 1788.

1788, Dec. 18. Inventory, £209.9.8, made by Samuel Shinn and Samuel Earl. Lib. 29, p. 546.

**1788, March 12. Riesller, Hontlel,** of Amwell, Hunterdon Co.; will of. Wife, Catharine, to live in my house and have what stock and goods she needs to keep house and carry on farming. If my family do not live there, then my plantation of 103 acres to be rented, and they to have the profit. Money I give to my wife and children, William, Jacob, Adam, Margaret, Catharine, Anna, Sarah and Elizabeth. My plantation in the swamp of 200 acres to be sold. Sons, Peter, William and Jacob, £20 each, and son, Adam, £40. Executors—son, William, and friend, Andrew Bearder. Witnesses—John Trimmer, George Trimmer, Jacob Bearder. Proved April 8, 1788.

1788, April 3. Inventory, £678.2.9, made by John Trimmer and George Trimmer. Lib. 31, p. 126.

**1787, Aug. 12. Rigans, Lazarus, Sr.,** of Maurice River Township, Cumberland Co., farmer; will of. Wife, Ellenar, my whole estate, and she is to pay to my children, 5 shillings each. Executrix—wife, Elenor. Witnesses—Barlow Williams, John Champion, Jonathan Badcock. Proved Sept. 25, 1787. Lib. 31, p. 71.

**1786, Oct. 31. Riggs, Daniel,** of Newark, Essex Co.; will of. My wife to have £50, and all she brought on the premises. Sons, Permenas and Benjamin, my homestead. Daughter, Phebe Terrall, 5 acres on the south corner and one acre of woodland of the Brown place; and the rest of said place to my son, Aruna Riggs. I have a place in Mendham Township, and one in Roxbury, in Morris Co., which I give to my sons, Permenas and Benjamin; and they are to have my salt meadow. Granddaughter, Phebe Riggs, £30. To my daughters, Phebe Terrel and Hanah Bruen, £30 each. Executors—sons, Permenas and Benjamin. Witnesses—John Dod, Jr., Joseph Brown, Job Brown. Proved Dec. 13, 1786. Lib. 28, p. 406.

**1787, Sept. 15. Riley, Griffiths [Griffen],** of Upper Precinct, Cape May Co. Int. Adm'x—Sarah Riley. Fellowbondsman—David Goff; both of said Co.

1787, Sept. 3. Inventory, £106.14.10, made by David Goff and Moses Williams. Lib. 29, p. 242.

**1787, Dec. 28. Risdon, John,** of Evesham Township, Burlington Co.; will of. Wife, Sarah Risdon, £50. Children, Hannah Ward, George Risdon, Jane Carr, Turner Risdon, Elizabeth Whiston and Samuel Risdon, 5 shillings each. Son, John, all my lands. Residue to my wife. Executors—son, Turner Risdon, and my son-in-law, Isaac Carr. Witnesses—John Hollinshead, Thomas Porter, William Cox. Proved Jan. 9, 1788.

1788, Jan. 7. Inventory, £76.12.6, made by Jacob Hollinshead and William Cox. Lib. 30, p. 4.

**1790, March 28. Roberson, Mary,** of Gloucester Township, Gloucester Co., widow; will of. Daughter, Lydia Roberson, a bed and land in Deptford Township, which my husband devised to me, when she is 18. Son, Ephraim, a gun. Children, Elizabeth Crawford, Sarah Denness, Ephraim Hillman and Joab Hillman, rest of estate. The clothing of my son, John, to be divided between Ephraim and Joab. Executors—sons-in-law, Samuel Crawford and Samuel Denness. Witnesses—Joseph Bolton, Isaac Tomlinson, Elizabeth Crawford.

1790, March 29. Codicil. All lands to be sold, and money put to interest for Lydia, till she is 18. Witnesses—Joseph Bolton, Elizabeth Tomlinson, Mary Harden. Proved April 20, 1790.

1790, April 3. Inventory, £105.18.4, made by Isaac Tomlinson and Ephraim Cheesman. Lib. 31, p. 456.

**1787, Sept. 24. Roberts, Richard,** of Black River, Morris Co. Int. Adm'rs—Anna Roberts and John Roberts. Fellowbondsmen—Robert Carlile and Jabez Mapes Sweezy; all of Roxbury, said Co.

1787, Sept. 6. Inventory, £199.13.9, made by Robert Carlile and Jabez Mapes Sweezy. Lib. 29, p. 473.

**1786, July 21. Robertson, John,** of Trenton, Hunterdon Co. Int. Adm'x—Mary Robertson. Fellowbondsman—Archibald William Yard; both of said place.

1786, July 21. Inventory, £31.9.0, made by Alexander Chambers and Benjamin Yard. Lib. 28, p. 246.

**1789, July 14. Robins, John,** of Alexandria, Hunterdon Co., yeoman; will of. My estate is to be turned into cash. Wife, Elizabeth, ⅓. The other ⅔ to my children, Jonathan, Robert, Mary, Lydia, Rachel and John Robins, when they come of age. The four younger children to stay with their mother. Executors—friend, Daniel Moore, and my brother, Jonathan Robins. Witnesses—Nathan Lacock, Samuel Shannon, John Houghton. Proved Nov. 19, 1789.
Lib. 32, p. 52.

**1786, Nov. 27. Robins, Nathaniel,** of Nottingham, Burlington Co.; will of. Daughter, Theodosia Rulon, £15. Daughter, Ann Stewart, £10. Daughter, Susannah Borden, £10. Daughter, Ruth Robins, £40, and £10 that her grandmother left her. Land and moveable estate to be sold, except what I have given to Job and Ruth Robins. Son, Vanroom Robins, 10 shillings. Sons, Nathaniel, Obadiah and Job, the residue. Executors—sons, Vanroom and Nathaniel. Witnesses—David Rulon, Daniel Hendrickson, Nathaniel Rulon. Proved Dec. 7, 1786.

1786, Dec. 6. Inventory, £324.11.6, made by Daniel Hendrickson and David Rulon. Lib. 28, p. 19.

CALENDAR OF WILLS—1786-1790　　　191

**1789, Aug. 25. Robins, Richard,** of Island of St. Johns. Int. Adm'r—Isaiah Robins, of Nottingham, Burlington Co. Fellowbondsman—Nathan Beakes, of Trenton, Hunterdon Co.
　　1790, Jan. 21. Inventory, £1,394.14.2, of the estate of Richard Robins, of Upper Freehold Township, Monmouth Co., made by Joseph M. Lawrie and Samuel Abbott.　　　Lib. 32, p. 55.

**1789, Oct. 14. Robins, Thomas,** of Mansfield Township, Burlington Co. Ward. Son of Aaron Robins, of said place. Said Ward makes choice of his father, the said Aaron Robins, as his Guardian.
　　1789, Oct. 14. Guardian—Aaron Robins. Fellowbondsman—Jacob Wolcott; both of said place.　　　Lib. 31, p. 322.

**1786, June 21. Robins, William,** of Essex Co. Adm'rs—Isaac Clark and Hannah Robins; both of said Co. Whereas the said William Robins in his will, dated July 24, 1776, appointed his son, Lewis Robins, Thomson Stelle and David Coriell as Executors, and the son, Lewis, is not in these parts, and Thomson Stelle and David Coriell renounced.
　　1786, June 17. Renunciation by Thomson Stelle and David Coriell.
　　　　　　　　　File No. 6420 G. (See Lib. 36, p. 497).

**1789, Aug. 15. Robinson, Dominick,** of Bergen Co. Int. Adm'x—Catherine Robinson. Fellowbondsman—Joseph Bound; both of said Co.　　　Lib. 30, p. 247.

**1790, Jan. 20. Robinson, Fransintye,** of Bergen Co. Int. Adm'rs—Cornelas Van Saan and Jacob Van Saan. Fellowbondsman—Isaac J. Van Saen; all of said Co.　　　Lib. 31, p. 543.

**1789, Dec. 12. Robinson, Martha Elizabeth,** of Gloucester Co. Ward. Daughter of John Robinson, of said Co., deceased. Joseph Turner and Samuel Black apply for a Guardian to be appointed.
　　1789, Dec. 12. Guardian—Joseph Turner. Fellowbondsman—Samuel Cozens; both of said Co.　　　Lib. 30, p. 139.

**1788, March 17. Robinson, William,** of Deerfield, Cumberland Co., yeoman; will of. Wife, Sarah, £20, and household goods. Son, William, my lands, and mulatto boy, Cain. Daughter, Ann Nieukirk, wife of Isaac, £25, and negro girl, Jude. Daughter, Mary Du Bois, wife of Benjamin, £25, and negro girl, Ratch. Son, William, and my youngest daughters, Catherine Robinson and Rebeckah Robinson, rest of estate. Son, William, is to be supported while an apprentice to Doct. Hugh McKee. Executors—friends, Eleazar Mayhew and Isaac Nieukirk. Witnesses—Jacob Nieukirk, Abigal Tullies, Ruth Titas. Proved Aug. 23, 1788.
　　1788, June 24. Inventory, £683.13.3, made by John Mayhew and Samuel Ogden.　　　Lib. 31, p. 69.

**1786, Nov. 25. Robson, Sarah,** of Deptford Township, Gloucester Co., widow; will of. Sister, Mary Lippincott, £5 and an ancient Bible. Cousin, Hannah Sharp, daughter of William Sharp, deceased, £5. Cousin, Benjamin Sharp, son of said William, £5. Cousin, Sarah Sharp, daughter of said William, £5; all to be paid them when they come of age. Cousin, Robert Cook, a note for £12 which I have against him. To Hannah Sharp, widow of William, and Bathsheba

Morgan, wife of Jonathan Morgan, my apparel. To Rachel Morgan, eldest daughter of Jonathan Morgan, my bed; and to his daughter, Rebecca Morgan, a chest of drawers. Bathsheba Morgan, daughter of said Jonathan, £6. To the 3 children of William Sharp, books. Executor—Jonathan Morgan. Witnesses—Jonathan Morgan, Jr., Elizabeth Morgan, Jacob Wood. Proved Dec. 25, 1789.
1789, Nov. 20. Inventory, £105.5.3, made by Samuel Webster and Joshua Hopper. Lib. 30, p. 123.

**1787, March 22. Rockefeller, Peter,** of Amwell Township, Hunterdon Co.; will of. Wife, Elizabeth, £60 and money I agreed to give her when we were married. She is to have the use of the land where Henry Lawshe lives, joining lands of William Belles and John Jewel. After she does not use said land, it is to be sold, and the money given to all my children, Peter, Godfree, John, Henry, William, Jacob, David, Mary and Elizabeth. Son, Peter, the plantation where he lives, bounded by lands of John Arwine, and Cornelius Williamson, of 150 acres. Son, Godfree, the plantation where he lives, in Kingwood Township, bounded by Philip Grandin and Charles Cox, and joining on the South branch of the Rarraton river, of 150 acres. Son, John, the plantation where he lives, bounded by lands of Frances Bersons and Henry Dils and Christopher Lawbocker, of 132 acres. Son, Henry, plantation I lately bought of John Emley, attorney of Thomas and John Marston, being the farm where Abraham Young lives, in Alexandria Township, of 180 acres. Son, William, £60. Sons, Jacob and David, the farm where I live, bounded by John Jewel, William Andresson and others, being bought in two parts, of 105 acres in each purchase; and David is to have the south part. Daughters, Mary Belles and Elizabeth Hoppock, £150 each. Grandson, Peter Rockefellor, son of David, £25, when 21. Executors—son, Peter, and Paul Kuhl. Witnesses—John Aller, Samuel Furman, Elizabeth Johnson. Proved May 14, 1787.
1787, May 7. Inventory, £259.19.1, made by Samuel Williamson and Samuel Furman.
1803, Aug. 3. Account by Executors. Legacies paid to Mary Belles, Elizabeth Rockafellar, John Hoppock, William Rockafellar and Peter Rockafellar.
1812, Feb. 7. Account by Paul Kuhl, surviving Executor. Paid Godfrey Rockafellar, $161.61. Paid Mary Bellis, $161.61. Paid Jacob Rockafellar, in part, $80.80. Paid David Rockafellar, $161.61. Paid Henry Rockafellar, $161.61. Paid John Rockafellar, $161.61. Paid James Larew, $26.93. Paid Abraham Rockafellar, $26.93. Paid Jacob Rockafellar, Jr., $26.93. Paid Daniel Rockafellar, $26.93. Paid Philip Rockafellar, $26.93. Paid David Fox, $26.93. Paid Enoch Ayerse, $23.08. Paid Israel Ayers, $23.08. Paid John Cox, $23.08. Paid William Decker, $23.08. Paid John Hoppock, $23.08. Paid William Hoppock, $23.08. Paid Henry Avery, $143.66. Paid Henry Avery, $17.95. Paid Peter Hoppock, $23.08. Lib. 29, p. 260.

**1789, March 16. Rockhill, Edward,** of Chesterfield Township, Burlington Co., yeoman; will of. Wife to have £20 a year, paid by my son, Nathan. Son, Edward, the plantation where he lives. Son, Nathan, rest of plantation where I live, and he shall find his mother her living, and pay to my daughters, Tobitha Field, and Elizabeth Bullock and Mary Smith, £25 each, and to Amy Rogers, £100. Executors—sons, Edward and Nathan, and my son-in-law, Isaac Bullock.

Witnesses—Caleb Rockhill, Edward Robbins, Nathan Robbins. Proved Dec. 17, 1789.
1789, Dec. 17. Renunciation by Edward Rockhill.
1789, June 22. Inventory, £507.4.5, made by Joseph Bullock and Nathan Robbins. Lib. 31, p. 295.

1787, Nov. 14. **Rockhill, John,** of Burlington Co. Int. Adm'r—Thomas Rockhill, of Mansfield Township, said Co. Fellowbondsman—James Craft, of Burlington.
1788, May 9. Inventory, £65.0.5, made by Joseph Craft and Thomas English. Lib. 29, p. 78.

1788, April 9. **Rodenbaugh, John, Sr.,** of Hunterdon Co. Int. Adm'rs—John Rodenbogh and Elizabeth Rodenbaugh. Fellowbondsman—Elias Wyckoff; all of said Co.
1788, March 28. Inventory, £140.1.0, made by Elias Wyckoff and Daniel Dunham. Lib. 31, p. 145.

1788, Dec. 16. **Rose, John,** of Lebanon Township, Hunterdon Co. Int. Adm'r—Andrew Rose. Fellowbondsman—David Frazer; both of said Co.
1788, Nov. 18. Inventory, £277.6.5, made by David Frazer and Adam Runkle. Lib. 31, p. 145.

1786, May 1. **Rosenkrans, John,** of Walpack Township, Sussex Co., yeoman; will of. Wife, Margerate, my real estate, until my youngest son, Simeon, is 21; after which she is to have £30. First-born son, John, a negro. Eldest daughter, Ariantie, wife of Abraham Van Campen, £150. Second daughter, now Cathrine Woodard, £150. Youngest daughter, Maria Rosekrans, £150. Sons, John, Jacob, Alexander, Cherrick, Elijah, Livi, Joseph, Benjamin and Simeon, real estate. Wife to have £15 yearly. Executors—sons, John, Jacob, Alexander, Cherrick and Elijah. Witnesses—Joseph Chestnor, Cornelius Van Vleer, John Henry. Proved Nov. 27, 1786.
1786, Aug. 4. Inventory, £881.0.5, made by Peter Van Neste and Harmanis Cole. Lib. 28, p. 451.

1786, May 1. **Ross, George,** of Essex Co. Int. Adm'rs—John Craig and Isaac Ross; both of said Co. Lib. 28, p. 425.

1786, July 1. **Ross, George,** of Essex Co. Int. Adm'x—Elizabeth Ross. Fellowbondsman—John Craig; both of said Co.
Lib. 28, p. 428.

1787, April 30. **Rouse, John,** of Freehold, Monmouth Co.; will of. Wife, Mary, real and personal estate, during her life; then what remains to my daughters, Catherine Toner and Mary Rituer. Executors—George Smock and John Vanderver, Sr. Witnesses—John Baird, Andrew Baird, Peter Baird. Proved Nov. 11, 1789.
1789, Nov. 16. Inventory, £52.8.9, made by Hendrick Smock and William Vanskoick. Lib. 30, p. 164.

1787, Feb. 10. **Rowe, Daniel,** of Essex Co. Ward. Son of Stephen Rowe, of said Co., deceased. Said Ward, being out of wardship of Martha Rowe, Guardian in Soccage, and having real and personal estate, makes choice of Joseph Tomkins as his Guardian.

**1787, Feb. 10.** Guardian—Joseph Tomkins. Fellowbondsman—Isaac Freeman; both of said Co. Lib. 29, p. 419.

**1786, Sept. 11. Rowen, Cleften,** of Gloucester Co. Int. Adm'x—Susannah Rowen (widow of said deceased and yeoman). Fellowbondsman—James Lord; both of Greenwich Township, said Co. Witness—Thomas Hendry. Lib. 28, p. 122.

**1789, May 6. Rowzer, Jacob,** of Amwell, Hunterdon Co. Int. Adm'rs—Mary Rowzer, of said place, and Jonathan Woolverton, of Kingwood, said Co. Fellowbondsman—Uriah Bonham, of Kingwood.
1789, May 5. Inventory, £329.19.10, made by Uriah Bonham and William Hoogland.
1792, Feb. 22. Account by Adm'rs.
1796, May 5. Account by Peter Fox and Mary, his wife, late Mary Rowzer. The intestate left 4 infant children, all of whom are yet under 10 years of age. Lib. 32, p. 55.

**1790, Sept. 27. Runnels, John,** of Gloucester Co. Int. Adm'r—James Avise. Fellowbondsman—Jacob Shires; both of said Co.
1790, April 17. Inventory, £28.6.3, made by James Avise and Jacob Shires. Lib. 31, p. 480.

**1786, Aug. 25. Runyon, Rezia,** of Middlesex Co. Int. Adm'r—John Thomson. Fellowbondsman—William Burnet; both of said Co.
Lib. 28, p. 339.

**1787, Nov. 16. Russell, William,** of Fairfield, Cumberland Co., yeoman; will of. Wife, Abigail, use of real and personal estate, except hereafter stated. Son, Edward, 10 shillings. Daughters, Rebekah, Kezia and Mary, 10 shillings each. Daughter, Abigail Buck, my lands. Executor—son-in-law, Ephraim Buck. Witnesses—Isaac Harris, Ephraim Harris, Aaron Peterson. Proved March 9, 1789.
1788, March 14. Inventory, £162.2.11, made by Ephraim Harris and John Bower. Lib. 30, p. 143.

**1787, March 14. Ryan, James,** of Burlington Township, Burlington Co. Int. Adm'r—Andrew Rowan, of Middlesex Co. Fellowbondsman—John Lawrence, of Burlington.
1787, March 14. Inventory, £72.10.10, made by Abraham Scott and Joseph Scott. Lib. 29, p. 79.

**1787, July 10. Ryerson, Martin,** of Totowa, Bergen Co. Int. Adm'rs—Richard Stanton, Theunis Ryerson and Isaac Vanderbeek. Fellowbondsmen—Garret Hoppe and John Hoppe; all of said Co. Witness—Roelef Westervelt.
1787, July 11. Inventory, made by Corneles Stagg and Cornelius Westervelt. [The above Martin Ryerson is sometimes called Martin F. Ryerson]. Lib. 29, p. 536.

**1790, Sept. 2. Ryerson, Martin,** of Readingtown, Hunterdon Co. Int. Adm'r—Ebenezer Cowell, of Philadelphia. Fellowbondsman—John Armstrong, of Hardwick, Sussex Co. Lib. 30, p. 316.

**1786, Jan. 27. Ryon, Joseph,** of Morris Co. Int. Adm'r—Mulford Martin. Fellowbondsman—Peter Layton; both of Morristown said Co.

CALENDAR OF WILLS—1786-1790

1786, Jan. 25. Renunciation by Sophia Ryon, widow of Joseph, in favor of Mulford Martin. Witnesses—Hannah Martin and Abegal Steward. Lib. 28, p. 486.

**(No date.) Sandford, Robert,** of Pequanack, Morris Co.; will of. Children, Robert, Elizabeth, Janne, Thomas and Mary, £5. Children, Sarah, Rachel, Catherine, Mary Stiles, Nancy and William, rest of estate. Executors—wife, Catherine, and friend, Aaron Kitchel. Witnesses—Mathew Baldwin, Daniel Farrand, Aaron Kitchel. Proved Aug. 22, 1786.

1786, June 8. Inventory, £86.16.3, made by Bethuel Farrand and Amos Young. Lib. 28, p. 480.

**1790, Sept. 25. Sansbury, Richard,** of Kingston, Somerset Co. Int. Adm'r—Ralph Sansbury. Fellowbondsman—Joshua Higgins, Sr.; both of said Co.

1790, Sept. 7. Renunciation by Walter Kearney and his wife, Eleanor, in favor of their son, Ralph Sansbury. Witnesses—Christopher Hoagland and Enoch Elbersen.

1790, Sept. 11. Inventory, £23.17.4, made by Henry Silvers and John Rule. Lib. 31, p. 530.

**1787, Nov. 15. Satterthwaite, Samuel,** of Chesterfield Township, Burlington Co., yeoman; will of. Children, Reuben, Joseph, Benjamin and Elizabeth Satterthwaite, all personal estate. Son, Reuben, two adjoining tracts in Mansfield Township; the first held by deed from John Hamel, and dated Dec. 29, 1770; and the other by deed from William Satterthwaite, dated Oct. 30, 1773. Son, Benjamin, a tract in Chesterfield, laying east of the road that leads from Recklesstown to Upper Springfield, of 100 acres, given to me by my father, Samuel, by deed Jan. 28, 1761, which he had by deed from Samuel Woodward, Sheriff of Burlington Co., Feb. 22, 1752. Daughter, Elizabeth Satterthwaite, £300, to be paid by my son, Joseph. Son, Joseph, the rest of real estate. Executors—sons, Reuben, Joseph and Benjamin. Witnesses—William Satterthwaite, Jane Satterthwaite, Benjamin Linton. Proved Nov. 17, 1789.

1789, Oct. 19. Inventory, £410.5.11, made by Nathan Robbins and Lawrence Minor. Lib. 31, p. 306.

**1789, March 16. Sawins, Henry,** of Gloucester Co. Int. Adm'rs— Jennet Sawins and Joseph Sawins. Fellowbondsman—Joshua Smith; all of said Co.

1789, March 12. Inventory, £131.0.7, made by Joshua Smith and Amos Ireland. Lib. 30, p. 138.

**1787, Oct. 24. Sayre, Sarah, Noah and Betsey.** Wards. Children of Ezra Sayre, deceased. Said Wards, having an estate of £100, make choice of Joseph Freeman, Jr. as their Guardian.

1787, Oct. 24. Guardian—Joseph Freeman, Jr. Fellowbondsman— Joseph Freeman, Sr. Lib. 31, p. 245.

**1790, Aug. 23. Scantling, Charles,** of Gloucester Co. Int. Adm'r— Anthony Warrick. Fellowbondsman—Joseph Crawford; both of said Co.

1790, Aug. 3. Inventory, £20.13.3, made by Joseph Crawford and David Henry. Lib. 31, p. 481.

**1789, Oct. 24. Scattergood, Caleb,** of Mansfield Township, Burlington Co.; will of. Son, Joshua, that part of my farm where I live, on the north side of the brook. Son, Caleb, the part of the farm next to Joshua's. Son, Benjamin, the rest of the farm. All sons to have their lands when 21. Said sons are to have my cedar swamp. Daughters, Sarah Folwell, Mary Scattergood and Martha Scattergood, my moveable estate. Wife, Mary, to be paid £20 by son, Caleb. Wife, Mary, £30. Executors—sons, Caleb and Joshua. Witnesses—Jonathan Barton, Jacob Wheeler, John Pope. Proved Nov. 5, 1790.
1790, Oct. 14. Inventory, £253.7.4, made by William Wright and Jonathan Barton. Lib. 32, p. 79.

**1786, May 15. Schenck, Albert,** of Penns Neck, Windsor Township, Middlesex Co.; will of. Wife, Agnis, all the legacy that her father, Nicholas Van Brunt, left her. Eldest sons, Garret and Nicholas, several lots as numbered on a map made by Joseph Skelton, being part of my homestead. Son, Garret, house and lot where Jacob Hawk lives. To my two second sons, Hendrick and John, the land I bought of William Cox, on Assanpink Creek, where they live. To my two third sons, Abraham and Isaac, my homestead, of 25 acres, joining the Stony Brook. Daughter, Mariah, wife of John Cox, price of lot No. 6. Wife to have use of homestead, and she is to support my 3 younger children and my 3 grandchildren that live with me. Youngest daughter, Rachel, £80. Grandson, Ace Cox, £50. Daughters, Ann, widow of John Voorheis, £200; Elnoer, widow of Peter Shuman, £200; Mariah, wife of John Cox, £200; Catharine, widow of Martine Schenck, £200; and Rachel, £200. Executors—son, John, and son-in-law, John Cox. Witnesses—Robert Taylor, Jacob Hawk, Joseph Olden. Proved June 10, 1786.
1786, June 2. Inventory, £1,716.8.11, made by Ezekiel Smith and Garret Schenck. Lib. 28, p. 325.

**1787, Feb. 24. Schenck, Jacob,** of Penns Neck, Windsor Township, Middlesex Co. Int. Adm'rs—Mary Schenck and Joseph Stout. Fellowbondsman—John Schenck, Jr.; all of said Co.
1787, Feb. 27. Inventory, £740.0.2, made by Ezekiel Smith and Garret Schenck. Lib. 29, p. 363.

**1787, May 8. Schermerhorn, John,** of Pequannock, Morris Co. Int. Adm'r—Aaron Schermerhorn. Fellowbondsman—John Schermerhorn; both of said place.
1787, April 26. Renunciation by Eve Schermerhorn, John Schermerhorn, Thunes Speare, John Adams, Fightty Speare, Angle Adams and Hannah Schermerhorn, in favor of Aaron Schermerhorn. Witness— John Adams.
1787, April 30. Inventory, £167, made by John Mandeville and Samuel Berry. Lib. 29, p. 474.

**1788, Sept. 29. Schuyler, Aaron,** of Burlington, Burlington Co. Int. Adm'rs—William Norcross and Daniel Hancock. Fellowbondsman— Jacob Perkins; all of said Co.
1788, Sept. 28. Renunciation by Hester Schuyler, widow of said Aaron, in favor of William Norcross and Daniel Hancock. Witness— Benjamin Dey.

CALENDAR OF WILLS—1786-1790 197

**1788, Sept. 29.** Inventory, made by Abraham Stockton and John Folwell. Lib. 30, p. 59.

**1788, March 22. Schuyler, Charles and Abraham,** of Burlington, Burlington Co. Wards. Sons of Arent Schuyler, of said place, deceased. Said Wards, having real and personal estate, make choice of Joseph Crozer as their Guardian.
**1788, March 22.** Guardian—Joseph Crozer. Fellowbondsman—John Folwell; both of said Co. Lib. 30, p. 61.

**1786, May 4. Scott, Archibald,** of Woolwich Township, Gloucester Co., Esq. Int. Adm'r—Robert Brown. Fellowbondsman—John Smith; both of said place.
**1786, April 24.** Inventory, £95.13.11, made by John Vandyke and John Smith. Lib. 28, p. 121.

**1786, Oct. 7. Scott, Jane,** of Shrewsbury, Monmouth Co. Int. Adm'x—Hannah Pintard. Fellowbondsmen—William Pintard and John Scott; all of said Co. Witness—Samuel Forman.
**1786, Oct. 7.** Renunciation by John Scott, brother of Jane Scott, deceased.
**1786, Oct. 9.** Inventory, £89.13.6, made by Thomas Borden and Mauritz Dehaert. Lib. 28, p. 292.

**1786, Dec. 22. Scott, John,** of Greenwich Township, Gloucester Co. Int. Adm'r—Jeffery Clark. Fellowbondsman—George Vanneman; both of said place, yeoman. Witness—John Griffyth.
**1786, Dec. 19.** Inventory, made by William Lippincott and David Brown. Lib. 28, p. 123.

**1786, April 17. Scott, Richard,** of Princeton, Somerset Co.; will of. Wife, Lydia, my house and goods, while my widow, and then to my children, Susannah, Job and Mehettable, when of age. Executors—wife, Lydia, and brother, Samuel Scott. Witnesses—Ruth Scott, Archebel Maccolm, Joseph Skelton. Proved Nov. 8, 1786.
Lib. 29, p. 191.

**1789, Dec. 16. Scudder, Abijah,** of Essex Co.; will of. Wife, Lucy, some household goods and livestock. Brothers, Benjamin, Joseph, John and Noah, rest of personal and real estate. Sister, Jane Badgly, £6. Sister, Liddy Badgly, £6. Sister, Anne French, £6. Sister, Rachel, £6. Niece, Jane Scudder Hole, daughter of my sister, Mary, £6. Executors—Jesse Clarke and my brother, Joseph Scudder. Witnesses—Cornelius Williams, Christopher Denman, Andrew Denman. Proved Dec. 26, 1789. Lib. 30, p. 213.

**1790, June 22. Scudder, Joseph,** of Essex Co. Int. Adm'r—Jesse Clarke. Fellowbondsman—Joseph Scudder; both of said Co.
Lib. 30, p. 360.

**1786, March 3. Scull, David,** of Egg Harbor Township, Gloucester Co. Int. Adm'r—Joseph Scull, of Great Egg Harbor, yeoman. Fellowbondsman—John Davis, Gent.; both of said Co.
**1786, Feb. 22.** Inventory, £144.13.1, made by Jeremiah Smith and David Sayrs. Lib. 28, p. 121.

**1786, March 27. Scull, John,** of Cape May Co. Int. Adm'x—Deborah Scull, widow. Fellowbondsman—Jesse Scull; both of said Co. Witnesses—Shamgar Hewit and Eli Eldredge. Lib. 38, p. 79.

**1787, Sept. 24. Searing, John,** of Elizabeth Borough, Essex Co., yeoman; will of. Wife, Ann, the use of ⅓ of my homestead and ⅓ of my moveable estate. Son, John, 4 acres of salt meadow, which I bought of Elias Woodruff. Sons, Simon and Jacob, my homestead farm, and land at Canoe Brook, and the rest of the salt meadow. Granddaughter, Sarah Marsh, £12, and, if she do not live, then it is to descend to my 2 daughters hereafter named, and my granddaughter, Anna, daughter of my daughter, Mary Clason, deceased. Granddaughters, Janet and Betsey Marsh, 20 shillings each. Daughters, Susannah Pool and Nancy Townly, and my granddaughter, Anna, the daughter of Mary Clason, deceased, rest of moveable estate. Executors—friends, James Carpenter and Jonas Wade. Witnesses—Daniel Wade, Joshua Winans, Daniel Sayre. Proved Feb. 25, 1788.

Lib. 31, p. 240.

**1786, March 27. Sebring, Cornelius,** of Hillsborough Township, Somerset Co.; will of. Wife, Onche (Holchey), use of real and personal estate, and, after her death, to my children, Rulif Sebring, Honche, wife of Denice Bice, Catharine, wife of Harmonus Vanderipe, and Christena, wife of Peter Cornine; but Rulif is to have the lands and Dutch Bible. Executors—son, Rulif, cousin, Rulif Peterson, and son-in-law, Harmonus Vanderipe. Witnesses—Ryneer Staats, John Nevus, John Davison. Proved Aug. 17, 1786.

1786, Aug. 2. Inventory, £597.3.6, made by Ryneer Staats and John Nevus. Lib. 29, p. 192.

**1788, Jan. 21. Sedam, Peter,** of Six Mile Run, Middlesex Co., shoemaker; will of. Real and personal estate to be sold. Son, Rick, £5. Son, Lowrance, £20. Son, Peter, £20. Son, Abraham, £20. Wife, Sarah, and children, Rick, Ginne, Anne, Lowrance, Peter and Abraham, rest of estate, share and share alike. Executors—brother-in-law, Peter Pumyea, my son-in-law, William Williamson, and my brother, Rick. Witnesses—Peter Stoothoff, Simon Addis, Derick Merrell. Proved Aug. 22, 1788.

1788, June 21. Inventory, made by Peter Stoothoff and Simon Addis.

Lib. 31, p. 221.

**1786, Nov. 25. Seed, Isaac,** of Chester Township, Burlington Co. Int. Adm'x—Rachel Seed. Fellowbondsman—Hezekiah Garwood; both of said Co.

1786, Oct. 31. Inventory, £468.9.7, made by Abraham Hewlings and Nathaniel Middleton. Lib. 28, p. 75.

**1789, Nov. 24. Seeley, Henry,** of Deerfield Township, Cumberland Co. Int. Adm'x—Rachel Seeley. Fellowbondsman—Mark Ryley; both of said Co.

1789, Oct. 7. Inventory, £136.6.9, made by David Moore and Adam Terryl. Lib. 30, p. 163.

**1786, Feb. 28. Senteny, John,** of Hillsborough, Somerset Co. Int. Adm'rs—Samuel Stout and Jane Senteny; said Samuel being of Hunterdon Co. Fellowbondsman—Joseph Hageman, of Somerset Co. Witness—William Maxwell.

CALENDAR OF WILLS—1786-1790       199

1786, Feb. 27. Inventory, £213.18.8, made by Joseph Hageman and Johanes Ditmars.  Lib. 29, p. 196.

**1787, Oct. 20. Seypart, Michael,** of Greenwich, Sussex Co., yeoman; will of. Son, Jacob, plantation I live on, and he is to pay the legacies. Daughters, Catharine Seypart and Sarah Seypart, each a good cow, and they are to live in the house while they are unmarried. Daughter, Margaret Steeley, £40. Daughter, Anne Elizabeth Hachenbery, £40. Daughter, Elizabeth Dietrick, £40. Daughter, Catharine Seypart, £100. Daughter, Christean Minier, £40. Daughter, Catharine Horn, £40. Daughter, Anne Winters, £50. Daughter, Sarah Seypart, £60. Executors—son, Jacob Scyphers, and friend, Jacob Welch. Witnesses—Paul Shipman, Mathias Shipman, Thomas Parry. Proved Jan. 17, 1789.
1789, Jan. 13. Renunciation by Jacob Welch. Witnesses—Tunis Young and Jesse Barber.  Lib. 30, p. 194.

**1790, Oct. 25. Shackleton, Richard,** of Knowlton, Sussex Co. Int. Adm'x—Mary Shackleton, widow of Richard. Fellowbondsman—Benjamin Shackleton; both of said place.
1790, Oct. 22. Inventory, £29.3.6, made by Charles Crisman and Abraham Besherer.  Lib. 30, p. 438.

**1788, Feb. 18. Sharp, Amos,** of Evesham, Burlington Co., yeoman; will of. Wife, Deborah, £50, to be paid by my son, Thomas; also household goods. Son, Daniel, to have an equal share of personal estate with my 3 sons, Aaron, Enoch and George. Son, Levy, the land I bought of Thomas Grunnel, and 10 acres of meadow in the lower end of my plantation. Son, Thomas, my plantation of 124 acres, except the 10 acres. Son, Barzillai, the land where he lives. My sons to have the Leader Swamp. Sons, Levy, Thomas and Barzillai, to provide food and clothing for my son, Daniel, during his life. Sons, Aaron, Enoch and George, £50 each. Executors—wife, Deborah, and my son, Thomas. Witnesses—Samuel Sharp, Joseph Sharp, Joshua Sharp. Proved May 24, 1788.
1788, May 22. Inventory, £438.18.6, made by Joseph Willcox and Amos Strattan.  Lib. 30, p. 13.

**1788, July 5. Sharp, John,** of Evesham, Burlington Co.; will of. Son, Isaac, plantation where he lives, bounded by Samuel Ballenger and Samuel Sharp. Son, Samuel, land beginning at an oak, corner to his uncle, Samuel Sharp, and brother, Isaac, and runs by line of Isaiah Haines. Son, John, the plantation where he lives. Son, Amos, land along Jacob Lamb and son John's line. Son, Samuel, a meadow along the line of Barzillai Sharp. Son, Isaac, land along Barzillai Sharp's line. Son, Mahlon, my homestead. Wife, Dinah, use of some furniture. Daughter, Dinah, use of some furniture. Daughter, Anna Sharp, bed and bedding. Daughter, Deborah Sharp, bed and bedding. Daughter, Hannah Sharp, bed and bedding. Daughter, Mary Sharp, bed and bedding. Daughter, Presillah Sharp, bed and bedding. Wife to have the profits of Mahlon's plantation, for support of my unmarried children. Executors—wife, Dinah, and son, Isaac. Son, Amos, shall have my share of the deed rights that was given between me and my brother, Amos. Witnesses—Samuel Sharp, Thomas Sharp, Joseph Sharp. Proved Aug. 15, 1788.
1788, July 18. Inventory, £710.19.10, made by Joseph Sharp and Amos Strattan.  Lib. 30, p. 36.

**1790, July 22. Sharp, Thomas,** of Gloucester Co. Int. Adm'r—James Stratton. Fellowbondsman—George W. Campbell; both of said Co. Lib. 31, p. 480.

**1790, March 25. Shaver, Adam,** of Deerfield, Cumberland Co.; will of. Wife, Margret, real and personal estate, during her life, and, after her death, I give it to the heirs of my brother, George Shaver, and to my wife's brother's, Adam Filsmire's heirs. Executors—Samuel Odgen and Martin Ott, who are to sell the land in Salem Co. that I bought of William Monigal. Witnesses—Henry Buck, Dayton Buck, Ephraim Buck. Proved Oct. 12, 1790.
1790, May 14. Inventory, £470.12.4, made by Adam Saull and Adam Hinman. Lib. 30, p. 279.

**1787, July 17. Shaw, Francis,** of Middlesex Co. Int. Adm'r—Adam Shaw. Fellowbondsman—James Patton; both of said Co.
1784, Dec. 5. Inventory of goods found at Spotswood at time of his death. Lib. 29, p. 363.

**1789, May 2. Shaw, Isaiah,** of New Brunswick, Middlesex Co.; will of. Wife, Ruth, use of the homestead, and she is to bring up the children. Isaiah to be bound to my son-in-law, William Nutton. When wife dies, land to be sold and money given to children. Executors—wife, Ruth, and James Patton. Witnesses—William Egbert, Jr., Ruth Disbrow, Peter Dewiot. Proved April 6, 1790.
1790, March 27. Inventory, £38.5.0, made by George McAroy and Richard Standley. Lib. 30, p. 528.

**1790, July 22. Shaw, Joshua,** of Cape May Co. Int. Adm'rs—Rachel Shaw and Elijah Shaw. Fellowbondsman—David Hildreth; all of said Co. Witnesses—Jeremiah Hand and Sarah Hand, Jr.
1790, Oct. 22. Inventory, £415.14.3, made by Philip Cresse and David Hildreth. Lib. 32, p. 106.

**1787, April 19. Shaw, Obadiah,** of Cape May Co. Int. Adm'x—Deborah Shaw. Fellowbondsman—Gideon Kent; both of Lower Precinct, said Co. Witnesses—Aaron Hand and Sarah Hand, Jr.
1787, April 18. Inventory, £175.2.9, made by Abraham Woolson and Gideon Kent. Lib. 29, p. 241.

**1788, May 5. Shaw, Thomas,** of Middletown Township, Monmouth Co.; will of. Sister, Elizabeth Stillwell, use of £600. To James Stillwell, son of my said sister, £240, after my sister's death. To Samuel Stillwell, son of said sister, £240, after sister's death. To Rebekah Stillwell, daughter of said sister, £120. To Thomas Shaw, son of my brother, Hennery Shaw, £200, when 21. Sister, Sarah Coreyel, interest of £150, and, after her death, the said £150 to her son, Tunis Coreyel. Brother, John Shaw, rest of my estate. Executors—brothers, John and Henry, and Crineyoance Vanmatre. Witnesses—Elbert Swart, William Crawford, John Schanck. Proved Oct. 22, 1789.
1790, Feb. 15. Inventory, £2,467.16.6, made by Hendrick Hendrickson and Richard Crawford. Lib. 30, p. 173.

**1786, Feb. 6. Shaw, William,** of Greenwich Township, Gloucester Co. Int. Adm'x—Cathrine Townsend. Fellowbondsman—William Lippincott; both of said place.
1785, Oct. 17. Inventory, £46.10.0, made by John Rambo and Martin Cox. Lib. 28, p. 120.

**1786, Oct. 15. Shedaker, Jacob,** of Burlington Co.; will of. Son, Jacob, two lots in Burlington, which I purchased of Joseph Elles and Thomas Smith, with the house. Daughter, Rachel Shedaker, a lot joining the last named, westward, which I bought of Daniel Elles, with the house. Step-daughter, Elizabeth Esdall, ½ of her mother's apparel. Sister, Elizabeth Gallagher, the rents on the said houses till my 2 children are of age. Executrix—sister, Elizabeth Gallagher. Witnesses—Alexander McMullin, Matthew Willson, Stacey Cook. Proved Dec. 19, 1786.

1786, Dec. 19. Inventory, £9.14.0, made by Abraham Scott and Joseph Scott. Lib. 28, p. 12.

**1787, Sept. 28. Sheperd, Catherine,** of New Barbadoes, Bergen Co. Int. Adm'r—John Sheperd. Fellowbondsman—Peter Cadmus; both of said place. Witness—Catherine Miller. Lib. 29, p. 536.

**1787, Jan. 29. Sheppard, Ananias,** of Cumberland Co. Int. Adm'x—Anne Sheppard. Fellowbondsman—Daniel Maskell; both of said Co. 1787, Jan. 2. Inventory, £170.12.0, made by Abraham Vanwinkle and Abner Woodruff. Lib. 29, p. 183.

**1786, March 17. Sheppard, Daniel,** of Cumberland Co. Int. Adm'rs—Sarah Sheppard and David Gilman (the younger). Fellowbondsman—Thomas Maskell; all of said Co. Witness—David Mulford. 1786, March 9. Inventory, £264.13.8, made by James Sheppard and David Mulford. Lib. 28, p. 182.

**1788, Nov. 30. Sheppard, James,** of Fairfield, Cumberland Co., yeoman; will of. Wife, Prudence, to have the use of my estate, and, if I have no child, then, at her marriage, my real and personal estate are to go to my brother, John Sheppard, and sisters, Mary Westcoat and Charlotte Sheppard. Executors—wife, Prudence, and my brother, Jehiel Westcoat. Witnesses—Levi Bond, Smith Bowen, Thomas Sheppard. Proved Jan. 6, 1789.

1788, Dec. 30. Inventory, £340.16.5, made by Thomas Daniel and Obadiah Caruthers. Lib. 30, p. 161.

**1786, Sept. 29. Sheppard, John,** of Cumberland Co. Ward. Son of Elias Sheppard, of said Co., deceased. Said Ward, having real and personal estate, makes choice of James Sheppard as his Guardian.

1786, Sept. 29. Guardian—James Shappard. Fellowbondsmen—David Sheppard and Dan Bowen; all of said Co. Witnesses—Benjamin Dare and Samuel M. Shute. Lib. 28, p. 183.

**1786, Jan. 16. Sheppard, Jonadab,** of Cumberland Co. Ward. Son of David Sheppard, of said Co., deceased. Said Ward makes choice of Hosea Sheppard, yeoman, as his Guardian.

1786, Jan. 16. Guardian—Hosea Sheppard. Fellowbondsman—Lansilet Sockwill; both of said Co. Lib. 28, p. 182.

**1786, Dec. 1. Sheppard, Thomas,** of Cumberland Co. Ward. Son of Daniel Sheppard, of said Co., deceased. Rachel Robbins, grandmother and next of kin, asks for a Guardian to be appointed for said minor.

1786, Dec. 1. Guardian—Daniel Maskell. Fellowbondsman—Job Sheppard; both of said Co. Witness—Samuel Wood. Lib. 28, p. 184.

**1788, April 25. Sheppardson, Thomas,** of Middletown, Monmouth Co., son of Ebenezer. Int. Adm'r—John Griggs, Jr. Fellowbondsman—Matthias Halstead; both of Middlesex Co. (?) Witness—Rachel Henderson.
Lib. 30, p. 102.

**1790, Aug. 18. Shinn, Barzillai,** of Burlington Co. Int. Adm'x—Hannah Shinn. Fellowbondsman—Amos Sharp; both of said Co.
1790, Aug. 6. Inventory (not added) made by Ruleff Voorhes and Amos Sharp.
Lib. 32, p. 95.

**1789, Oct. 31. Shinn, Isaiah, and Susannah,** of Burlington Co. Wards. Children of Vincent Shinn, of said Co., deceased. Said Wards, having real and personal estate, make choice of William Budd as their Guardian.
1789, Oct. 31. Guardian—William Budd. Fellowbondsman—Levi Budd; both of New Hanover Township, said Co. Witness—Thomas Adams.
Lib. 31, p. 322.

**1787, Oct. 18. Shinn, Sarah,** of Pilesgrove, Salem Co. Int. Adm'r—Isaiah Shinn. Fellowbondsmen—Benjamin Cripps and Edward Burroughs; all of said Co.
File No. 1954 Q.

**1789, Nov. Shinn, William, Israel and Vincent,** of Burlington Co. Wards. Children of Vincent Shinn, of said Co., deceased. Elizabeth Shinn, widow of Vincent Shinn, desires that William Budd and George Budd may be appointed Guardians of said minors, till they are 14.
1791, April 18. Guardians—William Budd and George Budd. Fellowbondsman—James Sterling; all of said Co. Witness—William Budd.
Lib. 32, p. 187.

**1788, April 19. Shirts, Johannis,** of Lebanon, Hunterdon Co., yeoman; will of. Wife to have the plantation I live on, and the wood lot which I bought of Benjamin Low, while my widow. Son, Michal, to find the provisions. Son, John, plantation where he lives, in Readingtown, which my father left to me in his will. Son, Michal, plantation where I live, and said wood lot. My daughters, Rachel and Elizabeth, the furniture, and £200. Executors—sons, John and Michal. Witnesses—Ezekiel Cole, Abraham Shirts, Michael Shirts, Jr. Proved Jan. 20, 1789.
1788, June 12. Inventory, £188.8.1, made by George Gearhart and Ezekiel Cole.
Lib. 32, p. 30.

**1788, April 18. Shotwell, Daniel,** of Woodbridge, Middlesex Co.; will of. Wife, Margit, a horse. Youngest daughter, Sarah, a bed. Rest of personal and real estate to be sold. Son, Titus, £130. Son, Daniel, £130. Daughter, Hannah Moores, £40. Daughter, Mary Thorn, £40. Daughter, Elizabeth Marsh, £40. Daughter, Sarah Shotwell, £70. Executors—son, Titus, and son-in-law, Daniel Moores. Witnesses—Nathaniel Heard, William Heard, Joseph Shotwell, Jr., Joseph Shotwell. Proved May 13, 1788.
Lib. 31, p. 220.

**1788, Dec. 27. Shotwell, David,** of Sussex Co. Int. Adm'rs—Elizabeth Shotwell, Hartshorn Fitz Randolph and Richard Fitz Randolph.
1789, March 16. Inventory, £318.18.2, of the estate of David Shotwell, of Roxbury, Morris Co., made by Isaac Hance and James Brotherton.

CALENDAR OF WILLS—1786-1790 203

1790, June 19. Inventory, £124.19.1, of the estate which was in the hands of Elizabeth Shotwell, who removed from Morris to Essex Co., where the deceased formerly lived, made by Isaac Hance and Benjamin Shotwell. Lib. 31, p. 201.

**1790, April 8. Shotwell, Sarah,** of Elizabeth Borough, Essex Co.; will of. What I have I give to my brother, Caleb Shotwell and David Shotwell, deceased, and Elizabeth Bills, my sister, wife of Thomas Bills, deceased, among their children. Executors—Uncle, Marmaduke Hunt, and my cousin, Jeremiah Shotwell, son of Abraham. Witnesses—Jacob Shotwell, Rhoda Morris, James Shotwell. Proved June 7, 1790.
1790, July 1. Inventory, £7.10.0, made by Samuel Marsh.
1790, July 17. Amount of Vendue, £4.16.10, held at the house of Elizabeth Shotwell, late widow of David Shotwell. Goods were sold to Elizabeth Shotwell, Sarah Townsend, Elizabeth Bills.
Lib. 30, p. 338.

**1790, June 16. Shreeve, Joshua,** of Waterford, Gloucester Co., miller; will of. My real estate at Aires Town, in Burlington Co. to be sold. Wife, Hope, the goods she brought with her, and £100. Children, Elizabeth, Joseph, Enoch, Caleb and Stacy, rest of estate. Executors—wife, Hope, and friend, Amos Strattan, of Evesham. Witnesses—John Parkam, Thomas Brasington, Thomas Redman. Proved July 1, 1790.
1790, June 30. Inventory, £275.0.1, made by John Gill and John Middleton. Lib. 31, p. 465.

**1786, Sept. 10. Shreve, Caleb,** of Mansfield, Burlington Co., farmer; will of. Son, Joseph, the land I bought of my brother, Thomas, and to son, Isaac, the land bounded by Joseph Talman, Joseph Shreve, William White, Caleb Newbold, deceased, John Branin and Samuel Quicksall, deceased. Son, Job, 10 shillings. Son, Caleb, rest of land. Granddaughters, Charrity Antram, Ann Antram and Abigail Antram, £10 each, when 18. Daughter, Rebekah Field, £30. Daughters, Penelope Shreve, Mercy Shreve and Sarah Shreve, £50 each. My wife to have the rest of the money, if any there be. Executors—sons, Joseph and Isaac. Witnesses—Joseph Hutchin, Amey Quicksall, Rebekah Quicksall. Proved Nov. 2, 1786.
1786, Oct. 19. Inventory, £480.7.1, made by Joseph Talman and Lawrence Minor. Lib. 28, p. 8.

**1787, March 27. Shriner, John,** of Lebanon, Hunterdon Co. Int. Adm'rs—Lena Shriner and John Shriner. Fellowbondsman—Jacob Gearhart; all of said Co. Witness—David Frazer.
1787, March 26. Inventory, £410.10.7, made by Philip Grandin, Adam Runkle and David Frazer. Lib. 29, p. 295.

**1786, Jan. 5. Shull, Jacob,** of New Jersey. Ward. Son of Bostian Shull, of said State, deceased. Said Ward, having real and personal estate, makes choice of Joseph Penton as his Guardian.
1786, Jan. 5. Guardian—Joseph Penton. Fellowbondsmen—Reuben Jarman and Eaton Harwood; all of said State. Witness—Thomas Parvin. Lib. 28, p. 182.

**1790, April 8. Shull, Reuben,** of Deerfield, Cumberland Co.; will of. Wife, Naomi, my moveable estate, in order to bring up the children. Daughter, Nancy, 15 acres of my plantation in Salem Co., bounded by land of William Davis. Son, Jacob Parvin Shull, rest of said plantation. Executors—wife, Naomi, and David Moore. Witnesses—David Moore, Hosea Snethen, Jacob Shull. Proved Sept. 29, 1790.

1790, April 15. Inventory, £166.14.11, made by Josiah Parvin and Hosea Snethen. Lib. 30, p. 269.

**1789, Oct. 31. Shute, William,** of Chester Township, Burlington Co. Int. Adm'r—Samuel Matlack. Fellowbondsman—Samuel Roberts, Jr.; both of said place.

1789, Oct. 27. Renunciation by Rachel Shute, widow of said William, in favor of Samuel Matlack.

1789, Oct. 19. Inventory, £130.10.4, made by Samuel Shute and Samuel Roberts, Jr. Lib. 31, p. 320.

**1786, Feb. 21. Sillomon, Alexander,** of Cumberland Co. Int. Adm'r—Joseph Ogden. Fellowbondsman—John Trenchard; both of said Co. Witness—Jonathan Elmer, Surrogate. Lib. 28, p. 180.

**1789, Sept. 30. Silver, Samuel,** of Pilesgrove Township, Salem Co., yeoman; will of. Wife, Rebekah, Bible, cow and warming pan, and £10 yearly for 5 years. Children, William, Samuel, Archabald, Ruth and Rebekah Silvers, rest of estate, when they come of age. Executors—friends, Seth Silvers and Isaac Eldridge. Witnesses—Abel Silver, William Wallace, Thomas Osborn. Proved Dec. 18, 1789.

1789, Nov. 4. Inventory, £272.14.3, made by John Barnes and William Wallace. Lib. 31, p. 352.

**1787, Jan. 24. Silver, William,** of Pilesgrove Township, Salem Co., yeoman; will of. Wife, Mary, lot in Pilesgrove that I bought of Thomas Thorn, while my widow, and £70. Daughter, Rhoda Dunn, ½ of plantation where I live, and ½ of said lot. Daughter, Mary Shores, the other ½ of said tracts. Brother Samuel's son, William, best coat. Executors—brother, Samuel Silver, and brother, Davis Bassett. Witnesses—Job Elkinton, Joseph Pimm, Jr., Daniel Bassett, Jr. Proved March 10, 1787.

1787, Feb. 15. Inventory, £453.17.9, made by John Barnes and Isaac Eldridge. Lib. 29, p. 139.

**1786, March 25. Simkins, John,** of Cumberland Co.; will of. Son, John, my title in a plantation in Fairfield Township. Son, Mark, £20. The place where I live to be sold, a part of which is in Cumberland Co., and a part in Salem Co. Sons, Uriah and Silvanus, £20 each, when 21. Wife, Phebe, a bed and cow. Daughter, Hope, £2, and to be brought up by her mother. Daughter, Heaster, £5. Two acres of marsh on the west side of Stow Creek, joining David Stretch, to be sold. Executors—sons, John and Mark. Witnesses—John Buck, Joseph Kelsay, Jacob Mulford. Proved July 10, 1786.

1786, June 16. Inventory, £119.13.7, made by William Mulford and Jacob Elwell. Lib. 28, p. 157.

**1786, March 3. Simonson, Aaron,** of Hanover, Morris Co. Int. Adm'r—Cornelius Genung. Fellowbondsman—Daniel Burnet; both of said place. Witnesses—Caleb Russell and Ebenezer Pierson.
Lib. 28, p. 486.

**1786, May 5. Simpson, John,** of Essex Co.; will of. Wife, Sarah, a cow and riding beast. Eldest son, John, and son, Isaac, my homestead, and John is to have 10 acres more than my son, Isaac. Son, Abraham, the house and land in Morris Co., on Long Hill, where he lives; also a lot in the Great Swamp of 29 acres, formerly the property of Isaac Jones, deceased; and he is to pay to my daughter, Margret Orsburn, wife of Howel Orsburn, £30. To my 4 younger sons, Jacob, Elexander, Ephraim and William, £25 each, when they are 21. Daughter, Margret, £30. Daughters, Magdelien Waldron, wife of Samuel Waldron, and Anna Simpson, £25 each. Granddaughter, Mary Badgley, £5, when 18 or at her marriage. Executor—son, John. Witnesses—William Drake, Timothy Crane, Jeremiah Crane. Proved Nov. 11, 1786. Lib. 28, p. 393.

**1787, Jan. 27. Sinclare, George,** of Windsor Township, Middlesex Co.; will of. Wife to have all to bring up my youngest daughter, Rhoda, and, if said child die, then to my 3 daughters, Annah, Elizabeth and Ann. If they marry, they are to be made equal to our daughter, Mary Cubberly. Son, John, 10 shillings. Daughter, Mary Coberley, 10 shillings. Executors—sons, John Sinclare and William Cobberley. Witnesses—David Rulon, John Pearson, Vanroom Robins. Proved Feb. 28, 1787.
1787, Feb. 17. Inventory, £237.6.0, made by Vanroom Robins and David Rulon. Lib. 29, p. 354.

**1787, March 27. Sipple, Nathaniel,** of Egg Harbor Township, Gloucester Co. Int. Adm'r—Martinus Sipple, of Kent Co., Delaware. Fellowbondsman—Edmond Ireland, of Galloway Township, Gloucester Co., yeoman. Witness—Joseph Hugg, Jr.
1787, March 24. Inventory, £83.17.0, made by Edmond Ireland and John Steelman. Lib. 29, p. 119.

**1787, Dec. 3. Skinner, Amos,** of Essex Co. Int. Adm'x—Margaret Skinner. Fellowbondsman—Marmaduke Hunt; both of said Co.
Lib. 29, p. 418.

**1787, Aug. 14. Skinner, Britton,** of Middlesex Co. Int. Adm'r—Cornelius Baker. Fellowbondsman—Henry Marsh; both of said Co.
1787, Aug. 14. Renunciation by Anne Skinner, in favor of Cornelius Baker. Witness—Henry Marsh.
1787, Aug. 2. Inventory, £69.16.0, made by William Moores and Icebod Thorp. Lib. 29, p. 363.

**1787, Feb. 12. Skinner, William,** of Perth Amboy, Middlesex Co., minister. Int. Adm'r—Philip A. Schuyler. Fellowbondsman—Arent J. Schuyler; both of Bergen Co.
1787, Feb. 8. Renunciation by J. Skinner, one of the sons of William Skinner. Witness—Ravaud Kearny.
Lib. 29, p. 416.

**1790, Sept. 6. Skirm, Joseph,** of Burlington Co. Ward. Son of Abraham Skirm, of said Co., deceased. Said Ward makes choice of Nathan Middleton as his Guardian.
1790, Sept. 6. Guardian—Nathan Middleton. Fellowbondsman—Daniel Ellis; both of said Co. Lib. 32, p. 98.

**1789, Jan. 19. Sleeper, Jonathan,** near Mount Holly, Burlington Co.; will of. Children, Joseph, Betsy, Leah, Polly, Jonathan, James and Ebenezer, all estate, when they come of age. Real estate to be sold. Executors—friend, Uriah Woolman, and my son, Joseph. Witnesses—Buddell Shinn, William Sleeper, Adin Kindell. Proved Feb. 23, 1789.
Lib. 31, p. 301.

**1786, May 27. Sloan, William,** of Cranbury, Middlesex Co. Int. Adm'rs—Mary Sloan and John Sloan. Fellowbondsman—George McAroy; all of said Co.
1786, May 30. Inventory, made by Nathaniel Hunt and David Chambers. Lib. 28, p. 342.

**1789, April 29. Smith, Abraham,** of Middletown Township, Monmouth Co. Int. Adm'r—Thomas Seabrook. Fellowbondsman—Tunis Vanderveer; both of said Co. Witness—Euphamia Clayton.
1789, Sept. 20. Inventory, £61.7.6, made by John Taylor, Jr. and John Stillwell. "Bond against John and Joseph Smith for £50."
Lib. 30, p. 189.

**1786, April 22. Smith, Baltser,** of Cumberland Co. Int. Adm'x—Catharine Smith. Fellowbondsman—George Hichner.
1786, Feb. 25. Inventory, £284.19.3, made by Thomas Brown and Isaac Brown. Lib. 28, p. 182.

**1789, March 20. Smith, Christian,** of Roxbury, Morris Co. Int. Adm'rs—William Smith and John Smith. Fellowbondsman—Jacob Thompson; all of said Co. Witnesses—Sally Pierson and Daniel Woodruff.
1789, March 19. Renunciation by Margret Wise, mother of Christian Smith. Witnesses—Daniel Woodruff and Jacob Smith.
1789, March 13. Inventory, £386.8.8, made by Jacob Drake and George Walldorff. Money due from John and William Smith.
Lib. 30, p. 234.

**1786, Aug. 28. Smith, Dougald,** of Wantage, Sussex Co. Int. Adm'rs—John Smith, of Baskenridge, Somerset Co., yeoman, and George Smith, of Wantage, yeoman. Fellowbondsman—Gilbert Smith, of Wantage, yeoman.
1786, Aug. 16. Inventory, £189.7.6, made by Hugh Haggerty and Silvanus Southworth. Lib. 28, p. 470.

**1789, Dec. 20. Smith, Elijah,** of Egg Harbor Township, Gloucester Co.; will of. Sons, Elijah and Enoch, farm where I live. Son, Elijah, my meadow on west side of Egg Harbor River. Son, Enoch, to have the south side joining to Isaack Smith's land, when he is 21. Son, Daniel, £8. Son, Philip, £8. Sons, Philip and Daniel, to be put to trades. Daughter, Jane, goods. Wife, Jane, ⅛ of my estate. Executors—brother, Elias, and my son, Elijah. Witnesses—Joseph Sharp, Jonathan Badcock, Isaac Smith. Proved June 16, 1790.
1790, Feb. 1. Inventory, £132.17.9, made by Joshua Smith and Isaac Smith. Lib. 31, p. 458.

**1788, June 13. Smith, Elisha,** of Gloucester Co. Int. Adm'r—Isaac Smith. Fellowbondsman—Noah Smith; both of Great Egg Harbor Township, said Co. Witness—William King Hugg. Lib. 31, p. 36.

## CALENDAR OF WILLS—1786-1790

**1786, Dec. 6. Smith, Hannah,** of Evesham, Burlington Co. Int. Adm'r—Job Prickitt. Fellowbondsman—Jacob Prickitt; both of said place.
1787. Jan. 2. Inventory, £136.18.7, made by Lawrence Webster and Thomas Hollinshead. Lib. 28, p. 74.

**1788, March 8. Smith, Hilche,** of Middlesex Co. Int. Adm'r—William Updike. Fellowbondsman—David Stonaker; both of said Co.
Lib. 31, p. 224.

**1788, Sept. 29. Smith, Isaac,** of Cumberland Co. Ward. Son of Daniel Smith, of said Co., deceased. Said Ward makes choice of Norton Ludlam as his Guardian.
1788, Sept. 29. Guardian—Norton Ludlam. Fellowbondsman—Eli Elmer; both of said Co. Witnesses—Jonathan Elmer and S. M. Shute. Lib. 31, p. 77.

**1786, Jan. 25. Smith, James,** of Monmouth Co. Int. Adm'x—Ann Smith. Fellowbondsman—John Brinley; both of said Co. Witness—Rebecah Dennis.
1785, Dec. 19. Inventory, £289.12.6, made by John Brinley and James Green. Lib. 28, p. 295.

**1787, March 6. Smith, James,** of Burlington, Burlington Co.; will of. Son, Richard, house and land where I live, on east side of High Street. Son, William, my plantation where my son, Richard lives; also a lot and blacksmith shop on High St. Daughter, Sarah Few, wife of Joseph Few, £400. Grandson, Thomas Rodman, Jr., a lot fronting on the Delaware, on which my bake house formerly stood. Granddaughter, Sarah Rodman, £40. Grandson, James Hopkins, £40. Grandchildren, the children of my daughter, Elizabeth Hopkins, one guinea each, the above James excepted. Sons, Richard and William, and my son-in-law, Pearson Rodman, and grandson, Thomas Rodman, Jr., my apparel. Executors—sons, Richard and William, and my grandson, Thomas Rodman, Jr. Witnesses—Thomas Smith, Nathaniel Coleman, Thomas Adams. Proved June 8, 1789.
1789, June 8. Renunciation by Richard Smith and Thomas Rodman, Jr. Witness—William Smith.
1789, Dec. 8. Inventory, £568.4.1, made by Robert Smith and Thomas P. Hewlings. Lib. 31, p. 308.

**1789, March 18. Smith, Jonathan,** of Gloucester Co. Int. Adm'x—Mary Smith. Fellowbondsmen—John Hyde and John Blackwood; all of said Co. Lib. 30, p. 137.

**1787, June 23. Smith, Joseph,** of Bellmont, Hopewell, Hunterdon Co., farmer. Int. Adm'r—Andrew Smith. Fellowbondsman—John Van Cleve; both of Hopewell, said Co. Witness—Furman Yard.
1787, March 15. Inventory, £134.14.1, made by John Van Cleve and John McKinstry. Lib. 29, p. 295.

**1789, June 10. Smith, Legget,** of Downe Township, Cumberland Co.; will of. Daughter, Sarah, live stock, household goods and carpenter tools. Lands to be sold. Son, Benjamin, 5 shillings. Granddaughter, Nelly Holeman, in East Jersey, £20, when 18; and, if she die, then to my 2 daughters, Sarah and Mary. Daughters, Sarah and Mary, the

residue. Executors—Ichabed Cumpton, and my daughter, Sarah. Witnesses—John Sutton, William Cobb, Peter Drummond. Proved Sept. 21, 1790. Probate to Sarah Embley.
1789, Nov. 21. Inventory, £85.14.7, made by James Blizard and Ziba Blizard. File No. 6034 F.

**1786, June 20. Smith, Mary,** of Lower Alloways Creek, Salem Co.; will of. To Richard Garrison the £14 that he has. Elizabeth Thompson, Hannah Dicson and William Plumer, rest of moveable estate. Richard Garrison, my lands. To Mary Stretch, Deby Plumer, Mary Dicson, Ann Dicson and Elizabeth Garrison, £15 each. To John Garrison, £5. All to be paid when they are of age. Executor—Richard Garrison. Witnesses—John Stewart, Edward Bradway, Elizabeth Bradway. Proved Sept. 10, 1786.
1786, Aug. 29. Inventory, £29.11.6, made by Edward Bradway and Joseph Hildreth. Lib. 28, p. 145.

**1787, May 9. Smith, Mary,** formerly of New York, but now of Somerset Co.; will of. Sister, Ann Jero, £100. "Nephew, Mary Murry," £25. To Margaret Staats, daughter of Abraham Staats, £25. To Mary S., daughter of said Abraham, £25. To Philip Curtenius, of New York, son of Peter Curtenius, £25. Margaret Staats, wife of Abraham, some goods. Sister, Ann Jero, and my "nephew, Mary Murry," my linnens. Nephew, Mary Murry, Margaret Staats and Mary S. Staats, daughters of said Abraham Staats, rest of estate. Executor—friend, Peter Curtenius, of New York. Witnesses—Abraham Staats, Hendrick Vannortwick. Proved Dec. 15, 1788. Lib. 31, p. 168.

**1786, Nov. 27. Smith, Nicholas,** of Oxford, Sussex Co. Int. Adm'r—Henry Smith. Fellowbondsmen—George Emrod and William Emrod; all of said place. Lib. 28, p. 471.

**1790, March 12. Smith, Noah,** of Great Egg Harbor, Gloucester Co.; will of. Daughter, Susanna Steelman, part of back land, joining Daniel Lake and Nathan Lake, of 30 acres; also ½ of Whirlpool Island. Grandson, Job Carr, the west part of land I bought of Francis Haddock; also ½ of Whirlpool Island. Daughter, Naomi Murphey, back land that joins Jonas Adams, and, at her death, to her son, Mahlon Murphey. Daughter, Judeth Smith, rest of back land bought of Amos Ireland; also ½ of the marsh which I bought of Nehemiah Nickelson, laying opposite to Alexander Fishes Island. Daughters, Naomi Murphey and Judeth Smith, ½ of the cedar swamp at Swan Bay. Granddaughters, Ann, Judeth, Melisent and Susannah Steelman, ¼ of cedar swamp at Swan Bay. Grandchildren, Melisent Carr and Noah Leeds, ¼ of the cedar swamp at Swan Bay. Daughters, Naomi Murphey and Judeth Smith, and my granddaughter, Melisent Carr, (after my daughter, Judeth, is made equal with that that Cate and Naomi had), rest of personal estate, except the apparel which I give to my son, John. Sons, Samuel and John, rest of real estate. Grandson, Noah Murphey, a small lot of woodland, on west side of Ingersuls road. Executors—son-in-law, William Murphey, and my daughter, Judith. Witnesses—David Scull, Daniel Leeds, Rachel Scull. Proved Dec. 25, 1790.
1790, Dec. 11. Inventory, £87.7.6, made by Joseph Johnson and Daniel Leeds, media. Lib. 31, p. 460.

CALENDAR OF WILLS—1786-1790          209

**1787, Jan. 31. Smith, Robert,** of Galloway Township, Gloucester Co.; will of. Homestead to be sold. Sons, Sylvanus, Daniel, Joshua and Robert, 300 acres of woodland on the Absecon road. Wife, Rebecca, ⅓ of moveable estate. Daughters, Sarah and Mary, ⅔. Executors—wife, Rebecca, and Richard Price. Witnesses—Richard Collins, Catharine Woodward, Henry Woodward. Proved March 22, 1787.
 1787, March 17. Inventory, £118.6.0, made by Micajah Smith, Daniel Leeds and Henry Woodward.                            Lib. 29, p. 99.

**1789, Nov. 7. Smith, Samuel,** of Burlington Co. Int. Adm'r— Thomas Smith. Fellowbondsman—John Neale; both of Burlington.
                                                          Lib. 31, p. 320.

**1789, Nov. 21. Smith, Samuel,** of Salem, Salem Co., yeoman; will of. Sisters, Hannah, Elizabeth and Rebeccah, my plantation in Manington. To Salem Monthly Meeting of Friends, £100. I am entitled by the will of my father, Pile Smith, as heir-at-law, to ½ of 10,000 acres, called Pilesgrove Tract, in Salem Co., which was illegally sold; but they are to have deeds for the same. Cousins, Thomas Carpenter and Samuel Sharp, rest of lands. Executors—friends, John Redman and John Denn. Witnesses—James Mason Woodnutt, David Bassett, John McGee. Proved Aug. 15, 1790.
 1790, April 13. Inventory, £375.9.3, made by James Mason Woodnutt and Whitton Cripps.                                   Lib. 31, p. 492.

**1789, Feb. 26. Smith, William,** of Middletown, Monmouth Co. Ward. Son of Abraham Smith, of said place, deceased. Said Ward makes choice of Thomas Seabrook as his Guardian.
 1789, Feb. 26. Guardian—Thomas Seabrook. Fellowbondsman— James Frost; both of said place. Witness—John Stillwell.
                                                          Lib. 30, p. 189.

**1790, Oct. 16. Smith, William,** of Rahway, Essex Co. Int. Adm'r— Richard Hartshorne. Fellowbondsman—Joseph Shotwell; both of said Co. Witness—Joseph Stackhouse.
 1790, Oct. 16. Renunciation by Elizabeth Smith, widow of said William, in favor of her son-in-law, Richard Hartshorne.
 1790, Nov. 20. Inventory, £5,743.5.5, made by Joseph D'Camp and James FitzRandolph.                                     Lib. 30, p. 361.

**1790, July 2. Smith, William Ames,** of Morris Co. Ward. Son of William Smith, of said Co., deceased. Said Ward makes choice of Dr. Jonathan Cheever as his Guardian.
 1790, July 2. Guardian—Jonathan Cheever. Fellowbondsman— Benjamin Freeman; both of Morristown, said Co.   Lib. 30, p. 481.

**1786, Nov. 2. Smith, Zebulon,** of Monmouth Co. Int. Adm'x— Hannah Smith. Fellowbondsman—Richard Longstreet; both of said Co. Witness—Ette Clayton.
 1786, June 19. Inventory, £152.2.2, made by Garret Longstreet and Richard Longstreet.                                   Lib. 28, p. 488.

**1786, July 28. Smock, Hendrick,** of Freehold, Monmouth Co. Int. Adm'r—Barnes H. Smock. Fellowbondsman—John Lloyd; both of said Co.
 1786, July 27. Inventory, £984.6.10, made by John Lloyd and Hugh Newill.                                               Lib. 28, p. 292.

**1786, Jan. 11. Snethen, Joseph,** of Deerfield, Cumberland Co.; will of. Eldest son, John, that place where Able Whitacar lives, on the southwest corner of my plantation. To Hosea Snethen, my grist mill, and the land and swamp on the east side of Cohansey Creek, and, for want of his leaving an heir, to go to Waitel Snethen's heirs, and, if he have no heirs, to go to Annanias Snethen's heirs. Son, Annanias, ⅔ of my land at the bottom of the fork. Youngest son, Waitel, the rest of the plantation where David Elwell lives, and ⅓ of the land at the fork. Daughter, Zepporah Lawrence, £15. Son, Joseph, £15. Daughter, Phebe Snethen, is to be maintained by my sons, Waitel and Hosea. Executor—son, Waitel. Witnesses—David Elwell, Cornelius Elwell, Jacob Elwell. Proved Nov. 26, 1788.
1788, Sept. 23. Inventory, £144.13.5, made by David Moore and Ephraim Foster, of estate of Joseph Snethen, of Hopewell Twp.
Lib. 31, p. 73.

**1786, June 22. Snider, Charity,** of Amwell, Hunterdon Co. Ward. Daughter of Peter Snider, of said place, deceased. Said Ward makes choice of Daniel Pursel as her Guardian.
1786, June 22. Guardian—Daniel Pursel. Fellowbondsman—Jeremiah Thatcher; both of said Co. Witness—David Everitt.
Lib. 28, p. 248.

**1790, Feb. 8. Snyder, Harman,** of Middletown, Monmouth Co. Int. Adm'r—Mathias Vanbrakel. Fellowbondsman—Aaron Vanderbelt; both of said Co. Witness—Job Clayton.
1790, Feb. 1. Renunciation by Anne Snyder, daughter of Harman, in favor of her friend, Mathias Vanbrackel. Witness—Jacob Allen.
1790, Feb. 1. Inventory, £155.12.6, made by Aaron Vanderbelt and Stephen Vanbrackel, Sr.
Lib. 30, p. 419.

**1787, Dec. 14. Snyder, John,** of Amwell, Hunterdon Co. Int. Adm'rs—Margaret Snyder and Nicholas Groenendyck. Fellowbondsman—William Hoogland; all of said Co.
1787, Dec. 13. Inventory, £251.8.5, made by William Hoogland and Jonathan Woolverton.
1794, June 25. Account by Isaac Van Camp, and Margaret, his wife, late Margaret Snyder, Adm'x of John Snyder, Jr.
Lib. 29, p. 295.

**1786, July 22. Somers, Esther,** of Great Egg Harbor Township, Gloucester Co., widow of John Somers. Inventory, £223.9.9, made by Joseph Scull and David Badcock.
File No. 1755 H.

**1790, Feb. 12. Somers, Hannah,** of Great Egg Harbor, Gloucester Co., widow; will of. Daughter, Zillah Smith, mare, 2 cows and loom. Daughter, Mary Somers, some goods. She is to have schooling and live with her aunt, Abigal Risly. Daughter, Zillah Smith, ½ of Japhet Ireland's note, and other ½ to daughter, Mary. Executors—friend, Thomas Somers. Witnesses—Joshua Smith, Dorcus Birdeleen, Joshua Smith, J. P. Proved June 18, 1790.
1790, Feb. 20. Inventory, £188.6.6, made by Joshua Smith, Esq., and Joshua Smith.
Lib. 31, p. 463.

**1787, June 20. Somers, Japhet and Eunice,** of Great Egg Harbor Township, Gloucester Co. Wards. Children of Jacob Somers, of said place, deceased. Said Wards make choice of Samuel Somers as their Guardian.

CALENDAR OF WILLS—1786-1790   211

1787, June 20. Guardian—Samuel Somers. Fellowbondsman—Thomas Somers; both of said place. Witnesses—John Taylor and Joseph Hugg. Lib. 29, p. 120.

**1788, Nov. 13. Southard, Uriah,** of Stafford, Monmouth Co., yeoman; will of. My heir, 10 shillings. My mother, all of estate, except to my brother, Amos, the land where he lives. Sister, Elizabeth Southard, a good living. Brother, Hezekiah Southard, £25, and to Joseph Southard, £5. Brother, John, £10. Executors—Amos Southard and Nathan Bartlett. Witnesses—Dennis Crawford, Samuel Brown, Job Southard. Proved March 23, 1789.
1788, Dec. 9. Inventory, £159, made by Job Southard and Israel Penington. Lib. 30, p. 179.

**1788, March 31. Spader, William,** of Hillsborough, Somerset Co. Int. Adm'r—John Spader. Fellowbondsman—Abraham Van Neste; both of said Co. Lib. 31, p. 177.

**1786, Dec. 25. Sparks, Joseph,** of Greenwich Township, Gloucester Co. Int. Adm'x—Ann Sparks, widow of said Joseph. Fellowbondsman—Robert Currie; both of said place. Witness—Joseph Hugg, Jr.
1786, June 8. Inventory, £67.19.6, made by Jacob Middleton and Daniel Sutherland. Lib. 28, p. 124.

**1787, Sept. 4. Sparks, Simon,** of Gloucester Co. Int. Adm'r—Joseph Hugg. Fellowbondsman—John Wilkins; both of said Co. Witness—Thomas Adams. Lib. 29, p. 118.

**1788, Aug. 4. Spear, Abraham,** of Bergen Co. Int. Adm'r—Thunes Spear. Fellowbondsman—Herman Rutan; both of said Co. Witness—David Ackerman. Lib. 31, p. 257.

**1787, May 10. Spear, Tunis,** of Acquackanonk, Essex Co.; will of. Wife, Angletie, ⅛ of the personal estate, while my widow. Son, Thomas, the said ⅛, and other ⅔ of personal estate. Son, Henry, 5 shillings, for his birthright. I give my wife ⅛ of 460 acres of land, provided it ever be recovered, which I do claim by deed from Peter Sunmans; and, after her death, to fall to my son, Thomas. Son, Thomas, and Abraham Ryerson, the other ⅔ of said 460 acres. Executors—son, Thomas, and Richard Mourison. Witnesses—Jonas Force, Moses Kent, Michael Vanderhoof. Proved Dec. 29, 1787.
Lib. 29, p. 381.

**1790, Jan. 28. Squire, Nathaniel,** of Essex Co. Int. Adm'rs—Mary Squier, widow of said Nathaniel, Ellis Cook and Enoch Beach. Fellowbondsman—Elijah Squier.
1789, Dec. 28. Inventory, made by Elijah Squier and Darling Beach. Lib. 30, p. 363.

**1787, Oct. 1. Stackhouse, Samuel,** of Burlington, Burlington Co. Int. Adm'x—Esther Stackhouse. Fellowbondsman—John Neale; both of said place. Lib. 29, p. 75.

**1787, Nov. 21. Standly, Andrew,** of Lower Penns Neck, Salem Co.; will of. Son, Onesiphrous, plantation where I live. Son, Sinnick, £350. Son, Henery, £350. Son, Nathaniel, plantation joining the

woods. Daughters, Jane, Anne and Margret, moveable estate. My wife to have use of all estate while she lives. Executors—sons, Onesiphorus and Nathaniel. Witnesses—Mary Trouss, Margret Sinnickson, Allen Congleton, Jr. Proved Dec. 20, 1787.
1787, Dec. 3. Inventory, £948.14.11, made by Andrew Sinnickson, Jr., and Allen Congleton, Jr. Lib. 29, p. 151.

**1788, April 2. Stateser, Isaac,** of Shrewsbury, Monmouth Co. Int. Adm'r—Garrit Hendrickson, of Freehold, said Co.
1788, April 2. Renunciation by Zilpha Stateser, widow of Isaac. Witnesses—Joseph Wainwright and John Lefferts.
1788, March 25. Inventory, £168.17.0, made by John Polhemus and Cornelius Van Mater. Lib. 30, p. 104.

**1789, Jan. 28. Statham, Hannah,** of Greenwich, Cumberland Co.; will of. Son, Thomas Statham, £5. Daughter, Deliverance Ewing, some apparel. Daughter, Rebecka Dare, some apparel. Daughter, Dorcas Mills, a table. Daughter, Naomi Ewing, some apparel. Sons, Philip and Ananias Statham, rest of personal estate. Executors—son, Thomas Statham. Witnesses—Sarah Statham, Israel Stathem, Thomas Remington. Proved June 15, 1789.
1789, Feb. 9. Inventory, £115.7.9, made by Job Butcher and Thomas Maskell. Lib. 30, p. 152.

**1787, Dec. 14. Steelman, Andrew, Jemima and John,** of Gloucester Co. Wards. Children of James Steelman, of said Co., deceased. Catharine Steelman, widow of said James, desires that Ebenezer Adams may be appointed Guardian of said children.
**1788,** Jan. 22. Guardian—Ebenezer Adams. Fellowbondsman—Daniel Sutherland; both of Greenwich Township, said Co., yeomen. Witness—Joseph Paul. Lib. 31, p. 426.

**1788, Jan. 25. Steelman, Edmond and Leah,** of Greenwich Township, Gloucester Co. Wards. Children of John Steelman, of said place, deceased. Said Wards, having real and personal estate, make choice of Abraham Dilkes as their Guardian.
1788, Jan. 25. Guardian—Abraham Dilkes. Fellowbondsman—William Tatem; both of Deptford Township, said Co. Witness—William K. Hugg. (The said John Steelman died about 12 years ago.)
Lib. 31, p. 38.

**1788, Jan. 22. Steelman, Elizabeth,** of Greenwich Township, Gloucester Co. Ward. Daughter of James Steelman, of said place, deceased. Said Ward makes choice of Ebenezer Adams as her Guardian.
1788, Jan. 22. Guardian—Ebenezer Adams. Fellowbondsman—Daniel Sutherland; both of said place, yeoman. Witness—William K. Hugg. Lib. 31, p. 38.

**1786, April 3. Steelman, James,** of Greenwich, Gloucester Co., yeoman; will of. Wife to have the profits of ⅓ of the real estate. Son, James, the 100 acres where he lives; also the 50 acres where Thomas Cooper lives; also 10 acres of meadow that join on Repaupo Creek. Son, Isaac, that land in the tenure of Andrew Derickson, and 19 acres that join the same; also 2 acres down the creek, now in the tenure of Andrew Steelman. Sons, John and Andrew, plantation where I live, and the one where Christopher Arnold lives, including 50 acres where James Noils lives; also the meadow over against Andrew Homan's house, of 36 acres. Daughters, Sarah, Elizabeth and Jemime, rest of real and personal estate, when they are 18. Executors—friend, Thomas Clark, and my son-in-law, Daniel Sutherland. Witnesses—Garrot Clark, Thomas Clark, Jr., Mary Clark. Proved Jan. 22, 1788.

    1787, Sept. 30.   Inventory, £413.13.5, made by Joseph Paul and Ebenezer Adams.   Lib. 31, p. 19.

**1790, Jan. 2. Steelman, James,** of Woolwich Township, Gloucester Co. Int. Adm'rs—Eleanor Steelman and James Codd. Fellowbondsman—Ebenezer Adams; all of said Co.

    1789, Dec. 31.   Inventory, £123.12.6, made by Peter Lock and Ebenezer Adams.   Lib. 31, p. 480.

**1786, June 21. Steelman, John,** of Great Egg Harbor Township, Gloucester Co. Int. Adm'x—Sarah Steelman. Fellowbondsmen—Luke Sooy and Joseph Ingersul, Jr.; all of said place. Witness—Richard Price.

    1786, April 25.   Inventory, £209.13.9, made by Joseph Ingersul, Jr.
    Lib. 28, p. 124.

**1790, Feb 15. Steelman, Zepheniah,** of Galloway, Gloucester Co. Int. Adm'x—Rebecca Steelman. Fellowbondsman—John Steelman; both of said Co.

    1790. Jan. 23.   Inventory, £82, made by Edmon Ireland and John Steelman.   Lib. 31, p. 480.

**1787, Jan. 2. Stephens, John,** of Freehold, Monmouth Co., blacksmith; will of. My saw mill to be sold. Son, James, land on line of John Antram, of 3 acres, when he is 21. Son, Apollo, land joining his brother, James. Son, Thomas, land along the Island meadow. Son, Edward, land along Thomas'. Son, John, also land. Son, Samuel, house I live in. Son, Stacy, rest of home place. Wife, Fanny, all she brought with her, and £10 yearly. Executors—son, Samuel, and my wife, Fanny. Witnesses—John Antram, William French, Thomas Walling. Proved March 23, 1787.

    1787, March 19.   Inventory, £192.19.2, made by John Antram and Francis Shinn.   Lib. 29, p. 303.

**1790, March 3. Stevens, William,** of Shrewsbury, Monmouth Co. Int. Adm'r—Obadiah Sears. Fellowbondsman—Jacob Wardell; both of said place. Witness—Peter Baird.

    1790, Feb. 26.   Inventory, made by Jacob Wardell and Stephen Woolley.   Lib. 30, p. 419.

**1787, May 15. Steward, William,** of Chesterfield Township, Burlington Co. Int. Adm'r—John Thorn, Sr. Fellowbondsman—John Thorn, son of Benjamin; both of said place.

    1787, May 7. Renunciation by William Steward, Bickley Steward, Ann Bunting, Mary Steward, Sarah Steward and Rebeccah Steward, legatees of William, deceased, in favor of John Thorn.

    1787, May 8.   Inventory, £63.18.6, made by Nathan Middleton and Jeremiah Smith.   Lib. 29, p. 76.

**1787, April 13.** Stewart, Charles Alexander, of Hunterdon Co. Int. Adm'rs—Samuel Robert Stewart and Aaron Dunham. Fellowbondsman—Charles Stewart; all of said Co. Witness—Joseph W. Shippen.
Lib. 29, p. 295.

**1788, Dec. 1.** Stewart, John, of Great Egg Harbor Township, Gloucester Co., yeoman; will of. Wife, Sophia, ⅛ of the moveable estate. Son, John, the homestead, and ⅛ the swamp. Son, William, the land above the road and ⅛ the swamp. Son, Joel, ⅛ of the swamp; also 30 acres which I own at Channel Run. Daughter, Jane, 5 shillings. Daughter, Sarah, 5 shillings; they both had their portions. Daughter, Hannah, a bed and desk that are up in the country. Son, Scobe, £20; and to be put to a trade. Son, Isaac, £5. Grandson, Ely, £3. Children, Hannah, Scoby, Isaac and Ely, residue. Executors—sons, John and Joel. Witnesses—David Sayrs, John Taylor, Nathaniel Burton Mills. Proved Feb. 18, 1789.
1789, Feb. 18. Inventory, £54.9.0, made by Thomas Champion and David Sayrs.
Lib. 30, p. 129.

**1787, May 23.** Stillwill, Anna, of Cape May Co. Ward. Daughter of Enoch Stillwill of said Co., deceased. Guardian—Richard Somers, of Phila. Co. Fellowbondsman—Richard Townsend, of Cape May Co. Witnesses—David Hand and Jesse Hand.
Lib. 29, p. 242.

**1788, June 12.** Stillwill, David, of Great Egg Harbor Township, Gloucester Co. Int. Adm'x—Jean Stillwill, widow of said David. Fellowbondsman—James Willets, Jr.; both of said place. Witness—Elizabeth Hugg.
1788, July 12. Inventory, £33.10.8, made by Andrew Godfrey and Contantine Smith.
Lib. 31, p. 36.

**1787, Feb. 27.** Stillwill, Enoch, of Cape May Co. Int. Adm'rs—Phebe Stillwill and Eli Eldredge. Fellowbondsmen—Zebulon Swain and Henry Stites; all of said Co. Witnesses—Richard Townsend, Sarah Hand and Mary Bowen.
1787, July 3. Inventory, £2,552.9.10, made by Jesse Hand and Thomas Shaw.
Lib. 29, p. 241.

**1788, May 28.** Stillwill, Savage, of Cape May Co. Ward. Son of Enoch Stillwill, of said Co., deceased. Said Ward makes choice of Richard Somers as his Guardian. Witnesses—Nicholas Stillwill and Jesse Hand.
1788, May 28. Guardian—Richard Somers, of Philadelphia. Fellowbondsman—Richard Townsend, of Cape May Co. Witnesses—Sarah Hand and Jesse Hand.
Lib. 31, p. 94.

**1787, May 23.** Stillwill, Sophia, of Cape May Co. Ward. Daughter of Enoch Stillwill, of said Co., deceased. Guardian—Richard Somers, of Philadelphia. Fellowbondsman—Richard Townsend, of Cape May Co. Witnesses—David Hand and Jesse Hand.
Lib. 29, p. 242.

**1787, May 11.** Stilwell, John, of Middletown, Monmouth Co.; will of. Wife, Rebecah, £15 and use of plantation till my son, John, is 21, in order to bring up my 3 daughters. Son, John, the plantation; also the purchase I made of my father, Thomas, deceased; out of which my wife, Rebacah, and 2 youngest daughters, Martha and Elizabeth,

are to be supported. Daughters, Nancy, Martha and Elizabeth, rest of estate. Executors—brother, William Stillwell, and friend, Joseph Stillwell. Witnesses—John Stillwell, Samuel Hoffmire, Sarah Stillwell. Proved June 23, 1787.
1787, June 19. Inventory, £245.5.6, made by John Stillwell and Elnathan Field. Lib. 29, p. 317.

**1787, Dec. 7. Stites, Jacob,** of Cape May Co. Int. Adm'x—Silvytha Stites. Fellowbondsman—Thomas James Curtis; both of said Co. Witnesses—Abraham Woolson and Jacob Schellinger.
1787, Dec. 5. Inventory, £122.19.10, made by Abraham Woolson and Jacob Schellinger. Lib. 29, p. 241.

**1787, April 18. Stockton, David,** of Springfield, Burlington Co., yeoman; will of. Son, Job, plantation where I live, which was conveyed to me by my brother, Benjamin. Son, Obadiah, my house and lot at Penny Hill, which I bought of Samuel Wright; also a lot laid out for him, it being part of the plantation given me by my father, David Stockton, and is to contain 26¾ acres. Son, Obadiah, to have my smith shop and tools, when he is 21. Son, Samuel, plantation given me by my father, except the said lot. Sons, Job and Samuel, my cedar swamp. Daughter, Mary Stockton, £200. Daughter, Mercy Stockton, £200. Daughter, Elizabeth, £200. Wife, Elizabeth, £100 and £10 yearly. Executors—wife, Elizabeth, and sons, Job and Obadiah. Witnesses—Henry Ridgway, Asher Gauntt, William Earl. Proved May 18, 1787. Lib. 29, p. 47.

**1788, Dec. 20. Stockton, Job,** of Springfield, Burlington Co.; will of. Son, Jonathan, the plantation where Joseph White lives, called White plantation. Son, William, the land I bought of my cousin, Richard Stockton. Son, Stacy, plantation where I live. Son, Monrow Stockton, the land called Middleton plantation. Son, William, £500. Son, John, £3. Rest of real and personal estate I give to son, William, Mary Bishop, and my other daughter, Margaret Stockton. Executors—sons, Jonathan and William. Witnesses—Stacy Budd, Joseph Pancoast, John Ridgway. Proved Feb. 28, 1789.
1789, Jan. 22. Inventory, £2,179.18.5, made by John Wright and Thomas Earl. Lib. 31, p. 299.

**1789, May 19. Stockton, Margaret,** of Burlington Co. Ward. Daughter of Job Stockton, of said Co., deceased. Said Ward makes choice of John Bishop as her Guardian.
1789, May 19. Guardian—John Bishop. Fellowbondsman—Thomas Rogers, Jr.; both of said Co. Lib. 31, p. 322.

**1787, March 7. Stoll, John,** of Newtown, Sussex Co.; will of. Wife, Jane, all lands and goods. Daughters, Mary and Anna, same as my sons. Executors—wife, Jane, and my son, Andrew. Witnesses—John Dunlop, Levi Lewis, Jr., James Colver. Proved April 4, 1787.
1787, March 22. Inventory, £183.9.0, made by Francis Price and David Phillips.
1795, Feb. 20. Adm'rs—John Stoll and Henry Stull. Fellowbondsman—Samuel Westbrook; all of Newtown. Both Executors have also died. Lib. 29, p. 477.

216   NEW JERSEY POST-REVOLUTIONARY DOCUMENTS

**1787, Aug. 24. Stone, William,** of Woodbridge, Middlesex Co.; will of. Grandson, William Stone, son of my son, Benjamin, deceased, 10 shillings. Granddaughter, Margaret Sayre, daughter of my son, Robert, deceased, 10 shillings. Wife, Lucy, use of land where I live, which I bought of Jonathan Jacques, and interest of £100; also what she had at our marriage. Grandson, Samuel Williams, £20. Land to be sold. Daughter, Ann Coddington, widow, ½ of the residue. Friend, William Smith, the other ½, who is to invest the same and pay the interest to my daughter, Elizabeth Williams, wife of Benjamin, during the life of her husband, and, after his death, to pay all to her. If she die first, then to her children. Executors—friends, William Smith, of Ash Swamp, Essex Co., Dr. Moses Bloomfield, Thomas Edgar and James Edgar, of Woodbridge. Witnesses—Daniel Shotwell, Jonathan Freeman, Samuel Bloodgood.
1788, May 28. Codicil. I commenced action against Samuel Sayre, which my Executors are to prosecute. Witnesses—Titus Shotwell, Jonathan Freeman, John Thomson. Proved Oct. 14, 1788.
1788, Sept. 19. Inventory, £1,318.8.4, made by Joseph Shotwell and Isaac Freeman. Lib. 31, p. 215.

**1787, April 20. Stout, Benjamin,** of Amwell Township, Hunterdon Co., farmer; will of. Wife, Mary, and daughters, Mary Prall, Rachel Hill and Anne Stout, rest of estate, after debts are paid, except hereafter mentioned. Sons, Judiah and David, lands where I live, as held by a deed from my late father; also land bought from Nathaniel Leonard, Rebecca Cox, Ralph Drake and Jacob Keshaw, at different times. Son, Benjamin, £60. Son, David, is under age. Executors—wife, Mary, and my eldest son, Judiah. Witnesses—Christopher Weart, Joseph Ferguson, John Weart. Proved June 16, 1789.
1789, June 1. Inventory, £435.1.1, made by John Weart and Derrick Sutphen. A debt against Garrison Prall. Lib. 32, p. 1.

**1788, Sept. 17. Stout, Benjamin,** of Lebanon Township, Hunterdon Co. Int. Adm'rs—Hezekiah Stout and Samuel Stout. Fellowbondsman—John Bray; all of said Co.
1788, Sept. 1. Renunciation by Martha Stout, widow of said Benjamin. Witnesses—Thomas Jones and John Bray.
1788, Sept. 1. Renunciation by Samuel and Hezekiah Stout, sons of said Benjamin. Witnesses—Thomas Jones and John Bray.
1788, Sept. 2. Inventory, £942.17.11, made by Thomas Jones and John Bray. Lib. 31, p. 145.

**1787, Feb. 26. Stout, David,** of Amwell, Hunterdon Co.; will of. Wife, Sarah, £60, and silver watch, and to have money as needed to bring up our children. What estate is left I give to my 2 daughters, and the child yet to be born. Executors—Joseph Ott and Abraham Runkle. Witnesses—Nathan Stout, Moses Stout, Philip Servis. Proved April 20, 1787.
1787, April 19. Inventory, £658.16.11, made by Nathan Stout and Philip Servis.
1791, Nov. 26. Account by Executors. A silver watch was delivered to Joshua Higgins, in right of his wife, agreeable to the will.
Lib. 29, p. 288.

**1789, Feb. 5. Stout, Eli,** of Hunterdon Co. Ward. Son of Abraham Stout, of said Co., deceased. Said Ward makes choice of Jediah Stout as his Guardian.

CALENDAR OF WILLS—1786-1790 217

**1789, Feb. 5.** Guardian—Jediah Stout, of Amwell. Fellowbondsman—Nathan Drake, Jr., of Hopewell. Lib. 32, p. 57.

**1790, Nov. 6. Stout, James,** of Middlesex Co. Int. Adm'r—Jonathan Stout. Fellowbondsman—James Jenkins; both of said Co. Witness—Minne V. Voorhies. Lib. 30, p. 535.

**1790, June 7. Stout, John,** of Amwell, Hunterdon Co.; will of. Grandson, Joab Stout, £5. To Mary Prall a bed. Wife, Rachel, the household goods, and, after her death, to be sold, and money given to my daughters, Cathrine Stout, Anne Manners and Rachel Prall. To my 2 surviving sons, Nathan and Moses, all my lands, and Nathan is to have the west part. Executors—sons, Nathan and Moses. Witnesses—Azariah Higgins, Philip Young, Mary Prall, Grace Stout. Proved June 17, 1790.
1790, June 15. Inventory, £238.4.4, made by Azariah Higgins and Philip Servis. Lib. 30, p. 284.

**1786, Feb. 6. Stout, Richard,** of Freehold, Monmouth Co.; will of. Son, John, land where he lives, and my son, Stephen, place where I live, and he is to support my wife, Hannah; and he is to pay to my daughter, Anna Barkalow, one of the best cows, and £8. Son, David, the land where he lives, which I bought of Nathan Tilton; and he is to pay to my daughter, Sarah Parker, £3, and to my grandchild, Silvenus Bills, £30, when 21. Son, John, is to pay to his eldest son, Joseph, £3. Executors—sons, John and Stephen. Witnesses—James Johnson, Aaron Brewer, Derick Barkalow. Proved Feb. 18, 1786.
1786, Feb. 16. Inventory, £160.2.6, made by James Johnson and Aaron Brewer. Lib. 28, p. 268.

**1789, April 19. Stout, Sarah,** of Hopewell Township, Hunterdon Co.; will of. Daughter, Mary Herrington, £6. Daughter, Martha Dollas, £3. Daughter, Sarah Merrel, some goods. Grandson, Aaron Dollas, 5 shillings. Granddaughter, Effa Merrel, 6 sheep. Brother, Joab Houghton, my Bible. Son-in-law, John Merrel, rest of estate. Executors—Joab Houghton and John Merrel. Witnesses—David Merrell, Andrew Merrell, John Merrell. Proved May 7, 1789.
1789, May 13. Inventory, £118.0.8, made by Nathan Drake and Benjamin Parke. Lib. 32, p. 27.

**1787, Oct. 25. Stout, Thomas and Louiza,** of Hunterdon Co. Wards. Children of James Stout, Jr., of said Co., deceased. Petition of Jacob Pecker and Ann Pecker for appointment of John Schank as the Guardian of her children by her late husband, James Stout, Jr.
1787, Oct. 25. Guardian—John Schanck. Fellowbondsman—Jacob Schenck, both of Amwell, said Co. Lib. 29, p. 298.

**1788, April 7. Stout, Zebulon,** of Somerset Co.; will of, being advanced in age. Eldest son, John, 37 acres in Hunterdon Co., which he now has; also 2 lots in this Co.; also a lot in Amboy conveyed to me by James Leonard. Youngest son, Zebulon, homestead where I live. Daughter, Ann Leigh, ¼ of personal estate; that is, to her heirs, deducting £50 for a negro, which Ann had in her lifetime. Daughter, Rachel Barton, also ¼ during her life, and, after her death, to her heirs and my grandsons, Stout Brinson and Zebulon Brinson; allowing the bond I have against her husband, Stephen

Barton, as part of said legacy. Daughter, Sarah Stout, also ¼, and, after her death, to her heirs and my grandchildren, Lorany Bryant and Charity Sortor; allowing a bond I have against her husband, Natte Stout. Daughter, Mary Corbine, also ¼, and, after her death, to her heirs and my granddaughter, Ann (Amy) Rodgers; allowing a bond I have against her husband, Francis Corbine, in part of said legacy. Sons, John and Zebulon, debt I have against Thomas Allen, John and Peter Nephew, Daniel McCarty and Jessey Hart. Executors—sons, John and Zebulon. Witnesses—Nathaniel Stout, Sr., Susanna Gordon, Peter Gordon. Proved Sept. 10, 1788.

1788, Sept. 12. Inventory, £918.6.6, made by Samuel Stout and Peter Gordon. Lib. 31, p. 166.

**1789, Jan. 8. Strattan, Josiah,** of Woolwich Township, Gloucester Co., cordwainer; will of. Real and personal estate to be sold. Wife, Mary, £70; but provision is to be made to bring up the children to the age of 7 years, and then to be bound out. Children, Beththual, William, Isaiah and Elias, to have a full portion, when of age. Executors—wife, Mary, and Samuel French, of Greenwich Township. Witnesses—Matthew Allen, Jacob Gosling, Abel Nicholson. Proved June 19, 1789.

1789, Feb. 21. Inventory, £335.13.2, made by Jacob Gosling and Enoch Allen. Lib. 30, p. 117.

**1789, Nov. 9. Stretch, David,** of Lower Alloways Creek Township, Salem Co.; will of. Son, David, silver buckles, when 21. Daughter, Elenor Stretch, silver spoons, when 18. Rest of personal estate to my daughters, Sarah Right, Margaret Evins, Elenor Stretch, Prudance Stretch and Mary Stretch, and my granddaughter, Feeby Thompson, when they are 18. Land in Cumberland Co. to be sold. Son, David, 100 acres of land lying at the lower end of my brother James' land. Son, John, rest of land whereon Daniel Trasey lives. Executor—son, John, and my friend and brother, Benjamin Corlis, to assist him. Witnesses—Jonathan Butcher, Daniel Tracy, Edward Bradway. Proved Nov. 1789.

1789, Nov. 27. Inventory, £166.12.10, made by Hugh Peddrick and Edward Bradway. Lib. 31, p. 350.

**1786, July 25. Strickland, Samuel,** of Galloway Township. Gloucester Co. Int. Adm'x—Diadamy Strickland. Fellowbondsman—Robert Morss, Esq.; both of said place. Witness—William Hugg, Jr. Lib. 28, p. 123.

**1786, Sept. 27. Stringham, Mary,** of Bergen Co. Int. Adm'r—James Stringham. Fellowbondsman—George Doremus; both of said Co. Witness—John Van Emburgh.

1787, Sept. 17. Inventory, made by James Stringham, the Adm'r. Two legacies bequeathed to the deceased and her sister, Feytie, deceased, by her father, Barent Van Horn, which was to be paid by their brothers, Barent and John; amount £300. Also 2 shares out of 5 of the personal estate of Barent Van Horne, and was bequeathed to said Mary and her sister, Feytie, the amount of which is not known, before a settlement with the Executors of said Barent Van Horne.
Lib. 29, p. 223.

CALENDAR OF WILLS—1786-1790 219

**1786, April 24. Stryker, Hendrick,** of Sowerland, Somerset Co., yeoman. Int. Adm'rs—Catharine Stryker and Thomas Skillman, of Western Precinct, and Abraham Van Arsdalen, of Hillsborough; all of said Co. Fellowbondsman—Jacob Vanarsdalen, of Western Precinct, said Co. Witness—Jacob Probasco.
1786, April 20. Inventory, made by Joseph D. Hageman and Jacob Van Arsdalen. Lib. 29, p. 196.

**1788, Feb. 1. Stryker, Jacobus,** of Alexandria, Hunterdon Co., yeoman; will of. Wife, Gitty, all real and personal estate, during her widowhood. Executors—wife, Gitty, and my son, John. Witness—Stephen Yard, Abraham Stryker, Peter Stryker. Proved June 13, 1789.
1789, May 9. Inventory, £164.14.9, made by Asa Titus and Adam Lennard. Lib. 32, p. 7.

**1786, Feb. 17. Stryker, John,** of Millstone, Somerset Co., yeoman; will of. Wife, Lydia, use of all estate, except the farm at Readingtown, in order to bring up my children that are under age. My 6 sons to have money from sale of personal estate, and my 3 daughters to have ½ as much. Son, Peter, farm at Readingtown, of 245 acres, which I bought of Cornelius Waldron, when he is 21. Daughter, Maria, £200. Son, John, farm I bought of Peter Schenk, which formerly belonged to Brogan Brokaw, of 170 acres. Daughter, Anne, £200. Sons, Hendrick, Abraham, Jacobus and Daniel, farm where I live, of 400 acres. Daughter, Lydia, £105. Executors—wife, Lydia, my brother, Peter, and my uncle, Daniel Perrine. Witnesses—John Stryker, Jr., Simeon Van Nortwick, Edmond Christopher. Proved June 7, 1786.
1786, June 2. Inventory, £138.5.6, made by Ernestus Van Harlingen and James Leonard. Lib. 28, p. 489.

**1786, March 6. Summerl, John,** of Salem Co. Int. Adm'x—Naomi Summerl. Fellowbondsmen—Thomas Carney and Robert Kitts; all of said Co. Witness—Sarah Dick.
1786, Feb. 11. Inventory, £574.0.6, made by Robert Kitts and Thomas Peterson. File No: 1961 Q.

**1787, Feb. 13. Sutphin, Peter,** of Somerset Co. Ward. Son of Peter Sutphin, of said Co., deceased. Said Ward makes choice of Robert Blair as his Guardian.
1787, Feb. 13. Guardian—Robert Blair. Fellowbondsman—Matthias Lane, Jr. Witness—Aaron Malich. Lib. 29, p. 440.

**1789, Oct. 26. Swain, Samuel,** of Burlington Co. Int. Adm'rs—Micajah Willets, of Northampton, and John Swain, of Evesham. Fellowbondsman—William Wilkins, of Evesham; all of said Co.
1789, Oct. 20. Renunciation by Hannah Swain, widow of said Samuel, in favor of her friend, Micajah Willets. Witnesses—Abraham Haines and William Wilkins.
1789, Oct. 20. Inventory, £41.3.3, made by William Wilkins and Abraham Haines. Lib. 31, p. 321.

**1788, Dec. 10. Swallow, Jacob,** of Amwell, Hunterdon Co. Int. Adm'r—Obadiah Hunt. Fellowbondsman—John Reed.
1788, Dec. 6. Inventory, £91.1.10, made by John Reed and Samuel Hill. Lib. 31, p. 145.

**1786, Nov. 17. Swanton, William,** of Lower Penns Neck, Salem Co.; will of. Wife to have my house and lot during her life. Executor—Henry Firth, of Mannington; and Benjamin Abbot and William Bilderback to be overseers. Witnesses—John Holliday, John Shaw, Shoures Bright. Proved Dec. 11, 1787. Lib. 40, p. 542.

**1788, May 14. Swayze, Jonathan,** of Oxford Township, Sussex Co. Int. Adm'r—Joseph Swayze, of said place. Fellowbondsman—William Honywell, of Knowlton, said Co.
1788, May 19. Inventory, £45.19.3, made by John Cline and Croust Mann. Lib. 31, p. 157.

**1788, July 6. Sweezey, Jabish Mapes,** of Roxbury, Morris Co. Int. Adm'rs—Mary Sweezy and John Sweezey. Fellowbondsmen—Daniel Budd and David Brown; all of said place. Witness—William Corwin.
1788, Aug. 6. Inventory, £130.16.6, made by Abraham Dickerson and Daniel Budd. Lib. 31, p. 201.

**1787, March 19. Talbert, Rachel,** of Mansfield Township, Burlington Co.; will of. Husband, William Talbert, all my estate which was left me by my father. Executor—husband, William Talbert. Witnesses—John Pope, Caleb Scattergood, Jr., Sarah Scattergood. Proved June 8, 1789. Lib. 31, p. 312.

**1790, March 6. Tallman, John,** of Shrewsbury, Monmouth Co., yeoman; will of. To Elias, the first born son to Mary Croxson, £110; and to Lydia, the first born daughter, £100. Brother, Stephen, residue. Executor—brother, Stephen. Witnesses—William Grinding, William Little, Mary Tilton. Proved June 21, 1790.
1790, June 21. Adm'rs—James Tallman and Thomas Seabrook; both of said Co. Witness—Peter Knott. Stephen Tallman also dead.
1790, June 22. Inventory, £280.0.2, made by William Parker and Thomas Little. Lib. 30, p. 383.

**1787, Nov. 28. Tallman, Oliver,** of Shrewsbury, Monmouth Co.; will of. Son, Daniel, ½ of the land that was bought of William Burns, and the other ½ to my daughter, Jemime. I also give them the land I bought of my brother, Jeams. To Daniel, Jemime, Molley and Hannah, ¼ of my wheel, to each. Son, William, £5. Daughter, Molley, £5. Executor—George Howlog. Witnesses—Cornelius Lane, Joseph Tallman, Sarah Cooper. Proved Jan. 11, 1788.
1788, Jan. 11. Adm'r—William Tallman, son of the deceased. Fellowbondsman—Joseph Tallman; both of said Co.
1788, Jan. 11. Renunciation by George Howland.
1788, Jan. 11. Inventory, £84.17.6, made by Cornelius Lane and William Cooper. Lib. 30, p. 66.

**1786, Feb. 28. Tallman, Peter,** of Burlington Co. Int. Adm'rs—Joel Gibbs and Jacob Wolcott. Fellowbondsmen—Martin Gibbs and Thomas Kerlin; all of Mansfield Township, said Co.
1786, Feb. 27. Renunciation by Margaret Tallman, widow of said Peter, in favor of Joel Gibbs and Jacob Wolcott. Lib. 28, p. 77.

**1788, Dec. 8. Tallman, Samuel,** of Shrewsbury, Monmouth Co. Int. Adm'x—Rachel Tallman. Fellowbondsman—James Tallman; both of said place.

CALENDAR OF WILLS—1786-1790   221

1789, Feb. 2. Inventory, £560.19.8, made by Joseph Parker and James Tallman. These are goods that Mary Williams and Nancy Tucker hold, and valued at £136.18.8. Lib. 30, p. 103.

**1790, June 21. Tallman, Stephen,** of Shrewsbury, Monmouth Co. Int. Adm'rs—James Tallman and Thomas Seabrook, both of said Co. Witnesses—Peter Knott and William Little.
1790, June 21. Renunciation by Rachel Tallman, Martha Seabrook, Polly Williams, Pattey Tallman and Mary Tallman, in favor of Thomas Seabrook and James Tallman. Witness—Thomas Little.
1790, June 23. Inventory, made by William Parker and Thomas Little. Lib. 30, p. 418.

**1790, March 6. Talmage, Thomas,** of Middlesex Co. Int. Adm'r—Thomas Talmage. Fellowbondsman—Benjamin Cook; both of said Co.
1790, March 5. Inventory, £555.16.6, made by William Van Duerson and William Letson. Lib. 30, p. 534.

**1787, Jan. 25. Tanner, John,** of Evesham, Burlington Co., weaver; will of. Wife, Susannah, to have the profits of my estate, and, after her death or marriage, to my children as follows:—to Esther Miller, £5; to Samuel Reeves' wife, Lydia, house and lot where she lives; to Job Burden, £7; to Martha, wife of Christopher Wylia, 30 shillings; to Phebe Goslin and Susannah Sands, their equal parts that remain, after Esther Miller and Job Burden are paid their shares. Executrix—wife, Susannah. Witnesses—Isaac Haines, John Rakestraw, John Walker. Proved April 12, 1790.
1790, April 12. Adm'r—Samuel Reeves. Fellowbondsman—Abraham Kinsey. The Executrix has since died, before having proved the will. Witness—Isaac Haines.
1790, April 6. Inventory, £24.0.1, made by Solomon Haines and Abraham Kinsey. Lib. 32, p. 83.

**1788, Jan. 31. Taylor, Benjamin,** of Cape May Co. Int. Adm'rs—James Hildreth and Artis Seagreave. Fellowbondsman—Thomas Yates; all of said Co., gentlemen. Witnesses—Jeremiah Hand and Aaron Hand.
1788, Feb. 25. Inventory, £1,373.5.8, made by John Cresse and Joseph Hildreth. Lib. 31, p. 93.

**1786, March 7. Taylor, Edward,** of Middletown, Monmouth Co., yeoman; will of. Wife, Susan, £100, and use of ½ of real estate. The other ½ for bringing up my daughter, Abigail. Executors—friends, Garrat Hendrickson and Hendrick Hendrickson. Witnesses—Richard Cox, Mercy Cox, John Robins. Proved Jan. 23, 1787. Lib. 29, p. 335.

**1790, July 20. Taylor, Elias,** of Deptford Township, Gloucester Co.; will of. Wife, Ann, all my goods, effects and property, to be disposed of as she sees fit. Executors—wife, Ann, and my friend, Uriah Paul. Witnesses—William Keais, Amy Wood. Proved Sept. 13, 1790.
Lib. 31, p. 469.

**1789, Oct. 9. Taylor, Elisha,** of Bridgewater, Somerset Co. Int. Adm'rs—Anne Taylor, of Bridgewater, and Joseph Taylor, of Monmouth Co. Fellowbondsman—Lewis Bond, of Bridgewater.
Lib. 31, p. 414.

**1787, Feb. 27. Taylor, George,** of Cape May Co., senior; will of. Son, George, the place where I live; also the land I bought of Amos Johnson and Salathiel Foster; which tracts join each other; all 3 tracts being in Lower Precinct; and he is to pay for the use of my granddaughter, Sophia Corgeia, £20, which is to be put to interest till she is 21. Daughter, Elizabeth Taylor, land I bought of Jacob Hand, in Middle Precinct, and ½ of the Beach below the said tract, which I bought of Jacob Spicer; also a part of woodland bought of Jacob Spicer, and being by lands of Elijah Hand, and a log house wherein Pheabe Matthews lives. Daughter, Jane Taylor, land I bought of Christopher Church, in Middle Precinct; also ½ of the Beach bought of Jacob Spicer; also some woodland bought of said Spicer. Wife, Rhodah, use of the best room in my house, and the chamber over it, and she may keep cattle, horses and sheep; also she is to have ⅛ my moveable estate. Daughter, Lydia Corgeia, £25, and in case her husband, Robert Corgeia, should bring in any account against my estate, then that amount shall be taken from the £25. Grandson, Robert Corgeia, £20, when 21. Grandson, John Corgeia, £20, when 21. Daughter, Judith Taylor, £100, when she is 21. Rest of moveable estate to my 4 daughters. Nephew, John Taylor, land in Lower Precinct, lying between Joshua Shaw and the plantation I live on, being the tract his father, John Taylor, deceased, lived upon. My wearing apparel I give to my son, George, and my son-in-law, Robert Corgeia. Executors—wife, Rhodah, my friend, Philip Cresse, and my son, George. Witnesses—J. Hinan, Ellis Hughes, Jr., Judith Hughes, Elijah Hughes. Proved Oct. 22, 1787.
1789, Jan. 27. Inventory, £1,260.12.3, made by Elijah Hughes and Ellis Hughes, Jr. Lib. 29, p. 224.

**1787, Oct. 17. Taylor, George, Sr.,** of Middletown, Monmouth Co. Int. Adm'r—William Tapscott. Fellowbondsman—Daniel Hendrickson; both of said Co. Witnesses—Tunis Vanderver and Tobias Hendrickson. Whereas, George Taylor, Sr. by a will appointed Executors, who have neglected to qualify.
1787, July 6. Renunciation by John Taylor, son of the deceased.
File No. 5969 M.

**1786, March 27. Taylor, Joseph,** of Shrewsbury Township, Monmouth Co. Int. Adm'r—Aaron Brewer. Fellowbondsman—John Richmond; both of said Co. Witness—Jonathan Forman.
1786, Feb. 23. Inventory, £58.6.6, made by John Richmond and John Stout, at the request of Mary Taylor. Lib. 28, p. 294.

**1789, Jan. 12. Taylor, Robert,** of Greenwich Township, Gloucester Co.; will of. Wife, Susannah, all real and personal estate. Executrix—wife, Susannah. Witnesses—Nathan Weatherby, Edmond Weatherby, Thomas Carpenter. Proved March 18, 1789. Lib. 30, p. 109.

**1788, July 18. Taylor, Zephaniah,** of Burlington Co. Int. Adm'x—Rachel Taylor. Fellowbondsman—Aaron Kille; both of said Co.
1788, July 17. Inventory, £85.13.9, made by Barzil Ridgway.
Lib. 30, p. 59.

**1786, March 7. Teeter, Jacob,** of Knowlton Township, Sussex Co.; will of. Wife to have the goods she wants, and rest to be sold for the benefit of my children. Wife, Cattrean, to live on the place for

8 years, after which it may be sold and money given to wife and 3 sons and 4 daughters. Eldest son, Henry, £30, when 21. Son, Conerod, £30, when 21. Son, Zachariah, £30. Rest of personal estate to my wife and sons, Henry, Conerod and Zachariah, and my daughters, Elizabeth, Cattreen, Cristean and Rachel. Executors—wife, Cattrean, Elles Teater and Jacob Main. Witnesses—Gabriel Ogden, John Seperlin, Peter Youngun. Proved May 25, 1786.
1786, May 18. Inventory, £103.2.6, made by Andrew Rose and John Dils. Lib. 28, p. 448.

**1789, Nov. 24. Tenbrock, Tierck,** of Western Precinct, Somerset Co. Int. Adm'rs—Jacob Tenbroeck and Reoloff Tenbrook. Fellowbondsman—Jacobus Lake; all of said Co.
1789, Nov. 23. Inventory, made by Jocobus Lake and Abraham Stryker. Lib. 31, p. 414.

**1790, March 13. Ten Broeck, Cornelius,** of Somerset Co., farmer; will of. Children, Cornelius, John, Peter, Abraham, Catharine, Hannah, Elizabeth and Helena, personal estate, as also real. Executors—sons, Cornelius and Abraham. Witnesses—Jacob Tenbroeck, William Hunt, Wessel Tenbroeck, John Tenbroeck, Jr. Proved Sept. 27, 1790.
1790, Sept. 6. Inventory, made by Cornelius Whitenack and Jacob Tenbroeck. Lib. 31, p. 522.

**1790, Feb. 15. Ten Brook, John,** of Hunterdon Co. Int. Adm'rs—Peter Ten Brook and Renselaer Ten Brook. Fellowbondsman—Cornelius Hoff; all of Kingwood Township, said Co.
1790, March 17. Inventory, £3,052.2.1, made by Joseph Chamberlin and Cornelius Hoff. Lib. 30, p. 317.

**1789, Aug. 12. Ten Eick, Peter,** of Hillsborough, Somerset Co. Ward. Son of Coanrod Ten Eyck, of said place, deceased. Said Ward makes choice of Jacob C. Teneyck, as his Guardian.
1789, Aug. 12. Guardian—Jacob C. Ten Eyck, of Bedminster. Fellowbondsman—John H. Schenk, of Hillsborough, both of said Co.
Lib. 31, p. 415.

**1790, May 3. Ten Eick, Peter,** of New Brunswick, Middlesex Co. Int. Adm'r—Peter Ten Eick. Fellowbondsman—Abraham Schuyler; both of said Co.
1790, June 29. Inventory, £84.12.3, made by George Hance and John Lyle. Lib. 30, p. 534.

**1786, May 24. Ten Eyck, Frederick,** of Hillsborough, Somerset Co. Int. Adm'x—Anne Ten Eyck. Fellowbondsman—Jacob Ten Eick; both of said place. Witness—Peeter Davis.
1786, April 29. Inventory, £301.6.1, made by Peeter Davis and Isaac Davis. Lib. 29, p. 195.

**1786, July 31. Terhune, Aeltje,** of Hillsborough, Somerset Co. Ward. Daughter of Roeleff Terhune, of said place, deceased. Said Ward makes choice of Gerret R. Gerritson as her Guardian.
1786, July 31. Guardian—Garrit R. Garretson, of said place. Fellowbondsmen—Rem Gerretson and Daniel Polhameus; both of said place. Witness—Peter Ditmars. Lib. 29, p. 198.

**1787, Dec. 5. Terhune, Aeltje,** of Somerset Co. Ward. Daughter of Roelef Terhune, of said Co., deceased. Said Ward makes choice of Coert Williamson, as her Guardian.
1787, Dec. 5. Guardian—Court Williamson. Fellowbondsman—Garret Terhune; both of said place. Witnesses—Joseph Cornell and Peter Nevious. Lib. 29, p. 440.

**1786, Jan. 4. Terhune, Gilyam,** of Pequanack, Morris Co. Int. Adm'x—Mary Terhune. Fellowbondsman—Henry Mandeville, Jr.; both of said place.
1785, Nov. 19. Inventory, £634.3.8, made by Henry Mandeville, Jr., and John Dumodt. Lib. 28, p. 486.

**1786, April 12. Terhune, John,** of New Brunswick, Middlesex Co.; will of. Eldest son, Albert, £5, as his birthright. Wife, Ellener, interest of £200 yearly. Son, Garret, all my lands, and he is to pay the interest to my widow. To the heirs of my daughter, Aeltje, deceased; daughter, Magdalen; daughter, Ellener; daughter, Anne; daughter, Elizabeth, £200. Executors—son, Garret, and my sons-in-law, Barnt Johnson and Simon Relect. Witnesses—Frances Costegan, John Schuurman, Isaac Slover. Proved July 19, 1786. Lib. 28, p. 316.

**1789, Dec. 10. Terhune, John,** of New Barbadoes, Bergen Co., blacksmith; will of. Wife, Ann, £100. Daughters, Mary and Elizabeth Terhune, £130, to be paid to my wife, Ann, their mother. Rest of personal and real to my granddaughter, Catharine Zabriskie, daughter to Christian A. Zabriskie, and my daughters, Mary Terhune and Elizabeth Terhune. Executors—wife, Ann, and my brother, Rolef Terhune, and Christian A. Zabriskie. Witnesses—Gabreal Haymar, Peter Vorhis, William Hammell, Jr. Proved Feb. 16, 1790.
1790, Feb. 16. Inventory, £769.8.0, made by Jacob Terhune and John Van Norden. Lib. 30, p. 547.

**1789, Dec. 9. Terril, Adam,** of Pittsgrove, Salem Co.; will of. Wife, Phebe, all estate while my widow; but, if she marries, then ⅓ to my widow, and ⅔ to my daughter, Phebe Prudence Terril and the other children. Daughter, Mary Terril, to be bound to Nethaniel Demmont, and Newcom Terril to be put to a trade. Executors—Phebe Terril and James Reeve. Witnesses—James Terril, Butler Thompson, James Bateman. Proved May 22, 1790.
1790, June 15. Inventory, £45.10.11, made by Obadiah Caruthers and Thomas Bateman. Lib. 40, p. 538.

**1789, March 24. Terril, Thomas,** of Bernerdstown, Somerset Co. Ward. Son of Thomas Terril, of said place, deceased. Said Ward makes choice of Jedidiah Swan, as his Guardian.
1789, March 24. Guardian—Jedidiah Swan, of Elizabeth Town, Essex Co. Fellowbondsman—Ezra Woodden, of Bernards Town. Lib. 31, p. 415.

**1787, June 7. Terry, Isaac,** of Monmouth Co. Int. Adm'r—David Wright. Fellowbondsman—Caleb Ivins; both of said Co.
1787, June 4. Renunciation by Mary Terry, widow of said Isaac, in favor of her relation, David Wright, Jr. Witnesses—Caleb Ivins and William Burtis.
1787, June 4. Inventory, £213.3.7, made by William Burtis and Caleb Ivins. Lib. 29, p. 340.

**1790, Aug. 20. Terry, Jeremiah,** of Upper Precinct, Cape May Co., gentleman; will of. Wife, Elizabeth, ⅓ of my estate. Son, Ashberry, my land in Jerusalem Neck, which was bought of Hezekiah Weaver, and by him of Willets. To the child not yet born, ½ of my plantation. My eldest sister, Phebe Boyd, and her 3 children, to have a home with my wife. Executors—wife, Elizabeth, and Richard Townsend. Witnesses—Enoch Hughes, Nathan Penington, Christopher Stafford. Proved Sept. 23, 1790.
1790, Sept. 23. Inventory, £156.0.6, made by Parmenas Corson and Eli Townsend. Lib. 32, p. 103.

**1790, Feb. 13. Teunison, Sarah,** of Bridgewater, Somerset Co.; will of. My sons and daughters to have an equal share in a legacy bequeathed to me by my father; my children are Cornelius, Dirck, Denis, Mary, Sarah and Anne. They are to have the residue. Executor— John Sebring. Witnesses—Samuel Bishop, Albert Bulmore, Daniel Castner. Proved March 29, 1790. Lib. 31, p. 520.

**1789, March 7. Thackray, Jacob,** of Lower Penns Neck, Salem Co.; will of. Brother, Joseph, my apparel. To the child yet to be born, all estate, when it is of age. Wife, Margaret, the legacy left her by her father, and in the hands of Mark Thackray. Executors— Mark Thackray, of Gloucester Co., and my brother, Joseph. Witnesses—John Tuft, Jesse Newark. Proved Aug. 29, 1789.
Lib. 40, p. 539.

**1790, Dec. 28. Thackrey, Mark,** of Newton Township, Gloucester Co. Int. Adm'x—Elizabeth Thackrey. Fellowbondsmen—James Sloan and Isaac Thackray; all of said Co.
1791, Jan. 3. Inventory, £238.0.11, made by Samuel Eastlack and James Sloan. Lib. 31, p. 481.

**1786, Dec. 25. Tharp (Thorp), Jonathan,** of Woodbridge Township, Middlesex Co. Inventory, £90.19.3. File No. 7063 L.

**1790, June 3. Thatcher, Jeremiah,** of Kingwood, Hunterdon Co.; will of. Wife, Nancy, use of homestead, except 50 acres where Doctor George Cambel lives; but my Executors are to dispose of the profits of the land to support my daughter, Rachel Cambel or my wife, Nancy, or my daughter, Nancy Everitt. Moveable estate and land in Sussex Co. to be sold, and the money to be let to my children, Daniel, Mary, Grace, Nancy and Rebeka. My Executors are to take out a deed for the land my son, Edward Thatcher, lived lately on in Pennsylvania. Edward's wife to live on the land and educate Edward's children; but, if my son, Edward, is alive and should return, I give the land to him. Executors—sons-in-law, Richard Opdike and Job Thatcher. Witnesses—Machal Stack, Jan Barkeloo, James Vannetter. Proved Sept. 4, 1790.
1790, Aug. 13. Inventory, £495.18.6, made by Elijah Allen and Hezekiah Waterhouse. Lib. 30, p. 292.

**1789, March 28. Thatcher, Thomas,** of Greenage Township, Sussex Co.; will of. Eldest son, Thomas, the rents of 120 acres of land which Samuel Sempleton and Peter Petty live on; and to him forever. Second son, Samuel, 200 acres where William Willis lives. Son, Elisha, 200 acres that are also rented. Daughter, Hannah, 110 acres joining Elisha's land. Daughter, Clorenda, 100 acres where John Smith lives. I did give my daughter, Susannah, 104 acres. Daughter, Elizabeth, the plantation that was surveyed to her. Youngest daughters, Sarah, Abigail and Rebecca, £300 when they are 21. Wife, Susannah, the profits of Elisha's land until he is 21. Executors—wife, Susannah, and my sons, Thomas and Samuel. Witnesses—Peter Pettey, Philip Wolever, Elias Jones. Proved May 21, 1789.

1789, May 19. Inventory, £66.3.0, made by Peter Pettey and Philip Woolever. Lib. 30, p. 196.

**1789, March 21. Thomas, Edward,** of Elizabeth Town, Essex Co.; will of. That lot at the Landing, which was released to me by son, Edmund D., is to be sold. "To my youngest, George Cummins," £100. To my wife, a wench, who lives with my daughter, Mrs. Ruecastle; also a silver tankard, which I bought at her father's vendue; also £200 in goods. Sons and daughters, rest of personal estate; except my daughter, Phebe, wife of Mr. Roucastle, and my son, George Cummins Thomas. Daughters, Margaret, Sally and Elizabeth, use of a room. Wife to have the use of the house and lot which was given me by my mother. Son, Robinson Thomas, the land which lies between the two lots I bought of Barnaby Shute, and his wife, Mary Ann; also ½ of my mountain lot; also ½ of my salt meadow; also ¼ of ¹⁄₂₀ part of a right in Lamaton purchase, which was given to me by my father-in-law, Ephraim Terrill; also the house, lot and dock, where my father and mother formerly lived. Son, Henry G. Thomas, the rest of land south of land of Robinson; also ½ the mountain lot, and ½ the salt meadow. Son, George Cummins Thomas, house and lot where I live; also the meadow which I bought of John Ramsden and John Price, on south off Oyster Creek. Daughter, Phebe Ruecastle, lot which I bought of Robert Ogden, Jr., and Matthias Ogden; but, if she die without heirs, then to my sons, Robinson, Henry and George. Daughters, Margaret, Sarah and Elizabeth Jelf, the 12 acres which I bought of George Badgley; also the 3½ acres I bought of Aaron Hetfield, Jr. Executors—my wife, my son, Robinson, and my son-in-law, Job Hains. Witnesses—Matthias Williamson, Benjamin Williamson, Isaac H. Williamson.

Lib. 36, p. 10.

(The above will is a copy, and was not proved.)

**1787, Oct. 25. Thomas, William,** of Mount Holly, Burlington Co., mason; will of. Friend, Elizabeth Cogehill, £10. Friend, John Stackhouse, some apparel. Friend, Samuel Clark, Sr., £5. Friend, Samuel Spragg, £5. To St. Andrews Church in Mount Holly, rest of estate. Executors—friends, John Clark, Sr., and Joseph Bennett. Witnesses—Joseph Brumley, John Crooks, Samuel Clark, Jr. Proved May 5, 1788.

1788, April 15. Inventory, £19.6.0, made by Peter Shiras and Joseph Brumley. Lib. 30, p. 8.

**1788, May 13. Thompson, Alexander,** of Amwell, Hunterdon Co. Int. Adm'r—Joshua Corshon. Fellowbondsman—John Singer; both of said Co. Witness—Richard Throckmorton, Surrogate.

1788, May 12. Renunciation by Catherine Thompson, widow of Alexander. Witness—John Brooks.

1789, Jan. 31. Inventory, £161.16.3, made by Nathaniel Tobin and **Francis Witt.** Lib. 31, p. 146.

CALENDAR OF WILLS—1786-1790         227

(No date.) **Thompson, Benjamin,** of Connecticut Farms, Essex Co.; will of. Wife, Esther, all that she brought to me. My wife appears to be pregnant, and I give to that heir my real estate, when it is 21; but, if said heir should die, then I give ½ to Moses Thompson (the third), son of my brother, Moses, deceased, and, if he should reform, then the other ½; he paying to his sisters, Phebe Wade, wife of Caleb, £25; to Abigail Lum, wife of Stephen, £25; to Rhoda Smith, wife of Stephen, £25, and to the children of Hannah Townly, deceased, wife of Charles, £25. To the Parish of Connecticut Farms, £20. Executors—friends, David Crane and Jonas Wade. Witnesses—Nehemiah Ball, Isaac Wade, Noah Wade. Proved June 19, 1786.
1786, June 19. Inventory, £76.3.6, made by Capt. Matthias Potter and Cornelius Williams.                                    Lib. 28, p. 380.

**1788, March 7. Thompson, Daniel, Jr.,** of Essex Co. Int. Adm'r—Daniel Thompson. Fellowbondsman—Thomas Thomson; both of said Co.                                                       Lib. 31, p. 244.

**1789, May 6. Thompson, James,** of Bernards Town, Somerset Co., yeoman; will of. Brother, Alexander Thompson, 10 shillings. Stepfather Isaiah Price, money from sale of livestock. Sisters, Mary Price and Sarah Price, residue. Executors—friends, Nathaniel Ayers and David Triphagen. Witnesses—Thomas Burgie, Thomas Kirkpatrick, John Nevill. Proved Nov. 21, 1789.
1789, June 11. Renunciation by Nathaniel Ayers and David Traphagen.
1789, Nov. 21. Adm'r—Isaiah Price. Fellowbondsman—Thomas Burgie; both of said place.
1789, Sept. 22. Inventory, made by Thomas Burgie and John Nevill.                                                        Lib. 31, p. 412.

**1786, Feb. 6. Thompson, Moses,** lately of Island of St. Croix, in West Indies, but now of Woodbridge Township, Middlesex Co.; will of. Kinsman, Thompson Steele, my gold watch. Friend, Isaac Cotheal, negro Harry, for his care of me in my illness. Friends and kinsfolks, James Thompson, son of my brother, Alexander, deceased; Moses Thompson, son of my nephew, Alexander Thompson; Thompson Martin and Rachel Martin, children of Samuel Martin, the residue. Executors—friends, Isaac Cotheal and John Ross. Witnesses—Crowell Evens, James Ross, Jr. Proved June 15, 1789.       Lib. 31, p. 387.

**1786, May 19. Thompson, Moses,** of Connecticut Farms, Elizabeth Town, Essex Co., weaver; will of. Wife, Dorcas, various household goods. Lands to be sold, and money put to interest for the support of my children, Aaron, Sarah and Moses Thompson. Oldest son, Aaron, £30. Daughter, Sarah Thompson, £20. Son, Moses, £30, and my Bible. Executors—friends, Enoch Miller and Charles Townly. Witnesses—Jonathan Thompson, Henry Lyon, Samuel Woodruff. Proved June 19, 1786.
1786, June 24. Inventory, £36.7.3, made by Joseph Tucker, Jr., and Joshua Winans.                                          Lib. 28, p. 384.

**1786, June 19. Thompson, Moses,** of Essex Co. Ward. Son of Moses Thompson, of said Co., deceased. Said Ward, being out of wardship of Benjamin Thompson, and having real and personal estate of £100, makes choice of Stephen Crane as his Guardian.

1786, June 19. Guardian—Stephen Crane. Fellowbondsman—Enoch Miller; both of said Co. Lib. 28, p. 428.

**1790, May 21. Thomson, Charles,** of Greenwich Township, Gloucester Co., yeoman; will of. Sons, John, Thomas, Joseph and Isaac, all my estate. Real and personal estate to be put to interest, and children brought up and given schooling. Executors—father, Thomas, and brother, Isaac. Witnesses—William Hooff, Abishai Chattin, Philip Ford. Proved June 16, 1790.
1790, June 14. Inventory, £2.8.8, made by Samuel Mickle and David Brown. Lib. 31, p. 466.

**1790, July 8. Thomson, George,** of New Brunswick, Middlesex Co. Int. Adm'r—David Williamson. Fellowbondsman—James Johnston; both of said Co.
1790, July 8. Inventory, £103.9.0, made by Jonathan Combs and James Johnston. Lib. 30, p. 535.

**1787, May 15. Thorn, Benjamin,** of Chesterfield Township, Burlington Co. Int. Adm'r—John Thorn, son of Benjamin. Fellowbondsman—John Thorn, Sr.; both of said place.
1787, March 8. Inventory, £73.11.6, made by Isaiah Robins and Nathan Middleton. Lib. 29, p. 73.

**1786, Jan. 2. Thorn, Thomas,** of Nottingham, Burlington Co.; will of. Nephew, Charles Thorn, £5. Nephew, Ezekiel Wright, 21 acres off the west end of the land I bought of David Hendrickson, and £150. To Joseph Thorn, son of my brother, William, the farm I bought of my brother, Joseph, and the rest of the above named tract, containing in the whole about 60 acres. Nephew, John Wright, £50. Niece, Jemima Bullock, £150. Brother, William's granddaughter, Ann Barber, £20. Nephew, Neal Curry, £20. To Isaac Thorn, son of said Joseph, £20. To Jemima Thorn, daughter of said Joseph, £10. Executors—brother-in-law, Joseph Bullock and John Wright. Witnesses—Samuel Middleton, Jacob Middleton, Amos Wright. Proved June 30, 1787.
1787, June 29. Inventory, £1,054.11.9, made by Samuel Middleton and Jacob Middleton. Lib. 29, p. 38.

**1787, Nov. 26. Thorp, Jonathan,** of Woodbridge, Middlesex Co. Int. Adm'r—James Bonney. Fellowbondsman—Peter Lott; both of said Co.
1786, Feb. 25. Inventory. Lib. 29, p. 365.

**1786, Oct. 10. Thurston, Benjamin,** of Middlesex Co. Int. Adm'r—James Bonney. Fellowbondsman—Samuel Force; both of said Co. Witness—William Hyer, Jr. Lib. 28, p. 338.

**1786, April 15. Thurston, David,** of Elizabeth Borough, Essex Co.; will of. Wife, Mary, the land where I live, and 2 acres near Westfield, joining lands of Benjamin Williams, which I bought of Col. Jacob Crane. Daughter, Hannah Thurston, all her late mother's apparel, and £17 in notes which are signed by Jeremiah Oliver, when she is 18. Executors—wife, Mary, and my brother, Benjamin Thurston. Witnesses—John Craig, William Cossen, Cornelius Roberts.
1786, April 20. Codicil. To John Morris, my wife's son, a colt. Witnesses—Benjamin Haviland, Cornelius Roberts. Proved April 28, 1786. Lib. 28, p. 375.

....., Oct. 4. **Tice, Christeon,** of Franklin Township, Bergen Co.; will of. My eldest brother's son, Henry Tice, £4. To Lane Ward, my eldest sister, Margaret Dill, Christeen Robison, Anne Slott, Mary Allen, my sisters, to each £4. To my cousin or my sister, Margaret Dill's son, Philip Reddock, £4. Brothers, John Tice and Dederick Tice, all real and rest of personal estate. Brother-in-law, John Allen, the interest of a bond, due me from him. Executors—brother, Dederick Tice, and my brother's, John Tice's son, John. Witnesses—Charles Moncrief, Isaac Williams, Garret Haulenbeek. Proved Dec. 12, 1788.
1788, Dec. 10. Inventory, £78.7.9, made by John Hogan and Thomas Mills. Lib. 31, p. 247.

**1787, May 31. Tichenor, David,** of Newark, Essex Co., mason; will of. Son, John, £40. Son, Jabez, £20. Son, Zenus, £60. Son, David, £60, when he is 21. Daughter, Mary, £20. Daughter, Hannah, £15. Daughter, Susanna, £40. Son, Caleb, rest of moveable and real estate. Executors—sons, John and Caleb. Witnesses—Thomas Williams, Matthias Pierson. Proved Aug. 28, 1788. Lib. 38, p. 92.

**1786, June 7. Tindall, Thomas,** of Maidenhead Township, Hunterdon Co. Int. Adm'x—Mary Tindall. Fellowbondsman—William Tindall; both of said Co.
1786, June 5. Inventory, £184.10.8, made by John Phillips and Gershom Lee. Lib. 28, p. 246.

**1786, June 10. Titus, Richard,** of Salem Co. Ward. Son of Philip Titus, of said Co., deceased. Said Ward makes choice of Ebenezer Lummis as his Guardian.
1786, June 10. Guardian—Ebenezer Lummis, yeoman. Fellowbondsmen—Ezekiel Foster and Ephraim Foster; all of Deerfield, said Co. Lib. 28, p. 183.

**1790, Jan. 2. Titus, Samuel,** of Cumberland Co. Int. Adm'x—Abigail Titus, of said Co. File No. 6181 F.

**1787, March 27. Todd, Isaac,** of Hunterdon Co. Ward. Son of Andrew Todd, of said Co., deceased. Said Ward makes choice of his mother, Sarah Todd, as his Guardian.
1787, March 27. Guardian—Sarah Todd. Fellowbondsman—Revd. John Hanna; both of said Co. Lib. 29, p. 298.

**1790, April 12. Todd, James,** of Hardwick, Sussex Co.; will of. Wife, Elizabeth, profits of plantation to bring up my 2 children. Son, James, the farm I live on of 150 acres, when he is 21. Daughter, Jane, £100, when 18. Executor—friend, George Armstrong. Witnesses—Uriah Dildine, Abraham Dildine, Dennis Stull. Proved June 17, 1790.
1790, June 3. Inventory, £287.3.3, made by Uriah Dildine and Isaac Lanning. Lib. 30, p. 432.

**1788, March 12. Tomlinson, Ann,** of Waterford Township, Gloucester Co., widow; will of. Brother, Samuel Burrough, a book. Nieces, Hannah Roberts, Ann Pine and Mary Pine, apparel. Niece, Ann Thorne, gold sleeve buttons. Nephews, Isaac and Samuel Pine, £100 each, when 21. Nieces, Ann and Mary Pine, £100 each, when 18. Niece, Rachel Davis, silver tankard. Niece, Ann Cooper, daughter of

Sarah Cooper, silver can. Niece, Sarah Cooper, £100. Niece, Hannah Roberts, £50. Niece, Ann Thorne, £50. Niece, Beulah Haines, £50, when 18; but, if she die, then to her brothers, Samuel, Jacob and Abel. Nieces, Mary and Abigail Thorne, £10 each, when 18. Nephews, Samuel, Jacob and Abel Haines, £10 each, when 21. To the Preparative Meeting of Friends, at Haddonfield, £20. Residue to nieces, Hannah Roberts, Ann Thorne, Mary Thorne, Abigail Thorne, Beulah Haines, Ann Pine and Mary Pine. Executors—brother, Samuel Burrough and my brother-in-law, Thomas Thorne. Witnesses—John Parham, Thomas Redman.

1789, March 6. Codicil. Niece, Beulah Haines, to have an equal share of apparel. Witnesses—Mary Dubree, Joseph Stokes. Proved March 31, 1789.

1789, March 23. Inventory, £1,270.12.2, made by Joseph Champion and Joseph Stokes. Lib. 30, p. 134.

**1789, July 5. Tomlinson, Catherine,** of Newton Township, Gloucester Co., widow; will of. Son, John Garner, and my daughter, Ann Olden, my apparel and household goods. Grandsons, Joseph, Ephraim and James, sons of my son, James Garner, deceased, the residue. Executors—grandsons, Joseph, Ephraim and James Garner. Witnesses—Thomas Githens, John Parhem, Thomas Redman. Proved Jan. 4, 1790.

1790, Jan. 4. Inventory, £306.5.10, made by Thomas Redman and John T. Glover. Lib. 31, p. 468.

**1788, May 8. Tomlinson, Charles and Francis,** of Hunterdon Co. Wards. Sons of Francis Tomlinson, of said Co., deceased. Said Wards make choice of Henry Waterhouse as their Guardian. They are joined in their petition with Joseph Hart and William Tomlinson, and say that their mother before her death spoke of said Henry Waterhouse as a proper person. And we request that Luther Opdyke, act no longer as our Guardian, as he became such in an improper manner.

1788, May 8. Guardian—Henry Waterhouse. Fellowbondsman—Joseph Hart. Witness—William Tomlinson. Lib. 31, p. 146.

**1788, Feb. 6. Tomlinson, Francis, Dinah and Sarah,** of Kingwood Township, Hunterdon Co. Wards. Children of Francis Tomlinson, of said place, deceased. Whereas, the widow and her son administered on the estate, and the widow since died, and left the said children and estate in the hands of one administrator. We, the legatees, pray that Luther Opdycke may be appointed Guardian. Signed, Mary Shearman, Rebeckah Tomlinson and Elizabeth Snyder.

1788, Feb. 7. Guardian—Luther Opdycke. Fellowbondsman—Jonathan Woolverton; both of said Co. Witnesses—Thomas Shearman and Nicholas Hendrickson.

1788, Feb. 7. Petition of Luther Opdycke, Guardian of Francis, Dinah and Sarah Tomlinson, and also Thomas Shearman, one of the heirs of the estate, praying that the shares may be divided, of lands left by Francis Tomlinson, deceased.

1788, May 6. Petition of us, the legatees and Guardian of the orphans of Francis Tomlinson, deceased; showing that Jeremiah Thatcher, Jonathan Woolverton and Absalom Runyan were appointed to divide the lands among the legatees and orphans, but Absalom Runyan refused to appear; therefore we desire another person to take his place. Signed, Luther Opdycke, Thomas Shearman and Henry Snyder.

CALENDAR OF WILLS—1786-1790        231

1789, May 15. Account of Luther Opdycke, Guardian of Francis, son of Francis and Dinah Tomlinson. Received from William Tomlinson, surviving Adm'r, £64.15.8.
1796, Feb. 4. Account by Luther Opdycke, Guardian of Dinah Tomlinson. Received ⅙ part of the personal estate of Francis Tomlinson, deducting the widow's ⅛, £29.2.4. Lib. 31, p. 146.

**1787, Dec. 24. Tomlinson, Thomas,** of Hunterdon Co. Ward. Son of Francis Tomlinson, of said Co., deceased. Said Ward makes choice of Luther Opdycke as his Guardian.
1787, Dec. 24. Guardian—Luther Opdycke, yeoman. Fellowbondsman—Thomas Shearman; both of said Co.
1792, Feb. 6. Account by Guardian. Received ⅙ part of the personal estate of Dinah Tomlinson, £29.2.4. Lib. 29, p. 298.

**1789, Feb. 11. Tomson, James,** of Alexandria, Hunterdon Co. Int. Adm'r—John Tomson. Fellowbondsman—Joseph Chamberlin; both of said place.
1789, Feb. 11. Renunciation by Yanna Tomson, widow of James. Witnesses—Lefferd Tomson and Mary Alexander.
1789, April 10. Inventory, £297.1.1, made by Joseph Chamberlin and Elijah Allen.
1800, Feb. Citation to John Tomson, Sr., to render an account unto Joseph Moore and Joanna, his wife, late Joanna Tomson.
Lib. 32, p. 54.

**1787, April 24. Tomson, Samuel,** of Monmouth Co. Int. Adm'r—Jacob Preston. Fellowbondsman—Richard Cox; both of said Co.
1787, April 3. Inventory, £38.9.5, made by Richard Cox and Nathaniel Britton. Lib. 29, p. 338.

**1786, May 19. Tonkin, Mary,** of Springfield Township, Burlington Co.; will of, being aged and infirm. Daughter, Bathsheba Clayton, £100. Daughter, Susannah Taylor, £100. Daughter, Mary Carpenter, £100. Daughter, Martha Tallman, £100. To each of my grandchildren, £5. Granddaughter, Mary Tonkin, daughter of my son, John Tonkin, a bed. Granddaughter, Harriett Clayton, case of drawers. Granddaughter, Mary Tonkin, daughter of my son, Israel Tonkin, the bed in her father's possession. To St. Mary's Church in Burlington, £10. Executor—John Tonkin, my son. Witnesses—John Ridgway, Israel Tonkin, Daniel Ellis. Proved Oct. 31, 1788.
1788, Oct. 31. Inventory, £681.11.8, made by David Ridgway and John Ridgway. Lib. 29, p. 548.

**1787, Nov. 28. Toomey, Henery, Sr.** Inventory, £45.4.10, made by Richard Burdge and Jacob Hart. File No. 6617 G.

**1789, June 29. Townsend, Henry Young,** of Cape May Co. Int. Adm'rs—Richard Townsend and Reuben Townsend. Fellowbondsman—Eli Townsend; all of Upper Precinct, said Co. Witnesses—Sarah Hand and Mary Harris.
1790, June 24. Inventory, £481.19.8, made by Eli Townsend and Parmenas Corson. "Debt due from the estate of Tobitha Willits, as allowed on the settlement." Lib. 31, p. 373.

**1786, May 18. Townsend, Joshua,** of Cape May Co. Int. Adm'rs—John Townsend and Jacocks Swain. Fellowbondsman—Richard Townsend; all of said Co., gentlemen. Witnesses—Henry Y. Townsend and Eli Townsend.
Lib. 38, p. 79.

**1788, Feb. 28. Townsend, Silvanus,** of Cape May Co.; will of. To be buried near my wife, in Friends' burying ground in Upper Precinct. Son-in-law, William Hawkins, my right in a note of £28 due to me from Drusilla Townsend, of Currytuck Co., North Carolina. To Augustus Hawkins and his brother, Immanuel, £92, which is due me from a statement of accounts from John Townsend, late husband to the said Drusilla. My only child, Rachel, the residue of estate. Executors—son-in-law, William Hawkins, and my friend, Richard Townsend. Witnesses—Nathan Cresse, Jeremiah Sayre, Henry Y. Townsend, William Thomas. Proved March 29, 1788.

1788, March 28. Inventory, £150.18.9, made by Henry Y. Townsend and Nathan Cresse.
Lib. 31, p. 89.

**1790, May 15. Towser, Richard,** of Upper Precinct, Cape May Co. Int. Adm'x—Hannah Towser. Fellowbondsman—John Goff; both of said place. Witnesses—Daniel Stites and Sarah Hand, Jr.

1790, May 14. Inventory, £59.18.1, made by John Goff and Moses Williams.
Lib. 32, p. 105.

**1787, April 10. Toy, James,** of Chester Township, Burlington Co., yeoman; will of. Son, James, my plantation, and he is to pay to my son, Elijah, when he is 21, £25; but, if he die, then to be paid to his brothers, Caleb, Andrew and Peter. Daughter, Patience, £5. Son, Elias, £5. Daughter, Rebeckah Toy, £5. Sons, Caleb, Andrew and Peter, moveable estate. Grandson, William Toy, one and ½ acres where his father, Richard Toy, died. Executors—sons, Caleb, Andrew and Peter. Witnesses—Grace Fish, William Brown, Joseph Morgan, Jr. Proved July 30, 1787.

1787, June 18. Inventory, £100.4.0, made by Joseph Morgan, Jr., and Hezekiah Toy.
Lib. 29, p. 59.

**1789, Nov. 10. Treadway, Henry,** of Deptford Township, Gloucester Co., yeoman; will of. Wife, Ann, £18 yearly and some goods. I give one acre of land, bounding on the line of the plantation late William Wood's and the road leading to Woodbury, to include the graves now fenced, for the only one of a Burying Ground for all my descendents. Sons, Henry, Nathan, John, Jessee and Matthew, my plantation, except the stated acre. Daughters, Ann Hewet and Hannah White, £35 each. Daughter, Sarah Amlin, £1, and to her children, £3 each. To my late daughter, Amy White's children, £35. To my late daughter, Azubee's son, George, £10. Executor—friend, John Hopkins. Witnesses—John Wilkins, Nathan Kinsey, William Wood. Proved April 27, 1790.

1790, April 27. Adm'r—John Tredway, of said Co. Fellowbondsman—Henry Treadway.

1790, April 26. Renunciation by John Estaugh Hopkins. Witnesses—John M. Hopkins and Zetthu Treadway.

1790, April 29. Inventory, £400.10.10, made by James Brown and John Wilkins.
Lib. 31, p. 472.

CALENDAR OF WILLS—1786-1790 233

**1786, Dec. 28. Treat, Joseph,** of Alexandria, Hunterdon Co.; will of. Eldest son, Richard Samuel Treat, ⅛ of real and personal estate. Youngest son, John Thomas Treat, ⅛. Wife, Elizabeth, ⅛. Executors—friends, John Thomson, Ebenezer Hazard, Revd. Azael Roe and Malachi Treat. Witnesses—Malachi Treat, Robert Johnston. Proved Feb. 10, 1787.
1787, Feb. 2. Inventory, of estate of Revd. Joseph Treat, £865, made by Peter Kenney, Sr., and Robert Johnston. Lib. 29, p. 269.

**1789, May 6. Trembles, Isaac,** of Bernards Town, Somerset Co. Int. Adm'rs—Samuel Downer and Nancy Trembles. Fellowbondsman—Jabez Potter; all of said Co.
1789, May 5. Inventory, £221.3.9, made by Moses McCollum and Thomas Kirkpatrick. Lib. 31, p. 414.

**1788, Aug. 28. Trembly, Renoni,** of Essex Co.; will of. Son, Benjamin, a loom. Sons, Jonathan and Abraham, a note of £28, and one of £21. Wife, Mary, residue. Executors—Mary Trembly, Jonathan Trembley and Abraham Trembley. Witnesses—David Woodruff, Isaac Martin, Ezekiel Wright. Proved Oct. 11, 1788.
1788, Oct. 10. Renunciation by Mary Trembly, the widow, and Abraham Trembly, in favor of Jonathan Trembly. Witnesses—Isaac Martin and Ezekiel Wright. Lib. 38, p. 90.

**1789, Nov. 2. Troth, Job,** of Burlington Co. Ward. Son of Isaac Troth of said Co., deceased. Said Ward, having real and personal estate, makes choice of Benjamin Pine as his Guardian.
1789, Nov. 2. Guardian—Benjamin Pine. Fellowbondsman—Samuel Leeds; both of Evesham Township, said Co. Lib. 31, p. 322.

**1788, April 7. Trowbridge, Javish,** of Hanover, Morris Co. Ward. Son of Shubel Trowbridge, of said place, deceased. Said Ward, being out of wardship of Mary Williams, makes choice of Joseph Beers as his Guardian.
1788, April 7. Guardian—Joseph Beers, of Morristown, said Co. Fellowbondsman—Absalom Trowbridge, of said Co. Witness—John Dalrimple. Lib. 31, p. 201.

**1787, April 2. Tucker, Elizabeth,** of Trenton, Hunterdon Co., wife of Samuel Tucker, Esq.; will of. To be buried at the old Church. My Aunt, Elizabeth Gould, late of Exeter, England, in her will, dated Aug. 23, 1766, devised to me ⅛ of the residuary of her estate in the hands of her Executor, William Hawker, Esq., to be at my disposal in my lifetime or at my death, and ⅓ of her plate; which I give to my nieces, Elizabeth Gould White and Sarah Phillips Margatroyd and their children, to them, Elizabeth Gould White, Frances White, John Gould White, Mary White, Elizabeth Gould White, Jr., Sarah P. Margatroyd, Samuel Margatroyd, Daniel Margatroyd, Elizabeth Gould Margatroyd and Mary Margatroyd. Executors—David White, Esq., of Island of Jamaica and Thomas Margatroyd, merchant of Philadelphia. Witnesses—Lydia Hankinson, Samuel Tucker, Sarah Bellerjeau. Proved Oct. 22, 1787. Lib. 29, p. 257.

**1788, Oct. 9. Tucker, Samuel,** of Trenton, Hunterdon Co., Esq.; will of. I give my brick house in which I live, and the lot of land I bought of Joseph DeCow, and the garden lots bought of Moore

Furman, Sheriff, and the Assignees of Ephraim and Samuel Bonham, the Iron Works lot, of 5 and ½ acres, and a lot adjoining which I bought from the estate of Captain John Anderson, to my brother, William Tucker, until his son, Ellit, is 21. I give my house and lot in King Street, which I hold as heir-at-law to my father, with the orchard which I bought of my sister, Charity Britton, of 4 acres, to my grandnephew, Samuel Tucker Bellerjeau, but my nephew, Samuel Bellerjeau, is to possess the house and orchard until his son, Samuel, my grandnephew, is 21. I give my house and lot in Morristown, Morris Co., to my nephew, Samuel Tucker, son of my brother, Phillip. Brother, William Tucker, my plantation in Somerset Co., where Nicholas Goulder lately lived, of 172 acres. Brothers-in-law, Samuel and Nathaniel Leonard, my other plantation in Somerset Co., now in possession of Joshua Anderson, on the road leading from Pennington to Rocky Hill, and bounded by the College, heirs of Richard Stockton, Dr. John Witherspoon and John Hedger, of 180 acres. Nieces, Elizabeth Gould White and Sarah Phillips Margatroyd, my blacksmith shop and lot on corner of Queens Street and Water Street, and £400 to each. Sister, Charity Britton, £200. Niece, Jane Jenkins, interest of £200 yearly, and, at her death, to pay the £200 to my grandnephews and nieces, children of Samuel Bellerjeau. Nephews, Samuel Bellerjeau, Joseph Britton, William Tucker, Jr., Ellit Tucker and my niece, Mary Marshett, brother and sisters children, £200 each. Nephews, Joseph Tucker, Richard Tucker, George Tucker, and my niece, Elizabeth Tucker, children of my brothers, George and Phillips Tucker, £100 each. Grandniece, Sarah Bellerjeau, £300. Grandniece, Elizabeth Gould White, £100, to be paid to her by her father, David White, when 21. Grandniece, Hannah Bellerjeau, £100. Grandnephew, Samuel Tucker Bellerjeau, £100. To the Presbyterian Church of Trenton and Lamberton, £50. To the Episcopal Church in Trenton, £30. Several negros to have their freedom. A deed is to be made to Doctor John Witherspoon for the plantation sold to Elias Woodruff, of 220 acres. I have agreed to sell a lot of land in Sussex Co., of 9 acres, to Solomon Keasby, for which he is to have a deed. The orchard which I bought from the Executors of David Pinkerton I give to my nephew, Samuel Bellerjeau. My lot between said orchard and a lot of George Davis to my nephews, William Tucker and Ellit Tucker, children of my brother, William. My new lot, which I bought of Isaiah Yard, to my grandnephew, John Bellerjeau. The meadow which I bought of Joseph Peace to my nephews, Joseph Tucker and Richard Tucker. Grandniece, Sarah Bellerjeau, some household goods and plate. Nephew, Isaac Britton, the money he owes me. Brother, William, my apparel. Land in Alexandria, Hunterdon Co., laying in 2 farms, of about 527 acres, to be sold. To my aunt, Mary Phillis, and to my cousin, Mary Phellps, of Boston, and my friend, John Lawrence, and friend, John Dunnis, 2 guineas each. Grandniece, Hannah Bellerjeau, a bed. Grandniece, Sarah Bellerjeau, silver spoons. I appoint my friends, Abraham Hunt and Benjamin Smith, Trustees of this will, and my Executors are to account to them. Executors—brother, William, my nephew, James Marshett, and nephew, Thomas Margatroyd, merchant of Philadelphia. Witnesses—Samuel R. Stewart, Cornelius P. Wyckoff, Eseck Howell.

1789, Jan. 12. Codicil. Benjamin Smith is to be an Executor. To grandniece, Sarah Bellerjeau, a pair of silver candlesticks. Niece, Mary Marshett, a pair of silver plated candlesticks. To David White,

and Elizabeth, his wife, a silver pot. To Samuel Leonard my family Bible, to whose father it formerly belonged. Witnesses—John Lawrence, Thomas Lowrey, Aaron D. Woodruff. Proved Jan. 24, 1789.
1789, Jan. 20. Inventory, £5,977.15.1, made by Capt. John Douglass and William Tindall. Lib. 31, p. 6.

**1789, Jan. 29. Tucker, Samuel,** of Trenton, Hunterdon Co. Ward. Nephew of Samuel Tucker, of said place, deceased. Said Ward makes choice of his brother, George Tucker, as his Guardian.
1789, Jan. 29. Guardian—George Tucker, of Morris Co. Fellowbondsman—William Tucker, of said Trenton. Lib. 32, p. 57.

**1789, Sept. 7. Tucker, William,** of Trenton, Hunterdon Co., cordwainer; will of. Wife, Mercy, the interest of my money. Son, William, all my tools, when he is 21. Son, Ellet, the stock, buttons and buckles, which were given to me by the will of my brother, Samuel. Son, William, the house and lot where I live, that I bought of Joseph Higbee; also lot I bought of Assignees of Andrew Reed, of 8 acres; also lot I bought of Stacy Potts, of 3 acres. Son, Ellet, land I bought of Stacy Potts, that joins Nathan Beakes and Hezekiah Howell, of 6 acres. Daughter, Mary Machett, farm in Somerset Co., that was given to me by the will of my brother, Samuel, of 170 acres. Sons, William and Ellet, meadow which I bought of Charles Axford, of 15 acres. Executors—wife, Mercy, and friends, Ellet Howell and Joseph Britton, of Trenton. Witnesses—Benjamin Woolsey, Charles Tomkins, Joseph Phillips, Jr.
1789, Nov. 30. Codicil. I give my negro man to my wife. Witnesses—William Tindall, Charles Tomkins, Aaron Howell. Proved Feb. 8, 1790.
1790, Jan. 25. Inventory, £315.5.4, made by William Tindall and William Smith. Lib. 30, p. 303.

**1787, Nov. 27. Tumey, Henry,** of Monmouth Co. Int. Adm'r—James Newill. Fellowbondsman—Hugh Newill; both of said Co.
1787, April 4. Renunciation by Samuel Tumey and Jemima Tumey, children of said Henry. Witnesses—Daniel Jagors and Prudence Patan. Lib. 29, p. 340.

**1787, Nov. 14. Tunison, Cornelius I.,** of Bridgewater, Somerset Co. Int. Adm'r—Aaron Lane, of Essex Co. Fellowbondsman—Dennis V. Duyn, of Somerset Co. Lib. 29, p. 439.

**1788, Feb. 18. Turner, Elijah,** of Maple Town, Albany Co., New York. Int. Adm'r—William Cheney, during the absence of Ebenezer Arnold, and Esther, his wife, late Esther Turner. Fellowbondsman—John Hollinshead, of Greenwich, Cumberland Co., farmer.
Lib. 30, p. 57.

**1787, May 5. Tuttle, John,** of Hunterdon Co., Soldier. Int. Adm'r—Nathaniel Leonard. Fellowbondsman—George Beatty; both of said Co. Witness—John Polhemus.
1787, Dec. 29. Inventory, £25.6.8, made by John Polhemus and William Tindall. John Tuttle was a private in the Jersey Brigade, and had 2 notes given for the depreciation of pay. Lib. 20, p. 294.

**1790, Sept. 30. Ulrich, Philip,** of Salem Co. Int. Adm'r—Thomas Britton, of Philadelphia. Fellowbondsmen—John Redman and William Parrot; both of Salem, Salem Co. Whereas, Philip Ulrich, died intestate, and Thomas Salter, of Philadelphia, was made Adm'r, who has also died, and left goods unadministered.
1787, Nov. 10. Inventory, £4,306.3.0, made by Thomas Norris and R. Whitehead, of the goods in the hands of Thomas Salter, at Philadelphia. Lib. 31, p. 505.

**1786, Jan. 3. Urion, Thomas,** of Woolwich Township, Gloucester Co. Int. Adm'x—Mary Urion. Fellowbondsman—Aquilah Barber; both of said place.
1785, Dec. 28. Inventory, £40.13.6, made by Aquilah Barber and Joseph Shute. Lib. 28, p. 120.

**1786, April 10. Van Alst, Aeltje,** of Hillsborough Township, Somerset Co. Int. Adm'r—Abraham Brokaw. Fellowbondsman—Isaac Brocaw; both of said place.
1786, May 9. Inventory, £243.15.4, made by George Van Neste and Isaac Davis. Lib. 29, p. 195.

**1786, March 3. Van Artsdalen, Rev. Simeon,** of Reading Township, Hunterdon Co.; will of. Wife, Magdalene, all she brought, and all she made since our marriage, and £100. Son, John, my apparel and library, and real estate in Northampton Township, Bucks Co., Pa., being ¼ part of a farm belonging to my father, John, but now in possession of my brother, Garret; which ¼ I give to my son, John. If John die under age, then of his part I give ¼ to my wife, Magdalene, ¼ to my mother, Elizabeth Van Artsdalen, ¼ to my brother, Garret, and ¼ to my 2 sisters, Ariantia and Lamache Lefferts. Executors—wife, Magdalene, my brother, Garret, of Bucks Co., and cousin, John Simonson, of Somerset Co. Witnesses—Michal Demott, Reynear Smock, Abraham Vanhorn, Jr. Proved June 13, 1786.
1786, June 12. Renunciation by Magdalene Vanartsdalen, widow of Reverend Simeon Van Artsdalen. Witness—Michal Demott.
1786, June 12. Inventory, £468.7.4, made by Edward Bunn, Michal Demott and Reynear Smock. Lib. 28, p. 210.

**1790, Feb. 22. Vanatta, Peter,** of Oxford Township, Sussex Co., farmer; will of. Wife is provided for. Eldest daughter, Tonica, £3. Son, Peter, £15. Daughter, Ann, wife of Jacob Riser, £10. Daughter, Margret, £5. Son, Benjamin, £10. Daughter, Hannah, wife of Joseph Coplin, £5. Daughter, Mary, wife of Jacob Sigler, and Peter Vanatta, son of my eldest son, Samuel, my lands. Executors—Mary Sigler and Peter Vanatta. Witnesses—Isaac Lerrowe, Thomas Hayes, Margaret Hayes. Proved June 22, 1790.
1790, June 16. Inventory, £118.16.6, made by James Davison and Peter Young. Lib. 30, p. 421.

**1790, Jan. 14. Vance, John,** of Gloucester Co. Int. Adm'r—John Vandyke. Fellowbondsman—Joseph Harker; both of said Co. Witness—Franklin Davenport. Lib. 31, p. 481.

**1787, Nov. 21. Vance, Samuel,** of Salem, Salem Co.; will of. Son, James, all real estate, and some goods. Rest of personal estate to be sold, and money given to son, James, and my daughters, Mary Dickey and Elizabeth Clark. House and lot to be rented until James is 21. Executor—neighbor, Anthony Keasbey. Witnesses—William Worth, Joseph Swabey, Dennis Sayre, Ezekiel Foster, Jr. Proved Sept. 10, 1788. Lib. 31, p. 51.

**1790, March 5. Van Culin, John,** of Upper Alloways Creek Township, Salem Co.; will of. Son, John, plantation I live on, which joins Howell Smith and Tyler Scroggens, of 112 acres. Daughters, Elizabeth, and Hannah Van Culin, my share in the lands, grist and saw mill that I bought of David Evens. Moveable estate to be sold, and divided between my wife, Sarah, daughters, Elizabeth and Hannah, and son, John. Executors—daughter, Elizabeth, and William Tyler, tanner. Witnesses—John Smith, Azariah Reeves, Jacob Scoggin. Proved May 15, 1790.
1790, April 7. Inventory, £967.4.1, made by Samuel Stewart and John Smith. Lib. 31, p. 496.

**1789, Jan. 24. Van De Linde, Benjamin,** of Bergen Co., minister in the Congregations of Paramus and the Ponds; will of. Wife, Elizabeth, a lot of land in Harrington Township, at or near Saddle River Meeting House, of about 60 acres, and the rest of real and personal estate, during her life. To my only child and daughter, Adriantye, now wife of Adrian Brinkerhoof, all my estate, after death of my wife. Executors—wife, Elizabeth, and my friends, Abraham Westervelt and Albert Zabriskie. Witnesses—Jacobus Bogert, Steven Bogert, George Warren Chapman. Proved Aug. 31, 1789. Lib. 30, p. 239.

**1787, April 7. Vanderbeek, Benjamin,** of Nottingham Township, Burlington Co. Int. Adm'x—Rachel Vanderbeek. Fellowbondsman—John Curtis; both of said Co.
1787, April 4. Inventory, £130.17.1, made by Samuel Middleton and Jacob Middleton. Lib. 29, p. 77.

**1788, Jan. 19. Vanderhoof, Cornelius,** of Franklin Township, Bergen Co.; will of. Wife, Elizabeth, all real and personal while my widow. My uncle, Hessel Vanallen, is to have a good support out of my estate. My wife is to have the furniture she owned before we married. Daughter, Anne, £4. Daughters, Anne, Rachel, Elizabeth and Jaine, to have the whole estate, after wife's death, except the Dutch Bible, which Rachel is to have. Executors—Giles Mead, James S. Bogert and Peter Ward. Witnesses—Abraham Manning, Uzal Meeker, Harmanus Van Huysen. Proved April 21, 1788. Lib. 31, p. 248.

**1786, Feb. 14. Vanderipe, John,** of Freehold, Monmouth Co.; will of. Nephew, Matthias Vanderipe, Jr., personal estate. To the children of Matthias Vanderipe, Matthias, John, Marthy Vanderipe, Mary Hunsiryer, Ann Marlatte, Jane Prat, Rachel Vanderipe and Elizabeth Vandoripe, my real estate in New York and elsewhere. Brother, Matthias, has had ½ of my real estate in New York, by deed, which he is to have. My estate in New York, which I have bequeathed, is an estate which I am heir-at-law to, being an estate formerly occupied and possessed by Cornelius Van Teenhoven, a former Governor of New York State, from whose line I am descended, and my Executors are to pay to Richard Vanderipe, son of my brother, Richard, 5 shillings. Executors—brother, Matthias, and Jonathan Pease. Witnesses—Charles Axford, 3rd, James Rhea, Jonathan Rhea. Proved March 20, 1786.

**1786, March 25.** Inventory, £78.2.4, made by Jonathan Bowne and Adam Pease. Lib. 28, p. 271.

**1786, Aug. 28. Van Derveer, Henry,** of Bridgewater, Somerset Co. Ward. Son of John Van Derveer, of said place, deceased. Said Ward makes choice of Jaques Voorheese as his Guardian.
1786, Sept. 20. Guardian—Jaques Voorheese. Fellowbondsman—Abraham Van Doren; both of said Co. Lib. 29, p. 197.

**1786, Oct. 2. Vanderveer, Jacobus,** of Readington, Hunterdon Co.; will of. Son, Jacobus, the part of the plantation where I live, as far back as the brook. Wife, Famitie, to live in the house and be provided for by said son. Daughter, Catharine, a bed. The plantation I bought of Stephen Bunnel, and the rest of said farm where I live, to be sold. Personal estate to wife, Famitie, and 4 children; but the money from sale of land to wife, Famitie, daughter, Sarah Brokaw, daughter, Jane Stryker, and daughter, Catharine. My daughter, Jane Stryker, has had £100 the 15th of June, 1778. Executors—son, Jacobus, my son-in-law, Bergun Brokaw, and my son-in-law, Domenicus Stryker. Witnesses—Peter Schamp, Abraham Lane, Adam Jobs. Proved April 30, 1787.
1787, Jan. 2. Inventory, made by John Wyckoff and Peter Schamp. Lib. 29, p. 258.

**1789, May 14. Van Derveer, Jacobus, Jr.,** of Hunterdon Co. Int. Adm'r—Brogon Brocaw, of Readington, said Co. Fellowbondsman—Jacob Ten Eyk, Sr., of Bridgewater, Somerset Co.
1789, March 24. Inventory, £279.11.3, made by Peter Schamp, Jacob Ten Eyk, Sr., and Isaac Brokaw. Lib. 32, p. 54.

**1787, Aug. 9. Van Dike, Charity,** of Western Precinct, Somerset Co., widow of John; will of. Daughter, Jannitie, a negro. Daughter, Cathrin, a negro. Daughter, Elsie, a negro. Daughter, Sarah, a negro. The children who had no outsets are to have them. The portion left to me by my husband I give to my children. Son, Jacob, shall have ⅛ of the crop. Executors—son, Jacob, and my son-in-law, Hendrick Berrian. Witnesses—Catharine Van Dike, Gerardus Beekman, G. D'Camp. Proved Feb. 25, 1788.
1787, Aug. 24. Inventory, made by Henry Vandike and Thomas Skillman. "By will of Fredk Bergen, in the hands of Hendk Bergen, the sum of £150." Lib. 31, p. 170.

**1788, June 21. Vandike, Martin,** of Shrewsbury, Monmouth Co.; will of. Wife, Mary, use of all estate, and, after her death, I give to Susannah, wife of Christopher Halsted, my brass kettle. Daughter, Margaret, £1. Daughter, Patience, £3. Grandchildren, the children of my deceased daughter, Elizabeth, £3. To Mary Thorp, who lives with me, a calf. Residue to my daughters, Margaret and Patience, and my grandchildren. Executors—friends, John Polhemus and Thomas George. Witnesses—Richard Lawrence, Jesse Pater, Thomas Morford. Proved Jan. 6, 1790.
1790, Jan. 4. Inventory, £97.17.0, made by Jacob Fleming and Samuel White. Lib. 30, p. 382.

**1786, April 15. Van Dike, Roelof,** of Somerset Co., farmer; will of. Son, Henry, land which I bought of Aaron Beekman; also land I

## CALENDAR OF WILLS—1786-1790      239

bought of Christopher Beekman. Daughter, Rebeca, 10 acres from rear of land I bought of John Ver Kerk. Wife, Catherin, farm where I live, which I bought of John Ver Kerk; also land left to me by my father, John Van Dike; and, after wife's death, to be sold, and money given to my grandchildren by daughter, Rebecca, and the children of daughter, Sarah. Personal estate to be sold, and money given to son, Henry, and grandchildren by daughter, Rebecca, and children of my daughter, Sarah. Executor—son, Henry. Witnesses—Joseph Badcock, Jacob Van Dike, Jr., Gerardus Beekman. Proved Aug. 16, 1788.
1788, Aug. 11. Inventory, £1,191.6.6, made by Gerardus Beekman and Jacob Van Dike.
1800. Inventory, £266.0.3, made by Jacob Van Dike and Samuel Beekman, Jr., of all given by will of Roelof Van Dike, her husband, which remains after wife's death.    Lib. 31, p. 174.

**1788, April 30. Van Doren, William,** of Eastern Precinct, Somerset Co. Int. Adm'r—Jaques Voorheese. Fellowbondsman—Jacob Vosseller; both of said Co.
1788, June 1. Inventory, £23.1.9, made by Frederick Vanliew and Bernardus Gerritsen.    Lib. 31, p. 177.

**1790, March 5. Vandyke, Charles,** of Burlington Co. Int. Adm'r—George Anderson. Fellowbondsman—Okey Hoagland. Witness—William Newbold, Jr.    Lib. 32, p. 93.

**1786, Feb. 20. Vandyke, John,** of Shrewsbury, Monmouth Co.; will of. Wife, Sarah, real and personal estate, until my youngest child is 8 years old, when estate is to be sold, and money given to wife and my children, James, Isaac, Mary, Sarah and Elizabeth, and the child my wife is pregnant with. Executors—Daniel Hill and Joseph Stillwell. Witnesses—Elizabeth Huit, Gilbert Forster, Mary Foster. Proved July 13, 1787.
1786, May 24. Inventory, £42.1.0, made by James West and William Brinley.    Lib. 29, p. 319.

**1790, Sept. 14. Van Emburgh, Ann,** of Essex Co. Int. Adm'r—John Wandell (Wendle), of New York City. Fellowbondsman—Abraham Van Emburgh, of New Jersey.    Lib. 30, p. 360.

**1786, April 17. Van Emburgh, Simeon,** of New Barbadoes, Bergen Co., weaver; will of. Wife, Margret, all land and moveable estate, except £10 which my son, Abraham, is to have, when he comes of age. Sons, Gilbert, John and Abraham, all my lands, after death of wife. Daughter, Elizabeth, a two acre lot near Abraham Kingsland's land, except what I gave to daughter, Jane, by a deed. Executors—wife, Margrit, and my friends, John Wandel and Peter Cadmus. Witnesses—John Cadmus, Abraham Cadmus, Charles Hedenberg. Proved Oct. 11, 1786.
1786, Oct. 14. Inventory, £43.2.0, made by John Earl and Abraham Cadmus.    Lib. 29, p. 218.

**1789, March 16. Van Gieson, John,** of New Barbadoes, Bergen Co.; will of. Land to be sold, and money given to my son, Poulus, and my daughter, Rachel. Executors—John D. Romeyn and Henderik Bardon. Witnesses—James Van Blarcum, Jacobus Terhune, Aert Cuyper. Proved May 13, 1789.    Lib. 30, p. 241.

## 240 NEW JERSEY POST-REVOLUTIONARY DOCUMENTS

**1786, Sept. 22. Van Horne, John,** of Communipaw, Bergen Co., husbandman; will of. Wife, Balicah, all real and personal estate, while my widow. Son, John, a silver tankard, as his birthright. Son, John 1/3 of incomes of my farms, and the other 2/3 to be for the use of my wife. Son, Garret, to have 1/8 the incomes of my farms, when he is 21. Sons, John and Garret, to have my real estate, at the death of my wife. Daughter, Lenah, wife of Cornelius Garrabrants, my wench, Mary; daughter, Altie, a wench; daughter, Eleanor Van Horne, a wench. My daughters to have the monies. Executors—wife, Balicah, my son, John, and my brother-in-law, Daniel Van Reypen. Witnesses—Jacob Van Wagenen, Jasper Prior, Jr., Zacharius Sickels. Proved Jan. 23, 1787. Lib. 29, p. 509.

**1786, May 15. Van Iderstien, Tauda I.,** of Bergen Co., yeoman; will of. Wife, Theodicia, to remain mistress of my personal and real estate, while my widow. Sons, Johannis and Peter, my real estate. Daughter, Elizabeth, some household goods. Rest of personal estate to my children, Johannis, the heirs of my daughter, Steentye, Rachel, Peter, Annatye and Elizabeth. To the daughter of my said daughter, Steintye, namely, Elizabeth, £15. Daughter, Annatye, wife of Theodorus Van Winckel, £15. My wife to have the things she brought with her at the time of our marriage. Executors—Adrian A. Post, of Slotterdam, and Walling Van Winckel. Witnesses—Caspares T. Van Iderstine, Frances Van Iderstiene, Charles Slade Fullwood. Proved Oct. 4, 1788. Lib. 31, p. 250.

**1787, May 1. Van Mater, Cyrenius,** of Middletown, Monmouth Co.; will of. Advanced in years. Grandson, Joseph Van Mater, son of my deceased son, Chryneyonce, farm where I live, which I bought of the heirs of Tise Lane, and what part he may claim by gift from his grandfather, Joseph Van Mater, to be claimed by said Joseph, the elder, shall be accounted part of his half. Daughters, Mary, wife of John Polhemus; Nelly, wife of Daniel Hendrickson; Auhely, wife of William Bennet and Sarah, wife of Cornelius Van Mater, the farm and salt meadow, lately Oakey Lefferts', deceased. Daughter-in-law, Nelly Van Mater, widow of my said son, ½ of my bonds. Executors—sons-in-law, John Polehemus, Daniel Hendrickson, and my nephew, Ruluf Van Mater. Witnesses—Richard Lawrence, Sarah Lawrence, Mary Lawrence. Proved Jan. 15, 1788. Lib. 30, p. 71.

**1786, Sept. ... Van Mater, Daniel,** of Freehold, Monmouth Co.; will of. To my 3rd daughter, Mirah Polhemus, wife of Daniel, £100. My 2nd daughter, Sarah Van Mater, wife of Benjamin Van Mater, £100. Eldest daughter, Caty Disbrough, wife of Henry, the 1/6 part of my estate. Daughter, Mirah, interest of 1/6 part, and at her death to be paid to Benjamin Van Mater's children, Jacob and Daniel. Son, Gilbert, 1/6 of estate. Servant, Charles Lehatt, £50. Friend, Charles Cook, £50. Executors—brother, Henry, John Rappelyea and Charles Cook. Witnesses—none given.
1788, Aug. 7. Appeared Lieutenant Colonel Elisha Lawrence, of the Parish of Saint Ann, Westminster, in County of Middlesex [England], and Robert Cooke, of Parish of Saint James, Westminster, in said Co., and declared they knew Daniel Van Mater, formerly of Freehold, in Monmouth Co., N. J., but late of Parish of Saint John, Westminster; also knew his hand writing, and believe the above to be his will. Letters were granted to Charles Cooke, as Executor. Lib. 31, p. 98.

## CALENDAR OF WILLS—1786-1790

**1790, Feb. 9. Vanmeter, Ephraim,** of Pitts Grove Township, Salem Co., yeoman; will of. Wife, Sarah, £50. Son, David, the home place where I live, bounded by Eleazar Mayhew and Joseph Vanmeter. Son, Benjamin, plantation that is rented to Adam Shaver. Daughter, Elizabeth Greenman, wife of Thomas, £100. Daughter, Bersheba Garrison, wife of Joshua, £100. Executors—wife, Sarah, and David Vanmeter. Witnesses—John Moore, Martha Titus, Isaac Nieukirk. Proved Oct. 12, 1790.

1790, April 8. Inventory, £380.17.8, made by William Garrison and Obadiah Caruthers. Lib. 31, p. 498.

**1790, May 21. Van Meter, Joseph,** of Pitts Grove, Salem Co., yeoman; will of. Daughter, Elizabeth Greenman, 20 shillings. Son, Henry, like amount. Son, Isaac, like amount. Son, Joseph, like amount. Son, Abraham, like amount. Sons, John and Samuel, my plantation of 213 acres. Daughter, Mary Van Meter, a cow and bed. Daughter, Rebecca Van Meter, a cow and bed. Youngest sons, Joel and William £20 each, when 21. Executors—sons, John and Samuel. Witnesses—Benjamin Weatherington, James Davis, John Nelson. Proved Dec. 11, 1790.

1790, June 28. Inventory, £252.1.9, made by William Alderman and William Murphy. Lib. 31, p. 500.

**1789, Oct. 9. Vanneman, Joseph,** of Greenwich Township, Gloucester Co. Int. Adm'x—Mary Vanneman. Fellowbondsman—John Porch; both of said Co.

1789, June 26. Inventory, £354.7.2, made by Samuel Mickle and William White. Lib. 30, p. 138.

**1787, Jan. 19. Van Ness, Gene,** of Paquanack, Morris Co. Int. Adm'r—Isaac Poulesoun. Fellowbondsman—Richard Jacobeson; both of Essex Co.

1787, Jan. 1. Inventory, £179.1.3, made by William Mandeveal and John Mead. Lib. 29, p. 472.

**1788, June 21. Van Ness, Seijomon,** of Paquanack Township, Morris Co.; will of. Wife, Elizabeth, all real and personal estate while my widow. Eldest son, Henry, after wife is done with it, ½ of the farm where he lives, and to be the south side; also ½ of the lot on the mountain, and my Dutch Bible. Second son, Yellas, the north part of the farm, and ½ of the lot on the mountain. Youngest son, Jacob, the lot behind the meadows where the new house and saw mill stand. Executors—sons, Henry, Yellas and Jacob. Witnesses—William Mandeveal, Yellas Mandeviel, Isaac Mead. Proved Nov. 3, 1788.

1789, Feb. 13. Inventory, £1,046.19.7, made by John Dumodt and William Mandeveal. Lib. 31, p. 193.

**1787, May 29. Vannetta, John,** of Oxford Township, Sussex Co., yeoman; will of. Wife to have house where I live while my widow, and the lands and goods; and then to the children of my brother-in-law, Jacob Kiser. Executors—wife, Elizabeth, and Joseph Mackey. Witnesses—Jacob Kiser, James Davison, Charles Smith. Proved May 28, 1789.

1789, Jan. 12. Inventory, £93.11.3, made by Peter Smith and John Summers. Lib. 30, p. 190.

**1790, Dec. 6. Van Norden, Michael,** of Bridgewater, Somerset Co. Int. Adm'rs—Archibald Van Norden and Peter Van Norden. Fellowbondsman—Benjamin Blackford; all of said place.

1790, Nov. 15. Inventory, made by James Van Norden and Benjamin Blackford. Lib. 31, p. 530.

**1790, March 22. Vannoy, Andrew,** of Maidenhead Township, Hunterdon Co. Int. Adm'r—Cornelius Vannoy, of said place. Fellowbondsman—James Wilson, of said Co.

1790, Feb. 8. Inventory, £380.5.5, made by Stephen Titus and James Wilson. Lib. 30, p. 319.

**1786, June 27. Van Pelt, Hendrick,** of Western Precinct, Somerset Co. Int. Adm'r—John Van Pelt. Fellowbondsman—Christopher Vanpelt; both of said place. Witness—Garrat Dorland.
Lib. 29, p. 195.

**1787, Feb. 5. Van Pelt, Johannes,** of Sowerland, Somerset Co., yeoman; will of. Son, Johannes, £5 as birthright, and the farm I bought of Garret Dorland, where he now lives, of 236 acres. Son, Christopher, my silver tankard, and the farm where I live; also 80 acres on the mountains; also 6 acres which my 2 sons bought of Hendrick Van Pelt, and which I paid for. Grandson, Aurt Sutphen, son of my daughter, Annatye, a bond which I have against John Witherspoon, for £60. Rest of estate to be sold. Grandson, Aurt Sutphen, £300. To the 4 children of my daughter, Maria, £200. And if, after the death of my son-in-law, Johanes Croy, my daughter, Maria, should be living, then my sons, Johanes and Christopher, shall provide for her. Executors—sons, Johanes and Christopher. Witnesses—Peter Stryker, Abraham Kershaw, Frederick Blew. Proved Sept. 3, 1790. Lib. 31, p. 290.

**1786, July 1, Van Pelt, Walterus,** of Somerset Co. Int. Adm'rs—Garret Vanpelt, Elbert Monfort and Cornelius Whitenack. Fellowbondsman—Hendrick Gulick; all of Western Precinct, said Co. Witness—Joseph D. Hageman. Whereas, Joseph Hegaman, Sr., and Sarah Van Pelt, the Executors of Walterus Van Pelt, are both now deceased.

1786, June 29. Inventory, £278.5.9, made by John Hagerman and Court Williamson. Lib. 29, p. 194. (See previous bill; Lib. 26, p. 545.)

**1790, Jan. 2. Van Riper, John,** of Acquackanonk, Essex Co.; will of. Real and personal estate to be sold. Son, Thomas Van Ryper, 10 shillings. Daughter, Jane Van Ryper, £10. Of the rest of my estate my wife, Jane, and my sons, Thomas and John, shall each have ¼, and my daughters, Moritye Van Ryper and Sarah Van Ryper, shall each have ⅛. Executors—wife, Jane, and Richard Van Ryper. Witnesses—John R. Ludlow, Henry F. Post, Hanmer Ludlow. Proved [no date] by Hanmer Ludlow.

1792, April 13. Adm'r—John R. Ludlow. Fellowbondsman—Darik Van Riper; both of said Co.

1792, April 13. Renunciation by Jane Van Riper and Richard Van Riper. Witness—Hanmer Ludlow.

1792, April 14. Inventory, £30.19.0, made by John Sip and John Getschius. Lib. 34, p. 41.

**1788, Oct. 2. Van Rype, Jurye,** of Hillsborough, Somerset Co.; will of. Son, Thomas, 20 shillings as birthright. Son, Harmen, the farm he lives on. Son, John, farm I live on. Daughter, Magdelen, £30. Daughters, Sarah and Christian, £12 each. Daughters, Mary, Catharine, Charity, Judy, Sarah, Magdelen and Christian, rest of personal estate and £400. My wife shall have ⅛ the profits of real estate. Executors—son, John, Hendrick Dehart and John Low. Witnesses—Rulef Sebring, Richard Hall, Joseph Coshun, Proved Oct. 10, 1789.
1789, Oct. 7. Inventory, £432.9.0, made by Dirck Low and Ryneer Staats. Lib. 31, p. 410.

**1787, June 1. Van Ryper, Garrit, Sr.,** of Essex Co. Int. Adm'r—Garrit Van Ryper, Jr. Fellowbondsman—Peter Simmons; both of said Co. Lib. 29, p. 418.

**1790, June 4. Vansciver, Martha,** of Burlington, Burlington Co.; will of. Son, Abraham Vansciver, 5 shillings. Son, William Vansciver, 4 acres in Willingborough Twp., which I bought of Jacob Noble. Sons, John and Jacob Vansciver, house and lot where I live, when 21. Son-in-law, Thomas Potts, the use of said house till my youngest son is of age. Money to all my children, except sons, Abraham, Jacob and John. Grandson, John Potts, silver buckles. My 3 daughters to have my apparel. Executor—son-in-law, Thomas Potts. Witnesses—Ann Craft, Samuel Treat, John Abraham De Normandie. Proved June 24, 1790.
1790, June 24. Inventory, £30.15.0, made by John Rogers and Thomas M. Gardner. Lib. 32, p. 61.

**1786, Feb. 16. Van Veghten, Elizabeth,** of Bridgewater, Somerset Co. Ward. Daughter of Dirk Van Veghten, of said place, deceased. Said Ward makes choice of Moses Scott as her Guardian.
1786, Feb. 16. Guardian—Doctor Moses Scott, of New Brunswick. Fellowbondsman—Abraham Van Neste, of Eastern Precinct, Somerset Co. Witness—Michael Van Veghten. Lib. 29, p. 197.

**1784, July 16. Van Veghten, Michael,** of Somerset Co. Ward. Son of Derrick Van Veghten, of said Co., deceased. Said Ward makes choice of John Young Noel as his Guardian.
1784, July 16. Guardian—John Young Noel, of New Brunswick. Fellowbondsman—John Dennis, of New Brunswick. Witnesses—Nancy Dealing and Mary Dennis. Lib. M, p. 246.

**1786, Dec. 18. Van Wyck, Helena,** of New Barbadoes, Bergen Co., widow; will of. Daughters, Margaretta Van Wyck and Anna Maria Van Wyck, all household goods, except my clock, which I give to my daughter, Helena Bogart. My apparel to my daughters, Helena, Margaretta and Anna Maria, and my granddaughters, Helena and Margaret Mason, children of my daughter, Catharine, deceased. Real estate to my daughters, Helena Bogart, Margaretta Van Wyck, Anna Maria Van Wyck, and children of my son, Abraham Van Wyck, deceased, that is to say, my grandson, Theodore Van Wyck, and my grandson Pierre Courtlandt Van Wyck; and the children of my daughter, Catharine Mason, deceased, that is to say, my grandson, John Mitchel Mason, granddaughter, Helena Mason and granddaughter, Margaret Mason. Executors—daughters, Helena Bogart, Margaretta Van Wyck and Anna Maria Van Wyck. Witnesses—Susannah Darbe, Richard Zabrisky, John Varick, Jr. Proved Jan. 24, 1788. Lib. 31, p. 253.

**1786, Oct. 16. Vanzickle, Lambert,** of Morris Co.; will of. Son, John, £5. Grandson, Isaac Vanzickle, £2. Son, Jacob, £15. Son, Abraham, £15. Daughters, Mary Schuiler and Rachel Clawson, £5 each. Daughter, Meriam Hamler, £10. Daughter, Ann Vanzickle, £10. Wife, Ann, to remain on the farm with my son, Isaac, and I give Isaac my real estate. Daughter, Ann, is to remain with her mother. Executors—wife, Ann, and son, Isaac. Witnesses—Jacob Schuiler, Daniel Lowrance, Peter Heiel. Proved April 8, 1790.
1790, March 20. Inventory, £278.3.6, made by Daniel Lowrance and John Batson. Lib. 30, p. 447.

**1786, March 13. Vaughn, Samuel,** of Burlington Co. Ward. Son of David Vaughn, of said Co., deceased. Said Ward makes choice of William Wright as his Guardian.
1786, March 13. Guardian—William Wright. Fellowbondsman— Edward Collins; both of said Co. Lib. 28, p. 81.

**1787, Oct. 18. Venable, Phillip,** of Evesham Township, Burlington Co., yeoman; will of. Son, Thomas, 25 acres at the upper end of my plantation. Son, Joseph, 25 acres, next to Thomas'. Son, Jesse, rest of plantation, except mill and pond, Daughters, Rebecca, Esther and Ann, 30 acres, to include the mill and pond, when they are 21. To Wallace Libra and Elizabeth Libra, children of Rachel Libra, rest of my lands. To Rachel Libra my personal estate and use of plantation till her son, Wallace, is 21. Executors—friends, Thomas Evans and Levi Lippincott. Witnesses—Jacob Evens, Isaac Barton, C. Evans. Proved Nov. 7, 1787.
1787, Oct. 29. Inventory, £107.18.3, made by Joseph Eves and C. Evans. Lib. 29, p. 20.

**1786, June 14. Verbryck, Roelef,** of Bergen Co. Ward. Son of Rev. Samuel Ver Bryck, of said Co., deceased. Said Ward makes choice of Abraham Haring, Esq., as his Guardian.
1786, June 14. Guardian—Abraham Haring. Fellowbondsmen— Bernardus Verbryck, Henry V. D. Linde Verbryck and Samuel G. Verbryck; all of said Co. Witness—Joost Beam. Lib. 29, p. 224.

**1787, Nov. 27. Vermeule, John,** of Bernards Town, Somerset Co. Ward. Son of Adrian Vermeule, of said place, deceased. Said Ward makes choice of Luke Covert, as his Guardian.
1787, Nov. 27. Guardian—Luke Covert, of Elizabeth Town, Essex Co. Fellowbondsman—Frederick Vermeule, of Bernards Town.
Lib. 29, p. 440.

**1786, Sept. 22. Vickery, Hester,** of Salem Co. Ward. Daughter of Thomas Vickery, of said Co., deceased. Said Ward makes choice of Gamaliel Garrison, as her Guardian.
1786, Sept. 22. Guardian—Gamaliel Garrison. Fellowbondsmen— Andrew Standly and Andrew Sinnickson, Jr.; all of Lower Penns Neck Township, said Co. Lib. 28, p. 156.

**1786, Sept. 20. Vickery, Thomas,** of Lower Penns Neck, Salem Co. Int. Adm'rs—Phebe Vickery and Gamaliel Garrison. Fellowbondsmen—Andrew Standly and Ananias Elwell; all of Penns Neck.
1786, Aug. 1. Inventory, £258.12.9, made by Ananias Elwell and Andrew Standly. Lib. 28, p. 156.

**1789, Oct. 8. Vincent, Levi,** of Newark, Essex Co.; will of. Wife to have most of the moveable estate, and, at her death, to be given to my 4 daughters. Son, Frederick, my farming tools and horses. Daughters, Christian Riker, Susannah Garrison, Mary Vincent and Esther Johnson, £10 each. Son, Levi, the land that lies between Samuel Ward and Stephen Crane. Son, John ½ of the rest of my lands, to be on the north side, with the house he lives in. Son, Frederick, the other ½. Executors—son, Frederick, and my son-in-law, Caleb Johnson. Witnesses—John Dod, Jr., Yelles Mandevail, Christian Mandeval. Proved Feb. 6, 1790.
1789, Dec. 14. Inventory, £115.10.10, made by Thomas Cadmus and Yelles Mandevill. Lib. 30, p. 355.

**1789, June 1. Vocard, Christopher,** of Upper Alloways Creek Township, Salem Co.; will of. All real and personal estate to be sold, and all money to my wife, Judy. Executor—friend, John Smith. Witnesses—Jonathan Hannah, John Gosling, David Baird. Proved June 4, 1789.
1789, June 5. Inventory, £99, made by John Van Culin and Stephen Willis. Land sold to James Paterson, £60. Lib. 40, p. 540.

**1789, Oct. 5. Voorheese, Coert,** of Bridgewater, Somerset Co. Int. Adm'r—Jacobus Bergen. Fellowbondsman—John Schooley; both of said Co. Lib. 31, p. 415.

**1787, Dec. 15. Voorhies, Cornelous.** We David Stonaker and William Updyke, of the estate of Cornelous Voorhies, deceased, did make an inventory of the goods that were left at the decease of his wife, Hilche V. Smith, and had them appraised by Levi Updick and Joseph Story. File No. 7347 L.
[See Lib. 31, p. 224, for administration of Hilcha Smith, of Middlesex Co., with William Updike as Administrator].

**1789, June 18. Voorhies, Peter and Cornelius,** of Middlesex Co. Wards. Sons of Daniel Voorhies, of said Co., deceased. Said Wards make choice of Peter Gordon as their Guardian.
1789, June 18. Guardian—Peter Gordon. Fellowbondsman—John P. Hunt; both of Hunterdon Co. Lib. 32, p. 56.

**1788, Jan. 31. Vough, John,** of Hardwick Township, Sussex Co.; will of. Wife, Peggy, use of farm where I live, and 200 acres in possession of James Crawford, and 50 acres on Chestnut Ridge; and my mother is to be kept as my father's will directed me. Brother, Andrew, £60 in State notes. Sister, Elizabeth Hull, £10. Rest of estate to children, Caty Vough, Elizabeth Vough, Mary Vough, John Vough and Jacob Valentine Vough, after death or marriage of wife. Executors—wife, Peggy, and my brother, Andrew and friend, Abraham Shaver. Witnesses—George Armstrong, Joseph Hunt, Richard Hunt. Proved March 1, 1788.
1788, Feb. 25. Inventory, £443.2.2, made by Jacob Dodderer and William Armstrong. Lib. 31, p. 153.

**1789, Aug. 25. Vreeland, Michael,** of Acquackanonk, Essex Co.; will of. Son, Michael, all real estate, and the bonds which my brother, Elias, assigned to me and Thomas Post; that is, my right in them. Daughter, Geertye, a chest of drawers which I got by her

mother, and some live stock. My son and daughter to have the negros. Executors—son, Michael, and my son-in-law, Adrian Post, and my friend, Henry Garritse. Witnesses—Benjamin Helme, Harman Van Riper, Cornelius Doremus. Proved Feb. 8, 1790.
Lib. 30, p. 325.

**1787, Jan. 11. Vreelandt, Derick,** of Essex Co. Int. Adm'x—Sophia Vreelandt. Fellowbondsman—Derik Van Riper; both of said Co.
Lib. 29, p. 417.

**1788, Aug. 21. Waggoner, Andrew,** of Knowlton, Sussex Co. Int. Adm'r—Valintine Baker, of said place; blacksmith. Fellowbondsman—William Henry Haynse, of Greenwich, said Co. Witness—Samuel Kikendull.
Lib. 31, p. 158.

**1790, March 8. Waldorf, John,** of Morris Co.; will of. Wife, Eve, £14 yearly, and enough goods to keep house. Oldest son, Anthony, 5 shillings. Son, Phillip, a plow and harrow. Son, Daniel, £10. Son, William, £10. Daughter, Mary, £5. Children, Anthony, John, Morris, Martain, Phillip, Daniel William, Koonrod, Mary and Ann, rest of estate. Executors—Adam Kinsard, and my sons, Anthony and John, of Hunterdon and Sussex Counties. Witnesses—Joshua Mott, David Welsh, John Kern. Proved June 10, 1790.

1790, June 8. Inventory, £1,116.12.2, made by Christopher Kern and Cunrod Bunn.
Lib. 30, p. 453.

**1786, March 13. Waldron, Antie,** of Essex Co. Int. Adm'r—Peter Waldron, of Harlem, New York.
Lib. 28, p. 424.

**1786, June 14. Walling, Joseph,** of Hardyston, Sussex Co. Int. Adm'rs—Benjamin Lindsly and Abraham Kitchel. Fellowbondsman—Francis McCarty; all of Morris Co.
Lib. 28, p. 470.

**1787, Nov. 18. Walling, Ladis,** of Greenwich, Cumberland Co., yeoman; will of. Sons, Jonathan, Ladis and Joseph, all real estate. If my mother-in-law, Rebekah Brewster, confirms to my son, Jonathan, a deed for 5½ acres of land, it may be done. My children to be put to a good calling. Executors—sister, Mary Woodruff, Amos Woodruff and Joseph Brewster. Witnesses—Thomas H. McCalla, Enos Woodruff, Jr., George Garnett Tiddiss. Proved Dec. 1, 1787.

1787, Nov. 28. Inventory, £205.19.10, made by Enos Woodruff and John Laning.
Lib. 29, p. 173.

**1787, Nov. 5. Wambaugh, Henry,** of Amwell Township, Hunterdon Co. Int. Adm'x—Ann Wambaugh. Fellowbondsman—Philip Snook; both of said place.

1787, Oct. 29. Inventory, £161.6.9, made by Paul Kuhl and John Rockafellor.
Lib. 29, p. 294.

**1789, Feb. 9. Wannemaker, William,** of Bergen Co. Int. Adm'r—Fredrick Crimm. Fellowbondsman—George Defandorf; both of said Co. Witness—Catherine Miller.
Lib. 30, p. 248.

**1788, Feb. 8. Wardell, Joseph,** of Shrewsbury, Monmouth Co., yeoman; will of, being the son of Thomas. Son, Jacob, real estate. Daughter, Charity White, 10 shillings. Daughter, Elizabeth Wolley,

and my grandson, Joseph Cox, personal estate. Executors—son, Jacob, and son-in-law, Joel Wolley. Witnesses—Peter Brinley, Abraham Vandike, Solomon Wardell. Proved July 15, 1788.
1788, July 14. Inventory, £684.19.0, made by Samuel Longstreet and William Brinley. Lib. 30, p. 96.

**1788, Feb. 9. Wardell, Mary,** of Shrewsbury, Monmouth Co.; will of. Son, John Smith, 10 shillings. Son, Jessey Smith, same sum. Sons, Samuel, Peter and Joseph Wardel, plantation I live on, at Long Branch. Daughter, Survier Smith, £10. Daughter, Hannah Hall, £5. Children, John Smith, Jessy Smith and Hannah Hall, moveable estate. Executors—sons, Samuel, Joseph and Peter Wardell. Witnesses— Peter Slocum, Peleg Slocum, Ruth Lane. Proved Sept. 2, 1788.
1788, March 19. Inventory, £194.10.3, made by William Cooper and Joseph Wardell. Lib. 30, p. 87.

**1789, Sept. 14. Warne, George,** of Mansfield Woodhouse, Sussex Co.; will of. Wife to be supported. Son, George, £10. Son, Joseph, 130 acres along line of Thomas Thatcher. Sons, Thomas and John, plantation where John Lake lives, and the £500 in hands of Joseph Hart. Granddaughter, Elizabeth Vancamp, £70. Elija and Elisha, rest of farm where I live. Daughter, Mary Hews, 15 acres on north of Pohathung. Daughter, Elizabeth Probasko, 150 acres on road up the mountains. Grandson, Jesse Warn, a horse. Executors— sons, Elija and Elisha. Witnesses—Thomas Thatcher, Peter Pettey, John Emley. Proved Nov. 25, 1789.
1789, Nov. 11. Inventory, £843.17.1, made by David Johnston and Philip Weller. Lib. 30, p. 192.

**1790, March 23. Warne, John,** of Middlesex Co. Int. Adm'x—Mary Warne. Fellowbondsmen—William Brown and Thomas Lamberson; all of said Co.
1790, March 19. Inventory, made by Thomas Lamberson and William Hillyer. Lib. 30, p. 534.

**1788, Sept. 25. Waterhouse, Nathan,** of Hardwick, Sussex Co.; will of. Eldest son, Nathan, 40 acres of my plantation. Son, Asa, £11. Wife, Sarah, rest of estate; and, after her death, to be sold and money given to my other 3 sons, Elkanah, John and Gideon. Daughter, Sarah, £5. Daughter, Ester, £7. Daughter, Mary, £10. Executrix—wife, Sarah. Witnesses—Daniel Hunt, Barnid Oulp, Catren Olp. Proved May 15, 1790. Lib. 30, p. 430.

**1786, June 28. Watson, Mary,** of Burlington Co. Int. Adm'rs— William Shaw, of Phila., merchant. Fellowbondsman—James Sterling, of Burlington.
1786, Sept. 5. Inventory, £89.11.5, made by James Verree and Jonathan Quest. Lib. 28, p. 78.

**1787, May 17. Watson, William,** of Woolwich Township, Gloucester Co. Int. Adm'x—Patience Watson. Fellowbondsman—Felix Fisler; both of said place. Witness—George W. Campbell.
1787, May 5. Inventory, £421.19.7, made by Valentine Reynalds and Felix Fisler. Lib. 29, p. 120.

**1790, Oct. 25. Watt, Anna,** formerly of Delaware, but now residing in Philadelphia. Ward. Daughter of Robert Watt, of New Castell, Delaware, deceased. Said Ward, having lands, makes choice of Matthew Whildin as her Guardian. Witnesses—Rebeccah Leaming and Thomas Leaming, Jr.

1790, Oct. 25. Guardian—Matthew Whilldin. Fellowbondsman—Joseph Hildreth; both of Cape May Co. Witnesses—Richard Somers and Lydia Hand. Lib. 32, p. 107.

**1789, No. 17. Watt, James** of Cape May Co., minister; will of. I give all my salary due to me to the Presbyterian Church of Cape May Co., for the use of the Church. Niece, Ann Watt, who lives with me, the rest of my estate, except some books, but she is to have the family Bible. To Katharine Swain, wife of Nezer Swain, my small Bible. To Letty Ewing, my books of Favel. To Lydia Eldredge, wife of Jeremiah, some books. Executors—Matthew Whilldin and Jeremiah Eldredge. Witnesses—Roanna Stites, Jean Buck, Ellis Hughes, Jr.

1789, Nov. 17. Codicil. To Ann or Nancy Hughes, daughter of Elijah Hughes, six silver teaspoons, marked H. H. To Sarah Hughes, daughter of Elijah Hughes, six silver teaspoons, marked H. H. To Sarah Hand, daughter of Major John Hand, six silver teaspoons, marked R. H. Witnesses—same as above. Proved Dec. 28, 1789.

1789, Dec. 23. Inventory, £428.3.1, made by Ellis Hughes, Jr. and Nezer Swain. Lib. 31, p. 368.

**1787, May 19. Weaver, Joseph,** of Woolwich Township, Gloucester Co., yeoman. Int. Adm'r—Jesse Weaver, of said place. Fellowbondsman—Samuel Stokes, of Waterford Township, said Co.

1787, May 16. Inventory, £75.0.6, made by George Vanleer and James Lord. Lib. 29, p. 117.

**1790, May 3. Webster, John, Jr.,** of Essex Co. Int. Adm'rs—Taylor Webster and Hugh Webster. Fellowbondsman—Joel Dunn; all of New Jersey.

1790, May 1. Renunciation by Mary Webster, widow of said John, in favor of her brothers-in-law, Taylor Webster and Hugh Webster.

1790, May 4. Inventory, £44.6.0, made by Benjamin Blackford and Jacob F. Randolph. Lib. 30, p. 359.

**1786, Feb. 17. Webster, Robert,** of Piscataway, Middlesex Co.; will of. Daughter, Sarah, a bed. Couzen, John Webster, son of my brother, John, my blue coat. Wife, Mary, rent of the land at Ambros Brook; also use of land and house at Quibble Town, until daughter, Sarah, is 14. Land to be sold and money given to daughter, Sarah Webster, and daughter, Mary Webster, when 18. If my daughters die, then I give the above to my couzen, Hugh Webster, son of my brother, John, and my couzen, John Webster, son of my brother, Thomas. Executors—friends, John Runyon and Samuel Randolph. Witnesses—David Coriell, Peter Merselis, Isaac Pound. Proved July 18, 1786.

1786, April 20. Inventory, £28.8.1, made by David Coriell and John Smalley. Lib. 28, p. 312.

**1789, July 20. Weiss, Philip,** of Morris Co.; will of. I have divided my lands and mills among my children, which I confirm. Grandson,

John Weiss, son of Jacob, deceased, £10. Granddaughter, Elizabeth Neighbour, £30. To the other 4 grandchildren, children of my son, Jacob, deceased, namely, Catherine, Jacob, Andrew and Anna, £25 each. Of the rest of my estate I give my son, Philip, ¼, and daughter, Elizabeth Hoeger, ¼, and daughter, Margaret Neissor, ¼, and the other ¼ to the 5 youngest children of son, Jacob, deceased, namely, Elizabeth Neighbour, Catherine, Jacob, Andrew and Anna Weiss. Executors—son, Philip, and sons-in-law, William Neisser and John Hager. Witnesses—William Graff, Richard Morgan. Proved Dec. 21, 1790.
1790, Nov. 1. Inventory, £641.6.2, made by David Welsh and John Sharp. Lib. 30, p. 477.

**1788, Nov. 12. Weller, George,** of Mansfield Township, Sussex Co. Int. Adm'rs—Philip Weller and William Weller. Fellowbondsman—John Cline; all of said place.
1788, Oct. 17. Inventory, £217.9.11, made by John Cline and Jacob Wendling. Lib. 31, p. 158.

**1786, March 4. Wescoat, Rebekah,** of Cumberland Co. Ward. Daughter of David Wescoat, of said Co., deceased. Said Ward makes choice of Samuel Wescoat as her Guardian.
1786, March 4. Guardian—Samuel Wescot. Fellowbondsman—John Mulford; both of said Co. Witnesses—John Peck, Jr. and Jonathan Elmer. Lib. 28, p. 183.

**1787, June 17. West, James,** of Shrewsbury, Monmouth Co.; will of. Wife, Anne, all the goods she brought to me, and £50. Son, John, farm where I live, and the east part of the land I bought of Ephraim Allen; also the salt meadow on Raccoon Island. Granddaughter, Catherine, daughter of my deceased daughter, Audra, rest of land I bought of Ephraim Allen, and £200, when 18. Daughter, Sarah, wife of Jacob Fleming, £10. Rest of estate to son, John, and all my grandchildren. Executors—son, John, and friends, Timothy Corlies and Pontius Chandler. Witnesses—Stephen Fleming, Joseph Lovell, William Stephens. Proved Feb. 13, 1788.
1788, Jan. 21. Inventory, £1,539.10.11, made by George Corlies and Stephen Fleming. Lib. 30, p. 74.

**1788, March 22. West, Rebekah,** of Shrewsbury, Monmouth Co. Ward. Daughter of John West, of said place, deceased. Said Ward makes choice of John Errickson as her Guardian.
1788, March 22. Guardian—John Errickson, of Freehold. Fellowbondsman—John Hulsart; both of said Co. Witness—Rachel Henderson. Lib. 30, p. 104.

**1789, Jan. 5. Westcott, David,** of Fairfield, Cumberland Co., farmer; will of. Wife, Elizabeth, ⅛ of the moveable estate and the use of the place where I live, till my youngest son, Leonard, comes of age. If my wife should marry before my son, Leonard, is of age, then each of my sons, Annanias, David and Charles, shall have possession of their parts, when 21. Son, John, my cedar swamp at the foot of Parvins Branch, and the cedar swamp in Lebenon, joining Abinadab Westcott. Sons, John, Annanias, David, Charles and Leonard, a lot of land that joins Eleazar Smith. The plantation and marsh, and woodlands, joining lands of Zebulon Woodruff, I give my sons,

Annanias, David, Charles and Leonard. Son, John, one acre of cedar swamp in Lebanon. Daughters, Lidia and Elizabeth Westcott, £15 each. Executrix is to sell the woodland that joins lands of Odol Cubby and Abinadab Westcott; also a salt marsh, which is undivided between James Clark and I, in the marsh called Bridgestiks. Executrix—wife, Elizabeth. Witnesses—John Ogden, Amos Westcott, James Whitecar. Proved Jan. 27, 1789.

1789, Jan. 26. Inventory, £209.0.11, made by Amos Westcott and John Ogden. Lib. 30, p. 160.

**1787, Jan. 30. Westervelt, John,** of Harrington, Bergen Co. Int. Adm'rs—Maria Westervelt and Benjamin Blacklidge. Fellowbondsman—Benjamin Westervelt; all of said Co.

1787, Feb. 5. Inventory, made by Isaac Blanch, Esq. and Abraham Demarest. Lib. 29, p. 535.

**1787, Oct. 20. Westfall, Catharine,** of Knowlton, Sussex Co., widow. Int. Adm'r—John Westfall. Fellowbondsman—John Shannan; both of said place.

1787, Nov. 9. Inventory, £24.8.3, made by Edward Freeman and John Quick. Lib. 29, p. 489.

**1787, Nov. 10. Westfall, Samuel,** of Wantage, Sussex Co. Int. Adm'x—Margaret Westfall. Fellowbondsman—Joseph Van Aken; both of said Co. Witness—David Westfall.

1787, Nov. 15. Inventory, £211.19.0, made by Jacob Dewitt and Benjamin Coykendall. Lib. 29, p. 490.

**1786, March 27. Wetherill, Christopher,** of Burlington, Burlington Co.; will of. Wife, Mary, and my daughters, Anna and Sarah Wetherill, my personal estate, except what I give to my son, Isaac. My wife is to live in my house, and have wood from the woodland, and my 3 sons and 2 daughters are to provide her with a good living. Son, Isaac, 20 acres where he lives. Sons, Samuel, Joseph, Isaac, and my daughters, Anna Wetherill and Sarah Wetherill, my other lands in Burlington, and also in Counties of Hunterdon, Morris and Sussex. Executors—wife, Mary, and sons, Samuel, Joseph and Isaac. Witnesses—Daniel Smith, William Smith, Jr., Thomas Smith. Proved April 17, 1786. Lib. 26, p. 422.

**1786, Aug. 18. Wetherill, John, Jr.,** of Chesterfield Township, Burlington Co. Int. Adm'r—John Wright. Fellowbondsman—John Thorn; both of said Co.

1786, Aug. 17. Renunciation by Sarah Wetherill, widow of said John, in favor of John Wright. Witness—John Thorn.

1786, Aug. 14. Inventory, £151.12.4, made by Isaac Cowgill and John Butler. Lib. 28, p. 76.

**1786, March 14. Wheeler, Abraham,** of New York City. Int. Adm'r—Jonathan Stiles. Fellowbondsman—Benjamin Lindsly; both of Morristown, Morris Co.

1786, March 13. Renunciation by Margret Wheeler, widow of Abraham, late of Morristown, in favor of Jonathan Stiles.

Lib. M, p. 286.

CALENDAR OF WILLS—1786-1790   251

**1786, March 11. Wheeler, William,** of Prince Morris River Township, Cumberland Co., yeoman; will of. Wife, Rebeccah, all personal estate, except my gun, which I give to my friend, Amos Edwards. Executrix—wife, Rebeccah. Witnesses—William Price, Mary Dun, Priscilla Fortner. Proved Aug. 7, 1786.
  1786, Aug. 5. Inventory, £52.15.10, made by William Furniss and Abraham Hoffman. File No. 6025 F.

**1789, Nov. 27. Whitacar, Lemuel and Lewis,** of Cumberland Co. Wards. Sons of Lewis Whitacar, of said Co., deceased. Said Wards made choice of Nathaniel Whitacar as their Guardian.
  1789, Nov. 27. Guardian—Nathaniel Whitacar. Fellowbondsman—Butler Thompson; both of said Co. Lib. 30, p. 163.

**1786, July 15. Whitaker, Jonathan,** of Bernards Township, Somerset Co. Int. Adm'rs—Nathaniel Whitaker and Jonathan Whitaker. Fellowbondsman—William Logan; all of said Co.
  1786, July. Renunciation by Mary Whitaker, widow of Jonathan, in favor of Nathaniel and Jonathan Whitaker. Witness—Mary Whitaker.
  1786, July 1. Inventory, £143.18.8, made by David Kirkpatrick and William Logan. Lib. 29, p. 196.

**1786, Dec. 15. White, Alexander and William,** of Cumberland Co. Wards. Sons of John White, of said Co., deceased. Said Wards make choice of Jonathan Bowen as their Guardian.
  1786, Dec. 16. Guardian—Jonathan Bowen. Fellowbondsmen—David Bowen and David Potter, Esquire; all of said Co. Witness—Samuel M. Shute. Lib. 28, p. 184.

**1788, July 22. White, Isabella,** of New Brunswick, Middlesex Co.; will of. Brother, Anthony Walton White, a portrait. Sister, Johannah Bayard, a wench. Sister, Euphemia Paterson, a wench. To Mrs. Ann Kearney, wife of Ravaud, a wench. To Miss Susan R. Kearney, my watch. To Miss Nelly Mercer, daughter of Doct. Mercer, £50. To Miss Cornelia Paterson, silver coffee pot. Brother-in-law, William Paterson, £100. To Mrs. Mary Lawrence, widow of Thomas, of Philadelphia, interest of £300, and, at her death, to my brother. My brothers-in-law, John Bayard and William Paterson, to sell a negro. To Anthony Walton White Bayard, son of James, deceased, £150. My lot in New York I give to sisters, Johanna Bayard and Euphamia Paterson. I give my land in Alexandria Township, Hunterdon Co., now occupied by Frederick Apgar and Coonradt Apgar, of 370 acres, and 60 acres in Lebanon, and ½ of land in Kingwood, which my father bought of Nehemiah Dunham, of 140 acres, to my said brother. To Elizabeth, Matilda, Euphemia White, daughters of my brother, some land. Executors—my said brother, and my brothers-in-law, John Bayard and William Paterson. Witnesses—John Neilson, Jacob Dunham, Lewis Dunham. Proved Aug. 21, 1789. Lib. 31, p. 391.

**1790, April 28. White, John,** of Shrewsbury, Monmouth Co. Int. Adm'r—Job White. Fellowbondsman—Henry Perine; both of said Co. Witness—Daniel Hendrickson.
  1790, April 29. Inventory, £15.8.9, made by Samuel White and James Leffettro. Lib. 30, p. 419.

**1787, Jan. 4. White, John M.,** of Cumberland Co. Ward. Son of John White, of said Co., deceased. Said Ward having real and personal estate, makes choice of Joseph Bloomfield as his Guardian.
1787, Jan. 4. Guardian—Joseph Bloomfield, of City of Burlington. Fellowbondsmen—John Lawrence, of Burlington, and Jonathan Bowen, of Cumberland Co. Witness—Thomas Adams. Lib. 29, p. 80.

**1790, Sept. 28. White, Lydia,** of Monmouth Co. Int. Adm'r—Thomas Morford, of Shrewsbury, said Co.
1790, Sept. 27. Inventory, £4.8.0, made by Joseph Stillwell and John Eldridge. Lib. 30, p. 418.

**1786, March 2. Whitehead, Elizabeth,** of Elizabeth Borough, Essex Co.; will of. House and 7 acres of land where I live to be sold, and the money divided between my granddaughters, Elizabeth, Mary and Sarah Whitehead. Son-in-law, William Whitehead, the rest of said lot. Executors—friend, David Brant, and Enoch Moore. Witnesses—Benjamin Whitehead, John Winans, John Roberson. Proved Sept. 6, 1786. Lib. 28, p. 388.

**1786, July 18. Whitehead, Mary,** of Middlesex Co. Int. Adm'r—Benjamin Leforge. Fellowbondsman—David Pound; both of Piscataway, said Co. Witness—William Sickles. Lib. 28, p. 339.

**1790, Jan. 20. Whitekar, Thomas,** of Fairfield, Cumberland Co. Int. Adm'x—Rachel Whitekar. Fellowbondsman—Isaac Preston; both of said Co.
1790, Feb. 27. Inventory, £142.8.0, made by Amos Westcott and John Ogden. Lib. 30, p. 280.

**1786, March 13. Wick, Mary,** of Morristown, Morris Co., widow of Henry Wick; will of. My husband by his will Jan. 26, 1771, did devise to me all his estate, and to those of our children and grandchildren of us both that I should give it to; and our son, Henry, became a lunatic, and I give to his first born child, called Mary, (now Mary Tuttle), that land in Mendham Township, on line of Peter Kemble and Joseph Guering, of 160 acres; and to his 2nd born child, Chloe, called Chloe Wick, £25. Elizabeth, the wife of our son, Henry, has had, since his lunacy, children, since she forsook his bed and board, so I give to each of them only 5 shillings. Daughter, Mary Blachly, land in said town, of 250 acres. Grandson, Absalom Blachly, £50. Granddaughters, Hannah, Jude, Phebe and Temperance Blachly, children of my daughter, Mary, £50 each. Daughter, Phebe, called Phebe Leddel, land along line of Caleb Eady; also the lot in possession of Doctor William Leddel, her husband. Granddaughters, Temperance and Eliza Leddel, £50. Daughter, Temperance Wick, rest of real estate and moveables. Executors—friend, Ebenezer Drake, and daughter, Temperance Wick. Witnesses—Preserve Riggs, Clement Wood, Samuel Gordon. Proved July 20, 1787.
1787, July 20. Inventory, £4,670.8.8, made by Preserve Riggs and Joshua Guerin. Lib. 29, p. 450.

**1788, May 4. Wiggins, John,** of Hardwick, Sussex Co. Ward. Son of Samuel Wiggins, of said place, deceased. Said Ward makes choice of Montgomery Reading as his Guardian.
1788, May 4. Guardian—Montgomery Reading, of Independence. Fellowbondsman—Jonathan Willis, of Newtown, both of said Co.
Lib. 31, p. 158.

CALENDAR OF WILLS—1786-1790   253

**1787, Nov. 30. Wild, Samuel,** of Gloucester Township, Gloucester Co. Int. Adm'r—John Wild. Fellowbondsman—Richard Cheesman, Jr.; both of said place, yeomen. Witness—George Sparks.
1789, July 25. Inventory, £60.8.0, made by Peter Cheesman and Richard Cheesman. Lib. 29, p. 118.

**1790, June 17. Wiley, John,** of Gloucester Co. Ward. Son of Mary and Joseph Wiley, the said Joseph being deceased. Petition is made by Peter Wheaton, and Mary, his wife, late Mary Wiley, for appointment of Jacob Wood as Guardian of John Wiley, son of said Mary, and Joseph Wiley, deceased.
1790, June 17. Guardian—Jacob Wood. Fellowbondsman—Anthony Sharp; both of said Co. Lib. 31, p. 483.

**1790, Nov. 8. Wilkins, Benjamin,** of Gloucester Co. Ward. Son of Constantine Wilkins, of said Co., deceased. Said Ward makes choice of Thomas Wilkins as his Guardian.
1790, Nov. 8. Guardian—Thomas Wilkins. Fellowbondsman—Elisha Clark; both of said Co. Lib. 31, p. 482.

**1787, Jan. 6. Wilkins, Thomas, Jr.,** of Evesham, Burlington Co. Int. Adm'x—Esther Wilkins. Fellowbondsman—Enoch Evans; both of said place.
1786, Oct. 30. Inventory, £313.2.10, made by Lawrence Webster and Bethuel Moore. Lib. 29, p. 72.

**1787, Feb. 9. Wilkins, William,** of Deptford Township, Gloucester Co. Int. Adm'rs—John Wilkins and James Wilkins. Fellowbondsman—Joseph Low; all of said place. Witness—John Clement.
1787, Feb. 5. Inventory, £355.15.3, made by Joseph Low and John Stephens. Lib. 29, p. 118.

**1787, Dec. 8. Wilkinson, John,** of Greenwich Township, Gloucester Co. Int. Adm'x—Mary Wilkinson. Fellowbondsman—William White; both of said place. Witness—Thomas Stokes.
1787, Nov. 29. Inventory, £63.5.3, made by Samuel Mickle and William White. Lib. 29, p. 117.

**1790, Feb. 5. Willets, Tabitha,** of Cape May Co. Int. Adm'r—Richard Townsend. Fellowbondsman—Eli Townsend; both of said Co. Witnesses—Jonathan Leaming and Philip Cresse.
The Adm'r made return that there were no goods to administer, as the deceased had only an estate in lands. Lib. 32, p. 105.

**1789, May 10. Williams, Daniel,** of Shrewsbury, Monmouth Co.; will of. To David Lewis, and to Jane Estill, wife of William Estill, 7 acres of land, on south side of the Metetecunck Bridge. Brother John's 3 daughters, Susannah Frances, Elizabeth Wainright and Rebeckah Williams, all lands in Stafford Township, near Mannahawking. Wife, Hannah, all other lands and moveable estate, and, after her death, to Marget Johnson and Hannah Johnson, daughter of said Marget, ½ of said lands which I left my wife, and my wife is to dispose of the other ½ as she sees fit. Executors—wife, Hannah, John Richmond and John Lloyd. Witnesses—William Barnes, Samuel Forman, John Forman. Proved June 30, 1789.
1789, June 1. Inventory, £283.11.6, made by Aaron Brewer and James Johnson. Lib. 30, p. 165.

**1787, Nov. 5. Williams, John,** of Chesterfleld, Burlington Co. Int. Adm'r—Joel Williams. Fellowbondsman—Joseph Williams; both of said Co.
 1787, Nov. 10. Inventory, £112.12.2, made by Jeremiah Smith and John Hall.  Lib. 29, p. 79.

**1788, Oct. 21. Williams, John,** of Shrewsbury, Monmouth Co. Int. Adm'r—James Williams, of said place. Witness—Rachel Henderson.
 Lib. 30, p. 103.

**1788, Jan. 18. Williams, Jonathan.** Int. Adm'rs—Jonathan Williams and Thomas Williams; both of Hunterdon Co.  File No. 6780 G.

**1790, Oct. 29. Williams, Mathew,** of Shrewsbury, Monmouth Co. Int. Adm'r—Robert Hulitt. Fellowbondsman—Benjamin Jackson; both of said place. Witness—Euphamia Clayton.
 1790, Sept. 3. Renunciation by Daniel Williams.
 1790, Sept. 8. Inventory, £49, made by Benjamin Jackson and Henry Herbert.  Lib. 30, p. 418.

**1788, May 7. Williams, Obadiah,** of Shrewsbury Township, Monmouth Co. Int. Adm'r—Edmund Williams. Fellowbondsman—Joseph Throckmorton; both of said place. Witness—Samuel Forman.
 1788, May 6. Inventory, £124.3.4, made by Jacob Fleming and Joseph Throckmorton.  Lib. 30, p. 102.

**1789, Nov. 10. Williamson, Aaron,** of Essex Co. Int. Adm'r—Melanthon Freeman, of Middlesex Co. Fellowbondsman—Joseph Cole, of Essex Co. Witness—James Stevens.
 1789, Nov. 9. Renunciation by Sarah Williamson, widow of said Aaron, in favor of Melanthon Freeman. Witness—Matthias Freeman.
 1789, Nov. 17. Inventory, £659.2.11, made by Luke Covert and John Webster, Jr. Note against James Williamson, and one against Daniel Williamson, who died insolvent.  Lib. 30, p. 219.

**1787, May 7. Williamson, Nicholas,** of Hillsborough, Somerset Co. Int. Adm'rs—Peter Dumont, Jacobus Gerritsen and Joseph Williamson. Fellowbondsman—Garret R. Garritsin; all of said Co.
 1787, April 4. Inventory, £217.9.0, made by Garret R. Garretsen, Isaac Van Nuys and Tunes Covert.  Lib. 29, p. 438.

**1789, Sept. 17. Williamson, Platt,** of Somerset Co. Ward. Son of William Williamson, of said Co., deceased. Said Ward makes choice of Jedediah Swan as his Guardian.
 1789, Sept. 17. Guardian—Jedidiah Swan. Fellowbondsman—Benjamin Laing; both of Essex Co.  Lib. 30, p. 219.

**1789, April 7. Willis, Benjamin,** of Elizabeth Borough, Essex Co.; will of. Lands to be kept in hands of Executors, until two youngest sons, David and Elias, are 21, when said lands may be sold and money given to my wife, Anna, and my sons, Benjamin, Abner, David and Elias. Daughter, Jane, wife of Ichabod Miller, £10. Wife to have the moveable estate. Executors—wife, Anna, and my son, Abner. Witnesses—John Craig, William Coffen, James Shotwell. Proved April 22, 1789.  Lib. 40, p. 517.

**1787, May 23. Willis, Isaac,** of Salem, Salem Co.; will of. Wife, Esther, some of the goods. Rest of goods and land in Alloways Creek Township to be sold, and, of the money, my wife is to have ¼, and daughter, Prudence Willis, the rest, when she is 18; but, if she die, then to Francis Asbury, who is Superintendent of the Methodist Society, for their use. Executor—friend, John Smith, son of James. Witnesses—Joshua Sims, Joseph Smith, Robert Tullis. Proved April 12, 1788.
1787, Oct. 1. Inventory, £118.5.9, made by Henry Firth and Richard Caruthers. Lib. 31, p. 52.

**1787, March 16. Willis, Thomas,** of Essex Co., yeoman; will of. Son, Nathaniel, 5 shillings. Son, John, 5 shillings. Daughter, Hannah Willis, has had a deed for 25 acres. Daughter, Anna Halsey, moveable estate, with Hannah having ½. Sons, James and William, rest of plantation. Executors—son-in-law, Joseph Halsey, and friend, Andrew Hetfield. Witnesses—Eli Miller, Noah Clark, William Coles. Proved Dec. 4, 1787. Lib. 29, p. 375.

**1786, May 19. Willits, Tabitha,** of Cape May Co., widow. Int. Adm'r—Henry Y. Townsend. Fellowbondsman—Elijah Townsend; both of said Co. Witnesses—James Townsend and Reuben Townsend. Lib. 38, p. 79.

**1789, Feb. 11. Willson, Jacob,** of Wantage, Sussex Co. Int. Adm'r— Joseph Willson. Fellowbondsman—Nevi Willson; both of said place, yeomen. Witness—Andrew Willson.
1789, Feb. 10. Inventory, £144.7.6, made by Evi Adams and Isaac Havens. Lib. 30, p. 200.

**1788, April 28. Willson, James,** of Middletown, Monmouth Co.; will of. Wife, Mary, use of personal and real estate, except a 9 acre lot. To Isaac Willson, son of my deceased brother, John, 20 shillings. Nephew, Samuel Carman, ½ of the 9-acre lot. To James Willson, son of Elizabeth Tippey, ½ of said 9-acre lot. William Willson, son of Andrew and Esther, rest of lands. Executors—wife, Mary, and William Willson, son of Andrew. Witnesses—John Smith, Nicholas Johnson, John Taylor. Proved Feb. 26, 1789.
1789, Feb. 11. Inventory, £149.15.0, made by John Taylor, Jr. and Jacob Covenhoven. Lib. 30, p. 175.

**1790, Jan. 12. Wilson, Elijah,** of Gloucester Co. Int. Adm'rs— Elizabeth Wilson and Anthony Warrick. Fellowbondsman—James Hurley; all of said Co.
1790, Jan. 11. Inventory, £193.19.10, made by John Wild and James Hurley. Lib. 31, p. 482.

**1789, Jan. 30. Wilson, Joseph,** of Windsor Township, Middlesex Co. Int. Adm'rs—Peter Wilson and Daniel Wilson. Fellowbondsman—Jacob Fisher; all of said Co.
1789, Jan. 29. Renunciation by Hannah Wilson in favor of her sons, Peter and Daniel Wilson.
1789, Jan. 29. Inventory, made by William Tindall and Jacob Fisher. Account against the estate of James Wilson, £113.8.4. Account against Rachel Hight, for an outset, £50. Lib. 31, p. 395.

**1788, May 1. Wilson, Josiah,** of Woodbridge Township, Middlesex Co., Doctor. Int. Adm'x—Jannet Wilson. Fellowbondsman—Thomas Laing; both of said Co.

1788, May 24. Inventory, £533.2.5, made by Enoch Moore and Edward Moore. Lib. 31, p. 224.

**1789, March 3. Wilson, Margaret,** of Middlesex Co. Int. Adm'r—Hopewell Wilson. Fellowbondsman—Benjamin Willson; both of Piscataway, said Co.

1789, March 11. Inventory, £12.0.3, made by William Harris and Hendrick Bownn. Lib. 31, p. 395.

**1789, Jan. 20. Wilson, Robert,** of Salem, Salem Co.; will of. Son, William, £150. Son, Isaac, £600, when he is 21. My daughters, Mary, Ann and Hannah Wilson, £400 each, when 18. Real and personal estate to be sold. Executor—son, William. Witnesses—John Redman, William Daniel, Jacob Hufty. Proved Sept. 17, 1790.

1789, Jan. 30. Inventory, £889.8.2, made by Samuel Stewart and John Redman. Lib. 31, p. 502.

**1789, April 24. Wilson, Samuel,** of Hunterdon Co. Ward. Son of Andrew Wilson, of said Co., deceased. Said Ward makes choice of James Wilson as his Guardian.

1789, April 24. Guardian—James Wilson. Fellowbondsmen—John Wilson, Jr., and Walter Wilson; all of Amwell, said Co.
Lib. 32, p. 58.

**1786, Nov. 20. Wilson, Savil,** of Deptford Township, Gloucester Co.; will of. Wife, Susannah, a bed, horse and 2 cows, and the rest to be sold, and the money to be paid to my daughter, Elizabeth Wilson. Son, Savil, plantation where I live, with the lower lot of meadow near Delaware River, and between Biddle Reeves' and Thomas Wilson's meadow; and 300 acres of back land, which I bought of the Trustees of Coll. Alford, including the cedar swamp I bought of Isaac Dilks. Sons, Edward and Jesse, rest of back lands and cedar swamp; also the meadow between Thomas Wilson and Biddle Reeves' meadows, on Ramboe Run. Wife, Susannah, the profits from the plantation until Savil is 21; also £15 yearly. Daughter, Elizabeth, £300. Youngest sons to be put to trades. Executors—said wife, and my friend, David Eldridge. I give the graveyard on the east side of the orchard, on my plantation, to be laid off 40 feet square, for a burying-ground for all my descendants, to be kept in good fence by them. Witnesses—John Wilkins, Jesse Chew, James Wood, Samuel Carpenter. Proved Jan. 30, 1787.

1786, Dec. 4. Inventory, £434.8.9, made by Biddle Reves and John Jessup. Lib. 29, p. 83.

**1787, Feb. 10. Wilson, Susanna,** of Deptford Township, Gloucester Co.; will of. My right in this plantation where I dwell, and my moveable estate, to be sold, and money to go to my sons, Edward and Jesse Wilson, when they come of age. Daughter, Elizabeth, and to each of my 4 children my apparel. Executor—friend, David Eldridge. Witnesses—James Wood, Jacob Wood, Jesse Chew. Proved June 15, 1789. Lib. 30, p. 108.

## CALENDAR OF WILLS—1786-1790

**1789, Jan. 5. Winans, Elias, Jr.,** of Essex Co.; will of. Wife, Esther, use of land. Daughter, Abigail, £15. Son, Abner, house and land where I live, and part of a salt meadow. Son, Hosea, £50. Daughter, Paty, £20. Son, Abraham, that place I got of Hosea Winans, and the woodland I got of Benjamin Winans, Jr. Son, Hosea Riosen, £40. Daughter, Anna, £40. Son, Elias, the place in Woodbridge. If my father leave anything, it is to go to my sons. Daughter, Nabi, is mentioned. Executrix—wife, Esther. Witnesses—Abraham Winans, Jr., William Paul, Elias Tucker. Proved Nov. 16, 1789. Lib. 30, p. 204.

**1789, Oct. 11. Windes, William,** of Mendham Township, Morris Co.; will of. Wife, Ruhamah, real and personal estate while my widow; and, after her death, to Abigail, Huldah and Susannah Beeman, daughters of Josiah Beeman, £15 each. To Barnabas Windes and his brother, Samuel, ½0 of my estate. To William Windes, Jr., son of Barnabas, ⅒. To William Windes, son of Abijah, ⅒. To William Ross, son of William, ⅒. To Mehetable Gouldsmith, daughter of Jonah, ½0. To John Corey, all he owes me. To the Presbyterian Church at Rockaway, rest of estate. Executors—William Ross and Samuel Lindsley. Witnesses—Joel Phelps, Josiah Goldsmith, Abraham Lyon. Proved Dec. 9, 1789.

1789, Oct. 30. Inventory, made by Andrew King and Job Allen.
Lib. 30, p. 226.

**1786, Feb. 21. Winne, Nicholas and Leah,** of Essex Co. Wards. Children of Abraham Winne, of said Co., deceased. Said Wards, having an estate of £300, make choice of Henry Rutan and John Van Riper, as their Guardians.

1786, Feb. 21. Guardians—Henry Rutan and John Van Riper.
Lib. 28, p. 429.

**1786, July 24. Witherill, Vincent,** of Middlesex Co. Int. Adm'r—Azariah Dunham. Fellowbondsman—James Dunham; both of said Co. Witness—John Van Horne. Lib. 28, p. 340.

**1789, May 20. Woglum, Abram,** of Nottingham Township, Burlington Co.; will of. To Abraham Woglum, son of my brother, Peter, the house and lot where I live, joining Abraham Hunt and Joseph Milnor; also ½ of my 72 acres, in which James Mathis and myself are concerned, in said Twp., and joins William Watson, Samuel Henry and others. To Sarah Woglom, £40, when she is 18, to be paid by her brother, Abraham. Executors—said Peter and Abraham Woglum. Witnesses—Rowland Hall, John Clunn, Stephen Carter. Proved July 22, 1789.

1789, July 21. Inventory, £111.5.0, made by James Mathis and John Clunn. Lib. 31, p. 313.

**1787, March 25. Wood, Anna,** of Gloucester Co. Ward. Daughter of William Wood, of said Co., deceased. George Ward, and Hannah Ward, his wife, which Hannah is the mother of Anna Wood, desire that Samuel Ladd may be appointed Guardian of said Anna Wood.

1787, March 25. Guardian—Samuel Ladd. Fellowbondsman—Joseph Gibson; both of Deptford Township, said Co., yeomen. Lib. 29, p. 121.

**1789, Oct. 5. Wood, Charlotte,** of Gloucester Co. Ward. Daughter of Jehu Wood, of said Co., who appointed Aaron Hewes as Guardian of his said daughter, and the said Aaron Hewes is dead; therefore Charlotte makes choice of Jeremiah Wood as her Guardian.
1789, Oct. 5. Guardian—Jeremiah Wood. Fellowbondsman—Thomas Reeves, Jr.; both of said Co. Lib. 30, p. 138.

**1789, Oct. 5. Wood, Hannah,** of Gloucester Co. Ward. Daughter of Jehu Wood, of said Co., deceased. Petition of Mary Wood, the mother of said Hannah Wood, asking that Jeremiah Wood may be appointed Guardian of said Hannah.
1789, Oct. 5. Guardian—Jeremiah Wood. Fellowbondsman—Thomas Reeves, Jr.; both of said Co. Lib. 30, p. 139.

**1790, July 24. Wood, Howell,** of Gloucester Co. Int. Adm'r—Benjamin Wood, of Penna. Fellowbondsman—Samuel Black, of Gloucester Co. Lib. 31, p. 481.

**1789, Aug. 25. Wood, John,** of Essex Co. Int. Adm'r—Daniel Smith Wood. Fellowbondsman—Theodorus Johnson; both of said Co. Lib. 30, p. 219.

**1789, Oct. 17. Wood, Joseph,** of Elizabeth Town, Essex Co. Int. Adm'r—Samuel Wood, of said place. Fellowbondsman—Samuel Sayre, of Newark, said Co.
1789, Oct. 14. Renunciation by Mary Wood, widow of said Joseph.
1789, Oct. 28. Inventory, £249.16.10, made by John Wood and Joseph D'Camp, of all goods of Joseph Wood, one of the sons of Samuel Wood. Lib. 30, p. 218.

**1789, Oct. 5. Wood, Marmaduke,** of Gloucester Co. Ward. Son of Jehu Wood, of said Co., deceased, who appointed Aaron Hewes as Guardian of his said son, and the said Aaron Hewes is dead; therefor Marmaduke makes choice of Jeremiah Wood as his Guardian.
1789, Oct. 5. Guardian—Jeremiah Wood. Fellowbondsman—Thomas Reeves, Jr.; both of said Co. Lib. 30, p. 139.

**1788, Aug. 1. Wood, Rachel,** of Deptford Township, Gloucester Co.; will of. Granddaughters, Ann Mickle and Sarah Mickle, daughters of James Mickle, my apparel and furniture, when 18. Grandsons, Joshua Wood Thompson and Aaron Thompson, sons of Samuel Thompson, deceased, £40, being now in hands of Henry Tredway; when 21. Said granddaughters to have the residue. Executor—friend, James Wilkins. Witnesses—David Wood, Aaron Hewes. Proved Feb. 16, 1789.
1789, Feb. 16. Adm'r—Phinehas Lord. Fellowbondsman—James Mickle; both of said Co.
1789, Feb. 7. Renunciation by James Wilkins.
1789, Feb. 2. Inventory, £238.18.3, made by James Wilkins and Aaron Hewes. Lib. 30, p. 127.

**1789, Nov. 1. Woodard, Nathaniel,** of Bernards Town, Somerset Co. Int. Adm'rs—Rachel Woodard and Jonathan Penington. Fellowbondsmen—Oliver Woodward and William Compton; all of said place. Witness—Aleser Rodgers.
1789, Nov. 4. Inventory, £206.0.3, made by John Lewis and Clement Wood. Lib. 31, p. 530.

CALENDAR OF WILLS—1786-1790 259

**1787, Aug. 24. Woodruff, John,** of Elizabeth Town, Raway, Essex Co. Ward. Son of Hezekiah Woodruff, of said place, deceased. Said Ward makes choice of Hezekiah Stites Woodruff, as his Guardian.
 1787, Aug. 24. Guardian—Hezekiah Stites Woodruff, of Hunterdon Co. Fellowbondsman—Ogden Woodruff. Witness—William Tindall.
 Lib. 29, p. 299.

**1790, Feb. 24. Woodruff, Josiah,** of Elizabeth Township, Essex Co.; will of. Wife, Patience, use of real and personal estate. Children, Robert, Josiah, Benjamin, Noah, Sarah Woodruff, Nancy Woodruff, Daniel and Abigail Woodruff, the said real and personal estate, after paying the following legacies, except Nancy, the wife of William Bonnel, and she is not to have as much as my other children by £16. Son, Benjamin, £5 more. Son, Ichabod, £5. Executors—wife, Patience, and friends, James Carpenter and John Potter. Witnesses—Samuel Norris, Jonas Wade, Silas Potter. Proved Sept. 21, 1790.
 1790, Aug. 9. Inventory, £122.12.0, made by Cornelius Williams and Matthias Potter.  Lib. 30, p. 350.

**1789, Nov. 10. Woolf, George,** of Roxbury Township, Morris Co. Int. Adm'x—Mary Woolf. Fellowbondsman—John Wolfe; both of said place. Witness—Jacob Schuiler.
 1789, Oct. 16. Inventory, £195.7.10, made by Jacob Schuiler and Richard Stephens. Value of plantation, £100.  Lib. 30, p. 233.

**1786, July 8. Woolley, Sarah,** of Burlington, Burlington Co.; will of. To George Eyre, son of John Eyre, late of Kensington, Penna., deceased, my house and lot where I live, fronting on the Delaware. To Anthony Taylor, son of John, my land known as the Pott House, on the said river, joining Abraham Hewling, Sr., and occupied by Amos Hutchin. To said John Taylor land on Burlington Island, of 2½ acres. To Lydia Eyre, widow of said John, my orchard lot of 3 acres. To Hannah Taylor, wife of John, £50. To Lydia Moore, wife of Thomas, £50. To Mary Marks, of Philadelphia, daughter of Henry Marks, £25. To Sarah Boin, of New York, £15, and to her sister, Hannah Giddington, £10. To Mary Lovett, the daughter of Mrs. Rigdon, £10. To Mary Bryant, widow, £5. To Ann Kimble, £5. Rest to Hannah Taylor, Lydia Moore and Lydia Eyre. Executor—friend, John Taylor, merchant in Bordentown. Witnesses—Abraham Hewlings, George Painter, Allan McCollins. Proved Jan. 22, 1787.
 1787, Jan. 22. Inventory, £743.9.1, made by Abraham Hewlings and Amos Hutchin.  Lib. 29, p. 5.

**1789, Oct. 6. Woolston, Joseph,** of Northampton, Burlington Co. Int. Adm'x—Mary Woolston. Fellowbondsman—Samuel W. Woolston; both of Northampton Township, said Co.
 1789, Sept. 21. Inventory, £38.8.0, made by Phinehas Kirkbride and William Burr.  Lib. 31, p. 321.

**1786, Feb. 27. Woolston, William,** of Northampton Township, Burlington Co.; will of. Son, William, a part of my land where Isaac Pippet formerly lived, and Edward Cotton now lives, and to be 30 acres. Son, Samuel, the rest of said land. Two oldest sons, George and Joseph, 20 shillings each. Four oldest sons, George, Joseph, William and Samuel, my cedar swamp. Daughter, Elizabeth Wool-

ston, goods to make her equal with that I gave my daughter, Mary Budd. Youngest son, Daniel, 20 shillings. Wife to have all the goods I had with her, and ¼ of the personal estate. Daughters, Mary Budd, Elizabeth Woolston and Rachel Woolston, rest of personal estate. Executors—sons, George, Joseph, William and Samuel. Witnesses—Joseph Eayre, Thomas Moore, Phinehas Kirkbride. Proved Aug. 30, 1788.
1788, Aug. 29. Inventory, £338.17.6, made by Phinehas Kirkbride and Thomas Moore. Lib. 29, p. 538.

**1787, Jan. 6. Woolston, William, Jr.,** of Northampton Township, Burlington Co. Int. Adm'rs—George Woolston and Samuel Woolston. Fellowbondsman—Levi Eayre; all of said place.
1786, Sept. 12. Inventory, £165.5.7, made by Levi Eayre and Enoch Haines. Lib. 29, p. 72.

**1786, April 10. Woolverton, Daniel,** of Kingwood, Hunterdon Co. Int. Adm'x—Hannah Woolverton. Fellowbondsman—Derrick Hogeland; both of said Co.
1786, April 21. Inventory, £220.2.9, made by Tunis Quick and Alexander Thompson. Lib. 28, p. 247.

**1786, March 4. Worrall, Peter,** of Burlington, Burlington Co.; will of. Nephew, Henry Young, and to my half brother, Thomas Bromfield, son of John Bromfield, £10 each. Niece, Hannah Hall, wife of David Hall, silversmith of Philadelphia, £10. Daughter-in-law, Mary Bowd, a silver tankard, that formerly belonged to Samuel Blunston. To Ann Stoute, daughter of my niece, Hannah Hall, £5. Susannah Dillwyn, daughter of my son-in-law, William Dillwyn, £50. Hannah Cox, daughter of my son-in-law, John Cox, £10. Henry Willis, son of Wiliam Willis, deceased, £5. Friends, Robert Willis, of Rahway; Benjamin Jones, of Springfield; Joseph Williams, half brother of Enion Williams, late of Bristol, deceased; Joseph Speakman, late of Falls Township, Pa., tinman; Abraham Griffith, Sr., of Pennsylvania, miller, formerly of Mount Holly; David Estough, of Philadelphia, Peter Yarnell, son of Mordecai Yarnell; and to Thomas Pryor, of Burlington, to each £5. Friends, Rebecca Jones, of Philadelphia, and Hannah Cathrall, of same place, £5 each. Friends, Grace Buchanon, of Burlington; Mary Humphrys (formerly Franks), wife of Benjamin Humphrys, of Philadelphia, and Margaret Porter, of Pennsylvania, £5 each. To Elizabeth Hicks, widow, now residing with Doctor Charles Moore; Mary Allen, of New York, widow, sister of John Cox, of Trenton, and to Edith Carty of Burlington, widow, £5 each. Whereas, my former wife, Sarah Worrall, deceased (whose maiden name was Blunston), had 15 acres ¾ of land, as heir to her uncle, Samuel Blunston, the same being part of 31½ acres, near Lancaster, which was transferred by my wife to Gasper Shaftner, and by him to me, and was sold by me in 2 lots, for about £164, and I desire that said sum may return to the descendants of my wife; therefore I give to the children of Samuel Bethel, and the children of Mary Bowd (the said Samuel and Mary being children of my said wife, by her former husband, Samuel Bethel), the said sum of £164. All the real and personal estate to be sold. Whereas, a part of a lot in Lancaster, which I bought of John Foulke, who bought of Michael Shank, is part of my estate, which lot the heirs of said Shank by his Warrantee are bound to support a good title.

CALENDAR OF WILLS—1786-1790        261

Rest of estate I give to my sons-in-law, George Dillwyn and William Dillwyn, my daughter-in-law, Ann Cox, and my kinsman, Richard Wells. Executors—sons-in-law, George Dillwyn and William Dillwyn, and my kinsman, Richard Wells, of Philadelphia, merchant, and Doctor Charles Moore, of Montgomery. Witnesses—John Hoskins, Daniel Smith, Robert Smith. Proved March 29, 1786.
1786, March 28. Inventory, £941.16.10, made by Daniel Smith and Robert Smith. "Interest on bond to the time of Peter Worrall's death, viz, the 23rd instant." Lib. 27, p. 526.

**1787, Jan. 5. Wright, Isaiah,** of Burlington Co. Int. Adm'rs—John Allen and William Duff. Fellowbondsman—John Mott; all of Northampton, said Co. Witness—Thomas Adams.
1787, Jan. 5. Renunciation by Rhoda Wright, widow of said Isaiah, in favor of John Allen and William Duff.
1787, Jan. 3. Inventory, £59.7.4, made by Daniel Gaskill and Samuel Parker. Lib. 29, p. 75.

**1786, March 24. Wright, Joseph,** of Chester Township, Burlington Co. Int. Adm'rs—John Haines, Jacob Merrit and Joshua W. Satterthwaite. Fellowbondsmen—Josiah Gaskill and Andrew Craig; all of said Co.
1786, March 31. Inventory, £1,027.13.5, made by John Ridgway and David Ridgway. Lib. 28, p. 77.

**1786, May 9. Wyatt, Bartholomew,** of Mannington Township, Salem Co., yeoman; will of. Daughter, Elizabeth Carpenter, all real and personal estate, and, if she die, then all to be sold and money given to children of my deceased sister, Sarah Wistar. To Mark Miller, and John Redman, £200, and they are to pay it to the Friends' Free School of Salem. Executors—son-in-law, William Carpenter, and my nephew, John Wistar. Witnesses—Samuel Austin, Josiah Miller, Ebenezer Miller. Proved Aug. 20, 1788. Lib. 31, p. 56.

**1787, May 28. Wyckoff, Jacobus,** of Reading Township, Hunterdon Co., yeoman; will of. To the Dutch Reformed Church of North Branch, £200. Brother, Cornelius, shall live on the place with my wife, Cornelia, and give her ⅛ of what he raises. Wife, Cornelia, use of real and personal estate during her life, and ½ thereof to her forever, and the other ½ to my brother, Cornelius, and to my brother's son, Jacobus. Best horses and cows to be kept on farm for use of family. Executors—wife, Cornelia, and brother, Cornelius, and Cornelius Johnson. Witnesses—Martin Wyckoff, Jr., Henry Garrabrants, John Wyckoff. Proved July 13, 1787.
1787, June 25. Inventory, £575.2.8, made by Martin Wyckoff, Jr., and Nicholas Wyckoff. Lib. 29, p. 251.

**1786, March 13. Wyker, Philip,** of Sussex Co. Int. Adm'x—Mary Wyker, widow of said Philip. Fellowbondsman—Phillip Wyker; both of Newtown Township said Co. Witness—Jonathan Willis.
1786, March 28. Inventory, £22.5.0, made by Charles Roszel and Joseph Roszel. Lib. 28, p. 469.

**1788, Feb. 8. Yard, Benjamin,** of Burlington Co., late of Santacruz. Int. Adm'r—Thomas Yard. Fellowbondsman—John Rozell; both of Trenton, Hunterdon Co. Lib. 30, p. 57.

**1790, March 26.** **Yard, Mary,** of Trenton, Hunterdon Co. Int. Adm'r—John Yard. Fellowbondsman—Benjamin Yard; both of said place. Lib. 30, p. 314.

**1786, June 21.** **Young, Daniel,** of Morris Co.; will of. My children to be decently brought up, and, if anything is left, they are to have it when they are of age. Executors—friends, Prudden Alling and David Bedford. Witnesses—Abigail Cooper, Prudden Alling, Othniel Looker. Proved June 29, 1786.
1786, June 27. Inventory, £292.7.3, made by Ananias Halsey and Ebenezer Sayre. Lib. 28, p. 479.

**1787, May 10.** **Young, Stephen,** of Newark, Essex Co.; will of. Wife, Joannah, all personal and use of ½ of the real estate. Son, Jonas, 6½ acres of land at the Mill Brook swamp. To the children of my son, Daniel, deceased, land bounded on Thomas Eagles. Daughter, Abigail Alling, £80. Son, Aaron, my homestead. Executors—wife, Joannah, and son, Aaron. Witnesses—David James, Jotham Harrison, Nathaniel Farrand. Proved May 10, 1790.
Lib. 30, p. 336.

**1788, Jan. 7.** **Young, William,** of Amwell, Hunterdon Co.; will of. Wife, Anna, use of house, live stock and goods. Son, Peter, plantation which I bought of him. Son, William, place where I live. Sons, Peter and William, to give their mother, ⅙ of all raised; at end of her widowhood, if any thing is left, it is to be given to my children, Peter, William, Catherina, and my 2 grandchildren, Mary and Paul Kuhl. Daughter, Catherina, £200. Executors—sons, Peter and William, and Paul Kuhl. Witnesses—Roleff Schanck, John Williamson, John Sutphen (Jacob's son).
1788, Jan. 30. Codicil. Witnesses—Roleff Schanck, Jacobus Diets, John Sutphen (Jacob's son). Proved Feb. 20, 1788.
1788, Feb. 13. Inventory, £574.18.0, made by Roleff Schanck and John Williamson. Lib. 31, p. 134.

**1789, March 21.** **Youngs, Joseph,** of Hanover, Morris Co., yeoman; will of. Wife, Isabella, £50. Sons, Grover and John ⅙ of estate. Daughter, Deliverance Youngs, ⅙. Daughter, Joannah Youngs, ⅙. Daughter, Keturah Youngs, now Marsh, ⅙. Son, John, ⅙. Estate to be sold. Wife, ⅙ of estate. Executors—Joseph Tuttle, Benjamin Lindsly and Jesse Cutler. Witnesses—Richard Johnson, Joseph Hallsey, James Youngs. Proved Nov. 14, 1789.
1789, Sept. 30. Inventory, £239.9.7, made by Richard Johnson and Joseph Hallsey. Lib. 30, p. 223.

**1786, March 30.** **Zabriskei, Jacob,** of Hackensack, Bergen Co.; will of. To Lenah Zabriski, widow of my late son, John, £40. My grandchildren, Sarah Zabriski, John Lansing Zabriski and Catharine Zabriski, children of my son, John, deceased, my real and personal estate, but that which I bought out of the estate of Nicholas Romine, to be sold; as also the land near David Berdan; and woodland in Kallie Koon Neck. My grandchildren are to be educated. If my granddaughter, Sarah Lansing, shall remain with her grandfather, John Lansing, at Albany, she shall not have any support out of my estate. Executors—brother, Peter Zabriskie, and my friends, Jacob Terhune and Albert C. Zabriskie. Witness—Yan Vanderbeeck, James Bertholf, John Zabriski.

1786, March 30. Codicil. Witnesses—as above. Proved Jan. 24, 1787. Lib. 29, p. 513.

**1790, Dec. 1. Zabriskie, Andrew,** of Bergen Co. Ward. Son of Andrew Zabriskie, of said Co., deceased. Said ward having real and personal estate, makes choice of Aert Cuyper as his Guardian.
1790, Dec. 1. Guardian—Aert Cuyper. Fellowbondsman—Isaac Vanderbeek, both of said Co. Lib. 31, p. 543.

**1790, Oct. 18. Zabriskie, Caty,** of Bergen Co. Ward. Daughter of Christian Zabriskie, of said Co. Said Ward makes choice of Christian Zabriskie, as her Guardian.
1790, Oct. 18. Guardian—Christian Zabriskie. Fellowbondsman—Andris Zabriski; both of said Co. Witness—William Ross Smith.
Lib. 31, p. 543.

**1786, March 21. Zabriskie, Hendrick C.,** of New Barbadoes; will of. Children, Abraham and Elizabeth, to be educated. Daughters, Mary, Elizabeth, Maregreat, Sarah, and my son, Abraham, £50 each, after they are 21. Wife, Mary, to have the interest of the money, and, after her death, said money to be paid to my children, Abraham, Lea, Martenje, Marregreatje, Sarah, Elizabeth and Mary, and children of my daughter, Gertje. Executors—my brother-in-law, Cornelius Haring and Christian A. Zabriskie. Witnesses—Garret Oldis, John Pervost, Jr. Proved June 13, 1786.
1786, May 23. Inventory, £996.11.0, made by John Pervost and George Doremus. Lib. 29, p. 208.

**1789, March 31. Zabriskie, Joost,** of Bergen Co. Int. Adm'r—William M. Bell. Fellowbondsman—Garret Hoppe; both of said Co. Witnesses—Albert Westervelt and Abram Westervelt. Lib. 30, p. 248.

**1788, March 12. Zane, Isaac,** of Woolwich Township, Gloucester Co., yeoman; will of. Wife, Azaubah, plantation I live on. Son, Brusilah, said plantation, after her death; also 5 acres of meadow on Oldmans Creek. Son, Henery, my swamp and small plantation, joining lands of Mathew Gill, of about 35 acres. Rest of lands on Oldmans Creek to my wife and children, Robert, Isaac, Wilkins and Lettis Zane and Azaube Zane. Daughter, Amey Biles, £5. Five acres of cedar swamp which join John Kille and others to be sold. Executors—wife, Azubah, and my sons, Barzillai and Henry. Witnesses—James Talman, Samuel Denny, Thomas Denny. Proved Sept. 27, 1788.
1788, Sept. 27. Renunciation by Henry Zane. Witness—Thomas Denny.
1788, April 2. Inventory, £263.12.2, made by Thomas Denny and Matthew Gill, Jr. Lib. 31, p. 1.

**1787, July 30. Zane, Nathan,** of Greenwich Township, Gloucester Co., yeoman; will of. Wife, Rachel, £10 yearly and some goods. Land to be rented out until my oldest son, Redmon, is 21, to bring up the children. Son, Redmon, the plantation and land up the woods; also old mill tract. Son, Nathan, the grist mill, which I bought of William Wriggons, part of the Commissioners, and part of Sheriff, Thomas Denny; except 2 acres that I sold. Nathan also to have plantation now in possession of William Wood. Daughter, Abigail Zane, 20 shillings. Executors—wife, Rachel, and Aaron Pancoast.

Witnesses—Joseph Zane, Jacob Gosling, George Hellerman. Proved March 1, 1788.
1788, Jan. 19. Inventory, £190,12.2, made by Samuel French and Jacob Gosling.
Lib. 31, p. 2.

**1787, April 17. Zane, William,** of Woolwich, Gloucester Co. Int. Adm'r—William Zane, Jr., of said place, yeoman. Fellowbondsman—Jacob Cozens, of Greenwich Township, said Co., yeoman. Witness—William Hollinshead.
1787, April 13. Inventory, £814.9.6, made by William Hollinshead and Samuel French.
Lib. 29, p. 117.

# INDEXES

I. INDEX OF NAMES OF PERSONS
II. INDEX OF PLACE NAMES

# Index of Names of Persons

NOTE—The names of testators, intestate persons or wards, printed in heavy type in the preceding text, are not repeated in this Index, as a rule. Where maiden names can be ascertained from the body of the will, they are included.

Where surnames in common use to-day, or at least with well-known spellings, are unusually or curiously used in the text, the current modern spelling is substituted in this Index, to facilitate reference. An exception is made where proper spelling is uncertain. To a lesser extent the same rule has been applied to Christian names.

## A

Aaronson (Aronson), Benjamin, 7
  George, 7
  John, Jr., 7
  Joseph, 7
  Mary, 13
  Rebecca, 7
  Samuel, 7
  Thomas, 7
Abbott (Abbit, Abit, Abot, &c.)
  Abdon, Jr., 7
  Anna, 7
  Benjamin, 220
  Elizabeth, 7
  Hannah, 36
  Jeptha, 99
  John, 7, 73, 134, 146, 175
  Martha, 7
  Mary, 7
  Samuel, 191
  Sarah, 7
Aborn, Jonathan, 7
Acken, Phebe, 7
  *See also* Akin
Acker, William, 67
Ackerman, David, 211
  Garret, A., 7
  Garrit, 70
Acton, Hannah, 7
  John, 7
Adams, Alexander, 74
  Andrew, 161
  Angle, 196
  Anne, 8, 76
  Barbara, 8
  Benjamin, 127
  Catherine, 8
  Christiana, 8
  Daniel, 150
  David, 81
  Ebenezer, 47, 50, 52, 106, 108, 115, 128, 150, 183, 212, 213
  Elizabeth, 8
  Evi, 61, 67, 80, 255
  Hannah, 8, 50
  Henry, 8
  Jacob, 8
  John, 196
  Jonas, 208
  Joseph, 127
  Lemuel, 8
  Margaret Beatson, 76
  Mary, 187
  Philathea, 8
  Samuel, 127
  Thomas, 8 11, 14, 16, 27, 32, 33, 35, 39, 54, 57, 86, 87, 100, 105, 114, 117, 121, 122, 124, 127, 129, 146, 148, 183, 202, 207, 211, 252 261
  William, Jr., 8
  *See also* Addoms
Addis, Simon, 198
Addoms (Addams), Jonathan, 69
  Mary, 69
  Silvanus, 39
  William, 21
  *See also* Adams
Akin, Abiel, 34
  *See also* Acken
Albertson, Aaron, 8, 9
  Deborah, 8
  Hannah, 18
  Isaac, Jr., 8
  Jacob, 8, 63
  John, 18
  Josiah, 8
  Keziah, 8, 15, 65, 123, 159
  Nathan, 8
  Nehemiah, 8
  Rachel, 8
  Reckliff, 8
  Samuel, 8
  Thomas, 8
  *See also* Elberson
Alderman, William, 241
Alexander, Mary, 231
Allen, Aaron, 9
  Abigail, 9
  Ann, 24
  Charles, 164
  David, Jr., 9

Allen, Dorothy, 9
  Elijah, 13, 225, 231
  Enoch, 218
  Ephraim, 249
  Erazamos Kent, 9
  Hannah, 9
  Hope, 9
  Isaac, 9, 58, 61
  Jacob, 210
  James, 9
  James, Jr., 9
  Job, 257
  John, 9, 41, 44, 74, 129, 229, 261
  Margaret, 10
  Margery, 10
  Martha, 10
  Mary, 9, 229, 260
  Matthew, 218
  Rachel, 9
  Ralph, 9
  Rebecca, 9
  Samuel, 9, 10
  Sarah, 9, 10, 172
  Silas, 9
  Sulfphias, 9
  Thomas, 9, 38, 41, 218
  William, 9
Aller, John, 192
Alling, Abigail, 262
  Isaac, 58
  Prudden, 262
Allinson, Mary, 38, 139
  Samuel, 36, 38, 129, 139
  William, 38, 139
Allison, Burgiss, 148
Allpock, Catharine, 184
  William, 184
Alston, Thomas, 18
Amerman, Eleanor, 10
Amlin, Sarah, 232
Anderson (Andresson), Aaron, 11
  Abel, 11
  Abigail, 11
  Abraham, Jr., 11
  Andrew, Jr., 11
  Anna, 11, 12
  Elizabeth, 11, 12
  Ely, 11
  Enoch, 11
  George, 11, 239
  Isaac, 11
  Jacob, 11
  James, 12, 75
  Jane, 12
  Jannett, 11
  John, 16, 30, 90, 234
  John Scott, 11
  Joshua, 11, 234
  Josiah, 11
  Mary, 11, 12
  Mary O., 106
  Mercy, 11
  Phebe, 11
  Samuel, 11, 21
  Sarah, 12
  Susanna, 11
  Thomas, 12, 24, 38, 39, 90, 106
  William, 39, 88, 192
  William Alexander, 131
Andrass, Nathaniel, 61
Andres, Catherine, 12
Andrews, Hannah, 176
  Paul, 176
  Peter, 100, 163, 186
  Rebecca, 76

Angur, Abraham, 91
Annin, Joseph, 60, 144
  Samuel, 60
Antram (Antrim, Antrum), Abigail, 203
  Ann, 97, 203
  Charity, 203
  Elizabeth, 104
  Hannah, 12
  Isaac, 12, 124
  John, 12, 64, 213
  Martha, 12
  Susannah, 12
  Thomas, 97
  Zacheriah, 64
Apgar (Apger), Adam, 77
  Coanrod, 77, 251
  Frederick, 251
  Mary, 77
Applegate (Apelgate), Andrew, 111
  Ann, 12
  Bartholomew, 116
  Charles, 16
  Elizabeth, 12
  Hannah, 12
  Israel, 12
  John, Jr., 12
  Joseph, 111
  Keziah, 12
  Lydia, 12
  Rebecca, 12
  Richard, 13
  Samuel, 12
  Sarah, 12
  William, 12, 71
  Zebulon, 12
Appleton, Henry, 166
Archer, Jacob, Jr., 115
Arey, William, 166
Armitage, John, 152, 153
Armstrong, Alley, 13
  Elizabeth, 13
  Ephraim, Jr., 13
  George, 140, 141, 168, 229, 245
  John, 13, 140, 141, 168, 194
  Joseph, 13
  Mary, 13
  Samuel, 13
  William, 116, 245
Arnet, Samuel, 111
Arnold, Christopher, 213
  Ebenezer, 235
  Esther, 235
  Jacob, 19, 20, 41, 149
  John, 113, 132, 176
  Samuel, 41
  Sarah, 13
Aronson—*see* Aaronson
Arrison, Elizabeth, 14
  Euphame, 14
  Grace, 14
  Jonathan, 14
  Mary, 13, 14
  Richard, 14
  *See also* Harrison
Arrowsmith, Joseph 78
Arwine, John, 192
  William, 73
Asa, Mary, 14
Asbury, Francis, 255
Ashcraft, Gibson, 83
Ashley, John, 35
Ashmore (Ashmoor), Anthony, 143
  Eleanor, 143
  James, 143
  Thomas, 63, 187

# INDEX OF NAMES OF PERSONS 269

Ashton, Joseph, Jr., 37
Atchley, Abraham, 145
Aten, John, 55
Atkinson, Aden, 14
  Ann, 14
  Benjamin, 14
  Elizabeth, 112, 139
  Hannah, 14
  John, 14, 74, 81, 112, 156
  Joseph, 14, 112
  Moses, 7
  Samuel, 14, 15, 139, 156
  Sarah, 7
  William, 39
Attmore, Caleb, 45, 62
Austin, Amos, 47
  Caleb, 10, 27
  Francis, 37
  Mary, 74
  Nathan, 74
  Samuel, 261
  Seth, 57
Auten—*see* Aten
Avery, Henry, 192
Avise (Avis), Agnes, 15
  Ann, 15
  James, 15, 194
Axford, Charles, 29, 235, 237
Ayers (Ayars, Ayres), Caleb, 72, 153
  David, 27, 72, 121, 153
  Dugal, 24
  Enoch, 192
  Israel, 192
  Job, 15, 72
  John, 70, 80
  Joshua, 37
  Lydia, 15
  Michael, 97
  Moses, 63
  Nathaniel, 60, 227
  Obadiah, 100
  Philip, Jr., 15
  Sarah, 15
  Silas, 84, 89, 92, 137
  Susannah, 152
  William, 63

## B

Babbit, Daniel, 120
Babcock—*see* Badcock
Backster, George, 32
Bacon, Daniel, Jr., 32, 38
  Job, Jr., 19
  John, 19
  John, Jr., 19
  Joseph, 72
  Mary, 15
  Samuel, 15
  Uriah, 27
Bacorn, Dennis, 159
Badcock, Christean, 15
  David, 210
  Enoch, 15
  Jacob, 15
  John, Jr., 15
  Jonathan, 189, 206
  Joseph, 239
  Margaret, 15
  Mary, 15
  Rebecca, 15
  Sarah, 15
Badgley (Badgly), George, 77, 226
  Isaac, 67

Jane, 16, 197
Lydia, 197
Mary, 205
Bailey, Eleanor, 16
  Hannah, 16
  John, 16
  *See also* Baley
Bainbridge, Abigail, 16
  Azubah, 125
  Richard, 125
  William, 16
Baird, Andrew, 193
  David, 48, 245
  John, 48, 193
  Peter, 31, 133, 193, 213
  *See also* Bayard
Baker, Aaron, 17
  Abner, 17
  Ann, 17
  Catharine, 17
  Cornelius, 17, 205
  Daniel, 16, 17, 49
  Elizabeth, 16
  Hannah, 17, 116
  Henry, 16, 17, 93, 128, 179
  Janet, 17
  John, 16, 17
  Jonathan, 17
  Joshua, 17
  Jude, 17
  Judith, 17
  Looe, 143
  Mariam, 17
  Martha, 16, 17
  Mary, 16, 17
  Nathan, 17
  Phoebe, 17
  Rachel, 17
  Sarah, 17
  Susannah, 17
  Thomas, 17, 164
  Timothy, Jr., 17
  Valentine, 246
  William, 17
Bald, Mercy, 84
Baldwin, Abraham, 169
  Bark, 150
  David, 53
  Dodok, 102
  Isaac, 50
  Jesse, 111
  John, 58, 69
  Jonathan, 58
  Joseph, 184
  Josiah, 169
  Lewis, 39
  Lydia, 169
  Martha, 53
  Mary, 58
  Matthew, 195
  Moses, 58
  Phebe, 17
  Rachel, 169
  Stephen, 187
  Thomas, 16, 69
  William, 35
Baley (Baly), Ann, 128
  Henry, 129
  *See also* Bailey
Ball, Esther, 164
  Ezekiel, Jr., 176
  Nehemiah, 227
  Samuel, 33
  Uzal, 89
Ballinger (Ballenger), Enoch, 128
  Isaac, 18

Samuel, 199
Thomas, Jr., 63
Bancroft—*see* Bencroft
Banks, David, 111
Barber, Ann, 228
　Jesse, 199
　Rebecca, 19
　Susannah, 62
　Uquilah, 236
Barclay, John, 146
Bard, John, 111
Bardon, Hendrik, 239
Barhight (Barhyt), Daniel, 37, 57
　Elizabeth, 37
Barkalow (Barcalow, Barrikelow), &c.)
　Anna, 217
　Cornelius, 179
　Derick, 180, 217
　Jan, 225
　Sarah, 179
Barkley, Christian, 18
　Elizabeth, 18
　Hugh, 18
　Isabel, 18
　John, 18
　Martha, 18
　Nancy, 18
　Rebecca, 18
Barlow, John, 169
Barnes, Isaac, 24, 139, 152, 153
　John, 19, 65, 204
　John, Jr., 19
　William, 253
Barnet, Oliver, 18
Barracliff, George, 19
　Ruth, 19
Barratt (Barrett, Barrot), Betsy, 154
　Caleb, 19
　Elijah, 19
　John Miller, 154
　Thomas, 154
Barrick, Elizabeth, 19
　Mary, 19
　Samuel, 19
Barron, Ellis, 105
Bartlett, Nathan, 211
Bartolf—*see* Bertholf
Barton, Gabriel, 164
　Isaac, 244
　John, 164
　Jonathan, 88, 196
　Joseph, 63
　Rachel, 217
　Stephen, 218
　Uriah, 63
Bartrim, Anthony, 138
　Joseph, 138
Bassett (Basset), Abigail, 10
　Ann, 19
　Beuley, 19
　Daniel, Jr., 19, 204
　David, 19, 209
　Davis, 204
　Elisha, 19
　Elizabeth, 19, 129
　Isaac, 19
　Jeremiah, 10
　John, 19
　Joseph, 19
　Josiah, 19
　Samuel, 129
　Sarah, 129
　William, 129
Bate, Esther, 114
　Japhet, 114
　Phebe, 114
　Sarah, 114
　Sibillah, 114
　Thomas, 114
Bateman, James, 224
　John, 27, 122
　Thomas, 224
Bates, David, 164
　Joshua, 157
　Phebe, 185
Batson, John, 244
Baxter—*see* Backster
Bayard, Anthony Walton White, 251
　James, 251
　Johannah, 251
　John, 251
　*See also* Baird
Beach, Daniel, 58
　Darling, 92, 211
　Enoch, 92, 211
　Epenetus, 20
　Gabriel, 20
　John, 140
　Noah, 92
　Sarah, 20
Beakes, Nathan, 152, 191, 255
Beakman—*see* Beekman
Beam, Anthony, 138
　Joost, 138, 244
Bearder, Andrew, 189
　Jacob, 189
Beasley—*see* Beesley
Beaston, William, 19
Beatty (Beaty), E., 145
　George, 235
　John, 94, 145
　Reading, 94
Beavers, Joseph, 46
Bebout, Hannah, 170
Beck, Hannah, 20
　John Scholey, 20
　Mary, 20
Beckett, Peter, 52, 130
　Samuel, 52, 81
Bedell (Bedeal), Abraham, 20
　Agnes, 77
　Catharine, 20
　Chateren, 20
　Deborah, 164
　Eleanor, 20
　John, 163
　Martha, 20
　Michael, 168
Bedford, David, 92, 96, 137, 262
　Jonas, 29
Bee, Ephraim, 128
Beekman (Beakman), Aaron, 238
　Ariony, 20
　Christopher, 239
　Cornelius, 20
　Garret, 20
　Gerardus, 238, 239
　John, Jr., 20
　Samuel, 153, 239
Beeman, Abigail, 257
　Huldah, 257
　Josiah, 257
　Susannah, 257
　*See also* Beman
Beers, Azubah, 20
　John, 104
　Joseph, 20, 233
　Nathaniel, 84
Beesley (Beasley), Catharine, 21
　Elizabeth, 21
　Johnson, 20, 21

## INDEX OF NAMES OF PERSONS 271

Joseph, 42
Morris, 150
Bell, Abigail, 21
  Abraham, 21
  Catharine, 21
  Deliverance, 21
  Elizabeth, 18, 21
  Hannah, 21
  John, 48, 110
  Mehitabel, 21
  Susannah, 21
  Unice, 21
  William, 21, 24, 138
  William M., 263
  William Tenant, 21
Bellangeau, Henry, 30
  Samuel, 30
Bellerjeau, Hannah, 234
  John, 234
  Samuel, 234
  Samuel Tucker, 234
  Sarah, 233, 234
Belles, Mary, 192
  William, 192
Bellvill, Ann, 30
Beman, David, 142
  Josiah, 142
  *See also* Beeman
Bemer, Elizabeth, 106
Bencroft, Phebe, 163
Bennet (Bennett, Bennit), Aaron, Jr., 12
  Abraham, 134
  Altee, 22
  Auhely, 240
  Benjamin, 22
  Catharine, 22
  Garrit, 103
  Hendrick, 22
  Jacob, 22
  Joseph, 226
  Margaret, 22
  Mary, 22
  Rachel, 22, 25
  Richard, 121
  Sarah, 22
  Thankfull, 22
  Thomas, 138
  William, 21, 22, 240
  William, Jr., 22
Benson, John, 129
Berdan, David, 262
Bergen (Bergon), Frederick, 238
  Hendrick, 181, 238
  Jacob G., 118
  Jacobus, 31, 245
  John, 94
  *See also* Burgin
Berrien (Berean), Major, 188
  Elizabeth, 128
  Hendrick, 238
Berry, Catalinety, 22
  Elizabeth, 147
  Jemima, 22
  Samuel, 196
  Sarah, 22
  Thomas, 18, 101, 180
Berson, Francis, 122, 192
Bertholf (Bartolf, Bertolf), Albert, 180
  Elseye, 180
  Gyles, 22
  James, 262
  Jemima, 22
  John, 22, 83
  Marietie, 22

Marey, 147
Marregreetie, 22
Bescherer (Besherer), Abraham, 10, 117, 199
Besson, John, 172
  Margaret, 172
Bethel, Mary, 260
  Samuel, 260
Betts, Samuel, 172
Bevins, Ann, 23
Bice, Denice, 198
  Honche, 198
  *See also* Boice, Buys
Bickham, Dinah, 182
Biddle, Joseph, 169
  Thomas, 75
Biddleman (Bidleman), Valentine, 46, 77, 131, 148, 174
Biglow, Aaron, 130
Biggs, William, 90
Bilderback (Bilderbeck), Charles, Jr., 23
  John, 23
  Jonathan, 23, 96
  Malcom, 23
  Sarah, 23
  Susannah, 23
  William, 114, 220
Biles, Amy, 263
  Henry, 17
  William, 71
Billings, Joshua, 23
  Temperance, 101
Bills, Elizabeth, 203
  Sarah, 23
  Silvanus, 217
  Thomas, 23, 203
Bilyew, Isaac, 114
Binge, William, 125
Bingham, Anne, 118
  Charles, 118
Bird, Abigail, 23
  Charles, 23
  Elizabeth, 23, 84
  Jeremiah, 23, 172
  John, 68
  Joseph, 172
  Mary, 68
  Samuel, 23
  Sarah, 23
  Ursula, 23
Birdeleen, Dorcus, 210
Bishop, James, 55, 70, 148
  Japheth, 181
  John, 215
  Joseph, 9, 24, 131
  Margaret, 96
  Mary, 215
  Moses, 24
  Samuel, 225
  William, 35
Bispham, Benjamin, 112
  Elizabeth, 112
  Hannah, 95
  Hinchman, 112
  John, 38, 112
  Joshua, Jr., 47
  Sarah, 112
  Thomas, 95, 112
Blachley (Blachly), Absalom, 252
  Ebenezer, 111
  Hannah, 252
  Jude, 252
  Mary, 252
  Phebe, 252
  Temperance, 252

Black, Edward, 156
  Ezra, 127
  John, 39, 47, 166
  John, Jr., 167
  Samuel, 191, 258
  William, Jr., 167
Blackford, Abigail, 25
  Benjamin, 49, 242, 248
  David, 165
  Mary, 25
Blacklidge, Benjamin, 250
Blackwell, Andrew, 34
  Ann, 24
  Jacob, 34
  Thomas, 125
Blackwood, John, 44, 97, 129, 153, 207
  Joseph, 159
Blair, James, 24
  Jane, 24
  Robert, 18, 180, 219
Blanch, Isaac, 250
Blanchard, John, 31, 137
  Margaret Burt, 37
Blauvelt, Abraham, 157, 158
  Harmon, 81
Blaw, Cornelius, 24
  Elizabeth, 24
  John, 24
  Leah, 24
  Mary, 24
  Michael, Jr., 24
  Samuel, 24
  Sarah, 24
  *See also* Blew, Blue
Blew, Frederick, 242
  *See also* Blaw, Blue
Blizzard (Blizard), James, 208
  Ziba, 208
Bloodgood, Samuel, 216
Bloomfield, Jonathan, 152
  Joseph, 29, 148, 252
  Moses, 216
  Samuel, 47, 166
Blue, Isaac, 24, 90
  John, 90
  *See also* Blaw, Blew
Blunston, Samuel, 260
  Sarah, 260
Board, Joseph, 75
Bockoven, George, 77
  John, 42
  Peter, 42
Bodine, John, 68
Bogert (Bogart), Gisbert, 24
  Helena, 243
  Jacob, 20, 66
  Jacobus, 237
  James S., 237
  Steven, 237
Boggs, Ann, 24
  Rachel, 37
Boice (Boyce, Boys), Jacob, 135
  John, 182
  Mary, 25
  Robert, 61
  *See also* Bice
Boin, Sarah, 259
Bollen, Unis, 25
Bolton, Joseph, 147, 190
Bond, Jacob, 17, 49
  Levi, 201
  Lewis, 221
Bonham, Ephraim, 234
  Hezekiah, 121

Samuel, 234
Uriah, 68, 118, 144, 183, 194
Bonnel (Bonnell), Abigail, 25
  Abraham, 25, 133
  Affa, 25
  Benjamin, 17, 25, 164
  Daniel, 25
  Hannah, 25
  Henry, 25
  James, 25, 125
  Jemima, 25
  Joseph, 25
  Mary, 25
  Mary Magdalene, 119
  Nancy, 259
  Phebe, 25
  Samuel, 119
  Sarah, 25
  Stephen, 25
  William, 259
  *See also* Bunnel
Bonney, James, 228
  Joseph, 71
Borden, Aaron, 26
  Amos, 26
  Carstine, 25
  Eliza, 26
  Elizabeth, 26
  Grietye, 26
  Hannah, 26
  Joel, Jr., 26
  John, 25, 26
  Joseph, 22
  Lydia, 26
  Mary, 26
  Philip, 26
  Rachel, 26
  Rebecca, 26
  Samuel, 26
  Sarah, 26
  Susannah, 190
  Thomas, 197
  Thomas, Jr., 26
Borradaill, William, 138
Borton, Abigail, 138, 139
  Caleb, 27
  John, 27
  Joshua, 27
  Martha, 138, 139
  Nathaniel, 139
Boudinot, Catharine, 33
  Elias, 111, 118
  Elisha, 33, 58, 61, 140
Bound, Joseph, 191
Bowd, Mary, 260
Bowen, Abigail, 101
  Abraham, 27, 87
  Dan, 201
  Dan, Jr., 27, 87
  David, 100, 101, 251
  David, Jr., 101
  Elijah, 100, 101
  Enoch, 27
  Ephraim, 27
  Jonathan, 100, 101, 115, 157, 251, 252
  Landal, 147, 148
  Lydia, 27
  Mark, 27, 87
  Mary, 27, 101, 214
  Miriam, 129
  Rachel, 27
  Rebecca, 27, 101
  Ruhamey, 27
  Samuel, 168
  Seth, 101, 129

## INDEX OF NAMES OF PERSONS 273

Smith, 201
*See also* Bowne
Bower, Anna, 187
  Jacob, 162
  John, 194
Bowker, Jemima, 28
  Uriah, 28
Bowlby, Thomas, 72, 106, 107, 132, 172
Bowman, Ann, 28
  Edward, 28
  Elizabeth, 28
  Hannah, 28
  Mary, 28
  Richard, Jr., 28
  Samuel, 28
  Sarah, 28
Bowne (Bownn), Hendrick, 256
  Jonathan, 238
  Samuel, 28
  *See also* Bowen
Boyce—*see* Bice, Boice
Boyd, Adam, 104
  Phebe, 225
Boylan, John, 42, 135
Boyles, Joseph, 60
Boys—*see* Bice, Boice
Brackney, Joseph, 26
Bradbury, Abner, 10
Braddock, Adam, 35
  Mary, 34, 35
  Phebe, 35
  Tryvena, 35
Bradford, Schuyler, 105
Bradshaw, Sarah, 94
Bradway, Aaron, 28
  Edward, 28, 62, 81, 208, 218
  Elizabeth, 67, 208
  Hannah, 28
  Jonathan, 37
  Thomas, 28
Brand, Audry, 128
  William, 128
Brandroff (Brandriff), Elizabeth, 119
  Timothy, 119
Branin (Brannon), John, 62, 203
Branson, David, 181
  Joseph, 159
  Moses, 26, 147
Brant, Anne, 160
  David, 168, 252
  Sarah, 28
Brasington, Thomas, 203
Bratton, David, 28
Bray, Andrew, 29
  Anne, 28
  Deliverance, 28
  Huldah, 28
  John, 28, 29, 71, 127, 181, 184, 216
  Sarah, 28
  Thomas, 29
  Tulalon, 29
Brearley, David, Jr., 29
  Elizabeth, 29
  Esther, 29
  George, 29
  Joseph, 29
  William, 29
Brewer, Aaron, 83, 217, 222, 253
  Catharine, 29
  David, 22, 29, 144
  Peter, 29
Brewster, Anne, 115
  Joseph, 246

  Rebecca, 246
  Samuel, 121
Brian, Haren, 165
Briant, Andrew, 29
  Cornelius, 29
  Mary, 29
  Phebe, 29
  Rachel, 29
  Simeon, 31
  Thomas, 29
  *See also* Bryant
Brick, John, 36, 181
  Joshua, 61
  William, 175
Bridges, John, 168
Briggs, Abel, 179
  John, 9, 29
Bright, Anne, 30
  Elizabeth, 30
  George, 30, 157
  Levi, 30
  Shoures, 220
  William, Jr., 30
Brinkerhoff (Brinkerhoof), Adrian, 237
  Adriantye, 237
  Necausy, 29
Brinley, John, 73, 207
  Peter, 247
  William, 239, 247
Brinson, Stout, 217
  Zebulon, 217
Britten (Brittain, Britton, Briton, &c.)
  Charity, 234
  Elizabeth, 30
  Isaac, 30, 234
  Joseph, 30, 234, 235
  Nathaniel, 25, 231
  Samuel, 173
  Susannah, 30
  Thomas, 236
  William, 152
Broadwell, David, 25
  Nathaniel, 54
Brocaw—*see* Brokaw
Brock, John, 142
  Uriah, 11
Brodrick (Broderrick), James, 25, 130
  Thomas, Jr., 30
Brognard, John, 127
Brokaw (Brocaw), Abraham, 31, 236
  Anne, 31
  Bergon, 31, 219, 238
  Caspares, 30, 31
  Catherine, 30
  Catlintje, 31
  Isaac, 31, 236, 238
  John, 30, 31
  Mary, 31
  Phebe, 31
  Sarah, 31, 238
Bromfield, John, 260
  Thomas, 260
Brook, Samuel, 93
Brookfield, Job, 49
  Noah, 47
Brooks, Edward, 183
  Elizabeth, 31
  Hannah, 31
  John, 31, 172, 226
  Philip, 31
  Rebecca, 182

Brorgard, John, 40
  John Smith, 40
  Sarah, 40
Brotherton, James, 202
Brown (Browne), Abraham, 34
  Agnes, 33
  Anne, 32
  Ashar, 34
  Benaiah, 32
  Beuley, 19
  Catharine, 118
  Christian, 33
  Clayton, 34
  Daniel, 86
  David, 39, 42, 81, 89, 153, 197, 220, 228
  Deliverance, 21
  Eleazer, 33, 39
  Fanny, 33
  Frances, 33
  George, 32, 140
  Hannah, 32, 33
  Henry, Jr., 32
  Isaac, 122, 206
  Jacob, 27
  James, 33, 51, 133, 232
  Jane, 143
  Job, 33, 189
  Joel, 32
  John, 32, 33, 34, 118, 181
  Joseph, 34, 114, 189
  Joseph, Jr., 28
  Mary, 118
  Nathaniel, 32
  Obadiah, 10
  Pain, 51
  Patience, 32
  Peter, 156, 157
  Philip, 33
  Preserve, 156
  Prudy, 32
  Rachel, 32, 187
  Richard, 31, 32, 114
  Robert, 137, 169, 197
  Samuel, 32, 211
  Sarah, 32, 84, 149
  Stephen, 21
  Thomas, 32, 89, 90, 115, 206
  Ursula, 33
  William, 33, 118, 232, 247
  Zacheus, 27
  Zephenia, 141
Browning, Jacob, 62
Bruen, David, 131
  Hannah, 189
Brumley, Joseph, 226
Brundage, Phebe, 170
Brush, Ann, 33
  Ard, 33
  Bashti, 33
  Benjamin, Jr., 33
  Edward, 33
  Hannah, 33
  Lorinal, 33
Bryant, Ann, 34
  Benjamin, 34
  Elizabeth, 34
  John, 34
  Lorany, 218
  Mary, 33, 34, 259
  Rebecca, 33, 34
  Samuel, 31
  Sarah, 34
  Susannah, 145
  William, Jr., 34, 145
  *See also* Briant

Buchanon (Buchannon), Grace 260
  John, 18, 122
Buchner, Henry, 38
  Jacob, 38
Buck, Abigail, 194
  Dayton, 200
  Ephraim, 168, 194, 200
  Henry, 200
  Jean, 248
  John, 204
  Margaret, 34
  Theoda, 74
  Thomas, 99, 172
Buckelew (Buckelow), Abraham, 92
  Frederick, 84
  Isaac, 22
Budd, Daniel, 220
  Deborah, 34
  Eli, 30, 169
  George, 202
  Isaac, 29, 169
  Joseph, 10, 156
  Levi, 169, 202
  Mahlon, 156
  Margaret, 34
  Mary, 260
  Samuel, 83
  Sarah, 155, 156
  Stacy, 155, 156, 189, 215
  William, 202
Buffin, Abigail, 35
  Levina, 35
  Mary, 34, 35
  Michael, 35
  Penelope, 35
  Richard, 35
  Sarah, 35
Bullman, Thomas, 25, 53, 128, 145
Bullock, Elizabeth, 192
  Isaac, 124, 192
  Jemima, 228
  Joseph, 88, 193, 228
Bulmore, Albert, 225
Bunn, Cunrod, 246
  Edward, 162, 236
  Joshua, 93
  Nathan, 33
Bunnel, Abigail, 35
  Hannah, 35
  Jacob, 35
  Joanna, 35
  Mary, 35
  Phebe, 35
  Stephen, 238
  Susannah, 35
  *See also* Bonnel
Bunting, Ann, 213
  Benjamin, 124
  Mary, 166
  Phineas, 166
Burch, James, 133
Burden, Job, 221
Burdge (Burdg), Jacob, 15, 126
  Richard, 231
Burgie, Thomas, 227
Burgin, John, 124
  Reuben, 79
  *See also* Bergen
Burman, Samuel, 41
Burnet, Daniel, 25, 204
  Elizabeth, 39
  Gertruyde, 90, 91
  Henry, 42
  Isaac, 90
  James, 131
  John, 111

## INDEX OF NAMES OF PERSONS 275

Justus, 184
Moses, 161
Staats Gouverneur, 91
William, 39, 109, 179, 194
Burns, William. 220
Burr, Henry, Jr., 188
John, 35
John, Jr., 135
Joseph, 156
Phebe, 139
Sarah, 139
Thomas, 35
William, 9, 10, 130, 173, 259
Burrough, Benjamin, 36
Casandria, 18
David, 36
Elizabeth, 36
Isaac, 36
Isaac, Jr., 13, 181
Jacob, 18
John, 36
Joseph, 8, 9, 13, 26, 36
Joshua, 36
Rebecca, 13
Reuben, 13
Samuel, 229, 230
Samuel, Jr., 9
Youryah (Uriah), 36
Burroughs, Benjamin, 36
David, 36
Edward, 202
Hannah, 36
Isaac, Jr., 36
John, 36
Joseph, 36
Patience, 36
Sarah, 36
Uriah, 36
Burrows (Burrowes), Ebenezer, 36
Eden, 37
Fanny, 36
Foster, 16
Hannah, 37
Michael, 30
Nathaniel, 36
Sarah, 36
Stehen, 36, 37
Stehen, Jr., 36
Burtin, William, 224
Burton, Charles, 158
Bush, Ephraim, 155
John, 15
Butcher, Elizabeth, 112
James, 37
Job, 21, 37, 76, 119, 185, 212
Jonathan, 37, 218
Phebe, 37
Thomas 37, 186
Butler (Butlar), Israel, 182
James, 182
John, 26, 100, 148, 182, 250
Joseph, 182
Rachel, 182
Rebecca, 182
Samuel, 182
Butterfield, Richard, 129
Buxton, Hannah, 37
Buys, Fulcert, 88
*See also* Bice, Boice
Buzby, Ann, 139
Benjamin, 139
Grace, 139
Hannah, 38, 96, 112
Jabez, 139
Martha, 139
Mary, 38, 139

Nathaniel, 139
Sarah, 76
Susannah, 38
Thomas, 57, 189
Byram, Naphiah, 154
Byron, Richard, 184

C

Cadmus (Cadmes), Abraham, 66, 239
John, 239
Peter, 201, 239
Phebe, 58
Thomas, 245
*See also* Codimus
Caldwell, Abraham, 82
*See also* Calwall
Calhoun, Alexander, 43
*See also* Colhoun
Callender, Hannah, 38
Calvert, William, 156
Calwall, William, 82
*See also* Caldwell
Cambel (Camble), Esther, 114
George, 225
Rachel, 225
*See also* Campbell
Cameron, Elizabeth, 39
Camp, Caleb, 39
Hannah, 39
Isaac, 39
Job, 39
John, 39
Joseph, 39
Mary, 39
Nathaniel, 39
Samuel, 39
Stephen, 39
Campbell (Campbel), Archibald, 144
David, 171
George W., 32, 161, 200, 247
James, 144
Rebecca, 15
Thomas McElrath, 144
William, 39, 157, 185
*See also* Cambel
Campfield, Hannah, 137
Jabez, 27, 30, 40, 47
Sarah, 30
William, 19, 42, 83, 90, 178
*See also* Canfield
Campion, Joseph, 44
Mary, 44
Canfield, Abiel, 111
Abner, 40
Abraham, 40
Abraham, Jr., 19, 47, 86, 90
Anna, 40
David Seely, 40
Hannah, 39, 48
Isaac, 40
Israel, 39, 40
Mary, 27, 39
Nathaniel, 61
Phebe, 40
Sarah, 39
Timothy, 90
*See also* Campfield
Cannady, Hannah, 125
*See also* Kennedy
Canned, John, 100
Carlile, Robert, 190
Carll, Constantine, 83, 150
John, 27
William, 40

Carman, Abigil, 41
  Caleb, 183
  Joseph, 41
  Samuel, 255
  Stephen, 41
Carney, Hannah, 41
  Ruth, 41
  Thomas, 219
  Thomas, Jr., 41
  *See also* Kearney
Carpenter, Elizabeth, 261
  James, 198, 259
  John, 36, 93, 157
  Mary, 231
  Samuel, 41, 256
  Thomas, 209, 222
  William, 261
Carr, Catharine, 140
  Isaac, 190
  James, 140
  Jane, 190
  Job, 208
  Martha, 41
  Melisent, 208
  *See also* Karr
Carslake, Abigail, 35
  William, 34, 35, 88
Carson, Levi, 104
Carter, Aaron, 25, 131
  Elizabeth, 41
  George, 131, 154
  Phebe, 131
  Stephen, 257
Carty (Cartey), Daniel, 11
  Edith, 260
Caruthers, Obadiah, 201, 224, 241
  Richard, 255
Cary, Beriah, 42
  Hannah, 42
Casaday, John, 106
Case, Daniel, 89
  Sarah, 19
  Tunis, 19
Cashley—*see* Keatsley
Cassels, William, 50
Cassidy—*see* Casaday
Castner (Casner), Barbara, 42
  Cathrind, 42
  Coonrod, 42
  Daniel, 42, 225
  John, 20
  Mary, 42
Cathrall, Hannah, 260
Cattell (Cattle), Elizabeth, 18
  Jonas, 12, 18, 176
Cawood, James, 42
Chadburn—*see* Chatburn
Chadwick, Thomas, 174
  William, 174
Chamberlain (Chamberlin), Enoch, 43
  John, 43, 56, 133
  Joseph, 223, 231
  Lydia, 42
  Mercy, 42
  Serviah, 79
  William, 70, 111
Chambers, Abraham, 125
  Alexander, 190
  Alexander, Jr., 30, 56
  David, 206
  Fanny, 185
  Mary, 111
  Rachel, 43
  Susannah, 43
  Thomas, 26

Champion, John, 141, 189
  Joseph, 46, 159, 230
  Thomas, 214
Champneys, Joseph, Jr., 43
Chandler, David, 178
  Pontius, 249
  Stephen, 178
Chapman, George Warner, 237
  Henry, 166
  James, 154
Charlot, Stephen, 89
Chatburn, Jonas, 68
Chattin, Abishi, 153, 228
  James, 36, 176
Cheesman (Chessman), Alexander, 43
  Christian, 43
  Deborah, 43, 44
  Drusilla, 43, 44
  Elijah, 43
  Ephraim, 41, 43, 44, 159, 190
  Isabella, 44
  Jemima, 43
  John, 43
  Lettia, 44
  Margaret, 43
  Mary Ann, 43
  Peter, 253
  Richard, 43, 176
  Richard, Jr., 43, 44, 253
  Tamer, 44
  Thomas, 43
  Uriah, 43
  William, 43
Cheever, Jonathan, 209
Cheney, R. W., 16
  William, 235
Chery, Henry, 144
Chessman—*see* Cheesman
Chester, Elizabeth, 183
Chestnor, Joseph, 193
Chetwood, John, 37, 174
  Margaret, 44
Chew, David, 29, 187
  Jesse, 41, 256
Christie, James, 166
Christopher, Edmond, 219
  Jesse, 93
  Mercy, 93
Church, Christopher, 222
  Lydia, 44
  Naomi, 44
  Patience, 44
  Silas, 44
  Ssannah, 44
  Thomas, 44
Clap, George, 44
  John, 44
  Jonathan, 44
  William, 44
Clark (Clarke), Abraham, 18, 154
  Adrial, 161
  Alexander, 45
  Ananias, 21
  Arthur, 154
  Carney, 45
  Catherine, 45
  Charles, 45
  Cornelius, 91
  Elisha, 161, 253
  Elizabeth, 160, 237
  Esther, 171
  Garrot, 213
  George, 45
  Hannah, 154, 171
  Henry, 45

## INDEX OF NAMES OF PERSONS 277

Isaac, 35, 96, 97, 104, 191
Isabella, 45
Israel, 104
James, 41, 45, 106, 250
James, Jr., 41, 45
Jeffery, 197
Jeremiah, 23, 147, 172
Jesse, 77, 197
John, 45, 165, 171, 226
Joseph, 140, 171
Julia, 171
Mary, 91, 213
Nathan, 142
Nicholas, 49
Noah, 45, 176, 255
Peter, 45
Rebecca, 140
Robert, 45
Sally, 154
Samuel, 226
Samuel, Jr., 226
Sarah D., 63
Susannah, 45
Thomas, 45, 213
Thomas, Jr., 213
William, 45, 171
William, Jr., 171
Clason, Anna, 198
  Mary, 198
Clawson (Clauson), Cornelius 135
  Mary, 135
  Mehitabel, 21
  Rachel, 244
Claypool, Thomas, 109
Clayton, Bathsheba, 231
  Ette, 209
  Euphamia, 22, 91, 103, 131, 206, 254
  Harriett, 231
  Job, 210
  John, Jr., 48
  Joseph, 55, 56
Clemans, Edwart, 46
  Elizabeth, 45
  Enoch, Jr., 45
  Esther, 45
  John, 45
  Samuel, 62
Clement, Ann, 18
  Casandria, 18
  Elizabeth, 18, 28
  David, 46
  Hannah, 18
  Jacob, 46
  John, 46, 253
  Joseph, 18, 51
  Mary, 46
  Ruth, 18
  Samuel, 43, 181
  Sarah, 18
  Thomas, 7
  William, 46, 93
Clements, Thomas, 149
Clifford, Elizabeth, 157
  John, 46, 134
Cliffton (Cleffton), Henry, 45, 118
  Nathan, 112
Cline, Catharine, 46
  Elizabeth, 46
  Jacob, Jr., 46
  John, 46, 220, 249
  *See also* Kline
Clover, Mary, 51
Clunn, John, 187, 257
Clutch, Margaret, 14

Coate, Barzillai, 47
  Daniel, 20, 47
  Deborah, 46
  Henry, Jr., 46
  Hetty, 46
  John, 46
  Lucy, 46
  Robert, 46
  Sarah, 46
Coates, William, 96
Cobb, John, 27
  William, 208
Coberly—*see* Cubberly
Cochey, Miriam, 47
Cock, Idah, 180
  Richard, 180
  Thomas, 180
Codd, Eleanor, 47
  James, 213
  Jeames, 47
  John, Jr., 47
  Joseph, 47
  Mary, 47
Coddington, Ann, 216
  Experience, 80
  Francis, 188
Codimus, Thomas, 184
  *See also* Cadmus
Coeks, Catherine, 170
Coffen, William, 254
Cogehill, Elizabeth, 226
Cole, Benjamin, 111
  Ezekiel, 202
  Harmanis, 193
  Joseph, 254
Coleman, Catharine, 21
  John, 47
  Nathaniel, 207
  William, 47
Coles, Barent, 66
  Mary, 167
  Samuel, 93, 137, 138, 167
  Sarah, 157
  William, 25, 49, 140, 255
Colhoun, Alexander, 145
  *See also* Calhoun
Colie, Anna, 47
  Daniel, 47
  Hannah, 47
  Mary, 47
Collier, Eleanor, 48
  Elizabeth, 48
  Isaac, 48
  Jemima, 48
  Joseph, 48
  Margaret, 48
  Mary, 48
  Rachel, 48
  Sophia, 48
  Susannah, 48
Collins, Amos, 41
  Edward, 122, 244
  Isaac, 117
  John, 93, 138
  Joseph, Jr., 13
  Richard, 209
  Stephen, 35
  Zebedee, 117
Colsen, George, 86
Colver, Amos, 48
  James, 215
  Lydia, 48
  Robert, 48, 142
  Simon, 48
  Thomas, Jr., 48

Combs (Combes), Jonathan, 23, 43, 70, 94, 120, 228
  Jonathan, Jr., 70
  Susannah, 177
  Thomas, 177
Commans, Huldah, 28
Compton, Daniel, 48
  Gabriel, 48
  Hannah, 48
  Jacob, 48, 176
  James, 48
  Luis, 48
  Mary, 48, 55
  Nancy, 48
  Samuel, 148
  Sarah, 48
  Ursula, 48
  William, 48, 258
  *See also* Cumpton
Conaroe, Caleb, 74
  Patience, 74
  *See also* Conrow
Condict (Condit), Joel, 170
  John, 58
  Matthew, 69
  Silas, 20, 92, 111
Conely—*see* Connelly
Coney, Jonathan, 80
Conger, John, 71, 160
  Joseph, 90
  Mary, 71
Congleton, Allen, Jr., 38, 125, 178, 212
Conine, Jacob, 51
Conklin (Conkling) Elizabeth, 49
  John, 84
  John, Jr., 84
  Lewis, 84
  Rachel, 49
  Stephen, 49, 77, 164
  William, 130
Connelly (Conely, Connoly), Briant, 49
  Ephraim, 49
  Temperance, 49
  William, 33
Connet, Abigail, 49
  Anne, 49
  Betsy, 49
  Daniel, 49
  Edward, 49
  Mary, 49
  Moses, 49
  Phebe, 49
  Rhoda, 49
Connor (Conner), Joseph, 21, 108
  Sarah, 114
Conover, Elias, 187
  Rebecca, 149
  *See also* Covenhoven
Conrey, Amy, 49
  Caty, 49
  John, 49
  Nancy, 49
  Peggy, 49
  Peter, Jr., 49
Conrow, Jacob, 49
  Sarah, 50
  *See also* Conaroe
Consolyee, Arie, 48
Cook (Cooke), Aaron, 50
  Abigail, 50
  Benjamin, 221
  Caseandre, 50
  Charles, 240
  Daniel, 62
  David, 42
  Ebenezer, 136
  Edward Paterson, 22, 26, **131, 159,** 160
  Eleanor, 50
  Elias, 50
  Elisha, 50, 93
  Elizabeth, 50
  Ellis, 92, 211
  George, 34, 116, 117
  Hannah, 50, 174
  Henry, 50
  Job, 28, 50, 167
  John, 49
  Joseph, 50
  Joshua, 21
  Martha, 21
  Mary, 174
  Michael, 69
  Peter, 26, 130
  Richard, 50
  Robert, 50, 191, 240
  Samuel, 50
  Sarah, 50
  Stacey, 201
  Susannah, 174
  William, 50, 92, 165
Cooker, John B., 92
Cookes, Sawrah, 116
Cool, Ann, 50
  Hannah, 50
  John, 50, 51
  Kesiah, 50
  *See also* Kuhl
Coolbaugh, William, 172
Coon, Azariah, 148
  Stephen, 55
Cooper, Abigail, 52, 262
  Ann, 36, 51, 52, 229
  Benjamin, 51
  Charles 52
  Daniel, 52
  Daniel, Jr., 51
  Davenport, 51
  David, 12, 15, 108
  Elizabeth, 52, 78
  Esther, 51, 160
  Hannah, 51
  Henry, 51
  James, 51
  John, 51, 160
  Joseph, 51, 127, 159
  Joshua, 161
  Marmaduke, 159
  Mary, 51, 52, 160
  Nathan, Jr., 51, 164
  Peter, 51
  Phebe, 51
  Philip, 26
  Prudence, 159
  Rebecca, 51, 52, 159, 160
  Richard, 52, 78
  Robert, 52
  Samuel, 51, 52, 129, 159
  Sarah, 52, 220, 230
  Thomas, 13, 212
  William, 14, 51, 160, 220, 247
  *See also* Cuyper
Cope, John, 140
Copeland (Copland), Cowperthwaite, 37, 148
Coplin, Hannah, 236
  Joseph, **236**

# INDEX OF NAMES OF PERSONS 279

Corbin (Corbine), Francis, 218
  George, 21
  Mary, 218
Corcelius, George, 52
  Peter, 52
Corgeia (Corgie), John, 222
  Lydia, 222
  Robert, 52, 53, 222
  Sophia, 222
Coriell (Coryell, Coreyll), David, 25, 191, 248
  John, 67
  Sarah, 200
  Tunis, 200
Corlis (Corlies), Ann, 53
  Asher, 53
  Benjamin, 26, 53, 218
  Elizabeth, 53
  George, 249
  John, 53
  Rachel, 53
  Timothy, 249
  William, 53
Corneilson, Andrew, 41
Cornelius, Garrison, 142
Cornell (Cornel), Abraham, 53
  Albert, 53
  Anne, 53
  Barnt, 53
  Benjamin, 53
  Cornelius, 53
  Edward, 53
  Eleanor, 53
  Elizabeth, 53
  Jannetje, 53
  John, 53
  Jonathan, 53
  Joseph, 53, 224
  Maria, 53
  Mary, 53
  Roelof, 53
  Samuel, 53
  William, 53
Cornine, Christene, 198
  Peter, 198
Cornish, Lydia, 152
Corshon, Joshua, 172, 226
Corson (Corsen), Abel, 80
  Eli, 54
  Jacob, 54
  James, 59
  Jesse, 54
  Margaret, 15
  Martha, 54
  Parmenas, 54, 85, 225, 231
  William, 228
  *See also* Courson
Cortelyou, Hermanus, 53
Cortis—*see* Curtis
Corwin (Corwine), Abner, 54
  Experience, 54
  Mary, 54
  Ruth, 54
  Sarah, 54
  Susannah, 54
  William, 54, 220
Cory (Corey), Aaron, 54
  Abraham, 54
  Benjamin, 54, 164
  David, 54, 165
  John, 54, 257
  Mary, 54
  Nancy, 54
  Naomi, 54
  Rachel, 54
  Sarah, 54
  Susannah, 54
Coryell—*see* Coriell
Cosad, Aaron, 55
  Anthony, 49, 148
  Catherine, 55
  Elizabeth, 55
  Hannah, 55
  Jacob, 55
  John, 55
  Mary, 55
  Samuel, 55, 62, 136
  Thomas, 55
Coshun, Joseph, 243
Cosort, Nelly, 31
Costegan, Frances, 224
Cotheal, Isaac
Cotton, Edward, 259
Courson (Coursen, Courssen), Abraham, 106
  Isaac, 89
  Jacob, 168
  Mary, 168
  *See also* Corson
Cous, Mary, 184
Covenhoven (Couwenhoven, Kovenoven), Abraham, 120
  Albert, 56
  Benjamin, 55, 56
  Cornelius, 56, 155
  Daniel, 41, 85
  David, 24, 55, 56
  Eleanor, 55, 56
  Elizabeth, 55, 56
  Garret, 55
  Hendrika, 56
  Idah, 55
  Isaac, 55, 56
  Jacob, 255
  John, 55, 187
  John D., 32
  Joseph, 55, 56
  Mary, 55, 56
  Minicus, 104
  Nelley, 155
  Nicholas, 55
  Peter, 56
  Sarah, 55
  Thomas, 55
  William, 55, 56, 104
  William B., 141
  *See also* Conover
Covert, Jacob, 31
  Luke, 244, 254
  Tunes, 254
Coverly—*see* Cubberly
Coward, Jacob, 141
Cowell, Ebenezer, 194
  Eunice, 56
  John, Jr., 56
  Mary, 56
Cowgill, Isaac, 61, 100, 169, 250
  Joseph, 57, 186
Cowperthwaite William, 166
Cox, Abel, 56
  Ace, 196
  Andrew, 168
  Ann, 261
  Catherine, 56
  Charles, 192
  David, 57
  Elisha, 56
  Elizabeth, 57
  Esek, 56
  Hannah, 260
  James, 56

Jane, 57, 187
John, 33, 85, 96, 137, 192, 196, 260
Jonas, 57
Joseph, 56, 247
Joshua, 56
Kezia, 114
Lydia, 57
Mariah, 196
Martin, 52, 200
Mary, 56, 57
Mercy, 221
Moses, 57
Rebecca, 57, 216
Richard, 14, 78, 141, 155, 221, 231
Richard, Jr., 156
Sarah, 57, 95
Willemina, 56
William, 11, 56, 57, 123, 190, 196
Coykendall Benjamin, 250
*See also* Kikendall
Cozens, Benjamin, 115
Jacob, 264
Joshua, 71
Samuel, 15, 191
William R., 126
Craft, Ann, 243
James, 75, 76, 125, 193
Joseph, 75
Craig (Craige), Andrew, 38, 76, 112, 261
James, 57, 143
John, 23, 56, 145, 154, 193, 228, 254
Mary, 40, 57
Timothy, 23
William, 143
Crammer, Rachel, 9
Crandal, Rebecca, 57
Crandlemire, Peter, 180
Crane, A., 61
Abigail, 58
David, 57, 58, 152, 227
Drake, 57
Elias, 57
Elihu, 58
Elijah, 58
Elizabeth, 58
Hannah, 58
Isaac, 163
Jacob, 178, 228
James, 58
Jane, 57
Jedediah, 58
Jeremiah, 205
Job, 69
John, 57, 58
John Haight, 58
Jonas, 58
Jonathan, 58
Joseph, 163, 174, 184
Lucy, 58
Mary, 58
Nathaniel, 57, 174
Oliver, 184
Paul, 58
Phebe, 58
Phineas, 58
Rachel, 58
Rebecca, 58
Sarah, 58
Sayre, 58
Sephen, 227, 228, 245
Timothy, 61, 205
William, 184
Zadock, 184

Crater—*see* Creator
Craven, Joseph, 148
Thomas, 53, 128
Crawford, Dennis, 211
Elizabeth, 190
James, 245
John, 133
Joseph, 195, 196
Richard, 200
Richard, Jr., 25
Samuel, 190
William, 200
Creator, Morris, 155
Creen, Elizabeth, 59
Crequi, Abram, 73
Cresse, Amos, 59, 149
Ann, 59
Daniel, 59
David, 59
Elizabeth, 59
Ellenner, 59
Hannah, 59
Israel, 59
Jacob, 59, 185
John, 59, 150, 221
Lewis, 59
Marcy, 59
Mary, 59
Nathan, 59, 232
Philip, 59, 98, 110, 200, 222, 258
Rachel, 59
Zebulon, 59
Crimm (Crim), Frederick, 246
Peter, 18, 141, 123
Sarah, 18
Cripps, Benjamin, 202
Whitton, 209
Crisman, Charles, 199
Crispin, Bathsheba, 62
Jonathan, 9, 87
Paul, 138
Selane, 62
Criter, Philip, 184
Croefoot, Sarah, 58
Crooks, Hetty, 46
John, 226
Crosby, William, 94
Choshaw (Crowshaw), George, 60
Hannah, 60, 87
Isaiah, 59
Joseph, 60
Cross, Bryan, 60
Catherine, 60
James, 60
John, 60
John Leferty, 60
Joseph, 60
Martha, 60
Mary, 60
Robert, 60
William, 60
Crow, David, 48
Josiah, 60
Samuel, 159
Crowell (Crowel), Daniel, 42, 99
Experience, 60
Henry, 62
John, 173
Josiah, 60
Recompence, 89
Ruth, 60
Seth, 174
Temperance, 60
Croxson, Elias, 220
Lydia, 220
Mary, 220

## INDEX OF NAMES OF PERSONS

Croy, Johannes, 242
Crozer, Joseph, 197
Crugh, Eve, 91
  Sarah, 91
  Valentine, 91
Crum, Abigail, 60
  Elizabeth, 60
  Isaac, 60
  Mary, 60
  Susannah, 60
  William, 60
Crusee, Cornelius, 61
  Elizabeth, 61
  Lukas, 61
Crusher, Rachel, 161
  Thomas, 161
Cubberly (Coberly, Coverly, &c.)
  David, 73
  Mary, 205
  William, 43, 97, 205
Cubby, Odol, 250
Cudaback, James, 32
Cuff, James, 18
Culver—see Colver
Cummings, John N., 92
Cummins, Robert, 29, 94
Cumpton, Ichabod, 208
  See also Compton
Current, William, 183
Curry (Currey, Currie), Abigail, 61
  Betsy, 61
  David, 61
  Hannah, 61
  Israel, 61
  Johanna, 61
  Neal, 228
  Phebe, 61
  Robert, 211
  Ruth, 49
  Samuel, Jr., 61
  Thomas, 61
Curtenius, Peter, 208
  Philip, 208
Curtis (Cortis), David, 22
  John, 22, 61, 183, 237
  Jonathan, 13, 103
  Thomas, 7, 22
  Thomas James, 215
  Walter, 103
Cutler, Jesse, 262
Cutter, Ford, 119
  Hannah, 84
  Kelsey, 84
  Samuel, 84
Cuyper, Aert, 26, 239, 263
  see also Cooper

### D

Dacker, Aaron, 61
  Charity, 61
  Jeremiah, 61
  Mary, 61
  Moses, 61
  Sarah, 61
  Temperance, 61
  see also Decker
Dalbow, Andrew, 41
Dalles (Dollas), Aaron, 217
  Jonathan, 61
  Martha, 217
  Rebecca, 61
Dalrimple (Dalrymple), Andrew, 29
  Dennis, 62
  Hannah, 62

John, 233
Joseph, Jr., 62
Mahlon, 62
Rachel, 62
Silas, 62
William, 62
Damer (Domar), Balser, 46, 106
Danbury, Samuel, 111
Daniel (Daniels), Aaron, 62
  Charles, 62
  Elizabeth, 62
  George, 62
  James, 62
  John, 85, 183
  Joseph, 69
  Owen, 62
  Thomas, 201
  William, 10, 62, 256
Danily, James, 108
D'Anterroches, J. L. Chr., 18
Darby (Darbe), Ephraim, 22
  John, 140
  John, Jr., 184
  Susannah, 243
  William, 25, 31, 96, 154
Dare, Benjamin, 201
  David, 62
  Gamaliel, 62
  Jeremiah, 62
  John, 62
  Mary, 62
  Rebecca, 212
  Robert, Jr., 62
Darnel, Edmund, 62, 63
  Jane, 62
  Samuel, 62
Daten, Ephraim, 63
  Joseph, 63
  Leonard, 63
  Mary, 63
  Sarah, 63
  See also Dayton
Davenport (Davinport), Abraham, 162
  Francis, 30, 35
  Franklin, 7, 123, 149, 150, 236
  Mercy, 63
  Samuel, 85
Davies, Comfort, 58
Davis, Abigail, 63, 123
  Ann, 124
  Arthur, Jr., 63
  Benjamin, 63
  Daniel, 63, 86
  David, 19, 45
  Earl, 63
  Ebenezer, 72
  Elijah, 63, 164
  Elizabeth, 19, 63, 103
  Elnathan, 15, 37, 90, 157
  Esther, 63
  Eunice, 86
  Gabriel, 62
  George, 234
  Hannah, 86, 123
  Isaac, 15, 63, 124, 223, 236
  Israel, 151
  Ivins, 123
  Jacob, 19
  James, 18, 21, 241
  Job, 123
  John, 103, 197
  Jonathan, 123
  Joseph, 17
  Joshua, 64
  Lydia, 64

Martha, 63
Mary, 63, 123
Meribah, 123
Naomi, 63
Othniel, 63
Peter, 223
Rachel, 81, 229
Richard, 19
Ruth, 63
Sarah, 18
Stephen, 151
Thomas, 19, 64
Uriah, 80
William, 103, 123, 204
Davison, James, 236, 241
John, 12, 93, 171, 198
William, 128
Dawson, Aaron, 64
Lydia, 64
Walter, 32
Day, Amos, 120
Artemas, 62
Ezekiel, 64
Jane, 120
Jehiel, 42
John, 72
Nehemiah, 120
Stephen, 137, 140
Dayton, Eli, 64
Elias, 64
Jonathan, I., 18, 64
*see also* Daten
Deacon, Barzillai, 95
John, 64
Rachel, 64
Susannah, 64
Theodocia, 64
William, 127
Dealing, Nancy, 243
Dean (Deane), Elizabeth, 90
Elkanah, 90
Mary, 33
Rebecca, 33
William, 33
Deanis—*see* Dennis
DeCamp, Aaron, 170
G., 238
John, 65
Joseph, 102, 127, 148, 172, 209, 258
Mary, 65
Moses, 77
Decker, Charity, 65
Dan, 65
Sarah, 66
William, 192
*See also* Dacker
DeCow, Achsah, 65, 66
Clayton, 65
Isaac, 24, 65
Jacob, 65
John, 65
Joseph, 65, 233
Sarah, 65
Thomas, 65
Dederer, Sally, 66
Deel, Elizabeth, 62
Defandorf, George, 246
Degarmo, Peter, 75
DeGroot, William, 123, 146
DeHart (DeHaert), Hendrick, 243
John, 31, 70
Mauritz, 197
Mauritz, Jr., 27
William, 20
DeKay, Charles, 13

Demarest (Demaret, Demare, &c.), Abraham, 250
David B., 66
Gerret D., 66
Jacobus, 66
Joast, 29
Johannes, 66
Peter, 29, 66
Samuel, 66
Soekke, 66
Demmont, Nathaniel, 224
*See also* Dumont
Demott, Catherine, 66
Derick, 66, 162
Elizabeth, 66
Michael, 66, 136, 236
Sarah, 66
Stinety, 66
*See also* Dumodt
Dendlesbeck—*see* Tentelpeck
Deniack, Samuel, 33
Denise, Denise, 136
Denman, Andrew, 197
Christopher, 77, 197
Denn, John, 15, 209
Dennelsbeck—*see* Tentelpeck
Dennis (Deanis, Dennes), Cateren, 106
Charles, 44, 159
George, 41
Jesse, 67
John, 243
Jonathan, 62
Joseph, 66
Mary, 243
Naomi, 62
Rebecca, 207
Samuel, 190
Sarah, 190
Denny, Samuel, 263
Thomas, 115, 150, 263
DeNormandie, John Abraham, 243
Denton, Margaret, 67
Depue, Nicholas, 17
Derickson (Dirickson), Andrew, 212
Thomas, 67
Deviney, John, 37
DeWitt (DeWidt, DeWit), Jacob, 250
Luke, 145
Peter, 200
Sarah, 67
Dey, Benjamin, 67, 196
David, 67
Esther, 67
Jane, 67
John, 48, 67, 128
Peter, 67
Philip, 67
Richard, 67
William, 48, 128, 186
*See also* Dye
Dick, Samuel, 9, 15, 38
Sarah, 38, 219
Dicker, Elizabeth, 67
Hannah, 67
Lydia, 67
Dickerson, Abraham, 54, 220
Daniel, 42
Dickeson, Catharine, 123
Mary, 123
William, 41, 45, 184
Dickey, James, 33
Mary, 236
Dickinson, Caleb, 67
John, 59
Philemon, 67

## INDEX OF NAMES OF PERSONS

Dicson—*see* **Dixon**
Dietrick, Elizabeth, 199
Diets, Jacobus, 262
Dildine, Abraham, 229
 Uriah, 229
Dilks (Dilkes), Abraham, 212
 Isaac, 256
 William, 122
Dill, John, 44
 Margaret, 229
Dillwyn, George, 261
 Susannah, 260
 William, 260, 261
Dils, Anne, 68
 Catherine, 68
 Charity, 68
 Elizabeth, 68
 George, 68
 Harmanus, 68
 Henry, 192
 Jacob, 68
 John, 68, 223
 Joseph, 68
 Mary, 68
 Peter, 68
 Philip, 102
 William, 68
 *See also* Dilts
Dilshaver, John, 153, 154
Dilts (Diltz), Anna, 68
 Catherine, 68
 Juliana, 68
 Mary, 68
 Peter, 68
 Sarah, 68
 Urie, 68
 *See also* Dils
Dirickson—*see* Derickson
Disbrow (Disbrough), Caty, 240
 Henry, 240
 Joseph, 162
 Ruth, 200
Dishan, Catharine, 77
 Elizabeth, 77
 Henry, 77
 Mary, 77
 Peter, 77
Ditmars, Johanes, 199
 Peter, 223
Dixon (Dicson, Dixson), Ann, 208
 Elizabeth, 69
 Hannah, 68, 69, 208
 John, 33
 Mary, 69, 208
 Tamson, 69
 Urban, 69
Dobbins, James, 155
 Joab, 82
Dod (Dodd), Abigail, 69
 Alling, 69
 Daniel, 69
 Ebenezer, 69
 John, 69
 John, Jr., 101, 170, 189, 245
 Joseph, Jr., 69
 Lebbeus, 42, 136
 Lydia, 69
 Mary, 69
 Mathias, 69
 Molly, 170
 Moses, 69, 184
 Rachel, 69
 Samuel, 17
 Sarah, 69
 Thomas, 22
Dodderer, Jacob, 245

Dods, Thomas, 70
Dole, Hannah, 69
 Joseph, 69
 Mary, 69
 Peter, 28
 Rebecca, 69
 Sarah, 69
 Surviah, 69
Dollas—*see* Dalles
Domar—*see* Damer
Donaldson, Hannah, 80
Done, John, 21
Donington, John, 154
Doremus, Abraham, 69
 Cornelius, 69, 70, 246
 David, 69
 George, 218, 263
 Jacob, 69, 70
 Margaret, 69
 Mary, 70
 Orecha, 69
 Peter, Jr., 69, 70
 Polly, 69, 70
 Rachel, 69
 Richard, 69, 70
 Sarah, 69, 70
 Simeon, 70
 Thomas, 70
Dorland, Garrat, 242
Dormer, Philip, 184
Dorsett, Joseph, 161
Doty, Isaac, 70
 Nathaniel, 62, 136
 *See also* Doughty
Dougherty, Robert, 26, 100
Douglass, Hannah, 104
 John, 104, 235
 *See also* Duglass
Doughty, Thomas, 19
 *See also* Doty
Downer, Samuel, 233
Downey (Downney), Elizabeth, 70
 John, 70
 Peter, 116
Downing, Dillon, 149
 Elizabeth, 149
Drake, Ebenezer, 252
 Francis, 101
 Jacob, 206
 James, 86, 132, 184
 Jane, 170
 John, 70
 Joseph, 70
 Nathan, 217
 Nathan, Jr., 217
 Ralph, 216
 Richard, 28
 Samuel, 64
 Silas, 48
 William, 205
Driver, Samuel, 130
Drummond, Peter, 208
 Rachel, 76
 Robert, 70
 William, 70
DuBois, Abraham, 36, 166, 167
 Benjamin, 191
 David, Jr., 36, 166
 Mary, 191
 Thomas, 166
Dubree, Mary, 230
Duff, William, 261
Duffield, Mary, 33
 Samuel, 33
 William B., 33
Dufford—*see* Tufford

Duglass, Joseph, 71
*See also* Douglass
Dukemaneer, Kitturah, 71
  Mary, 71
  Rhoda, 71
  Samuel, 71
Duley, Sarah, 170
Dumodt, John, 224, 241
*See also* Demott
Dumont, Elizabeth, 180
  Peter, 254
*See also* Demmont
Dunham, Aaron, 29, 214
  Abraham, 71
  Amy, 72
  Ann, 71
  Azariah, 257
  Benyou, 18
  Daniel, 193
  David, 18, 71
  Elizabeth, 18
  Francis, 72
  Hannah, 71
  Helen, 71
  Hezekiah, 72
  Hugh, 72
  Jacob, 71, 170, 251
  James, 71, 257
  Jane, 71
  John, 71
  Jonathan, 71
  Lewis, 71, 251
  Martha, 18, 71
  Mary, 71
  Nancy, 71
  Nehemiah, 251
  Sarah, 71
  William, 71
Dunlap (Dunlop), Charity, 19
  Edward, 184
  James, 57
  John, 215
Dunn (Dun), Anna, 72
  Benjamin, 71
  Catrine, 72
  Christian, 72
  Daniel, 72
  Elizabeth, 80
  Hugh, 72
  Isaac Budd, 187
  James, 72, 80
  James Thompson, 72
  Joel, 25, 248
  John, 72
  Jonathan, 136
  Justus, 72
  Mary, 251
  Rachel, 72
  Renne, 72
  Rhoda, 204
  Sarah, 80
Dunning, Benjamin, 61
Dunnis, John, 234
Durant, Briant, 89
  Elijah, 89
Durie, Gerrit, 66
Dusinbery, George, 72
  Henry, 72
  Johanna, 72
  Samuel, 72
  Silvanus, 72
  William, 72
Duyckinck, Christopher, 90
Dye, John, 70
  Thomas, 114
*See also* Dey
Dyer, Josiah, 92

## E

Eady, Caleb, 252
Eagles, Alexander, 58
  Thomas, 262
Eakin, Nancy, 182
  Susannah, 182
Earl (Earle), Caleb, 46, 47
  Close, 72
  Edward, 28, 101
  Edward, Jr., 72
  Hester, 46
  John, 72, 124, 239
  John E., 72
  Mary, 72
  Richard, 72
  Rynier, 72
  Samuel, 189
  Sicilia, 72
  Tanton, 20, 156
  Thomas, 20, 108, 140, 215
  William, 215
Earley, John, 99
Eastlack (Estlack), Francis, 109
  Joseph, 89
  Samuel, 115, 225
Eayre, Asa, 72
  Hosea, 33, 130, 173
  Joseph, 72, 260
  Levi, 260
*See also* Eyre
Eckerson, Cornelius, 100
  Garrit, 100
Eckley, Thomas, 92
Edgar, James, 105, 216
  Phebe, 17
  Thomas, 80, 216
  William, 17
Edison, Sarah, 170
Edmunds, Robert, 83
Edsall, Benjamin, 61
Edwards, Abier, 73
  Amos, 251
  George, 109
  John, 82
  Margaret, 73
  Reece, 137
  Richard, 112
Egan, John, 143
Egbert, William, Jr., 200
Eggman, Elizabeth, 13
Elberson, Enoch, 195
*See also* Albertson
Eldridge (Eldredge), Aaron, 134
  Abigail, 73, 74
  Abraham, 74
  Agnes, 159
  Amy, 74
  Ann, 73
  Daniel, 73
  David, 41, 256
  Eli, 59, 110, 119, 148, 169, 198, 214
  Elijah, 73
  Elizabeth, 73, 74
  Enoch, 179
  Esther, 73, 74
  Ezekiel, 73
  Hannah, 74, 76
  Isaac, 204
  Jacob, 73
  Jean, 73, 74
  Jeremiah, 44, 60, 73, 74, 98, 99, 248
  John, 73, 74, 252
  Jonathan, 74
  Jonathan, Jr., 73

INDEX OF NAMES OF PERSONS 285

Judith, 73, 74
Lamuel, 73
Levi, Jr., 73, 74, 99
Lois, 73
Lydia, 73, 248
Martha, 73
Mary, 73
Nathan, 73
Noah, 74
Obadiah, 11, 73
Prudence, 73
Tobitha, 73
William, 94, 181
Wilson, 73
Elkines, George, 186
Elkinton, George, 50
Job, 204
Ellis (Elles), Aaron, 149
Daniel, 11, 78, 95, 117, 124, 169, 201, 205, 231
Isaac, 43
Joseph, 143, 201
Priscilla, 129
Thomas, 112
William, 149, 188
Ellison, Lewis, 22, 103
Elmer, Ebenezer, 79, 115, 134
Eli, 40, 64, 157, 163, 207
Jonathan, 163, 204, 207, 249
Timothy, 63, 163
Elston (Elstun), Andrew, 105, 152
William, 25
Elton, John, 138
Revel, 138
Elwell (Elwill), Abraham, 75
Alexander, 74
Ammariah, 74
Ananias, 244
Cornelius, 210
David, 100, 185, 210
Ephraim, 74
Evin, 74
Jacob, 204, 210
Joseph, 125
Lurainy, 74
Margaret, 125, 175
Mary, 74
Rebecca, 74
Samuel, 74
Sawtel, 74, 90
Ely (Eley), Allison, 43, 75
John, Jr., 75
Joshua, 56, 75
William, 75, 92
Emans, James, 75
Sarah, 75
William, 75
Emley (Embly, Emlay), Jason, 158
John, 128, 192, 247
Robert, 46, 106
Sarah, 75, 208
Emrod, George, 208
William, 208
Endecott—see Indecut
Engle, Joseph, 158
Robert, 158
English, Ann, 34, 35
James, 75
James R., 75
Jonathan, 75
Mercy, 75
Thomas, 193
William, 97
Enoch (Enock), Thomas, 78, 130
Ernst, John Fred, 46

Errickson (Ereckson, Erickson), John, 249
Thomas, 34
Erwin (Ervin), John, 62, 143
Perynetie, 75
Peter, 75, 152
Samuel, 62
Sarah, 75
Susannah, 75
Esdale (Esdall), Elizabeth, 201
James, 114
John, 112
Estill, Jane, 253
William, 253
Estlack—see Eastlack
Estough, David, 260
Evans (Evins), C., 54, 244
Elizabeth, 76
Enoch, 76, 253
Esther, 76
Hannah, 76
Isaac, 62
John, 57
Joshua, 155
Lewis, 23, 32, 86
Lot, 43
Margaret, 218
Mary, 76
Rebecca, 76
Samuel, 47, 76
Thomas, 244
William, 76, 95
See also Evens
Eveland, Samuel, 72
Evelman, Mary, 76
Robert, 76
Evens, Crowell, 227
David, 237
Jacob, 244
See also Evans
Everitt, David, 126, 134, 210
Nancy, 225
Eves, Joseph, 244
Ewan, Evan, 76
Ewing, Abner, 76
Deliverance, 212
Enos, 40
James, 29, 63, 117
John, 157
Letty, 248
Maskell, 24, 117
Naomi, 212
Thomas, 43
Eyre, Ann, 76
Benjamin, George, 76
Elizabeth, 76,
George, 76, 138, 139, 259
Hannah, 76
Jehu, 76
John, 259
Lydia, 259
Mary, 76
Nathan, 76
Samuel, 72, 78
Samuel, Jr., 76
Samuel B., 76
See also Eayre

F

Faesch, John Jacob, 142
Fairchild (Fearchild), Abner, 40
Caleb, 77
David, 84
Elizabeth, 21, 76, 165

Jonathan, 42, 77
Joseph, 40
Moses, 92
Nathaniel, 165
Rebecca, 77
Stephen, 77
Farber, Elizabeth, 77
George, 77
Margaret, 77
Paul, 77
Philip, 77
Susannah, 77
Farley, Barbara, 77
Caleb, 77
Isaac, 77
John, 77
Joshua, 77
Mary, 77
Farnham, Isaac, 28
Farquar, Sarah, 119
Farrand, Bethuel, 195
Daniel, 195
James, 101
Nathaniel, 262
Farrington, Samuel, 165
Faulkner, Catherine, 180
Fearchild—*see* Fairchild
Featherer, Jacob, 130
Feit, Catharine, 77
Daniel, 77
Mary, 77
Fenimore (Fennemore), Abraham, 78
Elizabeth, 78
Henry, 159
James, 35, 78
John Hutchin, 78
Joseph, 16, 78
Joshua, 78
Mary, 78
Pearson, 12, 78
Rebecca, 78
Samuel, 78
Thomas, 78, 130
Fenton, Eleazer, Jr., 78
Elizabeth, 78
Hannah, 78
John, 78
Samuel, 78
Ferguson, Diana, 143
Joseph, 216
*See also* Forgason
Ferrell (Ferrol), John, 176
Nathaniel, 48
Sarah, 48
Fershee, Cornelius, 66
Fervier, Stephen, 79
Few, Joseph, 207
Sarah, 207
Fiddiss, George Garnett, 37
Field, Benjamin, Jr., 79
Dennies, 79
Elnathan, 215
Isaac, 79
Jacob, 79
Jeremiah, 79
John, 79
Margaret, 79
Rebecca, 203
Richard, 79
Richard, Jr., 79
Tobitha, 192
Fields, Grace, 168
John, 41
Rodman, 72
Sicilia, 72

Filsmire, Adam, 200
Margaret, 200
Firth, Henry, 220, 255
Fish, Alexander, 208
Caleb, 25
Grace, 232
Peter, 152
Fisher, Elizabeth, 79
George, 9
Grace, 149
Jacob, 255
Jonathan, 89
Mary, 79
Moses, 13, 14
Fisler, Felix, 247
Fitch, Rebecca, 53
Sarah, 53
Fithian, Amos, 157
David, 79
Elizabeth, 79, 80
Isaac, 80
Israel, 80
John, 79
John, Jr., 80
Lot, 69, 80
Lovece, 79
Molly, 80
Phebe, 79
Ruth, 62
Samuel, 80
Serviah, 79
Thomas, 80
Unis, 80
Wade, 79
William, 80
FitzPatrick, Archibald, 187
FitzRandel, Hartshorn, 62
FitzRandolph, Asher, 33
Elizabeth, 80
Esek, 148
Experience, 80
Hartshorn, 202
James, 209
Jephtha, 80
Joseph, 48
Nathaniel, 80
Phineas, 72
Reuben, 80
Richard, 202
Rosanah, 80
Samuel, 24
*See also* Randolph
Fitzsimmons, John, 45
Sarah, 45
Flack, Andrew, 48
Flaningam, Isaac, 120, 122, 150
Fleming, Benjamin, 118
Jacob, 80, 81, 238, 249
Sarah, 249
Stephen, 32, 249
Fletcher, William, 23, 172
Flock, John, 81, 104
Margaret, 81
Mary Margaret, 184
Philip, 81
Flummerfelt, Cornelius, 180
Fogg, Mary, 81
Samuel, 81
Folwell, Ann, 81
John, 81, 197
Mary, 81
Nathan, 81, 82, 171
Samuel, 81, 149
Sarah, 196
Thomas, 81
William, 81

## INDEX OF NAMES OF PERSONS

Force, Abigail, 82
  Jonas, 211
  Samuel, 23, 228
  Sarah, 23
  Squire, 82
  Thomas, 82
Ford, Benjamin, 128, 130
  David, 27
  Elizabeth, 82
  Philip, 228
  William, 57, 96, 162, 169
Fordham, Lemuel, 156
Forgason, John, 10
  Patience, 10
  William, 10
  *See also* Ferguson
Forker, Sarah, 177
Forman, Aaron, 118, 144
  Caty, 82
  Effy, 82
  John, 187, 253
  John, Jr., 135
  Jonathan, 83, 222
  Lewis, 82
  Margaret, 160
  Mary, 82
  Samuel, 31, 55, 115, 120, 174, 197, 253, 254
  Samuel P., 56
  Samuel T., 83
  Thomas, 76
  Ursilla, 82
  *See also* Furman
Forrest (Forest), Edward, 116
  John, 181
Forrester, John, 68, 77
Forster, Gilbert, 239
  William, 34
Forsyth, Andrew, 52
  Joseph, 63
Fort, Anne, 82
  Hannah, 82
  Jean, 82
  John, Jr., 82
  Joseph, 82
  Lettice, 82
  Levinia, 82
  Marmaduke, 82
Fortinor (Fortenor), Drusilla, 82
  Elizabeth, 149
  Priscilla, 251
Foss, Philip, 82
Foster, Allehanson, 83
  Benjamin, 71
  Christopher, 98
  Constantine, 44
  Elisheba, 83
  Ephraim, 63, 83, 86, 133, 210, 229
  Ezekiel, 63, 86, 229, 237
  Ezekiel, Jr., 82, 83
  Jeremiah, 82
  Josiah, 9
  Martha, 83
  Mary, 239
  Nathaniel, 73
  Patience, 83
  Rachel, 83
  Ransellor, 83
  Reuben, 83
  Salathiel, Sr., 83, 222
Foulke, John, 260
Fowler, Elizabeth, 83, 95
  Isaac, 114
  Joseph, 38
Fox, David, 192
  Hannah, 35
  Mary, 194
  Patrick, 35
  Peter, 194
  William, 59
  William, Jr., 83
Francis, David, 83
  John, 83
  Martha, 83
  Nehemiah, 83
  Richard, 116, 117
  Robert, Jr., 83
  Susannah, 83, 253
Francisco, Ann, 147
  Henry, 48
Franks, Mary, 260
Frazee, Survia, 140
Frazer (Fraser), David, 126, 127, 193, 203
Freas, Frederick, 43, 57
  *See also* Freese
Frederick, Henry, 83, 84
  Margaret, 83
  Mary, 162
  Rachel, 83
Frederickson, Frederick, 138
Freeman, Alpheus, 173
  Amos, 84
  Benjamin, 209
  Benjamin, Jr., 19, 20, 84
  Edward, 250
  Elijah, 41
  Elizabeth, 84
  Esther, 84
  Gilman, 84
  Henry, 84
  Isaac, 84, 158, 173, 194, 216
  Jacob, 84
  Jedidiah, 84
  Jonathan, 84, 216
  Joseph, 173, 195
  Joseph, Jr., 54, 195
  Matthias, 254
  Melanthon, 173, 254
  Phebe, 84
  Rachel, 84
  Samuel, 84
Freese, Jacob, 126
  *See also* Freas
Frelinghuysen, Frederick, 24, 136
  Getty, 24
French, Anna, 123, 197
  Charles, 112, 114
  Edward, 84, 85
  George, 84
  Samuel, 179, 218, 264
  Sarah, 84
  Uriah, 84
  William, 213
Frost, Esther, 85
  James, 85, 209
  Mary, 85
  Sarah, 85
Fry, Richard, 150
Fullwood, Charles Slade, 240
Funk, Hannah, 177
Furman, Aaron, 46
  Adrian R., 54
  Agur, 85
  Barzillai, 35
  Jonathan, 85
  Mary, 85
  Moore, 54, 70, 90, 116, 233, 234
  Robert, 50
  Samuel, 192
  Sarah, 85
  *See also* Forman
Furniss, William, 251

## G

Gale, Alexander, 152
  Cornelia, 91
Gallagher, Elizabeth, 201
Gano, Daniel, 32
  Stephen, 108
Gard, Charity, 86
  Daniel, 9
  Gershom, 9, 165
  Jacob, 76, 77
  Job, 86
Gardiner (Gardner, Gardener), Abraham, 138, 182
  Affe, 86
  Christopher, 86
  James, 86
  Jeniah, 86
  John, 117
  John, Jr., 47, 134
  Joseph, 86
  Mary, 86
  Thomas M., 243
  William, 86, 177
Garner, Ephraim, 230
  James, 230
  John, 230
  Joseph, 230
Garrabrants (Gerrebrantse), Cornelius, 184, 240
  Garrabrant, 66, 184
  Garrabrant A., 86
  Henry, 261
  John, Jr., 86
  Lenah, 240
  Marritye, 66
Garretson (Gerretson), Anne, 88
  Bernardus, 239
  Daniel, 16
  Garret, 88
  Garret R., 223, 254
  Jacobus, 53, 254
  Mary, 88
  Rem, 223
  Samuel, 16, 87, 88
Garrigus, David, 179
Garrison, Andrew, 142
  Azel, 86
  Bersheba, 241
  Daniel, 151
  David Ogden, 86
  Elizabeth, 86, 142, 208
  Ephraim, 7
  Gamaliel, 244
  George, 72, 126
  Joel, 86
  John, 72, 127, 151, 208
  Joseph, 151
  Joshua, 241
  Josiah, 86
  Mary, 7, 86
  Richard, 208
  Ruth, 63
  Susannah, 245
  William, 36, 57, 151, 166, 168, 241
Garritse (Gerritse), Catriena, 86, 87
  Ebegel, 86
  Henry, 87, 246
  Jacob, 87
Garton, Jonathan, 87
Garwood, Hezekiah, 198
  Japheth, 87
  Rebecca, 69
Gaskill, Daniel, 261
  Jennings, 87
  Job, 64
  John, 34
  Josiah, 177, 261
  Samuel, 10, 34
  Sarah, 34
  Theofela, 34
Gauntt (Gaunt), Asher, 87, 215
  Elihu, 87
  Elizabeth, 87
  Hannah, 87
  John, 188
  Peter, 87
  Reuben, 87
  Sarah, 87
  Sarepta, 87
  Uz, 87
Gearhart, George, 116, 120, 202
  Jacob, 203
  Margaret, 120
  Matthias, 120
Gearing, Zuba, 143
Gee, Marcy, 151
Genung, Benjamin, 25
  Cornelius, 204
  John, 25
  Moses, 25
George, Thomas, 238
Gerhart—see Gearhart
Gerrabrantse—see Garrabrants
Gerretson—see Garretson
Gerritse—see Garritse
Getschius, John, 242
Gibb, John, 88
  Richard, 88
Gibbs, Abel, 88
  Elizabeth, 88
  Hannah, 88
  Joel, 63, 220
  Joseph, 12
  Lucas, 46
  Martin, 220
  Richard, 46
Gibson, James, Jr., 88
  Joseph, 257
Giddington, Hannah, 259
Gifford, Abraham, 136
  Anna, 91
  John, 58
Gildersleeve, Daniel, 88
  Ezra, 89
  John, 88
  Joseph, 88, 89
  Lois, 88
  Phebe, 88
  Ruth, 88
  Sarah, 88
Giles, James, 89
Gill, John, 91, 93, 114, 149, 203
  Matthew, 263
  Matthew, Jr., 109, 130, 137, 263
  Sarah, 112
  Thomas, 38, 87
Gillman, David, 8, 129
  David, Jr., 201
Githens, George, 132
  Joseph, 161
  Thomas, 93, 230
Givens, George, 25
Glan, Gabriel, 30, 105
Glover, Francis, 92, 168
  Isaac, 71
  Jacob, 71
  John, 71
  John T., 230
  Joseph, 71
  Margaret, 172
  Mary, 71

Rachel, 71
Samuel, 71
Goble, Jonathan, 178
Goddard, William, 13
Godden, Abraham, 89
　David, 89
　Elizabeth, 89
　Hopestill, 89
　John, 89
　Joseph, 89
　Providence, 89
Godfrey, Andrew, 214
　James, 99
Godown, Evans, 89
　Jacob, 89
　John, 89
　Thomas, 89
Goetschius—see Getschius
Goff, David, 176, 189
　John, 176, 232
Golden, Alpheus, 89
　David, 90
　Elizabeth, 90
　Joanna, 90
　John, 54
　Joseph, 90
　Ledreme, 90
　Loanna, 90
Golder, Abraham, 90
　Catherine, 90
　John, 150
Goldsmith (Gouldsmith), Jonah, 257
　Josiah, 257
　Mary, 90
　Mehetable, 257
Goldy, John, 10, 56, 60, 82
　Samuel, Jr., 169
Goleker, Margaret, 83
Goodfellow, Thomas, 119, 160
Goodwin, Elizabeth, 10
　John, 149
　Susannah, 149
　William, 10, 52, 102
Gordon, Charles, 83
　Franklin, 133
　Peter, 102, 121, 152, 218, 245
　Samuel, 29, 252
　Susannah, 218
Gosling (Goslin), Jacob, 50, 179, 218, 264
　John, 245
　Phebe, 221
Gould, Elizabeth, 48, 233
　Encrease, 48, 175
　Jacob, 136
　Josiah, 48
　Samuel, 48
　William, 171
Goulden, Samuel, 90
Goulder, Nicholas, 234
Gouverneur (Gouveneur), Alida, 90
　Gertruyda, 90, 91
　Isaac, 90, 91
　Isaac, Jr., 91
　Mary, 90, 91
　Nicholas, Jr., 91
Grafenperger, Ignatius, 149
Graff, Sebastian, 91
　William, 249
　See also Groff, Gruff
Graham, William, 155
Grandin, Daniel, 31
　Mary, 91
　Philip, 120, 192, 203
　Rachel, 91

Sarah, 91
William, 91, 136
Grant, Isaac, 148
Gray, Elizabeth, 91
　Garret, 35
　Isaac, Jr., 91
　Rebecca, 104
Green, widow, 185
　Abigail, 92
　Adam, 91
　Anne, 92
　Ashbel, 92
　Calvin, 92
　David, 137
　Dorothy, 92
　Elizabeth, 92
　George, 91, 92, 121, 147, 185
　Jacob, 137
　James, 92, 207
　John, 168
　John Wickliffe, 92
　Joseph, 92
　Keturah, 92
　Mary, 92
　Pierson, 92
　Richard, 109
　Samuel, 118
　Sarah, 61
　Thomas, 47
　William, 21, 65
Greenman, David, 145
　Elizabeth, 241
　Mary, 182
　Thomas, 241
Gregeon, Thomas, 32
Gregory, Seth, 92
　William, 96
Griffee, Samuel, 178
Griffing, Betsy, 23
Griffith (Griffyth, Gruffyth), Abel, 79
　Abraham, Sr., 260
　Edward, 132
　Elizabeth, 39
　John, 114, 166, 197
　Joseph, 95
　Lydia, 39
　Nathaniel Camp, 39
　William, 95
Griffitts, James, 63
Griggs, Daniel, 79
　Elizabeth, 79
　Joakim, 12
　John, 12, 14, 105
　John, Jr., 202
　Samuel, 105, 106
Grimes, George, 130
Grinder, Christian, 129
Grinding, William, 220
Grinslade, Elizabeth, 93
　John, Jr., 93
Griscom, Deborah, 93
　Hannah, 93
Groenendyck, Nicholas, 210
Groff, John, 57
　Mary, 187
　See also Graff, Gruff
Groom, Mary, 93
　Stacy, 93
Grover, Joseph, 69
Grubb, Robert, 40
Gruff, Richard, 57
　See also Graff, Groff
Grumman (Gruman), Ichabod, 61, 170
Grunnel, Thomas, 199
Gruson, Mrs., 94

290   NEW JERSEY COLONIAL DOCUMENTS

Guerin (Guering), Joseph, 252
  Joshua, 252
Guest, Henry, 51
  Moses, 71
Guild, Benjamin, 93
  Charity, 93
  Esther, 93
  John, 16, 185
  John, Jr., 93
  Margery, 93
  Mary, 93
  Mercy, 93
  Phebe, 93
  Ralph, 93
Guinip (Gwinnup, Guinnup), Jabez, 42, 51, 76, 131, 140
  Sally, 81
Guisbertson, Mary, 116
Gulick, Hendrik, 242
  Henry, 113
  Joacham, 146
Gumersall, Mary, 93
Gustin, John, 52
Gwin, William, 15
Gwinnup—*see* Guinip

H

Hackenbery, Anne Elizabeth, 199
  *See also* Hockenbery
Hacket (Hackett), Elizabeth, 94
  John, 94
  Joseph, 28
  Patrick, 94
  Richard, 94
  Thomas, 94
Hackney, Ann, 18
  Mary, 18
Haddock, Francis, 208
Hagaman (Hegeman), Joseph, 132, 198, 199, 242
  Joseph D., 219, 242
  Jost, 24
Hager (Hoeger), John, 48, 249
  Elizabeth, 249
Hagerman, Garret, 94
  John, 242
  Nice, 94
  Ruth, 94
  *See also* Hagaman
Hagerty (Haggerty), David, 106, 107
  Hugh, 206
  John, 94
  Robert, 94, 106, 107
  William, 94
Haines (Hains, Haynes), Aaron, 38
  Abel, 38, 230
  Abigail, 95
  Abraham, 219
  Amos, 138
  Benjamin, 136
  Beulah, 230
  Caleb, 74, 95, 158
  Carlile, 158
  Catherine, 95
  Daniel, 78
  Dorcas, 95
  Elizabeth, 38, 95
  Enoch, 260
  Ephraim, 96
  Henry Pendergrass, 95, 166
  Isaac, 87, 221
  Isaiah, 126, 199
  Jacob, 36, 87, 230
  James, 164
  Jeremiah, 62, 95
  Job, 226
  John, 88, 95, 96, 261
  Jonathan, 95
  Joseph, 38, 95, 166
  Josiah, 64
  Keziah, 166
  Marian, 166
  Marion H., 166
  Mary, 13, 38, 78, 95, 139
  Nathan, 95
  Nathan, Jr., 166
  Rachel, 95
  Richard, 138
  Samuel, 38, 189, 230
  Sarah, 95, 166
  Solomon, 88, 221
  Thomas, 64, 95, 112
  William, 38, 62, 95, 112, 153
  William Henry, 246
Hall, Abraham, 162
  Daniel, 20, 21
  David, 260
  Edward, 7, 21
  George, 162
  Gervas, 46
  Hannah, 247, 260
  Jacob, 29
  Jesse, 29
  John, 52, 139, 254
  Richard, 162, 243
  Rowland, 102, 257
  Sarah, 111
  William, 162
Halladay, James, 96
  John, 96
  Mary, 96
  Samuel, 96
  Susannah, 96
Halsey (Hallsey), Ananias, 262
  Anna, 255
  Ichabod, 96
  Ichabod, B., 96
  Isaac, 96
  Jacob, 96
  Joseph, 96, 255, 262
  Margaret, 96
Halsted (Halstead), Christopher, 238
  Mary, 94
  Matthias, 102, 202
  Susannah, 238
Hamilton, Abraham, 96
  Ann, 96
  Arthur, 96
  Charles, 96
  Deborah, 96
  Elizabeth, 96
  Isaac, 96
  Jacob, 96
  James, 96, 169
  John, 96
  Margaret, 96, 159
  Mary, 96
  Priscilla, 96, 97
  Sarah, 96
  Susannah, 96
  William, 96
Hamler, Meriam, 244
Hamlinton, John, 159
Hammell (Hamel, Hammil), James, Jr., 11
  John, 195
  Susanna, 11
  William, Jr., 224
Hammitt, Elias, 24
Hampton, Abraham, 97
  Daniel, 181

INDEX OF NAMES OF PERSONS 291

Susannah, 97
William, 167
Hamson, Robert, 97
Hance, David, 53
  George, 223
  Hannah, 103
  Isaac, 202, 203
  Jacob, 53
  John, 27
Hancock, Ann, 97
  Daniel, 124, 139, 196
  Elizabeth, 37
  Godfrey, 97
  Isaac, 97
  John, 97
  Thomas, 10
  William, 97
Hand, Aaron, 73, 164, 185, 200, 221
  Absalom, 97
  Daniel, 97
  David, 214
  Deborah, 98
  Eleazer, 73, 98, 99
  Elihu, 73, 74, 168
  Elijah, 98, 222
  Elijah, Jr., 83
  Elizabeth, 73, 98, 99, 150
  Ezekiel, 98
  George, 60
  Hannah, 97, 98, 99
  Henry, 98
  Jacob, 222
  Jeremiah, 60, 98, 99, 200, 221
  Jesse, 52, 53, 60, 85, 98, 99, 110, 124, 134, 148, 169, 185, 214
  John, 83, 248
  Lydia, 99, 248
  Martha, 97, 98
  Mary, 98, 99
  Nathan, 98
  Nathaniel, 99
  Philip, 23, 59, 98, 119, 164, 185
  Rachel, 98
  Sarah, 23, 52, 53, 60, 85, 97, 98, 99, 110, 124, 142, 169, 172, 176, 214, 231, 232, 248
  Sarah, Jr., 85, 110, 200
  Seth, 97
  Thomas, 150
  Timothy, 98
  William, 85
Handsey, James, 29
Hankins, Elizabeth, 129
  Richard, 179
Hankinson, Aaron, 177
  James, 71
  Lydia, 233
  Sarah, 71
  William, 125, 187
Hanlon, Bernard, 21, 70, 108
Hanna (Hannah), John, 229
  Jonathan, 245
  Mary, 108
  Preston, 63
  Samuel, 62
  William, 108
Harden, Mary, 99, 190
  Rebecca, 97
Hardenburgh, John, 20
Harding, Dorothy, 100
  Hannah, 100
  Isaac, 100
  John, 100
  Richard, 100
  Samuel, 100
  Sarah, 100

Hardy, James, 100
Haring, Abraham, 244
  Fredericus, 81
  Frederick, 100
  Garri, 100
  Jacobus, 100
  Johannis, 100
  Margritie, 100
  Peter, 100
  Rensye, 100
Harker, David, 85
  John, 117
  Jonathan, 7, 140, 166, 176
  Joseph, 15, 126, 236
  Margaret, 8
Harling, Cornelius, 263
Harriman, Samuel, 154
Harriott—see Herriott
Harris, Abel, 41
  Benjamin, 17
  Ebenezer, 80
  Ephraim, 63, 194
  Euphamia, 100
  Francis, 125
  Isaac, 101, 194
  James, 45
  Jonathan, 27
  Mary, 100, 101, 123, 231
  Meriam, 101
  Ogden, 86
  Robert, 88
  William, 256
  William, Jr., 137
Harrison, Abigail, 101
  Amos, 102
  Arabella, 102
  Azuba, 101
  Elizabeth, 102
  Frazee, 102
  George, 101, 102
  Isaac, 101, 102
  James, 102
  Jonas, 61, 102
  Joseph, 170, 171
  Jotham, 262
  Martha, 102
  Mary, 101
  Phebe, 101
  Rachel, 102
  Robert, 102
  Samuel, 52, 63, 102
  Simeon, 102
  Stephen, 170
  Thomas, 102
  William, 28, 88
  See also Arrison
Harsel, Christopher, 102
Hart, Elijah, 11
  Enoch, 102
  Jacob, 118, 231
  Jesse, 218
  Joseph, 230, 247
  Kaziah, 102
  Nathaniel, 102
  Ralph, 102
Hartley, Anthony, 102
  Catharine, 102
  Elizabeth, 102
  Esther, 102
  Hannah, 185
  Mark, 102
  Mary, 102
  Rebecca, 115
  Samuel, 102
  Susannah, 102
  Thomas, Jr., 102

Hartshorne, John, 53, 117
  Esek, 136
  Richard, 209
Harvey, Margaret, 103
  Samuel, 103
  Thomas, 103
  William, 103
Harwood, Eaton, 203
Hatcher, William, 78
Hatfield (Hetfield), Aaron, Jr., 226
  Andrew, 255
  Caleb, 159
  John, 67
  Joseph, 23
  Mary, 104
Hathaway, Sarah, 103
Hathorn, Hugh, 54
  *See also* Hawthorn
Hatso, Balser, 46
Haughawout, Peter, 113
Haulenbeek (Haulenbeck), Garret, 229
  Isaac, 75
Haun, John, 154
Havens, Anna, 103
  Daniel, 103
  Eavis, 103
  Elizabeth, 103
  Isaac, 255
  Jacob, 103
  Jesse, 103
  Moses, 103
Haviland (Heaviland), Abigail, 104
  Benjamin, 15, 34, 103, 104, 109, 160, 228
  Benjamin Winans, 104
  Elizabeth, 105
  Grace, 105
  Hannah, 105
  Jane, 103
  John, 104, 106
  Lettea, 105
  Mary, 103, 105
  Nathan, 105
  Rebecca, 105, 106
  Sally, 103
  Stephen, 56, 103
  William, 104
Hawk, Catharine, 104
  Frederick, 104
  Jacob, 104, 196
  Rachel, 99
Hawker, William, 233
Hawkins, Augustus, 232
  Immanuel, 232
  William, 143, 232
Hawthorn, Isaac, 8, **119**
  *See also* Hathorn
Hay, Stephen, 61
Hayden, Benjamin, 43
Haydock, James, 37
Haymar, Gabriel, 224
Haynes—*see* Haines
Hays (Hayes), David, 39
  Hannah, 104
  Margaret, 236
  Mary, 104
  Samuel, 103
  Thomas, 236
Haywood, Budd, 34
  Deborah, 34
  George, 34
Hazard, Ebenezer, 233
Hazen, Arthur, 100, 104
  Thomas, 104
  Thomas, Jr., 89

Hazlehurst, Joannah, 182
  Mary, 182
Hazlitt, Samuel, 122
  William, 110, 132
Headey, Oliver, 41
Headly, David, 152
Heard, Nathaniel, 158, 202
  William, 202
Hearty, Jemima, 25
  Jacob, 25
Heath, Jean, 132
  John, 132
Heaton, Anna, 105
  Aula, 105
  Daniel, 105
  Gideon, 30, 141, 142, 159
  Gideon, Jr., 105
  Hannah, 78
  Isaac, 48
  John, 105
  Jonathan, 105
  Levi, 86, 105, 153
  Mary, 105
  Mercy, 105
  Rachel, 105
  Rebecca, 105
  Richard, 78
  Samuel, 105
  Seth, 105
  Susannah, 21, 48
Heaviland—*see* Haviland
Heddy, Hannah, 140
Hedenberg, Charles, 239
Hedger, John, 44, 150, 176, 234
  Mary, 47
Hedges, Lemuel, 173
Hegeman—*see* Hagaman, Hagerman
Heiel, Peter, 244
  *See also* Hile
Hellebrant, William, 136
Hellerman, George, 264
Helloms, Mary 47
Helm (Helme), Benjamin, 246
Helms, Major, 94
  William, 94
Hemsey, Joseph, 158
Hendershot (Hendershet), Casper, 68, 106
  Cateren, 106
  Charity, 68
  Elizabeth, 106
  Jacob, 106
  John, 106
  Rachel, 106
  Sarah, 106
  Suffiah, 106
  William, 106
Henderson, Anna, 105
  David, 106, 107
  Elizabeth, 107
  James, 106
  John, 105, 107
  John, Jr., 106
  Mary, 106
  Rachel, 10, 28, 34, 55, 91, **131**, 133, 151, 202, 249, 254
  Sarah, 106
  Thomas, 9, 10, 83, 91, **131**, **174**
Hendricks, Abram, 179
  Isaac, 16, 57, 176
  John, 152
Hendrickson, Abraham, Jr., 107
  Cathrine, 107, 108
  Daniel, 190, 222, 240, 251
  David, 52, 106, 107, 108, 228
  Edy, 108

## INDEX OF NAMES OF PERSONS 293

Garret, 107, 212, 221
Hendrick, 28, 107, 161, 200, 221
  Henry, 108
  Jacob, 107
  Mary, 108
  Nelly, 240
  Nicholas, 11, 230
  Thomas, 107
  Tobias, 75, 222
Hendry, Thomas, 173, 194
Henn, Anna, 68
  Jacob, 68
Henry, David, 8, 196
  John, 88, 193
  Rhoda, 108
  Robert R., 181
  Samuel, 108, 257
  Thomas, 108
  William, 21
Henselbecker, Johannes, 108
Henszey, Isaac, 44
Hepburn, John, 184
Herbert, Henry, 254
Herbeson, Robert, 78
Heritage, Benjamin, 97
  Mary, 108
Herley—see Hurley
Herrington, Mary, 217
Herriott (Harriott), David, 32
  George, 80
  John, 28
Heston, Thomas, 129
Hetfield—see Hatfield
Heulings—see Hewlings
Heward, Joseph, 185
Hewes (Hews), Aaron, 97, 109, 128, 150, 166, 171, 258
  Caleb, 109
  Elizabeth, 109
  George, 109
  Isaac, 109
  James, 51
  Jane, 108
  John, 109
  Joseph, 108
  Josiah, 108
  Mary, 247
  Rebecca, 109
  Samuel, 109
  Ursilla, 171
  William, 109
  See also Hughes
Hewet (Hewit, Huit, Huet, &c.), Ann, 232
  Elijah, 98
  Elizabeth, 239
  Rachel, 98
  Shamgar, 98, 198
Hewlings (Heulings), Abraham, 11, 42, 139, 198, 259
  Abraham, Jr., 127, 129
  Joseph, 139
  Thomas, 32, 158
  Thomas P., 207
Heyer—see Hyer
Hichner, George, 206
Hickman, Peter, 178
Hicks, Deborah, 160
  Elizabeth, 260
  Hugh, 14
Hider, John, 150
Higbee, Absalom, 109
  Charles, 109, 143, 188
  Edward, 109
  Isaac, 109
  Jeremiah, 135

  John, Jr., 109
  Joseph, 29, 143, 235
  Josiah, 109
  Mary, 109
  Richard, 109
  Samuel, 109
  William, 109
Higgins (Higgens), Andrew, 73, 109
  Anne, 12
  Azariah, 183, 217
  Elizabeth, 109
  Jediah, 61
  Joshua, 195, 216
  Michael, 109
  Nathan, 183
  Nathaniel, 109
  Sally, 103
  William Brown, 104, 109, 160
Highland, Hendrick, 42
Hight, John, 61
  Rachel, 255
Hildreth, David, 60, 110, 200
  Dorcas, 110
  James, 221
  Jonathan, 59
  Joseph, 110, 208, 221, 248
  Joshua, 110
  Martha, 110
Hile, Catherine, 110
  Christian, Jr., 110
  Christophel, 110
  Elizabeth, 110
  Hannah, 110
  Henry, 110
  John, 110
  Margaret, 110
  Mary, 110
  Peter, 110
  Thomas, 110
  See also Heiel
Hiles, Anne, 109
  Jacob, Jr., 109
  William, 96
Hill, Abigail, 42
  Bearsheba, 111
  Charles, 111
  Daniel, 239
  Elizabeh, 111
  Francis, 38
  James, 111
  John, 111
  Paul, 111
  Peter, 42
  Phebe, 111
  Rachel, 216
  Samuel, 12, 14, 42, 105, 106, 111, 122, 176, 219
  William, 111
Hilliard (Hillyard, Hilyard), Frances, 112
  John, 87
  Jonathan, 87, 112
  Kezia, 165
Hillman, Drusilla, 43, 44, 159
  Ephraim, 190
  Joab, 44, 190
  John, 190
  Joseph, 26, 43, 45, 115, 150
  Josiah, 187
  Priscilla, 44
  Samuel, 45
Hillyard—see Hilliard
Hillyer, William, 22, 92, 247
Hinan, J., 222
Hinchman, Elizabeth, 112
  Hannah, 112

James, 112, 128, 186
Sarah, 112
William, Jr., 71
Hinds, Elizabeth, 112, 113
James, 112
Joseph, 112, 113
Margaret, 113
Mary, 112, 113
Rebecca, 112
Richard, Jr., 112, 113
Hindshaw——see Hyndshaw
Hiner, Catherine, 113
Charity, 113
Herbert, 113
John, 113
Margaret, 113
Mary, 113
Susannah, 113
William, 113
Hinman, Adam, 200
Hire—see Hyer
Hires—see Hyers
Hixson, Abner, 116
Hoagland (Hoogeland, Hogland, Hoguland, etc.)
Abraham, 55
Agnes, 172
Amos, 172
Christopher 195
Derrick, 260
Henry, 172
John, 172
Joshua, 172
Lucas, 180
Mary, 55, 113
Okey, 79, 82, 239
William, 116, 185, 194, 210
Hockenbery, John, 110
See also Hackenbery
Hodge, Andrew, 159
Hodgson, Thomas, 7, 14
Hoeger—see Hager
Hoff, Andrew, 145
Cornelius, 113, 145, 179, 223
Elizabeth, 113, 145
Gabriel, 87
Isaac, 113
Joseph, Jr., 113
Lydia, 113
Mary, 113
Thomas, 113
see also Hooff, Hough, Huff
Hoffman, Abraham, 251
John, 77
Thomas, 45
See also Huffman
Hoffmire, Samuel, 49, 215
Hogan, John, 229
Hogland, Hoguland—see Hoagland
Holcomb, Jacob, 109, 178
Thomas, 112
Hole, Jane Scudder, 197
John, 16, 20
Mary, 197
Holeman (Holman), Elizabeth, 114
Jacob, 114
Joseph, 114, 162
Margaret, 114
Nelly, 207
Holliday, Catharine, 114
James, 114
John, 220
John, Jr., 114
Joseph, 114
Rebecca, 114

Sarah, 114
William, 114
Hollinshead (Hollingshead), Ales, 47
Alice, 114
Edmund, 47, 114, 138
Eleanor, 114
Hannah, 47
Jacob, 47, 87, 114, 190
James, 47, 57
John, 47, 100, 126, 190, 235
Joseph, Jr., 75
Mary, 47, 165
Morgan, 137
Thomas, 47, 95, 112, 114, 132, 166, 207
William, 264
Holloway, Isabella, 114
James, 166
Holman—see Holeman
Holme, Hannah, 114
John, 184
Kezia, 114
Phebe, 114
Samuel, 114, 115
See also Hulme
Holmes, Anthony, 13
Asher, 115, 161
Daniel, 115
Deborah, 136
Hannah, 97
Hugh, 73
James, 161
John, 176
John, Jr., 161
Joseph, 133, 136
Josiah, 174
Mary, 115
Nathaniel, 97, 98
Obadiah, 161
Rachel, 115
Sarah, 161
Holsart, Peter, 118
See also Hulsart
Holston, Christian, 135
Holton, Andrew, 115
Deborah, 115
James, 115
William, 115
Homan, Andrew, 52, 213
Priscilla, 115
Vanderver, 115
William, Jr., 115
Hommer—see Hummer
Honeyman, John, 173
Honeywell, William, 220
Hood, James, 27, 116
William, Jr., 116
Hooff, William, 228
See also Hoff, Hough, Huff
Hoogland—see Hoagland
Hooper, Robert L., 116
Hooton, Deborah, 175
Thomas, 175
Hopkins, Elizabeth, 207
Hannah, 116
James, 51, 96, 207
John, 232
John Estaugh, 232
John M., 232
Jonathan, 116
Nathan, 116
Silas, 97
William, 116
Hoppah, Peter, 132
See also Hoppock

INDEX OF NAMES OF PERSONS 295

Hoppe, Garret, 194, 263
  John, 194
Hopper, Altye, 116
  Andrew A., 7
  Garret, 116
  John, 116
  John I., 116
  Joshua, 12, 192
Hoppins, Samuel, 85
  Sarah, 85
Hoppock, Cornelius, 109
  Elizabeth, 192
  John, 192
  Peter, 132, 192
  William, 192
  *See also* Hoppah
Horn, Catharine, 199
  Thomas, 116
Horner (Hornor, Hornner), Benjamin, 117
  Fuller, 117
  Hugh, 116
  Jacob, 114
  James, 117
  Job, 117
  Joseph, 171
  Joshua, 117
  Sarah, 116
  William, 117
Horton, Benjamin, 180
Hoshel, Michael, 63
Hosher, Jane, 117
  William, 117
Hoskins, John, 38, 40, 261
  John, Jr., 38
  Joseph, 38
Hough, Charlotte, 167
  Daniel, 59
  Joseph, 167
  Samuel, 134, 167
  *See also* Hoff, Hoof, Huff
Houghton, Joab, 217
  John, 152, 190
  Sarah, 217
Housel, William, 102
Houston, Churchill, 117
  George, 117
  George S., 117
  William Churchill, 117
Houten, Rachel, 180
How, John, 127
  Samuel, 117
Howard, Alexander, 88
Howell (Howel), Aaron, 235
  Absalom, 118
  Caleb, 40, 51
  Daniel, 102, 118
  David, 144
  Ebenezer, 94, 157
  Ellet, 235
  Eseck, 234
  Gideon, 9, 42, 86
  Hannah, 56
  Hezekiah, 235
  Isaac, 181
  James, 63, 100
  John, 93, 185
  Joseph, 118
  Joshua, 32
  Mary, 93, 118
  Reading, 118
  Richard, 3, 52, 129, 187
  Silas, 93, 94, 149
  Susannah, 118
Howland, George, 220

Howlog, George, 220
Hudson, Anna, 118
  Isaac, 118, 119
  Joseph, 118, 119
  Obed, 118
  Phebe, 118, 119
  Sally, 118
Huet—*see* Hewit
Hufey, John, 29
  Kesiah, 29
Huff, Cornelius, 183
  Isaac S., 126
  *See also* Hoff, Hoof, Hough
Huffman, Mary, 120
  Peter, 120
  *See also* Hoffman
Hufty, Jacob, 256
Hugg, Elizabeth, 74, 119, 214
  Isaac S., 106
  Joseph, 9, 50, 57, 74, 150, 166, 211
  Joseph, Jr., 9, 30, 36, 130, 173, 205, 211
  Sarah, 119, 150
  William, Jr., 50, 218
  William K., 57, 212
  William King, 206
Hughes, Ann, 248
  Charles John, 119
  Constant, 52, 53, 60
  Constantine, 99
  David, 73
  Elijah, 99, 134, 172, 222, 248
  Elisha, 134
  Elizabeth, 119
  Ellis, Jr., 44, 98, 99, 222, 248
  Enoch, 16, 225
  Hugh, 148
  Jacob, 73, 99
  James, Jr., 119
  Jedediah, 60
  John, 119, 120
  Judith, 222
  Martha, 119
  Memucan, 73
  Nancy, 248
  Robard, 119
  Ruth, 119
  Samuel, 119
  Sarah, 248
  *See also* Hewes
Huie, Elizabeth, 120
  James, 120
  Jane, 120
  Pierses, 120
  Sarah, 120
Huit—*see* Hewit
Huling, Samuel, 169
Hulit (Hulitt), George, 43
  Robert, 254
  Thomas, 120
  Timothy, 43
Hull, Benjamin, 8
  Elizabeth, 62, 245
  Hopewell, 120, 132
  James, 120
  John, 68, 132
  Machack, 80
Hulme, George, 38, 182
  *See also* Holme
Hulsart, John, 249
  *See also* Holsart
Humes, Robert, 116
Hummer (Hommer), Ann, 120
  Elizabeth, 116, 120
  Herbert, 116, 120

Herbert, Jr., 116
Jacob, Jr., 120
Margaret, 120
Mary, 120
Sarah, 120
Humphries (Humphreys), Abigail, 19
Benjamin, 260
John, 121
Mary, 121, 260
Nancy, 121
Sarah, 121
Hunsiryer, Mary, 237
Hunt, Abigail, 121
Abraham, 30, 234, 257
Amelia, 121
Ann, 121
Catura, 121, 144
Charity, 34
Daniel, 247
Edward, 121, 122
Edward, Jr., 121
Elizabeth, 34
Esther, 121
Hannah, 121
Jacob, 181
James, 40
James B., 40, 186
Jane, 121
John, 37, 93, 121
John P., 53, 93, 102, 121, 245
Jonathan, 82, 125
Joseph, 96, 245
Margery, 93
Marmaduke, 203, 205
Mary, 121, 125
Nathaniel, 111, 206
Nathaniel, Jr., 125
Noah, 17
Obadiah, 54, 219
Parmela, 122
Peter, 22, 133
Ralph, 34, 53
Rebecca, 121, 122
Richard, 245
Samuel, 121, 122
Thomas, 117
William, 121, 223
Hunter, Andrew, 161, 173
Huntsman, Abraham, 11
Hurley (Herley), David, 26
James, 8, 63, 71, 255
John, 8
Hurst, Londwick, 44
Hussey, Christine, 122
Elizabeth, 122
Eve Catharine, 122
Hannah, 122
John, 122
John Michael, 122
Samuel, 122
Susannah, 122
Ursilla, 122
Husted, Anne, 122
Content, 122
Elizabeth, 122
Joel, 140, 154
Joseph Newcomb, 122
Mary, 122, 154
Mirabeth, 122
Moraby, 122
Moses, 122
Rachel, 122
Reuben, 140
Ruth, 122
Samuel, 108
William, 122

Hutchin, Amos, 76, 97, 100, 259
Hugh, 122
Joseph, 203
Hutchins, Anna, 123
John, 123, 137
Mary, 123
Hutchinson, Robert, 124
Huysen, Harmanus, 29
Hyde, John, 207
Hyer (Hire), Catharine, 123
Elizabeth, 123
William, 70, 123
William, Jr., 34, 41, 45, 56, 61, 88, 102, 146, 152, 157, 159, 186, 228
Hyers (Hires), John, 136
Silas, 84
Walter, 22
William, 22
*See also* Ayers
Hyndshaw, James, 65

I

Ilor (Iler), Elizabeth, 123
George, 123
Hannah, 123
Henry, 123
Jacob, 123
Imlay, Nathaniel, 145
Peter, 56
Indecut (Endicott), Jacob, 15
John, 15
Mary, 15
Samuel, 15
Ingersull (Ingersul), Hannah, 69
Joseph, Jr., 213
Ingrum, Benjamin, 98
Naomi, 44
Inskeep, Hnnah, 123
John, 138, 150
Samuel, 123
Ireland (Irelan), Amos, 195, 208
Edmond, 205, 213
Japhet, 59, 210
Joseph, 154
Mary, 59
Reuben, 119
Thomas, 59
Iszard, Reeves, 134
Ivins, Aaron, 63, 64, 123, 124
Ann, 123
Barzillai, 124
Caleb, 224
Hannah, 124
Isaac, 123, 124, 158
Margaret, 124
Mary, 123, 166
Moses, 65
Samuel, 12, 123
Sarah, 123
Solomon, 124

J

Jackaway, Hugh, 145
Jackson, Benjamin, 22, 131, 134, 254
Hugh, 159
Mary Ann, 43
Nathan, 174
Rebecca, 159
Jacobeson, Richard, 241
Jacobus, Gileam, 67
Roelf, 147
Jagard (Jaggard), James, 128, 159

## INDEX OF NAMES OF PERSONS

Jagors, Daniel, 235
James, Abigail, 58
  David, 100, 262
  Patience, 83
  Richard, 179, 180
  Robert, 124
  Sally, 188
  Uriah, 58
Jaques, Charles, 173
  Jonathan, 124, 216
  Moses, 149
  Richard, 42
  Samuel, 124
  Samuel, Jr., 152
Jaquett (Jaquet), Edith, 178
  John, 125
  John Daniel, 121
Jarman, Beriah, 124
  Jonathan, 124
  Reuben, 203
Jay, Reuben, 151
Jeffers, Elizabeth, 12
Jeffery, James, 124
  Jarrold, 136
Jefferys, Rebecca, 37
Jelf, Elizabeth, 226
Jemson, Jacob, 114
Jenkins, Ephraim, 97
  George, 125
  James, 217
  Jane, 30, 234
  Paulin, 125
Jennings (Jenings), Ann, 18, 125
  Benjamin, 125
  Elizabeth, 125
  Helena, 125
  Jacob, 18
  John, 125
  Judith, 112
  Margaret, 125
Jero, Ann, 208
Jessup, John, 81, 187, 256
Job, Ezekiel, 156
Jobs (Jobes), Adam, 238
  Austin, 44
  David, 44
  Hannah, 125
  John, 13
  Joseph, 125
Johnes (Johns), David, 91
  Martha, 44
  Richard, 44
  Stephen, Jr., 104
  Timothy, 84
  William, 84
Johnson, Abraham, 113
  Amos, 222
  Ann, 36
  Azubah, 125
  Barent, 53, 224
  Benjamin, 36, 126, 170
  Caleb, 245
  Cornelius, 66, 261
  Daniel, 28
  David, 124
  Dorothy, 126
  Eliphalet, 28
  Elizabeth, 66, 84, 177, 192
  Enos, 126
  Esther, 245
  Ezekiel, 26
  Hannah, 58, 125, 253
  Henry, 106, 126, 176
  Idah, 126
  Jacob James, 183
  Jacobus, 126
  James, 103, 127, 179, 217, 253
  Jane, 186
  John, 82, 85, 99, 126, 177
  Joseph, 125, 208
  Jotham, 39
  Lydia, 126
  Margaret, 126, 253
  Mary, 125
  Matthias, 41
  Moses, 92
  Nathaniel, 126
  Nicholas, 126, 255
  Peter, 126
  Philip, 127
  Rachel, 126
  Richard, 262
  Robert, 21, 146, 233
  Samuel, 106, 117, 126, 143
  Sarah, 85, 125
  Theodorus, 258
  Uzal, 58, 61, 82
  William, 162
Johnston, David, 121, 126, 247
  James, 62, 228
  Peter, 49, 115
  Robert, 111, 144
  Samuel, 126
Joice—*see* Joyce
Joline, Andrew, 35
Jones, Aaron, 128
  Anne, 28
  Aquilla, 129
  Benjamin, 260
  David, 23
  Edward, 127, 149
  Elias, 226
  Elizabeth, 95, 127, 128
  Hannah, 128
  Henry, 57
  Hezekiah, 35
  Isaac, 44, 128, 205
  Jacob, 81
  John, 127
  Joseph, 128
  Joshua, 157
  Martha, 127
  Mary, 56, 95, 103, 127
  Nicholas, 147
  Polly, 179
  Rebecca, 128, 260
  Reginah, 81, 127
  Robert, 56
  Robert P., 117
  Samuel, 134
  Sarah, 127, 128
  Sylvia, 134
  Tamar, 44
  Thomas, 28, 127, 216
  William, 128
  Zebulon, 50
Joraleman, John, 146
Jordan, John, 130
Joslin, Jacob, 151
  Thomas, 108
Journey (Journy), Ann, 128
  Audrey, 128
  Cateron, 128
  John, 128
  Joseph, 128, 186
  Lydia, 128
  Massay, 128
  Peter, 128
  Samuel, 128
Joyce (Joice), Daniel, 10, 130, 173
  Dorothy, 9

## K

Kaighin, James, 137
  Joseph, 137
Kain, Mary, 101
Kamstar, John, 96
Kanine, David, 120
  Elizabeth, 120
Karr, John, 87
  *See also* Carr
Katcham (Ketcham), David, 136
  Elizabeth, 128
  Enoch, 128
  John, 128
  Levi, 128
  Penelope, 128
  Sarah, 128
  Wintiah, 128
Katts, George, 101
Kay, Hannah, 138, 139
  Job, 128
  Joseph, 128
Keais, Sarah, 141
  William, 141, 221
Kean, Samuel, 41
  Thomas, 145
  *See also* Keen
Kearney (Kearny), Ann, 251
  Eleanor, 195
  Ravaud, 205, 251
  Susan R., 251
  Walter, 195
  *See also* Carney
Keasbey (Keasby), Anthony, 184, 237
  Edward, 81
  Solomon, 234
Keath, William, 21
Keefe, Anna, 118
  Arthur, 118
  Lucretia, 118
Keen, Benjamin, 90
  Catharine, 129
  Daniel, 129
  Elijah, 129
  Elizabeth, 129
  James, 9, 42
  Jonas, 151
  Rebeah, 129
  Samuel, 129
  Sarah, 129
  Thomas, 59
  Unea, 84, 85
  *See also* Kean
Keens, Henry, 31
Keephart, Andrew, 126
Kein, George, 8
Kells, John, 55
Kelly (Kely, Kelley), Anne, 77
  David, 49, 55, 155
  James, 78
Kelsay (Kelsey), Daniel, 129
  David, 129
  Hannah, 21
  John, 105, 177
  Joseph, 129, 204
  Miriam, 129
  Robert, Jr., 129
  William, 129
Kemble, Edward, 78
  Levi, 88
  Peter, 252
  Robert T., 91
  Samuel, 13
  Susannah, 129
  Thomas, 129
  William, 129
  *See also* Kimble
Kemple, Hannah, 130
  Lawrence, 68
Kempton, Moses, 82, 119, 156
  William, 44, 56, 153
Kenady—*see* Kennedy
Kenard, Samuel, 149
Kennedy (Kenady), Jemima, 130
  Samuel, 140, 141
  Thomas, 129
  *See also* Cannady
Kenny, Bridget, 129
  Peter, 233
Kent, Erasmus, 9
  Gideon, 200
  Moses, 211
  Sarah, 130
Kerlin, Thomas, 220
Kern, Christopher, 81, 246
  John, 246
Kerns, John, 115
Kerr (Ker), Ann, 141
  James, 188
  William, 12, 144, 174, 183
Kershaw, Abraham, 242
Keshaw, Jacob, 216
Kester, Samuel, 46, 166
Ketcham—*see* Katcham
Key, John, 130
  Joseph, 130
  Mary, 51
  Sarah, 130
  Thomas, 130, 169
  William, 130
Kidd, William, 45
Kierstead, Aaron, 48
  Eleanor, 48
Kikendall, Samuel, 24, 246
  *See also* Coykendall
Kille, Aaron, 222
  John, 71, 169, 263
Kimble, Ann, 259
  Caleb, 130
  Joseph, Jr., 95
  *See also* Kemble
Kindell, Adin, 206
Kine, Luke, 116
King, Mr., 21
  Andrew, 257
  Anne, 169
  Constant Victor, 51
  Diockesian, 64
  George, 64
  Jeremiah, 46
  John, 18, 144
  Joseph, 46
  Nancy, 18
  Sarah, 14
Kingsland, Abraham, 239
  Joseph, 130
Kinnan, Richard, 24, 25, 141
Kinner, Anthony, 75
Kinney (Kinny), Abraham, 39
  Angleche, 162
  Hannah, 39
  John, 66, 109
  Peter, 162
Kinsard, Adam, 246
Kinsey, Abraham, 221
  Charles, 124
  James, Jr., 27, 112, 132, 135, 169
  Margaret, 102
  Nathan, 232
Kip (Kipp), Cornelius, 67
  Lea, 147

INDEX OF NAMES OF PERSONS 299

Kirby, Richard, 123
  William, 123
Kirkbride, Joseph, 145
  Phinehas, 130, 173, 259, 260
Kirkpatrick, Andrew, 71
  David, 251
  John, 144
  Thomas, 227, 233
Kiser, Jacob, 241
Kisler, Peter, 126
Kitchel (Ketchel), Aaron, 64, 92, 195
  Abraham, 130, 246
  Benjamin, 164
  Moses, 136, 164
  Phinehas, 136
  Uzal, 173
Kitchen, William, 131
Kitt, John, 130, 178
Kitts, Robert, 41, 219
Kline, Anne, 131
  Caty, 131
  Godfrey, 148
  Harmon, 131
  Herman, 131
  Jacob, 101
  Jenny, 131
  John, Jr., 130
  Lydia, 131
  Polly, 131
  Rachel, 131
  *See also* Cline
Knapp, Thomas, 39
Knot, Abigail, 131
  Anna, 131
  David, 131
  Eliza, 131
  John, 10
  Peter, 22, 79, 131, 220, 221
Knoup, Jacob, 77
Knowles, Jesse, 145
Koch, Jacobus, 83
Kotts, Conrad, 70
Kovenoven—*see* Covenhoven
Krank, Isaac, 22
Krom, Mary, 36
Kruson, Leticia, 185
Kuhl, Mary, 262
  Paul, 122, 192, 246, 262
  *See also* Cool

L

Lacy (Lacey), Abraham, 185
  Jacob, 131
  John, 10
  *See also* Lasey
Lacock, Nathan, 190
Ladd, Samuel, 176, 257
Ladner, Benjamin, 131
  John, 131
  Mary, 131
  Phebe, 131
Ladow, Ambrose, 141
Lafetra (Leffettro), Edmond, 134
  James, 251
Lafferty (Lefferty), Henry, 32
  Rachel, 135
Lafler (Lefler), Coonrad, 131
  Peter, 131
Laing, Benjamin, 254
  Jacob, 159
  Joshua, 112
  Thomas, 256
  *See also* Lane

Lake, Abraham, 131, 132
  Cornelius, 132
  Daniel, 208
  Eleanor, 131, 132
  Garret, Jr., 132
  Hannah, 132
  Jacob, 131, 132
  Jacobus, 223
  John, 18, 89, 132, 247
  Joseph, 131, 132
  Nathan, 208
  Sarah, 131, 132
  Thomas, 131, 132
Lamb, Jacob, 199
  Joseph, 20, 28, 156, 167
  Joseph, Jr., 167
Lamberson, Thomas, 247
Lambert, Areyantye, 147
  Josiah, 84
Lambson, William, 41
Lampree, Elizabeth, 55
Lance, George, 8, 12
  Jacob, 52
Land, Henry, 132
Landon, Samuel, Sr., 104
Lane, Aaron, 154, 164, 235
  Abraham, 238
  Cornelius, 155, 220
  Harmen, 75
  Matthias, 180
  Matthias, Jr., 219
  Ruth, 247
  Siny, 155
  Tise, 240
  *See also* Laing
Langstaff, George, 34
  John, 72
Laning (Lanning), Altye, 132
  Amy, 132
  Enos, 70
  Esther, 114
  Isaac, 229
  John, 246
  Joseph, 132
  Robert, 37
  Samuel, Jr., 176
Lansing, John, 262
  Sarah, 262
Lantis, Catherine, 137
Lapsley, David, 45
Larason, Andrew, 89
Lare (Lear), Andrew, 133
  Anna, 133
  Elizabeth, 133
  John, 68
  Mary, 133
  Matthias, 133
  Samuel, 133
  Sarah, 68
  William, 133
Larew, James, 192
  *See also* Lerrowe
Large, Samuel, 106
Lasey, James P, 170
  *See also* Lacy
Latourette, John, 144
Lawbocker (Lawbaugher), Christopher, 68, 192
Lawrence (Lawrance), Elisha, 133, 141, 240
  Elisha, Jr., 56
  Hosea, 143
  James, 179
  John, 69, 121, 133, 167, 194, 234, 235, 252
  Mary, 109, 240, 251

Mehetable, 133
Norton, 64, 133
Rebecca, 133
Richard, 238, 240
Robert, 56
Samuel, 22
Sarah, 240
Susannah, 133
Thomas, 251
William, Jr., 133
Zepporah, 210
*See also* Lowrance
Lawrie, Ann, 166
James, 64, 133
John, 88
Joseph M., 191
Joseph Murfree, 166
Mary, 166
Lawshe, Henry, 192
Lawson, William, Jr., 71
Layton, James, 134
Joseph, 134
Peter, 30, 194
Rebecca, 134
Thomas, 134
Leach, Timothy, 76
Leacy, Richard, Sr., 107, 132
Leahy, Penelope, 134
Leake, John, 98
Levi, 63
Nathan. 62
*See also* Leek
Leaming (Leamyng), Allison, 134
Christopher, 149
Deborah, 134
Esther, 134
Hannah, 134
Humphrey, 134
Jacob, 134
Jonathan, 110, 119, 148, 253
Persons, 73, 83, 119, 163
Rebecca, 248
Sarah, 98, 134
Thomas, Jr., 248
Lear—*see* Lare
Leats, Henry, 43
Leddel, Eliza, 252
Phebe, 252
Temperance, 252
William, 20, 103, 252
Lee, Gershom, 22, 122, 229
Hannah, 122
John, 112, 122
Joseph, 23, 54, 122
Levi, 122
Mary, 122
Nathan. 122
Paul, 83
Rebecca, 122
Thomas, 122
*See also* Leigh
Leeds, Abraham, 44, 156
Daniel, 135, 208, 209
Enoch, 109, 135
Nehemiah, 135
Noah, 208
Rebecca, 135
Robert, 109, 135
Samuel, 135, 233
Sarah, 135
Solomon, 135
Leek, Amos, 157, 163
Martha, 135
Samuel, 135
Thomas, 164
*See also* Leake

Lefferson, Arthur, 145, 179
Lefferts, John, 212
Lamache, 236
Oakey, 240
Leffettro—*see* Lafetra
Lefferty—*see* Lafferty
Lefler—*see* Lafler
Leforge, Benjamin, 135, 252
Catherine, 135
David, Jr., 135
Mary, 135
Nicholas, 135
Peter, 135
Lehatt, Charles, 240
Leigh, Anna, 135, 217
Daniel, 135
Elijah, 135
Elizabeth, 135
Isaac, 135
John, 113, 135
Joseph, 135
Naomi, 135
Samuel, 135
Zebulon, 135
*See also* Lee
Lennard—*see* Leonard
Leonard (Lennard), Abigail, 136
Adam, 219
David, 136
Deborah, 136
Hughs, 136
James, 217, 219
Joseph, 136, 156
Lucy, 136
Mary, 136
Moses, 136
Nathaniel, 169, 216, 234, 235
Samuel, 234, 235
Samuel, Jr., 136
Stephen, 136
Susannah, 136
Thomas, 156
Lequear, John, 79, 182
Lerrowe, Isaac, 236
*See also* Larew
Leslie, Elizabeth, 136
Letson, William, 221
Lewis, Abraham, 136
David, 253
Elijah, 136
Elizabeth, 137
Ezekiel, 161
Isaac, 137
Jane, 136
Jene, 136
John, 83, 132, 136, 258
Joseph, 93, 126, 127, 136
Levi, Jr., 215
Mary, 136
Matthew, 137
William, 83
Libra, Elizabeth, 244
Rachel, 244
Wallace, 244
Light, Agnes, 137
Mary, 137
Linberger, John, 123
John, Jr., 137
William, 137
Linch—*see* Lynch
Lindsly (Lindsley), Benjamin, 49, 64, 137, 246, 250, 262
Daniel, 131
David, 178
Eleazer, 163
Elizabeth, 137

## INDEX OF NAMES OF PERSONS 301

Jed, 69
Jemima, 137, 165
John, 170
Joseph, 149, 165
Moses, 170
Philip, 77
Samuel, 257
Line, Jedediah, 187
Lines, Abraham, 138
 Daniel, 138
 Eleanor, 138
Linton, Benjamin, 195
Lippincott (Lipencot), Abraham, 34
 Agnes, 149
 Aquilla, 138, 149
 Beulah, 138
 Caleb, 138, 139
 Elizabeth, 81, 138
 Grace, 139
 Hannah, 138
 Hope, 138, 139
 Jesse, 138
 John, 139
 Jonathan, 24
 Joseph, 140, 183
 Joshua, 76, 138, 139
 Levi, 54, 244
 Mary, 95, 138, 139, 191
 Peter, 188
 Samuel, 93, 159
 Seth, 138
 Solomon, 50
 Thomas, 149
 Wallace, 138, 139
 William, 49, 81, 160, 197, 200
Lishman, Hannah, 139
 Jacob, 139
 Sarah, 139
Littell, Ephraim, 140
 Hannah, 140
 Mary, 139, 140
 Nathaniel, 17, 20, 65, 164
 Rachel, 140
 Roberds, 70
 Survia, 140
 Temperance, 140
 William, 140
Little, Isabel, 18
 Joseph, 40
 Nathaniel, 16
 Robert, 18
 Samuel, 18
 Theophilus, 32
 Thomas, 151, 220, 221
 William, 220, 221
Livingston, Brockholst, 140
 Philip Philip, 140
 William, Jr., 32, 58
Lloyd (Loyd), Bateman, Jr., 140
 Caleb, 115
 David, 44
 Jacob, 140
 James, 126
 John, 187, 209, 253
 Rebecca, 140
 Thomas, 103
 William, 141
Lock (Locke), Andrew, 140
 Charles, 64, 107
 Francis, 140, 141
 John, 115
 Peter, 115, 213
 Priscilla, 115
Lockerby, Robert, 17
Loder (Lodor), Isaac, 120
 Sarah, 120
 William, 109, 151

Logan, John, 101
 William, 251
Long, Eleanor, 141
Longer, Hannah, 107
Longley, John, 185
Longstaff, John, 113
Longstreet, Aaron, 43
 Daniel, 141
 Eleanor, 141
 Garret, 209
 Helena, 141
 James, 141
 John, 141
 Rebecca, 141
 Richard, 209
 Samuel, 12, 128, 247
 Stoffell, 65
 William, 141
Longworth, Mary, 154
Looker, Othniel, 262
Loper (Looper), Ezekiel, 80, 151
 James, Jr., 89
 Mary, 27
 Phebe, 79
Lord, Benjamin, 141
 Benoni, 89
 Elizabeth, 141
 Isaac, 89
 James, 89, 128, 141, 194, 248
 Joshua, 130, 141, 153, 186
 Matthew, 108
 Phinehas, 51, 141, 258
 Sarah, 141
Lore, Anna, 142
 Dan, 142
 David, 61, 82, 142
 Ethen, 46, 141
 Eve, 141
 Hannah, 141
 Ichabod, 30, 105, 142
 Leusey, 141
 Nathaniel, 86, 105, 141
 Phebe, 141
 Rachel, 141
 Reuben, 158
 Temperance, 142
Lott (Lot), Fanny, 36
 Henry, 12, 109
 Peter, 228
Louderback (Loutherback), Adam, 45
 Sarah, 45
Love, James, 49
Loveland, Samuel, 135
Lovell, Joseph, 249
Lovett, Mary, 259
Low (Lowe), Alexander, 56, 187
 Ann, 120
 Benjamin, 202
 Cornelius, 120
 Dirck, 177, 243
 John, 67, 105, 120, 188, 243
 Joseph, 253
 Nicholas, 91
 William, 141
Lowes, James, 42
Lowrance, Daniel, 244
 Margaret, 142
 *See also* Lawrence
Lowrey, Mary, 122
 Thomas, 235
 William, 30, 113, 161
Loxley, Benjamin, 56
 Catherine, 56
 Jane, 56
 Mary, 56

Loyd—*see* Lloyd
Lucas, Robert, 142
  Seth, 142
  Simon, 33
Ludlam (Ludlum), Abraham, 86
  Amelia, 98
  Christopher, 97, 124, 142
  Henry, 164
  Norton, 207
  Providence, 118
  Rachel, 118
  Reuben, 142
Ludlow, Benjamin, 178
  Cornelius, 30, 178
  Daniel, 182
  Ezekiel, 178
  Hanmer, 242
  John, 180
  John R., 242
  Sarah, 178
Lum, Abigail, 227
  Sephen, 227
Lummis (Lummes), Ebenezer, 229
  Ephraim, 27, 151
  Lovica, 163
Lundy, Jacob, 105
  Jacob, Jr., 105
  Jonathan, 105
  Rebecca, 105
  Samuel, 177
Lupardus, Christianus, 70
Lupp (Luùp), Henry, 102, 170
Lupton, Benjamin, 15
Luse, Nathan, 21, 42
Luther, Perthana, 142
  Susannah, 54
Lyle, John, 223
  John, 3d, 181
Lynch (Linch), Rachel, 137
  Jesse, 137
Lyon, Abraham, 257
  Benjamin, 137
  Ebenezer, 140
  Henry, 227
Lyons, William, 68

## M

McAlister, Hugh, 126
  *See also* McCollister
McAroy, George, 200, 206
McBride, John, 142
  Elizabeth, 142
  Mary, 142
  Noami, 142
McCalla, Aulay, 129
  Thomas H., 246
  *See also* McCullough
McCarter, John, 100, 120
McCarty, Daniel, 218
  Francis, 246
  Mary, 173
  Phinehas, 173
McChesney—*see* Machesny
McClain (McClane, McClean, McLean), Diannah, 143
  Hannah, 21
  Sarah, 21
  William, 117
McClong, Hope, 143
  Jane, 143
  Mary, 143
  Samuel, 40, 143, 167
  William, 143
McCollin, Allen, 182, 259
  Ann, 182
  John, 182
  Mary, 182
  Rebecca, 182
  William, 182
McCollister, John, Jr., 143
  Rachel, 143
  *See also* McAlister
McCollough—*see* McCullough
McCollum, Cornelius, 161
  John, 43
  Moses, 233
McConel, James, 143
McCormick, Sarah, 111
McCorrey (McCurry), Malcolm, 84
  Rachel, 84
McCourney, Malm., 20, 21
McCoy, Garin, 130
  Lawrence, 143
  Mary, 143
McCracken, Joseph, 162
McCrea (McCray), Alexander, 106, 107
  Archibald, 106
  James, 16
  Jane, 107
  Jean, 106
  John, 106
  Nancy, 180
McCullough (McCollough), Benjamin, 121
  John, 43
  William, 144
  *See also* McCalla
McCully, George, 34
  Margaret, 34
  William, 34
McDonald, Richard, 78
McDowell, Thomas, 67
McDuffy (McDuffee), Mary, 144
  William, 31
McElkeran, Daniel, 111
McElrath, Janet, 144
  Mary, 144
  Samuel, 144
  Sarah, 144
McElroy, Herbert, 33, 105, 182
  John, 144
  Mary, 144
McFarland (McFarlin), George, 41
  Thomas, 144
McFarson (McFerson, McPherson), Anne, 144
  Daniel, 144
  David, 144
  Elizabeth, 144
  Hester, 146
  Rebecca, 144
  Reuben, 144
  Samuel, 118, 144
McGalliard, James, 104
  John, 82
  Rebecca, 82
  William, 104
McGee (McGhee), John, 209
  Martha, 108
  Robert, 144, 145
  *See also* Maghee
McGill, Neile, 36, 179, 185
McGinnis, James, 86
  *See also* Maginnis
McGonigle, James, 14
McHenry, Charles, 10
McIlwain (McIlvaine), Arthur, 65
McKean, Ann, 145
  Elizabeth, 145
  Joseph B., 145
  Letitia, 145
  Robert, 145

INDEX OF NAMES OF PERSONS  303

McKee, Hugh, 191
McKinney, Elizabeth, 68
  Mordecai, 68
  William, 182
McKinstry, John, 207
McKnight, Elizabeth, 145
  Robert, 181
McLean—*see* McClain
McLeese (McCleese), John, 126
  Peter, 126
McMichael, James, 146
  Nancy, 145
McMicken, Alexander, 146
  Elizabeth, 146
McMullen, Alexander, 138, 201
McMurtrie, Abraham, 162
  John, 163
McNicol, Duncan, 65
McPeak, Jane, 146
McPherson—*see* McFarson
McShane, Francis, 46
McVicker, James, 120
McWhorter, Alexander C., 16, 58
Maccolm, Archibald, 197
Machesny, William, 154
Machet—*see* Marshett
Mackay, William, 156
Mackey, Joseph, 241
Maginnis, Mary, 188
  *See also* McGinnis
Maghee (Meghee), John, 146
  Lydia, 152
  William, 146, 152
  *See also* McGee
Mahaney, Jeremiah, 100
Main (Maine), Jacob, 223
  John, 142
  *See also* Mane
Major, Joseph Budd, 34
Makuren, Matthias, 29
  Rachel, 29
Malich, Aaron, 219
  *See also* Melick
Mandeville (Mandeval, Mandeveal, etc.), Ann, 147
  Areyantye, 147
  Christian, 245
  Clawsey, 147
  David, 146, 147
  Elizabeth, 146, 147
  Henry, 147
  Henry, Jr., 146, 224
  John, 196
  Lea, 147
  Marcy, 147
  Peter, 146
  William, 146, 241
  Yellas, 241, 245
Mane, Thomas, Jr., 142
  *See also* Main
Manly, Aaron, 90
Mann (Man), Croust, 220
  John, 168
  Mary, 168
Manners, Anne, 217
Manning, Abraham, 237
  Benjamin, 41, 80
  William, Jr., 48
Mapes, Edmund, 147
  Mary, 147
  Melicent, 147
Margatroyd (Murgatroyd), Daniel, 233
  Elizabeth Gould, 233
  Mary, 233
  Samuel, 233
  Sarah Phillips, 233, 234

  Thomas, 233, 234
Marinor, Nathaniel, 70
  William, 70
Markel, John, 8
Marks, Henry, 259
  Mary, 259
Marlack, Caleb, 81
  Reuben, 161
Marlett (Marlatte), Ann, 237
  Marcy, 80
Marselis, John, 89
  *See also* Marsellis
Marsh, Alexander Hamilton, 50
  Benjamin, 147
  Betsy, 198
  Daniel, 37, 54, 127
  Elizabeth, 202
  Henry, 148, 205
  James, 147
  Janet, 198
  John, 25
  Keturah, 262
  Mary, 147
  Moses, 147
  Richard, 17
  Samuel, 203
  Sarah, 198
  Thomas, 49
Marshall (Martial), Anne, 147
  David, 147
  Elizabeth, 177
  Isaac, 21
  John, 147, 150
  Joseph, 26, 147, 175
  Randall, 147
  Samuel, 176
  Thomas, 11, 139
  Thomas, Jr., 147
  William, 147
Marshett (Machet), James, 234
  Mary, 170, 234, 235
Marston, John, 192
  Thomas, 192
Marthews, Samuel, 147, 148
Martial—*see* Marshall
Martin (Martain), Anne, 148
  Azariah, 80
  Betsy, 148
  Clarkson, 148
  Constant, 148
  Edmond, 32, 67
  Ephraim, 51
  Hannah, 149, 195
  Humphrey, 39, 80
  Isaac, 233
  John, 46
  Meric, 149
  Mulford, 148, 194, 195
  Nathan, 148
  Phebe, 148
  Rachel, 227
  Samuel, 227
  Stewart, 149
  Tamar, 168
  Thompson, 227
  William, 102, 148
Marvin, Catherine, 149
Masear, Harman, 175
Maskell (Maskill), Daniel, 201
  Thomas, 76, 80, 201, 212
Mason, Ann, 149
  Catharine, 243
  Elizabeth, 149
  Helena, 243
  James, 103, 112
  John, 155
  John, Jr., 149

John Mitchell, 243
Margaret, 243
Mary, 149
Richard, 94
Sarah, 149
Susannah, 149
Thomas, 149
William, 21
Masters, Rachel, 140
Mathis, James, 63, 257
James, Jr., 143
Matlack, Abraham, 175
  Annie, 149
  Hannah, 161
  James, 149
  Mary, 149
  Richard, 149
  Samuel, 150, 204
  Sarah, 149
Matson (Mattson), Andrew, 52, 115
  Benjamin, 14
  Rebecca, 150
Matthews (Mathews), Bethiah, 150
  Catharine, 77
  Charlotte, 150
  David, 182
  Elizabeth, 150
  Isaac, 150
  James, 77
  Judith, 150
  Margaret, 77
  Nancy, 77
  Peter, 77
  Phebe, 222
  Richard, Jr., 150
  Sarah, 150
Mattison, Elijah, 128
  Jacob, 70, 105
  John, 128
Mattocks, Jesse, 150
  Luke, 150
  Rebecca, 150
  Robert, Jr., 150
  Sarah, 150
Matts, John, 50
Maul (Maule), Alexander, 151
  Benjamin, 151
  David, 150
  Garrison, 151
  Jeremiah, 151
  Jeremiah, Jr., 151
  John, 151
  John Garrison, 150
  Phebe, 151
  Rachel, 151
  Robert, 151
  Sarah, 91
  William, 150, 151
Maxell, Caleb, 85
Maxson, Elizabeth, 151
  George, 32, 151
Maxwell, Daniel, 17, 93
  John, 7
  William, 198
Mayhew, David, 7
  Eleazer, 7, 191, 241
  John, 129, 175, 188, 191
  Sarah, 7
Mead, Giles, 237
  Isaac, 241
  John, 146, 241
Mearing, George, 151
  Mary, 151
Meeker, Aaron, Jr., 152
  Daniel, 152
  Elizabeth, 152

  Hannah, 152
  Henry, 152
  James, 152
  Job, 152
  John, 152
  Mary, 152
  Matthias, 152
  Michael, 152
  Moses, 164
  Samuel, 152
  Susannah, 152
  Uzal, 237
Meghee—see Maghee
Mehelm, John, 167
Meldrum, John, 67
Melick, Tunis, 155
  See also Malich
Mellet, Charity, 152
  Elizabeth, 152
  Rebecca, 152
  Thomas, 152
  William, Jr., 152
Melrose, John, 118
Mercer, Archibald, 135
  Nelly, 251
Merlet—see Marlett
Merrell (Merrel), Andrew, 217
  David, 217
  Derick, 198
  Effa, 217
  John, 152, 217
  Sarah, 217
Merrick, John, 153
  Sarah, 153
Merrit, Jacob, 261
  Joseph, 34
Merryman, Eliza, 131
Mersellis (Merseles), Jacob, 81
  John Holder, 11
  Peter, 248
  See also Marselis
Mershon, Andrew, 11
  Benjamin, 11
  Francinah, 11
  Henry, 11
  Timothy, 11
Meserol, Jacob, 53
Mettler, William, 113
Mickle, Ann, 258
  David, 153
  George, 153
  James, 258
  Joshua, 153
  Samuel, 143, 144, 171, 228, 241, 253
  Sarah, 153, 258
  Sibbea, 153
Middagh, Derick, 20
Middleton, Aaron Hewes, 160
  Dinah, 167
  Jacob, 120, 211, 228, 237
  Joel, 124
  John, 45, 150, 203
  John, Jr., 149
  Judith, 112
  Meriam, 167
  Nathan, 114, 205, 213, 228
  Nathaniel, 42, 49, 50, 198
  Patience, 167
  Samuel, 149, 228, 237
Mifflin (Miflin), Daniel, 160
  Mary, 160
  Samuel, 43
  Warner, 160
Miller, Abraham, 154
  Andrew, 19, 28, 154

INDEX OF NAMES OF PERSONS          305

Barbara, 154
Benjamin, 154
Betsy, 154
Catherine, 49, 70, 108, 154, 201, 246
Ebenezer, 261
Eli, 31, 255
Enoch, 31, 227, 228
Enoch, Jr., 31
Esther, 221
Frederick, 82
George, 153, 154
Hannah, 154
Ichabod, 154, 254
Jacob, 31, 154
Jane, 254
John, 19, 20, 100, 119, 131, 154, 163
Jonathan, 154, 157
Josiah, 261
Margaret, 154
Mark, 261
Marsh, 16
Michael, 41, 154
Moses, 17, 31, 154
Noah, 31
Phebe, 154
Philip, 42
Richard, 119
Sally, 119
Sarah, 154
Stephen, 80
Susannah, 154
Thomas, 173
Mills, Rev., 94
  Dorcas, 212
  John, 27, 49
  Jonathan, 59
  Mary, 94, 154
  Nathaniel Burton, 214
  Thomas, 229
  William, 23
Milnor, Joseph, 257
Minch, Adam, 69
  Peter, 154
Minier, Christian, 199
  Jacob, 77
  Mary, 77
Minor, Lawrence, 12, 195, 203
Minton (Mintun), Anna, 165
  Jacob, 9, 77, 86, 165
  Lemuel, 76
Mitchell, Abigail, 21
  George, 21
  James, 21
Moffit (Moffett), Ann, 187
  William, Jr., 155
Molleson, Gilbert, 165
Moncrief, Charles, 229
Moncy, Yost, 20
Monfort (Monfoort), Elbert, 181, 242
  Eleanor, 155
  Hannah, 155
  Isaac, 155
  Margaret, 155
  Mary, 155
  Peter, 155
  Sarah, 155
Monigal, William, 200
Monroe (Monrow), George, 156
  John, 78
  Margaret, 155, 156
  Rebecca, 155
  Sarah, 155
Monson—see Munson
Montanye, Abraham, 156

Bergon, 156
Isaac, 156
Jane, 156
John, 156
Joseph, Jr., 156
Rebecca, 156
Montgomery, Dr., 188
  Alexander, 175
  Elizabeth, 76
  Patience, 188
  Robert, 133
Mooney, Elizabeth, 157
Moore (More, Moores), Aaron, 151, 157
  Alexander, Jr., 157
  Benjamin, 158, 185
  Bethuel, 9, 157, 158, 253
  Charles, 260, 261
  Cleary, 179
  Cyrus, 158
  Daniel, 33, 190, 202
  David, 62, 79, 83, 133, 185, 188, 198, 204, 210
  Dicason, 158, 159
  Eber, 157
  Edward, 158, 256
  Ely, 25
  Enoch, 157, 160, 252, 256
  Enoch, Jr., 157
  George, 125
  Gershom, 152
  Hampton, 122
  Hannah, 202
  Helena, 158
  Israel, 157
  Jacob, 157
  Jacob T., 158
  James, 91, 158
  Job, 14, 117, 177, 179
  Johannah, 168, 231
  John, 13, 91, 121, 158, 177, 185, 241
  Joseph, 14, 157, 158, 231
  Joshua, 157
  Lydia, 158, 259
  Martha, 158
  Mary, 159
  Nathan, 85
  Patience, 158
  Polly, 82
  Rebecca, 157
  Ruhamey, 27
  Sacket William, 157
  Samuel, 158
  Samuel T., 157
  Sarah, 157
  Theophilus, 177
  Thomas, 148, 157, 158, 259, 260
  Thomas T., 158
  Unice, 21
  Uriah, 158
  William, 205
  William, Jr., 158, 159
Morehouse, David, 47
  Hannah, 47
Morford, Noah, 13
  Thomas, 26, 238, 252
Morgan, Agnes, 159
  Amy, 159
  Ann, 159
  Bathsheba, 192
  Benjamin, 37, 159
  David, Jr., 159
  Elizabeth, 192
  George, 159
  Hester, 37

James, 159
John, 22, 49, 92, 132, 159
Jonathan, 159, 161, 192
Jonathan, Jr., 192
Joseph, 159, 232
Joseph, Jr., 139
Margaret, 37, 159
Mary, 76
Michael, 159
Rachel, 192
Randel, 43, 159
Rebecca, 159, 192
Richard, 249
William, 92
Morris (Moris), Anna, 160
Cadwallader, 36
Christopher, 19
Deborah, 160
Israel, 129
James, 103, 159
John, 89, 103, 228
Jonathan Ford, 17, 144
Joseph, 59, 143
Lida, 159
Margaret, 160
Mary, 159
Moses, 8, 106
Nathaniel, 160
Rebecca, 159
Reuben, 160
Rhoda, 203
Richard, 160
Richard H., 160
Sarah, 103
Silfe, 159
Morrison (Mourison), Henry, 160, 162
Jacob, 162
Mary, 162
Morris, 160, 162
Richard, 211
Morrow, James, 168
*See also* Murrow
Morse, Isaac, 172
Morss, Amos, 23
Amos, Jr., 160
Anne, 160
Anthony, 23, 160
Elizabeth, 160
Isaac, 160
Joseph, 160
Nehemiah, 161
Robert, 160, 218
Sarah, 160
Susannah, 160
Morton, Ann, 161
George, 161
Mott, Anne, 161
Cornelia, 161
Gershom, 161, 183
Huldah, 161
James, 29, 117
James, Jr., 161
John, 161, 261
John Gershom, 157
Joshua, 246
Mary, 161
Sarah, 161
Solomon, 183
William, 32
Mount, Jean, 162
Jesse, 162
John, 43
Lydia, 162
Matthias, 94, 162

Richard, 162
William, 162
Mounteer, John, 112
Mourison—*see* Morrison
Mowerson, Angleche, 162
Elizabeth, 162
Mowra, Catherine, 162
Elizabeth, 162
Jacob, 162
Leah, 162
Marylis, 162
Philip, Jr., 162
Mulford, Ananias, 164
Anne, 164
Barnabus, 164
Benjamin, 164
Cornelius, 163, 164
David, 163, 164, 201
Deborah, 164
Esther, 164
Hannah, 164
Henry, 67, 101, 163
Isaac, 163
Jacob, 8, 40, 80, 163, 204
James, 164
Jane, 163
Jemima, 163
Jeremiah, 164
John, 163, 164, 249
Jonathan, 163
Jonathan, Jr., 163, 164
Lewis, 178
Lewis, Jr., 164
Lovica, 163
Marcy, 164
Mary, 164
Peremiah, 164
Phebe, 163
Sarah, 174
Stephen, 164
Temperance, 163
Thomas, 164
William, 163, 204
Mullen (Mullin), Edward, 155, 156, 165
Elizabeth, 165
Jean, 165
John, Jr., 165
Joseph, 165
Kezia, 165
Mary, 165
Samuel, 165
Sarah, 165
Mulword, Jacob, 40
Mun, Joseph, 58
Rachel, 69
Mundy (Munday), Abraham, 165
Asher, 165
Isabel, 165
Israel, 165
John, 165
Joshua, 165
Margaret, 165
Robert, Jr., 165
Sophia, 165
Thomas, 165
Munroe—*see* Monroe
Munson (Monson), Anna, 165
Daniel, 165
Elizabeth, 165
Ezekiel, 178
John, Jr., 165
Margaret, 165
Stephen, 92
Munyan, John, Jr., 165
Joice, 165

## INDEX OF NAMES OF PERSONS 307

Joseph, 165
Mary, 165
Sarah, 165
Siddonia, 165
Thomas, 165
Murdock, Sarah, 166
Murfin, Ann, 166
Murgatroyd—*see* Margatroyd
Murphy (Murphey), Mahlon, 208
  Naomi, 208
  Noah, 208
  Robert, 23
  William, 147, 208, 241
Murrell, Ann, 166
  Franklin, 166
  Joseph, Jr., 166
  Rachel, 166
Murrow, Charity, 33
  *See also* Morrow
Murry, Mary, 208
Muysinger, Margaret, 166
  Nicholas, 166

### N

Neal (Neale), John, 33, 76, 129, 144, 209, 211
Nealy (Neely), Elizabeth, 166
  John, 143, 166
  Joseph, 184
Nefius—*see* Nevius
Neighbour, Elizabeth, 249
Neilson, John, 251
  Samuel, 66
  *See also* Nelson
Neissor (Neisser), Margaret, 249
  William, 249
Nelson, Elizabeth, 74
  John, 36, 60, 74, 90, 168, 188, 241
  Rachel, 175
  Samuel, 43, 74, 75
  *See also* Neilson
Nephew, John, 218
  Peter, 218
  *See also* Nevius
Nevill, John, 227
Nevius (Nefius, Neafis, Nevious, etc.)
  Abraham, 167
  Albert, 167
  Deborah, 167
  John, 87, 198
  Peter, 224
  *See also* Nephew
Newark, Jesse, 114, 225
Newbold, Ann, 167
  Caleb, 166, 167, 203
  Charles, 167
  Cleayton, 65, 167
  Daniel, 75
  John, 167
  Joseph, 166
  Martha, 167
  Michael, 167
  Rachel, 167
  Samuel, 167
  Thomas, 167
  William, 167
  William, Jr., 239
Newcomb, Bayse, 122
Newell (Newel, Newill), Elisha, 133
  Hugh, 83, 209, 235
  James, 235
Newford, Thomas, 160

Newkirk (Nieukirk), Ann, 60, 191
  Cornelius, 36, 167, 168
  Elizabeth, 167
  Isaac, 60, 191, 241
  Jacob, 191
  John, 167
  Margaret, 167
  Matthew, 167, 168
  Sarah, 168
  Susannah, 168
Newton, Alice, 163
  Ebenezer, 163, 168, 172
  Isaac, 12, 78
  John, 83, 168
  Joseph, 85
  Margaret, 168
  Samuel, 78
  Thomas, 35
Nichol (Nickol), Mary, 27
  Phebe, 27
Nicholas, Catharine, 168
Nichols (Nickles, Nickols), Jedediah Johnson, 58
  Margaret, 58
  Robert, 39
Nicholson (Nickelson), Abel, 13, 218
  Hannah, 28
  Nehemiah, 208
Nieukirk—*see* Newkirk
Nixon, Allen, 168
  Ephraim, 168
  Grace, 168
  Isaac, 108
  Jeremiah, 69, 122, 168
  John, 168
  Margaret, 168
  Mary, 168, 177
  Oliver, 168
  Patrick, 168
  William, 168
Noble, Jacob, 243
  Sarah, 169
Noe, Abram, 170
Noel, John Young, 243
Noils, James, 213
Norbury, Mary, 169
Norcross, Anne, 169
  Jacob, 169
  Joshua, 169
  William, 155, 169, 196
Norris, Affe, 86
  Gershom, 25
  James, 169
  Mary, 169
  Samuel, 164, 259
  Thomas, 236
Norton, George, 148, 150
Nutt, Adam, 35
  Levi, 122
  William, 74, 146
Nutton, William, 200

### O

Oakley (Okly), David, 171
  Elizabeth, 171
  Ephraim, 171
  Hester, 171
  John, 171
  Mary, 171
  Nancy, 171
  Silvanus, 164
Odell, Ann, 91
  William, 91
Offley, Ann, 167

Ogden, Abraham, 182
Abraham, Jr., 169
Ann, 170
Catherine, 170
Charles, 170
Daniel, 170, 171
David, 170
David A., 111
Eleazer, 169
Elias, 170
Ezekiel, 170
Gabriel, 223
Hannah, 170
James, 170
Jane, 170
Jedediah, 170
Joannah, 170
John, 58, 170, 250, 252
Joseph, 204
Keziah, 170
Leah, 170
Lewis, 91, 170
Lydia, 169
Martha, 63
Mary, 169, 170
Matthias, 226
Molly, 170
Moses, 170
Phebe, 170
Robert, Jr., 226
Samuel, 62, 170, 188, 191, 200
Sarah, 170
Susannah, 170
Swain, 170
Thomas, 170
Uzal, 91
Okly—*see* Oakley
Olcraft, William, 74
Olden (Oldden), Amy, 171
Ann, 171, 230
David, 41
David, Jr., 171
Elizabeth, 171
Ephraim, 29, 171
Job, 171
Joseph, 118, 196
Joseph, Jr., 171
Samuel, 171, 173
Thomas, Jr., 171
Oldis, Garret, 263
Oliver (Olifer, Olliver), Elizabeth, 172
Jacob, 172
Jeremiah, 228
John, 71, 82, 104, 172
John Nicholas, 168
Jonathan, 160
Joseph, Jr., 172
Kelsey, 172
Mary, 136
Sarah, 160
William, 172
William, Jr., 160
Olp—*see* Oulp
Ong, Joseph, 156
Opdycke (Opdike, Opdyke), Benjamin, 107
Caty, 172
Elizabeth, 172
Frances, 172
Hannah, 172
Jean, 107
Joshua, 72
Luther, 172, 230, 231
Margaret, 172
Mary, 72
Richard, 13, 113, 172, 225
Sarah, 172
*See also* Updike
Oppie, Benjamin, 172, 173
Elizabeth, 172
Grace, 172
Isaac, 172
John, 172, 173
Mary, 172
Nancy, 172
William, Jr., 172
Oram—*see* Orum
Orin, Rebecca, 183
Orr, Amy, 173
Orum, Samuel, 16
Osborn (Orsburn, Osborne, Osburn), Howel, 205
Margaret, 205
Moses, 33, 89, 169
Smith, 17
Thomas, 17, 164, 204
Oselwean, John—*see* Kitt, John
Ott, Joseph, 183, 216
Martin, 200
Otto, Bodo, Jr., 173
Frederick, 173
Ougheltree, John, 92
Oulp (Olp), Barnid, 247
Catren, 247
Outwater, John, 22
Owen, Ebenezer, 61, 65
Lewis, 7

P

Packer, Basheba, 89
John, 89
Paddon, Samuel, 112
Sarah, 42
Padgett, Thomas, 37, 186
Page (Paige), David, 30
Lydia, 44
Paine, Abraham, 173
Elizabeth, 173
Hannah, 173
Peter, 173
Rachel, 173
Painter, George, 135, 259
Palmer, Jacob, 77
Joseph, 143
Sarah, 129
Pancoast, Aaron, 263
Joseph, 14, 65, 215
Thomas, 35
Pangborn, Samuel, 17
Parham, John, 230
Paris, Mary, 86
Parish, Robert, 52
Parkam, John, 115, 203
Parke (Park), Benjamin, 217
Daniel, 130
Joseph, 107
Parker, Abraham, 173
Catherine, 173
David, 112, 173
Deborah, 174
Elizabeth, 174
George, 160
Hannah, 174
Isaac, 173
Jacob, 173, 174
John, 173, 174
Joseph, 221
Mary, 174
Miln, 174
Moses, 173

INDEX OF NAMES OF PERSONS 309

Nancy, 173
Nathaniel, 174
Samuel, 261
Sarah, 23, 217
Solomon, 173
Stephen, 173
Tamar, 173
Thomas, 23
William, 53, 174, 220, 221
Parkhurst, Caleb, 39
Parks, Robert, 41
Parrot, Abigail, 174
Samuel, 92
William, 174, 235
Parry, Thomas, 199
*See also* Perry
Parsel—*see* Passel
Parselow, Mary, 29
William, 29
Parson, Uriah, 29
Parsons, Robert, 74, 168
*See also* Passons
Parvin, David, 15
Jeffery, 69
Josiah, 204
Thomas, 203
Passel, Abigail, 174
Abner, 174
Ann, 174
Mary, 174
Phebe, 174
Sarah, 174
Stephen, 174
Passons, Jehu, 142
*See also* Parsons
Pater, Jesse, 238
*See also* Potter
Paterson (Patterson), Cornelia, 251
Elizabeth, 167
Euphemia, 251
James, 245
William, 251
Patton (Patan, Pattan), James, 12, 144, 145, 146, 200
Prudence, 235
Paul, Joel, 128
John, 57
Joseph, 212, 213
Samuel, 128, 141
Uriah, 89, 183, 221
William, 257
Paullin (Paulin), Catherine, 175
David, 143, 175
Elizabeth, 175
Hannah, 175
Henry, 74
Henry, Jr., 175
Joseph, 175
Margaret, 175
Nathan, 175
Rachel, 175
Ruth, 175
Uriah, 175
Whitlock, 141
Paxson, Joseph, 34
Peace, Joseph, 234
*See also* Pease
Peachey, Anna, 7
Benjamin, 7
Peacock, Abner, 175
Abram, 175
Aletheia, 175
Amos, 175
Daniel, 175
Elizabeth, 175
Hannah, 175

Hooton, 175
Isaac, 175
John, Jr., 175
Joshua, 175
Levi, 175
Lydia, 175
Margaret, 175
Mary, 175
Melchizedek, 175
Rachel, 175
Sarah, 175
Susannah, 175
Thomas, 175
William, 175
Peake (Peak), Eliza, 182
John, 123
Pearce, Andrew, 175
Charlotte, 175
Edward, 175
Elizabeth, 175
George, 175
Henry, Jr., 175
*See also* Pierce
Pearson, John, 205
Robert, Jr., 121
Sarah, 175
*See also* Pierson
Pease, Adam, 238
Jonathan, 237
Samuel, 151
*See also* Peace
Peck, Benjamin, 129
John, 121
John, Jr., 87, 249
Pecker, Ann, 217
Jacob, 217
Pedrick (Peddrick), Elijah, 45
Elizabeth, 62
Hugh, 62, 218
Isaac, 45, 165
Jacob, 178
John, 178
Joshua, 96, 165
Rebecca, 45
Peer, Cornelius, 162
Peirce—*see* Pearce, Pierce
Peirson—*see* Pearson, Pierson
Pendergrass, Martin, 21
Penington—*see* Pennington
Penn, Richard, 43, 121
Thomas, 121
Pennington (Penington), Israel, 188, 211
Jonathan, 258
Nathan, 225
Pennock, Tallan, 12
Penton, Joseph, 203
Perce, Ammariah, 176
Hannah, 176
John, Jr., 176
Margaret, 176
Mary, 176
Ward, 65
Perrine (Perine), Daniel, 135, 180, 219
Henry, 251
Isaac, 114
James, 120
John, 70
Maria, 180
Nicholas, 49
William, 97, 106
Perkins, Jacob, 142, 196
Mary, 176
Samuel, 176
William, 176

Perry, James, 100
   Joseph, 181
   Thomas, 33
   See also Parry
Persong, Francis, 120
Pervost, John, Jr., 263
Peterse, Hessel, 66, 87, 180
Peterson, Aaron, 194
   Hance, 143
   Mary, 177
   Robert, 143
   Rulif, 198
   Thomas, 176, 219
   William, 57
Pettit, Aaron, 177
   Benjamin, 17, 82, 174
   Deborah, 177
   Elizabeth, 177
   Esther, 177
   Hannah, 177
   John, 177
   Jonathan, 177, 188
   Mary, 177
   Rachel, 177
   Sarah, 177
   Susannah, 177
Petty, Peter, 225, 226, 247
Pharo, Ann, 188
   Gervas, 79, 124, 177
   Hannah, 188
   Kesier, 188
   Robert, 188
   Samuel, 188
   Timothy, 177
Phelps, Joel, 257
Phillips, David, 215
   Henry, 77
   John, 77, 177, 229
   Jonas, 84, 89, 137
   Jonathan, 91, 92
   Joseph, 50, 235
   Lott, 77, 177
   Mary, 234
   Micajah, 11, 178
   Pallmer, 108, 178
   Peter, 77
   Samuel, 9
   Theophilus, 11
   Thomas, 178
Philpot, Anne, 178
   Edith, 178
   Hannah, 178
   Rebecca, 178
   William, 96
Piatt—see Pyatt
Pickle, Abraham, 178
   Baltis, 178
   Elizabeth, 120
   George, 120
Pierce (Peirce), Deborah, 43
   Henry, 43
   John, 111
   Margaret, 43
   William, 43
   See also Pearce
Pierson (Peirson), Abraham, 178
   Caty, 58
   Daniel, Jr., 176
   Darius, 178
   David, 37
   Ebenezer, 204
   Elihu, 178
   Elijah, 49, 178
   Elizabeth, 178
   Eunice, 178
   Isaac, 39
   Jabez, 39
   Jacob, 178
   John, 176, 178
   Jonathan, Jr., 178
   Julia, 58
   Ludlow, 178
   Mary, 178
   Matthias, 229
   Phebe, 178
   Rebecca, 179
   Rhoda, 178
   Sally, 125, 163, 206
   Sarah, 178
   Sineus, 178
   Squire, 176
   Tahpenis, 178
   See also Pearson
Pimm, Joseph, Jr., 204
Pine, Ann, 229, 230
   Benjamin, 233
   Isaac, 229
   Lazarus, 139
   Mary, 229, 230
   Samuel, 229
   See also Pyne
Pinkerton, David, 234
   Elizabeth, 179
   Henry, 11
   John, 179
   Keziah, 179
   Mehetable, 179
   Polly, 179
Pintard, Hannah, 197
   William, 27, 197
Pinyard, Jane, 179
   John, 179
   Joseph, 67
   Joseph, Jr., 179
   Mary, 179
   Sarah, 179
   William, 179
Pippet (Pipet), Hannah, 179
   Isaac, 259
Pitney, Benjamin, 20
   James, Jr., 84
Pittenger, Joseph, 179
   Margaret, 178
Plasket, William, 33
Platt, John, 124, 166
   Sarah, 165
   Thomas, 10, 56, 153, 155, 169
Plum, Joanna, 179
Plumer, Deby, 208
   William, 208
Polhemus (Polemus), Arthur, 179
   Benjamin, 179
   Daniel, 223, 240
   John, 212, 235, 238, 240
   Mary, 179, 240
   Mirah, 240
   Tobias, 179
Polk, James, 21
   Sarah, 21
Pool, Catherine, 180
   Susannah, 198
Pope, John, 35, 47, 65, 196, 220, 241
Porter, Catherine, 180
   James, 180
   John, 180
   Margaret, 260
   Nancy, 180
   Nathaniel, 180
   Thomas, 112, 190
   William, 180
Post, Adrian, 83, 138, 180, 246
   Adrian A., 240

## INDEX OF NAMES OF PERSONS 311

Christopher, 180
Elsie, 180
Henry F., 242
Idah, 180
Jacomeinty, 180
James, 48
John I., 180
Maike, 180
Margaret, 180
Maria, 180
Teunis, 180
Thomas, 245
William, Jr., 180
Potter, Mr., 172
Amos, 185
David, 251
Ellis, 180
Hannah, 17
Jabez, 233
John, 259
Matthias, 227, 259
Reuben, 31, 180
Samuel, 17, 164
Silas, 259
See also Pater
Potts, Abigail, 82
Amy, 82, 158
Gainer, 94
Hannah, 82
John, 243
Joseph, 26, 71
Joshua, 82
Mary, 26, 82
Richard, 124
Samuel, 16
Stacy, 235
Thomas, 82, 158, 243
William, 71
Pound, David, 252
Isaac, 248
Powell, John, 122
Reuben, 122
Powelson (Poulesoun), Abraham, 180
Catharine, 180
Cornelius, 180
Isaac, 180, 241
John, 180
Prall, Garrison, 216
George, 179
Isaac, 180, 181
Lewis, 181
Mary, 182, 216, 217
Peter, 182
Rachel, 217
Prat, Jane, 237
Pratton, Thomas, 59
Predmore—see Pridmore
Preston, Elizabeth, 181
Isaac, 252
Jacob, 231
Joseph, 181
Price, Abraham, 171
Absalom, 85
David, 34, 85
Francis, 25, 38, 52, 130, 215
Isabel, 91
Isaiah, 227
Joannah, 25
John, 126, 182, 226
Jonathan, 25
Joseph, Jr., 181
Margaret, 103
Mary, 161, 227
Nathaniel, 164
Richard, 209, 213

Robert F., 63
Samuel, 38
Sarah, 227
Tenrub, 18
William, 13, 82, 251
Prickett, Hannah, 62
Jacob, 9, 207
Job, 207
Zachariah, 175
Pridmore, Daniel, 106
John, 106
Prior—see Pryor
Probasco (Probasko), Caty, 181
Dinah, 181
Elizabeth, 247
Garrit, 181
Jacob, 181, 219
Martha, 181
Peter, 55, 113, 181
Rem, 181
Simon, 181
Tunis, 82
Provost—see Pervost
Pryor (Prior), Hannah, 182
Jasper, Jr., 240
Thomas, 260
Pullen, Samuel, 94
Pumyea, Peter, 88, 198
Pursel, Daniel, 210
Purviance, Andrew, 182
Joannah, 182
Sarah, 182
Pyatt (Piatt), Ephraim, 182
James, 165
William, 71
Pyne, Anna, 182
See also Pine
Pysong—see Persong

Q

Quest, Dinah, 182
Edward, 182
John, 182
Jonathan, 247
Rachel, 182
Thomas, 40, 182
Quick, Catherine, 182
Clara, 183
Cornelius, 126
Hannah, 183
John, 182, 250
John, Jr., 183
Martha, 183
Mary, 182
Mehetable, 183
Peter, 53
Ruth, 183
Sarah, 183
Tunis, 260
Quicksall, Aaron, 183
Amy, 203
Rebecca, 203
Samuel, 203
Quinby, Josiah, 102
Moses, 102

R

Radford, Mary, 93
Rague, Hannah, 25
John, 25
Rakestraw, John, 221
Ralsten (Rolston), John, 20, 51

Rambo, Benjamin, 52, 81
　Champneys, 183
　Elizabeth, 183
　Gabriel, 183
　Jacob, 183
　James, 141
　Jesse, 43, 183
　John, 200
　John, Jr., 183
　Margaret, 167
　Peter, 183
　William, 183
Ramsay (Ramsey), Margaret, 184
　Samuel, 67
Ramsden, John, 226
Randolph, Benjamin F., 135
　Davis, 15
　Elizabeth, 184
　Jacob F., 248
　James, 19
　Lewis F., 132
　Samuel, 248
　*see also* FitzRandolph
Range, Elizabeth, 184
　Mary, 184
Rapelye (Rappelyea), George, 184
　John, 184, 240
Rarick, Ann, 184
　Catharine, 184
　Conrad, Jr., 184
　Henry, 184
　John, 184
　Mary Catherine, 184
　Mary Margaret, 184
　William, 184
Ray, Mary, 159
　Rhoda, 185
　*See also* Rhea
Raymond, Abigail, 185
　Christiana, 185
　James, 185
　Mary, 54
　Seth, 54
Rayworth, Ann, 44
Read, Israel, 188
　*See also* Reed, Reid
Reading (Redding, Reding), Abigail, 121
　Ann, 185
　Charles, 122
　Henry, 121
　Jeremiah, 126
　John, 121
　Joseph, 185
　Montgomery, 94, 113, 252
　Samuel, 94
　Thomas, 122
　William, 7
　Wright, 176
Reddock, Philip, 229
Redman, John, 209, 236, 256, 261
　Thomas, 8, 18, 71, 91, 93, 99, 108, 112, 115, 149, 182, 203, 230
Redrake, Francis, 38
Reed, Andrew, 235
　Bowes, 74
　Charles, 175
　Isaiah, 20
　John, 22, 54, 219
　*See also* Read, Reid
Reeder, Abigail, 185
　Abner, 185
　Absalom, 185
　Amos, 185
　Andrew, 185

　Charles, 185
　Elizabeth, 185
　Fanny, 185
　Hannah, 185
　Isaac, 185
　John, Jr., 185
　Joseph, 140, 141
　Letitia, 185
　Mercy, 185
　Taphath, 185
Reemer, Mary, 107
Reeve, Abraham, 13
　Experience, 54
　Hannah, 185
　James, 224
　John, Jr., 163
　Josiah, 185
　Mark, Jr., 185
　Martha, 167
　Nathan, 64
　Samuel, 185
　William, 185
Reeves (Reves), Aaron, 186
　Abijah, 99
　Abraham, 35
　Ann, 187
　Arthur, Jr., 186
　Azariah, 237
　Biddle, 186, 256
　Clement, 187
　Desire, 187
　Elizabeth, 187
　Henry, 30
　Joseph, 186, 187
　Josiah, 187
　Lydia, 221
　Mark, 186
　Mary, 187
　Samuel, 221
　Sarah, 187
　Thomas, 186, 187
　Thomas, Jr., 258
　William, 186
Reid, Augustine, 94
　George, 186
　James, 186
　Jane, 186
　John, 44, 94, 186
　Joseph, 186
　Mary, 94
　Richard, 186
　William, 186
　*See also* Read, Reed
Reily—*see* Riley
Relect, Simon, 224
Remington, Hannah, 186
　Mark, 186
　Rachel, 186
　Sarah, 186
　Theodocia, 186
　Thomas, 37, 212
Remsen, Agnes, 187
Rettinghouse—*see* Rittenhouse
Reyerson—*see* Ryerson
Reynolds, John, 12
　Thomas, 155, 165
　Valentine, 247
Rhea, David, 175
　James, 186
　Jonathan, 141, 174, 237
　Mary, 91
　*See also* Ray
Rhodes, Anna, 187
　Charles, 8, 91, 125, 187
　Charles, Jr., 187
　Thomas, 90

## INDEX OF NAMES OF PERSONS 313

Ribbel, George, 10
Rice, Joseph, 126
Richards, Aaron, 39
  Elizabeth, 187
  John, 29
Richardson, Elizabeth, 98
  Jacob, 60, 99
  Jeremiah, 60, 164
  Susannah, 44
Richey, Elizabeth, 107
  John, 107
Richman, Abraham, 129
  Experience, 188
  Harman, 143, 188
  Jacob, 188
  Jonathan, 188
  Joseph, 188
  Priscilla, 188
  William, 129, 188
Richmond, Catharine, 188
  Emmy, 188
  John, 34, 83, 222, 253
  Mary, 188
  William, 67
Rickey, Joseph, 188
Ridgway, Abigail, 188
  Barzillai, 222
  Benjamin, 78, 188
  Beulah, 189
  Daniel, 188, 189
  David, 10, 14, 74, 78, 95, 129, 130, 188, 231, 261
  Elizabeth, 189
  Freedom, 189
  Hannah, 188
  Henry, 47, 87, 137, 188, 215
  John, 14, 15, 88, 139, 189, 215, 231, 261
  Joseph, 47, 188
  Lot, 189
  Lydia, 188
  Mary, 87, 188
  Miriam, 47, 188
  Robert, 87
  Solomon, 188
  Susannah, 189
  William, 47, 112, 188, 189
Rieslier, Adam, 189
  Anna, 189
  Catharine, 189
  Elizabeth, 189
  Jacob, 189
  Margaret, 189
  Sarah, 189
  Peter, 189
  William, 189
  See also Risler
Rigans, Ellenar, 189
Rigby, Joseph, 112
Rigdon, Mrs., 259
Riggs, Aruna, 189
  Benjamin, 189
  David, Jr., 186
  Permenas, 189
  Phinchan, 186
  Preserve, 252
  Phebe, 189
Right, Sarah, 218
Riker, Christian, 245
Riley (Reily, Ryley), Grace, 185
  James, 19
  Mark, 198
  Sarah, 189
Riosen, Hosea, 257
Risdon, Elizabeth, 190
  George, 190
  Hannah, 190
  Jane, 190
  John, 47, 190
  Samuel, 190
  Sarah, 190
  Turner, 190
Riser, Ann, 236
  Jacob, 236
Risler, Jacob, 172
  See also Rieslier
Risley (Risly), Abigail, 210
  Samuel, 147
Rittenhouse (Rettinghous), Lot, 185
  William, 118
Rituer, Mary, 193
Robbins—see Robins
Roberson, Ephraim, 190
  John, 252
  Lydia, 190
Roberts, Anna, 190
  Cornelius, 228
  Hannah, 229, 230
  John, 25, 39, 50, 76, 82, 93, 112, 161, 190
  Joseph, 95
  Samuel, 161
  Samuel, Jr., 138, 204
  William, 76, 93
Robertson, Charles, 70
  Mary, 190
Robeson, Morris, 102
Robins (Robbins), Aaron, 191
  Ann, 190
  Clayton, 23
  Edward, 193
  Elizabeth, 121, 190
  Hannah, 191
  Isaiah, 191, 228
  James, 42, 43
  Job, 190
  John, 103, 123, 190, 221
  Jonathan, 190
  Lewis, 191
  Lydia, 190
  Mary, 121, 190
  Nathan, 12, 35, 122, 127, 195, 193
  Nathaniel, 190
  Obadiah, 190
  Rachel, 190, 201
  Robert, 190
  Ruth, 190
  Susannah, 190
  Theodosia, 190
  Vanroom, 190, 205
Robinson (Robenson, Robison), Abraham, 27
  Ann, 191
  Catherine, 191
  Christine, 229
  Eli, 27
  Ellis, 27
  Francis, 89
  Hambleton, 23
  Hosea, 27
  John, 191
  Mary, 191
  Rachel, 27
  Rebecca, 27, 191
  Samuel, 154
  Sarah, 191
  William, Jr., 191
Rockafellar (Rockefeller, Rockafellow), Abraham, 192
  Daniel, 192
  David, 192
  Elizabeth, 12, 192

Godfrey, 192
Henry, 192
Jacob, 192
John, 68, 192, 246
Mary, 192
Peter, 12
Peter, Jr., 192
Philip, 192
William, 192
Rockhill, Amos, 35
  Caleb, 193
  Edward, 193
  Edward, Jr., 12, 127, 192
  Elizabeth, 192
  Mary, 192
  Nathan, 167, 192
  Thomas, 193
  Tobitha, 192
Rodenbaugh (Rodenbogh), Anne, 68
  Elizabeth, 193
  John, 193
  Peter, 68
Rodgers, Aleser, 258
  Ann, 218
  Elizabeth, 96
  John, 147
  See also Rogers
Rodman, Pearson, 207
  Sarah, 207
  Thomas, Jr., 207
Roe, Azael, 233
  David, 43
  Henry, 159
Rogers, Abner, 14, 135
  Abraham, 142
  Amy, 192
  David, 152
  Isaac, 43
  James, 175
  John, 21, 95, 112, 243
  Keziah, 10
  Margaret, 10
  Margery, 10
  Rhoda, 10
  Richard, 83
  Thomas, 127, 215
  William, 133
  William, Jr., 95
  See also Rodgers
Rolfe, Elisha, 42, 77
Rolston—see Ralsten
Romine (Romeyn, Romyn), Daniel, 26
  John, 26
  John D., 239
  Margarietje, 26
  Nicholas, 262
Roof, Sarah, 106
  Sufflah, 106
Roome—see Roomer
Roomer, Sarah, 22
Root, Jared, 162
Rope, Christopher, 49
Rose, Andrew, 193, 223
  Ebenezer, 185
  Ezekiel, 182
  John, 86
  Sarah, 36
Rosenkrans, Alexander, 193
  Ariantie, 193
  Benjamin, 193
  Catherine, 193
  Cherrick, 193
  Elijah, 193
  Jacob, 193
  John, Jr., 193

  Joseph, 193
  Levi, 193
  Margaret, 193
  Maria, 193
  Simeon, 193
Ross, David, 18
  Elizabeth, 193
  George, 44, 137, 172
  Isaac, 54, 193
  James, Jr., 227
  Joannah, 49
  John, 123, 137, 165, 227
  John, Jr., 137
  Joseph, 137
  Michael, 137
  Moses, 49
  Rachel, 185
  Robert, 181
  Robert, Jr., 148, 181
  William, 257
Rossell, Ann, 112
  Zach., 119, 155
  Zachariah, 156
Roszell—see Rozell
Rothero, John, 166
Roucastle—see Ruecastle
Rouse (Rowse), Catherine, 193
  Mary, 193
  Rebecca, 122
Rowand, John, 99
Rowe, Martha, 193
  Stephen, 193
Rowen (Rowan), Andrew, 13, 194
  Susannah, 194
Rowland, James, 41
Rowzer, Mary, 194
Royl, Hannah, 114
Rozell (Roszel, Roszell), Charles, 261
  John, 92, 261
  Joseph, 261
  Nathaniel, 73
Rue, Matthew, 152
Ruecastle (Roucastle), Mr., 226
  Phebe, 226
Rule, John, 195
Rulon, David, 190, 205
  Nathaniel, 190
  Theodosia, 190
Runk, William, 178
Runkle, Abraham, 216
  Adam, 193, 203
  William, 106, 107
Runyon (Runyan), Absalom, 108, 113, 172, 230
  Catherine, 182
  Hill, 32
  Hugh, 32
  John, 10, 123, 135, 165, 248
  Peter, Jr., 89
Russell (Russel), Abigail, 194
  Caleb, 204
  Daniel, 40, 143
  Edward, 194
  Ephraim, 79
  James, 115, 143
  Jane, 143
  Keziah, 194
  Mary, 194
  Rebecca, 194
  William, 143
Rutan, Abraham, 20
  Henry, 257
  Herman, 211
Rutgers, Anthony, 90, 91
  Anthony A., 91

# INDEX OF NAMES OF PERSONS 315

Herman, Gouverneur, 90, 91
Nicholas Gouverneur, 90, 91
Ryder, Ann, 170
  William, 53
Ryerson (Reyerse, Reyerson, etc.),
  Abraham, 22, 211
  George L., 147
  John, 8, 22, 97
  Martin, 8
  Sarah, 22
  Teunis, 194
Ryley—*see* Riley
Ryon, Joseph, 195
  Sophia, 195
Rype—*see* Van Rype

## S

Sacket, James, 13
Sackman, Elizabeth, 77
Salmon, John, 144
  Samuel, 21
Saltar (Salter), Huldah, 161
  James, 161
  Thomas, 64, 236
Sanders, Thomas, 181
Sandford, Abraham, 127
  Catherine, 195
  Elizabeth, 195
  Janne, 195
  Mary, 195
  Mary Stiles, 195
  Nancy, 195
  Rachel, 195
  Robert, Jr., 195
  Sarah, 195
  Thomas, 48, 195
  William, 195
Sands, Susannah, 221
Sansbury, Ralph, 195
Sansom, Hannah, 38
  Joseph, 38
  Samuel, 38
  Sarah, 38
  William, 38
Sapp, Isaac, 21
Saterly, Hannah, 51
Satterthwaite, Benjamin, 195
  Elizabeth, 195
  Jane, 195
  John, 65
  Joseph, 195
  Joshua W., 261
  Reuben, 195
  William, 35, 167, 195
Saull (Saul), Adam, 184, 200
Savage, Thomas, 94
Savereen, Anna, 184
Savoy, John, 41
Sawer, Hannah. 44
Sawins, Jennet, 195
  Joseph, 195
Sayre, Abner, 54, 154
  Abot, 62, 81
  Abraham, 168
  Daniel, 198
  Dennis, 237
  Ebenezer, 96, 262
  Ezekiel, 20, 140, 164
  Ezra, 195
  Francis Bowes, 167
  Jeremiah, 151, 232
  Job, 37
  Margaret, 216

  Samuel, 70, 216, 258
  Thomas, 9
Sayres (Sayrs), David, 197, 214
  Hannah, 62
  Matthias, 16, 17, 96, 126
Scank—*see* Schenck
Scattergood, Benjamin, 196
  Caleb, Jr., 196, 220
  Joshua, 196
  Martha, 196
  Mary, 196
  Sarah, 196, 220
Schamp, Henry, 75
  Peter, 66, 131, 238
Schanck—*see* Schenck
Schellinger (Schillinger), Cornelius, 98
  Jacob, 215
  James, 44
  Patience, 44
  Philomele, 74
  William, 73, 99
Schenck (Schank, Schanck), Abraham, 130, 196
  Agnes, 196
  Ann, 196
  Catharine, 196
  Garrit, 31, 61, 196
  Hendrick, 196
  Henry H., 49
  Isaac, 196
  Jacob, 24, 90, 217
  John, 118, 196, 200, 217
  John, Jr., 196
  John H., 223
  Joseph, 118
  Koert, Sr., 107
  Mariah, 196
  Martine, 196
  Mary, 196
  Nicholas, 12, 196
  P., 22
  Peter, 31, 219
  Rachel, 196
  Roleff, 262
  Rulef P., 44
  William, 10
  *See also* Shank
Schermerhorn, Aaron, 196
  Eve, 196
  Hannah, 196
  John, 196
Schillinger—*see* Schellinger
Schomp—*see* Schamp
Schooley, James, 73
  John, 245
Schoonover, Henry, 149
  Rebecca, 156
Schuiler, Jacob, 244, 259
  Mary, 244
  *See also* Schuyler
Schultz, Peter, 12
Schuurman, John, 224
Schuyler, Abraham, 223
  Adoniah, 87
  Arent, 197
  Arent J., 205
  Hester, 196
  Peter, 90
  Philip A., 205
  *See also* Schuiler
Scoggin (Scroggens), Jacob, 237
  Tyler, 67. 237
Scott, Abraham, 194, 201
  Alexander, 174
  Ann, 174

Barzillai, 76
Jane, 197
Job, 197
John, 27, 162, 197
Joseph, 69, 194, 201
Lydia, 197
Mehetable, 197
Moore, 102
Moses, 181, 243
Ruth, 197
Samuel, 27, 197
Susannah, 107
Scudder, Anne, 197
Benjamin, 152, 197
Daniel, 185
Jane, 197
John, 57, 77, 172, 197
Joseph, 16, 50, 126, 127, 197
Lucy, 197
Lydia, 197
Mary, 197
Moses, 172
Noah, 197
Phebe, 154
Rachel, 197
Samuel, 172
Susannah, 154
Scull, David, 208
Deborah, 198
Jesse, 198
Joseph, 197, 210
Rachel, 208
Sarah, 69
Scyphers (Seypart), Ann Elizabeth, 199
Catharine, 199
Christine, 199
Elizabeth, 199
Jacob, 199
Margaret, 199
Sarah, 199
Seabrook, Martha, 221
Thomas, 55, 79, 85, 206, 209, 220, 221
Seagrave (Seagreave), Artis, 90, 98, 221
Tarver, 96
Seamer (Seamers), Andrew, 75
John, 75
Searing, Ann, 198
Jacob, 198
John, Jr., 198
Mary, 198
Nancy, 198
Simon, 198
Susannah, 198
Sears (Seers), Jacob, 165
Obadiah, 213
Sebrey, Nathaniel, 67
Sebring, Catharine, 198
Christine, 198
Holehey, 198
Honche, 198
John, 225
John, Jr., 89, 146
Rulif, 198, 243
Sedam (Sadam), Abraham, 198
Anne, 198
Ginne, 198
Hendrick, 28
Lawrence, 198
Peter, 172
Peter, Jr., 198
Rick, 198
Sarah, 198
*See also* Suydam

Seed, Rachel, 198
Seeley, Josiah, 79
Rachel, 198
Selover—*see* Slover
Sempleton, Samuel, 225
Senteny, Jane, 198
Seperlin, John, 223
Sergent, Loman, 132
Service (Servis), David, 170
Philip, 216, 217
Seward, Daniel, 51
Scypart *see* Scyphers
Shackleton, Benjamin, 199
Mary, 199
Shaffer—*see* Shaver
Shaftner, Gasper, 260
Shank, Michael, 260
*See also* Schenck
Shannan, John, 250
Samuel, 190
Shapard, Shaphard—*see* Sheppard
Sharp, Aaron, 199
Amos, 202
Anna, 199
Anthony, 253
Barzillai, 199
Benjamin, 191
Daniel, 199
Deborah, 199
Dinah, 199
Enoch, 122, 199
George, 199
Hannah, 191, 199
Henry, 163
Isaac, 199
Jemima, 163
John, 51, 136, 176, 249
John, Jr., 199
Joseph, 136, 199, 206
Joshua, 175, 199
Levy, 199
Mahlon, 199
Mary, 199
Priscilla, 199
Samuel, 143, 175, 199, 209
Sarah, 191
Thomas, 9, 199
William, 191, 192
Sharps, Peter, 121
Skatts, James, 49
Shaver (Shaffer), Abraham, 8, 177, 245
Adam, 241
George, 200
Margaret, 200
Peter B., 187
Shaw, Aaron, 59
Abigail, 59
Adam, 200
Andrew, 29
Deborah, 200
Ebinezer, 59
Elijah, 200
Elizabeth, 200
Henry, 200
Hosea, 59
Isaiah, Jr., 200
John, 136, 200, 220
Joshua, 222
Matthias, 59
Nathan, 59
Phebe, 141
Rachel, 200
Richard, 60, 164
Ruth, 200
Sarah, 28, 200

## INDEX OF NAMES OF PERSONS 317

Stillwell, 42
Thomas, 98, 110, 119, 169, 214
William, 42, 247
Shearman (Sheerman, Sherman),
  James, 134
  Jene, 12
  Josiah, 9
  Mary, 230
  Oliver, 134
  Thomas, 230, 231
Shedeker, Elizabeth, 201
  Jacob, Jr., 201
  Rachel, 201
Sheldon, Joseph, 82
Shenfelt—*see* Shinefelt
Sheppard (Shapard, Shepherd, etc.),
  Mr., 185
  Anne, 201
  Charlotte, 201
  Daniel, 201
  David, 87, 186, 201
  Elias, 201
  Elisha, 80, 81
  Hannah, 61
  Hosea, 142, 201
  James, 8, 201
  Job, 201
  John, 186, 201
  John, Jr., 118, 186
  Luse, 62
  Lydia, 62
  Mary, 62, 185, 201
  Moses, 83, 136
  Prudence, 201
  Richard W., 186
  Ruth, 175
  Sarah, 201
  Thomas, 201
Sheppardson, Ebenezer, 202
Sherman—*see* Shearman
Sherrad, Robert, 20
Sherrerd, Joseph, 113
  Samuel, 174
Sherry, Samuel, 74
Sherwood, Isaac, 66
Shinefelt, Frederic, 44
Shinemann, Christopher H., 92
Shinn (Shin), Buddell, 34, 206
  Corliss, 44
  Earl, 34, 155, 156
  Elizabeth, 156, 202
  Francis, 213
  Hannah, 78, 202
  Isaiah, 123, 202
  Jacob, Jr., 78
  John, 156
  Rebecca, 155, 156
  Samuel, 59, 74, 83, 156, 189
  Sarah, 87
  Thomas, 156
  Vincent, 202
Shints, Ruth, 19
Shipman, Catharine, 46
  Jacob, 46
  Matthias, 106, 199
  Matthias, Jr., 46
  Paul, 199
Shippen, Joseph W., 214
Shiras (Shires), Jacob, 194
  Peter, 39, 95, 226
Shirts, Abraham, 202
  Elizabeth, 202
  John, 202
  Michael, 202
  Michael, Jr., 202
  Rachel, 202
  *See also* Shurts
Shivers, John, 13, 42
Shoemaker, Peter, 162
Shoot—*see* Shute
Shores, Mary, 204
Shotwell, Abraham, 203
  Benjamin, 31, 203
  Caleb, 203
  Daniel, 216
  Daniel, Jr., 202
  David, 203
  Elizabeth, 31, 202, 203
  Hannah, 202
  Jacob, 203
  James, 203, 254
  Jeremiah, 203
  John Smith, 25
  Johnson, 174
  Joseph, 202, 209, 216
  Joseph, Jr., 202
  Margaret, 202
  Mary, 202
  Sarah, 202
  Titus, 202, 216
Shourds, Benjamin, 23
Shreve (Shreeve), Caleb, 203
  Caleb, Jr., 203
  Elizabeth, 87, 203
  Enoch, 203
  Hope, 203
  Isaac, 203
  Job, 103, 203
  Joseph, 12, 203
  Joshua, 64, 129, 167
  Mercy, 203
  Penelope, 203
  Rebecca, 203
  Sarah, 203
  Stacy, 203
  Thomas, 203
Shriner, John, 203
  Lena, 203
Shropshire, Edward, 142
Shuff, Christopher, 156
Shul, Bostian, 203
  Jacob, 204
  John Parvin, 204
  Nancy, 204
  Naomi, 63, 204
Shuman, Elnoer, 196
  Peter, 196
Shurte, Adolphy, 84
Shurts, Andrew, 29
  Deliverance, 28
  *See also* Shirts
Shute (Shoot), Barnaby, 226
  John, Jr., 47
  Joseph, 236
  Mary Ann, 226
  Rachel, 204
  S. M., 207
  Samuel, 204
  Samuel M., 40, 61, 63, 64, 75, 201, 251
  Sarah, 51
  Thomas, 165
  William, 51
Sickels (Sickelse, Sickles), Antye, 66
  Robert, 66
  William, 13, 31, 61, 93, 171, 252
  Zacharius, 240
Siddons (Siddens), Edward, 149
  Jane, 139
Sigler, Jacob, 236
  Mary, 236

Sillcock, Isaac, 42
Silver, Abel, 204
  Archibald, 204
  Mary, 204
  Rebecca, 204
  Rhoda, 204
  Ruth, 204
  Samuel, Jr., 204
  Seth, 204
  William, 204
Silvers, Henry, 195
Silverthorn, Henry, 89
Simkins, Benjamin, 108
  Hester, 204
  Hope, 204
  John, Jr., 204
  Mark, 204
  Phebe, 204
  Silvanus, 204
  Uriah, 204
Simons (Simmons), Peter, **183**, **243**
Simonson, Cornelius, 24
  John, 131, 179, 236
Simpson, Abraham, 205
  Alexander, 205
  Anna, 205
  Ephraim, 205
  Isaac, 205
  Jacob, 205
  John, Jr., 205
  Magdalien, 205
  Margaret, 205
  Sarah, 205
  William, 205
Sims, Joshua, 255
Sinclare, Ann, 205
  Elizabeth, 205
  John, 205
  Mary, 205
  Rhoda, 205
Singer, John, 33, 70, 108, **117**, **226**
Sinnickson, Andrew, 125
  Andrew, Jr., 212, **244**
  Margaret, 212
  Sarah, 97
  Thomas, 97
Sip, John, 242
Sipple, Martinus, 205
Skelton, Hannah, 157
  Joseph, 196, 197
Skillman (Skilman), John, **174**
  Polly, 90
  Thomas, 219, 238
Skinner, Anne, 205
  J., 205
  James, 156
  Margaret, 205
Skirm, Abraham, 205
Slack, Samuel, 32
Slaght, Elizabeth, **177**
Slape, James, 103
Sleeper, Betsy, 206
  Ebenezer, 206
  James, 206
  Jonathan, Jr., 206
  Joseph, 206
  Leah, 206
  Polly, 206
  William, 206
Sloan, James, 62, 159, **225**
  John, 206
  Mary, 206
Slocum, Peleg, 247
  Peter, 247
Slott, Anne, 229
Slover, Isaac, 224

Small, Charity, 158
  John, 158
Smalley (Smally), David, 55
  John, 248
  Jonathan, 151
  Phebe, 151
Smallwood, Deborah, 44
Smith, Aaron, 156, 165
  Abel, 21
  Abigail, 58
  Abijah, 150, 169
  Abraham, 12, 163, 209
  Andrew, 37, 121, 207
  Ann, 207
  Belcher P., 33
  Benjamin, 10, 28, 30, 38, 56, **117**, 207, 234
  Catharine, 21, 72, 206
  Charles, 241
  Christopher, 96
  Constantine, 214
  Daniel, 38, 40, 72, 138, 166, **182**, 206, 207, 209, 250, 261
  Dougould, 32
  Eaton, 21
  Eleazer, 249
  Elias, 206
  Elijah, Jr., 206
  Elizabeth, 40, 45, 56, **123**, 179, 207, 209
  Enoch, 72, 85, 206
  Ezekiel, 45, 104, 157, 196
  Garret, 100
  George, 78, 206
  Gilbert, 133, 206
  Hannah, 179, 209
  Harriet, 85
  Henry, 179, 208
  Hilche V., 245
  Hill, 10, 28
  Howell, 237
  Isaac, 157, 163, 206
  Jacob, 48, 107, 186, 206
  James, 114, 119, 255
  Jane, 206
  Jemima, 151
  Jeremiah, **197**, **213**, **254**
  Jesse, 247
  Job, 72, 104
  John, 28, 96, 101, 102, 109, **164**, 188, 197, 206, 208, 226, 237, 245, 247, 255
  Jonathan, 85, 151
  Joseph, 40, 206, 255
  Joshua, 15, 195, 206, 209, 210
  Josiah, 171
  Judith, 99, 208
  Katherine, 38
  Legget, 75
  Mary, 38, 58, 85, 94, 192, 207, 209
  Mehetable, 179
  Micajah, 209
  Naomi, 208
  Noah, 69, 147, 206
  Peter, 67, 140, 151, **183**, **241**
  Phebe, 58
  Philip, 206
  Pile, 209
  Rachel, 182
  Rebecca, 27, 209
  Reynear, 236
  Rhoda, 227
  Richard, 28, 40, 97, 149, 207
  Richard, Jr., 19
  Richard R., 40

# INDEX OF NAMES OF PERSONS 319

Robert, 38, 109, 135, 155, 182, 207, 261
Robert, Jr., 209
Samuel, 40, 44, 64, 147, 186, 208
Sarah, 38, 58, 207, 208, 209
Seth, 40
Simeon, 80
Stephen, 227
Surviah, 247
Susannah, 208
Sylvanus, 209
Thomas, 20, 40, 92, 129, 201, 207, 209, 250
Walter, 47
William, 9, 21, 94, 113, 152, 153, 156, 206, 207, 216, 235
William, Jr., 40, 76, 250
William Lovett, 188
William Pitt, 33
William Ross, 263
Zillah, 210
Smock, Barnes H., 209
  Barnes I., 32
  George, 107, 193
  Hendrick, 193
  Matthias, 136
  Rynier, 136
Sneathen—see Snethen
Snedeker, James, 131
Snell, Samuel, 15
Snethen (Sneathen), Annanias, 210
  Hosea, 204, 210
  John, 62, 210
  Joseph, 62
  Joseph, Jr., 210
  Phebe, 210
  Waitel, 210
  Zepporah, 210
Snider, Sniter—see Snyder
Snook (Snuke), John, 8
  Philip, 246
Snowden, Richard, 94
Snuke—see Snook
Snyder (Snider, Sniter), Anne, 210
  Elizabeth, 230
  Henry, 230
  James, 68
  John, 29, 177
  John, Jr., 210
  Margaret, 210
  Peter, 76, 210
Sockwell (Socwell), Jonathan, 141
  Lansilet, 201
Somerlin, John, 41
  *See also* Summerl
Somers, Jacob, 210
  James, 147
  John, 147, 210
  Mary, 210
  Richard, 150, 214, 248
  Samuel, 210, 211
  Thomas, 210, 211
  Zillah, 210
  *See also* Summers
Sonmans—see Sunmans
Sooy, Luke, 213
Sortor, Charity, 218
  Hendrick, 24
Sotherlin—see Sutherland
Souder, Philip, 153
  Simon, 153
Soullard, John, 168
Southard, Amos, 211
  Elizabeth, 211
  Henry, 130
  Hezekiah, 211

Job, 211
John, 211
Joseph, 211
Southwick, Josiah, 156
Southworth, Silvanus, 206
Spader, John, 211
Sparks, Ann, 211
  Elizabeth, 181
  Gabriel, 42
  George, 123, 181, 253
  Isaac, 119
  John, 173
  Mary, 181
  Robert, 36
Speakman, Joseph, 260
Spear (Speer, Speare), Angletie, 211
  Elizabeth, 146, 147
  Fightty, 196
  Garrit I., 75
  Henry, 48, 146, 211
  Sophia, 48
  Thomas, 211
  Thunis, 48, 196, 211
Sperling, Daniel, 34
Spicer, Jacob, 59, 98, 168, 222
Spinning, Benjamin, 148
  John, 148, 160
Spraggs, Mary, 119
  Samuel, 119, 155, 226
Sprague, William Peter, 24
Springer, Samuel, 172
Sprowl, Thomas, 121
Squier (Squire), Elijah, 16, 92, 211
  Henry, 89
  Mary, 211
Staats, Abraham, 31, 55, 88, 136, 181, 208
  Margaret, 208
  Mary S., 208
  Peter, 153, 177
  Rynier, 198, 243
Stack, Machal, 225
Stackhouse, Esther, 211
  John, 226
  Joseph, 209
Staffon, James, 93
Stafford, Christopher, 225
Stagg, Cornelius, 174
Stanberry, Sarah, 154
Standly (Standley), Andrew, 244
  Anne, 212
  Henry, 211
  Jane, 212
  Margaret, 212
  Nathaniel, 211, 212
  Onesiphrous, 211, 212
  Richard, 200
  Sinnick, 211
Stanton, Daniel, 49
  Jane, 180
  Leonard, 51
  Richard, 194
Stark (Starke), George, 125
  Isaac, 94
  Pauline, 125
  Sarah, 125
Starkey, Abel, 88
Stateser, Isaac, 212
  Zilpha, 212
Statham (Stathem), Ananias, 212
  Deliverance, 212
  Dorcas, 212
  Israel, 212
  Naomi, 212
  Philip, 212
  Rebecca, 212

320   NEW JERSEY COLONIAL DOCUMENTS

Sarah, 212
Thomas, 212
Steele, John, 137
Josiah, 170
Thompson, 227
Steeley, Margaret, 199
Steelman, Ann, 208
  Catherine, 212
  Eleanor, 47, 213
  Elizabeth, 213
  Isaac, 47, 212
  James, 212
  James, Jr., 212
  Jemima, 213
  John, 205, 212
  Judith, 208
  Milicent, 208
  Rebecca, 213
  Sarah, 213
  Susannah, 208
Stelle (Stell), Oliver, 72
  Thomson, 72, 191
Stephens, Alexander, 154
  Apollo, 213
  Edward, 213
  Fanny, 213
  James, 213
  John, 57, 123, 183, 184, 253
  John, Jr., 213
  Richard, 259
  Samuel, 213
  Stacy, 213
  Thomas, 213
  William, 249
  See also Stevens
Sterling, James, 202, 247
Stevens, James, 254
  John, 187
  See also Stephens
Stevenson, Amelia, 166
  John, 166
  Juliana, 68
  Margaret, 167
  Martha, 167
Steward, Abigail, 195
  Bickley, 213
  Mary, 213
  Rebecca, 213
  Samuel, 88
  Sarah, 213
Stewart, Ann, 190
  Archibald, 88, 119
  Charles, 214
  Ely, 214
  Hannah, 214
  Isaac, 214
  Jane, 214
  Joel, 214
  John, 10, 208
  John, Jr., 214
  Samuel, 15, 102, 237, 256
  Samuel, R., 234
  Samuel Robert, 214
  Sarah, 214
  Scobe, 214
  Sophia, 214
  William, 214
  See also Stuart
Stiers, John, 133
Stiles (Styles), Abigail, 174
  Ebenezer, 89, 179
  Ebenezer, Jr., 89
  Ephraim, 162
  George, 29
  John, 162
  Jonathan, 40, 137, 174, 250

Thomas, 138
William, 174
Stillwell (Stilwell, Stillwill), Elizabeth, 200, 214, 215
  Enoch, 214
  James, 200
  Jean, 214
  John, 13, 41, 49, 85, 107, 206, 209, 215
  John, Jr., 214
  Joseph, 215, 239, 252
  Martha, 214, 215
  Nancy, 215
  Nicholas, 124, 214
  Phebe, 214
  Rebecca, 200, 214
  Samuel, 200
  Sarah, 215
  Thomas, 214
  William, 13, 215
Stinson, Archibald, Jr., 140
Stites, Benjamin, 23
  Daniel, 142, 232
  Elizabeth, 98
  Henry, 172, 214
  Humphrey, 59
  John, 73, 99
  John, Jr., 74
  Mary, 59
  Philip, 98
  Roanna, 248
  Sarah, 98
  Silvytha, 215
  William, 31
Stockton, Abraham, 72, 129, 197
  Benjamin, 95, 215
  Elizabeth, 215
  Job, 155, 156, 215
  Job, Jr., 87
  John, 156, 215
  Jonathan, 156, 215
  Margaret, 155, 215
  Mary, 155, 215
  Mercy, 215
  Monrow, 156, 215
  Nancy, 156
  Obadiah, 215
  Richard, 215, 234
  Samuel, 87, 215
  Samuel W., 116
  Stacy, 215
  Susannah, 129
  Thomas, 171
  William, 95, 133, 156, 215
Stokes, David, 78
  Hannah, 112
  Jacob, 161
  John, 138
  John H., 96
  John Hinchman, 112
  Joseph, 46, 96, 132, 133, 161, 230
  Judith, 112
  Mary, 112
  Samuel, 9, 57, 112, 138, 248
  Sarah, 112
  Thomas, 123, 139, 166, 253
Stoll (Stull), Andrew, 215
  Anna, 215
  Dennis, 229
  Henry, 215
  Jane, 215
  John, 36
  Mary, 215
Stonaker, David, 207, 245
Stone, Ann, 216
  Benjamin, 216

## INDEX OF NAMES OF PERSONS 321

Elizabeth, 216
Lucy, 216
Margaret, 216
Robert, 216
Stonebanks, Joseph, 123
Stoothoff, Peter, 198
Story, Joseph, 93, 245
  Rebecca, 16
Stout, Abraham, 216
  Andrew Bray, 29
  Anne, 216, 217, 260
  Benijah, 180
  Benjamin, Jr., 216
  Catherine, 217
  David, 216, 217
  Elizabeth, 12
  Freegift, 133
  Grace, 217
  Hannah, 217
  Hezekiah, 216
  James, 133
  James, Jr., 217
  Jediah, 216, 217
  Joab, 217
  John, 111, 218, 222
  Jonathan, 217
  Joseph, 196, 217
  Joshua, 112, 113
  Judiah, 216
  Martha, 216, 217
  Mary, 111, 112, 113, 216, 217, 218
  Moses, 216, 217
  Nathan, 79, 111, 182, 183, 216, 217
  Nathaniel, 218
  Natte, 218
  Rachel, 216, 217
  Richard, 24
  Samuel, 86, 152, 198, 216, 218
  Sarah, 216, 217, 218
  Stephen, 217
  Zebulon, Jr., 135, 217, 218
Stoutenborough, John, 115
Stow (Stowe), Ann, 20
  Isaac, 20
  John, 21
Strang, Andrew, 130
  Eleanor, 169
Strattan (Stratton), Amos, 199, 203
  Bethuel, 218
  Elias, 218
  Fithian, 151
  Isaiah, 218
  James, 71, 140, 200
  Mary, 218
  William, 218
Stretch, David, 204
  David, Jr., 218
  Eleanor, 218
  James, 218
  John, 218
  Margaret, 218
  Mary, 208, 218
  Prudence, 218
  Sarah, 218
Strickland, Diedamy, 218
  Samuel, 109
Stringham, James, 218
Struble, Daniel, 151
Stryker, Abraham, 219, 223
  Anne, 219
  Catharine, 219
  Christopher, 162
  Daniel, 219
  Domenicus, 238
  Gitty, 219

  Hendrick, 219
  Jacobus, 219
  Jane, 238
  John, 219
  John, Jr., 219
  Lydia, 219
  Maria, 219
  Peter, 136, 180, 219, 242
Stuber, Henry, 188
Stull—*see* Stoll
Stuart, Daniel, 100
  *See also* Stewart
Sturges, Ebenezer, 173, 174
  Rhoda, 173
Styles—*see* Stiles
Sullivan, Thomas, 154
Summerl, Naomi, 219
  *See also* Somerlin
Summers, John, 241
  *See also* Somers
Sunmans, Peter, 211
Sutherland (Sotherlin), Daniel, 41, 47, 107, 115, 123, 128, 143, 211, 212, 213
Sutphen (Sutfen, Sutfin), Annatye, 242
  Aurt, 242
  Derick, 79, 111, 131, 216
  Guisbert, 70, 180
  Jacob, 262
  John, 262
  Peter, 181
Sutton (Sutten), Cornelius, 128
  Elizabeth, 7
  Henry, 71, 160
  James, 7
  John, 208
  Jonathan, 94
Suydam (Suidam), Jacob, 25
  *See also* Sedam
Swabey, Joseph, 102, 237
Swaim, Catharine, 29
  Richard, 54
Swain, Aaron, 12
  Catherine, 98, 248
  Hannah, 219
  Jacocks, 42, 99, 232
  John, 134, 219
  Nezer, 98, 163, 248
  Zebulon, 134, 149, 214
  *See also* Swen
Swan, Jedidiah, 96, 97, 224, 254
Swart, Elbert, 200
Swartwelder, Martin, 8
Sway, Mary Green, 177
Swayze (Swayzey, Sweezy, etc.),
  Caleb, 116
  Henry, 68
  Jabez Mapes, 190
  John, 220
  Joseph, 220
  Joshua, 116
  Mary, 220
Swen, Matthias, 167
  *See also* Swain
Swett, Benjamin, 91
  Joseph Cooper, 91
  Mary, 91
  Sarah, 91
Swiney, Thomas, 173
Swing, Samuel, 166
Swisher, Abraham, 10, 117
Swoop, Walter, 122
Sykes, Anthony, 166
  Samuel, 167

## T

Taggert, Jacob, 161
John, 161
Talbert, William, 220
Tallman (Talman), Benjamin H., 159
Daniel, 220
Hannah, 220
James, 79, 220, 221, 263
Jeams, 220
Jemima, 220
John, 78, 79
Joseph, 7, 75, 79, 203, 220
Margaret, 220
Martha, 231
Mary, 221
Molly, 220
Patty, 221
Peter, 7
Rachel, 220, 221
Samuel, 94
Stephen, 78, 79, 220
William, 220
Tanner, Esther, 221
Lydia, 221
Martha, 221
Phebe, 221
Susannah, 221
Tappan, Jacob, 103
Tapscott, James, 56
William, 222
Tatem (Tatum), John, 18, 51
William, 212
Taylor, Aaron, 139
Abigail, 221
Amy, 82
Ann, 221
Anthony, 259
Benjamin, 85
Beriah, 10
Edward, 56
Elizabeth, 133, 222
George, 52, 53, 60, 85
George, Jr., 222
Hannah, 259
James, 85, 133
Jane, 222
Joel, 183
John, 61, 65, 99, 100, 155, 158, 180, 211, 214, 222, 255, 259
John, Jr., 66, 206, 255
John V. K., 18
Jonathan, 189
Joseph, 221
Judith, 222
Lydia, 158, 222
Mary, 222
Nathaniel, 54
Rachel, 222
Rhoda, 222
Robert, 196
Stacy, 65
Susan, 221. 222, 231
Thomas, 127
William, 103
Teal (Teel), Jacob, 42
Mary, 98
Teeter (Teater), Cattrean, 222, 223
Conrad, 223
Cristean, 223
Elizabeth, 223
Ellis, 223
Henry, 223
Rachel, 223
Zachariah, 223
Tenbrook (Ten Broeck), Abraham, 223
Catharine, 223
Cornelius, Jr., 141, 223
Elizabeth, 223
Hannah, 223
Helena, 223
Jacob, 223
John, 134, 223
John, Jr., 223
Peter, 223
Roeloff, 223
Wessel, 223
Ten Eyck (Ten Eick, Ten Eyk), Anne, 223
Conrad, 136, 223
Elizabeth, 136
Jacob, 28, 223, 238
Jacob C., 223
Janet, 17
Renselaer, 223
Richard, 17
Tunis, 79
Tentelpeck, Fratrick, 188
Terhune, Albert, 22, 224
Anne, 224
Eleanor, 224
Elizabeth, 224
Garret, 224
Jacob, 224, 262
Jacobus, 239
Magdalen, 224
Mary, 224
Roeleff, 223, 224
Terrill (Terrell, Terryl, etc.), Abraham, 169
Adam, 198
Ephraim, 226
James, 224
Mary, 224
Newcom, 224
Phebe, 189, 224
Phebe Prudence, 224
William, 161
See also Tyrrel
Terry (Terrey), Mr., 21
Ashberry, 225
Elizabeth, 225
Jonathan, 30
Mary, 224
Nathaniel, 21, 84
Phebe, 225
Test, Zacheus, 26
Teunison—see Tunison
Thackray (Thackrey), Elizabeth, 225
Isaac, 225
Joseph, 225
Margaret, 225
Mark, 225
Tharp—see Thorp
Thatcher, Abigail, 226
Bartholomew, 87
Clarenda, 226
Daniel, 89, 225
Edward, 225
Elisha, 225, 226
Elizabeth, 226
Grace, 225
Hannah, 225
James, 87, 124
Jeremiah, 87, 124, 210, 230
Job, 225
Mary, 225
Nancy, 225
Rachel, 225

INDEX OF NAMES OF PERSONS 323

Rebecca, 225, 226
Samuel, 225, 226
Sarah, 226
Susannah, 226
Thomas, 226, 247
William, 87
Thixton, Jane, 71
Joseph, 71
Thomas, Edmund D., 154, 226
Edward, 70
Elias, 74
Elizabeth, 226
George Cummins, 226
Henry G., 226
Margaret, 226
Phebe, 226
Robinson, 226
Sally, 226
Seth, 38
Solomon, 14
William, 232
Thompson, Aaron, 149, 227, 258
Abigail, 227
Alexander, 226, 227, 260
Benjamin, 136, 227
Butler, 224, 251
Catherine, 226
Charles, 123
David, 51, 120
Dorcas, 227
Elizabeth, 136, 208
Esther, 227
Hannah, 227
Jacob, 164, 206
James, 39, 101, 227
Janet, 144
John, 102
Jonathan, 227
Joshua Wood, 258
Margaret, 144
Moses, 227
Petero, 8
Phebe, 218, 227
Rhoda, 227
Samuel, 140, 258
Sarah, 227
Thomas, 15, 94, 128
Uriah, 28
William, 21, 61, 136
*See also* Thomson, Tomson
Thomson, Charity, 72
Isaac, 228
James, 72
John, 109, 194, 216, 228, 233
Joseph, 23, 124, 160, 228
Mark, 30, 65, 121
Thomas, 169, 227, 228
*See also* Thompson, Tomson
Thorn (Thorne), Abigail, 230
Ann, 229, 230
Benjamin, 213
Charles, 228
Henry, 44
Isaac, 228
Isabella, 44
Jemima, 228
John, 43, 44, 61, 71, 74, 79, 123, 158, 213, 228, 250
Joseph, 228
Mary, 202, 230
Thomas, 26, 36, 45, 158, 204, 230
William, 228
Thornal, Israel, 159
Thorp (Tharp), Icabod, 205
John, 102, 124, 181
Mary, 103, 238

Throckmorton, James, 136
Joseph, 118, 136, 174, 254
Richard, 118, 161, 162, 226
Thurston, Benjamin, 228
Hannah, 228
Mary, 160, 228
Tice, Anne, 229
Christine, 229
Dederick, 229
Henry, 229
Jacob, 31
John, 26, 229
Margaret, 229
Mary, 229
Tichenor, Caleb, 229
David, 229
Elizabeth, 39
Hannah, 229
Jabez, 229
John, 229
Jonathan, 9, 86
Mary, 229
Sarah, 58
Susannah, 229
Zenus, 229
Tiddiss, George G., 186
George Garnett, 246
Tilton, Mary, 79, 220
Nathan, 217
Thomas, 22
Tindall, Mary, 229
William, 30, 102, 139, 229, 235, 255, 259
Tippey, Elizabeth, 255
Titus (Titas), Abigail, 229
Asa, 219
Benjamin, 185
Martha, 241
Philip, 229
Ruth, 191
Stephen, 11, 242
Tobin, Nathaniel, 226
Todd, Andrew, 229
Elizabeth, 229
James, 24, 229
Jane, 229
John, 18
Sarah, 229
Tomkins (Tompkins), Charles, 235
Isaac, 76, 160
Joseph, 58, 84, 193, 194
Samuel, 171
Tomlin, William, 141
Tomlinson, Ann, 230
Dinah, 230, 231
Elizabeth, 190
Ephraim, 26, 43, 147
Francis, 230, 231
Isaac, 26, 43, 44, 159, 190
Rebecca, 230
Sarah, 230
William, 230, 231
Tompkins—*see* Tomkins
Tomson, James, 231
Joanna, 231
John, 113, 231
Lefferd, 231
Yanna, 231
*See also* Thompson, Thomson
Tone, Hannah, 103
John, 103
Toner, Catherine, 193
Tonkin, Bathsheba, 231
Hepzibah, 189
Israel, 32, 231
John, 231

Martha, 231
Mary, 81, 231
Samuel, 81
Susannah, 231
Tooker, Abraham, 160
  Charles, 174
  Jane, 103
  Lewis, 104
  Mary, 174
  Phebe, 160
  Sally, 103
  Susannah, 160
  *See also* Tucker
Toomey, Henerey, Sr., 231
  *See also* Tumey
Totten, John, 118
Townley (Townly), Charles, 227
  Hannah, 227
  Nancy, 198
  Richard, 32, 170
Townsend, Catherine, 200
  Cresse, 59
  David, 59
  Drusilla, 232
  Eli, 99, 134, 225, 231, 232, 253
  Elijah, 59, 85, 143, 255
  Henry Y., 85, 134, 232, 255
  James, 255
  John, 232
  Jotham, 59, 110
  Keturah, 18
  Rachel, 59, 232
  Reuben, 59, 231, 255
  Richard, 54, 59, 99, 143, 214, 225, 231, 232, 253
  Sarah, 203
Towser, Hannah, 232
Toy, Andrew, 232
  Caleb, 232
  Elias, 232
  Elijah, 232
  Hezekiah, 11, 232
  Isaiah, 14
  James, 232
  Patience, 232
  Peter, 232
  Rebecca, 232
  Richard, 232
  William, 232
Traphagen (Triphagen), David, 227
Trasey, Daniel, 218
Traubles (Trembles), Nancy, 233
Treadway (Tredway), Amy, 232
  Ann, 232
  Hannah, 232
  Henry, 232, 258
  Jesse, 232
  John, 232
  Matthew, 232
  Nathan, 232
  Sarah, 232
  Zetthu, 232
Treat, Elizabeth, 233
  John Thomas, 233
  Joseph, 233
  Malachi, 233
  Richard Samuel, 233
  Samuel, 243
Treen, William, 98
Trembles—*see* Traubles
Trembly (Trembley), Abraham, 233
  Benjamin, 233
  Hannah, 148
  Jacob, 160
  Jonathan, 233
  Joseph, 148
  Mary, 148, 233
Trenchard, John, 154, 204
Trimmer, George, 120, 189
  John, 189
Triphagen—*see* Traphagen
Troth, Isaac, 233
  Paul, 62
Trotter, William, 164
Trouss, Mary, 212
Trout, George, 122
Trowbridge, Absalom, 233
  Shubel, 233
Tucker, Elias, 257
  Elizabeth, 234
  Ellit, 234, 235
  Ezekiel, 92
  George, 234, 235
  Joseph, 234
  Joseph, Jr., 227
  Mercy, 235
  Nancy, 221
  Philip, 234
  Richard, 234
  Samuel, 30, 63, 233, 235
  Sarah, 84
  Wessels, 178
  William, 30, 234, 235
  *See also* Tooker
Tufford, Matthias, 81
Tuft, Brathwaite, 41, 178
  John, 225
Tullis (Tullies), Abigail, 191
  Daniel, 86, 105
  Robert, 255
Tumey, Henry, 235
  Jemima, 235
  Samuel, 235
  *See also* Toomey
Tunis, Samuel, 85
Tunison, 116
Tunison (Teunison), Anna, 20, 225
  Cornelius, 225
  Dennis, 225
  Dirck, 225
  Mary, 225
  Tunis, 102
Turner, Elizabeth, 52
  Esther, 235
  John, 41
  Joseph, 191
Tuthill, Samuel, 84
  Samuel, Jr., 84
Tuttle, David, 92
  Ephraim, 3d, 48
  John, 127
  Joseph, 262
  Mary, 252
  Phebe, 29
  Phinehas, 29
  Timothy, 173
Tyler, Job, 119, 163, 186
  Samuel, 67
  William, 237
Tyrrel, Robert, 49
  *See also* Terrill

U

Ulp—*see* Oulp
Ulrich, Philip, 236
Updike (Updick, Updyke, etc.), Lawrence, 107
  John, Sr., 107
  Levi, 245

## INDEX OF NAMES OF PERSONS 325

William, 207, 245
See also Opdycke
Urion, Mary, 236

### V

Vactor, John, 173
Vail, Benjamin, 51, 60
  Noah, 125
  Thomas, 125
Valentine (Vallentine, Volintine), Jonathan, 171
  Joseph, 140
  Mary, 164
  Obadiah, 171
  Temperance, 140
Van Aken, Joseph, 250
Van Allen, Hessel, 237
Van Anglèn, John, 80
Van Arsdalen (Van Arsdale, Van Artsdalen), Abraham, 176, 219
  Ariantia, 236
  Cornelius, 12
  Elizabeth, 236
  Garret, 236
  Jacob, 64, 219
  John, 176, 236
  Lamache, 236
  Magdalene, 236
  Philip, 20
  Simeon, 236
Vanatta, Ann, 236
  Benjamin, 236
  Hannah, 236
  Margaret, 236
  Mary, 236
  Peter, 236
  Samuel, 236
  Tonica, 236
  See also Vannetta
Van Blarcum, James, 239
Vanbrakel (Vanbrackel), Matthias, 210
  Stephen, 49, 115, 210
Van Brunt, Agnes, 196
  Nicholas, 196
Van Buskirk (Vanbuscark, Van Buskark, etc.), Hester, 110
  John, 7
  Thomas. 110
  Thomas L., 83
Van Camp, Elizabeth, 247
  Isaac, 210
  Margaret, 210
Van Campen, Abraham, 17, 193
  Ariantie, 193
Vance, Elizabeth, 237
  James, 236, 237
  Kennedy, 16, 30, 82, 174
  Mary, 236
Van Cleve (Van Cleaf, Van Cleave), Aaron, 50, 61
  Benjamin, 23, 117
  Ishi, 179
  John, 207
Van Culin, Elizabeth, 237
  Hannah, 237
  John, 67, 237, 245
  Sarah, 67, 237
Vandergrift, John, 16
Van de Linde, Arriantye, 237
  Elizabeth, 237
Vanderbeek (Van Derbeck), Annatye, 25
  David, 25
  Isaac, 25, 194, 263
  John, 25
  Rachel, 237
  Yan, 262
Vanderbilt (Vanderbelt), Aaron, 210
  Cornelius, 53
  Jacob, 153
Vanderhoof, Anne, 237
  Elizabeth, 237
  Jane, 237
  Michael, 211
  Rachel, 237
Vanderipe, Catharine, 198
  Elizabeth, 237
  Harmonus, 198
  John, 180, 237
  Jurrie, 180
  Martha, 237
  Matthias, 237
  Rachel, 237
  Richard, 237
Vanderveer, Catharine, 238
  David, 44
  Familie, 238
  Garrit, 55, 56
  Hendrick, 118
  Jacobus, 238
  Jane, 238
  John, 115, 187, 193, 238
  Sarah, 238
  Tunis, 44, 55, 206, 222
Vandervoort, Gabriel, 55
Van Dike—see Van Dyke
Van Doren, Abraham, 238
  David, 162
  Joseph, 162
Van Duerson, William, 170, 221
Van Duyn, Cornelius, 88
  Dennis, 235
  James, 88
  Martin, 22
Van Dyke (Van Dike), Abraham, 247
  Catharine, 238, 239
  Elizabeth, 238, 239
  Elsie, 238
  Frederick, 102
  Henry, 238, 239
  Isaac, 239
  Jacob, 238, 239
  James, 239
  Janitie, 238
  John, 74, 197, 236, 238, 239
  Margaret, 238
  Mary, 238, 239
  Patience, 238
  Rebecca, 239
  Roelof, 239
  Sarah, 238, 239
Van Emburgh, Abraham, 239
  Elizabeth, 239
  Gilbert, 130, 239
  Jane, 239
  John, 82, 218, 239
  Margaret, 239
Van Gieson (Vangeson), Isaac, 72
  Poulus, 239
  Rachel, 239
Van Harlingen, Ernestus, 219
Van Horne (Van Horn), Abraham, 236
  Altie, 240
  Balicah, 240
  Barent, 218
  Eleanor, 240

Feytie, 218
Garret, 240
James, 179
John, 49, 218, 257
John, Jr., 240
Lenah, 240
Mary, 218
Van Houte, John I., 66
Van Huysen, Harmanus, 237
Van Iderstein (Van Iderstine),
　Annatye, 240
　Caspares T., 240
　Elizabeth, 240
　Frances, 240
　Johannis, 240
　Peter, 240
　Rachel, 240
　Steentye, 240
　Theodocia, 240
Van Kirk, John, 17
Vanleer, George, 248
Van Liew (Van Leuwe), Frederick,
　239
　Jeremiah, 181
　Johannes, 153
Van Mater (Van Meter), Abraham,
　241
　Auhely, 240
　Benjamin, 36, 57, 60, 168, 182,
　　240, 241
　Bersheba, 241
　Caty, 240
　Cornelius, 212, 240
　Chryneyonce, 200, 240
　Daniel, 240
　David, 241
　Elizabeth, 36, 241
　Gilbert, 240
　Henry, 240, 241
　Isaac, 241
　Isaac Burroughs, 36
　Jacob, 36, 240
　Joel, 241
　John, 241
　Joseph, 240, 241
　Joseph, Jr., 241
　Mary, 240, 241
　Mirah, 240
　Nelly, 240
　Rebecca, 241
　Ruluf, 240
　Samuel, 241
　Sarah, 168, 240, 241
　William, 241
Van Middleswart (Van Middles-
　worth, Van Middleswaert),
　Andrew, 24, 176
　Andrias, 153
　Antje, 153
　Ariantje, 153
　Femmetje, 153
　Henricus, 153
　Jannetje, 153
　Jeneke, 153
　John, 153
　Neltje, 153
　Susannah, 153
　Teunis, 153
　Teunis I., 153
Vann Edward, 121
Vanneman, George, 197
　Mary, 241
Van Ness, Elizabeth, 241
　Henry, 70, 241
　Jacob, 241
　Yellas, 241

Van Neste, Abraham, 211, 243
　George, 24, 236
　Peter, 193
Vannetta, Elizabeth, 241
　James, 225
　See also Vanatta
Van Norden, Archibald, 242
　James, 242
　John, 224
　Peter, 242
Van Nortwick (Van Noortwyck),
　Hendrick, 208
　Simeon, 31, 219
Vannoy, Cornelius, 145, 146, 242
Van Nuys, Isaac, 254
Van Orden—see Van Norden
Van Pelt, Annatye, 242
　Christopher, 242
　Garret, 242
　Johannes, Jr., 242
　John, 242
　Maria, 242
　Sarah, 242
Van Rype (Van Reype), Catherine,
　243
　Charity, 243
　Christian, 243
　Harmin, 66, 243
　John, 243
　Judy, 243
　Magdalen, 243
　Mary, 243
　Sarah, 243
　Thomas, 243
Van Rypen (Van Reypen), Daniel,
　240
Van Ryper (Van Riper), Darik, 242,
　246
　Garret, 87
　Garret, Jr., 243
　Harman, 246
　Jane, 242
　Jerry, 87
　John, 257
　Moritye, 242
　Richard, 242
　Sarah, 242
　Thomas, 242
Van Saun (Van Saán, Van Saen),
　Cornelius, 191
　Eva, 25
　Giesy, 25
　Isaac, 67
　Isaac J., 191
　Jacob, 191
　Lucas, 26
Van Sciver, Abigail, 35
　Abraham, 243
　Jacob, 35, 243
　John, 243
　William, 243
Van Sickle, Mary, 140
　Zachariah, 140
　See also Vanzickle
Vanskoick (Vanskoyke), Perthenia,
　179
　William, 193
Van Teenhoven, Cornelius, 237
Van Tuyl, Hermanus, 49
　Isaac, 155
Van Veghten, Derrick, 243
　Dirk, 243
　Michael, 243
Van Vleer, Cornelius, 193

INDEX OF NAMES OF PERSONS        327

Van Voorhees (Van Voorhose),
    Albert, 108
    Peter, 24
    *See also* Voorhees
Van Wagenen, Jacob, 240
Van Waggoner, Henry, 138
Vanwey, Jane, 156
Van Winkle (Van Winckel), Abraham, 201
    Annatye, 240
    Cornelius, 180
    Simon, 49
    Simon, Jr., 180
    Theodorus, 240
    Walling, 240
Van Wyck, Abraham, 243
    Anna Maria, 243
    Catharine, 243
    Margaretta, 243
    Pierre Courtlandt, 243
    Theodore, 243
Vanzant, Isaac, 135
Vanzickle, Abraham, 244
    Ann, 244
    Isaac, 244
    Jacob, 244
    John, 244
    Mary, 244
    Meriam, 244
    Rachel, 244
    *See also* Van Sickle
Varick, John, Jr., 243
Vaughn, David, 244
Veal, Elizabeth, 62
Venable, Ann, 244
    Esther, 244
    Jesse, 244
    Joseph, 244
    Rebecca, 244
    Thomas, 244
Verbryck, Bernardus, 244
    Henry V. D. Linde, 244
    Samuel, 244
    Samuel G., 244
    William, 111
Ver Kerk, John, 239
Vermeule, Adian, 244
    Frederick, 244
Verree, James, 182, 247
Verseilus, Andrew, 75
Vickery, Phebe, 244
    Thomas, 244
Vincent, Christian, 245
    Elizabeth, 169
    Esther, 245
    Frederick, 245
    John, 245
    Levi, Jr., 245
    Mary, 245
    Susannah, 245
Vocard, Judy, 245
Volintine—*see* Valentine
Von Phull, Katherine, 01
    William, 91
Voorhees (Voorhies, etc.), Abraham, 90, 135, 173, 181
    Ann, 196
    Cornelius, 71
    Daniel, 245
    Eleanor, 180
    Garret, 12
    Hendrick, 141
    Henry, 29, 30
    Hilche, 245
    James, 16, 123
    Jaques, 238, 239
    John, 24, 90, 135, 155, 180, 196
    John, Jr., 141
    Koert, 94
    Minne V., 217
    Peter, 135, 224
    Ruleff, 202
    Stephen, 12
    *See also* Van Voorhees
Vosseller, Jacob, 239
Vough, Andrew, 245
    Caty, 245
    Elizabeth, 245
    Jacob Valentine, 245
    John, Jr., 245
    Mary, 245
    Peggy, 245
Vreeland (Vreland, Vreelandt),
    Elias, 245
    Elias I., 66
    Elizabeth, 66
    Geertye, 245
    John E., 86
    John I., 66
    Michael, Jr., 245, 246
    Sophia, 246
Vroom, Peter D., 31

W

Wade, Caleb, 227
    Daniel, 198
    Isaac, 227
    Jonas, 152, 198, 227, 259
    Nehemiah, 7
    Noah, 227
    Phebe, 227
Wadington, Sarah, 28
Waer, William, 15
    *See also* Ware
Wagner (Waggoner), Andrew, 24
    Henry, 144, 145, 146
Wainright, Elizabeth, 253
    Joseph, 212
Waiscot—*see* Westcott
Waitman, Almoran, 8
Waldorf (Walldorf), Ann, 246
    Anthony, 246
    Daniel, 246
    Eve, 246
    George, 206
    John, 184
    John, Jr., 246
    Koonrod, 246
    Martain, 246
    Mary, 246
    Mary Catherine, 184
    Morris, 246
    Philip, 246
    William, 246
Waldron, Adolph, 22
    Cornelius, 219
    Magdalene, 205
    Peter, 246
    Samuel, 205
Walker, Elizabeth, 82
    George, 82
    John, 221
    Lucy, 82
    Lydia, 82
    Phebe, 154
    Rebecca, 18
    Samuel, 41
    Thomas, 18
    Ursilla, 82
Wall, John G., 66

Wallace, Joshua M., 105
Samuel, 11
Sarah, 91
William, 123, 204
Walling, Daniel, 77
  Jonathan, 246
  Joseph, 246
  Ladis, Jr., 246
  Mary, 246
  Thomas, 213
  Thomas, Jr., 13
Walmsley, William, 96
Walton, Elisha, 55, 175
  William, 65
Wambaugh, Ann, 246
Wandell (Wendell, Wendle), John, 91, 239
Wane, Patience, 158
Wannamaker (Wanamaker), Derck, 166
  Henry, 22
  Marietie, 22
Ward, Abraham, 50
  Benjamin, 176
  David, 25, 131
  David, Jr., 131
  Deborah, 161
  Ebenezer, 187
  George, 161, 171, 257
  Hannah, 190, 257
  James, 18
  Jesse, 50
  John, 50
  Lane, 229
  Peter, 75, 237
  Rachel, 176
  Samuel, 245
  Sarah, 18
  Timothy, 175
Wardell (Wardel), Charity, 246
  Elizabeth, 246
  Jacob, 213, 246, 247
  Joseph, 247
  Joseph, Jr., 53
  Peter, 247
  Samuel, 247
  Solomon, 247
  Thomas, 246
Ware, Asa, 34
  Elizabeth, 37
  Hannah, 37
  John, 113, 122
  Margaret, 168
  *See also* Waer
Warman, John, 183
Warne, Benjamin, 172
  Elijah, 247
  Elisha, 247
  Elizabeth, 247
  George, Jr., 247
  Jesse, 247
  John, 247
  Joseph, 247
  Joshua, 22
  Mary, 247
  Thomas, 247
Warner, William, 20
Warrick, Anthony, 195, 255
Warrington, John, 50
Waterhouse, Asa, 247
  Elkanah, 247
  Esther, 247
  Gideon, 247
  Henry, 230
  Hezekiah, 13, 113, 225
  John, 247
  Mary, 247
  Nathan, Jr., 247
  Sarah, 247
Watley, Mary, 188
Watson, Aaron, 106, 172
  Edward, 36
  Howel, 186
  John, 73, 134, 143, 187
  Marmaduke, 104
  Patience, 247
  Sally, 118
  William, 257
Watt, Ann, 248
  Robert, 248
Waycoff—*see* Wyckoff
Weart, Christopher, 216
  John, 216
Weatherby—*see* Wetherby
Weatherington, Benjamin, 241
Weaver, Ann, 161
  Hezekiah, 225
  Jesse, 248
  Joseph, 161
  Thomas, 161
Webb, Zebulon, 156
Webley, Ann, 27
Webster, Hugh, 248
  John, 248
  John, Jr., 254
  Lawrence, 10, 63, 87, 175, 207, 253
  Mary, 248
  Samuel, 8, 192
  Sarah, 18, 248
  Taylor, 248
  Thomas, 248
Weck, Hunagal, 87
Weidman, Joseph, 130
Weiss, Andrew, 249
  Anna, 249
  Catherine, 249
  Elizabeth, 249
  Jacob, 249
  John, 249
  Margaret, 249
  Philip, Jr., 249
  *See also* Wise
Welch—*see* Welsh
Weller, Philip, 247, 249
  William, 249
Welling, Esther, 93
  John, 36, 93
  John, Jr., 25
Wells, Abraham, 47
  Henry, 21
  Richard, 76, 261
  Thomas, 21
Welsh (Welch), David, 246, 249
  Jacob, 199
  Maurice, 21
Wendell—*see* Wandell
Wendling, Jacob, 249
Wescoates, Wescot—*see* Westcott
West, Anne, 249
  Audra, 249
  Jacob, 23
  James, 80, 239
  John, 62, 73, 249
  Matthew, 33
  Sarah, 249
  William, 73, 162
Westbrook, Samuel, 215
  Wilhelmus, 125
Westcott (Waiscot, Wescot, Wescoates), Abinadab, 249, 250
  Amos, 27, 63, 69, 100, 170, 250, 252

## INDEX OF NAMES OF PERSONS

Annanias, 249, 250
Arthur, 76
Charles, 249, 250
David, Jr., 249, 250
Elizabeth, 249, 250
Jehiel, 201
Joel, 149, 153, 166, 176
John, 249, 250
Leonard, 249, 250
Lydia, 250
Mary, 201
Philip, 87
Rhoda, 170
Richard, 119
Samuel, 249
Westervelt, Abraham, 237, 263
Albert, 66, 263
Anne, 116
Antye, 166
Benjamin, 250
Cornelius, 194
Johannes, 66
Jury, 26
Maria, 250
Roelef, 194
Westfall, David, 250
John, 250
Margaret, 250
Westlake, Priscilla, 152
Wetherby (Weatherby), Benjamin, 128
Edmond, 222
Nathan, 222
Wetherill, Anna, 250
Isaac, 64, 250
John, 146, 152
Joseph, 250
Mary, 250
Samuel, 250
Sarah, 250
Wheaton, Isaac, 134, 186
John, 37
Joseph, 85
Mary, 253
Molly, 80
Peter, 253
Reuben, 8
Wheeler, Abiel, 29
Jacob, 196
John, 109
Margaret, 250
Rebecca, 251
Whilldin (Whildin), James, 44, 73
Matthew, 73, 248
Whiston, Elizabeth, 190
Whitaker (Whitacar, Whiteacre, etc.), Able, 210
Diament, 108
Eleanor, 19
James, 250
Jonathan, 251
Lewis, 251
Mary, 251
Nathaniel, 251
Rachel, 252
Whitall (Whital), Benjamin, 7, 32, 128, 132, 153, 175
James, 52
James, Jr., 18, 51, 57
John S., 153, 166
Whitas, Sarah, 129
White, Amy, 232
Ann, 153
Anthony Walton, 251
Charity, 246
David, 233, 234
Elizabeth, 68, 235, 251
Elizabeth Gould, 233, 234
Euphemia, 251
Frances, 233
Hannah, 89, 152, 171, 232
Jane, 84
Job, 251
Johannah, 251
John, 174, 251, 252
John Gould, 233
Joseph, 215
Josiah, 165
Mary, 233
Matilda, 251
Robert, 45, 152, 171, 174
Samuel, 238, 251
William, 107, 128, 144, 153, 203, 241, 253
Zephaniah, 85
Whitehead, Benjamin, 252
David, 147
Jacob, 9
Mary, 252
R., 236
Samuel, 135
Sarah, 252
William, 252
Whitenack, Cornelius, 223, 242
Whithers, Grace, 19
Wick, Chloe, 252
Elizabeth, 252
Henry, 252
Phebe, 252
Temperance, 252
Wicoff—see Wyckoff
Wiggins, Samuel, 252
Thomas, 152
Wikoff—see Wyckoff
Wilcocks (Willcoks, Willcox, etc.), Deborah, 164
Joseph, 199
Levi, 126
William, 126, 171
Wild (Wildes), John, 253, 255
Joseph, 124
Wiley, Joseph, 253
Mary, 253
See also Wylia
Wilkins, Constantine, 253
Esther, 76, 253
James, 57, 123, 184, 187, 253, 258
John, 108, 173, 211, 232, 253, 256
Mary, 112
Thomas, 253
William, 219
Wilkinson, Mary, 253
Willard, Parr, 123
Willets (Willits), Mr., 225
Jacob, 54
James, 141
James, Jr., 214
Joseph, 28
Micajah, 219
Tabitha, 231
Willgus, William, 73
Williams, Abbott, 38, 182
Barlow, 189
Benjamin, 69, 216, 228
Caleb, 69
Cornelius, 197, 227, 259
Daniel, 254
Daniel, Jr., 33
Edmund, 133, 136, 254
Elizabeth, 216, 253
Enion, 260

330    NEW JERSEY COLONIAL DOCUMENTS

Enos, 170, 171
Hannah, 253
Isaac, 229
Jacob, 43
James, 254
Joel, 254
John, 43, 253
Jonathan, 8, 152
Joseph, 44, 254, 260
Margaret, 80, 81
Mary, 61, 69, 221, 233
Moses, 189, 232
Polly, 221
Rebecca, 253
Renseeler, 188
Ren., Jr., 70
Samuel, 216
Sarah, 135
Susannah, 170, 253
Thomas, 69, 229, 254
Williamson, A., 118
  Benjamin, 226
  Cornelius, 66, 133, 192
  Court, 224, 242
  Daniel, 254
  David, 161, 228
  Elizabeth, 11
  Isaac H., 226
  James, 254
  John, 11, 262
  Joseph, 254
  Matthias, 226
  Peter, 18
  Samuel, 18, 192
  Sarah, 254
  Stinety, 66
  William, 198, 254
Willis, Abner, 254
  Anna, 254, 255
  Benjamin, 168
  Benjamin, Jr., 254
  David, 254
  Elias, 254
  Esther, 255
  Hannah, 255
  Henry, 260
  James, 255
  Jane, 254
  John, 255
  Jonathan, 131, 177, 187, 252, 261
  Nathaniel, 255
  Prudence, 255
  Robert, 260
  Stephen, 245
  William, 177, 225, 255, 260
Willits—*see* Willets
Willmington, Fenimore, 78
  Paul, 78
  Rebecca, 78
Wills, Aaron, 38
  Daniel, 64
  Ephraim, 73
  Jacob, 54
  Moses, 38, 114
  Samuel, 51
Wilmerton—*see* Willmington
Wilson (Willson), Andrew, 170, 178, 255, 256
  Ann, 256
  Benjamin, 123, 256
  Daniel, 116, 255
  Edward, 256
  Eli, 169
  Elias, 155
  Elizabeth, 255, 256
  Esther, 255

  Hannah, 255, 256
  Hendrick, 87
  Henry, 90
  Hopewell, 256
  Isaac, 255, 256
  James, 23, 133, 146, 242, 255, 256
  Jennet, 256
  Jesse, 256
  John, 255
  John, Jr., 256
  Jonathan, 105
  Joseph, 255
  Josiah, 168
  Mary, 255, 256
  Matthew, 201
  Mercy, 105
  Mordecai, 105
  Nevi, 255
  Peter, 29, 255
  Robert, 188
  Sarah, 25
  Savil, Jr., 256
  Susannah, 256
  Thomas, 57, 256
  Walter, 256
  William, 94, 140, 255, 256
Winans, Abigail, 257
  Abner, 257
  Abraham, 257
  Abraham, Jr., 257
  Anna, 257
  Benjamin, 55
  Benjamin, Jr., 257
  Elias, 3d, 257
  Esther, 257
  Hosea, 257
  Jacob, 54
  John, 185, 252
  Joshua, 198, 227
  Matthias, 160
  Nabi, 257
  Patty, 257
  Susannah, 160
Windes (Winds), Abijah, 257
  Barnabus, 257
  Ruhamah, 257
  Samuel, 257
  William, Jr., 257
Winkle, Mrs., 90
Winkler, Lydia, 48
Winne, Abraham, 257
  Claesye, 66
  John, 66
  Lavynis, 66
Winner, Abraham, 26
  John, 147
  Joseph, 147
  Melicent, 147
Winter, John, 77
  Peter, 77
Wintermut, George, 187
Winters, Anne, 199
Wise, Margaret, 206
  *See also* Weiss
Wiser, Catharine, 109
Wistar, John, 261
  Sarah, 261
Witherspoon, John, 234, 242
Witt, Francis, 226
Woglum (Woglom), Abraham, 143, 188, 257
  Peter, 257
  Sarah, 257
Wolcott, Jacob, 35, 191, 220
Wolever—*see* Woolever

# INDEX OF NAMES OF PERSONS 331

Wolfe (Woolf), Elisha, 76
John, 259
Mary, 259
Woolley—see Wooley
Wood, Amy, 221
Benjamin, 258
Clement, 39, 252, 258
Daniel, 86
Daniel Smith, 258
David, 258
Hannah, 257
Henry, 62
Jacob, 171, 176, 192, 253, 256
James, 256
Jehu, 258
Jeremiah, 258
John, 27, 147, 166, 185, 186
Jonathan, 53
Mary, 86, 258
Richard, 37, 100, 186
Richard, Jr., 19, 100, 186
Samuel, 39, 176, 201, 258
Sarah, 39
William, 50, 232, 257, 263
Woodard, Catherine, 193
Rachel, 258
*See also* Woodward
Woodden, Ezra, 224
Woodhull, John, 91, 92
William, 54, 81, 156, 184
Woodnutt, James Mason, 209
Woodruff, Aaron D., 235
Abigail, 259
Abner, 201
Amos, 246
Benjamin, 33, 84, 259
Daniel, 206, 259
David, 233
Elias, 198, 234
Elizabeth, 33
Enos, 157
Enos, Jr., 246
Ezekiel, Jr., 178
George, 29
Hezekiah, 259
Hezekiah Stiles, 53, 128, 145, 259
Ichabod, 259
Isaac, 171
John, 47, 92
John C., 57
Josiah, Jr., 259
Mary, 143, 246
Matthias, 185
Michael, 152
Nancy, 259
Noah, 259
Ogden, 259
Patience, 259
Robert, 259
Samuel, 47, 54, 185, 227
Sarah, 259
Simeon, 143
Thomas, 16, 152
Thomas, Jr., 54, 57
Timothy, 178
William, 57, 174
Zebulon, 249
Woodward, Acsah, 76
Alice, 76
Catharine, 209
Elizabeth, 76
Henry, 209
John, 76
Mary, 76
Oliver, 258
Samuel, 195
Susannah, 76
*See also* Woodard
Woolever (Wolever), Philip, 226
Wooley (Wolley, Woolley), Adam, 181
Catharine, 188
Elizabeth, 246
Joel, 247
Samuel, 188
Stephen, 213
Woolf—*see* Wolfe
Woolman, Jane, 13
Jonah, 95, 165
Mary, 13
Samuel, 13
Sarah, 13
Uriah, 13, 35, 158, 206
Woolsey, Benjamin, 93, 235
Woolson, Abraham, 60, 200, 215
Charity, 74
Woolston, Daniel, 260
Elizabeth, 259, 260
George, 29, 179, 259, 260
Jacob, 30
John, 29
Joseph, 260
Mary, 259, 260
Newbold, 28
Rachel, 260
Samuel, 259, 260
Samuel W., 259
William, Jr., 259, 260
Woolverton, Hannah, 260
John, 118
Jonathan, 29, 194, 210, 230
Worrall, Peter, 261
Sarah, 260
Worth, William, 188, 237
Wright, Amos, 228
Caleb, 60
Daniel, 142, 224
Ebenezer, 171
Ellis, 76
Ezekiel, 228, 233
John, 51, 167, 215, 228, 250
Joseph, 87
Nathan, 88
Rhoda, 261
Samson, 166
Samuel, 215
William, 125, 196, 244
Wriggons, William, 263
Wurts, John, 44
Wyatt, Elizabeth, 261
Sarah, 261
Wyckoff (Waycoff, Wikoff, etc.), Cornelia, 261
Cornelius, 261
Cornelius P., 234
Elias, 46, 193
John, 131, 238, 261
Martin, Jr., 261
Nicholas, 261
Peter, 53, 107, 177
Simon, 131
Wyker, Mary, 261
Wylia, Christopher, 221
Martha, 221
*See also* Wiley

## Y

Yard, Archibald William, 177, 190
Benjamin, 25, 190, 262
Furman, 207

Isaiah, 234
John, 262
Lewis, 188
Pamelia, 177
Stephen, 219
Thomas, 261
Yarnell, Mordecai, 260
  Peter, 260
Yates, Abraham, 44
  Thomas, 149, 221
Yawger, Philip, 120
Yeomans—*see* Youmans
Yorke, Andrew, 21, 97
  Eleanor, 97
Youmans (Yeomans), Aaron, 121
  Benjamin, 177
  James, 172
Young (Yung), Aaron, 50, 262
  Abigail, 262
  Amos, 195
  Anna, 262
  Catherine, 262
  Daniel, 262
  Henry, 163, 260
  Jacob, 111, 131
  James, 103, 170
  Joannah, 262
  Jonas, 262
  Peter, 116, 120, 236, 262
  Philip, 217
  Robert, 103
  Sarah, 94
  Tunis, 199
  William, 159, 192
  William, Jr., 262
Youngs, Brown, 30, 153
  Deliverance, 262
  Grover, 262
  Isabella, 262
  James, 262
  Joannah, 262
  John, 262
  Jonathan, 153
  Keturah, 262
Youngun, Peter, 223

## Z

Zabriskie (Zabrisky), Abraham, 263
  Albert, 237
  Albert C., 104, 262
  Andris, 263
  Catharine, 224, 262
  Christian A., 224, 263
  Elizabeth, 263
  Gerrit, 39
  Gertje, 263
  John, 262
  John Lansing, 262
  Lee, 263
  Lenah, 262
  Margaret, 263
  Martenje, 263
  Mary, 263
  Peter, 262
  Richard, 243
  Sarah, 262, 263
Zane, Abigail, 263
  Amy, 263
  Azubah, 263
  Barzillai, 263
  Benjamin, 50
  Henry, 263
  Isaac, 67, 109, 263
  Joseph, 264
  Lettis, 263
  Nathan, Jr., 263
  Rachel, 50, 263
  Redmon, 263
  Robert, 50, 263
  Simon, 50
  Wilkins, 263
  William, Jr., 264
Zantzinger, Esther, 91
  Paul, 91
Zelley, Daniel, 78
  Silvanus, 74

# Index of Place-Names

NOTE.—This Index has the modern spelling as a rule. Where towns and townships have the same name it is not always certain which is intended. Names of counties of New Jersey are omitted.

A

Abbett's Island, 68
Accomack (Va.), 188
Acquackanonk township, 70, 86, 180, 211, 242, 245
Airestown, 203
Albany (N. Y.), 33, 262
Alexandria township, 46, 113, 126, 190, 192, 219, 233, 234, 251
Allentown (Allintown, Allenstown), 73
Alloways Creek, 51
Alloways Creek township, 178, 184, 185, 255
Amboy, 217, *see also* Perth Amboy; South Amboy
Ambros Brook, 248
Amwell township, 10, 11, 14, 18, 37, 46, 54, 67, 68, 70, 79, 89, 105, 109, 111, 112, 116, 118, 120, 121, 126, 132, 133, 146, 172, 177, 182, 183, 185, 189, 192, 194, 210, 216, 217, 219, 226, 246, 256, 262
Ardstraw Parish (Ire.), 116
Arneystown, 133
Ash Swamp, 148, 216
Assunpink Creek, 196

B

Back Neck, 185
Barnegat, 188
Basking Ridge, 206
Batavia (N. Y.), 90
Bear Swamp, 142
Beaver Dam Brook, 22
Bedford (Pa.), 115
Bedminster township, 18, 42, 135, 181, 223
Bellmont, 207
Bergen, 66, 72
Bernards township, 148, 251
Bernardstown, 55, 70, 71, 130, 155, 224, 227, 233, 244, 258
Bethlehem township, 19, 46, 72, 80, 106, 107, 131, 132, 133, 172
Big Miami River, 178
Billings Port, 183
Black Horse, 35
Black Meadow, 156
Black River, 190
Blackman's Branch, 147

Bloomsbury (Blomborough), 24
Boiling Spring, 61
Bordentown, 82, 100, 124, 145, 158, 259
Boston (Mass.), 234
Bridgeton, 80
Bridgetown, *see* Rahway
Bridgewater township, 24, 28, 49, 78, 101, 144, 162, 179, 180, 181, 221, 225, 235, 237, 238, 242, 243, 245
Bridgesticks, 250
Bristol township (Pa.), 260
Brunswick, *see* New Brunswick
Bucks county (Pa.), 16
Buckshutem, 69
Burlington, 24, 32, 38, 40, 64, 72, 75, 76, 79, 82, 95, 97, 105, 112, 117, 121, 125, 127, 129, 138, 144, 182, 193, 194, 196, 197, 201, 207, 211, 231, 243, 247, 250, 252, 259, 260
Burlington Island, 259

C

Calcoon Neck, 262
Callen (Ire.), 129
Camps Point, 39
Canfields Creek, 39
Canoe Brook, 198
Cape May, 163
Catluss' Plantation, 22
Cedar Swamp Bridge, 97
Channel Run, 214
Chester (Pa.), 160
Chester township, 11, 42, 47, 49, 50, 93, 96, 114, 137, 138, 161, 198, 204, 232, 261
Chesterfield township, 35, 61, 65, 71, 79, 104, 114, 123, 127, 139, 167, 192, 195, 213, 228, 250, 254
Chestnut Ridge, 245
Chillasquake Hills (Pa.), 95
Cohansey, 45
Cohansey Creek, 79, 151, 210
Colestown, 161
Communipaw, 184, 240
Connecticut Farms, 227
Coopers Creek, 52, 138
Cranbury, 152, 206
Crane Town, 184
Crosswicks, 71
Currytuck county (N. C.), 232

## D

Deerfield township, 27, 62, 63, 79, 82, 86, 90, 133, 150, 151, 154, 191, 198, 200, 204, 210, 229
Delaware, 23, 248
Delaware Bay, 59
Delaware River, 159, 183, 207, 256, 259
Dennis's Neck, 134
Deptford township, 12, 18, 41, 43, 44, 51, 56, 122, 123, 140, 141, 159, 166, 171, 173, 176, 186, 187, 190, 212, 221, 232, 253, 256, 257, 258
Devon county (Eng.), 182
Dey's Slip, 67
Dismal, 80
Dividing Creek, 30, 105
Downe township, 30, 105, 141, 142, 158, 207

## E

Eagle Island, 122
Eastern Precinct (Somerset county), 135, 181, 184, 239, 243
Egg Harbor, 19
Egg Harbor River, 206
Egg Harbor township, 197, 205, 206
Elizabeth (Elizabethtown), 16, 17, 18, 23, 31, 37, 47, 54, 57, 67, 103, 126, 147, 152, 154, 163, 164, 168, 172, 174, 176, 178, 185, 198, 203, 224, 226, 228, 244, 252, 254, 258, 259
Elsinborough township, 28, 94, 97, 102, 149
Erexon Point, 163
Evesham township, 9, 10, 27, 37, 47, 54, 62, 72, 76, 87, 95, 112, 126, 132, 157, 158, 175, 190, 199, 203, 207, 219, 221, 233, 244, 253
Exeter (Eng.), 233

## F

Fairfield township, 63, 68, 100, 122, 154, 185, 194, 201, 204, 249, 252
Falls township (Pa.), 260
Finns Point, 114
Fish's Island, 208
Forks of Susquehanna (Pa.), 95
Four Mile Branch, 44
Franklin township, 138, 166, 229, 237
Freehold township, 48, 55, 75, 83, 91, 92, 107, 115, 120, 124, 126, 187, 193, 209, 212, 213, 217, 237, 240, 249

## G

Galloway township, 109, 135, 161, 205, 209, 213, 218
Garrets Hill, 49
Georgia, 188
Gibbs Meadow, 7
Gloucester (and township), 26, 36, 43, 63, 71, 74, 88, 147, 181, 190, 253
Grand Isle, 90

Great Britain, 93, 112
Great Egg Harbor township, 15, 24, 59, 69, 119, 147, 197, 206, 208, 210, 213, 214
Great Meadows, 164, 174
Great Island, 178
Great Swamp, 61, 169, 205
Green Branch, 27, 90
Green Swamp, 63
Greenstadt (Germany), 137
Greenwich township (Cumberland county), 19, 76, 80, 100, 118, 186, 212, 235, 246
Greenwich township (Gloucester county), 29, 30, 47, 57, 65, 89, 106, 107, 123, 128, 130, 140, 143, 153, 168, 169, 179, 183, 194, 197, 200, 211, 212, 218, 222, 228, 241, 253, 263, 264
Greenwich township (Sussex county), 12, 46, 77, 121, 131, 148, 172, 174, 177, 199, 225, 246

## H

Hackensack, 22, 39, 66, 262
Hackensack River, 100, 188
Hackettstown, 94, 100
Haddonfield, 93, 99, 114, 139, 149, 230
Hanover township (Burlington county), 74, 123, 125
Hanover township (Morris county), 9, 25, 27, 33, 42, 64, 69, 71, 76, 77, 83, 84, 86, 89, 92, 96, 103, 125, 131, 136, 137, 164, 165, 173, 179, 204, 233, 262
Hardwick township, 8, 24, 38, 89, 91, 116, 125, 140, 141, 144, 149, 168, 177, 187, 194, 229, 245, 247, 252
Hardyston township, 25, 28, 39, 65, 80, 149, 160, 246
Harlem (N. Y.), 246
Harrington township, 66, 100, 237, 250
Harrison county (Va.), 94
Heavytree Parish (Eng.), 182
Hillsborough township, 24, 31, 87, 131, 135, 136, 176, 198, 211, 219, 223, 236, 243, 254
Hopewell township (Cumberland county), 8, 15, 30, 89, 154, 210
Hopewell township (Hunterdon county), 11, 16, 25, 34, 36, 37, 53, 77, 93, 102, 121, 128, 145, 152, 153, 177, 178, 179, 207, 217
Horseneck, 48, 98, 175

## I

Independence township, 104, 105, 113, 252
Indian Branch, 43
Ireland, 45, 111, 116, 129, 145
Iron Works Land, 156, 165
Island Meadow, 213

## J

Jacobs Creek, 157
Jamaica (W. I.), 233
Jerusalem Neck, 225

# INDEX OF PLACE-NAMES 335

## K

Kallie Koon Neck, *see* Calcoon Neck
Keese Lot, 178
Kensington (Pa.), 259
Kent county (Del.), 205
Kilkenny county (Ire.), 129
Kingston, 195
Kingwood township, 13, 14, 28, 29, 46, 68, 87, 108, 113, 117, 118, 124, 134, 144, 166, 172, 177, 178, 183, 185, 192, 194, 223, 225, 230, 251, 260
Knowlton township, 10, 24, 116, 117, 199, 220, 222, 246, 250

## L

Lake Champlain (N. Y.), 90
Lamberton, 63, 143, 187
Lancaster (Pa.), 91, 188, 260
Landing, The, 79
Leader Swamp, 199
Lebanon township, 29, 68, 82, 90, 102, 110, 116, 120, 126, 193, 202, 203, 216, 249, 250, 251
Lematon Purchase, 226
Leonards Causeway, 98
Lieningen (Germany), 137
Little Ease Branch, 183
Little Egg Harbor township, 109, 126, 135, 156, 188
Little Mantua Creek, 183
Little Miami River, 178
Little Neck, 39
London (Eng.), 166
Long Beach, 156
Long Branch, 247
Long Hill, 205
Long Point, 143
Lower Alloways Creek township, 9, 20, 27, 62, 67, 81, 97, 102, 149, 208, 218
Lower Penns Neck township, 38, 41, 114, 125, 178, 211, 220, 225, 244
Lower Precinct (Cape May county), 44, 52, 53, 73, 83, 200, 222
Lyman township (N. H.), 90

## M

Maidenhead, 50, 82, 85, 91, 92, 125, 145, 146, 177, 229, 242
Manasquan, 22
Mannahawking, 253
Mannington township, 16, 19, 23, 94, 96, 103, 178, 209, 220, 261
Mansfield township, 7, 12, 32, 34, 35, 61, 65, 67, 75, 88, 122, 127, 139, 191, 193, 195, 196, 203, 220, 249
Mansfield Woodhouse township, 28, 144, 247
Mantua Creek, 51
Maple Island, 39
Maple Island Creek, 39
Mapletown (Albany Co., N. Y.), 235
Maurice River, 30, 105, 163, 185
Maurice River township, 189, 251
Mendham township, 19, 20, 42, 62, 101, 103, 120, 136, 142, 170, 189, 252, 257

Metetecunck Bridge, 253
Middle Precinct (Cape May county), 59, 110, 142, 149, 169, 222
Middletown township, 13, 22, 41, 49, 83, 85, 103, 107, 126, 133, 161, 200, 202, 206, 209, 210, 214, 221, 222, 240, 255
Mill Brook Swamp, 262
Miller's Mill, 41
Millstone, 53, 219
Montague township, 125
Montgomery county (Pa.), 261
Moorestown, 84, 93, 137, 138
Morris Neck, 58
Morris River, *see* Maurice River
Morristown, 19, 20, 30, 39, 49, 51, 64, 67, 82, 86, 137, 143, 149, 154, 173, 178, 194, 209, 233, 234, 250, 252
Mount Airy, 71
Mount Holly, 112, 119, 158, 165, 206, 226, 260
Moyack, 146

## N

Neshanic, 180
New Barbadoes township, 29, 146, 201, 224, 239, 243, 263
New Brunswick, 42, 70, 71, 88, 120, 200, 223, 224, 228, 243, 251
New Castle (Del.), 248
New Hampshire, 90, 91
New Hanover township, 10, 20, 28, 56, 59, 60, 83, 88, 155, 167, 169, 202
New Market, *see* Quibbletown
New Mills, 10, 44
New Providence, 171, *see also* Turkey
New Shanneck, *see* Neshanic
New York City, 13, 67, 111, 186, 140, 144, 166, 170, 171, 182, 188, 208, 237, 239, 250, 251, 259, 260
New York State, 71, 93
Newark (and township), 13, 33, 39, 50, 58, 61, 69, 88, 90, 101, 102, 111, 118, 169, 170, 178, 189, 229, 258, 262
Newton township (Gloucester county), 8, 52, 93, 115, 129, 159, 161, 225, 230
Newton township (Sussex county), 8, 25, 28, 38, 52, 88, 97, 109, 130, 144, 168, 174, 176, 177, 180, 183, 184, 215, 252, 261
North Branch, 261
North Carolina, 108
Northampton township, 9, 13, 14, 29, 34, 35, 44, 62, 72, 82, 87, 95, 112, 135, 155, 165, 179, 219, 259, 260, 261
Northampton township (Pa.), 236
Nottingham township, 11, 31, 61, 73, 74, 86, 97, 134, 143, 146, 162, 166, 187, 188, 190, 191, 228, 237, 257

## O

Oldmans Creek, 50, 263
Oxford township, 12, 106, 109, 116, 162, 208, 220, 236, 241
Oyster Creek, 226

336  NEW JERSEY COLONIAL DOCUMENTS

## P

Parsippany (Persipining), 69
Parvins Branch, 151, 249
Passack (Paskack), 100
Passaic River, 163
Pennington, 53, 234
Penns Neck township, 51, 196, 244
Pennsylvania, 28, 29, 36, 160, 225, 258, 260
Penny Hill, 215
Pequannock township, 41, 67, 69, 90, 130, 146, 162, 195, 196, 224, 241
Pequest, 65
Perth Amboy, 22, 80, 205
Pettys Island, 159
Philadelphia (Pa.), 21, 33, 35, 38, 45, 52, 56, 91, 112, 118, 129, 135, 138, 139, 143, 145, 146, 161, 194, 214, 233, 236, 247, 248, 251, 259, 260, 261
Piersons Creek, 61
Pilesgrove township, 19, 41, 45, 62, 71, 93, 123, 129, 143, 202, 204, 209
Piscateway township, 24, 25, 41, 48, 64, 70, 71, 72, 79, 80, 119, 123, 132, 135, 146, 165, 248, 252, 256
Pittsgrove township, 7, 36, 43, 49, 57, 60, 74, 90, 166, 175, 182, 188, 224, 241
Pohathung, 247
Portsmouth (N. H.), 91
Preakness (Preckinus), 69
Preston Marsh, 63
Prince Morris River, *see* Maurice River
Princeton, 145, 169, 171, 197
Prodder's Pond, 43

## Q

Queenstown, 118
Quibbletown, 248

## R

Raccoon, 81
Raccoon Island, 249
Rahway, 17, 37, 54, 172, 209, 259, 260
Rainbow Island, 78
Ramapo, 83
Ramboe Run, 187, 256
Rancocus, 78
Rapapo Creek, 212
Raritan, 153
Raritan Landing, 181
Raritan River, 192
Readington township, 66, 75, 131, 136, 155, 167, 178, 179, 194, 202, 219, 236, 238, 261
Recklesstown, 195
Roadstown, 105, 163
Rockaway, 257
Rocky Hill, 173, 234
Rogerstown (Ire.), 129
Roxbury township, 20, 21, 42, 47, 48, 51, 54, 81, 116, 142, 156, 163, 164, 184, 189, 190, 202, 206, 220, 259
Rumson, 26
Russels Neck, 86

## S

Saddle River township, 67, 138
St. Ann (Parish, Eng.), 240
St. Croix (V. I.), 227
St. James (Parish, Eng.), 240
St. John (Parish, Eng.), 240
St. Johns Island, 191
Salem, 7, 10, 15, 28, 140, 146, 149, 209, 236, 255, 256, 261
Salem Creek, 19, 41
Santacruz (Mex.?), 261
Scotland, 32
Seacaucus, 72
Second Branch, 186
Sedge Island, 78
Shilo, 15
Shrewsbury (and township), 9, 10, 22, 26, 53, 56, 73, 78, 79, 83, 103, 120, 124, 131, 133, 134, 136, 159, 160, 174, 197, 212, 213, 220, 221, 222, 238, 239, 246, 247, 249, 251, 252, 253, 254
Six Mile Run, 198
Slotterdam, 240
Sourland, 219, 242
South Amboy, 49, 66, 92, 128
South Carolina, 188
South River, 55, 170
Spotswood, 200
Springfield township, (Burlington county), 14, 46, 74, 78, 87, 129, 130, 134, 139, 188, 189, 215, 231, 260
Springfield township (Essex county), 29, 47, 61
Squan River, 136
Squancum, 26
Stafford township, 188, 211, 253
Stony Brook, 196
Stow Creek (and township), 27, 37, 72, 121, 129, 149, 204
Stow Neck, 37
Swan Bay, 208
Swedesborough, 183
Swimming-over, 135

## T

Tewksbury township, 77, 101, 155
Timber Creek, 52, 187
Toms Point, 69
Toms River, 34
Totowa, 194
Trenton, 24, 29, 30, 33, 43, 63, 70, 92, 108, 111, 116, 117, 139, 143, 145, 152, 157, 177, 185, 190, 191, 233, 235, 260, 261, 262
Turkey, 17, 126, 164, *see also* New Providence
Turnip Hill, 178
Two Mile Beach, 134
Tyrone county (Ire.), 116

## U

Upper Alloways Creek township, 67, 143, 167, 237, 245
Upper Freehold township, 56, 65, 76, 117, 133, 145, 162, 179, 191
Upper Penns Neck township, 41, 45, 50, 165
Upper Precinct (Cape May county), 16, 54, 59, 176, 189, 225, 231
Upper Springfield township, 195

INDEX OF PLACE-NAMES 337

**V**

Virginia, 21, 34

**W**

Walpack township, 17, 198
Wantage township, 32, 39, 67, 206, 250, 255
Waterford township, 9, 13, 36, 43, 45, 46, 62, 91, 114, 115, 123, 138, 159, 161, 166, 203, 229, 248
Weasel, 111
West Point, 63
Western Precinct (Somerset county), 82, 219, 223, 238, 242
Westfield, 33, 35, 57, 176, **228**
Westminster (Eng.), 240
Whippany River, 92
Whirlpool Island, 208
White Oak, 150

Willingborough township, 12, 38, 47, 78, 142, 188, 243
Willow Meadow, 92
Wilmington (Del.), 161
Windham, 149
Windsor township, 42, 93, 94, 104, 114, 162, 171, 196, 205, 255
Woodbridge township, 33, 48, 71, 102, 124, 148, 152, 158, 159, 160, 180, 181, 202, 216, 225, 227, 228, 256, 257
Woodbury, 7. 18, 32, 51, 96, 108, 149, 153, 166, 171, 232
Woolwich township, 15, 50, 51, 52, 67, 71, 81, 101, 106, 108, 109, 115, 126, 127, 128, 137, 150, 169, 188, 197, 213, 218, 236, 247, 248, 263, 264

**Y**

Yorktown, 29

www.ingramcontent.com/pod-product-compliance
Lightning Source LLC
Chambersburg PA
CBHW060552230426
43670CB00011B/1798